Eros and Eris

Eros and Eris

Love and Strife In and Beyond the Greco-Roman World

Ori Z Soltes

Washington, DC

Copyright © 2020 by Ori Z Soltes
New Academia Publishing, 2021

All rights reserved. No part of this book may be reproduced or transmitted in any form or by any means, electronic or mechanical, including photocopying, recording, or by any information storage and retrieval system.

Printed in the United States of America

Library of Congress Control Number: 2021937222
ISBN 978-1-7359378-3-0 paperback (alk. paper)

New Academia Publishing, 4401-A Connecticut Ave. NW, #236,
Washington, DC 20008
info@newacademia.com - www.newacademia.com

In memory of

Joshua David Kadish

amicus optimus

et figulus amicitiae significativae

Contents

List of Figures	viii
Preface and Acknowledgments	ix
Introduction: Language and Literature from Greek Thought to Roman Religion	1
Chapter One: Hesiod's *Theogony*: The Beginning of Reality	17
Chapter Two: The *Iliad*: The *Eros*-filled War at Troy	29
Chapter Three: The *Odyssey*: The Last Homecoming and Love Delayed	65
Chapter Four: Lyric and Tragic Journeys Out and Back, from Sappho and Pindar to Aiskhylos and Euripides	145
Chapter Five: *Eros* and *Eris* in Sophokles and Euripides Beyond the Trojan War	191
Chapter Six: Comic, Platonic, and Visual *Eros* and *Eris*	221
Chapter Seven: Greek Epic Becomes Romanized: Vergil's *Aeneid*	263
Chapter Eight: From Latin Epic to Lyric	345
Chapter Nine: From Roman Philosophy to Comedy and Satire	417
Chapter Ten: An Epilogue of Sorts: From the Bible to the Baghavad Gita++	443
Chapter Eleven: The Western Return to Epic and the Epilogue of Music: From Nikos Kazantsakis and Derek Walcott to *West Side Story*	475
Notes	513
Bibliography	545
Index	551

List of Figures

Fig 1 Black-figure amphora: *Herakles and the Nemean Lion* (Munich Glyptothek; ca 510 BCE)   253

Fig 2 Red-Figure Kalyx Krater by Euphronios: *Death of Sarpedon* (Archaeological Museum of Cerveteri; 515 BCE)   254

Fig 3 Red-figure Kylix by Sosias Painter: *Akhilleus Binding the Wound of Patroklos* (AltesMuseum, Berlin; ca 500 BCE)   255

Fig 4 Red-figure kylix by Penthesilea Painter: *Akhilleus and Penthesilea* (Munch Glyptothek; ca 470-460 BCE)   256

Fig 5 Polyklitos: *Doryphoros* (ca 450-40 BCE; Roman copy)   257

Fig 6 Praxiteles: *Apollo Sauroktonos* (ca 340-30 BCE; Roman copy)   258

Fig 7 Praxiteles: *Knidian Aphrodite* (ca 340-30 BCE; Roman copy)   259

Fig 8 *Augustus of Prima Porta* (Vatican Museums; ca 20 BCE/15 CE)   260

Fig 9 *Laookon* (Vatican Museums, ca 200-175 BCE)   261

Preface and Acknowledgments

The history of the *polis*—the Greek city-state, definable in short-hand as a community large enough to be self-sufficient but small enough so that pretty much everybody (of consequence, at least) knows everybody (of consequence) and, one might suppose, everybody knows everybody's business—and of ancient Greece in general, might be fairly summarized as one largely "of dissent and disunity, of war between Greek cities and within the cities themselves."[1] The reasons for that history may be sought both in its events and personages and in the psychology of the unique configuration of people(s) from which those personages derive. Conclusions reasonably drawn regarding the psychological circumstances of what we call ancient Greece might, in turn, be expected to cast their reflections not only onto the progression of historical events, but also onto the works of art and literature that remain to us as the cultural legacy of ancient Greece—as well as in the literature and art of Rome, which offers the most immediate and direct reflection and continuation of that Hellenic legacy. Moreover, that legacy may be seen to trickle down through the ages, encompassing Western literature and art all the way into the twenty-first century. Indeed, apposite to that legacy, some of its key aspects will be found in non-Western culture, as well.

The narrative that follows, therefore, has three related intentions. The first, and primary in sheer volume of discussion, is to consider Greek and Latin literature as a prism through which Greco-Roman civilization may be understood, but through the specific lens of the interweave of two concepts, *eros* (love) and *eris* (strife). The idea is that neither of these apparently opposed modes of human behavior is presented without the other; that the two are repeatedly intertwined with each other, from the description of how our world came into being to the various threads of epic and lyric poetry that offer accounts of human-divine, divine-divine and human-human interaction. Thus, beginning with Hesiod's *Theogony* ("The Coming into Being of the Gods") and the surviving Homeric epics, (the *Iliad* and the *Odyssey*), I will go on to consider Greek lyric, tragic and comic poetry and in turn observe how the issue of *eros/eris* further plays out in Roman poetry.

A briefer discussion of the visual arts will single out a handful of works in which this theme is particularly well represented, offering a complement to the literary articulation. My intention is to draw conclusions regarding this aspect of Greco-Roman culture while recognizing differences inherent in Greek versus Roman thinking that mark them both as a continuum and as distinct from each other.

In what amounts to an extended epilogue, the third component of my narrative will briefly (by no means exhaustively) trace the *eros/eris* theme as it continues to play out in Western literature, suggesting this theme as one of the many instruments through which Western civilization erects a complex edifice built on Greek and Roman—and Hebrew biblical (included in this epilogue)—foundations. More simply put—given my brief discussion of the *Baghavad Gita* with respect to this theme—I will ask how all of this might reflect more broadly and deeply on what humans are about, across the panoply of our cultures and civilizations.

This project had a treble inception-point. When I taught Freshman English at Cleveland State University in 1980-81, I decided to shape the course as a class on the theme of "Love"—and so my students honed their composition skills while reading and being inspired not only by a handful of critical essays, but by Plato's *Symposium*, Euripides' *Medea*, and St Augustine's *Enchiridion on Faith, Hope, and Love*. That course and the discussions that it generated in turn inspired me, when I was asked to teach a class at CSU a few summers later, to contrive one called *"Eros* and *Eris* in Greek Literature and Art." In part through a long conversation with one of my students, Pam Eyerdam, I had by then begun to see those two antithetical ideas tangled in a constant interweave in Greek culture—never the one without the other—but by the end of the summer I had begun to think of how far that double motif extended: not only into Roman literature and art, but further into Western culture and beyond the West.

When, for reasons beyond this discussion (certainly more *eris* than *eros*), my PhD dissertation on Plato's *Cratylus* at Princeton University was turned down by my advisor, Michael Frede, who had begun to lose his hold on the sane world, the head of the graduate program in Classics, J. Arthur Hanson, sat down with me to consider other options. This was 1985, and I already had an idea of what I might try: *Eros and Eris in Greek Epic Poetry*—limiting my focus to the *Iliad*, the *Odyssey*, and Hesiod's *Theogony*. Art thought this a splendid idea, and even had an idea of who could be my adviser: Anne Carson—at that time, an Assistant Professor in the Department, with an interest in just this sort of subject. The three of us sat down and she agreed—albeit she did so, I will admit, with some questions, as opposed to unbridled enthusiasm. I did not know that her own PhD dissertation four years earlier had been called *Odi et Amo ergo sum* ("I Hate and I Love and Therefore I Am"), a play on the opening three words from an important short poem by Catullus followed by two of Descartes' most famous three words (*"Cogito ergo sum"*: "I am thinking, therefore I am/exist").

I am not sure if the limited enthusiasm was because she was interested in continuing to write on that sort of subject and felt that working with me on my project might be a kind of conflict of interest or because it was too close to but different from her interest and therefore too distracting. I never will know. Within the following half year, I provided her with my introduction and an outline of where I proposed to go from there. When I had not heard from her in what seemed like too long a time, I called her, and she informed me that Art Hanson had died suddenly of an embolism, and that, since we had nothing in writing and she was junior faculty, she could not continue to work with me. That was that—although interestingly, her first book came out a year later, entitled *Eros the Bittersweet*, which made me wonder.

I bought the book, but like this project, which I shelved for years, that small, beautiful volume lay on my shelf unread until after I finished my own manuscript. Anne Carson went on to become renowned as a poet while continuing her career as a classicist—the two roles often interweave in her work, as they did in that first published book of hers—and I myself became preoccupied with a range of teaching, lecturing, curating, and writing projects, not returning to this subject until a year or two ago. In having finished my manuscript and finally turning to *Eros the Bittersweet*, I see how it moves toward some of the same outcomes as does my work but along a very different path: at once narrower and yet broader, less detailed and yet with certain specific details that are other than those that I offer, and, above all, both scholarly and, more than my volume, poetic. Our relatively brief encounter may or may not have influenced her thinking; I know that it did not influence mine at all. And yet, who knows?

I want to acknowledge my students at CSU who first inspired my thinking in this direction more than 35 years ago, and to honor the memory of J. Arthur Hanson for his support at the time when I was thinking of repurposing a light summer course into a serious dissertation. Thanks, also, to Caitlin Mannering, whose perceptive reading of my not-quite-finished manuscript earlier, and to Perry Flores, whose equally careful reading of the completed manuscript later, not only caught many small errors of spelling and syntax, but raised a number of questions that forced me to improve the quality of my narrative. I also wish to thank Adrianne Pierce, a superb classicist and even better friend for her many insightful suggestions that have improved this manuscript. So, too, the extraordinary philosopher and artist, Alex Shalom Kohav, for his own potent thoughts.

I am dedicating this work to the memory of an old and very dear friend who passed away too soon and too suddenly of brain cancer 2 years ago: Joshua Kadish, with whom I spent a good number of hours when we were college seniors laughing and slogging through Heidegger (and debating whether his writing was more difficult and obscure in English translation or its German original), and philosophizing about life and love from the hills of Berkeley to Quadra Island to the "Philosopher's Way" across the river from Heidelberg. Those were magical times. No strife, man, only love.

Summer, 2020

Washington, DC

Introduction

Language and Literature from Greek Thought to Roman Religion

Robert J. Littman, in the first chapter of his classic volume, *The Greek Experiment*, reviews theories that account for what he calls the *disunity* of the Greek character: the geographic isolation of community from community—which he wisely terms "simplistic"[2]—and competition, upon which he focuses approvingly:

> Everything was made into a contest, from athletics to the great drama festivals, such as the Dionysia at Athens, where playwrights vied for prizes. Competition was formalized in the great *agones*, public festivals at which competitors contended.[3]

Littman turns further to an anthropological summary of the Greek competitive urge. In observing the often non-productive nature of their competitions in the concrete sense, he observes that "the Greeks had a shame culture rather than a guilt culture"[4]— that their sense of worth was dependant entirely upon the opinion of others, rather than on any sort of internalized standards. And because the internal results of one's efforts are the only obvious basis for one's being judged by others, "the Greeks regarded any kind of defeat as disgraceful, regardless of circumstances... the glory of winning accrued to the victor from the lost glory of the defeated"[5]—as if there were a finite volume of glory to be gained from any given competition that had to be shared in greater and lesser measure by the victor and the victim.

In turn, the psychological foundation of this anthropological commentary is based on narcissism, "which led them into a continuing struggle for personal glory and fame, as well as for the wealth and power by means of which these were to be acquired. Personal ambitions were unquenchable."[6] Against such a backdrop, Littman notes that treason and betrayal were common enough to be considered "national pastimes." Greek history with its disunity and dissent, both within and without the *polis*, might be said then to derive from these marked propensities.

In an attempt to explain the depth and basis of the narcissism that he finds foundational to Greek culture—for it requires explanation as much as does the competitive nature of which it is part of an explanation—Littman refers to Philip E. Slater's psycho-sociological study, *The Glory of Hera*. Slater traces the etiology of narcissism—particularly in Greek males—to the structure of the family as it develops within the structure of the *polis*.[7] His focus, indeed, is on the *polis* and people within it at the time of its peak of developmental prowess, the fifth century BCE. But his psycho-sociological interest is based on his consideration of the mythological and literary background of the great works produced, primarily in Athens, at that time.

Slater begins by observing an apparent paradox in the role of women in fifth- and fourth-century Athens:

> On the one hand, one is usually told that the status of women in fifth-and fourth-century Athens achieved some kind of nadir. They were legal non-entities, excluded from political and intellectual life, uneducated, virtually imprisoned in the home, and appeared to be regarded with disdain by the principal male spokesmen whose comments have survived. (Kitto, 1960, pp 219-22; Bluemner, n.d., passim). On the other hand, as Gomme points out: "There is, in fact, no literature, no art of any country, in which women are more prominent, more important, more carefully studied and with more interest, than in the tragedy, sculpture, and painting of Fifth-century Athens" (Gomme, 1937, p. 92).[8]

Slater goes on to note Gomme's subsequent rejection of the first half of this perspective as a valid view of women's role in fifth-century Athens, and then proceeds to adjudicate between the "dissenting voices of Gomme and Kitto" in the discussion that follows.

He begins by observing that the position of women inside and outside the home are two very different aspects of their sociopsychological role vis-a-vis males—that their powerlessness out in the workings of the *polis* is, paradoxically, the basis of extreme power in the household where the males who will run the *polis* undergo their most potent psychological development: "The Athenian male fled the home, but this meant that the Athenian male child grew up in a female-dominated environment. As an adult he may have learned that women were of no account, but in the most important years of his psychological development he knew that the reverse was true."[9]

It is the consequence of this state of affairs, and of the relationship between sons and mothers in particular that Slater outlines in his book. "The [ancient] Greek male's contempt for women was not only compatible with, but also indissolubly bound to, an intense fear of them, and to an underlying suspicion of male inferiority. Why else would such extreme measures (of limiting what is permitted to females) be necessary?"[10] Therefore, Slater suggests, "the low status of women and the male terror of women were mutually reinforcing in Hellenic society"[11] and traceable to the societal configuration that engenders a particular account— what the Greeks before the fifth century simply called *mythos*—of mother-son relationships within that society.

Slater continues his analysis with reference to the kind of women portrayed in Greek drama in the context of the often-present theme of intra-familial conflict, as well as with a discussion of homosexuality as "an essential part of a total pattern of response"[12] to mother-son, female-male conflicts present in classical Athenian society. His conclusions are astute; he fills out a theoretical Freudian understanding with concrete instances drawn from modern psychoanalytic literature.

Accordingly, he furthers the starting point of Freud's (and others') conclusions regarding the psychological bases of Greek (and other) myths, focusing that furtherance on Greek myth, literature, and society at its cultural zenith. These Slater sees as largely a consequence of male fear of the female resulting in and from circumstances that leave the female largely unfulfilled and with little other direction to exorcise and exercise her male-induced frustration than toward her son(s). While it is important to note that, like most non-classicists, Slater confutes "Athenian" with "Hellenic"—using the most culturally prominent *polis* at its apogee to represent Greece at large, and thus ignoring, most obviously, Sparta and its far more equal genderal ways—for our purposes we can and shall follow his lead, *because* Athens was so culturally and politically pre-eminent.

The ultimate consequence of the familial-societal configuration of fifth- and fourth-century Athens as perceived by Slater is the narcissism that Littman, in turn, places in the foundation of his analysis of the development of the *polis* in evolving Greek history. But it seems to me that one may seek still further for the etiology of that familial-societal configuration in the tension between two apparently contradictory forces: love and strife. It is the pervading dynamic tension between these apparently opposed forces that, perhaps as a universal, will be found at the root of the Hellenic matter, and which reveals itself throughout the length and breadth of Greek mythology and literature.

No opposition is more compelling than that between love and strife—in Greek, *eros* and *eris*. In Greek literature—and beyond it, Latin literature (and Western literature well beyond the time of the Romans)—these two apparently antithetical concepts are consistently glued to each other: you rarely find one depicted in action without the other involved. Interestingly, Euripides, the fifth-century BCE playwright who again and again, like other Greek writers, exemplifies this truth, made the offhand observation in a work of which only fragments have survived, that the terms "*eros*" and "*eris*" derive, linguistically-speaking, form the same root. They look at first glance as if they could, but it turns out that they don't; Euripides is wrong (he was, after all, a playwright, not a linguist). What is interesting is that he thought so: it was apparently not just the identical first syllable and last phoneme in each word that led him to think this, but what he saw around him and read in prior Greek poetry. The interwoven relationship between these two ideas evidenced as early as Homer's epic *Iliad* would continue with the *Odyssey*, Hesiod's *Theogony*, subsequent lyric poetry, the tragic theater of Aiskhylos, Sophokles, and Euripides three hundred years after Homer; and with Greek comedic playwrights from Aristophanes to Menander in the generations after Euripides.

Moreover, the dynamic of this tension pervades Latin literature—on both Greek-borrowed and distinctly Roman terms— as, in fact, it will be seen to move forward through the sweep of Western thought and literature, as they build on the legacy of the Greeks and Romans. We can see it in Dante and Shakespeare, identify it in Cervantes and Melville, and find it on Broadway in *West Side Story*.

Littman's conclusions are not diminished by recognizing that the narcissism to which he calls attention is not the point of *origin* of *polis* development as he discusses it, but in large part a *consequence* of the problematic mother-son relationship that Slater discusses (and that, to repeat, Littman acknowledges). Similarly, the significance of Slater's argument is by no means diminished by the suggestion that I shall put forth. In effect, my argument will be that what Slater describes is part of a larger psychological condition; that the mother-son complications that he analyzes are merely an aspect of a struggle visible in Greek (and Latin) literature on all levels of gender and generation relations; that what one finds in the literary tradition may well, as Slater observes, "mirror directly the modal patterns of the culture;"[13] and, indeed, reflects precisely the tensions between contradictory psychological forces to which Slater himself alludes in his preface and beyond.[14]

What follows, then, is a study of the interweave of *eros* and *eris* in the key works of Greek and Latin literature—from epic to lyric, tragic and comedic poetry, with reference to Plato's very relevant prose. As such, I will be offering psychological and therefore cultural conclusions regarding the society in which those literary works were created. I will further propose, in arriving toward the concluding chapter of this volume, that this interweave and the conclusions to which we arrive for the Greeks and Romans have ongoing implications in thinking both laterally toward the Hebrew Bible as another foundation stone in the edifice of Western thought and literature and forward to the long sweep of that thought and literature (and not only in the West) that leads to our own time and world.

Two further notes are essential before one moves forward. The first pertains to the Greek vocabulary with which we begin. Our starting point is *eros* and *eris* and the mistaken presumption of a relationship between those two terms etymologically that reflects and is reflected in the interwoven relationship between the concepts underlying the terms. Were this a study of a different sort, it would be imperative not only to limit ourselves to those two terms as the poles that must sustain the discussion, but to clarify the distinctions between them and other Greek terms that are near synonyms. We would thus be following the course apparently laid out by the great sophist and contemporary of Sokrates, Prodikos, whose process of synonymy was well-known and well-regarded in the Athens of the late fifth and early fourth pre-Christian centuries.

In Plato's *Kratylos*, however, it becomes clear that Plato's own interest—even as he references Prodikos early on—is not in comparing terms in order to parse sometimes subtle distinctions of nuance, but to focus on any given term with regard to understanding in a definitive manner its essential conceptual underpinnings. Not "what is the difference between near-synonyms 'x' and 'y'?" but "what is the true meaning of 'x' and what is the true meaning of 'y'?"[15] Thus the discussion that follows is more Platonic than Prodikean, and when, say, the term *philia* is used in an *eros*-bound context, the fact that *philia* rather than *eros* is the term of use will not alter the direction of the discussion.

The second further note is this: given both the first, lateral, part of the epilogic assertion regarding the Hebrew Bible and the fact that most of the Greek and Latin literature under discussion includes within its pages the imputation of an important role to the gods in *eros/eris* as in other aspects of human affairs—and in the case, for instance, of Greek theater, every drama is understood to take place under the patronage of gods—our narrative requires a few further introductory comments pertaining to religion and its concomitants, by way of specific vocabulary derived from the Romans.

Religion presupposes a dichotomy to reality. On the one hand, the realm in which humans operate in the everyday sense—the realm, in time, from sunrise to sunset (daytime) and from birth to death; the realm, in space, of the community in which I am comfortable and safe, whether I construe that community to be my small village or planet earth; the realm that encompasses humanity and its preoccupations—all of this diversely construed realm is what the Romans termed the *profanus*. It is that aspect of reality that we know—or believe we can or do know—and in which time moves in a reliable, linear manner and distance is measurable in agreed-upon, consistent units.[16]

The other side of reality is called the *sacer*. This term refers to the realm of sleep and dreams, of night, of death, and of the unknown vastnesses beyond the community: the ocean, the woods, the mountains, the desert, outer space. The *sacer* is that which is not human: it is the realm of animals, particularly wild animals, and above all, it is the realm of divinity. As such, the *sacer* does not conform to our patterns of pre-expectation; rather than offering safe circumscription it operates unpredictably—sometimes with positive results (thus it is a realm embedded with hope) and sometimes with negative outcomes (thus it is a realm fraught with fear).

This understanding of a fundamental dichotomy to reality is endemic to human thought, across the entire panoply of our cultures and civilizations, even as myriad differences of detail distinguish one culture or civilization from another. Moreover, within this dichotomous thinking, the *sacer* offers a two-fold possibility in its relationship to the *profanus*. For it is intrinsically neutral in its disposition toward the *profanus* but potentially positive or negative in its interaction with us, a source of help and harm, of obstruction and promotion. Moreover, while all aspects of the *profanus* and the *sacer* are analogues of each other, the most profound and profoundly disturbing aspect of the *sacer* is divinity—for the obvious reasons: if divinity, as humans believe, has created us, it has the power to destroy us; if it can help us and it can also harm us—further or hinder us, bless or curse us; it can exercise the potential of the *sacer* to affect the *profanus* in either positive or negative ways more extremely than is true of other aspects of the *sacer*.[17]

Particularly in its divine aspect, the *sacer* is a realm of paradox, beyond straightforward understanding. It is ultimately eternal, and fundamentally spaceless in our sense of "space" and timeless in our sense of "time." Every inch of reality is part of the continuum of its awareness; all of time is present tense to its consciousness—in contrast to our limited spatial sightlines and our senses of easily forgotten past and invisible future. Yet we establish precisely—emphatically precise—circumscribed times and spaces in attempting to engage the *sacer*. The times are most often border times (for their very being as borders connotes our intention to cross a border in engaging the *sacer*)—sunrise, sunset, noon, midnight—from which we diverge at the minimal peril of the inefficacy of our rituals and the maximal peril of disaster.

We define precise spaces in which to interact with the *sacer*: locations that are known or believed to offer a point of contact with the *sacer*; border places where that interaction has a maximal chance of success. Each of these places functions as a kind of center—a sacred center—around which our *profanus* reality revolves, and that connects us to the *sacer*. Thus the *omphalos* at Delphi—the Greek word is cognate with the Latin "umbilicus"—suggests a consciousness of that site as propitiously connected to that particular aspect of the *sacer* that offers guidance to human petitioners, divinity articulated, in this case, as the god Apollo.

Similarly, when in Genesis 28, Jacob flees the wrath of his brother Esau, his first night away from home on the way to his uncle's home in Haran is spent in the wilderness—the *sacer*. At night—a *sacer* time—he has a *sacer* experience—a dream—in which he sees some sort of ladder-like entity connecting heaven (*sacer*) and earth (*profanus*) with beings going up and down (moving between *profanus* and *sacer*) on it. When he awakens he is astonished regarding what he has understood to have been a message to him from the *sacer* and asserts that "I did not know that the God of my fathers, Abraham and Isaac dwelt here." He takes the stone upon which he had slept and other stones and creates a tangible marker of that experience to indicate this site as propitious of divine-human contact: a high place—an *altar* (from the Latin *altus*, meaning "high"—see the English word "altitude")—and to his descendants, that place, called *Beit-El* (Hebrew for "House of

God") will be an important spatial point of *sacer-profanus* contact forever thereafter.

Moreover, to repeat, the *sacer* is inherently neutral in its disposition toward the *profanus*, while its response to and interaction with us is *potentially* either positive or negative. We may sleep and have no dreams, or we may dream and the dreams are not particularly memorable, or they can be so sweet that we don't wish to wake up or so nightmarish that we cannot wait to get out of them and remain profoundly disturbed by them long after we are awake. In the woods my fairy-god-mother may touch me on the shoulder and give me three wishes that transform my life wonderfully—or wild beasts may attack me and tear me apart. When we die nothing may happen—or we may go to a wonderful place called heaven or paradise or a horrific place called hell. When we seek contact with divinity, it may not respond at all, or it may respond in an altogether positive way by giving us precisely what we need or in an enraged manner that is intensely destructive to us.

So: the *sacer* is that which is outside and beyond the *profanus*. The *profanus* may be understood as the community, and the *sacer* is beyond and outside the community. It is not only the realm of gods and animals and foreigners—friend or foe—but even a member of the community who becomes estranged from it is by definition *sacer*. Some individuals are habitually half out of the community: prophets and seers, priests and pharaohs: beings who are both part of the community but stand apart from it and possess a unique connection to the *sacer*. Such beings are termed *sacerdotes* (*sacerdos* in the singular)—a word that attaches the suffix "-*dos*," from the Latin "*do, dare*," meaning "to give"—to the noun/adjective "*sacer*."

Thus such individuals can give to us what the *sacer* would have us be (its instructions) and give to the *sacer* what we need from it (our petitions). Differently, heroes are also *sacerdotes*: Akhilleus is literally comprised of both divine (*sacer*) and human (*profanus*) elements; Odysseus, while fully human, has an unusual connection to the divine *sacer*—Athene—who makes it possible for him to accomplish and to survive dangers that ordinary humans cannot (and in the case of his crew, do not) accomplish or survive. Even—symptomatic of the inherently paradoxic nature of the *sacer*—among the *sacer* gods, a divinity like Hermes is also a *sacerdos*: a liminal character who, as a messenger and *psychopompos* (guide of souls into Hades), straddles the *sacer* and *profanus* realms.

Religion is that construct that articulates this understanding of reality and seems to have existed as long as humans have. Its purpose is to bind us back to divinity as that aspect of the *sacer* that is the source that has made us. We can see this in the Latin term from which the word itself derives: *religio*, whose three etymological components are *re-*, (meaning "back" or "again"); *l-vowel* (usually "i" or "e" and in this case "i")-*g*, meaning "binding" (as in *lig*aments, or *lig*atures); and the suffix, *-io*, indicating that it is a grammatically feminine-gendered noun. The purpose *within* the purpose of "binding us back"—to the source that we believe has made us—is survival. Based on the belief that that which has created something can destroy it—can hinder or further it, help or harm it, curse or bless it—religion has, as far back as humans have existed, sought to ensure that the relationship between divinity and ourselves has a positive and not a negative outcome.

Religious rite and ritual regulate the separation between *sacer* and *profanus*, and guide us toward the appropriate times, places and manner of transgressing the boundaries between realms. One might ask how we know what the proper rituals are and where and when to perform them so that divinity is pleased and not offended by our performance. The answer resonates with the larger problematic of religion, and not just its rites and ceremonies. Every religious tradition offers revelation as its starting point; every tradition believes that there are individuals—*sacerdotes*; prophets and priests—to whom and through whom divinity communicates, revealing itself and instructing them with regard to guiding their constituents in general terms as they relate to the *sacer* and specifically with regard to rituals and ceremonies, whether communal or individual, on a defined periodic basis or occasionally.[18]

This entire matrix of ideas can be understood in a succinct manner by considering the Roman inscription in which the term "*sacer*" first appears (albeit in a pre-classical form); this is the earliest Latin inscription available to us. It is found on an object called the *lapis niger*—the black stone—that, as early as the seventh pre-Christian century, marked the boundary between the amorphous center (the old forum) of the early town (village, really, at that point) of Rome and an area that was separate and dedicated to a goddess, perhaps Diana.

The inscription indicates that whoever upsets this boundary stone—together with his cattle (presumably a symbol of wealth and well-being)—will be *sacer*. The inscription offers us three obvious questions: What exactly does "*sacer*" mean in this context? Why would someone who upset the stone become *sacer*? What might that individual do, assuming that the condition of being *sacer* is not a desideratum, to reverse that condition? The intention is obviously to curse the individual—so "*sacer*" means "cursed"—but in practical, actualized terms it means "not be part of the *profanus*." Since the *profanus* is, in effect, the community, the individual so-labeled, no longer part of the *profanus*, is estranged from the community. As a further practical consequence, s/he is no longer protected by that which binds a community together—its *religio* and its *leges* (laws)— and may be assumed to be at potential risk: if she has enemies, this condition will offer them a chance to do her in.

So the offender had better leave town quickly, for his own protection. But that departure has a more profound motivation: to protect the community. The offending individual must be separated from those around him because, within the reality of *sacer/profanus* relations as they are governed by religion—a realm of analogues—every boundary connotes the ultimate *sacer-profanus* boundary. Thus, to upset any boundary (particularly one that marks the separation between an area set aside for a goddess and the area of human action) is potentially to upset the ultimate boundary between the community and its gods—or in this case, a particular goddess—thereby inviting their (her) wrath upon the entire community. So the offender must disconnect himself from the community in order to draw the anger of the goddess onto him and away from the community of which he was formerly part.

This situation is well exemplified in the Greek story of Oidipos. At the outset of Sophokles' play, *Oidipos the King*, the city of Thebes of which Oidipos is the ruler has been decimated by plague. By the end of the play, he, they and we have learned that Oidipos is himself the unwitting source of the plague, because he has—again, unwittingly—killed his own father and married his own mother, producing four children with her, and thereby offended the gods. In order for the plague to be removed, Oidipos leaves Thebes, going into exile accompanied by the more loyal of his two daughters.

The last of the three loosely-linked plays on this topic that Sophokles (ca 497/6-406/5 BCE) wrote (*Oidipos at Colonus*) presents Oidipos years later, having made amends to the gods, having assuaged the gods' anger, permitting him to die in peace, albeit never having returned, and never having desired to return, to Thebes. But what of the offender who has disturbed a goddess by disturbing the *lapis niger*—what if, unlike Oidipos, she wishes to return to the community? How is it possible for her to make amends to the offended goddess and to return? She must first of all consult someone who will be able to answer that question: a *sacerdos*.

The *sacerdos* will inevitably instruct him along three lines all of which converge on the principle of precision. At a precisely prescribed sacerdotal place, at a precisely prescribed—almost inevitably, a border-type—time, he must perform a precisely prescribed ritual. Any number of rituals may fill out this third aspect of the process, but more than likely it will involve making something other than herself *sacer*. "To make *sacer*" in Latin is "*sacer facere.*" Certainly a very common sort of ritual would involve taking some animal—perhaps a lamb, or a goat, or a bull—and then slaying it (in a precisely prescribed manner), thus making it *sacer*, since death is an aspect of the *sacer*.

This must have happened pretty frequently, under diverse conditions, since ultimately the two words, *sacer facere*, coalesced to produce one word: *sacrificare*—that becomes "to sacrifice" in English. But the Latin term, meaning "to make *sacer*" does not only or necessarily mean to slay—although to go to the gods, while it implies going to immortal life (a positive outcome), at the same time, does mean "to die" in the sense of being separated from human affairs (a presumably negative outcome in most people's view).[19] In any case, the animal that is slain (if that is the process) by the one who disturbed the *lapis niger* is both *sacer* in being a gift to the goddess to atone for the offender's guilt and, if it has indeed been killed, is also *sacer* in that death is an aspect of the *sacer* realm.

It is very likely that part of the process—before slitting the animal's throat—will be to touch it; to lay one's hands upon it, transferring the guilt for the offense from the *sacer* individual to the animal by physical contact. We may recognize this sort of process in the account of what happened on the annual Day of Atonement in the courtyard of the Jerusalem Temple of the Israelites and Judaeans. The High Priest, who was understood to have taken upon his shoulders a year's worth of God-offending sins from the entire people, laid his hands on a goat—the *Azaz-El*, as it was called in Hebrew, rendered in English as "scapegoat"—that was then pushed off the precipice of the Temple Mount into the valley below that led out into the Judaean wilderness. Put otherwise, then, the *Azaz-El*, to which those sins had been transferred by the laying on of the High Priest's hands, was made *sacer*—protecting the *profanus* by being made *sacer*—in the sense either of perishing (assuming that it died in the fall into the valley) or of wandering out into the wilderness (if it did not die). Or both. Either way, the sins were conveyed into the *sacer*, away from the *profanus*.

Of course, we must distinguish a ceremony that was an annual event—or periodic according to whatever timetable—and enacted by a *sacerdos* on behalf of the community, from one that involved an individual who has committed a one-time offense that requires expiation, as in the *lapis niger* context. But in both cases the same fundamental methodological issue is operative—precision with regard to time, space and ritual act, and border/boundary contexts for all three aspects of that precision—and the same fundamental goal: to protect the communal *profanus* from the potentially negative action toward it by the *sacer* in its overwhelming aspect as divinity. The need for precision offers an inherent paradox. For the realm of the *sacer* is by definition spaceless and timeless—it may not be boxed in with *profanus*-style borders—yet our engagement of it with such precision does just that.

Moreover, both the communal/periodic and the individual/occasional types of situations underscore the above-noted paradox of the *sacer*: that it is inherently neutral but potentially negative or positive in its disposition toward the *profanus*. For the animal that is sacrificed—made *sacer*—particularly if that means that it is killed, may be assumed by us to experience a negative fate, if we understand death as a fate that is negative. But if we think that death is "going to a better place" then that fate is positive. To become one with the gods, since they are also *sacer*—assuming that the gods are at least partly good if not mostly good; and if there is only one God, that that God is even understood to be all-good—can only be a positive experience, while at the same time most of us are likely to prefer to live than to die, which means that it is perceived to be a negative experience.

There remains at least one further pressing question evoked by this discussion: how do the *sacerdotes* whom we consult about all of this know what they know so that they may instruct us as to what to do under whatever *sacer*-related circumstances we encounter? How are they privy to the information that they provide for us? It is *revealed* to them. Every religious tradition, as we have observed above, offers as its starting point the conviction that there are certain individuals who are particularly conducive to s*acer-profanus* contact, as there are certain times and places that are.

The beliefs concerning revelation carry within them a layered complication that pertains to the second part of the process of religion: interpretation. We might ask how precisely divinity communicates with the sacerdotal individuals to whom it reveals itself and through these individuals communicates to the *profanus*. Does it have a voice as we do? Does it shape words with a throat, tongue, teeth and lips? When in Exodus 3 Moses "encounters" God at/through the Burning Bush, how exactly does Moses perceive the God that pushes him to return to Egypt and engage the Pharaoh toward allowing the Israelites to go free? And did Moses correctly understand the Lord—standing before the Burning Bush, and later on, when he and the Israelites were standing at the edge of the Sea of Reeds (Ex 14:16), or later still when, following the death of his sister, Miriam, he would importune God on behalf of the people to provide them with water and is told to speak to the rock (Numbers 20:8)?

For Moses—even Moses—is not infallible in his understanding of God's word. In his hurry to return to Egypt from the wilderness of Midian, he completely forgets to circumcise his son—God almost slays Moses for this omission, his error corrected through the remedial action of his wife, Tzipporah (Ex 4:24-7). And instead of speaking to the rock, Moses hits it—twice—with his staff (Num 20:11), provoking the anger of God, and thus, "because you did not trust me enough to demonstrate my holiness to the people of Israel, you will not lead them into the land I am giving them! (Num 20:12)" Thus the greatest of Israelite prophets will be denied entrance into the Promised Land toward which he leads his flock for 40 years in the wilderness, for having misconstrued the word of the Lord.

So a prophet, however great, is still human and humans make mistakes, including that of misinterpreting revelations. And what happens when the prophet is gone? The texts that eventuate—for example, the Torah, the Gospels, the Qur'an—are all written down well after the events that they describe and the oral shaping of those texts by the prophets to whom their content has been revealed by God. How incontrovertibly accurate are such texts, written down after the prophet has left us—and thus reliant in part, at least, on the memory of those writing it all down?

As often as not, the text as we receive it in writing may be sufficiently obscure that we need to interpret it carefully in order to understand God's intentions. What exactly does it mean "not [to] seethe a kid in its mother's milk" (Ex 23:19) for the purposes of an everyday traditional Jew in the twenty-first century? Why and how does it come to mean that he may not eat a cheeseburger, or either drink a glass of milk with her steak or follow that steak immediately with an ice cream sundae? A series of interpretations pertaining to the underlying intent of the commandment and also connecting it to a different commandment—to "build a fence around the roof of your house that you may not bring guilt of bloodshed on your household if anyone should fall from it" (Deut 22:8)—and its own interpretative chain lead, in combination, to this post-steak, sundae-less conclusion.[20]

This issue of distinguishing revelation from interpretation and correct interpretation from false may be seen in any number of contexts. It is not limited to the Abrahamic traditions that include Judaism, Christianity and Islam, for instance, but encompasses other faiths, as well. The issue, in short, carries far and wide.

In ancient pagan Greece, these issues center in particular on that most important of sites, Delphi, with its *omphalos* and its Pythian *sacerdos*. She sat on her tripod over a cleft in the earth from which noxious fumes apparently emerged, enveloping her and in-spiriting her—causing her to babble in a manner well-nigh incomprehensible to ordinary people. It fell to the priests to interpret her ravings and transmit the messages of the god, Apollo, to those inquiring of the oracle. In turn, the statements of the priests might be obscure, so the inquirer, departing the site, would have to decide what exactly the words of the god had been and had meant.

Perhaps the most notorious instance of a misinterpretation is that recorded by Herodotos in his *Histories*. In that work the "Father of History" tells the story of Croesus, the enormously wealthy King of Lydia, who is not sure whether or not to wage war against the Medo-Persians and their shah, Cyrus the Great, in 547 BCE. The oracle informs him that if he does so, he "will destroy a great kingdom." It is only after being defeated by Cyrus that Croesus realizes that he had misinterpreted the oracle: the great kingdom that he destroyed was his own.

Moreover, both the sense of how the divine *sacer* is configured and of what awaits us in the *sacer* of afterlife are not a constant throughout Greek history and culture; perceptions and beliefs and interpretations evolve. If, for instance, a Homeric audience understood death to be an intense condition of deprivation, as suggested in *Odyssey* 11, Sokrates and hopefully his audience saw it as offering wonderful opportunities for learning about the Truth that the *profanus* of life made more difficult to access.

All of this in any case, as we shall see, offers important and interesting contexts within which the problematic of *eros* and its relationship to *eris* may be seen to play out for the Greeks and Romans in their literary legacy—and to reverberate from that legacy down through the centuries.[21]

Chapter One

Hesiod's *Theogony*: The Beginning of Reality

The question of creation is an inherently vexing one, for at least two reasons. One, that no human was around when it began, to witness it, so that knowledge of it can only have come from a divine source that vouchsafes the information to some human—a prophet, like Moses, or a poet like Hesiod (that is: a *sacerdos*). Two, if the Creator is by definition something other than what we humans are—even if we assume, by paradox, that some of the Creator is breathed into us and that therefore there is a bit of us that is like the Creator and conversely a bit of the Creator that is like us—then anything we say about It/Him/Her/Them—*anything*—is said from our own perspective, our own understanding, our own reality. Thus, if I say, for example, that God is all-powerful and all-just, I must understand these descriptives as metaphors: I have no way of knowing what "power" and "justice" truly mean in God's terms, only my own.

    Language, which so extends our species beyond others, is nonetheless a limited and limiting instrument: if someone could even come up with a definitive account of a fairly common aspect of human reality, parental love, for instance, or beautiful sunsets, then poets would stop writing about these things. How much the more so if the object of our description is beyond anything within our reality. So everything we say about divinity falls short of being absolute; every attribute that we ascribe to (the) God(s) is an approximation at best, derived from our own sense of things.

    The earliest work of surviving Greek literature that addresses the question of how the world—the *kosmos*, or "order"—came into being is Hesiod's *Theogony*: "The Coming to Be of the Gods." Hesiod (fl ca 700-650 BCE), a poet who also wrote on very down to earth topics as they relate to the history of humankind in its relationship to the gods, as in his *Works and Days,* cannot obviously have been there when the gods came into being. So he is a poet whose work may be understood as analogous to that which adherents to the Abrahamic religions associate with prophecy. Both prophets and poets are *sacerdotes* in-spirited—inspired—by divinity with the other-worldly knowledge that they possess and which they share in their utterances. Not surprisingly, Hesiod spends the first 115 lines of his poem invoking the gods, by way of their handmaidens, the muses, to inspire him not only with the skill to tell their story effectively but with a true understanding of the details that shape the story that he is about to tell.[22]

When the poet arrives past that long invocation to the substance of his tale he informs us that *Khaos* came into being first. This Greek term—from the verb, *khaomai,* meaning "to yawn," and cognate with the English word, "chasm"—implies a vast emptiness, although if one considers its English-language derivative, "chaos," one realizes that *kosmos* could be understood as the filling of the void with physical matter as much as organizing a radically disorganized mess into order; it ends up at the same place. The point is that this beginning is followed by a rapid filling in: Earth (*Gaia*) first, and then *Eros,* "the most beautiful of the immortal gods," and then Darkness, Night—out of which came Light and Day; after which Earth produced Heaven (*Ouranos*), "to cover her on all sides" (126).

Earth and Heaven together produce a whole slew of offspring, from Ocean (*Okeanos*) to Memory (*Mnemosyne*), culminating with Kronos, "the youngest and boldest of her [Earth's] children" (137). There are three things that stand out as the narrative proceeds. One is the absence of a simple, straightforward, linear chronology of creation, as we shall see more fully shortly. Two is the way in which both abstract concepts and natural elements begin to assume anthropomorphic qualities. Three is how quickly relationships among these beings that we might expect to be dominated by love are instead dominated by strife. For *Ouranos* "their father hated them from the beginning," and, as the last of them emerged into the light—three huge creatures, each with a hundred arms and fifty heads—"he hid them all away in the bowels of Mother Earth; Heaven took pleasure in doing this evil thing" (154-5).

This ultimately became unbearable for Gaia, for "in spite of her enormous size, [she] felt the strain within her and groaned." She came up with a plan, however, and using a new metal—iron—that she produced, she fashioned a huge sickle.

> Then she laid the matter before her children, the anguish in her heart making her speak boldly: "My children, you have a savage father; if you will listen to me, we may be able to take vengeance for his evil outrage: he was the one who started using violence" (163-7).

All of her children are afraid to take up the challenge, however—except Kronos, the youngest of the group later (as we shall see) called the Titans. So

> She hid him in ambush and put in his hands the sickle with jagged teeth, and instructed him fully in her plot. Huge Heaven came drawing night behind him and desiring to make love; he lay on top of Earth stretched all over her. Then from his ambush his son reached out with his left hand and with his right took the huge sickle with its long teeth and quickly sheared the organs (*medea*) from his own father and threw them away, backward over his shoulder (174-82).

So between generations and genders—husband-wife and father-son—two genres of relationship where we might hope for and expect love, instead we encounter strife of a rather extreme variety. The context—a reality before our reality has come into existence—also interweaves natural forces and their anthropomorphization. Thus we might understand that Kronos hides in a cave in mother earth, which we may also understand to be the entrance to her womb—her vaginal orifice. So, too, Heaven, self-evidently spread over the earth as night falls and the separation between them—

the horizon line—disappears, follows (or sets an example for) the human custom of love-making at night, male lying on top of female.

The Greek verb that is rendered above as "sheared"—*emese*—also connotes the idea "harvested," (as grain would be cut down/harvested with a sickle such as Kronos wields)—appropriate to an eristic act that yields a very fertile outcome. For while out of the bloody drops that were a by-product of this act, the Erinyes (Furies, but more literally, "Strife-bound ones") were eventually born, the organs were thrown by Kronos into the sea, where they floated around for a while until "white foam (*aphros*) issued from the divine flesh, and in the foam a girl began to grow" (191-2).

> First she came near to holy Cythera, then reached Cyprus, the land surrounded by sea. There she stepped out, a goddess, tender and beautiful, and round her slender feet the green grass shot up. She is called Aphrodite by gods and men, because she grew in the foam (*aphros*), and also Kytherea, because she came near to Kythera (Cythera), and Kyprogeneia, because she was born in watery Kypros (Cyprus), and also Philommedea (organ-loving), because she appeared from organs (*medea*). Eros and beautiful Himeros (Passion) were her attendants both at her birth and at her first going to join the family of the gods (192-202).

So out of the eristic act of castration, the goddess of love and beauty is born. Moreover, she is born during the time of the Titans, a "generation," one might say, before the other Olympians will be born, although she will be one of them, underscoring for us that we cannot understand the chronology of the narrative in the linear terms that are standard in our reality. This is what we might expect from a time that, in being pre-time as we know it, is *sacer* and not *profanus*, and which deals entirely with *sacer* creatures, for whom time is an altogether different construct from what it is for us humans. The non-linearity is further underscored by the presentation of Eros as attending her washing up onto the shores of Kypros, having been referred to as coming into existence at the same time Gaia did, right after *Khaos* came into being—yet in the classical Greek tradition Eros will be treated as if he is the son of Aphrodite.²³

This, too, is the point at which the dominant group within the generation of supernatural, pre-human-time beings led by Kronos is first called by the term "Titans,"—so-named by Ouranos, "because of his feud with them: he said that they blindly had tightened/strained [from the Greek verb, *titaino*] the noose and had done a savage thing for which they would have to pay in time to come."

That time is, in pre-time terms, not far off. Another series of concept-creatures is produced by Night, such as Destruction (*ate*), Specter, Death, as well as Sleep and Dreams, and next, Blame and Grief, as well as Retribution, "then Deceit and Love and accursed Old age and stubborn Strife. So Love (*Eros*) and Strife (*Eris*) are born at the same time—although Eros was also already created earlier on, and although Aphrodite is the personification of Eros, even as she presides over Eros and even as Eros is present at her birth but also her son. There follows a long delineation of others born in the timeless time stretching forth, in which, to repeat, creatures share qualities of being abstract, being forces of nature and being anthropomorphic. Among those birthed during the next several hundred verses are the gods.

With them, the drama of *eris-eros* interweave moves into the next act. For

> Rhea submitted to the embraces of Kronos and bore him children with a glorious destiny: Hestia, Demeter, and Hera… Hades… Poseidon… and Zeus the lord of wisdom, the father of the gods and men, whose thunder makes the broad earth tremble. As each of these children came out of their mother's holy womb onto her knees, great Kronos swallowed them. His purpose was to prevent the kingship of the gods from passing to another one of the august descendants of Ouranos; he had been told by Gaia and starry Ouranos that he was destined to be overcome by his own son.

Once again, then, inter-genderal and inter-generational strife where we might hope for love prevails. For the Greek verb that is here rendered as "submitted" (*dmetheisa*, from *damao*) can imply a forced/subdued/conquered condition, as opposed to one done in mutual affection or passion. And this time the paternal perpetrator swallows up each of his would-be off-spring as soon as he or she is born. Interestingly—in another example of how divine behavior mirrors human behavior (or is it that *we* emulate *them*?)—Rhea turns to both her parents, Gaia and Ouranos, the would-be grandparents of her children, to assist her against her husband, Kronos, the obstructive parent of those children. So one might say that, in the case, at least, of Ouranos (who is apparently quite reconciled with Gaia; they are a pair that doesn't age, yet grows old together, peacefully) a bit of revenge against the son who castrated him is made possible: they formulate a plan, together, "whereby she [Rhea] might bear her children without Kronos' knowing it, and make amends to the vengeful spirits of her father Ouranos" (471-3).

Heaven and Earth tell Rhea what destiny has in store for

> Kronos and his bold son. When she was about to give birth to great Zeus, her youngest child, they sent her to the rich Cretan town of Lyktos [a town that somehow, already existed]. Huge Mother Earth undertook to nurse and raise the infant in the broad land of Create. Dark night was rushing on as Gaia arrived there carrying him, and Lyktos was the first place where she stopped. She took him and hid him in an inaccessible cave, deep in the bowels of holy earth, in the dense woods of Mount Aegaeon (477-84).

One of the first things we might notice is how limited the knowledge of Kronos is regarding things future and even things in the present: the would-be victim of his fearful voraciousness can be spirited away and hidden from him without his realizing that it has happened, much less where the victim is hidden. Moreover, Gaia then "wrapped a huge stone in baby blankets and handed it" to Kronos, who swallowed it without realizing "that a stone had replaced his son, who survived, unconquered and untroubled, and who was going to overcome him by force and drive him from his office and reign over the gods in his place" (488-91).

The fear of being overtaken by his son is what generated Kronos' eristic behavior toward his offspring and in turn generated the plot against him by his wife and his own parents. Years later, in fact, Kronos was again tricked by his mother, Gaia, and vomited up the stone and all the gods that he had swallowed as infants; Kronos' brothers were also set free by Zeus "from the cruel chains in which their father Ouranos had in foolish frenzy bound them." These victims of paternal *eris* would of course be grateful to their nephew, giving him the thunderbolt and the lightning flash in gratitude.

Shortly after this part of the narrative, humans enter the picture, without much explanation as to exactly when, where or why, but the story of Prometheus' gifts to humans—most importantly, fire—and Zeus' anger as a consequence; and the creation of the spectacular human female, Pandora ("all-gifts," for the immortals seem to have given her every gift that would make her perfect); suggests if not a less-than-wonderful birth, a quickly diminishing condition for humans. Woman is blamed for bringing into being all things catastrophic for humankind, a far-from-unique perspective within the realm of creation stories shaped by men.

Meanwhile the long-incarcerated "Hundred-Armed ones—Briareos, Kottos, and Gyges... restored to the light by Zeus and the other gods born of the loves of Kronos and fair-haired Rhea" (617, 624-5) decide, in gratitude, to join Zeus and the gods as they continue to fight a war against Kronos and the Titans—the gods from Mount Olympos and the Titans from the top of Mount Othrys—that had been going on for ten years, with the two sides fully balanced. "Then the Olympians provided the Hundred-Arms [Briareos, Kottos, and Gyges] with full equipment, with nectar and ambrosia, the gods' own food, and restored their fighting spirit,[24] ... [t]he limitless expanse of the sea echoed terribly; the earth rumbled loudly; and the broad area of the heavens shook and groaned" (640-1, 678-80). The decision of these huge monsters to support Zeus, combined with his decision, finally, not "to restrain his own power [any] longer, [so that] a sudden surge of energy filled his spirit, and he exerted all the strength he had... [caused] the whole earth's ocean-streams and the barren sea to begin to boil... The sight there was to see, and the noise there was to hear, made it seem as if the Earth and vast Heaven were colliding" (687-8, 695, 701-3), and in the end the Titans were finally beaten, and tied up deep beneath the earth—in the lowest region of Tartaros—with "cruel chains."

The further outcome of this victory, "when the Olympian gods had brought their struggle to a successful end" was that Earth suggested that they invite Zeus "to be king and lord over the gods," which they did. He in turn distributed among the gods their various rights and privileges. We are then presented with a review of all of Zeus's consorts, from Metis (Wisdom) to Themis (Law) to Eurynome (of Broad Pastures), the daughter of Okeanos; and then Demeter (Earth Mother—but not to be confused with the Earth herself, Gaia)—followed by Mnemosyne (Memory) and then Leto, which last union yielded the twin Olympians Apollo and Artemis; and finally, Hera (with whom, among others, he fathered Ares, God of war), who would be his enduring consort.

That said, the relationship between Zeus and Hera is depicted as fraught with both love and strife. He produces Athene out of his own head, without a consort, and "Hera, in turn, in resentment and jealousy, without union with her husband, produced famous Hephaistos, the master craftsman..." (929-32).[25] Hera's resentment might certainly be understood, given the continuum of Zeus' extramarital dalliances: with Maia, Atlas' daughter (who gave birth to Hermes) and also with mortal women, such as Semele, who bore Dionysos, and Alkmene, who gave birth to Herakles—the figure with whom our own narrative began, as it were.

Other stories then briefly focus on mortals who had particularly strong connections to the Olympians, by blood-line or otherwise. Thus, toward the end of the poem both Kirke (Circe) and Kalypso are mentioned, both minor goddesses who had relations with Odysseus, the Akhaian hero from Ithake who was forced to wander for ten years after the end of the Trojan War—seven of which years he spent with the second of these goddesses and one year with the first—who survived the long journey home thanks to his being favored by Athene, and whose story will shape the third chapter of this narrative.

Aside from the reference to Odysseus that comes at the end of the *Theogony*—and not all scholars agree that the last 74 verses in which that reference is embedded were actually originally part of the poem—the only mention of humans is the occasional, somewhat anachronistic mention of them, as we have noted. They would seem to be an afterthought, as far as the *Theogony* is concerned, but make a fuller-fledged appearance in a second work by Hesiod, the *Works and Days*, which, within the context of what is ostensibly a treatise advising humans—directed in form to the poet's brother, Perses, (who is thus a stand-in for all of us), regarding how to be in the world and how, most specifically, to farm properly—presents a precis of human history as a process of degeneration.

A more detailed elaboration in the *Works and Days* of Prometheus' gift of fire to humans, against the will of Zeus, and the shaping of Pandora as punishment—through the false gift brought to her by Epimetheus (the brother of Prometheus) from Zeus, the jar filled with sicknesses and troubles—underscores the admonition that "[t]here is no way to avoid what Zeus has intended" (105). From this prelude comes the human genealogy that moves from a generation of gold, followed by one of silver, "far worse than the other" (128), and in turn by a generation of bronze. The generation of heroes that follows is presented as better and nobler than that of bronze, "but of these too, evil war and the terrible carnage took some" (161)—some at Thebes (the story of the offspring of Oidipos) and others at Troy, while others were settled by Zeus in "a country of their own, apart from humankind, at the end of the world... in the islands of the blessed by the deep-swirling stream of the ocean" 167-9).

Hesiod's own—our—generation is referred to as an age of iron, the most degenerate of the five, "yet here also there shall be some good things mixed with the evils. But Zeus will destroy this generation of mortals also, in the time when children, as they are born, grow grey in the temples, when the father no longer agrees with the children nor the children with the father, when guest is no longer at one with host, nor companion to companion, when your brother is no longer your friend, as he was in the old days" (180-5). In that era that is fast-arriving, "men will deprive their parents of all rights as they grow old... (185). There will be no favor for the man who keeps his oath, for the righteous and good man… (190). The spirit of Envy, with grim face and screaming voice, who delights in evil, will be the constant companion of wretched humanity … (195). And there shall be no defense against evil" (200).

It is a dark vision of humankind, its evolution and its fateful direction—but not altogether surprising in a world the very shaping of which, from the advent of *khaos* to the assumption of power by the Olympian gods, is understood to be marked by such violent expressions of strife, even—particularly—in contexts where we might hope for love to dominate. If the coming into being of the gods is dominated by the presence of *eris* interwoven with *eros* at its most potentially powerful, then what can one expect of the world of humans?

As the narratives of the lives of the Olympians expand into a rich and complex tapestry, further threads underscoring this interweave will reveal themselves. Most directly will be the betrayal by Aphrodite, goddess of love and beauty, of her husband, Hephaistos, impelled by Eros itself who is both a witness to her birth and her son: she engages in an intense affair with Ares, god of war—whose sister is Eris. If love may be said to conquer war, in fact that conquest yields both laughter (when Hephaistos captures the naked Ares and Aphrodite in an unbreakable golden net, and all the gods come to seem them thusly humbled) and strife among the gods.

Laughter, because ultimately the gods never pay a price for what they do wrong: they don't grow ill, don't grow old, and don't die, so they have all the time in the world to correct any mistakes that they might make. Mortals, on the other hand, live lives that are relatively short, and are constantly confronted with choices in which, when they mis-choose, they only find out the error when it is too late to avert the disasters that mis-choices yield for humans. This is one of the ways in which the early Greeks perceived the human condition to be ironic: that we achieve the kind of knowledge that might save us when it is too late to be saved because of the mistake(s) made in ignorance.

Cognate with this sense of paradox is the co-existence of ideas that, in our reality, cannot co-exist—like mortality and immortality. So: like all non-divine species, we die; but unlike the other species we wonder and worry about what immortality might be, and express a yearning for it. The most stupendous of the characters in the heroic age of which Hesiod speaks exemplify this *in extremis*, which is why, in large part, they are heroes: they are like you and me, only more so, and that "moreness" is facilitated by their connections—that you and I don't possess—to divinities.

Within the Theban narrative centered around Oidipos that Hesiod specifically references, that character (as we shall discuss more fully later, in Chapter Five), exemplifies the irony of human ignorance in the face of choice-making. He stands—literally—at a cross-roads—twice, in fact. At one he meets and kills his father, not knowing that it is his father; at a second he meets the Sphinx and solves her riddle, saving Thebes of her murderous presence. At a crossroads one must choose: does one go to the right or to the left? Were we gods looking from above, we would recognize that there is a third choice: to go back whence we came. In graphic terms, (picture a kind of wish-bone seen from above), this particular aspect of irony is to mistake the number of choices: one thinks that there are two when there are three, or where there is really one; or thinks that there is only one when there are two. The human experience is fraught with these, all along the paths of our lives.

The further narrative of the human experience in *Works and Days* suggests how thoroughly Zeus keeps an eye on our activities (232), so that those who commit evil acts ultimately find that the evil recoils back upon them, for unlike the wild beasts who simply feed on each other, humans were gifted by Zeus with justice (279). Thus, he has set before us two roads, the road toward evil, which is smooth and easy; and "[t]he road to virtue, [which] is long and goes steep up hill, hard climbing at first, but the last of it, when you get to the summit, (if you get there), is easy going after the hard part" (290-91). The poet enjoins Perses (and through him, us) to work hard, for the gods don't favor idleness; and poverty, derived from laziness, is disgraceful. Mistreating family and friends draws the anger of Zeus, who loves the pious.

Hesiod's instructions continue: "when you deal with your brother, be pleasant, but get a witness, for too much trustfulness, and too much suspicion, have proved men's undoing" (371-2)—in other words, don't trust anyone. And start your work before dawn and early in the season—whether to sow or to reap. Plan ahead. Take good care of your (farming) equipment. Make your prayers to Zeus and to Demeter. And if instead of farming you have to go to sea (against which he advises), he suggests the best time to sail—not from experience, but from inspiration, "for the Muses have taught me to sing immortal poetry" (661). We are reminded, therefore, of the source of the poet's knowledge of matters both divine and human.

He concludes with a run-down on which days of the month are best for what, within the context of reminding Perses to be pious, to pray to the gods, to limit the number of friends he makes, to marry at an ideal time (age 30, to a woman of 18) and to raise a family properly—while noting that everything is, ultimately, unpredictable within the human experience, but those who follow the kind of advice that he has laid out are most likely to succeed and be happy.

Within the Trojan War narrative to which Hesiod specifically refers in the course of what is intended as an everyman's sermon-narrative, the consummate hero-symbol is Akhilleus: the son of a goddess (the sea-nymph, Thetis) and a mortal father, Peleus. He will be confronted with the choice of choices when Odysseus comes along to push him to join the other Akhaians in the great war at Troy. Unlike ordinary mortals—thanks to his divine connection—he knows something about his death: that if he goes and fights at Troy, he is fated to die there; but he will gain a kind of immortality: *kleos aphthiton* ("undying glory") on that battlefield. His reluctant choice—to go to Troy and fight—helps form the backdrop of the most majestic of Greek epics, the *Iliad*, in which the intersplicing of love with strife reflected in divine reality in the *Theogony* is explored in the great conflict in which gods participate with men. It is to this epic that we turn in the chapter that follows.

Chapter Two

The *Iliad*: The Eros-filled War at Troy

I Gods, Humans and Fate

While with regard to the chronology of the shaping of a *kosmos* inhabited by both gods and humans, we have considered Hesiod's *Theogony* and *Works and Days* first, the *Iliad* is the earliest extant epic Greek poem available to us. In the *Iliad* (ca 750-700 BCE) we recognize the key issues and ideas that will obsess the Greeks and speak through their literature over the centuries. In the "chronology" of the universe, however, its narrative follows Hesiod's narratives.

We might keep in mind several aspects of this magnificent work of verbal art. One is that the events it describes took place long before the poem was committed to a definitive written form. For various reasons beyond this discussion, we can understand that the Trojan War—however its precise historical details did or did not accord with the tradition looking back at it—took place toward the end of the Bronze Age (ca 1200-1150 BCE), and that the destruction of Troy at that time coincided with a good deal of unrest and destruction throughout the Aegean and East Mediterranean worlds. What we call "Greek culture"—with its literature and its art and the socio-economic entity referred to by the term, "polis"—emerged gradually, beginning two or three centuries later.

So, too, the world of the Late Bronze Age in the Aegean and Eastern Mediterranean possessed, among other things a syllabic writing system, commonly referred to as Linear B, which disappeared from knowledge and use in this period of transition toward an Age of Iron. Thus, whatever the details may have been, the Trojan War era was certainly marked by cataclysm. The culture that we might associate with the likes of Agamemnon, Akhilleus, Odysseus, Aias and Hektor, and with substantial fortified inhabitations contrived with gargantuan blocks of stone, at sites like Mykenai and Tiryns, disappeared.

As such, whatever memory of that era and the Great War that engaged so many figures and their extended families, that we might imagine passed on from generation to generation, would have of necessity been transmitted orally. On the one hand, this would help push the process of transmission to include a process of embroidery: each generation and each poet retelling the story could almost not avoid the inclination to add new details. On the other, the developing canons of epic composition would facilitate the twin processes of memory and embroidery. Thus a prescribed metrical system (known as dactylic hexameter) and a repeating pattern of applying epithets to the names of key characters and elements (swift-footed Akhilleus, long-suffering Odysseus, rosy-fingered dawn, and many others) would provide consistent structure and extra pre-shaped seconds of opportunity to move creatively from one line to the next.

Whether Homer existed or not is not a question for this discussion. What interests us is the poem that eventually achieved a canonical, written form, as did other epics that, however, did not survive, or survived only in fragments (also for reasons beyond this discussion). It offers us not only a beginning point for Greek literature, but a coalescence of whatever forces between the end of the Bronze Age and the evolving Iron Age led from the Mykenean world described, for the most part, in the *Iliad* to the time when "Homer"—whoever he (or they) was or was not—offered up this culminating version of the story as Greek art was emerging (sculpture) or changing significantly (vase-painting), and the *polis* was taking shape. As those we call the Hellenes (i.e., Greeks)[26] were becoming more adventuresome and, through the expansion of trade and colonial settlement both east and west, were coming into contact with other groups, they adopted and adapted a writing system from one of those groups—the Phoenicians—which instrument would make possible the writing down of both government decrees and long epic poems like the *Iliad*.

"Greek culture" undergoes development with extraordinary speed thereafter. The literature that moves from epic to lyric poetry and thence to full-fledged theater—as well as prose philosophy and historiography—expresses and explores certain broad ideas again and again that one finds first articulated in the *Iliad*. We might, in turn, consider several particular aspects of these broad, doted-upon ideas, which revolve around the question of how humans fit into the order of things. *Kosmos*—"order"—is the Greek word for this, so the universe is understood as an ordered reality, albeit one the order of which we don't always grasp.

In a nutshell, the human condition offers three aspects: tragedy, irony and nobility. That is: the human condition is tragic because human life is so brief in the scheme of things and because in the course of our lives, we humans are confronted again and again with choices, both small and large, and if we make the wrong choice(s), the consequences can be dire—for ourselves and for those around us—and, because our lives *are* so brief, we rarely if ever have the chance to rectify our errors and forestall the dooming outcomes of our mis-choices.

Our condition is a self-contradiction, a paradox—one of the modes of irony being the co-existence of mutually contradictory ideas. This is unique to us as a species since, like all the other beings in our world, from flowers and trees to cows and lions, we die—we are mortal—yet unlike them we wonder what immortality might be; we yearn for immortality, and conceive of or contrive different ways in which we may achieve it, particularly in our art and literature. This connects us to the gods, whose most obvious difference from us is that they *are* immortal: they don't grow ill, they don't grow old, they don't die.

The consequence of these two aspects of the human condition is a third: we are capable of the sort of nobility that even the gods lack. Whereas they can make whatever wrong choices they want—having all of time to rectify their errors and in any case are not (cannot be) seriously injured, much less killed by poor choices—we are always confronted with the price tag for our thoughts, words and actions. Given the high stakes, there is something inherently noble in the human experience.

This threefold matrix applies to all of us, but heroes are typically defined by the larger-than-life manner in which their stories play out with regard to these issues. The quintessence of this condition is someone like Akhilleus, a bigger version of all of us, and not only in his swiftness of foot or athletic strength. His entire life is lived under the shadow of a kind of foreknowledge of his own death—a preternatural knowledge which, like his preternatural fighting skills, is a function of what he is as a being: half-human and half divine—a combination in which each side will triumph over the other in a particular way, based on the choice that he makes at a particular juncture in his life.

That juncture is the question of whether to come to Troy to fight or not to do so. If he does, he knows that he will die (reach his human mortality) before the city is taken, but earn undying glory (achieve a divine-like immortality in the memory of humans down through the ages) as compensation for his early death.

The threefold matrix in which Akhilleus is entangled in a particularly intense manner is, in turn, enfolded within a second threefold matrix with regard to choices and the differences between humans and divinities. That is, that besides divine and human participants in the drama of the *kosmos* there is a third element that hovers over both: fate. The Greek concept of Fate is fraught with the tension between the idea that we truly do have choices and the notion that everything is ultimately either only illusorily choice-ridden or altogether pre-determined—that there is really no choice at all. Does Akhilleus really have the option not to come to fight at Troy? Yes, of course, in one sense he does—but in that case he would *not* be *Akhilleus*, the consummate warrior whose essence it is to be engaged where the fighting is thickest. And can he withstand the shame with which his failure to come and fight would envelop him? Presumably not, given the shape of Greek culture as a shame-culture.

The Greek word for fate is *"moira,"* and it might be explained in this way: *moira* is like a piece of pie, served up to each of us at birth. We cannot determine the nature of the pie—blueberry, cherry, banana, chocolate cream—for that is already determined. So is the size of the piece we are served. But we can determine whether we consume it with our fingers or a fork; whether we eat it carefully, so that it all goes slowly (or quickly) into our mouth and down our throat, or whether some of it dribbles down our chin or falls to our lap or onto the floor.

There is thus a constant—ironic—tension between the question of fate and free will, of pre-determination and choice—and we can never really know whether we are making the right or wrong choice, and whether (as later on, Sophokles will imply) we didn't notice a third option, or thought we had two when we only had one, when confronted with a particular situation, until, perhaps, it is too late. Akhilleus, to repeat, is the exception to that rule with regard to knowledge of where one specific and life-shaping choice will lead him, but is still caught in the web of the "do I really have a choice?" question.

Nor are the gods entirely free of this problematic. The difference is that their choices never directly affect them adversely; they affect the humans with whom the gods are involved and sometimes in love. Thus when Zeus wishes to save the life of Sarpedon, one of his sons by a human mother, Hera reminds him that, as the most powerful of gods, he certainly could do so—but he certainly cannot, since *moira* dictates that Sarpedon's time to die has come, specifically at the hands of Patroklos, and even Zeus cannot abrogate the dictates of *moira*. Or rather, he could, but, to be more specific, if he does so, other gods with children on the battlefield may wish to do the same, and the entire *kosmos* of things may be upset, with consequences that even he cannot foresee (*Iliad* XVI: 433-49).

Embedded within this larger series of treble issues, the matter of mutually contradictory, co-existent *eros* and *eris* play out throughout the entire narrative of the Trojan War cycle of which the *Iliad* relates merely part. The issue of love-strife tension as a means both to engender and to further a story line is present from a variety of perspectives on aspects of the Trojan War that once were found in a range of epic accounts. The two epics that have survived intact are, of course, the *Iliad* and the *Odyssey*. Indeed, while it has often been suggested that, in general terms, the *Iliad* is the epic of strife—a war epic—and the *Odyssey* the epic of love, both works are in large part a function of the alternation and interweave of both concepts.

In suggesting that the love-strife tension within early Greek literature is part of a love-strife unconscious that extends beyond literature in Greek culture, we also note the putative instances of epic poetry pertaining to the Trojan War that extend beyond the extant texts of the *Iliad* and the *Odyssey*. If the *Iliad*, for example, offers, actually, a record of barely two weeks in the last year of the war, accounts of other aspects of the story were undoubtedly present in the minds of Homer's audience—and found in those other works that have not survived. That Homer's audience would have been familiar with the significant details of the Trojan War *mythoi* we may infer from allusions to such details found in the *Iliad* itself—which allusions would be pointless without such familiarity.

Thus, for instance, when at II.158-62 reference is made to the carrying off of Helen as the cause of the war,[27] then, as Richmond Lattimore asserts, "the audience knew who Helen was, what she did."[28] Similarly, at the opposite end of the epic, at XXIV.25-30 the reference to the judgment of Paris would make sense only to an audience that had familiarity with that event.[29] In both instances, more description would be necessary from the poet were such awareness not present.

Furthermore, we might infer a broad and deep well of myth from which the poet draws given the plethora of material outside the direct scope of *Iliad*ic events that he introduces frequently— Glaukos' words in VI.144ff, for example, or the tale in IX.529ff adduced by Phoinix.[30] The specific existence of cyclic material beyond Homer is known, of course, via Photius' summary of Proklos' account of the cycle.[31] A number of no-longer extant works is said to have delineated the events leading to and from the *Iliad* and *Odyssey*. As much as the *Cypria*, the so-called *Little Iliad*, and others are understood to have been devised later than what we commonly refer to as Homer's works, yet the material was present earlier. Homer selected his particular subject along which he embroidered his particular details from the morass of oral traditions familiar to him and his audience regarding the war, its etiology and its outcome.[32]

Thus the account of love-strife as it emerges in the *Iliad* begins for us well outside that work, with reference to the beginnings of the war barely a few weeks of which the epic details. The very causes of the Trojan War are embedded in this *eros-eris* rubric. At a celebration of love—the wedding of Peleus and Thetis (a wedding with high inherent disaster-potential—for humans, at least—joining as it does divine and human realms that, by definition, ordinarily remain separate)[33]—the goddess, *Strife* (*Eris*), is not invited, as if to undercut that disaster potential. But as so consistently in Greek myth—and in human experience—the attempt to short-circuit forces greater than *both* gods and humans unleashes the power of those forces unpredictability.

The goddess Eris does what her name, expressing her essence, might be expected to do: inject strife into the midst of this feast of love. She lets fly a piece of fruit at the wedding celebration the curved erotic external form of which bears a potentially eristic message. It reads: "to the fairest of the goddesses"—instantly engendering the strife endemic to its author. While Eris chuckles, Aphrodite, Hera and Athene begin to argue over who among them should be regarded as most appropriate to receive the fruit.[34]

Also consistent with the patterns of Greek myth—which sees endless analogues between the divine and human realms—this strife among the gods and goddesses will yield strife on the human plane. With the assistance of Hermes, the three goddesses seek out the cowherd-prince, Paris (Alexandros) of Troy, to judge among them, on the hillocks of Mount Ida. In this contest, the solution to the strife among the three goddesses is sought through proffered gifts—i.e., bribes. Aphrodite, goddess of love and mother of *Eros*, is triumphant in the strife.

This secondary intersection of divine and human realms (the primary intersection was the love-affair of Peleus and Thetis that yielded the wedding feast on Olympos in the first place) at the meeting point of *eros* and *eris* in turn begets a tertiary intersection. The bribe that gains the victory for Aphrodite over her rivals is the promise of love to the judge: Paris/Alexandros is told that the goddess will gain the most beautiful woman in the world for him. This victory for love also of course brings to Paris the enmity and implied promise of strife from the goddesses who lose the beauty contest. Aphrodite's promise of love, moreover, will itself be inevitably strife-ridden. For the woman she promises him is Helen, who is unfortunately married. The abduction of Helen from Sparta and the court of Menelaos will not only yield strife but strife of the sort that will provide Hera and Athene with the perfect opportunity to enact their eristic inclinations toward the cowherd-prince as surely as Aphrodite fulfills her promise of *eros* for him.

Helen, with her various familial connections to divinity — her father is Zeus, who in the form of a swan had seduced her mother, Leda — is, in her possession of preternatural beauty, the analogue on the human plane of Aphrodite among the goddesses. Long before her meeting with Paris she has been a love-laced source of strife for others. She who is the fruit proffered to Paris had been, prior to her own wedding to Menelaos, a source of potential disaster through warfare among her wooers. Her father, in order to undercut that possibility, had suggested a solution: that whomsoever Helen would select to become her husband would be accepted by all the others as her spouse. More than that, they agreed that, should anyone ever attempt to take her from that fortunate man, they would all assist him in reclaiming her on his behalf. The suitor chosen by Helen was Menelaos — not only king of Sparta, but brother of Agamemnon, who was king of Mykenai and the most economically powerful of the Akhaians.[35]

Thus it is that, several years later, having pronounced Aphrodite the most beautiful of goddesses, Paris-Alexandros finds himself a visitor at Menelaos' court, with Aphrodite as his invisible side-man. With Menelaos conveniently off on Crete for his grandfather's funeral, the Trojan prince abducts Helen with the seductive assistance of the goddess. Helen, direct focus of so much *eros*, will become the direct cause of *eris*. All the Akhaian chieftains rally to Menelaos' assistance as, under Agamemnon's leadership, they set forth in warships for Troy.

All but one, that is, at first. The only Akhaian warrior who exhibits reluctance to join in is the greatest of them: Akhilleus. As the son of a goddess, he has access to certain information that is hidden from ordinary men — such as the matter of his own mortality-immortality. And so he knows that if he goes to Troy to fight — a fight not his own on behalf of a man whom he seems not to respect overly much, but in fulfillment of a pledge the ignoring of which would bring shame upon him — he will perish there. More precisely: he will be choosing death in his prime, but will gain undying glory—*kleos aphthiton*—rather than a long, obscure life back on the farm.

It requires the wiles and quick-wittedness of Odysseus to find Akhilleus and convince him to join the other Akhaians in the assault on Troy. But the interesting issue within the larger issues is this: Helen and Akhilleus are analogues and opposites of each other. She is the embodiment of *eros* and he personifies *eris*. But, due to their parallel kinds of parentage, both of them are more distinctly intermediating beings between divinity and humanity than virtually any other characters in the entire epic cycle—and each of them may be seen as a central "cause" of the war. After all, it was the wedding feast of the divine/human pair whose future progeny was Akhilleus that set in motion the conflict among the goddesses that led to Paris' judgment; and it was Helen, as the prize within that contest-judgment whose abduction led directly to the conflict that would encompass both humans and gods.[36]

The problem of love and strife soon manifests itself again in a completely different mode. Preparing to sail, the Akhaian ships are becalmed at Aulis, apparently as a consequence of offending Artemis.[37] Thus Agamemnon sends for his daughter Iphigenia under the pretext of wishing to present her to Akhilleus, his greatest warrior—again: *eris* incarnate—in marriage. The ostensive marriage (*eros*) with *eris* incarnate for Iphigenia leads, instead, to her sacrifice—which for Agamemnon begets the *eris* with Klytaimnestra (who, we must not forget, is Helen's half-sister), which will doom him a decade later.[38]

II The Passion of Akhilleus

All of these events precede the action detailed in the *Iliad* itself; yet there is ample evidence of their role in the tradition familiar to Homer and his audience. The subject matter of the *Iliad* is, in its entirety, of course, *strife*. The Trojan War is its context, as its purpose is to focus on an extended moment in that event that concentrates all the elements endemic to the human condition of which wars such as the Trojan War are so consistently a part. And the take-off point for the poem—the event that precipitates the action of the poem as the fabrication that permits the account of the action—

is strife: the confrontation between Agamemnon and Khryses that engenders the conflict between Akhilleus and Agamemnon.[39] They who would have been joined by love at the inception of the war are joined by strife at the inception of the poem.

Yet the *Iliad*, in broad strokes and small details, is as much occupied with love as it is with strife—love as both a *source* of strife and a condition *intertwined* with it. The bone of contention in the double-beginning of the poem is a woman—a love-object[40] of Agamemnon's which, when finally given up by him, leads him to usurp, as compensation to himself, a love-object of Akhilleus.[41] Naturally, the emphasis is more on the latter than on the former— since the ostensive subject of the poem is Akhilleus and his *menis*. Thus we are made aware of Briseis' feelings—"and the woman went with them all unwilling still" (I. 348)—indicating the most obvious aspect of "love-relationship" that she represents and the usurpation of which leads to Akhilleus' anger. And the epic is constantly, when focusing the words of its warriors, pre-occupied with love-objects as prizes—not only Helen, but women, particularly Trojan women, in general.[42]

But other layers of love are—not far beneath the obvious surface—at issue in the strife at the poem's beginning. As the women under consideration here *are* love-*objects*—not overly different from cattle, tripods and sackable cities—the issue is not love of *them*, really, but how they serve love of *self*. It is Agamemnon's love of *self* that is compromised as it is his self that is assaulted by Khryses, (father of Khryseis, who comes to beg for her back), which provokes that strife-ridden exchange at I.32. His honor, as leader of all the Akhaians, his status, his unequivocal sense of who he *is*, is threatened (I.118-19: "Then find me some *honor-prize* that shall be my own, lest I alone/ among the Argives go without, since that would be unseemly" (emphasis added). The parrying of that threat, in turn, *necessitates* (in the sense of *moira*—fate—with its plans for all of these characters), Agamemnon's assault on *Akhilleus'* self-love—love of his honor, his sense of who *he* is.[43] These are, to be sure, variations on a theme—in the one case, Agamemnon's stature as leader has been attacked; on the other, Akhilleus' stature as a warrior has been insulted[44]—but that shared theme is love: *self-love*. Each is willing to sacrifice his friends' well-being for love of the honor that each holds highest.[45]

Indeed, the very theme of the poem—Akhilleus' *menis* and its consequences—will, from this beginning point, be seen to be a passion (rather than, per se, a madness or an anger)[46] that intrinsically interweaves threads of love and strife. This is the nature of Akhilleus—to be passionate, *menis*-ridden—and the consequences of his actions go beyond himself: they affect the war at large as they create the poem at large. Akhilleus is an intense microcosm of humanity, as the Trojan War is, as is the *Iliad*, which delineates a crucial period/extended moment in the "life" of both. What is interwoven in Akhilleus is interwoven in the war, in the poem, in human experience—as well as echoed and echoing the experience of divinity, albeit, obviously, with less dire consequences for the immortals.

Indeed, in the architectonic of the poem and its place in the war, the divine love/strife interweave is clear: in the largest sense, love/Aphrodite created the action that precipitates the events of the poem; in the course of the poem, Ares and Aphrodite are intertwined as Troy's most visible divine patrons; beyond the poem, Troy will be destroyed, in the largest sense, by strife/war/Ares.

The gods are a reference point in the initial exchange between Agamemnon and Akhilleus: the first refers to the second as god-loved (I.176, 178) who loves strife (I.179). The strife between them, in turn—out of the need on the part of Akhilleus' loving mother (and of Fate and of the poem) to appease Akhilleus' injured self-love—leads to strife among the gods. In responding to Thetis' request to Zeus "[to] put strength into the Trojans until the Akhaians give my son his rights, and his honor is increased among them" (509-10), Zeus expresses dread at the consequences, which will "set me in conflict/ with Hera..." (518-19)—yet he agrees to fulfill her request. And indeed, verbal *eris* immediately follows on Olympos, echoing the strife between Akhilleus and Agamemnon on the Trojan plain below.

Here, on Olympos, its consequences for the principals are resolved by humor: Hephaistos, who "fears" for his mother's potential fate should Zeus get too angry with her (588: that she might be "struck down"—which could never really happen; gods and goddesses don't *get* struck down...), as the Kalkhas-like counselor, ends up as a source of loud divine laughter. The counterpart of human tragedy is divine comedy; the building-blocks are, in both places and their dramas, interwoven blocks of love and strife. Book I is dominated, for its human protagonists, by the strife the mood of which is still uppermost as the scene comes to an end (487-92). For the gods at the corresponding end, of a long day, love is uppermost (609-11):

> Zeus the Olympian and lord of lightning went to his own bed,
> where he always lay when sweet sleep arrived;
> there he went up and slept, with Hera of the golden throne beside him.[47]

Book Two offers a crucial double interlude. It describes the deception to Agamemnon, sent by way of a dream, which will set in motion—well, all the rest of the events in the epic; and includes the renowned and extensive descriptive listing of the different groups who participated in the Great War on the Akhaian side, and all their ships. That which to us is perhaps most boring in the epic would no doubt, as the post-Trojan War generations carried forward, been of keenest interest to auditors who hoped and expected to find their own tribal names within that descriptive listing.

Book Three returns us to the principals involved in the *larger* quarrel in which that of Akhilleus and Agamemnon is embedded, in *strife* regarding *love*. Alexandros/Paris ("on account of whom this strife has arisen..." (87) faces Menelaos ("to fight together for Helen and all of her possessions." 70). It is singularly appropriate that Helen, symbol of love—ultimate love-object of contention—and direct cause of the strife that is this war, should, at the moment she is called upon to come witness this contest, be shown in the midst of weaving at her loom. She is weaving the very scenes of strife of which she *is*, as direct cause, the weaver: "struggles that they endured on her behalf at the hands of Ares" (128). But it is *love* that saves Alexandros at the climactic moment of strife with Menelaos, when the latter is dragging Alexandros back to the Akhaian camp by his helmet. For Aphrodite, Helen's counterpart in the world of the gods and Alexandros' patron, "...broke the chinstrap, made from the hide of a slaughtered bullock/ and the helmet came away empty in the heavy hand [of Menelaos]." (375-6)[48]

Directly after his eristic failure with his lover's husband, Alexandros/Paris is wafted by Aphrodite into the bed-chamber whither Love brings Helen—as in Sparta, so in Troy, Paris will triumph over his opponent on the battlefield of the bed. Yet not without an initial setback: Helen, called by love, initially refuses. Her eristic tone to Aphrodite[49] is rebuked, however, as the goddess warns her of how easily divine love can turn to hate—so that, out of fear, Helen returns to the field of love. Alexandros, in responding to Helen's derision, asserts that "for this time Menelaos has beaten me with Athene's help;/ another time I shall beat him, for there are also gods on our side"—and, as if to underscore both positive assertions, commands: "but come now let us go to bed and turn to love-making..." (441), explicitly recalling how his love-conquest of her *is* his triumph, with divine assistance, over Menelaos, as he continues, that he has never felt so impassioned for her,

> not when I took you the first time from Lakedaimon the lovely
> and caught you up and carried you away in sea-faring ships,
> and lay with you on the island of Kranae in the bed of love,
> not even then, as now did I so love you and desire seize me.
> (443-6)

While Alexandros and Helen make love, Menelaos continues to rage down on the battlefield. But Agamemnon's words to close Book Three still seek a negotiated end to war-strife based on the ascription of singular victory to Menelaos.[50]

Naturally, Fate and the purposes of the gods, men and poets could not be fulfilled if events concluded as Agamemnon would wish. Helen is still in Alexandros' bedchamber, Akhilleus is still sulking, alive, in his tent—and twenty-one books of the *Iliad* remain to be sung. So, as Book Four opens, the gods, seated on Olympos as they imbibe nectar—that tasty liquid endemic to what they are as immortals[51]—are gathered around Zeus. Zeus asks, in balancing in his mind and those of the other deities, whether strife or love should be the next move in the game of human suffering (13-16):

> So now the victory is with Ares-loving Menelaos.
> Let us consider then how these these things shall be accomplished,

Whether again to stir up grim warfare and the terrible
Fighting, or to cast down love and make them friends with each
  other.

This query provokes, once more, strife between Zeus and Hera—which is resolved by Zeus' agreement to permit Troy's destruction and the responding agreement from Hera that Zeus may, in exchange, sack *her* favorite cities,[52] "Argos and Sparta and Mykenane of the wide ways, whenever [any of them] become hateful to your heart" (52-3). The resolution of divine strife is to renew strife among the humans below: so Athene, warrior-goddess "persuaded the fool's heart" (104) in the Trojan Pandaros, and he lets fly an arrow toward Menelaos, wounding him. While Menelaos is being tended by a physician, (Makharos), "the ranks of the armored Trojans came on/ The Akhaians again put on their armor, and remembered their own warcraft" (221-2). Gathered for battle, inspired by Agamemnon's admonitions and encouragements, the Akhaians—driven on by Athene, as the Trojans are by Ares. Both sides are driven by Terror and Fear and Eris "whose wrath is relentless,

> she the sister and companion of man-killing Ares,
> she who is only a little thing at first, but thereafter
> grows until with her head striking heaven she strides the earth,
> she then hurled down bitterness equally between both sides
> coming through the onslaught and making men's pain heavier.
> (440-45)

The description of the battle that fills out the rest of Book Four introduces—in particular, with regard to Odysseus—the motif of an Akhaian killing a Trojan to avenge the specific death of the former's "brave companion" (491), which anticipates, of course, the denouement of the poem. Odysseus strikes down Demokoon, a son of Priam (499-503), to avenge the death of Leukos, for whose "killing [by Antiphos, another son of Priam] Odysseus was stirred to terrible anger" (494). This turning point in the immediate action—causing the Trojans led by Hektor ro draw back—presages Akhilleus' slaughter of Hektor to avenge Patroklos' death, as it introduces a powerful reason for such killing. It is for love of Leukos, and for their friendship, that Odysseus becomes so furious as, suddenly, to "stride out among the great warriors (495), the Trojans gave way / before the spear-throwing man" (497-8). Love breeds an upsurge in the intensity of strife.

In Book Five, focusing on the eristic skills of Diomedes—this is his *aristeia*, his moment to shine; it is one of many moments in which the depiction of a warrior's glorious fighting talents anticipates the portrayal of Akhilleus in his conquest of Hektor—Athene and Ares initially withdraw, but Athene returns to support Diomedes. With such support, even wounded by a Trojan arrow he fights spectacularly—warned by Athene, however, not to *overstep* his bounds by battling against deities, which would be *hubris* and lead to his demise. Except for Aphrodite, that is: "her at least you may stab with the sharp bronze" (132). In his brief encounter with Aineias, the latter is rescued by Aphrodite, (his mother), whom Diomedes wounds, in turn—knowing her as a god without warcraft, not one of those goddesses who range in order among the ranks of men in the fighting (331-2). *Love,* not as a progenitor of strife, but as an interferor with its progress and consequences, is injured. She is *rescued* by strife—or more precisely the brother and male personification of Eris, who is also Aphrodite's lover, (as we may recall from a different thread within the tapestry of these stories)—Ares, god of war, who "gave her the gold-bridled / horses" (363), that carry her in Ares' chariot, driven by Iris, away from the battlefield and up to Olympos.

The fundamental difference between gods and humans could not be more evident here: Aphrodite was surely in no danger of more than a bit of pain, but that, too, is swiftly eliminated as she is healed by Dione. Nonetheless, Zeus warns the goddess of love to "concern yourself only with the lovely secrets of marriage" (429)—her proper battlefield. Hera and Athene join forces on behalf of the Danaans (aka the Akhaians) against the force of Ares' support of the Trojans. The culmination of this equation finds Athene assisting the resurgent Diomedes in a direct confrontation with Ares: the god is wounded by the man (846-63). As Love and War had both entered the fray on behalf of Troy, both are injured by great Diomedes.

There is considerable irony here: though Ares is pro-Trojan, he is, among the gods, most like Akhilleus the Akhaian: the consummate warrior.[53] Akhilleus' withdrawal from the battle makes possible the events that bring both Aphrodite and Ares directly into the action as Diomedes assumes the position of dominance (temporarily) vacated by Akhilleus. Zeus, king of gods as Agamemnon is king of men, in rebuking Ares—"most hateful are you to me of all the gods who hold Olympos. / For eternal quarreling is dear to your heart, wars and battles" (l. 890-91)—precisely repeats Agamemnon's very words of rebuke to Akhilleus back at I.177. Ares is then healed, at Zeus' order, by Paieon. All is calm on Olympos once more, as Book V ends—in profound contrast with the unhealed, bitter strife/love-engendered *menis* that attended Akhilleus' departure from Agamemnon's presence, and which creates the epic.

Beyond the famous encounter between Diomedes and Glaukos in Book Six, Hektor returns from the battle, first greeting his mother, then turning to his brother Alexandros' house, where he admonishes him for withdrawing to love while all outside the walls are engaged in the strife occcasioned by his theft of Helen/love/love object. Alexandros defends himself, stating that, indeed, Helen was just then urging him back into the fight with soft words (l. 337-8). Again the ultimate source of *eros* urges someone toward *eris*—as the equation between the battlefields of bed and plain is emphasized, together with Alexandros' varying degrees of success in each. Helen herself speaks characteristically: condemning herself as the source of strife, but reminding them and us, as frequently we *are* reminded, that "the gods brought it about that these vile things must be" (349) and again "us two, upon whom Zeus set a vile destiny (*moira*)..." (357). The events that precipitated the descent into war are known by all, as is the notion recognized that such events are the events with which epic poetry concerns itself: "...so that hereafter / we shall be made into things of song for the people of the future." (357-8). The actors in this drama, from Zeus to lowly Thersites, represent aspects of a human picture so complex that they are more significant *as* symbols than *qua* them*selves*: they will be sung about as humans and deities *because* they symbolize aspects of the human condition beyond themselves.

Hektor moves on, this time to his own wife, Andromakhe. A strong contrast is immediately suggested between the Hektor-Andromakhe relationship and that of Alexandros/Paris-Helen—even to Helen encouraging Paris to the battlefield, having expressed bitter desire for his death (in Book Three), while Andromakhe will beg Hektor to stay *out* of the battle, *lest* he die.[54] She does this while in fact offering concrete advice, based on her observations from the upper wall where Hektor finds her, as to how to engage the Akhaians successfully.[55] So, too, in the midst of the strife of war, whereas we have found Paris/Alexandros and Helen in an illusory *domestic* moment (321-4)—where in her quarters we and Hektor found him busy with his armor and Helen busy with her weaving, but each is *alone,* self-focused and self-engaged, post-sexual *passion*—by contrast Hektor and Andromakhe, in a scene far *removed* from the calm of home and hearth as well as from sexual passion, are, yet, engaged (in perhaps the most poignant scene in the *Iliad*) in husband-wife love (as opposed to mere passion) at its most profound.

What begins with Andromakhe's summary of all the aspects of love that Hektor is to her—"Hektor, you are thus father to me, and my honored mother/ you are my brother, and you are my young husband" (429-30)—culminates with the arrival of the fruit of their love, Astyanax. We are led to Hektor's tragic prayer to Zeus and the other gods on his son's behalf: his fatherly love culminates with the hope for his son's success in war-strife.[56] There surely is no passage more heart-breaking in all of literature, for every auditor and reader of the Trojan hero's heaven-flung words knows—because they have all heard this story so many times before—that not only are his hopes doomed not to be fulfilled. They know that Hektor will be defeated, his body dragged again and again around the city; that the city will fall; that Andromakhe will be enslaved to some Akhaian as his honor-prize—and that, at the command of Odysseus, Astyanax will be dashed from the walls of the burning citadel to the rocks below, lest he grow up and avenge his father's death: a far cry from the fate for which Hektor so urgently prays.

Perhaps even the players in the drama have some sense of this—yet they must continue to move forward with their lives, against whatever Fate has in store for them all, with whatever control they have, or believe they have. Andromakhe returns to her weaving and Hektor to his fighting. Each player has a particular role to play, even as their roles are often so excruciatingly interwoven, their threads running sometimes along parallel and sometimes along perpendicular patterns. Thus the interlude of these Book Six passages, particularly as they are juxtaposed in the memory of Homer's audience with those in Book Three (ls 320-448), above all present a contrastive view of the *strife*-ridden love of Paris and Helen with the *love*-ridden relationship of Hektor and Andromakhe.[57]

Yet, as Hijmans[58] and others[59] have noted, in the end, in the *Iliad*ic world, Helen and Andromakhe have more in common with each other than what separates them. As much as Helen is, at least in large part, trapped by circumstances greater than herself, so too is Andromakhe. Andromakhe's description of what Hektor is to her (ls 429-30) is not just metaphor: she was an object cast adrift by strife (Akhilleus, by irony, the perpetrator—413-28) before becoming a focus of Hektor's love. Indeed, "it would be far better for me/ to sink into the earth when I have lost you" (410-11), she says with conviction. Both women are alone, entirely dependant on the eristic success and survival of men. They remain part of the "object" situation that defined Khryseis and Briseis in Book I: their nature, their existence as love-objects—objects of sexual and male-ego-gratification—creates strife which reinforces their isolation. Homer's final simile in Book Six underscores the joyous eagerness—the love of strife—that drives Paris back into battle after his problematic love interlude:

> As when some stalled horse, that has been corn-fed at the manger,
> breaking free of his rope, gallops over the plain in thunder,
> to his accustomed bathing place in a sweet-running river,
> and in the pride of his strength holds high his head, and his mane floats
> over his shoulders; sure of his glorious strength, the quick knees
> carry him to the beloved sites and pastures of horses,
> so came Paris, son of Priam, from the height of Pergamon
> shining in all of his armor of war as the sun shines
> laughing aloud, and his quick feet carried him..." (506-14).

Honor is on both his and Hektor's minds, as they return, together, to the fray.

As Hektor's return from battle in Book Six had echoed—contrastively—that of Paris in Book Three, so, in Book Seven, Hektor's duel with Aias will echo that between Paris and Menelaos in Book Three. Once again, single combat is suggested as a means of resolving the strife—Helenos speaking to Hektor (46-53) and Hektor to the gathered Akhaians and Trojans (67-91)—again self-love and the concern for glory culminate the suggestion. In the end, Aias is selected by lot—by fate, indeed—to oppose Hektor. Among the details that separate this encounter from that between Alexandros and Menelaos is, of course, its conclusion: night, brought on by neither man nor god, is the reason for terminating the unfinished struggle. In strife where neither warrior has the personal enmity against the other that is endemic to the between Paris and Menelaos—or later, between Hektor and Akhilleus—not only can the contest end undecided, but it may end with recognition of each other's eristic skills and with gifts exchanged. Hektor's words go to the heart of the Iliadic chivalric code under such circumstances; he suggests to Aias that they exchange their gifts so that any of the Akhaians or Trojans may say of us: "These two fought each other in heart-consuming strife, but joined with each other in close friendship, before they parted." (300-302).

Again, then, a different side of love—the friendship derived from respect in turn derived from the kind of enthusiasm that had brought Alexandros and Hektor into battle at the end of Book Six and had brought the Akhaians out at the end of Book Two and that, in part, fueled the war as a whole—is embedded in the midst of strife. It is recognition of this kind of love—*warrior* love—and sadness at its consequences that fuels Antenor's speech to the assembled Trojans that evening: that Helen—*woman-as-object-love*—be given back in order to eliminate that source of strife. But Alexandros, "for whose sake this strife has arisen" (374, 388) will not give up that love-object which—he stands on common ground in this with Akhilleus and Agamemnon in Book One—is, in that refusal, the reflection of his *self*-love. Fittingly, this lengthy moment ends with the gathering and burial/burning of the dead—Akhaians and Trojans on their respective sides.

With this culmination of events and motifs we arrive, in Book Eight, at a kind of interlude that begins with the gods in debate and continues with Akhaians and Trojans dying on the battlefield. We are reminded in the midst of this carnage, by Athene (in her words to Hera) of the immediate reason for the fierce battle that gives the Trojans, briefly, the edge: "...Zeus has bent to the wish of Thetis/ who grasped his knees and stroked his chin in her hand/ entreating him to honor Akhilleus, sacker of cities" (370-2).[60] Akhilleus' self-love engenders the present configuration of strife. And so, Zeus adds later (to Hera): "For Hektor the huge will not sooner be stayed from the fighting,/ until there stirs by the ships the swift-footed son of Peleus... (473-4) — which succession will take place soon enough.

As if the epic has begun anew — having been reminded in Book Eight of Akhilleus' *menis* and its consequences — we are brought, as Book Nine begins, to a scene reminiscent of that in Book Two: Agamemnon is suggesting to the Akhaians that they return home. At this juncture it is the long-winded Nestor who, as so often, speaks up, reminding Agamemnon of his insult to Akhilleus "whom Zeus in his heart loves" (117). Agamemnon agrees to make good the insult with an array of gifts that include the — untouched — Briseis, in order to resolve the strife between them, which is limiting Akhaian success in their strife with the Trojans; Agamemnon is advised to restore Akhilleus' object of love and symbol of honor — which object is as much a symbol of self-love as it is a symbol of the love and honor accorded him by the Akhaians. Phoinix, Aias, and Odysseus are dispatched as an embassy to Akhilleus.

The hero is found playing music in his tent, attended by his "beloved ...companion" (205), Patroklos. Odysseus, all too prophetically, reminds him that "it will be an affliction to you hereafter, there will be no remedy/ found to heal the evil thing when it is done" (249-50). Most significantly, it will be his beloved friend Patroklos' death — aside from that of Danaans generally — that will be such an affliction. Odysseus invokes Akhilleus' father — who will be re-invoked when, so much later, Akhilleus will return Hektor's body to Priam. Friend-love and father-love are invoked to parry Akhilleus' strife with Agamemnon. And to parry Akhilleus' self-love: the honor implied by the list of gifts offered him, and the possibility, ultimately, of glory to be gained in a specific battle: "For now you might kill Hektor..." (304).

Yet Akhilleus refuses, referring, in response, to Briseis as "the bride of my heart" (336) taken from him by Agamemnon—and focusing, in fact, on the whole subject of love as the centerpiece of his resistance and of the whole war:

> ...was it not for the sake of lovely-haired Helen?
> Among mortal men who love their wives are the sons of Atreus alone? Since any who is a good man, and careful,
> loves her who is his own and cares for her, even as I now
> loved this one from my heart, though it was my spear that won her. (339-43)

Ironically enough, Akhilleus echoes his Akhaian nemesis' twice-used technique: he pretends to be ready to pick up his ships and return home (357-63).

Phoinix's entreaties repeat those of Odysseus from a slightly different angle, invoking father-imagery (438-95), prophesying (510-12), likening his supplication of Akhilleus to that typically directed toward the gods. Tales of victorious heroes who have yet lost much complete Phoinix's lengthy speech.[61] Briefly, bluntly, in dismay, finally, Telemonian Aias invokes the love of friends—and unwittingly, in alluding to the blood-price compensated for a brother or a child, offers us the irony of Akhilleus' future in this poem: to need to accept, too late, the "blood-price" for his "brother," Patroklos, for the child—Hektor—of the father—Priam—who will, in the end, recall Akhilleus' own father to Akhilleus. With the departure of Odysseus and Aias, Akhilleus and Patroklos each goes to sleep with a woman (663-68). In its dismal, unhappy brevity, the passage describing this lull of love contrasts strongly with the lengthy passages in Book Three and Book Six that refer to Paris and Hektor and *their* respective beloved women. Clinging to strife-ridden *menis*, the hero and his alter-ego have little space for that sort, or perhaps any sort, of love.

Book Ten offers the interlude of spies and Odysseus' and Diomedes' success against Dolon as well as Rhesos and the twelve Thracians. Book Eleven furthers the series of pre-Akhillean *aristeiai*: Agamemnon's and Aias' on the one hand; Hektor's on the other. Once more Diomedes and Odysseus work together; later, Odysseus is rescued by Menelaos and Aias in concert from surrounding Trojans. (Had they not done so, and had Odysseus perished, the story would have had a different outcome, given Odysseus' singular role in devising the stratagem of the great wooden horse to take Troy—and his silencing of his fellow Akhaeans in its belly when Helen almost tricked them into revealing themselves, as we will later hear from Menelaos himself in *Odyssey* 2:20).[62]

In the midst of all this, Akhilleus—for the first time we *watch* him *watching*—calls to Patroklos; and the narrator intones: "this is the beginning of the evil" (604). In his growing interest in the action, anticipating further supplication of him by the Akhaians, Akhilleus sends Patroklos to inquire into events—specifically into the apparent wounding of Makhaon. It is this expression of interest, of course, which will offer Nestor the opportunity to expound and to seek further to draw the drama on, via the suggestion to Patroklos that, if Akhilleus

> ...is drawing back from some prophecy known in his own heart
> and by Zeus' will, his honored mother has told him of something,
> let him send you out, at least, and the rest of the Myrmidon people
> follow you, and you may be a light given to the Danaans.
> And let him give you his splendid armor to wear to the fighting,
> so that perhaps the Trojans will think you are he, and give way
> from their attack, and the fighting sons of the Akhaians get wind
> again after hard work... (793-800)

A fateful suggestion. Patroklos returns to Akhilleus, healing Eurypylos' wound along the way: Patroklos heals what, in a sense, his alter-ego, Akhilleus, has engendered (by his absence from the battlefield)—and also exhibits a skill at healing wounds that is ordinarily associated obliquely with Akhilleus himself, who was trained by the consummate physician, Kheiron the centaur. More significant, Akhilleus, in sending Patroklos out, has taken the first step toward the latter's death.

Book Twelve begins, on the other hand, with presages of *Hektor*'s doom, as his *aristeia* brings him toward the Akhaian ships: "who, as he had before, fought on like a whirlwind..." (40), "...and it is his own courage that kills him" (46). So, too, Sarpedon, as he exclaims to Glaukos that love of glory must push them on:

> But now, seeing that the spirits of death stand close about us
> in their thousands, no man can turn aside nor escape them,
> let us go on and win glory for ourselves, or yield it to others.

And on the Akhaian side, Telemonian Aias is solidly spectacular in holding his own as he protects the ships from destruction. Trojan fire is met, in Book Thirteen, by water—Poseidon himself encourages the Akhaians against the Zeus-powered Trojans. As the Aiantes *love* the fray—"…joyful in the delight of battle that the god had put into their spirits…" (82)—Zeus and Poseidon

> …had looped over both sides a crossing
> cable of strong discord and the closing of battle, not to be
> slipped, not to be broken, which unstrung the knees of many.
> (358-60)

Menelaos at a moment of his glory (520-39) reminds us of what drives *him*: anger at the theft of his wife and insult to the guest-host relationship. And indeed, that reminder that love is the source of strife and with it, death, comes forth once more in Hektor's rebuke to Paris:

> Evil Paris, beautiful, woman-crazy, cajoling:
> where has Deiphobos gone, and the strength of the prince
>   Helenos,
> Adamas, Asios' son, and Asios, son of Hyrtakos?
> Where is Othryoneos? Now all steep Ilion is lost
> entirely; now your own headlong destruction is certain. (769-73)

Surprisingly, Paris asserts his skill and success in the *eris* of the battlefield:

> … My mother bore me not entirely lacking in Warcraft.
> …. I think that we shall not
> come short in Warcraft, in so far as the strength stays with us.
> (777, 785-6)

If in Book Three, Paris failing on the battlefield was followed by his return to the bed of love-making, while Book Six—after his and Hektor's respective love-home situations have been contrasted—ended with the exultant return of both, in love of battle, to the battlefield; Book Thirteen ends with Paris' and Hektor's success on the battlefield: "They went on, to where the clamor and fighting were greatest... and now Zeus stirred them into the fighting" (789, 794), together with the others, "and Hektor led them, Priam's son, a man like the murderous war god..." (802-3).

This will be swiftly followed, at the beginning of Book Fourteen, by the march of Zeus and Hera into their Olympian bedroom. As Agamemnon considers a return to Akhaia once again, in the face of Hektor's and the Trojans' success against his troops—this time met in words, however, by no Thersites, but by Odysseus and Diomedes of the Great War Cry—Hera prepares herself to battle Zeus with love, in spite of the fact that in that strife-ridden moment of Trojan success, he seems "despicable in her eyes" (158):

> And perhaps he might be taken with desire to live in love with her
> Next to her skin, and she might be able to drift an innocent
> Warm sleep across his eyelids, and seal his crafty perceptions. (163-5)

She deceives the goddess of love in order to use *love* to deceive Zeus and to undercut his *eristic* plans—which deceptions are born of the strife between herself who "defend(s) the Danaans, while [he] help(s) the Trojans" (192). Under the pretext of needing something special to renew the love of Ocean and Tethys against the current strife within their relationship—"since for a long time, now, they have stayed apart from each other and from the bed of love..." (207-8)—she obtains from Aphrodite a special wrapping that gives her irresistibility in order most effectively to seduce Zeus.[63] She convinces Sleep to do her bidding—to agree to close Zeus' eyelids after lovemaking—by promising him love:

> Come now, do it, and I will give you one of the younger
> Graces for you to marry, and she shall be called your lady;
> Pasithea, since all your days you have loved her forever. (267-9)

—this after the promise of a golden throne had failed to convince him.

Zeus is bewitched ("desire was a mist about his close heart" (294)). In telling Hera how desirous of love-making he is, he compares this moment to seven instances when he had felt such desire, all paling in the memory by comparison to the moment — and each recollection that of a love-indiscretion that bred strife with Hera and disaster for the love-subject: the wife of Ixion, Danae, Europa, Semele, Alkmene, Demeter, and Leto.[64] Seven erotic sources of *eris* between himself and Hera form Zeus' plea to seduce the one who would seduce him!

Nowhere is such an obviously eristic tone to *eros* articulated as distinctly as in this scene: the litany from Zeus framed by the poet's own litany: "then with false lying purpose Lady Hera answered him" (300, 329). Nowhere else is the bed of love so clearly a form of battlefield — used for ends beyond itself, and here, specifically to further Hera's side in the *eris* of Trojan-Danaan conflict. Nowhere is the contrast between gods and humans more apparent: the divine love-making interlude on Olympos facilitates renewed war-making before the walls of Troy. Hera's success in love-battle is followed by Poseidon-induced success on the field of strife (as, so frequently, the divine cards are stacked against Hektor's ultimate success):

On the other side, glorious Hektor ordered the Trojans,
and now Poseidon of the dark hair and glorious Hektor
strained to its deadliest the division of battle, the one
bringing power to the Trojans, and the god to the Argives.
(388-91)

Can Hektor possibly win when he is opposed by Poseidon himself?

Strife continues to range the human stage below Olympos in tandem with death. This grows further into Book Fifteen, both in terms of the strife between Zeus and Hera with which the book opens — the aftermath of falsely used "love" is strife ("...see if your love-making in bed will help you/ that way you lay with me apart from the gods, and deceived me." (32-33)) — and in terms of the strife on the field below, as *aristeia* scenes for Hektor and Aias, respectively, intensify. The details of the denouement are being put into place—as Zeus specifically presents to Hera the fate to come of Patroklos and Hektor and, ultimately, Troy (64-71)—yet not before Akhilleus' honor will have been assuaged. Between the *aristeia* of Aias and that of Hektor, we get a glimpse of gentle Patroklos administering to Eurypylos, (as noted above), and then, distressed, running to bring Akhilleus back into battle.

This is where we locate Patroklos as Book Sixteen opens. This is, of course, the book that begins the fulfillment of Zeus' predictions made in Book Fifteen. At the heart of the matter is the focused weave of love and strife for which all the previous words and actions have been anticipatory. In permitting Patroklos to don his (Akhilleus') own armor and go into battle "disguised"—the reversal of all those incidents in which gods have disguised themselves as men (Patroklos assumes the *demas* and *aude* of godlike Akhilleus, as it were)—Akhilleus warns him not to go too far. Otherwise, (90), "you will diminish my honor"—and the gods might crush him (Patroklos) for his hubris. Akhilleus sends Patroklos out

> so that you can win great honor and glory for me
> before all the Danaans, so that they will bring back to me
> the lovely girl, and give additional shining gifts as well. (84-6)

What has always been at issue, then, *remains* at issue: Akhilleus' self-love, his emotional and egotistical needs—that send Patroklos into the field of strife. And to his death.

Two aspects of the Akhilleus-Patroklos relationship have been frequently discussed by commentators. Whether or not they were lovers and in what way, is one.[65] Ultimately, that question is irrelevant to this discussion. What is both obvious and significant—both in terms of the architecture of the poem and in terms of particular details—is that their relationship is unique, primary among the friend-love relationships that are so much an ongoing motif of the strife in the poem.

The second aspect of this relationship frequently discussed is the sense in which, after all, Patroklos is actually Akhilleus' alter-ego[66]—that he represents part of the complete Akhilleus: the gentler, more passive, more loving side. Their dynamic is, then, intrinsically one of love-strife interweave. It is for this reason, in the end, that Patroklos will be destroyed: he exceeds the reasonable bound of being the part (in both senses: drama and division) of Akhilleus that he is not. If, then, Patroklos is, finally, destroyed by Hektor, bringing to the surface a different aspect of Akhilleus' *menis*—grief mixed with anger, anger toward himself whom he well recognizes as Patroklos' killer as surely as Hektor was—which death will finally induce Akhilleus to pick up the arms of strife that he left so long aside, then Akhilleus' *eros*-induced return to strife is the mirror-image of his *eris*-ridden giving up of *eros* (personified by Briseis) in Book One.

It *is* an aspect of himself that has been killed with Patroklos' defeat and death or, more to the point, dishonored. His self-love has again been affronted—in a manner far more dire and immediately tragic than was so for Book One and the argument with Agamemnon that is so petty. Patroklos, the *eros* side of Akhilleus the warrior, goes forth in *eris*, culminating in the duel with Hektor that is the penultimate such pairing in the poem. He is killed, bringing Akhilleus back into *eris*. Patroklos' *aristeia* is short-lived and, in the end, a failure: his death undoes what he had initially accomplished in pushing the Trojans back and doesn't bring Akhilleus honor (except indirectly, in that his death forces Akhilleus back onto the field—but one could argue that Akhilleus' subsequent behavior, how he treats Hektor's body, *diminishes* whatever honor has accrued by his return to, and action in, the battle).

The high point of Patroklos' success is his killing of Sarpedon. This represents a series of incidents in which gods *are* indirectly hurt by the strife among humans: earlier on, Ares' son (Askalaphos) died, and here, Zeus's son, dies: fate—*moira*—overrules divine love of men engaged in such strife. Sarpedon is, of course, also a harbinger of Troy's fate and at the same time, because of his divine parentage, an anticipator of Akhilleus' fate, as he is a symbol of human fate—even god-sprung humans.

Such fate continues to operate through Book Seventeen, as, delaying the denouement, Homer builds so agonizingly slowly to the moment when Akhilleus will *know* of Patroklos' fate. Among the details of death, we encounter the fateful moment (194-7) when Hektor dons Akhilleus' armor stripped from Patroklos' body. It is the armor of doom—as even Zeus observes:

> ...Ah, poor wretched man!
> There is no thought of death in your mind now, and yet death stands
> close behind you as you put on the immortal armor
> of a surpassing man... (200-203)

Yet Hektor, too, must have his final *aristeia*—in order (as Zeus observes) to compensate him for the death that shall too soon reach him. So, too, another Trojan advance is necessary to set the appropriate eristic stage for Akhilleus' return to battle. (Had Patroklos fully succeeded there would have *been* no need for Akhilleus' return to the fray.) Appropriately enough, too, it will be Antilokhos who will actually bring the news to Akhilleus of Patroklos' death and its attendant disasters—Antilokhos who will, if anyone, succeed Patroklos in Akhilleus' affections.

So, suddenly, Antilokhos breaks the news to Akhilleus as Book Eighteen opens. Brilliantly, the poet presents from Akhilleus a wordless reaction, describing his gestures and finally his outcry—echoed beneath the depths of the sea by his mother: for now, indeed, the die is cast and the chain of events has begun to tighten, moving one link closer to Akhilleus' *own* death. The mother-son love-relationship that, from Book One—with Akhilleus' entreaty of Thetis to engineer the revenge for his affronted honor—had been the ultimate shaper of the strife of the poem, centers around the final moments of strife to come, as Thetis notes, with tears, to her son, that "then I must lose you soon, my child, by what you are saying/ since it is decreed that your death must come soon after Hektor's" (95-6).

That love that engineered strife will now be called upon to produce the weapons of strife that will bring about the final duel of the poem. The self-love-sourced *eris* that is the ruin of humans is what Akhilleus rues, in responding to his mother's comment and anticipating his own death (the first *third* of that death begun with Patroklos and, as we shall see, its second third to continue with the death of Hektor):

> ... would that strife would vanish away from among gods and mortals

and gall, which makes a man grow angry for all his great mind,
that gall of anger that swarms like smoke inside a man's heart
and becomes a thing sweeter to him by far than the dripping of
honey. (107-110)

At the same time, his *menis* assumes a new form, albeit hardly diminished in intensity from when it had been directed at Agamemnon, as he vows (336) twelve headless Trojans to Patroklos' ghost in "anger over [his] slaying."

In the context of the request for armor for her son from the smith-god, Hephaistos, Thetis reminds us of the ill-starred event that precipitated the chain of events leading to this moment and beyond: the grief of inter-marrying divinity and mortal; her love of now-aged Peleus (428-35).[67] That love, which had led to the birth of Akhilleus is, then, the precipitator of the strife in which, ultimately, her son, product of that love, must perish. The most noteworthy of the arms manufactured by Hephaistos for Akhilleus is, of course, the shield. In the long run, it can't prevent his death, as human activities can't step outside their description on its layers, as the human condition of which the poem offers a microcosm cannot be escaped: we are born, we love, we strife, we pray and sacrifice to the gods, we die—and if we are fortunate, our names live on after us.

The details of the shield are too rich (and have been discussed too effectively by others) for delineation here. For the purposes of our discussion, it is sufficient to note two things about its decoration. One: that that world within a world portraying the poem's world is a gift brought to Akhilleus as an act of love, which will yield the final stages of Iliadic strife. Two: that the paired primary images offer love and strife: a city celebrating a wedding and a city under siege—as if the one might recall the only wedding otherwise referenced in the Trojan War cycle, that between Peleus and Thetis, and the other the outcome of that wedding that accounts for this poem: the siege of Toy by the Akhaians.[68]

In Book Nineteen, Akhilleus formally renounces that initial aspect of the *menis* that Book One had engendered. Now he rues the love-object that had been the immediate source of that strife in a rhetorical question addressed to Agamemnon (56-60).[69] Forces beyond human powers are acknowledged as the truer sources of it all: *moira*, *atê*, the gods.[70] For Akhilleus, the renunciation of his *menis* toward Agamemnon is simply replaced by his passion for a return to the fighting: giving up one form of strife, he is eager for another. But Odysseus, voice of reason, stays that eagerness, calling for food, first, for the troops; the gifts for Akhilleus from Agamemnon to be assembled before the assembly, and an oath from Agamemnon "that he never entered her bed and never lay with her" (176)—never referring to the love-object, Briseis, by name as if she were a person. All this—in spite of Akhilleus' impatience to return to battle—is done, with propriety.

Underscoring the situation of women that had been suggested in Helen's and Andromakhe's speeches of Book Three and Book Six; as well as emphasizing what Patroklos *was*; Briseis laments in seeing the hero's body laid out when she is returned to Akhilleus' tent.[71] The tragic equation is suddenly focused: the trade-off in Akhilleus' *eris*-ridden self-love is Briseis for Patroklos. The price for one love-relationship is the other; to gain *her* back, he lost *him*—both losses are heavily strife-ridden. Significantly, the women mourn Patroklos while the men beseech Akhilleus to eat; these are the two sides of what the hero is. His armor, and the portentous words of his horse, Xanthos—

We shall keep you safe for this time, O hard Akhilleus,
and yet the day of your death is near, but it is not we
who are to blame, but a great god and powerful Destiny.
(408-10)

—and the hero's rueful response, that he knows he will die here far from home, yet will keep fighting until the Trojans have had enough of him, carry us into the end of the book.

The gods go forth to join the two sides in battle as Book Twenty opens, encouraging them. Akhilleus subdues Aineias—if not for his (Aineias') destiny, Akhilleus would have succeeded in killing him. The final battle with Hektor is delayed by the gods, as Akhilleus' *aristeia* against others must build his eristic stature. That sweeps him into Book Twenty-One where—so preternaturally *other* than the other heroes whose glory has been detailed before his—Akhilleus battles the very river-god, Xanthos, who waters the plain of Ilion. Akhilleus' *menis*, transformed, continues to fill him with furious love of this strife: with each spear thrust, he plunges at *himself*, burying himself ever deeper within his intense fury, neglecting the chivalric codes, even of battle and its suppliant and other aspects, guaranteeing the doom for himself that is, in any case, pre-ordained.

Again, the tragicomic contrast: the gods in strife that can result in momentary hurts; men in strife that ends in painful wounds and death—and Zeus (389) "...where he sat on Olympos, and was amused in his deep heart..." Again (recalling Book Five), the two gods notably intertwined (as he is again injured) are Ares and Aphrodite: Strife (or to be more precise: war, the brother of strife) and love (400-417).[72] By and large the gods who, by the advice of Apollo (466-7) "let the mortals fight their own battles," leave them to die their own deaths.

And so we are led toward that most significant of deaths in Book Twenty-two. Here the ultimate duel will be fought, ending with the final instance of Akhilleus' wrath-dominated lack of *sophrosune* (self-control)—particularly as it compares with that of his earlier stand-in, Diomedes. Perhaps Akhilleus might have climaxed his *menis* on the battlefield with mercy or at least chivalry—but Hektor wears the fateful, unmistakable armor, "bronze and splendid, that he stripped when he cut down the strength of Patroklos" (323). As much as this is armor that Patroklos had *worn*, it *is Akhilleus'* armor. Hektor is an aspect of Akhilleus, as Patroklos was. He and Akhilleus are both aspects of what killed Patroklos. The repeated fire images of Hektor, particularly as he nearly enflamed the Akhaian ships, were suddenly shifted to Akhilleus as he entered the fray, particularly as, Hephaistos-supported, he had battled the waters of Xanthos in Book Twenty-one.

This intertwining of personae is emphasized by the armor: two Akhilleoi, one false (as Patroklos in the same armor had been); one real, in terms of eristic capability. Hektor *as* Patroklos, the more emphatic love-side—as the Book Six presentation of Hektor with Andromakhe and Astyanax had shown, particularly (again) when re-invoked recently in Briseis' lament for Patroklos in Book Nineteen (and see above, **58**) as well as re-invoked in the pathetic interlude of Andromakhe's loving, unknowing preparations for

Hektor's return from strife (437-46).[73] It is this which intensifies Akhilleus' fury: it is the second stage of his death, in his strife with his own self-love. The book ends with Andromakhe's mourning: the strife that claimed her love will doom her son—as she well knows. She will be helpless to help Astyanax (it is an obvious irony that someone so-named—"Lord/Protector of the City"—should require help)—as helpless as Thetis, for all her divinity and the assistance it affords Akhilleus, will be to save her son in the end. No mother's love can prevent the strife and its consequences wrought by men, gods, and fate.

Book Twenty-three, of course, offers the "civilized" alternative to the human love of competition and strife in war: the funeral games—as it offers the culminating expressions of Akhilleus' *menis*, off the battlefield, in the sacrifices he offers to Patroklos' spirit. The preparations begin with the building of a funeral mound—"a huge grave mound, for himself and Patroklos" (126) that Akhilleus had chosen, anticipating their being rejoined in death who had been inseparable, except by cruel strife and madness, in life. As the fire is finally kindled, Akhilleus, tellingly, mourns "as a father mourns as he burns the bones of a son, who was married/ only now, and died to grieve his unhappy parents..." (222-23): it *is* himself he mourns, who will, too soon, be Patroklos. He drags himself by the fire (225) as he drags Hektor's body around the walls of Troy—the Hektor he drags is himself (wearing his armor)—he, who will, too soon, *be* Hektor.

The contests that follow illuminate, one last time, all of the key Akhaian heroes who have participated in the strife of war (and are still alive)—including Antolokhos, who had held Akhilleus' hands lest he cut his own throat in Book Eighteen (33-34) and who triumphs in the chariot race, albeit not by fully-proper driving protocol. This protocol issue provokes an argument in which Antilokhos, threatened with losing his prize, warns of his anger if "you intend to take my prize from me" (544)—echoing Akhilleus' words to Agamemnon at I.161. Indeed, Antilokhos is more Akhilleus than Akhilleus had been at that earlier point. For Antilokhos states that, should someone seek to take his honor-prize (a mare won in a game) the individual "must fight me for her with his hands before he can take her" (554); whereas Akhilleus had said in I.298-9 of *his* prize (won in battle):

> I will not fight with my hands for the girl's sake, neither
> with you nor any other man, since you take her away who gave her.

But this *is* a different Akhilleus, here in Book Twenty-three, from the Akhilleus back in Book One: Akhilleus has become the arbitrator-diplomat, moved outside the strife and argumentation of these games—that remain *games*. In both assuaging Antilokhos' and Menelaos' anger and in earlier stepping between Aias and Idomeneos to mediate *their* quarrel (490-91), he had withdrawn from strife into the love side of his personality that had hitherto only been visible in his alter-ego, Patroklos. Yet the poet weaves another strand into his tapestry: Antilokhos emerges clearly as a Patroklos-surrogate at this point as, in responding to his (Antilokhos') Akhilleus-like passion, Patroklos-like Akhilleus, "favoring Antilokhos, smiled, since he was [as Patroklos had been] his beloved companion" (555-6). And Antilokhos himself, his burst of *menis* having passed, recedes into a Patroklos-like graciousness as he assuagingly addresses Menelaos, speaking respectfully, younger man to older, and offering him not only the mare that he had won, but anything else from out of his house that Menelaos might choose.[74]

Each hero's role in the drama of the games is consistent with his role in the drama of the battle delineated in the overall poem, as has been frequently observed by commentators.[75] Book Twenty-three concludes perfectly: with the new Akhilleus addressing the son of Atreus, wide-powerful Agamemnon—to offer him one prize but to deny him another in discouraging one last contest—to which Agamemnon agrees, *larger* as king of Akhaian kings than such a contest and such a prize as other, lesser leaders, might find desirable. The last words of Akhilleus to Agamemnon are the last words of resolving strife and *menis*.

So in Book Twenty-four, all the gods who have participated in the drama—which for them has been one long game, albeit never, for them, *funeral* games—come before us. So the last phase of Akhilleus' *menis*, that toward himself/Hektor, must be resolved: he still drags the body around and around: there can be no end to his grief, as he tries to extend the moment of killing Patroklos/Hektor's killer into eternity. His grief can only end when his life does. But the *menis* that occasioned it may be resolved, just so the poem can end.

The form that the resolution takes has perhaps been prepared by Akhilleus' own father-like mourning in Book Twenty-two (220-25), as by the certainty of Akhilleus' own death that had attended his words in preparing to cut his hair by Patroklos' pyre (43-7). It will be Hektor's father who—in recalling to Akhilleus his (Akhilleus') own father and evoking Akhilleus' grief for his father's anticipated grief, his love for his father's love, the cruel fate for his father of outliving a son stuck down by strife—will bring Akhilleus' final *menis* to resolution. The poem's architecture completes its circle—alluding, as all the gods but Hera have pity on Hektor's corpse, to the *eros*-induced beginnings of the *eris* at Troy.[76] The gods pity, as in the end Akhilleus will be restored to pity; Zeus sends for Thetis (who is already mourning her son, Patroklos-Akhilleus) to go to Akhilleus to restore his pity—his humanity—as in the beginning, Akhilleus had sent Thetis to Zeus to manipulate events toward his god-like glory.[77] Priam arrives as a suppliant to Akhilleus, asking for his son back, as Khryses had arrived as a suppliant to Agamemnon in Book One, asking for his daughter back.[78]

The final aspect of *eris*, then, as the initial aspect, when it is resolved, will be resolved by reference to parent-child love and the unnatural balance of loss (sons pre-deceasing their fathers) that strife induces in the nature of gods and humans. Priam is accompanied/guided into Akhilleus' camp by Hermes—"beloved son" (333) of Zeus father—who addresses Priam (362) as "my father," saying, moreover: "you seem to me like a beloved father" (371). Priam's response is that "your parents are fortunate in you" (377)—as he was fortunate in Hektor and Peleus was in Akhilleus—yet they, in the end, are *not* fortunate, outliving their sons, which is the sort of painful fate that is irrelevant to divine Hermes' divine father.

The emphasis is all on fathers and sons. Maintaining his disguise as he tries to induce Priam to approach Akhilleus (to beg for the body of Hektor), Hermes identifies himself as the son of Polyktor, "…aged, as you are. He has six sons beside, and I am the seventh…" (398-99). Two further exchanges later, Priam responds "my child, surely it is good to give the immortals/ their due gifts; for my own son, if ever I had one,/ never forgot in his halls the gods who live on Olympos" (425-7). And when Hermes finally acknowledges who he is, "a god immortal, Hermes" he adds that "my father sent me down to guide and go with you" (461). The poet leads us by way of father-son love to the resolution of the confrontation between Akhilleus and Priam, and of their potential, unrealized strife. Priam reminds Akhilleus to "…remember your father, one who is of years like mine, and on the door-sill of sorrowful old age (486-7)… but honor the gods… and take pity on me/ remembering your own father (503-4)… [me, who has] put my lips to the hands of the man who has killed my children" (506).

Thus Akhilleus "wept now for his own father, now again/ for Patroklos" (511-12) — which brings the circle back to *both* its beginnings: grief out of self-love affronted, which spills out at the poem's inception; an allusion offered (as it had been, earlier, by Thetis) to the love between man and goddess that was the inception of both Akhilleus' *moira* and of the events at Troy that encompass that *moira*.

Resolution of the drama and of events for both deities and humans underlies the contrast between them ("that we live in unhappiness, but the gods themselves have no sorrows" (526)) — that guaranteed the catastrophe borne of a liaison between them, as between Peleus and Thetis. Akhilleus at his most sensitive, acknowledging the grief of father-love, commands that Hektor's body be prepared beyond the view of Priam — lest grief beget Priam's anger beget Akhilleus' renewed anger beget Priam's death at Akhilleus' hand beget divine anger: lest love re-engender a chain reaction of strife (581-6).

Agreeing to hold back the Akhaians himself for the time necessary for Hektor's funeral, Akhilleus offers Priam rest for the night, himself sleeping with "Briseis of the fair coloring" (676), reminder to us of the initial strife and *menis* of the poem and *its* resolution. But Priam leaves under divine aegis. Looking backward, the end looks forward, too: only Kassandra, "a girl like golden Aphrodite" (699) perceives the nighttime return of the king, from one of the fabled towers rising above the city — she who is doomed to be Agamemnon's Briseis — in a way — brought back to Mykenai as his prize, and to perish there at Klytaimnestra's hand. Her death will arrive in the long-delayed response of husband-wife strife to

Agamemnon's father-daughter deception, when a decade earlier he had offered Iphigenia not to Akhilleus as wife but to Artemis as sacrifice—so that his self-love-leading-the-Akhaians-in-the-glory-of-battle might be satisfied and the fleet sail under his command from Aulis to Troy.

The death of Astyanax—mourned in advance by Andromakhe as Thetis had mourned Akhilleus in advance—is presaged with precision:[79] strife will encompass yet one more instance of parent-child love. From Hektor's wife (710-45), the mourning moves to his mother (748-59), reviewing the Patroklos-Akhilleus details of his death. And lastly, Helen (762-5), sister-like, who, in her lament, completes the circle of multi-aspected love that, focused in Hektor's obsequies, has been interwoven with the strife that informs the poem.

Love and strife of different sorts alternate and interweave both in the chronology of events that engender the action that leads into the *Iliad* and that leads out and away from it, and in the complex weave, book by book and detail by detail, of the poem's tapestry. Nowhere do we find discussions or demonstrations of the one force without the other in attendance. From the viewpoint of the maker and audience of the poem, apart from the various layers of its fabric with which we have been concerned, they subscribe to a sense that Zeus and Themis had decided upon such a war already by the time of the wedding of Peleus and Thetis and the fruit tossed into the middle of the celebration by Eris.[80] So as the war is part of a larger "universal plan," it may not be unreasonable to understand the early Archaic Greek understanding of the workings of the universe to be substantially involved with the interplay of love and strife. Such a hypothesis may be corroborated by an examination of the second major Homeric text, the *Odyssey*.

Chapter Three

The *Odyssey*: The Last Homecoming and Love Delayed

The surviving records of the destroyed ancient libraries of Alexandria and Pergamon, among others, show us that there was once a number of epic poems focusing on aspects of the Trojan War and on its diverse heroes. For reasons beyond this discussion, however, most of these survive only in name or in an occasional fragment. While the *Iliad* offers us a magnificent insight into the Akhaian world by focusing its attention on a mere ten days in the last year of a ten-year-long war, the only surviving homecoming narrative—called a *nostos*—is the *Odyssey*, the account of the ten-year-long journey of Odysseus from the plain of Troy to his home in rocky Ithake.[81] Along the way, the hero has an extraordinary array of adventures and experiences, losing his flotilla and then the entire crew of his own ship before being gently deposited, asleep and laden with piles of gifts, in a cave on the edge of his home island by the Phaiakians.

The *Odyssey*, tale of tales, web of webs, in proceeding from an angle—along a different path drawn from the Trojan War cycle—different from that of the *Iliad*, in following the course described by Odysseus on his long journey home, in interweaving adventures of love and of battle for its hero, is ultimately focused on the bond of love between that hero and Penelope, the wife who waits for him for twenty years. As we follow him, we are drawn constantly back to the Ithake to which he seeks return, and to the strife pitting Penelope and those loyal to Odysseus against those who seek her hand in marriage—and with it, her husband's property. More fundamentally, it is against the backdrop of this unique love story that all of the epic's episodes of strife are played out.

The *Odyssey* is, in a sense, more narrowly focused than the *Iliad*, less philosophical: it is a tale of adventure focused upon a hero who, by means of his wits and divine assistance, overcomes whatever obstacles appear on his path and achieves his dual goal of adventure and return to his wife. Even in the notions of struggle to return and to find himself, to fulfill his nature, to be what his name is etymologized to mean, we find less pathos than in a tale of the inevitability of human mortality, of the futility of even divine machinations against fate. The *Iliad*'s heroes and, in particular, its central protagonist, Akhilleus, act against a backdrop that they and we share, of the brevity and sometimes the bitterness of human existence. The *Odyssey* is about reveling in human experience—and in fact preferring it to the ever-youthful immortality that is offered to the protagonist, perhaps even twice.

But even in its more limited ideational scope, the *Odyssey* offers a panoply of aspects of human relationships, situations, inclinations—within which array, *eros* and *eris*, in succession and in interweave, are dominant. So the opening of the first book announces to us in line 2 that the man whose tale is being told is a warrior (an exemplar of *eris*) who "had sacked the sacred citadel of Troy." It also tells us that love (*eros*) motivates him—"longing for his home and his wife (13)—while the delay in arriving at that goal is a function of the desire for him of a nymph (*eros*):

> [he] was delayed by the queenly nymph Kalypso, among goddesses,
> in her hollow caverns, desiring that he be her husband. (14-15)

—as it is by the hostility (*eris*) towards him of one god, Poseidon. So the first twenty lines offer strife-related parentheses in the middle of which, side by side, lie the love-related causes of both return and delay. *Eros* within *eris* will motivate the poem.

There is a direct allusion (in verses 30-31) to the Klytaimnestra-Agamemnon-Aigisthos-Orestes story that moves us from third-person narrator to a first-person protagonist—in this case, Zeus himself. We are thus offered a not-so-subtle reminder of Klytaimnestra's disloyalty and treachery to her far-away husband (and to her son) as a foil for Penelope, whom we shall meet shortly—

subtle in that Klytaimnestra herself is not actually mentioned and the ostensive focus is on Aigisthos, yet the chain of association that the auditor/reader must inevitably make, who knows the story all too well, inevitably leads to Klytaimnestra through the invocation of her lover's name. Aside from such an implication, the reference offers a direct comment by the Chief of the gods on the human condition: that it is strife-ridden—and in the specific context of Zeus' little speech, strife is interwoven with the ostensive love relationships ordinarily assumed of both husbands and wives and parents and children.[82]

As in the *Iliad*, then, the text reaches outside itself (with respect to implications for its narrative and for the aspects of the human condition addressed by its narrative) to carve the larger relief imagery into which this episode in Greek and human history is incised. This is all underscored, moreover, by the speech of Athene, Odysseus' patron (the Goddess of *war—eris in extremis—*who so well *loves* him). She informs us of the hero's condition: Odysseus is, as it were, in a love-situation that has buried him (as is suggested by the verb that is cognate with the name of the nymph in whose cave he has been residing for seven years—Kalypso, from *kalyptein*, meaning "to bury") albeit it has been only in the last of those seven years that he has begun to weep copiously about wishing to go home. Odysseus is reported to yearn for death if he cannot return to his home—which is to return, not only to Penelope, but to the hurly-burly of life which is so endemic to his very being, as opposed to dwelling forever outside that hurly-burly, which would be his fate (tantamount to death, in fact) as an immortal, eternally young, dwelling in Kalypso's cave.[83]

But the point is that one might surely imagine Agamemnon to have been similarly eager to get home. Both situations were/are exemplars of strife-bound love situations. Odysseus weeps outside Kalypso's cave and will come home to find a loyal wife and suitors whom he will choose to slaughter rather than simply drive away, perhaps, or accommodate by some other means. Agamemnon manages to come home far more quickly and uneventfully to find, however, a community of citizens afraid to speak a word of warning, and to further find, too late, that his wife is more than disloyal: she has not only acquired someone to share her bed while he has been gone but will murder him in the bath with the salt of the sea and the dust of the road—and beyond these, the salt and dust of battle and the charred smells redolent of a burning city—barely washed off him.[84]

Having obtained assurance from Zeus that Odysseus *will* return home safely in the end, Athene swoops down to Ithake—where we see the suitors, as well as both Telemakhos and Penelope, in action. Again, the foil—directly offered to Telemakhos by the disguised goddess—is presented, of Klytaimnestra-Agamemnon-Aigisthos-Orestes; this time the emphasis is on Orestes, running obliquely parallel to Telemakhos.[85] But this tale is told as the denouement of their dialogue, which is followed immediately by Penelope's entrance. Telemakhos, growing more assertive by the moment after Athene's departure, speaks sharply to his mother—and then harshly to the suitors—a verbally eristic culmination to the events of the day the postlude of which refocuses on love. Love, in a different key, that is: the central figure is Eurykleia, the nurse, loyal to the house of Laertes as Laertes had been loyal to his wife in never having slept with Eurykleia; loyal and loving now to Telemakhos in contrast to the strife which is depicted immediately prior to the moment when Eurykleia is brought into the narrative.

As the key players in the emerging drama—except Odysseus himself—have been presented in the course of the first book, Book Two carries forward two themes in particular: Telemakhos' coming into his own, and the suitors' outrageous behavior. The second of these two is dwellt upon mostly when, in responding to Telemakhos' speech of lines 40-79,[86] Antinoos twists the causes of difficulty toward Penelope. The desire for Penelope, "who has been denying the desire of the Akhaians (90)"—and who, no doubt, is not separable from the considerable "dowry" that marriage to her would bring to the successful suitor—has achieved a decidedly eristic tone, as Antinoos' refers responsibility for the unpleasant circumstances to her tricks:

> For she holds out hope to everyone, and makes promises to each man,
> sending us messages, but her mind has other intentions.
> And here is another stratagem of her heart's devising:

> She has set up a great loom in the palace, and has set to
>   weaving
> a web of threads long and fine. Then she has said to us:
> 'Young men, my suitors now that the great Odysseus has
>   perished,
> wait, though you are eager to marry me, until I finish
> this web, so that my weaving will not be useless and wasted.
> This is a shroud for the hero Laertes…'
> Thereafter in the daytime she would weave at her great loom,
> but in the night she would…undo it… [as]
> one of her women…. told us,
> and we found her in the act of undoing her glorious weaving.
> So, against her will and by force, she had to finish it (91-110).

So the trick of weaving and unweaving has finally been exposed through the treachery of one of Penelope's own maids, and she will now be forced at last to embrace one of the suitors as her groom.

The ugly eristic tone is yet stronger in Eurymakhos' words to Halitherses, an aged warrior and interpreter of omens, (who has just responded to a Zeus-sent pair of eagles that soar at length up in the sky, by warning the suitors that Odysseus is somewhere near and plotting their destruction), at 178ff:

> Old sir, better go home and prophesy to your children,
> for fear that they may suffer some evil to come… Odysseus
> is dead, far away, and how I wish that you had died with
>   him…
> But… if you… stir up a younger man [i.e., Telemakhos]
> and by talking him round with words, encourage his anger,
> then first of all it will be the worse for him…
> And on you, old sir, we shall pay a penalty and it will grieve
>   your
> mind as you pay it, and that for you will be a great sorrow.

Indeed, the paradox of a strife-ridden portrait of a bride-to-be is explicitly suggested in Eurymakhos' designation of the process as a "harsh courtship" (*mnestos argalees*; 199). Penelope is sophistically presented as the engenderer of strife, who is the object of love.[87] She *is*, as love-object, a source of strife—and again, of course, a kind of reflection of the image of Helen, love-object, source of strife, because of whom the action of both epic poems transpired. And we shall meet Helen, of course, in Book Four, whither the action at the end of Book Two—Telemakhos' sailing forth to find himself and news of his father—leads us.

Having set sail at the end of Book Two, Telemakhos arrives in Book Three to Pylos, where long-winded Nestor alludes to Odysseus' clever stratagem that finally took Troy in the tenth year of the war (118-23). So, too, once more, the murder of Agamemnon by Klytaimnestra and Aigisthos, and Orestes' revenge for it is all related by Nestor (194-98, 262-72, 303-8). The extended emphasis on this last story, with its focus on marriage twisted into a knot of *eris* again offers not only implicit comparison to that of long-lost Odysseus and ever-loyal Penelope and inspiration to Telemakhos to do something, but also implicit comparison with the story of Klytaimnestra's sister, Helen, and her husband, Menelaos—Agamemnon's brother—comfortably ensconced in Sparta, whither Telemakhos heads as his mini-adventure pushes into Book Four.[88]

So we meet Helen and Menelaos in Book four. At Sparta, back on the royal throne as queen, next to her husband, Helen presides: she who had been, in the direct sense, the inception point of the Trojan War cycle.[89] Like Penelope, she was the object over whom suitors *also* fought, but in a different context and under different, more appropriate circumstances—and she also (perhaps) betrayed her husband as Klytaimnestra did,[90] if with different, arguably more far-reaching, consequences: the overturning of the entire Akhaian world.

For not only was Troy destroyed and all of its significant inhabitants, save one, perhaps, (Aineias), killed or enslaved, but most of the key figures in the Akhaian world also perished or, in the case of Odysseus, wandered for another decade before making it home. Akhaian farms and palaces were left undefended for ten years, Akhaian wives left to fend for themselves and Akhaian sons left to grow up without fathers to tutor them in the ways of becoming adult men. But among those few to survive the war intact were none other than the not overly attractive Menelaos, for whose sake his brother and friends lost their lives or at least an easy homecoming.

And the wife for whose return they all suffered one way or another, Helen, we, along with Telemakhos, now see comfortably emerging "from her fragrant high-roofed bedchamber, looking like Artemis of the golden distaff (121-2). The likening of the queen to the chaste, virgin, goddess of hunting must carry a tone of irony—an irony that will be compounded by the contrastive retellings of events at Troy that are shortly offered by Menelaos and Helen. Specifically, in recalling the accomplishment of Odysseus with high praise, she singles out the time when

> He crept into the wide-wayed city of the men he was fighting,
> disguising himself in the likeness of somebody else, a beggar... (246-7)

> ...[and] I alone recognized him even in this form,
> and I questioned him, but he in his craftiness eluded me,
> but after I bathed him and anointed him with olive oil
> and put some clothing upon him, after I had sworn a great oath
> not to disclose before the Trojans that this was Odysseus
> until he had made his way back to the fast ships and the shelter,
> then at last he told me all the purpose of the Akhaians,
> and after striking many Trojans down with the thin bronze
> edge, he went back to the Argives and brought back much information.
> The rest of the Trojan women cried out shrill, but my heart
> was happy, my heart had changed by now and was for going back
> home again, and I grieved for the madness that Aphrodite
> bestowed when she led me there away from my own dear country,
> forsaking my own daughter, my bedchamber, and my husband... (250-63)

From her words we would infer that Helen felt duped, as it were, by Aphrodite, goddess of love and beauty, to run away with Paris/Alexandros, thereby setting a great war in motion, but that she came to her own senses by the time of Odysseus' mission, (nearly ten years after she left Sparta!), and was thrilled to be back home *now* with a husband "who lacks no endowment either of brains or beauty" (264).

That husband, however, responds with a rather different perspective, in telling the tale of the great wooden horse stratagem. For he, too, offers praise for Odysseus:

> Here is the way that strong man acted and the way he endured
> action, inside the wooden horse, where we who were the greatest
> of the Argives all were sitting and bringing death and destruction
> to the Trojans. Then you came there, Helen, you will have been moved by
> some divine spirit who wished to grant glory to the Trojans,
> and Deiphobos, a godlike man, was with you when you came.
> Three times you walked around the hollow ambush, feeling it,
> and you called out, naming them by name, to the best of the Danaans,
> and made your voice sound like that of the wife of each of the Argives. (271-9)

> ... and we heard you crying
> aloud, and Diomedes and I started up, both minded
> so go outside, or else to answer your voice from inside,
> but Odysseus pulled us back and held us, for all our eagerness.
> Then all the other sons of the Akhaians were silent:
> There was only one, Antiklos, who was ready to answer,
> but Odysseus, brutally squeezing his mouth in the clutch of his powerful
> hands, held him, and so saved the lives of the Akhaians
> until such time as Pallas Athene led you off from us. (281-9)

It is not just that Menelaos offers such a radically different portrait of Helen from her own self-portrait—this event would have transpired well after the event that she described, by which time, she had just asserted, she was eager for Akhaian success, so that she might return home—in which, far from seeming eager for that success, she strove to bring destruction upon the Akhaian warriors (and given her own tale of a few moments back, it might not be unreasonable even to suppose that the plans about which Odysseus informed her included this very wooden horse stratagem).

More significantly, the discontinuity between the two tales suggests either that Helen was lying about her about-face and/or that Menelaos maintained a very jaundiced view of her and of her role in her abduction and return to him. Put simply, a war had been fought for ten years—in which many men were wounded and killed, wives and children were left bereft of their husbands and fathers, a magnificent city was torched; and on the one hand, Menelaos' own brother, who organized the expedition on his (Menelaos') behalf, had been cut down upon his return home; while on the other, Odysseus continues to struggle to get home after nearly ten years of wandering and fighting against the anger of Poseidon toward him. All this, in order to bring this couple back together, but in our only active sight of them in their palace in Sparta, we find them radically unhappy with each other. Their love, whatever it may have been or might still be, is shot through with strife.

Menelaos goes on, in response to Telemakhos' query, to tell the story of how, while delayed without relief in his own homecoming, he managed to capture and hold Proteus, the Old Man of the Sea (351-70). From him he learned how to appease the god, Zeus, who was preventing his further progress homeward; he also learned of the fate of Agamemnon and Aias as well as of Odysseus, captive on Kalypso's isle. Thus Menelaos' tale within this long tale offers a lighter parallel to Odysseus' current condition—and one notes that the betrayal of Proteus by his own daughter, Eidothea, who instructs and assists Menelaos regarding how to capture and hold her father, echoes, albeit also in a much lighter manner, the stories of gendered and generational strife that define divine relations in Hesiod's *Theogony*.

On the other hand the narrator's turn back to Ithake, where we encounter the eristically-engaged suitors not only continuing their depredations of Odysseus' supplies but then setting sail to ambush Telemakhos on his return (625-72; 768-86; 842-7) contrasts significantly with the loving concern of Penelope for Telemakhos

(704-14), Euryklaia's reference to Telemakhos' loving concern for his mother (742-9), the concern expressed for Penelope by Athene and the goddess' shaping of an eidolon of Penelope's own sister to help comfort her (795-841)—and Penelope's reference to how wonderful Odysseus was (724-6).

These first four books are shot through, indeed, with references, from every conceivable angle, to the Odysseus whom we have not yet met. A long, dramatic wind-up, then, yields, at last, the pitch, in Book Five. Based on the discussion among the Olympians—except, of course, Poseidon, who was off visiting the Aithiopians at that strategic moment—back toward the beginning of Book One, Hermes is now dispatched with the message to Kalypso that she must let Odysseus continue on his journey home. The god finds the lesser goddess in her cave weaving on her loom and singing—an image reminiscent of that of Penelope through her long years of waiting.

While Odysseus is on the beach crying his heart out, Hermes and Kalypso chat, deity to deity, and in her response to his Zeus-driven command that she give Odysseus up she first makes the observation that the Olympian gods are hard-hearted. She specifically notes that, when a goddess loves a human man, as rosy-fingered Dawn did Orion the hunter (121-4), and Demeter of the lovely hair did Iasion (125-8), the Olympians destroy the man. In the first case it was Artemis and in the second Zeus—but in all such cases, *eros* involving a goddess and a human male is met by a destructive, eristic gesture derived from jealousy. And thus she views the divine insistence that she give up her plan of making Odysseus hers forever by making him immortal—"[for] I gave him my love and cherished him" (136)—as a cruel act.

One might wonder, too, how intentional the poet is in offering three abortive instances (including that of Kalypso-Odysseus) of such relationships against the larger epic backdrop of this moment. This is, after all, the beginning of the last phase of the last homecoming from a war, part of the beginning point of which war was the love relationship between a goddess, Thetis, and a human male, Peleus. It was at their wedding that the conflict begat by Eris actually set in motion the great Trojan War—to say naught of the fact that their offspring, Akhilleus, is the central tragic warrior figure in that war (whose eristic *aristeia* we wait an even longer time to actually see in the *Iliad* than we wait to see Odysseus take the stage in the *Odyssey*) in the consummate war poem.

After Hermes departs—warning Kalypso not to anger Zeus by disobeying him—she goes out to the beach to find Odysseus, weeping

> ...for a way home, since the nymph was no longer pleasing
> to him. By nights he would lie beside her, of necessity,
> in the hollow caves, against his will, by one who was willing,
> but all the days he would sit upon the rocks, by the seaside,
> breaking his heart in tears and lamentation and sorrow... (153-7)

We might note two things. One, of course, is this encapsulation of the tortured condition to which the love relationship between these two has arrived for Odysseus: *eros* has subsumed into something hardly short of *eris*. The poet seems to state without irony that obviously Odysseus was perfectly happy to cavort for several years with Kalypso, before the situation began to become increasingly oppressive for him. It has arrived to the extreme of its unhappy condition because the life force—the essence—of Odysseus has been draining out of him slowly, for seven years. To be Odysseus, son of Laertes, sacker of cities, is to be out in and *engaged* with the world, *our* world, the *profanus* world, with all of its issues and problems.

That he is "not himself" is underscored—and this is the second thing we might notice—by the fact that, having waited for four books and 150 lines to meet our hero, not only do we find him rather unheroically, crumpled in tears on the beach, but he, the consummate talker, says not a word when we first meet him. Kalypso does all of the initial talking; Odysseus' first words in the epic, arriving by verse 173 of this book, are words of fear that she is planning his destruction in anger at his rejection of her. Only gradually does his verbiage begin to suggest who he truly *is*. In the exchange that evening over dinner, when Kalypso calls to mind the suffering that he will still need to endure—and notes that, as a goddess, she must be at least as attractive as Penelope, a mere mortal—he responds diplomatically yet honestly, and bravely.

What she says is true, but he longs for home nonetheless, "and if some god betters me out on the wine-blue water, I will endure it, keeping a stubborn spirit inside me… so let this adventure follow" (221-4).

For the reader, of course, the adventure is just beginning. Not just anything that happens hereafter, but anything that happened before to Odysseus we will only hear about later—and much will happen, through the *eris*-driven anger of Poseidon, who will nonetheless not kill the hero, thanks to the *eros*-driven support of Athene and thanks to Fate that limits what any god can do. More precisely: after Odysseus spoke these last words, and the sun went down, he and Kalypso spent the night making love. The next morning, she showed him where the best wood for his raft was to be found and he spent four days expertly crafting it; she supplied him well with water, wine and victuals, he set sail for 17 days until arriving in sight of the island of the Phaiakians—which is when and where Poseidon, returning from his visit to the Aithopians, saw him from afar and swelled with anger, bringing up a terrific storm.

His raft overturned, he nearly drowns, "for the clothing that divine Kalypso had given him weighed him down" (321-2)—a gift of love almost causing him to be swallowed up by the sea-god's eristic furor. The former mortal, Leukothea, daughter of Kadmos, now a sea-bound goddess, sees and takes pity on Odysseus and instructs him on how—and helps him—to swim naked to the island. It takes more than two days—Poseidon makes sure of that just as Athene makes sure that it is no longer than that. Eventually he staggers ashore by way of a fresh-water stream flowing into the sea, finding a place in the bushes away from the water where he can pile up leaves as a bed and cover, and falls asleep.

Odysseus awakens, in Book Six, to the voices of young maidens, for Nausikaa, princess of the Phaiakians, and her handmaidens, have come down to the river and sea to do the royal laundry—a task suggested by Athene in a nighttime dream-disguise—in order to be properly prepared for marriage. When the maidens are down by the river, Odysseus, awakened by their chatter, comes out of his makeshift bed shielding his private parts with a leafy branch and the girls—all except Nausikaa—scatter in terror. She stands her ground, princess that she is, and he speaks at length, flattering her and then telling the story of the previous 19 days of his sea-born journey with its disastrous finale.

Her response, among other things, guarantees that, even if for some reason—romance, for example—he were inclined to stay for very long among the Phaiakians, he could not. Since they "live apart by ourselves in the wash of the great sea at the utter end, nor do any other people mix with us" (204-5), he would be back where he was with Kalypso: functionally dead, away from the excitement and action that define the human world of which he needs to be a part if he is to be Odysseus.

That reality clashes—ever so gently—with the following trio of moments. Nausikaa orders her servant girls to calm down, gather around her and then to lay out some beautiful garments and body oil for Odysseus, so that he can bathe in the fresh water of the river, anoint his skin with oil and dress well; Athene works her magic so that, when he is finished, Odysseus looks positively godlike in appearance, quite taking Nausikaa's breath away; and the princess quickly devises a plan that will bring the hero to her parents' feasting table, but explaining that she cannot simply ride into town with him by her side lest wagging tongues inappropriately ask

> who is this large and handsome stranger whom Nausikaa
> has with her, and where did she find him? Surely, he is
> to be her husband...? (276-8)

So the sandwich between which Odysseus makes his appearance—beginning as a naked mess and ending looking like a god to Nausikaa—offers the idea of the princess' marriageability as a theme: that she has come down to the river, in part because of this, and that she cannot be seen with Odysseus on the way back into town for the same reason. Given the stirring of her feelings, however gently, at virtually the same time when we are being reminded that Odysseus would never consider remaining in this place, the potential for pain within the levels of love—I am including those between Nausikaa's parents and between them and her—is being shaped.

Book Seven finds our hero wending his way into the city and to the palace of Alkinoos and Arete. Athene, as usual, lends a hand, casting a mist of invisibility around him—because "she cared for him lovingly" (42)—and appearing, disguised as a young girl, to lead him. We are again introduced, first by Athene's words to Odysseus, to a lovingly married couple, for (the disguised goddess explains), once Alkinoos married Arete, his niece, he "gave her such pride of place as no other woman on earth is given of such women as are now alive and keep house for their husbands" (66-8). Another foil in the ongoing positive and negative series for Odysseus and Penelope—and perhaps, too, another subtle hint that, on the one hand, a relationship between Odysseus and Nausikaa would not be amiss due to age-disparity, but would be the polar opposite of what obtains for the apogee of Phaiakian society, since Odysseus, as a stranger, could hardly be farther from Nausikaa in blood-line.

Odysseus follows Nausikaa's instructions and grasps the knees of Arete as a suppliant—only at this moment does the magical mist dissipate from around him—and begs to be conveyed homeward. After the shock of his sudden appearance wears off, and advised by the wise, elderly Ekheneos, Alkinoos places Odysseus on the seat of honor, next to himself (this is the seat on which his most-loved son sits) and offers a handsome welcoming speech, concluding with a speculative comment upon the as-yet-unnamed guest, that perhaps he is a god in disguise, observing that they don't typically disguise themselves but come openly to dine with the Phaiakians from time to time, for "we are very close to them, as are the Kyklopes and the savage tribe of the Giants" (205-6). For the audience that already knows the story that Odysseus has not yet told of his adventures, these last words must ring with irony, as we shall see.

Odysseus, meanwhile, is becoming more and more himself. His well-balanced response to Alkinoos (noting that he is by no means a god) brings praise from the assembled company. And when the clever Arete asks who he is—"what man are you and whence? And *who was it who gave you this clothing? Did you not say that you came here ranging over the water*?" (238-9; emphasis added)—he responds with only part of his story. We wait in suspense to hear who he is, meanwhile hearing of his arrival, after shipwreck, to Ogygia, Kalypso's isle, who held him a captive of her love for seven long years, "but [I was] forever drenching with tears that clothing, immortal stuff, that Kalypso had given me]..." (259-60). And we hear of his departure from Ogygia, and his long trip on the raft until it was destroyed by Poseidon, and of how he encountered Nausikaa, supplicated her, and how the princess gave him the clothing (that Arete could not fail to recognize, surely, so one might suppose that her question was, in part a test of Odysseus' honesty — and perhaps wondering about his relationship to her daughter).

The response by Alkinoos to this is first to criticize Nausikaa (lightheartedly) for not having simply brought Odysseus directly to their door, to which comment the hero responds in defense of that "blameless daughter," taking the responsibility for having been embarrassed to arrive that way to the palace. Alkinoos then, rather quickly, moves to *eros*: impressed by the stranger, he ruminates out loud: "how I wish that, being the man you are and thinking the way that I do, you could have my daughter and be called my son-in-law, staying here with me. I would dower you with a house and properties, if you stayed by your own good will" (312-25). But he knows that this is not likely to be Odysseus' wish, and quickly adds that on the morrow he will provide the necessary conveyance to get the traveler home.

And so the two converse until a comfortable bed has been made up for Odysseus and he goes happily to it; Alkinoos sleeps "in the inner room of the high house, and at his side the lady his wife served as bedfellow" (346-7) as, we are no doubt intended to hope, will Odysseus with Penelope by his side—soon. As Book Eight opens, on the next day, the Phaiakian leadership gathers in their hall of assembly to determine the specific course of action vis-à-vis Odysseus, whom Athene has again imbued with "a divine-seeming grace about his head and shoulders, and made him taller for the eye to behold, and thicker, so that he might be loved by all the Phaiakians" (19-21). To them Alkinoos proposes that they prepare a ship to ferry Odysseus home and then come to his (Alkinoos') palace for a great feast in honor of the wanderer before they carry him away.

Demodokos, the court singer—a blind poet like Homer himself is said to have been—is inspired by the Muse to sing:

about the Trojan War. That conflagration has already become a centerpiece of epic story-telling while Odysseus is still on his long way home. The poet begins with the argument between Odysseus (not Agamemnon!) and Akhilleus, and telling us how Agamemnon was pleased because this was fulfilling a prophecy regarding events that would transpire shortly before Troy was finally taken. It is an interesting choice of subject for the poet to reference, given who now sits in his audience as a guest. More oddly, we have no other source for such an argument outside this Odyssean scene, and yet it obliquely echoes, rather ironically, the argument between Agamemnon and Akhilleus that starts the *Iliad* on its course. It also so perfectly sets the stage for what immediately follows.

Odysseus wraps himself in his cloak, weeping (recalling for us, perhaps, how Telemakhos had wept at hearing about his father in Menelaos' court). Alkinoos is the only one who notices, and, with great sensitivity, simply suggests that they move on from poetry to sports, and go outside for some athletic competitions. As so often in Homeric epic, there are echoes and reflections between serious and lighter scenes. Laodamas, son of Alkinooos, after the Phaiakians have participated in running, wrestling, jumping, throwing the discus and boxing (in which Laodamas was best, by the way), suggests in what Odysseus takes to be a mocking tone that he show them what he can do in one or more of these sporting events. When Odysseus demurs, Euryalos (who had won the wrestling competition) more assertively mocks him: "You do not resemble an athlete!" (164).

These two interchanges may be seen to anticipate what will ultimately transpire between Odysseus and the suitors, in a manner somewhat reminiscent of how the various examples of Trojan and Akhaian *aristeia* in the *Iliad* anticipate the ultimate battle between Akhilleus and Hektor. And indeed, "darkly resourceful Odysseus" responds to Euryalos that "that was not well spoken; you seem like one who is reckless… now you have stirred up anger deep in the breast within me by this disorderly speaking…" (165-6; 178-9). And he jumps up without removing his mantle, and picks up a discus much heavier than those the Phaiakians used and threw it well beyond where any of theirs had landed.

It's not just that the exchange between Odysseus and the Phaiakian youths may be said to anticipate that with the suitors, but with a much more unfortunate outcome for the latter than for these athletes, who are merely stunned and stricken to silence. It is that, in Odysseus' self-assertive speech following the discus throw—while noting that, as a proper guest he would never challenge his hosts, but if challenged by them, he would defeat them—the first sport he mentions, (which had not been mentioned by the poet as one of those taking place on that bright Phaiakian afternoon) is this:

> I know well how to handle the polished bow, and would be
> first to strike my man with an arrow aimed at a company
> of hostile men…
> There was Philoktetes alone who surpassed me in archery
> when we Akhaians shot with bows in the Trojan country.
> (215-17; 219-20)

    The reader/auditor, well aware of where this narrative will end cannot not think ahead for a moment to the suitors whom he will shoot down with those arrows when, under rather different circumstances from those right here, he does throw off his cloak and his old beggar disguise, having easily strung a bow that nobody but Telemakhos can even come close to stringing, and shooting an arrow true through a line-up of axe-heads. One might also note the nuance: the reminder that he (they do not yet know who he is, of course!) fought at Troy—a ten-year-long war—while these kids were growing up by the hearth and playing mere games with and without weapons. So, too, the reference to Philoktetes might bring to mind to most that particular thread in the tapestry of the Trojan War story of how the war could only be won with the arms of Herakles, owned by Philoktetes who would be marooned by his fellow-Akhaians on the island of Lemnos due to a suppurating wound—and Odysseus' role in bringing Philoktetes and those semi-divine weapons back into the fray.[91]

    Once more Alkinoos, the consummate host, intervenes to cut through the potential tension and maneuvers in a particularly clever way. Odysseus noted that the one sport in which he would not fare well against the Phaiakians is the foot race, because "I have been through too much and shamefully battered on shipboard; because of this my legs have lost their condition" (232-3). Alkinoos suggests shifting back from sports to other entertainments and specifically boasts of how well the Phaiakians dance—so, aside from sailing, he suggests that fancy footwork (and not only foot-races) is their hallmark, and he wants to show this off to his guest before demonstrating Phaiakian skill at ferrying him home.

Demodokos is once again called for, this time with his lyre, and this time sings about the notorious affair between Ares and Aphrodite—*strife and love* divinely personified—in which they are captured in bed and trapped in an unbreakable snare by Aphrodite's husband, Hephaistos, the smith-god (who made the new armor for Akhilleus described in Book Eighteen of the *Iliad*). Once more a married couple, Olympian, no less, in which the wife betrays the husband, offers an implied comparison to the loyal Penelope, still awaiting the return of Odysseus while he is briefly detained by the hospitable Phaiakians. The sad victory that Hephaistos enjoyed over his dual betrayers contrasts both with the true, loving relationship we have observed between Alkinoos and Arete (whose very name means "virtue") and with what we recognize as the loving loyalty of Penelope to Odysseus.

The most important attribute of the Phaiakians, however, is how loving they are to a stranger who is their guest—the opposite of the suitors whom we saw and will see again who have been so immeasurably rude as guests in the house presided over by loyal Penelope while its master is so long away. When Alkinoos proposes that each of the twelve kings (he is the thirteenth) of the land offer a significant gift to Odysseus, each of course, does, but most significantly is both the gift and the apologetic words delivered, at Alkinoos' suggestion, by Euryalos, whose concluding words are to wish that "the gods grant you safe homecoming to your own country and wife, since here, far from your own people, you must be suffering" (410-11)—quite the opposite of the sort of behavior exhibited by the suitors, both earlier and later on. Odysseus responds with equal warmth, the sun goes down, they all repair to the palace, Odysseus' gifts are piled into a beautiful chest, he is bathed, oiled and dressed and Nausikaa has eyes full of admiration, as she asks that he not forget her nor, specifically, that she was "the first to whom you owed your life" (462).

A third time, as they sit down to feast, Demodokos enters—this time Odysseus makes a point of sending him a juicy cut of meat, noting that such singers should be cherished, whom "the Muse has taught her own way" 480-1). He also challenges him to tell more of the war at Troy—specifically the story of the horse stratagem and Odysseus' own role in effecting the sack of Ilion—for if he can add this to his narrative, as if he had been there himself, then praises for his divine gift will be carried far by Odysseus. Once again, however, as the singer sings his tale, Odysseus is overcome by weeping and once again it is only Alkinoos who notices, and who asks Demodokos to desist. This is the point, at last, when he turns to Odysseus and asks:

> Tell me the name by which your mother and father called you in that place....
>
> Tell me your land, your neighborhood and your city, so that our ships, straining with their own purpose, can carry you there. (550-1; 555-7)

Moreover, he asks:

> Tell me why you weep in your heart and make lamentation when you hear of the Argives' and the Danaans' venture, and hear of Ilion...
>
> Was there perhaps some kinsman by marriage, wife's father or brother, a brave man who perished before Ilion? (577-8; 581-2)

Book Eight ends with this dramatic request for information—sandwiched between the two parts is the unwitting prophecy of destruction to the ship that will end up carrying Odysseus home—and with still greater drama, Book Nine opens with Odysseus' response. It takes him 19 verses of declamation to arrive at the famous words:

> I am Odysseus son of Laertes, known before all men
> for the study of crafty designs, and my glory goes up to the heavens.
> I am at home in sunny Ithake ... (19-21)

This tale is devoted to delays, devised by fate, gods and humans. Most broadly, it is all about the delay in the homecoming of Odysseus, against the backdrop of which Penelope has been desperately delaying betrothal to one of the suitors. What she does primarily with her loom Odysseus does with the time he spends at each of the stopping points to which he has arrived by a combination of his own curiosity, divine anger (Poseidon) or assistance (Athene), and fate. So, too, the poet contributes, both broadly, in delaying our first genuine sighting of Odysseus and, in the context of the Phaiakian story, delaying his arrival to their court and then delaying the point at which Alkinoos asks who he is and then finally offering a response from Odysseus that still delays saying his name and his home.

With that statement, the Odysseus whom we saw at such a disadvantage on the beach of Kalypso's isle but who has gradually been returning to himself, finally arrives back at the full strength of his self-assertion. We have, as we shall see, arrived at the heart of the matter, which is the array of adventures that certify Odysseus as unique among heroes for all that he has seen, experienced, endured, enjoyed. The telling of the adventures will further delay the narrative from arriving at the point when the hero is carried to and safely deposited on his own shores. But that is to be expected. The adventures *are* Odysseus and to bring him home too quickly would prevent his being who he is, to say nothing of limiting the entertainment value of the poem for its multiple audiences.

Moreover, the narrative about to be spun by Odysseus will offer another thread in the tapestry of *eros*-bound linkage to Penelope: as she weaves the tales of the Trojan War adventures to the extent that she knows of them from visitors and travelers, he weaves the tales of his post-war *nostos* as a visitor and traveler. As she is forced to be hostess to obnoxious permanent visitors, the suitors who eat and drink without her permission, Odysseus has been nobly entertained by the Phaiakians and responds by being a good guest—not only, as he explicitly had put it, by not challenging their athletes with his own athletic skill, but by telling the tales that entertain and inform them of things beyond their self-isolating borders. In fact, although this is a separate matter, one might wonder how much of what the wily Odysseus tells is fact and how much of it is fiction designed to be more entertaining as well as to elevate his heroic status—in their eyes (confirming that his *kleos* goes up to the heavens), and in our eyes.

His tale begins by referencing the lovability of Ithake in comparison with the first two places along his way that he mentions—the home islands of Kalypso and Kirke. He starts briefly, then, one might say, with *eros*, since in both these cases he notes that each goddess wanted him as a husband (29-33)—and perhaps this might underscore the unlikelihood, were Alkinoos or Nausikaa (just in case!) to think seriously otherwise, that he would ever consider staying here as son-in-law and husband, without his ever having to say no to these people who have treated him so well and will continue to do so. His story immediately shifts gears in the opposite, more expected conceptual direction, leading directly, thanks to the winds, from the eristic plain of Troy to Ismaros and the Kikonians (39-40); he sacked the city, killed the people, and "out of their city taking their wives and many possessions we shared them out" (41-2)—but the survivors, escaping into the hills, called upon other Kikonian neighbors, and since Odysseus' men refused his advice that they leave quickly, but preferred to drink heavily, they were attacked at dawn and lost six men out of each of his ships before fleeing.

Hardly a noble beginning to the enterprise of getting home safely and well-laden with loot. Zeus compounded their misery with an enormous storm, but still, they seemed headed for home until a strong North Wind beat them off course, and they ended up in the country of the Lotus-Eaters—the first of Odysseus' more supernatural adventures and the second to offer a form of the ongoing question of whose fault it is that things happen as they do. That question, we have seen, applies to the entire Trojan War cycle; in this immediate subset—was it Odysseus or his men whose fault it was that so many got killed by the Kikonians?—the same question might be asked: is it fate, or Zeus, or Odysseus or his men because of whom this small second disaster almost befalls them all? Here Odysseus takes credit for not eating the lotus and for physically carrying back to the ship his men who had partaken, and getting away quickly (84-104): but the near-disaster is the opposite, in form, from that at the hands of the Kikonians: eat the lotus blossoms and you forget about home and lose all desire to return there.

These four contrastive events/experiences—Kalypso, Kirke, Kikonians, and Lotus-Eaters—form a series of preludes for the first major disastrous adventure, one that may be seen both to set so much else in motion for this *nostos* and to offer a direct contrast to Odysseus' experience with the Phaiakians. For from the island of the Lotus Easters they arrive at the land of the Kyklopes, a people who "have no institutions, no meetings for counsels... and each one is the law for his own wives and children, and cares nothing about the others" (112, 114-15). Odysseus arrives there with twelve ships that they beach across from the Kyklopes' island (by sheer luck—or fate—since they do not yet know where they are or who lives there), but, after a day of goat-and-wine feasting sandwiched between two restful nights, the hero proposes that he and his own ship reconnoiter across the bay. This time the opposite condition from that at Ismaros obtains: entering the cave of the one-eyed giant while he is out tending his flocks, Odysseus' men are desperate to take some cheeses and leave and then come back to take "the lambs and kids from their pens, and get back quickly to the ship again, and go sailing off across the salt water, but *I would not listen to them*—it would have been better their way—not until I could see him, see if he would give me presents" (226-9; emphasis added).

Odysseus is too curious, too eager to know about everything. He cannot just leave with his belly's needs satisfied. So he and those members of the crew who are with him set themselves up to await their gigantic host, and when he arrives, after doing his various chores and discovering his visitors, we are subtly informed that this fellow will not be following the usual host-guest behavioral code: he begins by asking them immediately who they are and where they are from, unlike Alkinoos who waits patiently for so very long before asking that question of Odysseus. The question, moreover, is asked with a negative suspicious nuance, asking whether they are marauding pirates of sorts. Odysseus, never caught short-handed for a response, presents his group as Akhaians coming from Troy who "are suppliants at your knees... respect the gods, O best of men. We are your suppliants, and Zeus the guest god, who stands before all strangers and honors due them, avenges any wrong toward strangers and suppliants" (266-7, 269-71).

Alas, that response receives a counter-response that lets us know that the situation is even worse than we might have supposed: "The Kyklopes do not concern themselves over Zeus of the Aegis, nor of any of the rest of the blessed gods, since we are far better than they..." (275-7). Words lead quickly to actions: the reversal of host-guest relational norms intensifies: rather than wining and dining his guests, the Kyklope dines *on* them, seizing two of them and smashing them against the rocky ground before cutting them up "limb by limb and got supper ready, and like a lion reared in the hills, without leaving anything, ate them, entrails, flesh and marrowy bones alike" (291-3).

Odysseus recognizes that, even if he were able to kill his gigantic enemy, even twenty of his men and he—all together—would not be able to remove the stone blocking the door and they would thus perish within this cave. Again a delay until we arrive at the inevitable: that Odysseus the wily one comes up with a stratagem that will both facilitate his escape and further his *kleos*. In one of the decisively eristic moments in the poem, Odysseus—with a good deal of irony—offers Polyphemos wine (after the latter had done his usual evening chores and slaughtered two more of Odysseus' men for his dinner), "[so that he might] see what kind of drink our ship carried inside her. I brought it for you, and it would have been your libation had you taken pity and sent me home..." (348-50).

The irony is double: not only will Odysseus use that wine to get his "host" drunk and sleepy, so that he can sear out his single eye with the well-sharpened, fiery-tipped log that he has spent the better part of a day preparing for the task, returning radically wrong host behavior with radically wrong guest behavior. But when the monster asks Odysseus his name—"so that I may give you a guest present to make you happy... [that] I will eat [you] after [your] friends" (356, 369), the hero answers "Nobody is my name. My father and mother call me Nobody, as do all the others who are my companions" (366-7). So the *kleos*-obsessed Odysseus is—temporarily—instinctively wise enough not to reveal his true name, literally reducing (for the moment) his *kleos*, his famous name, to nothingness: anonymity. It is as if he had never been born, much less achieving name-immortality.

The brutal blinding of the brutal kyklops yields his loud and pained cries, of course, but when he yells to his fellows, bellowing from within his cave, that "Good friends, Nobody is killing me by force or treachery" (408), naturally the others respond with a rhetorical question: why are you crying out, if nobody is hurting you—and they go on their way, leaving behind the suggestion that he pray to his father, Poseidon to cure whatever his ills are. The further trick—to get out of the cave alive and back to their ships—follows. As Polyphemos stands in the entrance to his cave, allowing his huge sheep to go out, Odysseus and his men strap themselves to the bellies of those animals, thereby slipping by his blindly feeling hands.

Odysseus and his men are able in fact to direct those fat sheep to their ship. Safe on board, the hero—perhaps unwisely, but his cleverness is not always synonymous with wisdom, and he believes himself well beyond the monster's reach—abandons his anonymous persona, and from the ship he taunts his victim, and, in spite of the efforts of his men to calm and quiet him, he culminates his tirade with the cry that, regarding "this shameful blinding, tell [whoever asks] that you were blinded by Odysseus, sacker of cities" (503-4). The mistake is that Polyphemos *is* the son of Poseidon, and he prays to his father that he avenge the loss of his eye to Odysseus. The affirmative response—carried out by a father who apparently loves his son regardless of the latter's stated contempt for all the gods, presumably including his own father (another little twist of the *eros-eris* thread)—will ultimately guarantee two things: a long and painful homecoming for Odysseus, alone; and the rest of the epic narrative within the poem with which Odysseus regales the Phaiakians—and us.

The question of where the responsibility resides for the demise of all of Odysseus' crew is addressed by events that begin in the following book of the *Odyssey*, Book Ten. They arrive at the island of Aiolos, who wines and dines his guests and then provides them with a perfect West wind to carry the flotilla home, but "we were ruined by our own folly" (27). For Odysseus was sleepless for nine days, trusting the steering of the lead ship to nobody else, but as he finally gave in to sleep, virtually in site of Ithake, his crew grew too suspicious of the bag given to him as a gift by Aiolos, convinced that it was filled with gold and silver (it contained all the winds needed for a safe journey home). They tore it open and all those winds, released, blew the ships back to the island where they had begun that ten-day journey.

This time, Aiolos, seeing what has happened, in response to Odysseus' plea—"my wretched companions brought me to ruin" (68)—responds that he must be someone whom "the blessed gods hate with such bitterness [and this time commands him] 'out! This arrival means that you are hateful to the immortals!'" (75). And the adventures of Odysseus seem to range back and forth like a barely controllable seesaw between *eros* and *eris*, or hospitality and hostility, as their next journey, seven days after leaving the comfortable island of Aiolos for the second time, brings them, disastrously, to the land of the Laistrygonians. These giants (reminiscent in their size of the Kyklopes) are cannibalistic (like Polyphemos). Only this time the outcome is worse: all of the men in all the ships except those on Odysseus' own vessel are destroyed and turned into a meal for these boulder-wielding brutes (112-32).

Filled with grief and also relief at being alive, this last member of the once majestic flotilla—that sailed and swashbuckled its way to glorious Troy and along the first part of its turn toward home—finds itself at the shore of Aiaia, the island of "Kirke of the lovely hair, the dread goddess who talks to mortals" (136), daughter of Helios, the sun-god. Her incipient *eris*—the turning of the men of Odysseus into swine (as we shall see) and the attempt to do the same to Odysseus—morphs into an entire year of *eros*. We thus arrive at the full story for which Odysseus had earlier provided a prelude. The goddess doesn't seem to like men who come from afar (and men can only come from afar, since her island is off in the middle of the middle which is the edge of the edge of nowhere—part of the amorphous *sacer* realm, indeed). She hosts the half of Odysseus' crew, led by Eurylokhos to scout the landscape, but turns them, with *pharmaka* (drugs—under other circumstances *pharmaka* can be medicines) and her magic wand, into pigs (230-43; I suppose that might not be so difficult to accomplish with many men who are already at least half-way there).

Eurylokhos, having hung back with some suspicion of the goddess, flees back to the ship and tells Odysseus, with horror, what has happened—or rather, simply, that all 22 of his men went into Kirke's palace and never came out again, though he sat and watched for quite some time (244-60). Naturally, the hero sets forth into the deep woods toward Kirke's house to see for himself and to see if he can find and if necessary save his men somehow. It is a moment potentially parallel in its uneven playing ground and thus inevitable outcome, to Hektor going up against Akhilleus in the *Iliad*: the one human and with human weapons, the other semi-divine and with divinely wrought weapons: however heroic Odysseus may be, he is merely a mortal, and he is about to go up against an immortal. However, love will overcome the eristic nature of Kirke, and shape his salvation: the love of a goddess, Athene.

For Athene dispatches Hermes, messenger god, from high Olympos, down into that forest to accost the hero before he draws too near to Kirke's house (280-306). Hermes lays out a plan for Odysseus, having told him exactly what has happened to his men, and culminates his speech by offering Odysseus a special *pharmakon* that he has dug out of the ground: "the gods call it *moly*. It is difficult for mortals to dig it up, but the gods have power to do all things" (305-6). This will serve as a prophylactic against the malignant *pharmaka* of Kirke—and it will tip the seesaw of the playing field in the opposite uneven direction. For Athene and Hermes are Olympians, the highest among god-types; Kirke is a lesser divine being than they, and thus her *pharmaka* are weaker than theirs.

The outcome is that when she hands the hero his drugged beverage and touches him with her wand, saying "go to your sty now and lie down with your other friends there" (319), not only is he not transformed, but he draws his sword—an image that Sigmund Freud would surely have had little difficulty appreciating, particularly given what follows immediately in word and action[92]—"[I] rushed forward against Kirke as if I were going to kill her, but she screamed aloud and ran under my guard, clasping both knees..." (321-22). As we may recall from chapter two, the word knees is "*gounon*" (in the genitive plural form)—derived from the same root that we might recognize in the English word, "gonad(s)."[93] So he pulls out his sword, rushes toward her and she grasps him by both of his...*gounon*...

"[A]nd [she] addressed me in winged words: 'What man are you and whence? Where are your city and parents? ...for no other man, *none*, could ever have stood up under my drugs... there is a mind in you no magic will work on. You are, then, many-turning Odysseus [about whom Hermes was forever telling me]" (325-50). Having been amazed—and, one might say, positively enchanted by the conqueror of her magic (rather than he having been negatively enchanted by hers)—she quickly continues her shift from *eris* toward straightforward and emphatic *eros*: "Come then, put away your sword in its sheath, and let us two go up into my bed so that, lying together in the bed of love [the Greek uses *philotes* here, and not *eros*, specifically], we may then have faith and trust in each other" (333-5).[94]

In order for that transformation to be reciprocated and thus consummated (in both senses of that term), Odysseus, following the instructions given to him by Hermes, demands of her that she "swear a great oath that there is no other evil hurt you might devise against me" (343-4)—which she does, willingly. Her handmaidens prepare everything for the creature comforts of the hero, from bath to bed. Never forgetful of the loyal men, the long-suffering companions whom he loves, he asks her to release them before he can comfortably eat, and so she does—and, recovering their forms, they look younger and taller and handsomer by far than before—and they and Odysseus all weep both for joy at their salvation and renewed grief over the many companions they had lost. The palace resounds with the voices of brotherly love—and all of this is a stepping-off point for a year-long love-fest between Odysseus and Kirke, until finally his men, getting ever more restless, prevail upon him to continue the journey home (to his loyal, long-suffering and forever-waiting wife, Penelope...).

Willing as she is to help Odysseus on the last leg of his journey home, Kirke, however, informs him that he has yet one more important stop to make—that will carry him even further to the edge which is the center which is the edge of nowhere (of *sacer* space): the border between our reality and the realm of death (which is *sacer*), where he will

> ...reach the house of Hades and of revered Persephone,
> there to consult with the soul of Teiresias the Theban,
> the blind prophet, whose senses stay unshaken within him,
> to whom alone Persephone has granted intelligence
> even after death, but the rest of them are flittering shadows.
> (491-5)

Embedded within the epic voyage home of Odysseus, this is the ultimate voyage; intertwined with the paradoxic interweave of *eros* and *eris* is the ongoing and ironic interweave of life and death, of mortality and immortality, of human and divine. Each of these pairs is an analogue of the others and all of them are part of the problematic of trying to understand what humans *are*, within the larger scheme of things. As a hero whose job it is, in part, to offer a more intense, larger-than-life version of what all of us are, the journey within the journey that takes Odysseus to the gates of Hades is the centerpiece of his ongoing effort not only to get home, but to find out who he really is: he, Odysseus, the hero, the warrior, the wanderer, the bigger-than-you-and-I symbol of humanity in its diverse aspects.

As Hermes had given the hero instructions that would help him overcome Kirke's *eris* and transform it into *eros*, Kirke offers him precise instructions—as every successful ritual encounter with the propitious and dangerous *sacer* must include—regarding where to go, and what to do when he gets there. The place to which his ship must take him is precisely indicated; it is where "Pyriphlegthon and Kokytos—which is an off-break from the water of the River Styx—together flow into the Acheron. There is a rock there and the junction of two thunderous rivers. There, hero, you must go close in and do as I tell you..." (513-16). The proper procedure is laid out in detail: the cubit-square pit, the drink-offerings of different types, the promises to the dead in general and to Teiresias in particular of sacrifices upon his return home; the warning not to allow any of the dead near the blood of the sacrificed sheep until Teiresias has drawn nigh and conversed with Odysseus.

There is one thing more—a sacrifice, as it were, to ensure a successful journey to Persephone's grove, of which Odysseus, (and perhaps even Kirke), remains unaware: the youngest of the crew, Elpenor, who fell asleep, drunk, on the roof of Kirke's palace during the long night of farewell eating and drinking and suddenly awoke as the voices of imminent departure grew loud, and forgetting where he was, fell to his death from the roof, breaking his neck.

All of this will play out in the next book (Book Eleven), which tells the story of this central adventure among the hero's adventures. For they arrive at the far limit of deep-running Okeanos, to the place of which Kirke had spoken. Odysseus follows her instructions, digging the pit, pouring in the drink offerings, making his promises, cutting the throat of the sheep, "and the dark-clouding blood ran in, and the souls of the perished dead gathered to the place, up out of Erebos..." (36-7), but he will not allow any of them to draw near to the blood until he has questioned Teiresias. The one exception—he did not need to drink the life's force-bearing blood in order to communicate with the living, since, having died without a funerary ritual he remained between realms—is Elpenor. Odysseus is shocked to see him there—on the other side—having "come faster on foot than I could in my black ship" (57). And so the story of the young man's fate is repeated in his own words, followed by the request that, on the way back Odysseus stop at Kirke's island and give him a proper burial, which the hero is more than happy to do.

The emotion-provoking individuals among the perished dead quickly spikes, when the next to appear is Antikleia, Odysseus' own mother, "whom I had left alive when I went to sacred Ilion" (86)—but he dares not allow her near the blood that would make conversation possible until Teiresias shows up. The Theban seer duly arrives next, however, asking Odysseus, rhetorically, why he is in this dread place, and then asking him to "draw back from the pit, and hold your sharp sword away from me [it is another paradox that the dead would fear and be driven back by a sword!], so that I can drink of the blood and speak the truth to you" (95-6). In lines 100-137 Teiresias speaks of the homecoming, explaining that much of his suffering is the result of Poseidon's anger at the blinding of Polyphemos, as we already, perhaps, suspected. He warns him to "contain your own desire, and contain your companions'" (105)—and we, the audience, so familiar with the story already, know, when he specifically mentions the island of Thrinakia and the cattle and sheep of Helios that he will fail at the latter half of this prescription, resulting in the demise of his entire crew.

We hear with the hero the stated right to "punish the violent acts" of the insolent suitors when he returns home—although whether or not that punishment necessarily means that he slaughter them all is certainly ambiguous. Most riddle-like is the description of what he must do and where he must go, eventually, on yet another journey—this one apparently inland (for he will arrive "where there are men living who know nothing of the sea" (121-22)—making peace with Poseidon through ceremonious sacrifices; and his eventual death "from the sea, in some altogether unwarlike way, and it [death] will find you in the ebbing time of a sleek old age" (134-6). Odysseus' response is to accept the seer's words as true and to turn quickly to the question of why his mother sits there patiently but with neither a word nor even a look in his direction. So apparently Odysseus has not understood the importance of the living blood of the dead sheep to facilitate communication between the dead and the living, since this is what Teiresias explains to him.

Antikleia drinks the blood and immediately recognizes Odysseus. The issue of mother-son love is what we hear next, as we learn from her of the ongoing challenges to his loving wife and of his son who, having come of age, is managing to administer his father's lands, and regarding Laertes, that he is living in depressed, self-chosen squalor out on the farm, away from the main estate, longing for his son's homecoming—and that she, Odysseus' mother, died of a broken heart when it appeared that her son was never coming home again: "it was my longing for you, your cleverness and your gentle ways, that took the sweet spirit of life from me" (202-3).

Odysseus, the poet asserts, responded first by "pondering in my heart" (204), but it is not clear exactly *what* he is pondering: does he really realize that the death of his mother and the grief of his wife, son and father are all directly connected to the adventures (albeit not without pain—but what true adventure lacks some pain?) in which he has thus far been engaged? If we acknowledge how he cannot be blamed for the blowing of his ships back to Aiolos' island or for the dire circumstances of the visit to Polyphemos' island and the aftermath anger toward him of Poseidon, we also cannot ignore the fact that he spent an entire year with Kirke, rather than, theoretically at least, choosing to continue on his homeward journey say, 360 or so days earlier. But the kind of sensitivity to which Akhilleus arrives in the last books of the *Iliad*, and the transformation from someone whose thoughts are only for himself into one who thinks of others does not seem to be part of Odysseus' story.

Its moments of poignancy are more slender, and scattered here and there through the epic—one of the more important ones being here, when, instead of spending much time on reflection or even with words, "three times [he] started toward [his mother], and my heart was urgent to hold her, and three times she fluttered out of my hands like a shadow or a dream, and the sorrow sharpened at the heart within me" (205-7), and in response to why she will not or cannot stay in his arms she informs him—and us—that this

> ...is only what happens, when they die, to all mortals.
> The sinews no longer hold the flesh and the bones together,
> and once the spirit has left the white bones, all the rest
> of the body is made subject to the fire's strong fury,
> but the soul flitters out like a dream and flies away... (218-22)

Having figured out both how the dead can communicate with the living and what it means, physically, to be dead, Odysseus converses, one after the other, with a series of women. The first, Tyro, was in love with the river-gold, Enipeus, but was seduced by Poseidon himself, which union produced a parcel of glorious offspring. The next, Antiope, bore two sons to Zeus. The third is the wife of Amphitryon, Alkmene, who was also seduced by Zeus—producing Herakles. Next he sees Megara, and then beautiful Epikaste, mother of Oidipos (known later, in Sophokles' dramas, as Jokasta) who unwittingly married her own son—the son who had unwittingly murdered his own father, her husband.[95]

Next Odysseus sees Khloris, whom Neleus (one of the sons of Tyro and Poseidon) married for her beauty, who bore him glorious children, including the beautiful Pero, courted by all the heroes—recalling in this the story of Helen and those pursuing her hand when she approached the age of marriage. Next he saw Leda, wife of Tyndareos (seduced by Zeus in the guise of a swan, but that detail is not mentioned here— nor is the fact that Helen resulted from that seduction); and after her, Iphimedeia, wife of Aloeus— "but she told me how she had been joined in love with Poseidon and bore two sons to him" (306-7), who grew gigantic and already as children threatened the Olympians and the order of things until Apollo slew them. "I saw Phaidra and Prokris and Ariadne… and Maira, Klymene, and Eriphyle the hateful, who accepted precious gold for the life of her own dear husband" (321, 326-7).

All of these women share in common some abnormality with regard to love, whether it is to have been seduced—perhaps raped would not be unfair as a term in at least some of these cases—by a god, or having betrayed her husband, or both, or having produced problematic offspring or having had problematic relations with them. There is thus an intensely eristic undertone to all of these figures, the stories of whose loves won and lost would have been well known to the poet's audience—and all of them further focus indirect yet very bright light on Penelope, Odysseus' own wife—and on Arete and the Phaiakian court in which, we are suddenly reminded, the tale of all of these encounters is being recited by Odysseus. For the hero, after these last lines, directs his words to that audience, telling them that he could not recount all of the "women I saw who were the wives and daughters of heroes, for before that the divine night would give out. It is time now for my sleep…" (328-31). And as they are all enthralled into silence, Arete speaks up in praise of his story-telling as well as his beauty and stature, and encourages her fellow Phaiakians to load him down with gifts when he departs.

The dramatic pause reminds us that we are hearing a tale within the tale of the *Odyssey*—thus reminding us, too, that issues that are raised in Odysseus' story to the Phaiakians should resonate not only to them but to us, who are listening, as it were, over their shoulders, to his recital. The account (*mythos*) of the human experience cast in an intensified, exaggerated form, with its paradoxes, contradictions and ironies—the issue and question of mortality and immortality, of human-divine (and more broadly, *profanus-sacer*) relations, of which the intertwining of *eros* and *eris* is a particular and particularly engaging part—resonates beyond the bounds of Odysseus' world and the culture of which he is part, and his time with its immediate audiences, to ourselves, however distant we are from him in time and space.

In any case, in the interlude begun by Arete, to which a warm response comes notably from Ekhenos, Alkinoos has the last words. Taking up first the call to load their guest with gifts—to which Odysseus responds with eloquence—he cannot resist the obvious question before calling it a night; however hospitable he is and considerate of his guest, his curiosity overcomes him, and so he asks: "Did you see any of your godlike companions, who once went to Ilion and there met their destiny? Here is a night that is very long, it is endless. It is not time yet to sleep in the palace. But go on telling your wonderful story…" (371-4)—and who knows, perhaps the wily story-teller had had this in mind all along, and was just testing the interest level of his audience. Whether it had been his plan or not, he responds "if you insist on hearing me still, I would not begrudge you the tale of these happenings…" (380-81)—and takes up his narrative, turning to the men who had sailed to Troy with him.

Not surprising, perhaps, the first of these whom he reports having encountered, after Persephone had scattered the women from the blood-pit, is the soul of Agamemnon, who throws himself into the arms of Odysseus, weeping—or rather, tries to embrace Odysseus, "but there was no force there any longer, nor any juice left now in his flexible limbs, as there had been in time past" (393-4). So we are reminded a second time that the dead retain the form that they possessed when alive but no substance at all. As surprised as he was to see Elpenor at the gate of Hades, he is dismayed to encounter Agamemnon. The son of Atreus tells the story of his demise (that the audience already knows, both from having heard a version of it with Telemakhos and because it is simply known), culminating with a reference to Klytaimnestra as having "splashed shame on herself and the rest of her gender, on women still to come, even on the ones whose acts are virtuous" (433-4).

Again the deep penetration of *eris* in what might be hoped for as a wife-husband relationship of *eros* is articulated—and again, in spite of Agamemnon's angry words, the stark contrast between the behavior of Klytaimnestra and Agamemnon's homecoming to her, and the behavior of Penelope and Odysseus' homecoming-to-her-to-be is shown in high relief. Agamemnon's words dig, further, from another angle, into this contrast: the loving son whom Odysseus will find ready to serve as an ally—who, unbeknownst to him, in fact, has set sail to seek word of his father at the courts of surviving Akhaian friends—who "will fold his father in his arms, as is right" (451) is directly contrasted to Orestes (who will arrive back home from his mother-imposed exile too late to do aught but weep at his father's tomb and then plan an unhappy revenge for his father's death), whom "[m]y wife never even let me feed my eyes [on]... before ... I myself was killed by her" (452-3).[96] Indeed, poignantly, Agamemnon asks whether perhaps Odysseus has heard any news regarding Orestes—is he alive or dead? (457-61)—but as much as, beyond the world of the living, Agamemnon does not know that Orestes is alive, having killed Klytaimnestra to avenge his father's death at her hand, neither does Odysseus know anything, having spent all the time since Troy beyond the bounds of the known world.[97]

While the dialogue with Antikleia had wrapped primarily around parent-child love, and the dialogue with Agamemnon was wrapped primarily around husband-wife and father-son (and mother-son) love, the next great figure, whose argument with Agamemnon set the *Iliad* in motion, is both implicitly about the love of the people for a hero and about self-love; it offers the culminating and most damning of the reflections on death that this poem and the larger pair of surviving epics of which it is part offer to their audience. The central figure of the *Iliad* engages in dialogue with the central figure of the *Odyssey*. For Akhilleus steps forth: hero of heroes, semi-divine—but his divine side and his divine mother, Thetis, could not save him from his human mortality, once he agreed to fight at Troy to earn the *kleos aphthiton*, the "immortal glory" that made him who he was.

Odysseus, seeing the soul of the swift-footed, powerful warrior, responds to the latter's query—what are *you* doing *here?*—with his own comment *cum* query: how goes it for one as glorious as you in these parts? "Before, when you were alive, we

Argives honored you as we did the gods, and now in this place you have great authority over the dead. Do not grieve, even in death, Akhilleus" (484-6). The latter's rueful response reverberates through the corridors of the entire Greek epic tradition:

> O shining Odysseus, never try to console me for dying.
> I would rather follow the plow as a slave to another
> man, one with no land allotted him and not much to live on,
> than be king over all the perished dead. (488-91)

So it's not only that death leaves one formally as one was in life but substanceless, but that the condition is a painful one: one of deprivation, presumably because one still yearns for things that only the living can possess.

In Akhilleus' case, as in Agamemnon's, that yearning is not necessarily to possess physical things—food, wine, precious garments, weapons, tripods, cities, women—but to be in contact with one's loved ones. Like Agamemnon, with whom (to repeat) he engaged in such intense *eris* at the beginning of the *Iliad*, the first question he asks Odysseus is regarding his own "proud son, whether or not he went along to war to fight as a champion [and also] tell me anything you have heard about stately Peleus" (492-4),

> whether he still keeps his position among the Myrmidon
> hordes, or whether in Hellas and Phthia they have diminished
> his state, because old age constrains his hands and feet, and I
> am no longer there under the light of the sun to help him,
> not the man I used to be once…(494-99).

Indeed, Akhilleus spends a full nine lines inquiring and worrying about his father and recalling how invincibly he had, in life, been able to protect Peleus from those who might seek to keep him "from his rightful honors" (503). We have picked up, as it were, where we left Akhilleus at the end of the *Iliad*, having sufficiently transcended his self-love (which does not mean that he has forgotten how great a warrior he was or how to reflect on or speak about it) in favor of love and concern for others, most particularly his aging, mortal father—who is, literally, the DNA source of the human side of this bicameral hero, a hero at once dead and yet so vibrantly alive in the imagination of the audience then and in the generations since.

Odysseus, whose love for life and for undying *kleos* is unparalleled, responds with a full report of the bravery and success of Akhilleus' son, Neoptolemos on the battlefield of Troy—for Odysseus himself fetched him from Skyros to join the Akhaian forces in the last phase of the war. Beyond that, of course, Odysseus could not say, since they will have parted ways after the war and Odysseus, like the dead, lost contact with all of his fellow-warriors heading home with their ships laden with booty—but at least Akhilleus' soul can walk away happy for the news of his son's heroic activity.[98] Appropriately in two ways, the next figure seen by Odysseus is Telemonian Aias: appropriate because he was regarded as the most powerful of the Akhaian warriors after Akhilleus and also because he offers an antithesis to the warm conversations between Odysseus and both Agamemnon and Akhilleus, refusing even to come near (apparently recognizing Odysseus without the benefit of the sheep-blood).

For he remains filled with anger toward Odysseus: after the death of Akhilleus, we are told, Thetis offered the arms of her son as a prize to the one considered most important in the defeat of Troy (the city, the eristic engagement with—thanks to the *eros*-motivated theft of Helen—took the life of her beloved son), and the Akhaians, with support (surprise!) from Athene, voted them not to Aias but to Odysseus. Regarding the focus of our narrative there is something more that is left unsaid here: that part of Aias' upset at having been denied the prize of Akhilleus' arms must be seen in the light of his great love for Akhilleus: he is the one who carried Akhilleus' dead body off the battlefield.[99] Odysseus addresses Aias with comforting words, saying that he, Aias, was indeed the greatest of the Akhaian warriors after Akhilleus, and that the Akhaians mourned him "as incessantly as for Akhilleus the son of Peleus at his death" (557-8)—but Aias merely turns away with quiet hostility.

Odysseus continues his tale of extraordinary meetings at the gates of Hades, with Minos, son of Zeus and judge of the dead; and Orion, the great hunter; and Tityos, son of Earth—described suffering in a manner reminiscent of Prometheus, with two vultures tearing at his liver—but the reason for this unique punishment is that he had raped Leto, "the honored consort of Zeus" (and mother of Apollo and Artemis) while she was on her way to Pytho.[100] The last few are mainly, in fact, individuals being subject to punishments: Tantalos—the ancestor of Agamemnon—who can never quite reach the water in which he stands, to drink, or the plentiful fruit of the tree with branches just above his head; and Sisyphos, soaked in sweat as he forever tries to push the boulder up the hill from the near-top of which it keeps rolling back down.

Lastly, Herakles—or rather, as the poet quickly tells us, his *eidolon* (his *image*), since "he himself [as everyone knows] is among the immortal gods enjoying their festivals, married to sweet-stepping Hebe, child of great Zeus and Hera of the golden sandals" (602-4). Mere image or not, Herakles recognizes Odysseus and addresses him, comparing his own sufferings through the twelve labors that he was forced to do for a man who was very much his inferior with what he assumes must be Odysseus' sufferings if he is down among the dead. It is at once a strange and fitting conclusion to this adventure within the larger adventure: strange in offering a grim way to think in comparative terms of Odysseus and prior heroes, yet fittingly focused on the ultimate heroic demi-god, and the only one among all those whom Odysseus encounters who in some real sense escaped death, since the true Herakles, and not a mere *eidolon*, resides among the immortals. Odysseus, his mirror opposite, is slowly, now, returning from the reality beyond the gates of adventure and death to everyday life: to Ithake, his beloved wife and beloved son and beloved father—and loving nurse and dog—and with that return, to the re-engagement of the storm and stress and hurly-burly of the real world.

He is suddenly caught by green fear that Persephone might send up some monster from Hades, so he hurries back to the ship, calls his companions on board and sets sail, as Book Twelve opens, making first for Kirke's island in order to burn the body of Elpenor with the proper funerary rites. This culminates with a grave mound crowned by a gravestone and the well-shaped oar planted in the top of it (10-15). We are perhaps reminded of the anticipated culmination of Odysseus' future post-*nostos* travel, when he will plant his oar in the earth and offer sacrifices to Poseidon—which is as it should be, since death and divinity are analogous aspects of the *sacer*, and our engagements of both run on parallel tracks.

Kirke and her attendants come down to the water's edge near which they have had the funeral—with sympathy for these poor mortals who will end up having visited Hades twice, not just once—bringing food and drink to sustain them. They spend the night there—Odysseus and Kirke apart from the others, as she tells him what to anticipate on the rest of the homeward journey. They will pass the beautiful but dangerous singing Sirens, and find themselves caught in the challenging choice of direction between Skylla and Kharybdis—that choice will be between the entire ship being sucked down into the depths of Kharybdis' whirlpool or losing six men to the multiple mouths of Skylla, extending down from the rocky cliffs above. Odysseus naturally wants to know if there is some way he can avoid even that loss. There seems to be naught that he can do, according to Kirke, except to invoke the mother of Skylla, Krataiis—which may prevent a second attack and the loss of another six men. So one might say that he is advised to make use of the love-relationship that is assumed between mother and daughter (even among monstrous immortals!) in order to avoid the strife/hate-driven action of Skylla.

Kirke's ongoing prophecy regarding what Odysseus will encounter, culminating with reference to the island of Helios, the sun-god and his magnificent cattle, continues until the dawn came up—not only the appropriate time to depart from Kirke's uniquely *sacer* space but for her to complete and terminate her *sacer*-inspired words to the hero. Moreover, as a *sacer* figure, with certain powers to affect the *profanus*, Kirke—the erstwhile eristic, would-be destroyer of Odysseus and his men, having become the hero's *eros*-bound companion and aid—is able to provide the ship with a strong following wind (149-50). Odysseus now shares the information that Kirke had imparted him during their last night together. Shortly, the ship passes the Sirens and Odysseus stops up his men's ears with beeswax and has himself tied firmly to the mast so that he can listen to their song, without being drawn to destruction. He cannot simply pass by beyond hearing's distance, for to be who he is he must *experience and know* what others have not—and the Sirens claim to "know everything that happens" over the entire earth—and survive.

The path between Skylla and Kharybdis is as horrible as Kirke had predicted, and six men are lost to the lustful appetite of Skylla. They arrive thereafter to the island of Helios (also called Hyperion), which evokes not only the warning of Kirke (who is the daughter of Helios) to the hero, but also a warning that he had been given by Teiresias, the blind *sacerdos*: to avoid the island that is so pleasant. There is some irony in the fact that the sailor who speaks up to convince Odysseus that they ought to stop at the island is Eurylokhos, the very one who led half of the crew into the lair of Kirke and its near-disaster. He accuses his leader of being a hard man, whose

> limbs never wear out. You must be made all of iron,
> if you will not let your companions, worn with hard work and wanting sleep,
> set foot on this island...
> ...[to] make ready a greedy dinner... (280-3)

Little does Eurylokhos know how precisely prophetic his words are—the fulfillment of which will lead to doom for everyone left in the crew except the "made all of iron" leader whose limbs "never wear out." Indeed, the events that follow underscore that ongoing Greek question that is so particularly well embedded within its epic poems: who is ultimately responsible for the outcome—particularly the tragic, unhappy outcome—of a given narrative? Not only is that answer shared across three realms—Fate (*moira*), the gods, and humans—but in this case, among humans, where any number of tragic outcomes for members of his crew can be traced to Odysseus himself, here he explicitly reminds them (and us) that he has acceded to their "force" for him to stop at a place that he was warned two times to avoid (297).

Moreover, he then extracts an oath from them that they not touch any sheep or cattle that they encounter, limiting their meal to the food provided already by Kirke (298-302). They agree, and he reminds them again—when their stay is lengthened due to a huge Zeus-provided storm that prevents their putting out to sea—that they keep their hands off the cattle that are "the cattle and fat sheep of a dreaded god, Helios, who sees all things and listens to all things" (322-3). Alas, however, the storm continues and adverse winds follow for an entire month, and their food runs out and they turn to hunting and fishing—until the gods to whom Odysseus has gone off to pray "shed a sweet sleep on [his] eyelids" (l 339), and Eurylokhos (again!) induces his companions to slaughter the *best*, no less, of the cattle, to make an offering to the gods and consume the rest.

When Odysseus awakens and, heading back toward the ship, realizes from the smell of cooking meat what has happened, he assails the gods for having lulled him "with a pitiless sleep, to my confusion" (372), while Helios Hyperion demands of Zeus punishment of and recompense from the companions of Odysseus for what they have done—threatening otherwise to "go down to Hades' realm and give my light to the dead" (383). Odysseus informs his audience that he was made privy to this *sacer* conversation later on, by Kalypso, who had heard it from Hermes (389-90).

In any case, for six days the men continue to feast on the cattle—Odysseus presumably does not, although nowhere is the text explicit that he did otherwise—and when the winds change and they sail, Zeus waits until they are out to sea to bring on the huge storm that destroys the ship and the remainder of the crew, while Odysseus himself survives—again, there is irony in the details: the windy sea drives him back to Kharybdis, where he is able to cling to the fig tree growing on the rocks near her inescapable whirlpool until it spits back up remnants of his ship that he can grab and use to convey himself away—thanks to Zeus, according to the hero's narrative—which last piece of journey carries him, nine days later, to the island of Kalypso. And "she befriended and took care of me" (450). So embedded in the human-vs-gods-vs-Fate and Odysseus-vs-his crew question with regard to responsibility for outcomes, in the conclusion of his tale, is a journey that extends from the angry eristic words of Helios and the destructive actions of Zeus to the loving behavior toward him (rather understated by him) of Kalypso.

Halfway through the epic, now, we are returned to the time and place in which Odysseus has been spinning this dynamic tale of his adventures, in Book Thirteen, and to the long-delayed conveyance of the hero back home, with the generous help of the

Phaiakians. In Odysseus' last speech to them — in particular to Alkinoos — while still in their halls, he lovingly hopes for a return to his house to find "a blameless wife" and wishes them comfort and cheer, in remaining at home, with "your wedded wives and your children" (43-5).

This is certainly the simplest and most straightforward, family-based moment of expressing love within the epic. It comes sandwiched between the end of the narrative of his adventures — culminating with a reference to Kalypso and its much more ambiguous love-contexts — and the final stage of his twenty-year journey itself. That journey will once again find our hero closing his eyes in "a sleep, gentle, the sweetest kind of sleep with no awakening, almost like death" (79-81) while others take the tiller. We might recall that the last time that this happened to him on board ship, after he had guided his ship for nine days and nights, his crew opened up the bag given to him by Aiolos, leading to a disaster that would ultimately encompass everyone, destroying every last one of them except Odysseus himself.

This time there will be another disaster — a double disastrous outcome: one for the hero's newest friends and one for his most recent enemies. The hero will be safely deposited, still deeply asleep, in a cave on the outskirt shore of Ithake, together with more than enough gifts to compensate him for all the loot that he has lost in the past decade of wanderings since Troy. This final act of Phaiakian love and respect for the guest who wove such wondrous tales of love and strife for them — of suffering and triumph across known and unknown worlds — is a prelude to the final act of *eris*-driven anger enacted by Poseidon, when he can, upon Odysseus, and upon those associated with him or helpful to him when Odysseus proves to be beyond his reach. It will come against the brave and skillful sailors who brought Odysseus and his gifts home, as they in turn return home to their own island.

For after conferring with Zeus about this, Poseidon goes off

> to Scheria, where the Phaiakians are born and live. There
> he waited, and the sea-going ship came close in, lightly
> pursuing her way, and the Earthshaker came close up to her,
> and turned her into stone and rooted her there to the bottom

with a flat stroke of his hand. And then he went away from her. (160-4)

That final act by Poseidon is either exceptionally cruel—he allows them to reach virtually to their own harbor before he strikes them down (and it is implied but not certain that all those on board the ship are turned to stone when their ship is)—or just the opposite. For to the dismayed Phaiakians on land who see this horrifying transformation, Alkinoos recalls an old prophecy that, he now understands, has been fulfilled. Not only, then, are the Phaiakians not left wondering what happened to their fellows as they might have been had Poseidon struck on the high seas, but, through the words and prescribed actions (the sacrifice of twelve bulls to Poseidon) of their king, they are able to arrive at a resolution with the god of the sea (170-87).

Meanwhile, Odysseus, unaware of the havoc that he has indirectly wreaked on his former hosts, awakens in that cave within his home country, and in a manner recalling his arrival into the home city of the Phaiakians, his patron goddess Athene, who so loves this hero, covers him with a mist so that he cannot be recognized—and makes his own homeland unrecognizable to him—as she waits for the opportunity to tell him exactly what has happened in Ithake and to assist him in formulating a plan to reclaim it all. That plan will culminate with the final eristic acts of Odysseus against those who sought to take it all from him.

He even curses the Phaiakians for having lied to him, as he thinks, and deposited him somewhere other than Ithake. So again, responsibility for outcomes: could we say that it is actually Odysseus who is responsible for the demise of that Phaiakian ship in that Poseidon, paradoxically, fulfills the wish expressed in the hero's uttered curse? In *sacer* time and space the fact that Poseidon would seem from a *profanus* perspective to have already acted might be irrelevant—but maybe the god's action came after Odysseus woke up and after he utters his curse. Odysseus in any case thinks that he is still somewhere in the *sacer* and not in the *profanus* homeland to which he has in fact finally arrived—awake now, whereas he slept through the journey. Surely it must have been confusing to him, however, when he counted up all the gifts and found nothing missing: why would the Phaiakians deceive him but not steal from him when they could have?

Athene can explain, if he can be patient—which he barely can, and in fact, even her explanation will arrive in the context of another deception, as she disguises herself as a young herdsman. The great dissimulator finds himself deceived for the first time since, perhaps, he mistakenly believed that Polyphemos would respect the gods of hospitality—but by his own patron!

As so often, there are small touches of irony interlaced with the larger ones that shape the Greek epics overall. Thus, when Odysseus encounters the goddess in her guise as shepherd boy, he is so thrilled to meet someone in what to him is a strange, unknown country that he bubbles over with the words "I make my prayer to you [to rescue his possessions and him] as to a god, and come to you and your dear knees as a suppliant" (230-1). S/he responds to his question regarding where he is by revealing that it is Ithake, the name of which "has gone even to Troy" (248-9)—and he, clearly gladdened by that news, responds by addressing "her in winged words; but he did not tell her the truth... [saying] 'I heard the name of Ithake when I was in wide Krete, far away, across the sea... I have fled, an exile, because I killed the son of Idomeneus, Orsilikhos, a man swift of foot... because he tried to deprive me of all my share of the plunder from Troy" (254-63)—contriving an entire fiction that concludes with the statement that he paid Phoinikian seamen to take him to Pylos or Elis, but they left him here.

If on the one hand we might appreciate some of the resonances from real events—swift-footed heroes who died (like Akhilleus) at Troy, but not at Odysseus' hand, or swift-footed Phaiakians whom he didn't deign to race, or Aias who perished indirectly due to Odysseus' being awarded the prize of swift-footed Akhilleus' armor after the latter's death—we might also, in some corner of our auditor/reader mind, wonder again regarding the tales he told the Phaiakians: how much of all of that was true and how much entertaining fabrication? Be that as it may, Athene responds (287ff) by resuming her recognizable guise and noting how clever he is: "it would be a sharp one, and a stealthy one, who would ever get past you in any contriving; even if it were a god against you!" (291-2).

So this duel of deceptions, which under other circumstances would certainly be considered eristic in nature—why would you feel obliged to lie to a loved one you trust?—resolves itself into a love-based recognition reunion between the hero and his patron goddess (who reminds him of that love, and of how she is always by his side, including back among the Phaiakians, when she "made you loved by all [of them]" (302). Even then, he doubts that he is truly in Ithake, thanks to her success at fogging it up for him, and their banter back and forth continues. She assures him that his wife has been waiting loyally for him—but recognizes that he will need to see that for himself—and explains that she did not wish to fight with her father's brother, Poseidon, and thus could not ease Odysseus' homecoming to the extent that she would have liked.

She finally scatters that mist and the land comes into a familiar focus for Odysseus: one might imagine him as if he were the viewer of an Impressionist painting, who steps back from the horsehair-laden globs of paint to the point where the colors and lines coalesce as the image of the depicted landscape. Then they enter the cave and begin planning the destruction of the suitors. When Athene exclaims on how for the past three years these guys have been pressing Penelope—while she continues to hope for the return of her husband, cleverly promising this to one and that to the other, while "her mind has other intentions" (381)—Odysseus observes how he might have suffered an ignominious fate like Agamemnon did. Once more, then, we are reminded of the contrast between Klytaimnestra's wait for her husband, plotting his destruction, and Penelope's wait for her husband, who is now finally in a position to plot the destruction of the suitors—and asks the goddess to "weave the design" (386) of that destruction in which he asks her to remain by his side. For her presence would raise his capacity to face down a multiplicity of enemies.

The beginning of the woven plot—its weave resonating with the three-year-long deceptive weaving project carried out by Penelope and of Odysseus' previous weaving, to the Phaiakians, and, we might suppose, with his future weaving to Penelope and Telemakhos, of tales of his sufferings and his ultimate victories—is, again, deception, and not at all related to standard warrior valor. For Athene changes his appearance to that of an old beggar and sends him to his loyal swineherd to ask questions and wait. Meanwhile, the goddess will head to Sparta to fetch Telemakhos. Yet another twist in this complex relationship, as Odysseus asks Athene why she never informed Telemakhos of his father's fate: "was it so that he too wandering over the barren/ sea should suffer pains, while others ate up his substance?" (418-19)—that he, we might say, could experience a smaller version of what his father was experiencing, and thus begin the growth process not only toward manhood, but toward being the man-son of a hero? Confirming this last aspect of Telemakhos' story, Athene adds that it was "so he would win reputation—*kleos*—by going there [to Sparta]" (422-3).

And so the two part ways. Odysseus finds Eumaios, as Book Fourteen opens, who hosts the anonymous beggar warmly—again contrasting the behavior of the suitors in a manner recalling obliquely how the hosting of the hero by the Phaiakians so strongly contrasted with the non-hospitality of Polyphemos. The swineherd's enduring loyalty—his love—for Odysseus is clearly articulated, as is his longing for the hero: "even when he is not here, my friend, I feel some modesty/about naming him, for in his heart he cared for me greatly/ and loved me (144-6). Eumaios prattles on, certain that Odysseus is coming home soon, and Odysseus responds with another tall tale about his disguised self—once more placing his origins in Krete (where Zeus, consummate patron of hospitality, was raised, after all). The false tale within our tale extends a full 170 verses—and embedded within it is the assertion that among the Thesprotians he had word of Odysseus, to wit that he "had gone to Dodoma, to listen to the will of Zeus" (327-8).

There is irony, yet again, in the response of Eumaios: that although he is not convinced about what the stranger has said regarding Odysseus, yet "why would such a man as you are lie recklessly to me?" (364-5)—a rhetorical question to which we know the answer: because Odysseus has an inordinately difficult time not telling tales, even with those he has reason to trust, especially when his survival is at stake and/or he is in the midst of a plot for which the time of truth has not yet arrived. Indeed, the conversation continues at length, and Odysseus continues to punctuate his part of it with references to himself that are and are not references to himself. Thus, for instance,

> I wish I were young again and the strength still steady within me,
> as when, under Troy, we formed an ambush detail and led it.
> The leaders were Odysseus and Atreus' son, Menelaos,
> and I made a third leader with them... (468-71)

How marvelous this detail on the poet's part—or on Odysseus' part! We, and presumably the poem's original auditors, well remember that important ambush, described in Book Ten of the *Iliad*. It was led, though, by Odysseus and Diomedes, not Odysseus and Menelaos, and there was no third leader, as this tale-teller of course knows, since it is Odysseus himself telling about it—because he was there, not as a nameless third figure but as himself. Nor does our Odysseus-disguised-as-old-beggar merely throw this off as a passing comment on his lost youth, but goes into considerable detail regarding the fabricated conversations that he, (the nameless beggar), alleges to have had with Odysseus.

We might also note the symmetry within the poem with regard to the play on the question of Odysseus' identity and the *kleos* of his name: After finally identifying himself to the Phaiakians as Odysseus, he told tales the centerpiece of which may be said to be his first and last interchange with Polyphemos—the first in which he calls himself "Nobody" and the last in which he perilously shouts out his real name to the angry, groaning, blinded giant. Here, at the beginning of the end of the hero's long adventure, disguised as a nobody beggar, this tale within the tale unraveled for Eumaios' benefit, reminds us obliquely of his great skill as a strategist and not merely as a straight-out warrior—who will shortly use both those skills to defeat his final enemies. And how perfect is it that Eumaios' response is to refer to the tale as "a blameless fable the way you told it" (508)? A strong bond—a loving friendship—is being forged between these two, at a different level from that bond of twenty years earlier between Eumaios and Odysseus.

Meanwhile—in Book Fifteen—Athene has swiftly come to Sparta, where we left Telemakhos in the emotionally charged and complex court of Menelaos and Helen, back in Book Four. Telemakhos has been engaged in a parallel search for his father, for words about and word of his father, and for his own identity, while his father has been searching for home and at the same time for adventure and his own identity and *kleos*. The goddess appears at the foot of Telemakhos' bed and suggests to him that it is time for him to head home, to begin thinking of marriage and of how to avoid the suitors waiting in ambush for him—weaving, then, the dual issues of *eros* and *eris*. Loaded with gifts from Menelaos that remind us yet again of that all-important guest-host relationship (and of how it has been abrogated for several years by the suitors in Odysseus' home), and accompanied by heaven-sent bird-portents and Helen's prophetic assertions, he begins the journey home, accompanied initially by Peisistratos, son of another of Odysseus' old friends, Nestor.

Telemakhos' own words (195-7) to Peisistratos as they arrive toward Pylos, Nestor's home, confirm that that friendship and love has been passed to his own generation. His words before boarding ship at Pylos—to Theoklymenos, a former fugitive for having killed a man, who became a prophet—identifying himself as an Ithakan, "and Odysseus is my father, if he ever lived" (267-8) reminds us, too, who have followed the hero through all of his adventures and recounted adventures, that for his son, having grown up without a father, that heroic figure is a virtual myth whose reality he has as much reason to doubt as do those who have waited so long for his return and heard so many false claims regarding where he is and when he is coming back to Ithake.

As always, the entertainment value of side stories serves also to delay the arrival—in this case, of the son of Odysseus, on a smaller scale than the story-generated delays of Odysseus himself—and offer a fleshier Telemakhos than a mere skin-and-bones character who arrives not home, but to Eumaios' hut, as instructed by Athene. There—further delaying Telemakhos' arrival for the reader/auditor—Odysseus the disguised is once again regaling the swineherd with, not a false tale but a faulty plan, in order to test the loyalty of this loyal retainer. Eumaios, in response, ends up telling his own story—of how he had once been a prince and was reduced to his present circumstances. While that long tale is being told, Telemakhos is being dropped off-ship nearby, and, after another conversation with Theoklymenos that underscores the disarray in the home of Odysseus, the prophet is dispatched for hospitality to the home of Telemakhos' best companion, Peiraios, to be cared for until Telemakhos can send for him—after the issues in his own home have been resolved—and the budding young hero hikes swiftly to the hut of Eumaios.

Book Sixteen thus begins with the approach of Telemakhos first noticed by the dogs, then by Odysseus and then Eumaios, who greets him as a father would a long-lost son, with embraces and kisses and strong statements of love. Odysseus himself has to hold back, of course, or lose his cover—the emotional strain is compelling, given the twenty years of separation and the awe with which the father must be struck by the fine young man who was an infant when he last saw him. He waits in the hut, rising only to offer his own seat to the ever-courteous Telemakhos who insists that the old man not move on his account. When Eumaios identifies the stranger as a suppliant for Telemakhos' hospitality, the young man is pained and honest about his fear that he cannot offer him appropriate protection, given the situation at home, so begs Eumaios to keep him on, for which he (Telemakhos) will happily bear all the costs.

This provokes the dialogue between Odysseus and Telemakhos (in which, of course, the son does not know that it is his father with whom he speaks, nor does he know that his father knows that it is the son of Odysseus, his own son, to whom *he* speaks) in which the son tells his father about his own genealogy and about the problems in the house. Eumaios is dispatched to tell Penelope that Telemakhos is back. Athene arrives, seen only by Odysseus and the dogs, who taps him with her golden wand, and he is transformed back to his own form—which is of course still not one familiar to the son who has not seen his father since infancy. Indeed, when Telemakhos is amazed at the change, and asks if he is a god, Odysseus identifies himself, and weeps and kisses his son—but Telemakhos does not believe his father: "No, you are not Odysseus my father, but some divinity/beguiles me, so that I must grieve the more, and be sorry" (194-5).

Identity is even more complicated than we thought up to this point, as are love and strife and their place in what we believe and what we recognize. Odysseus is a bit put out by his son's refusal to believe him, insisting that it is he—for "no other Odysseus than

I will ever come back to you" (203-4) — and explaining that Athene had indeed effected the transformation that he has seen. And now, convinced, Telemakhos breaks into tears and loud laments, joined shortly by his father — interrupted by Telemakhos' question (he *is* the son of ever-curious Odysseus, after all) as to how he arrived here. Odysseus briefly explains about the Phaiakians, before quickly turning to his own questions regarding the number of suitors and who and of what sort (presumably as potential warriors) they are.

The beginnings of the plan are being hatched, while meanwhile, the ship without Telemakhos is arriving into harbor, the suitors' intended ambush is foiled by the lack of the intended victim, the suitors confer — and we are reminded of their arrogance and moral ugliness — and for the first time since Book One Penelope not only appears but speaks. She singles out Antinoos, whose father's life was saved by Odysseus, calling upon him to desist from his despicable behavior and to encourage the other suitors to do so, as well. The one who responds to her, however, is Eurymakhos, who recalls how Odysseus used to hold him on his knees "and put roasted meat in my hands, and hold the red wine out to me. Therefore, of all men Telemakhos is the dearest to me by far" (443-5) — while planning Telemakhos' murder. This profession of son-like and bother-like love embedded within the knowledge that the speaker plans a maximal eristic act yield to the end of the book, with Eumaios back at the hut, Odysseus back in his old beggar disguise and "the gift of slumber" distributed to all.

Book Seventeen continues the slow but relentless push toward the poem's climax, with Telemakhos returning to his house, where he tells his mother about his adventures, including what he has heard regarding his father — most notably, in lines 142-4, that he is held in the palace of the nymph, Kalypso, (and one might wonder what Penelope or the audience thinks about that!). The prophetic assertion by Theoklymenos immediately follows: that Odysseus is already here, somewhere in Ithake, planning disaster for the suitors. Odysseus himself arrives, in his beggar disguise, together with Eumaios — encountering the nasty goatherd, Melanthios, on the way (a foil for Eumaios) — and recognized by his loyal dog, who, in his extreme old age, content at last to see that his master is home, dies quietly. Odysseus begs for food from the suitors, who further the ugliness of their character-depiction by mocking him: Antinoos in fact throws a footstool at him, hitting Odysseus in the back with it, causing him to prophecy the destruction of this leader among the suitors, for "if there are any gods or any Furies for beggars/ Antinoos may find his death before he is married" (ls 475-6). Eumaios tells Penelope about his still-unnamed guest who claims to be a friend by family of Odysseus, and she asks to speak to him, wishing that if her husband might return, he and his son could rid the palace of the pestilence of suitors: and Telemakhos' timely sneeze is interpreted hopefully by her as a prophecy of her wish's fulfillment.

We are led into Book Eighteen by way of further moments anticipating the final acts of violent strife in this palace in which familial love has held sway on so many levels during the years while Odysseus was gone and engaged in very different sorts of acts of love and strife. The still-disguised hero is challenged by the beggar Iros, goaded on by Antinoos, and Odysseus easily knocks his opponent down and out, to the cruel amusement of the suitors — the display reminiscent of a cock fight in some other part of the world in a different time — who toast the victor whom a moment earlier they had mocked. Unwittingly, of course, their prayers for his future success helps invoke their own oncoming demise. Inspired by Athene — and her beauty supernaturally enhanced, during a nap, by the goddess, with ambrosia — Penelope chooses to re-appear in the aftermath of the fight, criticizing Telemakhos for having permitted the new stranger to be so-treated. Telemakhos agrees with her that he should not have allowed the fight that, nonetheless, resulted in the stranger's victory over Iros — and invokes the gods, that they might bring the suitors to a condition similar to that of Iros. We cannot miss the irony — we who know that their fate will in fact be worse than his, and who also know that Telemakhos knows that the victorious stranger is the very Odysseus, disguised, who will effect that outcome.

Penelope is again verbally assaulted by Eurymakhos, and her response is recognized by her husband as fitting for someone who is his life-mate: she cleverly hints at marriage to one of them, while first seeking to exact from them competing courtship gifts, rather than consuming her own food and drink. It is as if she somehow knows, even as she does not yet know, that Odysseus is here, that these haughty and cruel men are doomed. The threads in the tapestry continue to multiply and intertwine. Odysseus the old beggar is berated by Melantho, the disloyal maid, who has been sleeping with Euymakhos—who then adds more insults to his soon-to-be killer. The verbal *agon*—the contest, in this case, of words—between Eurymakhos and Odysseus ends only when Telemakhos intervenes, commanding the suitors to go home to sleep, shocking them with his assertiveness. And, perhaps surprisingly, they leave for the night.

Book Nineteen opens with Odysseus suggesting to Telemakhos, after the suitors have left, that he hide away all of the weapons usually out in the hall of feasting, while Eurykleia, the old nurse, is commanded to keep all of the womenfolk out of the way. After Telemakhos goes up to bed, Penelope—"looking like Artemis or like golden Aphrodite" (l 54)—comes down from her chamber, surprised to see the old beggar still hanging around in the great hall. One of her servant girls—it is Melantho, a second time—snaps at him, and in response, Odysseus once again tells a brief tale (only a few verses, really) of who he was and is and warns of the demise of those who behave as she does, whether or not Odysseus returns. Penelope, overhearing the exchange, excoriates Melantho and asks a different servant-girl to pull up a comfortable chair for him, "so that the stranger may be seated, and tell me his story, and listen to what I have to say" (98-9).

This will be the first conversation between these two in two decades, and her first question to him is: "What man are you and whence? Where is your city? Your parents? (105)—the sort of question posed so directly only once before, by Alkinoos, king of the Phaiakians, but only after a considerable amount of time had passed after Odysseus' sudden appearance into his court. He responds by complimenting her—indeed asserting that her *kleos* goes up into the wide heaven—and asking her to ask him anything, "but do not ask who I am, the name of my country, for fear you may increase in my heart its burden of sorrow…" (116-17). She responds in turn by turning the subject back to herself, unburdening herself to this stranger and apologizing, really, for ignoring both strangers and suppliants because of her ongoing grief: "I waste away at the inward heart, longing for Odysseus. These men try to hasten the marriage. I weave my own wiles" (136-7). In one concise pair of verses she has underscored her undying love for the man who, unbeknownst to her, sits before her at her feet while also asserting her Odysseus-like cleverness at keeping the wild suitor-dogs at bay—but also, twenty verses later, expressing her fear that she has run out of tricks and will be forced into marriage with one of them.

Odysseus' response is—once again—to tell a partial, false tale of himself, various versions of which we have heard before: that he hails from Crete and that there he knew—and entertained—Odysseus. Where back in Book Fourteen Eumaios had responded to Odysseus' tale by noting what "a blameless fable [it was] the way you told it" (508), Penelope, more aggressively challenges him—she has heard too many people over the years asserting too often that they have seen or spoken with Odysseus—by giving him a test: if he indeed entertained him, then "tell me what sort of clothing he wore on his body, and what sort/of man he was himself, and his companions who followed him" (218-19). Odysseus plays his part well, for he notes that this was many years ago—and yet (of course) he remembers the hero's "woolen mantle of purple, with two folds" (225-6), and how it was decorated, and the golden pin that held it in place. Needless to say, the accumulation of details brings Penelope to tears—"For I myself gave him this clothing, as you describe it..." (255). And of course Odysseus arrives at the statement, offered "without deception, without concealment" (269), that Odysseus is nearly home, who, the sole survivor of his crew, was cast ashore onto the island of the Phaiakians, who, honoring him in their hearts, would have borne him safely home sooner than this, had he not wanted to go about, first, acquiring the valuable possessions for the gathering of which he has a unique, almost god-like skill.

Penelope's response to this extended semi-fabrication is also of the sort we have heard/read before from those dear to our hero: if all that you say prove true, "soon you would be aware of my love and many gifts given by me" (310)—but she doubts that Odysseus will ever come home again. Rather than responding to this, Odysseus redirects, suggesting to her that he is tired, and hinting that he has no desire for foot-washing hospitality—unless there might be some "aged and virtuous woman" who, having endured as he has, would handle his feet without disgust—which prompts Penelope to call upon Eurykleia (as Odysseus must have anticipated) to perform just that task. One of our three central concerns regarding this poem—the search for self-definition, identity, name-fulfillment by Odysseus; the violent strife that carries us from Polyphemos' cave to the slaughter of the suitors in Odysseus' dining room; and the interweave of strife with the ongoing theme of love as it is expressed in diverse forms and directions—is about to achieve one of its climaxes. Or perhaps the "Nobody" shoe dropped by Odysseus in the Kyklopes' lair is about to be dropped with Odysseus' foot suspended above the basin of bath water in which Eurykleia is washing it.

The old nurse begins by noting that

> [t]here have been many hard-traveling strangers who have come here,
> but I say that I have never seen one as like as you are
> to Odysseus, both as to your feet, and voice, and appearance.
> (379-81)

Indeed. This similarity he can pass off as an oft-noted detail—but then, as she pushes up his garment to wash his feet and legs,

> ...she at once recognized
> that scar, which the boar with his white tusk had inflicted
> on him... (392-4)

In that extended moment—almost *sacer* in its nature, in which, as time seems to stand still, Odysseus realizes that he has been recognized and reaches for Eurykleia's throat, fearful that she will expose him—a lengthy aside tells the tale of that scar, gained when, as a young boy, he had been allowed to participate with the grown men in the boar hunt. Being *Odysseus*, it was he, the mere boy, who got the boar; but it also gored him, at the moment in which he was killing it with his spear, ripping his leg and leaving it with a permanent scar. More to the point, this moment of giving and receiving intense pain simultaneously, encapsulated in that childhood moment, is used by the poet to articulate the essence contained within his name. For *'Odysseus'* is etymologized by the poet as coming from the Greek verb, *'odyein'*—meaning 'to give or receive pain.'

And we think: not only is Odysseus' most frequent epithet 'long-suffering,' and not only does he indeed suffer in the course of his long journey home from Troy, but *everyone* he encounters suffers as a consequence—from the Trojans whose city he destroys, obviously, to the goddesses he abandons when he is ready, to the Kyklops he blinds, to the Phaiakians who ferry him home, and, together with their ship, are turned to stone within sight of their own harbor; from the entire flotilla of his ships' crews who don't survive the journey with him, to the suitors he slaughters upon his return; from the wife who spends so many years fighting off the insistent interest of those suitors to the son who grows up without a father, to the mother who dies of heartbreak while he is gone and the father who moves back out to the old farm, living like a hobo, in grief and frustration. 'Giving and receiving pain' is indeed the essence of Odysseus, regardless of the technical correctness or not of the poet's etymologizing.

The ambiguous meaning of the hero's name is mirrored by the expression—as we exit the long side tale of how he got that scar—of Eurykleia: "Pain and joy seized her at once, and both eyes filled with tears… 'Then, dear child, you are really Odysseus…!'" (471-4). Athene succeeds in distracting Penelope at that moment, and when Odysseus, horrified, asks Eurykleia rhetorically why she is trying to kill him, she responds, equally horrified that he should imagine such an intention on her part—and furthermore telling him that she will provide him with a list of those women in the palace who are loyal and those who are not. Book Nineteen offers such a wonderful sequence of images: Odysseus' foot in mid-air, the tale of his name, then his hand reaching for Eurykleia's throat as Athene, invisibly, distracts Penelope, then immediately after the brief conversation between Master and Nurse, as she heads off to get another basin of water because virtually the entire contents of the first spilled onto the floor in the excitement—and Penelope, snapping out of a frozen trance, begins to talk again, telling the stranger that she "will stay here and talk to you, just for a little" (509) — clearly drawn to him, although she does not realize it or know why. Again she confides in him — not her long-lasting sorrow, but her indecision regarding what she must do *now*: continue to wait for her husband in spite of everyone's insistence (her parents, her people, even her son) that she trade the past for a present-future, or give in to everyone's insistence.

She asks the stranger to interpret a dream that she has had, regarding a great eagle that came down from the mountains and broke the necks of twenty geese around the house that she delighted in feeding. As she wept, the eagle perched on the gable of the house and spoke in a human voice, identifying himself as her husband and the geese as the suitors. The stranger observes that Odysseus himself has told her the meaning — but ever the doubter, Penelope notes the two kinds of gates through which dreams come, horn and ivory, and that she believes that this one may have issued thought the gate of ivory — that of false dreams, destined not to be fulfilled. The culmination of two decades of despair, it turns out, will yield the beginning of the salvational plan that Odysseus himself could not have devised any more effectively: she tells him that she will set up twelve axe-heads — the following morning — as a test for the suitors: whoever can most easily string the great bow in his hands and send an arrow through those axe-heads will be the one who will get to carry her off as his bride.

The *agon* — eristic as every *agon* must be — will lead her, alas, away from the house of love to one of a tolerated marriage, were it not for where that *agon* will *actually* lead: to bloodshed and a paradoxical (embedded as it is in *eris*) return of *eros* in the palace of Odysseus and Penelope. Knowing this, in fact, Odysseus suggests that she not wait a moment longer to arrange this contest. She does not respond to that insistence, but says that, as entertaining as he is — she could talk with him all night long — she must get some sleep, and goes up to her chamber, "and wept for Odysseus, her beloved husband, until gray-eyes Athene cast sweet slumber over her eyelids" (603-4).

Each of them sleeps without sleeping, she as she weeps for him, he as he worries about how to destroy so many suitors and how, if he succeeds, to get away with it — which issue he places before the goddess who so loves him, Athene, who descends from the sky to stand by his bedside to reassure him and scatter slumber over his eyelids as she had over those of his beloved wife a few minutes earlier. And so Book Twenty begins—and barely has Odysseus fallen asleep when Penelope is again awake and weeping, and praying to Artemis to bring her misery to an end with a divine arrow. As dawn arrives, Odysseus prays for a sign, and as the household begins to stir, Zeus thunders high above the clouds, and the hero recognizes this as the sign he seeks from without, echoed by one from within the house: a mill woman praying to Zeus that that clap of thunder be indeed an omen of the suitors' immanent destruction.

One by one, the key characters in the climactic drama unfolding make their appearance before us: Telemakhos awakens and immediately asks Eurykleia whether the stranger has been well taken care of, and she proudly notes how Penelope has seen to it that he be offered a proper bed—which he declined, preferring the hide of an ox as a kind of ancient sleeping bag, laid down in the forecourt. Telemakhos goes off to attend the assembly of the Akhaians—which means, essentially, the suitors and their coteries—and she to organize the maid-servants. Eumaios arrives with the three best pigs he has, and asks after the stranger, while Melanthios, the nasty goatherd, arrives and again speaks harshly to his disguised master.

A new figure is introduced, as well: Philoitios, "driving in for the suitors a barren cow and fat goats" (186); he asks Eumaios about the stranger, noting that "he is like a king and a lord in appearance" (194), offering Odysseus his right hand and wishing him well—and noting how Odysseus might well be somewhere in a condition of similar dilapidation as this stranger, or if he is dead, how he, Philoitios, mourns him. He notes how he might have left for another place and a new master, but could not do so, leaving the young Telemakhos' service—and Odysseus predicts for him that if he stays he will soon see Odysseus home and watch the slaughter of these suitors, to which Philoitios responds that, if that occurs, "you would see what kind of strength my hands have" (237).

So the very small army of allies is growing—just as "the suitors were compacting their plan of death and destruction for

Telemakhos, and a bird flew over them on the left side" (241-2). That this bird—an eagle—passes along the left side makes it clear to one of them, Amphinomos, that their plan is doomed, so he suggests that they drop it and head to Odysseus' and Telemakhos' house to continue their feasting.[101]

Telemakhos is there to pseudo-host them all, and provides a comfortable place for his disguised father—cleverly, within the hall and near where he will be at most advantage when the time for action arrives—pledging to protect him from the suitors' mistreatment—and speaks boldly to them, who are amazed at the suddenness with which this child has entered manhood (257-67). They are so impressed that they actually provide the beggar with decent shares of food—but Athene makes sure that their overweening haughtiness and arrogance grates fully upon father and son, lest they weaken in their resolve. Another suitor, Ktessipos, throws an ox hoof toward Odysseus, which he easily dodges; Telemakhos excoriates Ktessipos, noting that it is lucky that his throw missed, since otherwise "I would have struck you with my sharp spear fair in the middle" (305).

As so very often, the poet delays the outcome toward which his narrative drives. The suitors are stricken to silence by Telemakhos' words. Finally, another of them, Agelaos, advises him—almost kindly, lest the suitors in their entirety be oversimplified as dark—that since clearly Odysseus will never return, he would be best off giving up the fruitless wait and marrying his mother off. Telemakhos responds that he would never push her out, but would let her take her time choosing a suitor—but Athene causes them all to respond with uncontrollable laughter (to redarken this landscape of men gorging themselves on Odysseus' food).

And then Theoklymenos, who has apparently been with Telemakhos all along, utters a dark statement regarding ghosts huddling in the forecourt and how the heads and faces and knees of the suitors are all shrouded in night and darkness, with tears and blood all around on the walls—to which they merely laugh again. When Eurymakhos suggests sneeringly that someone escort him out, Theoklymenos answers that he will take himself out with his own feet, beyond the destruction coming upon them "for you are outrageous to men, and all your designs are reckless" (370). The book ends with the suitors preparing yet more food for themselves: a meal described by the poet as consummately unpleasant, given where it would end.

We auditors and readers can surely begin to smell and taste the blood of the suitors as surely as they do the blood of the meat that they are tearing apart with their teeth and greasy fingers. The final lead-up, as we enter Book Twenty-One, is singularly appropriate: the culminating act of *eris* will be arrived at by means of an *agon* designed, ostensibly, for the consummate act of *eros*: the choosing of a bride (or in this case, a groom) for marriage. Indeed, in the climax of the book's very first sentence, noting that Athene has placed in the mind of Penelope the thought to set up the contest, the setting-up is referred to as "the beginning of the slaughter" (4). Of course, Penelope herself is unaware of the real purpose of this *agon*; she thinks of it as a final acknowledgment of Odysseus' demise and her own capitulation to leaving her home as the bride of one of these suitors. So she weeps again, at length, as she takes down the great bow and lays it across her knees. At last she calms herself and speaks to the haughty suitors, telling them simply that, whoever is able to string it and shoot an arrow through the twelve axe-heads that she has lined up, shall carry her off as his prize.

Eumaios also weeps as he transfers the bow from his lady's hands to the contest location—but Antinoos mocks and scolds the two of them. Telemakhos acknowledges that he, too, will accept the verdict of the contest—but that he shall also try his hand, and that should he prove the victor, he will keep his mother protected within these halls, affianced to nobody among this group. For it would prove that he is ready to take up his father's mantle as master of this house.[102] He knows that Odysseus is here in disguise, of course, but he does not necessarily know exactly how this plan will play out. He actually arranges the axe-heads, and is the first to try the bow. Three times he fails, but on the fourth would have succeeded if not for the head-signal of Odysseus to desist: he is becoming his father's son but is not yet the man his father is, who can (and will) easily string the bow the first time.

The build-up continues, as one after the other of the suitors tries his hand and fails to string the bow, together with side comments and discussions: Leodes is first, after which they tried to heat the bow, which doesn't help as the young men trying, one after the other "were not nearly strong enough" (185). While they all struggle—both Antinoos and Eurymakhos, their leaders, hold back—Eumiaos and Philoitios both slip out into the courtyard and Odysseus follows and asks them which side they would take were Odysseus to suddenly show up—and their answers are unequivocally loyal. So Odysseus reveals that "I am he. I am in my house... and now I see that of all my men it was only you two who wanted me to come" (l 206-10). He promises them that, if he and they succeed, he will find them wives, build them houses next to his own and think of them "always as companions of Telemakhos, and his brothers" (216). As proof that he is who he claims to be, he shows them the scar that is his distinctive badge. They weep uncontrollably for joy—where the suitors laugh uncontrollably, those loyal to Odysseus weep uncontrollably, it seems.

The last touches on the plan are assuming their places: Eumaios is to be the one offering the bow around, so that he can place it in Odysseus' hands, thereafter telling the women to bar the hall doors tightly and keep them locked; Philoitios must secure the courtyard gates. The three amble back into the hall just as Eurymakhos takes up the bow. His failure is accompanied by a lamentation: that he realizes how far short all of them fall from the stature of Odysseus, "so that we cannot even string his bow. A shame for men unborn to be told of" (254-5). These are, after all, men in their prime—the same age as or older than Odysseus was when he sailed for Troy: we cannot underestimate the gigantic stature of the hero. Perhaps—too late—Eurymakhos and perhaps the others are beginning to realize how presumptuous they have been in courting his wife in the ugly manner in which they have been doing so.

Be that as it may, it falls, last, to Antinoos to try—but he suggests that it is the fault of the occasion, a holy feast for the gods that he suddenly remembers is in progress, and "who could string bows then?" (259). So he suggests that they put the bow away for now, leave the axe-heads in place, drink some more wine, pour a libation, and at dawn, sacrifice goats to Apollo—who is, after all, the far-darter—and try again. Everyone thinks that's a great idea, but Odysseus speaks up, of course, in admiration for Antinoos' words, but suggesting that, nonetheless they might permit him to give it a try, to see if his limbs retain any of their former strength. The suitors are all up in arms at the suggestion, and Antinoos tells him to sit back in his place if he does not want them to load him on a ship "and take you over to King Ekhetos, one who mutilates all men" (308-9).

The brief dialogue that follows pits Penelope who, having entered the scene, asks Antinoos what he is afraid of—that the stranger has no intention of carrying her off—to which Eurymakhos responds: but what if he could string the bow? Then we would be further humiliated for our inferiority! To which Penelope responds: You can fall into no deeper dishonor than that into which you have already thrown yourselves, for eating away and dishonoring the house of a great man. "But this stranger is a very big man, and is built strongly... so come then, give him the polished bow. Let's see what happens.... If he can string the bow, and Apollo gives him that glory, I will give him fine clothing to wear, a mantle and tunic, and give him a sharp javelin... sandals, a sword with two edges, and send him wherever his heart and spirit desire to be sent" (334-42).

Her astonishing assertiveness is met, not by a response from Eurymakhos or Antinoos, but from Telemakhos, who tells his mother to go back to her loom and to leave this business to him—which she does, amazed at her son's assertiveness. Eumaios picks up the bow and begins to offer it around and the suitors berate him but Telemakhos tells him to continue to wander around with it, for "you cannot do what everyone tells you. Take care, or, younger though I am, I might chase you out to the fields with a shower of stones..." (369-71)—which brings laughter once more to the suitors' lips, redirects their anger away from Telemakhos, and provides the cover with which Eumaios can arrive next to Odysseus and hand him the bow. He then instructs Eurykleia to bar the doors of the strong-built hall. Philoitios steps out to bar the courtyard gates—and meanwhile, Odysseus is examining the bow and the suitors mock him as one who admires bows or steals them. Suddenly he strings it, easily, and tests the bowstring, the singing sound of which draws the suitors into swift attention and panic. Zeus thunders in the distance once again, as Odysseus pulls out a swift arrow and, without even standing up, lets it fly cleanly thought the axe-heads. He announces out loud to Telemakhos that

> now is the time for their dinner to be served the Akhaians
> in the daylight, then follow with other entertainment,
> the dance and the lyre; for these things come at the end of the feasting.
> He spoke, and nodded to him with his brows, and Telemakhos,
> dear son of godlike Odysseus, put his sharp sword about him
> and closed his own hand over his spear, and took his position
> Close beside him and next the chair, all armed in bright bronze. (428-30)

The action commences immediately as we enter Book Twenty-Two with Odysseus throwing aside his rags, leaping onto the threshold, scattering the arrows at his feet and choosing his first target: Antinoos, in the midst of drinking from a golden vessel, (the quality of which is one final reminder of how he had so casually led the suitors to despoil Odysseus' household), oblivious to the danger, since how could one man, however strong, take them all on? He is hit in the throat. The suitors begin to scatter, looking for their arms, all of which, of course, have been hidden away, but still not really aware of the fate awaiting them — they believe that his killing of Antinoos was due to bad aim, until his words identifying himself make his intentions clear. Eurymakhos rises to attempt verbal reasoning: if you are truly Odysseus, you have punished the man who was really the ring-leader of all the inappropriate behavior, and

> now he has perished by his own fate. Then spare your own
> people, and afterward we will make public reparation
> for all that has been eaten and drunk in your halls, setting
> each upon himself an assessment of twenty oxen.
> We will pay it back in bronze and gold to you, until your heart
> is softened. Till then, we cannot blame you for being angry. (54-9)

Where, in a world dominated by love rather than strife, might the narrative have gone next? Might Odysseus have calmed his anger, assuaged by Eurymakhos' words and accepted the terms, or negotiated, as he is so skilled at doing, for a higher rate of reparation? After all, what had the suitors taken from him?

Food and drink, albeit loads of it. They imposed an oppressive and frustrating condition on his wife and son (it is true that they intended to kill him, but that plan was foiled first by Athene and next by one of the suitors suggesting that the plan would fail, and the assassination idea had only developed in the previous few weeks). They didn't actually kill *anyone*. They didn't *rape* anyone. They didn't even transfer precious objects from Odysseus' home to any of their homes.

And by the time they began their depredations, Odysseus had been gone *for seventeen years*, nobody had heard a *word* about or from him that could be verified, and many other Akhaian heroes—Akhilleus, Aias, Agamemnon, to name the most obvious—had perished either in the war or because of it. So that he was dead or not coming back—how much longer would he have stayed with Kirke, if his own troops had not gotten antsy? under ever-so-slightly different conditions, might he have chosen to stay longer with Kalypso?—would have seemed a very reasonable proposition. Was it so entirely unreasonable, however crude their methodology, for them to have spent the last several years trying to convince Penelope to marry one of them, and to give up her hope that her husband would return?

How, in a different world, might the poem have reached its conclusion? The world of Odysseus is, however, a world of epic poetry, in which—because of what humans are, ultimately, or because of what the gods impose, or because of what Fate decrees, that trumps both gods and humans, and in which maximum entertainment must be extracted from the tales being shared in that and subsequent generations—poet and audience demand that strife dominate love even as both features of human enterprise are always interwoven. As the paragon, the hero par excellence of this tale, he is too filled with anger to see reason, too dominated by *menis*—as Akhilleus was, through the first 22 books of the *Iliad*—to allow its resolution into something softer.

And perhaps in his world, giving in to negotiation instead of slaughter might have been perceived as fundamentally weak, allowing for some subsequent stab in the back from one of these fellows. And could even Odysseus have successfully negotiated with so *many* suitors? And if he failed, he would have lost the strategic advantage in which we find him, now, at the end of Book Twenty-One and beginning of Book Twenty-Two.

There is another thread of irony within this tapestry of contradictions: the *Iliad* is the supreme battle epic, the absolute *paragon* of articulated *eris*. Yet it resolves, as the fierceness of Akhilleus resolves, as we have seen, into a very specific softness, wherein the consummate warrior turns, finally, away from his self-absorption and his self-love, and in empathizing through his love of his own father with the grief of his slain enemy's father, gives the last word to that enemy: whereas the epic began with the words that refer to Akhilleus' *menis*, it ends with the words "Hektor, tamer of horses."

The *Odyssey*, by contrast, is often thought of as not only the supreme adventure story, but as the supreme love epic: as motivated by Odysseus' desire to get home to those he loves and by Penelope's insistent loyalty as she simultaneously mourns and waits for him, her love for him unabated and often re-stated. Yet—aside from the side love interests of Odysseus that might, in a society other than his, be seen by some to undercut the purity of his love for his wife—when the epic approaches its conclusion, here in the midst of Book Twenty-Two, and he is offered the chance to resolve the situation without further bloodshed (he has killed the one who is arguably the most obnoxious of the suitors, and the one who has been most insulting to him while he has been in disguise), he does not, and perhaps cannot choose that peaceful, softer, more loving-of-his-community path.

"Spare your own people," Eurymakhos implores him. But Odysseus responds, "looking darkly at him," that

...if you gave me all your father's possessions,
all that you have now, and what you could add from elsewhere,
even so, I would not stay my hands from the slaughter,
until I had taken revenge for all the suitors' transgression. (61-4)

The hero's next words are filled with yet another kind of irony, given the Hellenic obsession with the question of free will and choice: do we ever really choose freely, or are the outcomes of our actions, and even in many cases, those of the gods, pre-determined by *moira*? For he tells Eurymakhos, further, that the suitors have a choice: to run or to fight him. But he has barred the doors, so they can only run within the confines of the great hall. And he has hidden away most of their weapons, (each seems still to have a sword by his side) so their ability, even with their numbers, to fight him—and his few, but well-armed allies—is limited, to say the least, so when he concludes "I think not one man will escape from sheer destruction" (67), we can hardly doubt the truth of such a prophecy.

In despair, Eurymakhos cries to the others to overturn the table together as a refuge from the arrows and to rush him with their swords, but his fellows are not able to think quickly or act quickly enough in coordination to accomplish anything. Eurymakhos rushes Odysseus himself, sword drawn, and Odysseus guns him down quickly. Amphinomos follows quickly, but is struck down by Telemakhos' spear. Telemakhos runs to get armor and spears for Odysseus, Eumaios, Philoitios and himself, while Odysseus keeps the remaining suitors from the door, shooting them down, one by one.[103] Out of arrows, he dons his armor and grabs his spears as do his three associates—but the traitorous goatherd, Melanthios, manages to climb though a vent into the inner chamber where the arms and armor have been hidden away, and provide a dozen suitors with shields, helmets and spears. When he tries to get more, however, Eumaios and Philoitios catch him and string him up by the twisted arms, following Odysseus' instructions, so that "while he stays alive, he will suffer harsh torment" (177).

Odysseus and his crew are still significantly outnumbered by the remaining suitors, both armed and unarmed—but Athene appears in the form of Mentor, the herald (whom Odysseus nonetheless clearly recognizes as the goddess). Agelaos cries out, warning "Mentor" not to side with Odysseus, and threatening not only his life but the lives of his family—which only makes Mentor-Athene angrier. She asks Odysseus, rhetorically, where his ferocity has gone—he who destroyed so many Trojans, now confronted with defending his own home—and, now taking the form of a swallow, soars up to a roof beam to watch the action that she will in part influence. But not completely, for in her fierce love of the hero, "she was still putting to proof the strength and courage alike of Odysseus and his glorious son" (237-8).

To the suitors it appears that Mentor, after some empty boasting, has simply disappeared, and it doesn't occur to any of them to ask where he went or how he left. Agelaos suggests that six of the twelve armed suitors throw their spears at once—"but Athene made vain all their casts" (256), so that none of them reach Odysseus, who responds by suggesting that he and his cohort throw their spears—and each of the four kills a man. As the suitors retreat into a corner, Odysseus and his men rush to pull the spears out of their first group of victims. Once again, six spears are thrown by the suitors and once again Athene deflects them from reaching their targets. Once again Odysseus and his crew throw spears, which even more easily reach targets, since the suitors have crowded together. And now the four are able, with their second, longer spears, to approach the cowering crowd and stab them.

There are still many suitors, but Athene waves the Aegis, and "all their wits were bewildered/ and they stampeded about the hall, like a herd of cattle/ set upon and driven wild by a darting horsefly... (298-9). Leodes—the first, we may recall, to attempt to string Odysseus' bow earlier on this fateful and fatal day—rushes in and catches Odysseus by the knees, begging for mercy, and asserting that he never said or did anything wrong to the women of the house; that in fact he tried to stop any suitors who did misbehave that way, claiming, too, to have been merely the diviner for the group. Odysseus refuses that request, asserting that, as the diviner, he must have often prayed that the hero's homecoming never come about, and slits Leodes' throat with the sword dropped earlier by Agelaos when the latter had fallen. Phemios the singer—who was forced by the suitors to sing for them—also begs for mercy. Telemakhos comes quickly to his aid, asking his father to spare an innocent man, and so, too, to spare the innocent herald, Medon. Odysseus agrees, sending them quickly forth from the hall, albeit still in terror that they may yet be slain.

But the slaughter is over; there is none among the suitors still alive in the hall, and Telemakhos summons Eurykleia to oversee the clean-up. Seeing the suitors lying there dead she begins a paean of victory, but Odysseus stops her:

> Keep your joy in your heart, old woman; stop, do no raise up
> the cry. It is not piety to glory so over slain men.
> These were destroyed by the doom of the gods and their own
>   hard actions,
> for these men paid no attention at all to any man on earth
> who came their way, no matter if he were base or noble.
> So by their recklessness they have found a shameful
>   death. (411-17)

We might well challenge the severity of that summary by Odysseus. Be that as it may, Eurykleia offers him information regarding he women of the household—50 all told, 12 of whom "have taken to immorality" (l. 424, meaning, we learn 21 lines later, that they had sexual relations with some of the suitors), before suggesting that she go wake up Penelope, whom some god has enabled to sleep through the whole debacle, but Odysseus suggests letting her sleep, and then instructs Telemakhos, Eumaios and Philoitios to begin the clean-up process, together with the women— after which, they are further instructed, they should take the 12 traitorous ones to a place outside, between the roundhouse and the courtyard, and execute them with the sword. Telemakhos prefers to hang them. Melanthios, who has been hanging this whole time is, simply put, cut to pieces "in fury of anger" still unquenched—his nose, ears, private parts, hands and feet fed to the dogs. The palace is cleansed with sulfur and fire. Only then are all the (living, loyal) servant girls brought in to see the master now returned, amidst tearful kisses and rejoicing.

In a manner somewhat analogous to the narrative of the *Iliad*, were the story to end here, its drama could be said to have come to a conclusion, but essential emotional elements would remain unresolved, from the relationship between Odysseus and Penelope to that between his family and the Ithakan families whose sons he slew in his all-consuming rage. Book Twenty-Three opens with a joyful, laughing Eurykleia rushing into the upper chamber of the palace to awaken Penelope with the astonishing news that Odysseus is indeed, truly, really, finally here—in the palace. Not surprisingly, Penelope's initial response is disbelief—and annoyance that her sleep, the most satisfying that she has had in nearly 20 years, has been disturbed. But the nurse persists, telling her that it is in fact the unnamed stranger, and that Telemakhos has known for quite a while, but has kept quiet in order not to betray his father's plans.

At this, Penelope jumps up from her bed and asks whether this is really true, asking for details—which she has difficulty believing: rather, "it is one of the immortals who has killed the haughty suitors in anger over their wicked deeds and heart-hurting violence... but Odysseus has lost his homecoming and lost his life, far from Akhaia." (63-4, 68). To let go of her sorrow and leave behind the constant disappointments of false news of Odysseus-sightings over so many years is not an easy task. She descends into the freshly cleaned hall, where Odysseus, however, is still in his beggar's garments, and she stares and wonders and doesn't know—and Telemakhos accuses her of stubborn coldness, but she assures him that if indeed this is Odysseus, they will find ways to re-know each other. Their love can and will transcend the inevitable, strange distance derived from twenty years apart and all that each has endured during that time.

Odysseus knowingly smiles at this, and suggests to Telemakhos that he leave his "mother to examine me in the palace as she will, and presently she will understand better" (113-14), proposing that he (Telemakhos) turn to considering how they should handle their present circumstances—of not having killed one member of the community, which might well lead to exile, but having killed "what held the community together, the finest young men in Ithake. It is what I would have you consider" (121-2). Telemakhos responds—with words that no doubt delight both his parents—that Odysseus is the one with the best head for figuring their way out of this little jam.

Odysseus happily answers that the first part of his suggested plan is that they all go and wash up and put on fresh clothes and that the servant girls do the same, and that the singer (unnamed, but it must be the one whose life he had spared) begin a song to be accompanied by dancing, so that whoever is outside, "some one of the neighbors, or a person going/ along the street who hears us, will think we are having a wedding" (135-6). There is once again, a perfect *eris/eros* irony to this idea, since the stringing of the bow and setting of the axe heads in place was intended ostensibly, indeed, to be a contest (an *agon*) that, having been resolved by now would have led to the celebration (however grim) of a marriage—between Penelope and one of the suitors—but instead became the prelude to the slaughter of the suitors and the not-yet-fully-resolved reunion of Odysseus and Penelope, the enduring bride and groom.

The noise of the impermissible rejoicing over the death by slaughter of so many young men—and women—will be allowed in spite of its impermissibility in order to present a false tale to the outside world of what has happened and is happening within the palace of Odysseus. Passersby imagine, the poet tells us (in lines 146-51), that a raucous celebration of a marriage is indeed in process, and that Penelope has finally agreed to abandon hope and the long wait for her long-lost husband. But within those walls, a kind of love-*agon* proceeds: Odysseus continues to be mystified by his wife's reticence and she continues to test him, still uncertain that it is he and not some immortal playing a cruel trick on her. When he suggests that Eurykleia make him up a separate bed here in the hall, Penelope suggests that, indeed, Eurykelia should have their bed moved outside the bedchamber for him—the very bed which he himself built. This is indeed the consummate test, to which Odysseus responds in pain: what man could have put my bed in some other place than where it always was, or made it, in any case, movable at all, since he built the entire bedroom around an ancient olive tree, the trunk of which serves as one of the bed posts (189-204).

This is it, the final proof, for who but Odysseus could know the details of that bed's construction, and Penelope goes weak, begins to cry and rushes to his arms, begging him not to be angry at her, "since, beyond all men, you have the most understanding" (209-10). The choice of how to defend her reticence is both extraordinary and oddly appropriate, given both the place where the *Odyssey* began, with Telemakhos' visit to Sparta, and the larger context of the Trojan War narrative:

> For always the spirit deep in my very heart was fearful
> that someone from among mortal men would come my way
>   and deceive me

with words. For there are many who scheme for wicked revenge.
For neither would the daughter born to Zeus, Helen of Argos,
have lain in love with an outlander from another country,
if she had known that the warlike sons of the Akhaians would bring her
home again to the beloved land of her fathers.
It was a god who stirred her to do the shameful thing she did... (215-22)

So she feared being like Helen, if, tricked, she were to end up taking into her bed someone who was not really her husband! What a fascinating twist to the kinds of concerns one might imagine swirling though Penelope's mind. As for us, we are reminded of the entire epic of the Trojan War, the direct beginning point of which was Helen and her embrace of Paris/Alexandros, in which the suffering of Odysseus (and Penelope) is a fractional part; and we recognize a return full circle to the questions implied by the interaction between Menelaos and Helen back in Sparta, witnessed by Telemakhos, toward the beginning of the poem.

Even as now, at last, she can be unquestioningly in his arms (surely she will have the wisdom not to ask him too much about Kirke or Kalypso, and instead, direct her questions toward other adventures, like those with the Kyklops or the Laistrygonians or the Phaiakians), Odysseus reminds her and us that the journey is still not quite finished, recalling the words of Teiresias at the inner gates of Hades. For Odysseus must make yet one final, inland journey. He recounts for Penelope the entire prophecy, at her urging—delaying further their going to bed (265-84).

Their room prepared by Eurykleia and Eurynome, they finally turn in, going "glad[ly] together to bed, and their old ritual" (296)—a rather interesting and circumspect to say nothing of understated way for the poet to bring the expression of Odyssean-Penelopean *eros* to its climax, as it were. At the same time, the music and dancing down in the hall stops, and Telemakhos, Eumaios and Philoitios also turn in. The book ends with a post-lovemaking night for Odysseus and Penelope not, at first, of sleep but of talking—she about all that she had endured; and he about all that he had suffered and afflicted on others. He told her about the Kikonians, the Kyklops, Aiolos, the Laistrygones, the visit to the home of Hades and his talk with Teiresias, the Sirens, Kharybdis and Skylla and the cattle of Helios, and of the Phaiakians (about whose final, stony suffering he knows nothing).

He embeds within these tales mention, however brief, "of the guile and the many devices of Kirke" (321)—all of her devices, or only those pertaining to the destruction and salvation of his men, one might wonder?—and also of

> ...the nymph Kalypso
> who detained him with her, desiring that she should be her husband
> in her hollow caverns, and she took care of him and told him
> that she would make him ageless all his days, and immortal,
> but never so could she persuade the heart that was in him.
> (333-70)

Here, too, one might wonder how vague he was or was not regarding the care taken of him by Kalypso and the number of years he in fact spent with her before his weeping to go home came to the attention of the gods on Olympos—and whether that would really have mattered to Penelope, both in whatever, as a woman of her time and place, her expectations and understanding of appropriate male behavior might be, and more directly in terms of the distinct implications of these last two lines: that Odysseus in the end, however long it took him, chose a briefer life with Penelope into old age over immortality in the arms of an ageless goddess.

Their love offers the final word with regard to their lives and their *kleos*. But this is not the final word of the epic. For even before this book has ended, Athene, having decided that Odysseus has had enough of bedtime relaxation with his wife, and a long, deep sleep—she seems to have managed to delay the arrival of dawn itself, (347) reminding us of how powerful the gods truly are, even given how we have also seen their sometimes remarkable limitations—awakens our hero, who immediately reminds his wife of still-unfinished business. He tells her that he must go out to see his father on the old farm, instructing her to remain in the upper chamber with her attendant women, "looking at nobody and asking no questions," when the rumors of what happened the day before in the hall below start to spread (365). Donning his armor, he awakens Telemakhos, Eumaios, and Philoitios, and in a manner reminiscent, perhaps, of Hermes covering Priam in darkness so that he cannot be seen until he arrives into the camp of Akhilleus (and also of the time when Athene hid Odysseus in a cloud until he arrived before the main Phaiakian feast table), the goddess hides the four companions until they are out of the city—and Book Twenty-Three, briefer than most books in the poem, but densely packed, comes to an end.

The final book of the epic opens with Hermes, the *psykhopompos*, summoning the souls of the dead suitors and, golden staff in hand, leading them, gibbering, past "the Ocean stream, and the White Rock, and passed the gates of Helios the Sun, and the country of dreams, and presently they arrived in the meadow of asphodel. This is the dwelling place of souls, images of dead men" (11-14)—arriving, that is, to the place toward which Odysseus, having sent them, had himself once arrived, at the center of his journey into the outermost/innermost reaches of the *sacer*, encountering heroic Akhaians and the *sacerdos* whose words will be guiding him beyond the pages of this poem.

Indeed, there in the meadow the souls of the suitors find the souls of Akhilleus, Patroklos, Aias and others. Agamemnon comes along, and Akhilleus observes to him (in words evocative of Odysseus' words to Akhilleus when they first meet, back in Book Eleven), how

> Son of Atreus, we thought that all your days you were favored
> beyond all other heroes by Zeus who delights in the thunder,
> because you were lord over numerous people, and strong ones,
> in the land of the Trojans, where we Akhaians suffered hardships.
> And yet it was to you that the destructive doom spirit
> would come too early; but no man who is born escapes her.
> How I wish that, enjoying that high place of your power,
> you could have met death and destiny in the land of the Trojans.
> So all the Akhaians would have made a mound to cover you,
> and you would have won great *kleos* for your son hereafter.
> In truth you were ordained to die by a death most pitiful. (24-34)

To this Agamemnon replies: "Oh happy son of Peleus, Akhilleus, like the immortals, who died in Troy…" (36-7) and goes on to describe to Akhilleus his death's aftermath: the fighting over his body all day long, the carrying of it back to the ships and the anointing of it, the warm tears of the Akhaians and the weeping of Thetis and other sea nymphs so loudly that it terrified the troops, calmed by the wise Nestor. All nine Muses were there, singing in antiphony. The active weeping continued for 17 days and on the eighteenth the great fire of cremation was kindled with the sacrifice of countless sheep and cattle, and his bleached bones deposited, together with those of Patroklos, in an exquisite handled jar—a gift, Thetis said, from Dionysos, the work of Hephaistos (who had made Akhilleus the fine armor that he wore when he slew Hektor) and buried it in a great and perfect mound "on a jutting promontory there by the wide Hellespont, so that it can be seen from far out on the water by men now alive and those to be born in the future" (82-4). The most magnificent funeral games were celebrated, with prizes supplied by the gods themselves, through Thetis—more magnificent than any Agamemnon had ever seen in all his years of attending funerals for heroes and kings. He concludes his long, poignant speech by observing that:

> …You were very dear to the gods. So,
> even now you have died, you have not lost your name, but always
> in the sight of all mankind your *kleos* shall be great, Akhilleus;
> but what pleasure was there for me when I had wound up the fighting?
> In my homecoming Zeus devised my dismal destruction,
> to be killed by the hands of my cursed wife, and Aigisthos."
> (92-7)

This remarkable exchange that virtually opens the last book of the *Odyssey* accomplishes several tasks at once. Aside from recalling the discussion between Akhilleus and Odysseus back in Book Eleven—offering a kind of other shoe dropping not only with regard to Akhilleus but with regard to humankind in general and the gigantic paradox-laced question of mortality and immortality within which Akhilleus and Odysseus, each in his own way, figure as paradigms. It also offers one last time—recalling most obviously the stories shared with Telemakhos by Menelaos and Helen in their court at Sparta—a reminder of the contrast between Odysseus and Penelope and other husbands and wives, most extremely, Agamemnon and Klytaimnestra, who awaited her husband's return in her lover's bed and then slew the returning conqueror in his bath.

It offers a gentle and sweet reminder not only of the reconfigured Akhilleus of the end of the *Iliad*—his words to Agamemnon resound as genuinely felt, that the great king was cheated of the kind of glorious death on the battlefield that he merited. And Agamemnon's response is equally sincere in reminding Akhilleus and everyone else of how beloved the great warrior was, still is, and always will be, as the memory of his name is deathless.

The love that dominates the conversation, both between the conversants, and that to which Agamemnon alludes, of Akhilleus for Patroklos as well for Antilokhos, transcends not only the strife that initiated the *Iliad*, but that was encapsulated by the great war in which that epic poem and this, and the stories of all of these heroes—and of humanity in microcosm—is embedded. The fulfillment of the possibility for reconciliation and resolution that must somehow come between Odysseus and the suitors' families may also be seen to be anticipated in this dialogue of love between the two key eristic players in the epic tradition. And as these two converse, Hermes approaches, leading the souls of the dead suitors, one of whom, Amphimedon, is asked by Agamemnon how he got here—by shipwreck or in battle?

Amphimedon's response is not brief: he reviews—for us as a kind of summing up, as much as for Agamemnon's information—the story of their courting of Penelope and of her stratagem of the loom and its three-year-long web of constant weaving and unraveling and weaving again; of the end finally coming for that trick, when Odysseus, led by Telemakhos, arrived "in the likeness of a wretched vagabond" (156), who urged Penelope to set up the contest of the bow and the slaughter that resulted soon thereafter. Notably, he never refers to the suitors' behavior during the years when they took over Odysseus' house in his absence, and asserts that Penelope's withstanding of them through her loom-stratagem was part of her own plan for "our death and black destruction" (127). He concludes in dismay that their bodies lie piled in Odysseus' house, rather than being taken and properly washed and laid out as they should be. Agamemnon's response? To comment on how fortunate Odysseus is to have such a wife, the *kleos* of whose virtue will live forever—the opposite mirror of Klytaimnestra, whose song will be one of loathing forever.

And meanwhile, while the suitors' souls have arrived in Hades, Odysseus and his small crew have arrived at the farm of Laertes. Odysseus sends the others ahead to prepare sacrifices and dinner while he seeks out his father ("to see whether he will know me and his eyes recognize me, or fail to know me, with all this time that has grown upon me" (217-18). He finds his father in the orchard, in a squalid tunic, and "a cap of goatskin on his head, to increase his misery" (231). Ever Odysseus, the hero decides to test his father rather than presenting himself straightforwardly. He comments on the old man's skill tending to his orchard, but not to himself, culminating with the comment that his master doesn't take good care of him, and with the question "what man's thrall are you? Whose orchard are you tending" (257)? He asks him whether this is truly Ithake, as some passerby has told him, for he is looking for an old friend who used to live here—a friend who claimed to be from here and the son of Laertes.

Laertes weeps in response, saying that this is the place, but that the son in question is long gone and the land is possessed by violent and reckless men, and asks how long ago the stranger saw that son—and asks who he, the stranger, is and where he is from. One last time, Odysseus spins a tale—and one last time we are reminded that the line between fact and fable is sometimes thin or blurry or both for our hero—claiming to be from Alybos, and to be named Eperitos, and that he saw Odysseus (now mentioned by name for the first time in this conversation) about five years ago.

Laertes, submerged in "the black cloud of sorrow" (315) begins to pour earth on his own face, which finally drives Odysseus out of his game-playing mode and he rushes to Laertes, and embraces and kisses him and announces who he really is and that he has killed the suitors. Laertes—yet another member of this family of clever doubters—asks for an unmistakable sign, and for a third time, Odysseus shows his unmistakable scar, recalling its source, and then goes on to identify specific groups of trees in the orchard that Laertes had given him when Odysseus was a child.

A warm reunion follows and then immediately Laertes voices concerns regarding the families of the suitors, but Odysseus says not to worry, and they head over and into the house where Telemakhos and Philoitios and Eumaios are preparing a feast. Laertes bathes—and Athene is once again there to assure that he looks younger and stronger than ever when he emerges from the bath, to the amazement of his son. Soon the old and loyal retainer, Dolios, and his six sons, arrive from their work and are invited to join the feast.

Meanwhile, rumor has sped through the city, spreading the news of the suitors' deaths, and their corpses are carried out of Odysseus' house for burial by their families. The father of Antinoos, Eupeithes, addresses them all as they gather in assembly after the funerals, saying that Odysseus has wrought great evil upon the Akhaians—first taking many along on the journey to Troy during which they all perished, and now killing the best of the upcoming generation. He suggests that they all go out to get to him before he escapes over the sea to Pylos or someplace else. The final moment of strife is being organized, but not before Medon and the inspired singer, both of whom had been spared by Odysseus, arrive from Odysseus' palace, and the herald warns them that "Odysseus devised what he did, not without the consent of the immortal/ gods. I myself saw an immortal god who was standing beside Odysseus" (444-6)—so to go up against him might well mean going up against the gods. Green fear takes hold of them.

Further, Halitherses, Mastor's son, an aged warrior, speaks up, saying that he and Mentor had warned them to make their sons

> ...give over their senseless
> mood; for they, in their evil recklessness, did a great wrong
> in showing no respect to the wife, despoiling the possessions,
> of a lordly man. (457-60)

He counsels them not to go out to Laertes' farm and wreak more violence, but half of them ignore his plea and arm themselves and head out to the farm, with Eupeithes as their leader. Athene, witnessing this, asks Zeus what his intentions are:

> Will you first inflict evil fighting upon them, and terrible strife, or will you establish friendship between the two factions? (475-6).

Regardless of the answer, we are reminded of the ongoing and marvelous ambiguity with regard to who is ultimately responsible for the eristic events of the Trojan War: humans, gods or fate—or what combination of these three elements. Zeus' response is to ask Athene why she asks such a question, since it was always her intention to facilitate Odysseus' return and slaughter of the suitors, so "Do as you will; but I will tell you how it is proper" (481): that they achieve oaths of faith and friendship, that they somehow forget about the deaths of their brothers and sons and be friends as they had in the past.

The question is how that might be accomplished. For meanwhile, Odysseus and his crew are finishing their delicious meal and Eupeithes and his followers are approaching the farmhouse. So Odysseus and his force, now numbering twelve all told, quickly arm themselves and head outside. Not alone against the odds, however, since while Penelope was waiting for twenty years at home for Odysseus, the virgin goddess of wisdom and warfare, Athene, was always with him—sometimes more overtly than at other times—manifesting her undying love for him; and she is with him still, this time "likening herself [yet again] in appearance and voice to Mentor," and so joins them outside the house. This cheers Odysseus considerably, since by now he has come to recognize his patron goddess even in disguise.

Yet one more reminder of the interweave between strife and love, involving fathers and sons, is shown, on a note both light and, given the circumstances, serious. For Odysseus makes a little goading speech to Telemakhos about not shaming the blood of his fathers, who have been pre-eminent in warfare across the world, and Telemakhos replies to his father: just you wait and see. To an astute auditor or reader of both these epics, the interchange between father and son might evoke that very different exchange, toward the end of Book Six of the *Iliad*, between Hektor and Astyanax. Different indeed: Astyanax, the baby, is terrified of his father's war helmet, we recall, and so Hektor takes it off laughingly and picks up his son, holding him high and uttering that heartbreaking prayer to the gods for his son's future success—heartbreaking because of the purity of the father-love it expresses and because we all know that it won't be heard, and that both Hektor and Asytanax are doomed.[104]

But three generations, not two, are gathered here in the last book of the *Odyssey*, and Laertes rejoices:

'What day is this for me dear gods: I am very happy
my son and my son's son are contending over their courage.'
(514-5)

In this context so different from that of the *Iliad*'s Book Six—there the moment, in which Hektor's wife, Andromakhe, was also present, was a calm between storms, facilitated by the rescue of Paris by the goddess, Aphrodite, (more, it would seem, from a sense of obligation than of love) from the battlefield and near-death at the hands of Menelaos; whereas here in *Odyssey* 24, Penelope is again back home (and the intervening goddess operates out of love, not mere obligation)—for all the right reasons and in a very different way from the situation of Astyanax, Telemakhos won't get the opportunity to show his stuff and neither father nor son will really display their battle skills, *because* of divine intervention.

Indeed, assuming Mentor's form and voice, Athene instructs Laertes to make his prayer to Zeus and Athene and to cast his spear. The throw, assisted by the enormous strength breathed into his limbs by the goddess, strikes Eupeithes in the side of his bronze helmet, killing him. Thusly inspired, Odysseus and the others charge the front fighters with swords and stabbing spears,

And now they would have killed them all, and given none of them
homecoming, had not Athene, daughter of Zeus of the Aegis
cried out in a great voice and held back all the company:

'Hold back, men of Ithake, from the wearisome fighting,
so that most soon, and without blood, you can settle everything.'
(528-32)

    The rapid result of that vocal intervention is that green fear takes hold of them all, they all drop their weapons to the ground and all of the attackers turn tail and begin running back to the city. Odysseus gathers himself to begin pursuit, but Zeus now intervenes, throwing down a smoky thunderbolt that lands right in front of Athene. And the goddess bids her hero to desist, lest "Zeus of the wide brows, son of Kronos, be angry at you" (544).
    The epic ends a mere four lines later, Odysseus happily obeying the goddess's command. We must infer, for it is not stated, that the crowd returned after the thunderbolt struck and Athene's words were spoken, for the last three lines inform us that

pledges for the days to come, sworn by both sides
were settled by Pallas Athene, daughter of Zeus of the Aegis,
who had likened herself in appearance and voice to Mentor.
(546-8)

    The epic, like its sibling, ends on a note of resolution and reconciliation, but whereas the *Iliad*'s final emphasis may be seen to be on the transformation of Akhilleus, and generously gives the last word, as it were, to his defeated and previously humiliated opponent, Hektor[105]—that is to say, its emphasis is on the *profanus* and the beings who define the *profanus*; the *Odyssey*'s final emphasis is on a peace-process that, given the enormous slaughter that preceded it, is almost inconceivable without the intervention of the divine *sacer*.
    A peace is arrived at, literally negotiated by the goddess and, we can well believe, facilitated by her in psychological ways of which the protagonists are unaware. Like all of those phantasmagorical adventures in the *sacer*—those encounters with the supernatural that shape the epic—its conclusion has both a suddenness and a phantasmagorical quality to it.
    Eris is resolved in a peace that at least is expected to lead back to friendship: we might call it neighborly love, but the true *eros*

outcome—the reunification between Odysseus and Penelope as well as between Odysseus and Laertes and Odysseus and Telemakhos and Odysseus and the others near and dear to him—is not part of the vocabulary of the poem's ending, at least as we have it.

Where we know that after the end of the *Iliad* the war will go on for nearly a year, that Akhilleus will die by the unheroic hand of Paris/Alexandros, and Aias will die by his own hand, and a host of other events will take place before it ends, and where we also know, obviously, that Odysseus will end up wandering for another decade before getting home; we have no epilogue to the *Odyssey*, at least that has come down to us from antiquity. Do they all simply live happily ever after? Or do the neighbors get annoyed after a while, or Odysseus bored, or Telemakhos restive under his father's roof and rule? Or??[106]

Aside from the issue of other post-Troy stories—to be taken up by the tragic poets whose work we shall consider in the next chapter—and further explorations by Roman authors (most specifically, Vergil in his *Aeneid*, which we shall also consider three chapters hence), we can only guess about how the *eros/eris* story of Odysseus and those around him plays out between the end of the poem and the time when he experiences the last part of what Teiresias had prophesied to him in the *sacer-profanus* borderland where they spoke years earlier: his death at sea, fat in years.[107]

Chapter Four

Lyric and Tragic Journeys Out and Back, from Sappho and Pindar to Aiskhylos and Euripides

For reasons beyond our discussion, the era of great Greek epic poetry—defined in part by its heroic *sacer-profanus* subject matter, its wondrous similies and metaphors, its often stunning imagery, its dactylic hexameter rhythmic pattern, and its presentation in a single, unaccompanied voice—is succeeded by lyric poetry, with its first single and later combined single and choral voices, accompanied by the lyre (hence the term "lyric").[108] This transpires in the seventh and sixth centuries, just as the Hellenic world is more distinctly assuming its *polis*-form and several of those *poleis* are spreading their wings by beginning to sprout colonies along the Anatolian coast and up into the Black Sea, to the east; and along the coasts of Italy and Sicily and further, toward what are now France and Spain, to the west.

I Sappho and Pindar

Lyric poetry is associated with a range of figures, from Sappho—the first female artist of whom we are aware in the Greek literary tradition—to Pindar. They all make use of varied metrical schemes, their narratives are contemporary—but sometimes with references to the same traditions recorded in the epic poems—each offering his or her distinctive voice. In diverse ways, those voices often resonate with the interweave between *eros* and *eris* that are important threads in the larger fabric of the Greek literary tradition.

One may recognize our *eros/eris* theme in the work of any number of poets, but I shall limit myself to two: the just-mentioned Sappho and Pindar—each of whom addresses this idea in a manner very different from the other. Sappho (630-580 BCE) is, in fact, as Anne Carson points out, the one who first referred to eros itself as "bittersweet." "Eros seemed to Sappho at once an experience of pleasure and pain,"[109] in her poetic fragment LP 130:

> Eros once again limb-loosener spins me,
>   sweetbitter (*gkukupikron*), impossible to fight off, creature, stealing up…

I might have translated the first word of the second line as "sweetsharp," in order to underscore the need for thinking carefully about what the poet intends, and since the primary meaning of *pikros* is "sharp"—but the secondary meaning is "bitter," which makes more inherent sense in this context. As Carson notes, the Greek word-component order (versus the normative English order: "bittersweet") reflects the chronology of normative experience: it starts out sweet and ends bitterly. That, as we shall see, is, at any rate where both Greek and, even more so, Latin lyric poetry tends to take the subject—particuarly when it reflects the poet's personal experience.

Sappho is best known, among her many love lyrics, for her bittersweet address to one with whom she is infatuated, but can only watch from afar, suffering "being poor"—but this poem, like many others, explores the bittersweetness of love, rather than the strife-woven aspect of it.[110] Or at least one might suggest that the internal torture to which the poet reports herself subject—and the fire running through her system—is a more subtle instance of *eris* than the externalized form that we have considered in the epic context. In any case, she starts out sweetly before becoming, if not bitter, then at least tortured.

She writes:

> He seems to me equal to the gods
> who sits opposite you and
> hears you near as you speak
>   and softly laugh

in a sweet echo that jolts
the heart in my ribs. For now
as I look at you my voice
    is empty and

I can say nothing as my tongue
cracks and slender fire is quick
under my skin. My eyes are dead
    to light, my ears

pound with thunder, and sweat pours over me.
I convulse, paler than grass,
and feel my mind slip as I
    go close to death.

    The description is at once highly emotional and almost clinical: a depiction of a kind of catalyptic fit—with some tinnitus thrown in for good measure. The strife is entirely internal, in any case: the passion that the poet feels twists and turns her into one of the living dead, rather than—or simultaneous with and contradictory to—feeling reborn by the experience of love.

    The reason may be that the object of this *eros*-filled series of quatrains is unattainable. There is a Sapphic fragment that some consider to be part of the poem. It reads "but I must endure everything, since…"—and still others finish the fragment with "I am poor." Whether or not this last phrase is the continuation of the line and whether or not the line is the last part, or part of the last part, of the poem, we are left with a personal and painful meditation on unrequited love. The fuller strife-ridden consequences of unrequited love will await the Roman lyric poets to be expressed, however.[111]

    Somewhat more directly connected to our subject is Sappho's address to "Lady Hera, with her "graceful form" in which poetic invocation she references the Atreidai, who "accomplished many feats first at Ilion, and then on the sea on their voyage here…" So we might recognize an implied nod of the head toward *eris*—the Trojan War and its epilogic *nostoi*—within this loving invocation that is a request for help.

Such words referencing the Atreidai are, to repeat, only oblique in their interweave of love and strife, in not even playing out the entire double strand of Agamemnon's and Menelaos' homecoming stories: the first, (as we shall shortly discuss in more detail), murdered by his wife upon his return from Troy to Mykenai; the second, as we have seen in the previous chapter, home safe with his wife, Helen, because of whose beauty the entire debacle of the Trojan War was endured, but potentially engendering in the audience a strong doubt as to how happy they are now, back together—a passive-aggressive *eris* seems to drive their relationship—and therefore questioning whether that most eristic of *eros*-driven adventures was justified in the end.

There is an altogther diffferent way in which we may see Sappho offering a juxtaposition of *eros* and *eris*, which will be picked up upon by a number of key Roman lyric poets centuries later. In the sixteenth fragment, found on a second century CE papyrus in that extraordinary collection from Oxyrinchus (Oxy. 1231 fr. 1. Col i13-34), the poet writes

> Some say a host of cavalry, others of infantry,
> still others, of ships, is the most beautiful thing
> on the black earth—but I say it is whomsoever
> one loves.

By implication this may be seen to suggest that to write about those one loves is more worthwhile than to write about war. This contrast—not, per se, between love ands strife but between the importance of these two concepts as subjects for poetry and thus between two kinds of poetry—epic and lyric; war/strife-heroic and love-heroic—interestingly enough, immediately turns to a reference to that most renowned of Greek wars and that war most renowned as a subject for poetry, by way of referencing the love-object over whom the war was fought. For Sappho's poem continues:

> It is simple enough to make this understood
> by everyone: for she who so far surpassed all of
> humankind in beauty—Helen—left her
> most noble husband

and went sailing to Troy with no thought at all
for her child or her dear parents
but [love] led her astray
… lightly…

[and her story]
reminds me
now of Anactoria who
is not here:

I would prefer to see her lovely walk
and the bright sparkle of her face
than the chariots of the Lydians and
their armed infantry…

Here, then, the *eros-eris* duality pertains to which condition is both preferable in general and preferable as the subject of poetry. Love matters more than armies—and this extends from the mytho-historic past to the very actual present. And, one might add, Sappho underscores the irrelevance of same/other gender to the issue: *love is love.*[112]

By contrast with Sappho, who is ultimately best known for her verses that focus, one way or another, on love, Pindar (526/18-446/38 BCE), in his praise-poems for his clients, victors in this or that athletic competition, frequently likens them to this or that heroic forebear, occasionally placing our subject front and center in the heroic tales that he chooses to bring forward. In his first "Olympian Ode," written to laud Hieron of Syracuse for his vistory in the chariot race in the Olympic games—who hosted Pindar when he arrived on an extended visit to Sicily in 476—the poet invokes the story of Tantalos and Pelops and their family line.

At first glance this seems an odd choice, since the standard understanding of that story is that it carries disaster from one generation to the next, beginning with the attempt by Tantalos to fool the gods by serving them a meal that featured his son, Pelops, in a stew. But Pindar tells us in the midst of his second strophe that "I shall speak against what earlier poets assert of you," opining rather that Poseidon snatched Pelops away from the banquet, "his mind wild with desire, and on golden horses carried you to the high halls of Zeus." But some jealous neighbor spread the rumor, when Pelops disappeared, that "you had been cut up, limb from limb and...at the final course [they] divided and ate your flesh."

Pindar then follows the story of Pelops, re-angling his narrative toward the hero as a young man. With the help and support of both Poseidon and Aphrodite, Pelops manages to do what 13 (or 18, in another variant version of the tale) wannabees before him could not do (and indeed lost their lives trying to do): defeat Oinomaos, the father of Hippodameia, in a chariot race, in order to win her hand in marriage. And there, of course, the connection shifts suddenly into place: Hieron in his chariot victory is likened to Pelops in his; both have skills in this event that suggest divine support. Thus the athlete is likened to a mythological figure whose father, Tantalos, had been known as the best human friend of the gods and who was himself a favorite of the gods—who dined with them on Olympos and in his own home—as opposed to recalling the more common part of his story, of having wrecked his relationship with the gods through an act of cruel gastronomic tomfoolery.

More to the point of our own narrative: Oinomaos had tried to fend off the marriage day (the consummate symbol of *eros*) of his daughter because of a prophecy that her husband would kill him (the consummate expression of *eris*)—so he treated each one of the suitors for her *eros*-bound hand in an unusually and dangerously eristic manner. In the end, indeed, Pelops not only defeated Oinomaos because Poseidon provided him with a chariot drawn by winged horses, but because Pelops convinced Myrtilos, care-taker of Oinomaos's chariot, to sabotage the latter's vehicle. In the course of the race the chariot fell apart and Oinomaos, tangled in the reins, was dragged to his death. So a contest that had been eristic so many times, with *eros*—the winning of Hippodameia to wife—as its purpose, and in which the victor in this final iteration was assisted by the goddess of love and by the god who had once been his protective lover, (snatching him from the banquet table, rather than from a pot in which he had been cooked up as a meal (un)fit for the gods), ran its final iteration with an eristic pulse leading to the death of one of the protagonists.

There is more, of course. While Hippodameia and Pelops went on to have many children, the bribe that had been offered to Myrtilos for his help—either one night with Hippodameia or half the kingdom that came with her hand—was not only not paid by Pelops. Pelops killed Myrtilos when the latter came to claim his reward. As he lay dying, Myrtilos cursed Pelops and Hippodameia, which led not only to the demise of their children Atreus and Thyestes, but to the doom of their grandchildren: Aigisthos and Agamemnon.

The disaster involving these last two and those around them is the centerpiece of another Ode, the eleventh Pythian, written to honor Thrasydaios of Thebes for his victory in the footrace, and dating from either 474 or 454 BCE. He invites the muses and others to come to Delphi and the shrine of Apollo to honor the one who brought honor to his city with his victory there, "in the fields of Pylades"—which then leads him on a long side story regarding the best friend of Pylades and his family. So Thrasydaios was

> a victor in the rich fields of Pylades, the friend of Laconian Orestes,
> who indeed, when his father was murdered, was taken
> by his nurse Arsinoe, from the strong hands and bitter deceit
> of Klytaimnestra, when she sent the Dardanian daughter of
> Priam, Kassandra, together with the soul of Agamemnon,
> to the shadowy bank of the Acheron with her gray blade
> of bronze, the pitiless woman. Was it Iphigenia,
> slaughtered at the Euripos far from her fatherland,
> who provoked her to raise the heavy hand of her anger?
> Or was she vanquished by another bed
> and led astray by their nightly sleeping together?
> This is the most hateful error for young brides,
> and is impossible to conceal because other people
> will talk. Citizens are apt to speak evil,
> for prosperity brings with it envy as great as itself.
> But the man who breathes close to the ground roars unseen.
> He himself died, the heroic son of Atreus, when at last
> he returned to famous Amyklai, and he caused the destruction

> of the prophetic girl, when he had robbed of their opulent
>   treasures
> the houses of the Trojans, set on fire for Helen's sake.
> And his young son went to the friend of the family, the old man
> Strophios, who dwelled at the foot of Parnassos.
> But at last, with the help of Ares, he killed his mother
> and laid Aigisthos low in blood.
>
> My friends, I was whirled off the track at a shifting
> fork in the road, although I had been traveling on a straight
> path before. Or did some wind throw me off course,
> like a skiff on the sea? Muse, it is your task, if you undertook
> to lend your voice for silver, to let it flit now this way,
> now that: now to the father, who was a Pythian victor,
> now to his son Thrasydaios. (15-45)

Thus the name of Pylades causes the segue into the brief tale of Orestes and the complications to his life resulting from the murder of his father, Agamemnon, by his mother, Klytaimnestra. That side tale is a tale of multi-level *eros* and *eris*: the questioned love of Klytaimnestra and Aigisthos, the failed love of Klytaimnestra and Agamemnon, the failed love of Agamemnon and Iphigenia, the strife of Klytaimnestra and Agamemnon, the love of Klytaimnestra and Ihpigenia, the love of Orestes and Agamemnon, the strife of Orestes and Klytaimnestra and Aigisthos—and so on. Quite a weighty side-step for a foot race!

II Aiskhylos and the *Oresteia*

All of this brings us back again to the subject of the Trojan War and its homecoming tales (*nostoi*)—and specifically to the fate of Agamemnon and Klytaimnesta as yet another obvious instance of the interweave of *eros* and *eris*—and forward to the poetry of Aiskhylos (ca 525/4- ca456/5 BCE), first among the three great fifth-century BCE tragic playwrights from whom substantial works have survived to our own time. Seven of the plays of Aiskhylos still exist in a fairly intact form, (out of perhaps 80 that he wrote), of which three function as a trilogy (first produced in 458 BCE at the Festival of Dionysos, at which it won first prize) that follows the story of Agamemnon, Klytaimnestra his wife, Aigisthos his cousin and her lover, and Orestes his son, forward into the first few years following the successful end of the Trojan War.

That tale also in a certain way may be said to narrow the broader focus on the *eros/eris* interweave that punctuates the *Iliad* and the *Odyssey*: for it turns us to one family line, and therefore shapes *eros/eris* as an aspect of dysfunctional family life—or, rather, offers a dysfunctional family as a particular and particularly emphatic instance of the interweave of *eros* and *eris* as part of the human condition.

There is irony from the very beginning in Aiskhylos' telling of the tale of what happens next, after the war is over, to this specific clan. For in the opening scene of *Agamemnon*, the watchman, waiting for a sign from afar that Agamemnon is coming home succesfully from his now-ten-year-long mission, as he stares into the distance from the rooftop of the palace, likens himself, in the second and third lines of the play, to a dog, as he is "lying awake, elbowed upon the Atreidai's roof dogwise..." Two thoughts might occur to an astute member of the audience, barely settled into his seat: that dogs are supposed to be loyal and this play is, above all, about the failure of Klytaimnestra to be loyal to Agamemnon—and the impotence of anyone around who knows this and might wish to say something about it to the returning king—and perhaps more precisely to the moment when Odysseus, coming home disguised as an old beggar, is recognized immediately by his own very loyal and loving dog, Argos who, having seen his master finally return, can die in peace.

Dramatically speaking, Agamemnon in the *Agamemnon*, like Odysseus in the *Odyssey*, makes a late entrance onto the stage—in line 781, nearly half-way through the drama. In a manner more than a bit different from that of Odysseus, Agamemnon arrives home triumphantly, directly from Troy, and his wife, with irony, (for we know how firmly her tongue is beating against her cheek), welcomes him—"I take no shame to speak aloud before you all the love I bear my husband..." (856-7). She tells him a lie about why and where Orestes is, in admitting that their son "in whom my love and yours are sealed and pledged" is indeed elsewhere and not here at home in Mykenai (878-9). She lays out—quite literally—a red/purple carpet for him, again with irony commenting that "justice leads him along a crimson path" (911; alluding, as we well know, to the color of his blood that shall soon flow so freely, while punning on the idea of an exalted royal arrival connoted by a carpet thusly hued).

He commits at least two obvious errors in his behavior in his initial presence within the drama, which will help doom him. Surely the presentation to his wife, after ten years apart, of his new young concubine to host—a prisoner Trojan maiden, the unfortunate prophetess Kassandra—cannot be viewed as an act the emotional response to which by Klytaimnestra will be less than hostile—eristic—regardless of what deceptive words she may use in receiving this love-gift.

Perhaps more fundamental than this, in that it more directly should offend the gods and not just the hero's wife, is Agamemnon's decision—regardless of his own words that initially recognize the impropriety of it—to ascend to his palace gates by way of that crimson path, talked into doing so by his wife, for this is the sort of path reserved for gods and kings who have been properly *purified*. He graciously and egotistically follows the path that his wife has laid down for him, before he has washed the grime of the journey from his body, made appropriate offerings to the gods, and thus washed his soul clean.

So we understand even before the narrative has quickened that he has doomed himself; that the path up to the palace that he has chosen, on that carpet, is the sort of path along which a bull or ox about to be sacrificed might be led. Not surprisingly, as Kassandra begins to see impending doom and to cry out, language placed by the poet into her mouth references the bull, (1135) who, we understand, is Agamemnon. She conjures, further, images of the family past, "children almost killed by those most dear to them and their hand filled with their own flesh, as food to eat" (1219-20)—a recollection shared by the chorus: of "Thyestes' feasting upon the flesh of his own children" (1242).

Fundamentally, the *eros*-based husband-wife link that might and ideally should define this house (and that had defined the house in Ithake to which Odysseus returned, in spite of the eristic denouement involving Odysseus and the suitors) has been smashed by repeated blows from the hammer of *eris*.

For we know the back story. We know that Agamemnon's cousin Aigisthos had had it in for Agamemnon before the latter went off to the Great War, leaving Klytaimnestra behind and available, should she choose to be responsive to some suitor. And we know that she was available less because she was drawn by *eros* to Aigisthos than because of the eristic turmoil with which her soul had become infected toward Agamemnon. (Seriously, how drawn could a woman like her *be* to Aigisthos, a man who, alone, it seems, of all the men of his generation, stayed at home rather than going to fight at Troy? No reference there to flat feet, bone spurs, or some other physical flaw...)

We also know the key reason for her animosity toward her husband. For before sailing to Troy, all of the ships commanded by all of those heroes convened at Aulis. There, while gathered and preparing to depart, one of the troops inadvertantly killed a rabbit (or a deer in a slightly different version) in a grove sacred to Artemis — thereby killing an animal that was itself sacrosacnt, in being under the protection of the goddess. The anger of Artemis directed itself to the overall leader of all the troops, Agamemnon, who was told by his priestly advisors that he had a choice with regard to assuaging that anger. He could either give up his position as leader and hand it off to someone else — or he could offer up one of his daughters as a sacrifice to the goddess.

Consistent with the sense of Agamemnon and his ego that one derives from the *Iliad*, (and from his opening actions here, in the *Agamemnon*), he chose the latter course. So he sent a message home, to Klytaimnestra, instructing her to send down their daughter Iphigenia to Aulis — informing his wife that it was his intention to marry off their daughter to Akhilleus, pre-eminent among the Akhaian warriors. So what he presented to his wife as an *eros*-based mission was in fact a death-dealing mission occasioned by the *eris* toward him of the goddess. Whatever there was of *eros* in Klytaimnestra's feelings for her husband up to that point drained out of her, to be replaced by *eris*,when she found out what his true intention was and when he followed up on that intention.

Agamemnon's wife slays him by running him a nice hot bath and then entangling him—like a fish—in a net, to eliminate his ability to raise his very arms, much less really defend himself, as she stabs him to death: once, twice, thrice—the last time as an offering of thanksgiving to Zeus (who is almost, one might say, her father, since her mother, Leda, was once seduced by the god in the guise of a swan—and Leda thus bore her half-sister, Helen).

The eristic end of Agamemnon's life is facilitated by the once-upon-a-time presumed object of his erotic intentions. Indeed, she informs us, after she has slain her husband, as she stands on stage with blood-stained garments and perhaps a large bloody knife in her hand, speaking forth both to the chorus of Argives and to us, how "he [Agamemnon] slaughtered like a victim his own child, my pain grown into love, to charm away the winds of Thrace" (1417-18). And further, that "by my child's Justice driven to fulfillment, by her Wrath and Fury, to whom I sacrificed this man, the hope that walks my chambers is not traced with fear while yet Aigisthos makes the fire on my hearth..." (1432-5).

He does indeed warm her hearth, (and the intended use of that term as a metaphor for the entrance to her womb is fairly patent), but to whatever degree Aigisthos was part of her plan of *eris*-birthed vengeance, he was no more than an instrument, rather than anything resembling a full-fledged object of *eros* for her. Aigisthos is far less an erotic source for Klyaimnestra than the vision she describes, of Kassandra lying also dead, on the bed, "against his [Agamemnon's] fond heart, and to me has given a delicate excitement to my bed's delight" (1446-7).

She also references the legacy of familial blood—the book to which she has merely added another chapter—asserting that not she but vengeful justice struck him down: "his revel of hate struck down this man, last blood for the slaughtered children" (1500-02—although we know, too, that this is hardly the *last* blood). She again reminds the chorus and us of how her eristic act aginst the one-time partner and object of her love was justified by the death of Iphigenia at Agamemnon's hands: "The flower of this man's love and mine, Iphigenia of the tears he dealt with even as he has suffered" (1525-7).

Aigisthos, on the other hand—however he might wish to present himself as the man in charge at the end of the play, in a brief but nasty dialogue with the chorus of townspeople who warn him that his doom is not far off—is clearly her subordinate. He, too, however, had a dysfunctional family-based reason for participating in the doom of Agamemnon, recalling to the chorus how "Atreus, this man's father, King of Argolis—I tell you the clear story—drove my father forth, Thyestes, his own brother..." (1583-5), and when Thyestes returned to supplicate his brother, Atreus "served my father his own children's flesh to feed on" (1593-4). These would have been Aigisthos' older brothers. So he, who also suffered exile as a consequence of those events, asserts his own reasons for being involved—indeed claiming that "it was I who pieced together the fell plot" (1609).

We are not likely to believe that, in spite of the sense of his dominant role that the *Odyssey* had earlier provided. The chorus, in fact, mocks him as, "like a woman, you waited the war out here in this house" (1625-6), asking him rhetorically how, if he indeed planned the whole thing, he would now rule, who "could not dare to act it out, and cut him down with your own hand?" (1634-5). Klytaimnestra indeed has the last lines of the play, asserting that "we two shall bring good order to our house, at least," before the two of them go into the palace and the stage clears.

More to the point, the action that shaped the play—between its opening with the return of Agamemnon from Troy and that exit—is articulated by Klytaimnestra. For the centerpiece of the play—albeit offstage, lest it offend the god under whose patronage Greek tragedy rests—is his murder, not at the hands of some warrior like Hektor the Trojan, breaker of horses, nor even at the hands of his own unheroic cousin, but at the hands of a *mere* woman.

She is also the mother of the *outcome* of that erotic part of their relationship—daughters like the long-gone Iphigenia and the virtual shadow figure, Elektra, and a son, above all: Orestes, whom she and Aigisthos had sent away soon after Agamemnon left for Troy, lest he come of age in the house in which these two were having their adulterous daliance and in which she in particular was plotting the death of her husband. The chorus remembers that son, asking the ether whether he might still be alive, "somewhere in the sunlight still" (1646)—implying that if so, might he not return and avenge his father's death? and again warning Aigisthos that his position of dominance will not last long "if the god's guiding hand brings Orestes home again" (1667)

The fact that Orestes is alive and well and will indeed come home and avenge his father's death—at a huge and heavy cost: the murder of his own mother—becomes the basis for the second play in Aiskhylos' trilogy, *The Libation Bearers*. The first 651 lines of that play take place at Agamemnon's tomb, where Orestes, having returned—a young man, now, who left, sent away by his mother and her lover, as a boy—accompanied by his best friend, Pylades, places a lock of his hair. For having heard that his father had returned from Troy, he had hurried to Mykenai only to learned that, in coming home, his father had been slaughtered—by his wife, Orestes' mother. So the primary subject to which this first part of the play arrives is the conundrum in which the young hero finds himself: obligated by the laws of filial piety—filial love—to avenge his father's murder, but learning that that act of vengeance (an act of *eris*) must be carried out against his own mother, which will turn him into a matricide.

There is more, of course, in general and with regard to our theme. Orestes' loving sister, Elektra (whom he readily enough recognizes after ten years apart), accompanied by a chorus of women, arrives at the tomb a minute or two after her brother, (who hides himself while assessing the situation), not certain what sort of offering is appropriate for her murdered father's grave—and ruminates about how Orestes is doing, not realizing, of course, that he is right there and not still off in exile. But she sees that lock of hair, and recognizing its similarity to her own, wonders whether it is from Orestes—although how did it get here? she and the chorus wonder—and the only other candidate who would fit that lock is Klytaimnestra, "my mother, but no mother in her heart that has assumed the God's hate and hates her children" (190-1). If we had somehow missed this point, the usual love of mother for children has been subverted in Klytaimnestra's case by an inordinate hatred for her—surviving—children, no doubt shaped by the unquenched eristic feelings toward her husband and, one might suppose, her instinctive sense that their sympathies lay (and lie) with him and not with her in the chasm that Iphigenia's death opened up between their mother and father.

This issue is interwoven with an opposite one, that of brother-sister love that, it would further seem, is something that in particular Elektra has held onto for the past ten years, as she had also held onto the hope that her father, returning, would right the ship of their family and not (forgive the continued metaphor) be drowned in it. How quickly Elektra jumps to the still-hopeful conclusion that her brother has somehow managed to return—a hope reenforced by her identification of his footprints (205-6), which must have been made by feet like her own! (She is extraordinairly observant and deductive.) But then to whom, she wonders, does the second set of prints belong?

This is the moment when Orestes reveals himself, although it naturally takes Elektra awhile to believe that it is truly he who stands before her (somewhat reminiscent, albeit, of course, differently, of Penelope's suspicions regarding the returned Odysseus when he first reveals himself to her). But he shows her the garment that he wears, which she herself had woven for him, and his last words "I know those nearest to us hate us bitterly" (234) pushes against and directly into her first words of response: "Oh dearest one, treasured darling of my father's house, hope of the seed of our salvation..." (235-6). This reunion is accompanied by Orestes' prayer to Zeus to help them destroy their father's destroyers, they, "orphaned children" (247)—for they clearly no longer acknowedge their mother as a parent—"I, with my sister, whom I name, Elektra here, stand in your sight, children whose father is lost" (252-3).

By contrast, they turn to a more active and verbal mourning of that father, concerning whom,

> If only at Ilion,
> father, and by some Lykian's hands
> you had gone down at the spear's stroke,
> you would have left high fame [*kleos*] in your house,
> in the going forth of your children
> eyes' admiration... (345-50)

which sentiments the chorus continues without a missing a beat, that

> loved then by those he loved
> down there beneath the ground
> who died as heroes, he would have held
> state, and a lord's majesty, vassal on it to those most great,
> the Kings of the under darkness.
> For he was king on earth when he lived
> over those whose hands held power of life
> and death, and the staff of authority. (354-62)

Aiskhylos' audience may well have recognized the resonance back to Book Eleven of the *Odyssey*, and Akhilleus' words to Odysseus regarding his condition in death—and perhaps back, too, to the beginning of the *Iliad* and the quarrel between Akhilleus and Agamemenon, and where that quarrel ultimately led—and even to Book Twenty-Four of the *Odyssey* in which those two heroes were clearly reconciled, posthumously.

To the words of Orestes and the Chorus, Elektra adds that he should *not* have died at Troy.

> Sooner, his murderers
> should have been killed, as he was,
> by those they loved, and have found their death,
> and men remote from this outrage
> had heard the distant story. (367-71)

While the chorus asserts that "you are dreaming" yet it assures her and us that "power grows on the side of the children" (379). So this entire back and forth among these three protagonists is redolent of the problematic *eros/eris* interweave that defines the entire history of the House of Atreus up to the present moment: those who are—or should be—loved ones kill or are killed by each other. The shape of this interweave, which is both inter-genderal and inter-generational, is starting to be reconfigured: at least the intra-generational, inter-genderal aspect of it—Orestes and Elektra—seems less, shall we say, abberational. The most recent manifestaion of the abberation/dysfunction (Agamemnon and Klytaimnestra) has been intra-generational. But the turn, with power growing on the side of the children—who have been abused, up to this point, the one by being treated practically as a slave and the other by being cast into exile—will further the complex along inter-generational lines.

Orestes and Elektra both invoke the help of their dead father (479-509) to succeed in their plan—which is primarily focused on Aigisthos (482). How could it be otherwise? It is much easier to direct their righteous, murderous anger toward him than toward their own mother, regardless of how she has (also) treated them. Moreover, its seems, oddly, that she has herself sent libations to the tomb of the husband murdered by her own hand—an act that, not surprisingly, Orestes cannot understand. It is the chorus that explains it: her dreams—nightmares—of having given birth to a snake, suckled it and how "the creature drew in blood along with the milk" (533). So the offerings are being sent in the hopes of bringing such nightmares to an end.

It is in response to this that Orestes actually articulates for the first time that "I turn snake to kill her" (550). With the further delineation of his plan—and following a long choral interlude that references other mythic eristic betrayals of *eros*, to wit: Althaea and her son, Meleager; Skylla and her father, Nisus; and the Lemnian women and their husbands—the scene and its site shift to the gates of the palace, whither Orestes and Pylades have arrived, disguised as travellers seeking refuge for the night—and where they are met by Klytaimnestra.

If the heart of the deception is their disguising who they are, its soul is the news they bring: that Orestes is dead, news that, Orestes says, "I think his father should be told" (690). Klytaimnestra's response, to be filled with grief (or feigning the same) goes so far as to refer to her now-dead son as "the hope that was our healer once and made us look for a bright revel in our house"(698-9). Or perhaps there is nothing feigned here: one might imagine that Orestes was such a source of bright revel in the house when he was a child, a rambunctious little boy—before the Iphigenia episode poisoned everything—and it is this that, in a moment of genuine grief provoked by the onrush of such unexpected news, the queen recalls.

The screw of irony in any case is twisted another turn by Orestes, as he asserts that he would have prefered to have arrived with better news, especially to such an august house. "For what is there more kindly than the feeling between host and guest" (702-3)? Might the audience, or at least some of its members, think of the guest/lover of Klytaimnestra in Agamemnon's house, Aigisthos, and perhaps of Paris/Alexandros as a guest in Menelaos' home, years ago, from which home, his host's home, he abducted Helen—and even, perhaps, of Odysseus and his guest-host experiences: with Polyphemos, among the Phaiakians, with Kirke and Kalypso, and of course with regard to the suitors and his own wife, Penelope?

In any case, Klytaimnestra's response is that, in spite of the news he brings, the stranger will "not find that your reception falls below your worth, nor [will you] be any less our friend for this" (707-8). They exit, and Orestes' old nurse, Cilissa enters, according to the chorus, in tears—and from her we indeed hear the truth regarding the Queen's feelings: that "she put a sad face on before the servants, to hide the smile inside her eyes...[for] the pained story that the strangers have brought" (737-8, 741). Well, if that memory of the child, Orestes, and her grief were, for a moment, real, then it was only for a very brief moment. When Aigisthos arrives onto the stage, and similarly expresses pain at the news that he has already heard, he notes that he wants "to question, carefully, this messenger... [for] ...the mind has eyes, not to be easily deceived" (851, 854)—and with that exits into the palace. In the midst of the choral recitation that follows we hear a cry, and one of Aigisthos' loyal followers enters to tell us that he is dead—at the hand of a very much alive Orestes.

So the son/nephew returned from boyhood exile has slain the uncle who as his mother's lover and a—passive, background—participant in his father's murder had justified his own position by references to the pain of his own exile as a boy. That irony is almost lost, crowded out as it is by so many other ironies in the swift flow of events.[113]

Klytaimnestra, on stage again, calls for "an ax to kill a man" (889)—and so Orestes and Pylades return to the stage, swords drawn. His mother tries one last gambit to preserve her own life, bearing her breasts and reminding Orestes who they are to each other:

Chapter Four 163

Hold, my son. Oh, take pity, child, before this breast
where many a time, a drowsing baby, you would feed
and with soft gums sucked in the milk that made you strong.
(896-8)

And the ploy might have worked, had not Pylades been present, to whom Orestes turns, asking "what shall I do, Pylades? Be shamed to kill my mother" (899)? It is Pylades who, in response, reminds him of the oracle at Delphi and of the promises made to and by Apollo, which re-affirms Orestes' conviction to finish the task he had come to accomplish. Orestes turns to his mother—and the discussion is not yet over, although we might assume that its outcome will still be her death at his hand (even if we did not already know the story and know that this will indeed be the outcome).

The discussion is about love, at different levels: her greater love for Aigisthos—over whose body Orestes intends to kill her—than for her husband, his father, Agamemnon; about the mother-son relationship that she has functionally sacrificed to her relationship with Aigisthos—except for the too-late, hopeful and self-serving rhetorical flourishes in which she continues to engage—and through which we are reminded of the ever-present threefold matrix that defines the Greek sense of human experience: fate/destiny (*moira*), the gods, and human action.

Klytaimnestra
I raised you when you were little. May I grow old with you?
Orestes
You killed my father. Would you make your home with me?
Klytaimnestra
Fate had some part in that, my child.
Orestes
Why, then, Fate has so wrought that this shall be your death.
Klytaimnestra
A mother has her curse, child. Are you not afraid?
Orestes
No. You bore me and threw me away, to a hard life.
Klytaimnestra
I sent you to a friend's house. This was no throwing away.

Orestes
I was born of a free father. You sold me.... (907-15)
Klytaimnestra
... Take care. Your mother's curse, like dogs, will drag you down.
Orestes
How shall I escape my father's curse, if I fail here? (924-5)

There are at least three issues that this dialogue engages: One, given the family history, is the question: how much of what is about to happen was inevitable, before Orestes was born, before the war in Troy appeared on Agamemnon's horizon, before the sacrifice of Iphigenia: how much of this is a function of fate? Two, we are reminded that whatever obligations he might feel toward his mother nonetheless—or fears from her curse—are outweighed by his sense of obligation to his father and fear of being cursed by his father's immortal soul (and perhaps the gods with which it is now associated). Three, this eristic discussion—an *agon* or verbal contest of sorts—pits her attempts to conjure the mother-son love that might save her against the eristic anger that he retains, and, when it comes down to it, articulates as a kind of denouement that results from his painful exile: she took away his childhood of comfort, caused him to suffer for ten years—thus stripping herself of any "loving mother" claims on him. While he is avenging his father's murder and keeping his promises to Apollo, the tipping point is the personal suffering that he has endured.

Although the play continues for a few hundred more lines, and includes Orestes' display of his father's blood-stained robe—as well as his acknowledgment that although "I have won... my victory is soiled, and has no pride" (1017), the drama really ends with this *agon* and its off-stage aftermath. In case we did not know it, the chorus points out that "there is trouble here. There is more to come" (1020). The reference to a mother's curse makes the third play in the trilogy necessary—inevitable, if there is to be any true denouement to this narrative. As the play ends, Orestes is already experiencing torment, and the helpful and hopeful chorus—townspeople liberated by his double murder of a pair of tyrants—directs him to the temple of Apollo, where he can be cleansed.

The first 234 lines or so of *The Eumenides*, in fact, take place in Delphi at the sanctuary of Pythian Apollo. Even there, against the backdrop of the god's pledge to protect Orestes—asserting that "it was I who made you strike your mother down" (84), that lady's ghost makes an appearance, in the company of the sleeping Furies, to whom, as to us, she speaks, complaining that they sleep too much and have "no pity for my plight. I stand, his mother, here, killed by Orestes. He is gone" (121-2). They awaken as she exits, and howl, until Apollo enters and commands them to leave his sanctuary—but in an *agon* they assert that their pursuit of Orestes is legitimate. And so they will continue to do—but Orestes is gone because he has been directed by Apollo, and led by Hermes, to Athens and the Temple of Athene, patron goddess of the city. It is here that the narrative will achieve its conclusion, beginning with the ever more eager pursuit of Orestes by those Furies.

Whether they will continue to do this, driving their victim mad, or whether he can be somehow exonerated of the murder that he has commited, is discussed and decided in stages. Orestes states his case, reminding everyone that Agamemnon

> died without honor
> when he came home. It was my mother
> of the dark heart, who entangled him in subtle gyves
> and cut him down. The bath is witness to his death.
> I was an exile in the time before this. I came back
> and killed the woman who gave me birth. I plead guilty.
> My father was dear, and this was vengeance for his blood.
> Apollo shares responsibility for this…
> I am in your hands. Where my fate falls, I shall accept.
> (458-65, 469)

So a double tension pulses beneath the surface of Orestes' statement: the issue of divine versus human responsibility, and that of how to skew one's loving loyalty: more toward one's father or toward one's mother—for which Orestes had made a clear choice. What do the larger powers in the universe respond? Athene immediately acknowledges that

> [t]he matter is too big for any mortal man
> who thinks he can judge it. Even I have not the right
> to analyze cases of murder where the wrath's edge
> is sharp, and all the more since you have come, and clung
> a clean and innocent suppliant, against my doors... (470-74)

But the Furies, she points out, cannot simply be brushed aside. So—interestingly, and reflective no doubt of the time period in which the play was written, as Athens was assuming an increasingly hegemonic position in the Hellenic world in the context of the Persian Wars—she appoints "judges of manslaughter" in order to "establish a court into all time to come" (483-4): a jury of Athenians.

In the *agon* that shortly follows, between Orestes and the chorus of Furies, in which Orestes reiterates his full admission of having killed his mother, he asserts that that single act is outweighed by his mother's double act, for "she murdered her husband, and thereby my father, too" (602)—and her death was therefore justified: an *execution* for a *double* murder, rather than a *murder* for a *simple* murder, one might say.

Orestes twists back to ask the Furies, after her act, when she lived (as the Furies have observed that he does, now): "why did you not descend and drive her out?" to which they respond that "the man she killed was not of blood congenital" (604-5). So there are different kinds of love-relationships that, if they end up subverted by strife that leads to violence and the death of one of the protagonists, require different penalties. Presumably the answer to the question as to why Agamemnon was not pursued by Furies after sacrificing Iphigenia would be that she was an offering to a goddess and not the victim of murder—or perhaps that he *was* pursued by them, but only gradually, from the argument with Akhilleus to the revenge-murder at the hands of his wife.

This matter of a kind of hierarchy of love-relationships takes another turn as Apollo, speaking in defense and justification of Orestes, also in a back and forth *agon* with the Furies, culminates his defense with the assertion that

> the mother is no parent of that which is called
> her child, but only nurse of the new-planted seed
> that grows. The parent is he who mounts. A stranger, she
> preserves a stranger's seed, if no god interfere. (658-61)

The details of how Apollo proves this perspective on biological reality are not important for our purposes. What matters is what it reflects of the Greek understanding being expressed by Aiskhylos regarding the relative significance of the relationship between a child and his/her parents: the father is the only *real* parent—the offspring is the outcome of his seed, *period*, no ovular contribution from the mother is included in the make-up of the child—the mother is of distant secondary consequence, a pot in which the father's seed is kept warm so that it may germinate and grow.

If it could be argued that this is at least consistent with why a demi-god like Akhilleus ultimately dies—since his mother as an immortal contributes no DNA to him; it all comes from his mortal father—it may certainly be said to contradict the story of Sarpedon in *Iliad* Book Sixteen, who by this same logic should have defeated Patroklos and lived, bearing within him only his father's—Zeus's—DNA, and not his mortal mother's DNA. Even more so, it contradicts the mortal/immortal fate of that earlier hero of heroes, Herakles, who dies on his own pyre (although he *is* swooped up to Olympos and ultimately immortalized, anyway....)

Of course the point is not these sorts of inconsistencies; they are not what is at issue—Apollo is not teaching a biology class, after all, but arguing a case before the first-ever convened Athenian jury, and basing his argument on his own divine—*sacer*—logic, so to speak. What is at issue is the Greek understanding of things as represented by Apollo's words in Aiskhylos' play. For that understanding, Orestes' love for his father is infinitely more significant than his anger toward his mother and his murder of that woman is far less important than his having avenged his father's death—and, moreover, there really isn't a true blood-bond between mother and son, so the Furies have no right to be pursuing him, anyway.

Apollo promises Athene, at the end of his speech, that he will make her city great (668ff), if she judges in favor of his "client." She, on the other hand—a battle-dressed, male-like virgin female goddess, born from her father's head, without a mother involved (736) and who claims to always be "for the male ... and strongly on my father's side" (737-8)—in order to accede to his request to cast the deciding vote among the Athenian judges to exonerate Orestes, (the ballots of the Athenians are divided equally, when counted out), also makes an offer: to the very-upset Furies. She promises them a place of their own, "deep hidden under ground that is yours by right, where you shall sit on shining chairs beside the hearth to accept devotions offered by your citizens" (805-7). After a long back-and-forth discussion, they accept "this home at Athene's side" (916), and from being Furies they are transformed into the blessed ones—the Eumenides, for whom this play is named, who have the last words, in which they affirm that

> there shall be peace forever between these people
> of Pallas and their guests. Zeus the all-seeing
> met with Fate to confirm it.
> Singing all, follow our footsteps. (1044-7)

So love—some form of it, anyway—triumphs over strife as the trilogy comes to an end. One thread in the Great War tapestry is, for the time being at least, tied up in an elegant bow.[114]

The tapestry of the Trojan War narrative does not end here, however. Both Sophokles and Euripides will write various plays (a number extant even among the relatively few of their works that have survived out of antiquity) that focus on other threads within that narrative, including several works that focus on Orestes or on Elektra, as well as those that deal with characters outside the house of Atreus, such as Philoktetes or Aias (each of them the subject of a play by Sophokles), or surviving Trojan women, like Hekabe and Andromakhe, in plays by Euripides.

III Euripides and the Trojan War

Euripides (ca 480-406 BCE), in fact, was apparently so disturbed by the husband/wife/lover, *eros/eris* issue that led directly to the great war, that he devoted a play to Helen, in which she is, as it were, exonerated of the crime of betraying her husband, and spends the entire war in Egypt—an *eidolon* of the famous beauty is all that accompanies Alexandros to Troy—and is picked up in Egypt by Menelaos on his way home from the war.

He is even more disturbed, it seems, (in returning to the House of Atreus), by the idea that Agamemnon would so casually sacrifice his daughter or that a goddess would demand such a cruel sacrifice from him. So the playwright pushes against the standard-issue understanding of the story and in one play, *Iphigenia among the Taurians*, suggests that Artemis swept Iphigenia up from the altar at the last moment and wafted her to a distant place where she was put in charge of tending the goddess's shrine.

One could, of course, argue that, from the perspective of the broad categories of *sacer* and *profanus*, there is very little difference: to be dead and to be out in the middle of the middle of nowhere, far away from the Greek (Akhaian) world, amounts to the same thing as being dead—one is in both cases *sacer* and not *profanus*—which is why Odysseus, in the end, for example, didn't wish to remain with Kalypso for eternity, away from that world. But in common thought, there is certainly a difference between these two aspects of the *sacer*, from one of which there is no return (except for reincarnation) and from the other of which, return always remains a possiblity—which possibility is realized for Iphigenia in Euripides' play.

Artemis' Taurian shrine is devoted to virgin girls (like the goddess herself, in her classical configuration)—in fact, is so devoted to this principle that, should a male arrive on the premises, he must perish. Who should show up in his wanderings but Orestes—and so the play explores the female-male sibling love and how it ultimately triumphs over what may be seen as a divinely-ordained *eris* between genders. Orestes is not only spared but in the end is able to take his sister away from the isolated island and back to their *profanus* world.

Euripides' second play devoted to the fate of Iphigenia places her in the location where she is to be sacrificed in the first place—this is *Iphigenia at Aulis*—and poignantly examines daughter-father, father-daughter love in its hierarchic relationship not to the ego of the male father, nor to the mother-child or husband-wife relationship, but to his (and her) sense of obligation to the gods. One of his last plays—produced (by his son or possibly his nephew) at the Great Dionysia in March, 405 BCE, a few months after the playwright's death, (with some parts apparently unfinished and added in by the producer)—*Iphigenia in Aulis* presents a rather humble Agamemnon, who comments, when we encounter him toward the beginning of the drama, on how he envies those like his old servant, "who without peril pass through their lives, obscure, unknown... [for] glory (*kleos*) that is perilous, and will trip them as they walk" (17-19, 21-2).

This is of course the consummate theme that undergirds the epic tradition; it is what haunts the argument between Agamemenon and Akhilleus in the *Iliad* and also the traditional narrative of what happens with Agamemnon and Iphigenia at Aulis. Men like Agamemnon and Akhilleus crave for, strive for, yearn for—at virtually any cost—the *kleos* that reflects their own self-love above all. So the audience knows from the get-go that the Agamemnon shaped here by Euripides is a different one from that with which we have been so long familiar. In the dialogue with his old servant, Agamemnon then reviews—for him and for us, in case we've forgotten—the story of why they are still here at Aulis, (beginning with the genealogy of his own wife, Klytaimnestra and her sister, Helen), but noting that, when the prophet Kalkhas urged "that my daughter, Iphigenia, be sacrificed to the goddess of this place... I ordered our herald, Talthybios, to make a loud proclamation and dismiss the whole army. I would never have the cruel brutality to kill my daughter" (90-1, 95-7)!

After a good deal of pressure from his brother, though, he had agreed to do it, and wrote that letter to Klytaimnestra in which he asked that she send down Iphigenia, contriving the fiction that his daughter was to be married to Akhilleus. "Of the Akhaians who know, there are Kalkhas, Odysseus, and Menelaos, only... I did this wrong! Now in this letter I rewite the message and put down the truth... You must go to Argos. Of the message folded here I will tell you all, since you are loyal to both my wife and to my house" (105-9, 111-12). And the second message is to *not* send their daughter down, but that they must wait another season. When the servant worries that this will anger Akhilleus, Agamemnon reminds him that Akhilleus never knew of the original plan in the first place. He instructs his servant to be sure that on his way to Argos he isn't passed by Iphigenia's carriage—that if it is already in transit, he turn it back!

This is a very different Agamemnon, much more thoughtful and tortured—and much more loving of his daughter (and his wife) than the one we have encountered in prior depictions. What thickens and complicates events is that somehow Menelaos has managed to waylay Agamemnon's servant when he is barely out the door; he has opened and read this second missive intended for Klytaimnestra. They are fighting over this when Agamemnon re-enters onto the stage before his brother can beat the old servant, but in the *agon* that follows, he threatens Agamemnon with revealing to all the Akhaians what he considers to be treasonous—and culminates the back-and-forth with a lengthy speech about disloyalty and the changing of one's mind regarding friendships and actions. He concludes with the words:

> I groan for Greece in her affliction,
> for she was ready to act with honor,
> but on account of your girl and you,
> she lets the barbarians, even the basest
> of them, slip from her grasp and make her name
> a mockery! Oh may I never make
> any man ruler of my country or
> commander of her armies because I am
> in debt to him. No, a general
> must have wit; and a ruler, understanding. (370-5)

So Menelaos construes the matter as one of national honor—Hellenes versus barbarians—obscuring entirely his personal stake in the situation: that one of those "barbarians" managed to pry his wife away from him with ease; and parent-child relations have no meaning for him—one might imagine from his casual willingness to allow Agamemnon to sacrifice his daughter that he and Helen are childless—for he has absolutely no sympathy for Agamemnon's love for his daughter.[115] This is the sort of self-centered Menelaos we might expect from earlier views of him in the *Iliad* and the *Odyssey*.

It is this twisting of the facts into a different shape that forms the centerpiece of Agamemnon's equally lengthy retort, the first part of which asks rhetorically

> …Tell me, who
> has wronged you, what do you want? Are you
> burning to possess a virtuous wife? Well,
> I cannot procure her for you. The one you had
> you governed foully. Should I pay the price
> for your sins, when I am innocent? (382-4)

These inflaming words laser in on the truth of why the ships have been assembled at Aulis in the first place by Agamemnon: to reclaim, for Menelaos, the wife, Helen, that he could not hang onto through his own husbandly skills. Brother-love (currently turned to strife) has led to the current complication after the messy failure of wife-husband love (currently leading to the greater strife of war, albeit temporarily paused due to strife between a goddess and men). Agamemnon continues, that his brother is crazy, "for the gods, being favorable, rid you of a wicked wife, and now you want her back!" (389-90). In the service of such madness,

> I will not kill my children.
> Nor will your enterprise of vengeance upon
> an evil wife prosper against all justice.
> If I did commit this act, against law, right,
> and the child I fathered, each day, each night,
> while I yet lived would wear me out with grief
> and tears…" (397-400)

Fraternal love is being assailed by strife—to the extent that Menelaos challenges his older brother with the question "Where is the proof that you are our father's son, my brother?" (406), to which Agamemnon responds: "I am brother to you when you are sane, not mad" (407). Menelaos continues: "Greece is in grief and in trouble. Isn't it right that you should bear a part of the hardship?" (409-10)—remarkably, one might suggest, confusing his personal situation with a national crisis a second time within a very brief compass—and Agamemnon responds: "This is what I think: Greece, like yourself, some god has driven mad" (411).

The two most obvious issues here are first, (to repeat), the conflation of a personal with a national situation—which is to say that, Menelaos has managed to turn his situation into a national one (thanks to the oath all of Helen's suitors had once taken)—and second, within the emergent personal conflict between his brother and him, the weighing of husband-wife and brother-brother relations against a father-daughter relationship. In a sense the question of hierarchies of love and loyalty (as is so overt in the *Oresteia*) presents itself.

That question becomes irrelevant, however, since a messenger shortly enters with the news that Iphigenia has arrived in Aulis. Or is it irrelevant? Since only four people (including the old servant) know the real reason why she is here, (although everyone else suspects that her arrival at such a time to this place can only be because she is going to be married—but nobody knows to whom), the question still remains as to what will be done with her. The response to the news of her arrival has Agamemnon torn to emotional shreds—both because "what can I utter to my wife or with what countenance receive and welcome her when she appears, unsummoned, in the midst of my disaster?" (454-6) and because of his daughter: "the unhappy maiden! Maiden [i.e., unmarried virgin], no—soon, it seems, Hades will marry her. Oh piteous fate! I hear her cries to me: O Father, why do you kill me?... Beside her, Orestes the infant will cry out meaningless words, but full of meaning to my heart!" (460-33, 465-6). This is a compassionate and tender and broken Agmamemnon who bears little resemblance to the one we know from prior works!

And there is a further twist, as Menelaos, moved to pity by his brother's anguish—"the tears bursting from [his] eyes" (476)—turns 180 degrees from his previous stance and beseeches that

>...you do not slay the child
> to prosper me and to destroy yourself.
> It is against all justice that you should
> groan from the same cause that makes me
> fortunate or that your daughter die while
> all my children live and face the sun.
> What do I want? Could I not obtain
> a perfect marriage elsewhere, if I longed for
> marrying? But a brother whom I should
> most cherish, I was about to forfeit
> to gain a Helen, so bartering excellence
> for evil... (481-88)
> ...what has Helen
> to do with this girl of yours? Disband
> the host, I say, let it go from Aulis... (494-6)

> I have changed because I love a brother. (502)

    This is also not the Menelaos whom we have known from earlier texts, (or earlier lines in this text), who has been moved to a distinct selflessness by his brother's grief. The hierarchy of love has shifted its configuration, for the moment: in this mode, it is fraternal love as well as parent-child love that are both presented as more enduring and more important than that between husband and wife—particularly when in this case the wife has betrayed the spousal love, thus engendering the potentially wide-spread era of *eris* that, if things proceed, will shortly follow.

    The irony that mounts, therefore, is powerful: Agamemnon asserts that he cannot do what Menelaos now suggests: he cannot disband an army that is raring to go and waiting to fight—and will feel cheated from that opportunity for *kleos* and chaos if Agamemnon sends his daughter back to safety in Argos, and hugely angry at their erstwhile leader, for Kalkhas will tell them. Even if, as Menelaos proposes, they kill Kalkhas, Odysseus will reveal the whole scenario to the troops. So in the end, the two brothers exit the stage after tacitly agreeing that the most Agamemnon can do is to kill Iphigenia before Klytaimnestra knows what is going on and before too many pre-sacrifice tears have been shed.

The denouement comes in two stages, one might say. First, a cheerful Klytaimnestra—rejoicing in her daughter's imminent marriage—and that daughter arrive on stage, and Iphigenia runs ahead to throw herself into her father's arms. When she asks her mother whether her running to him makes her upset, Klytaimnestra responds

> No my child, this is rightful, and it is
> as it always has been. Of all the children
> I have borne your father, you love him most. (638-9)

We cannot not be moved by the irony of those last words, given what is presumably about to transpire between father and most-adoring daughter, and more broadly, the irony of the entire scene with its happy family reunion, both because of what will transpire soon and because of our knowledge of the longer outcome of the moment of reunion, having heard about it in the *Odyssey* and witnessed it in Aiskhylos' trilogy.

Irony persists, in line after line, as Iphigenia observes to her loving and much-loved father that "it is a good and wonderful thing that you have done—bringing me here!" (642). The love between Agamemnon and Iphigenia is intense, so we cannot fail to feel the increasing effort it must take Agamemnon to respond joyfully to the daughter whom he loves while knowing what he will shortly do to her—and while she (and her quiet mother) remain innocent of that plan. The playwright carries on an extensive and very different sort of *agon*: one which is not a contest or competition as much as an ever-expanding demonstration of love-based agony.

He pushes that agony further as Iphigenia leaves the stage (literally) to her parents, who discuss the impending marriage—Agamemnon having decided to continue the deception and Klytaimnestra continuing to be deceived—and with it, at his wife's request, the leader of the Akhaians recites the extraordinary heritage of Akhilleus and the immortal blood that flows through his veins. We can feel the perspiration accumulating on Agamemnon's whole body as Klytaimnestra's reasonable and innocent questions push him more and more deeply into the lie that he has not been happy about making since the beginning of the play: "What is the day set for the marriage?" (717)... and "Now I ask this, have you slain the victims to Artemis, the goddess, for our child?" (719)... and when the child is given away, "where must I be staying?" (730), to which last query he answers: "In Argos, where you must take care of your younger daughters" (731). And she asks: "Leaving the child? Who then will lift the marriage torch?"—which leads to an argument regarding the propriety of the mother giving away her daughter or not, over against the mother's obligation to be home with the younger daughters.

When he finally simply demands that she obey him, she refuses, leaves the stage, and Agamemnon once more bemoans his situation. And we, who know where this story ends, may be struck by this—presumably first—instance of Klytaimnestra's self-assertion against a powerful male: a harbinger of the story a decade later that we have already encountered in the *Agamemnon*.

A long choral interlude is followed by the arrival onto the stage of Akhilleus—at the door of Agamemnon's temporary quarters to inquire when the journey toward Troy will finally begin—and again his words are fraught with irony, as he notes that such a delay is not good, especially for those "of us [who] are unmarried" (805); particularly since he has no idea that he has been mis-presented as the soon-to-be married as son-in-law of Agamemnon in order to arrange for the slaughter of the daughter to whom he would, by that fiction, be wed, so that the ships can indeed sail. That irony is multiplied when the person who enters from inside the tent is Klytaimnestra.

For in their dialogue—in which Akhilleus is quite uncomfortable speaking alone with an attractive woman—when Klytaimnestra mentions that he will soon be wed to her daughter, he is surprised and she of course is troubled by that fact: she quickly concludes that the betrothal is a lie, perhaps a cruel joke. But then the same old servant whom we encountereed at the outset, enters from the tent, having overheard their brief conversation, and tells them—presumably in a trembling voice—that "her father plans with his own hand to kill your child" (873). Not surprisingly, Klytaimnestra's response is that the old man is crazy or, when the servant persists, that Agamemnon has gone crazy, and then asks (in part rhetorically, in part directly to the servant) why ever her husband would be planning such an outrage.

The outrage is to enable the fleet to sail, "so that Menelaos may bring Helen back" (882)—to which Klytaimnestra responds "Oh, Fate then, has bound Helen's homecoming to my daughter and her death" (883)—clearly, then, providing a comparative weight to the two relationships under question: brother-brother/ husband-disloyal wife versus father-daughter. The third element besides humans and Fate in the matrix—the gods—she recognizes in the next verse uttered by the old servant: that "it is to Artemis that her father will sacrifice the child."

It is at this moment that we realize that Agamemnon will be sacrificing not only his beloved daughter for the sake of his brother and his sister-in-law. The steely anger that overwhelms Klytaimenstra, as she realizes that the wedding to Akhilleus had been only a trick to have her bring down Iphigenia to Aulis, is the first stage in the destruction of Agamemnon's relationship with his wife—and since we all know the ultimate outcome of that expanding *eris*, regardless of how these intermediate details have been sensitively re-considered by the playwright, (who at this point allows the servant to explain how Agamemnon would have relented in his plan had not Menelaos intercepted the servant and obstructed that would-be change), it is his own life that Agamemnon will have sacrificed along with his wife's love.

But we are still 700 lines from the end of the play and Euripides is not finished with us. For Akhilleus has been standing there this whole time, never having left his post by the tent door, and is horrified, offering to Klytaimnestra, to "hurl my reproach upon your husband" (899). Klyaimnestra falls to her knees to beg him to intercede—to protect her daughter as is most appropriate for the heroic son of a goddess. He responds vehemently that he will do this—and then somewhat more calmly, perhaps, expresses annoyance that Agamemnon did not at least ask his permission to use his name in such a ruse (in which case, he might have agreed "for the sake of Hellas" (966))—but (in the end of his long soliloquy), he concludes that he will fight and kill fellow Akhaians, if need be, to preserve Iphigenia, a sentiment that he expresses in crescendoing tones.

No doubt the audience recognizes at least three moments, past and future, to which this one resonates. One, (past), the renowned reluctance of Akhilleus to go to Troy, given the inevitable death at a young age that such a voyage would mean, and here we play on a different sort of reluctance, pertaining to the dishonorable context of this time and place (and thus the matter of his honor). Two, (future), the argument that will open up the first book of the *Iliad*, between Agamemnon and Akhilleus, albeit very differently, yet also focused on the fate of a girl and the consequences for the honor of Akhilleus. Three, (future), that we will next encounter a female clinging to the knees of a male, begging for assistance when the goddess who is Akhilleus' own mother clings, also in *Iliad* I, to the knees of Zeus, asking for his help in the matter of her son's life, death, and honor.

In both cases a mother who loves and is upset by the fate of her offspring clings to the knees of a potential savior (or at least aid-giver) of that child: Zeus to Akhilleus (albeit, really, only with regard to Akhilleus' *kleos*, not his life); Akhilleus to Iphigenia. A Greek audience might also be sensitive to the pun allowed by the word "knees," (as we have previously noted), for which the root is the same as that for "gonads"—particularly when Klytaimnestra, raining praises on Akhilleus, offers to bring her daughter to him, "to clasp your knees" (992), if he needs further convincing that he ought to help her out. Akhilleus desists—his goal is the glory of saving Iphigenia; he does not need to see her and is not interested in the scandalous gossip that would endure were she to appear before him (998-1007).

So: the issue is how to convince Agamemnon to shift course. Akhilleus suggests that Klytaimnestra beseeach her husband as a suppliant, first—and if that succeeds then "I need not be a party to this affair" (1018); "so without me you and those dear to you may succeed in all" (1021-22). After a choral interlude, Klytaimnestra re-appears on the stage, and a moment later, Agamemnon, whom she had not been able to locate. He is continuing the deception, unaware that his secret is known to both his wife and his daughter, and asks her to

> send for the child from the army-tent
> to join her father. But first listen to me:
> The lustral waters have now been prepared

and the barley thrown on the cleansing fire;
bridal victims are ready—their black blood
soon to flow in honor of Artemis (1110-14)

—and we cannot miss the irony of his words, for indeed the victim is (almost) ready, whose black blood will soon flow, and the cleansing fire and lustral waters are no doubt ready, and all shall be done to honor Artemis, (an odd goddess to oversee the ceremony that is the prelude to sexual congress between man and woman, given her own emphatic virginal status), but the "bridal victim" is the bride.

Klytaimnestra's response is to begin to reveal what she knows—"...for the deed of your intention, I can find no good name for that (1116-7)—although Agamemnon does not pick up on this; she calls to Iphigenia to come out of the tent, carrying her baby brother, Orestes, in her arms. We arrive at the denouement of this family interaction within both the private and public spheres, as it were. Agamemnon asks his daughter why she is weeping, "and hood[ing] your eyes from me with your robe" (1123). It is Klytaimnestra who responds enigmatically—except for the punctuating word: sorrow. Again husband-father asks why they "both look at me with trouble and with terror in your eyes" (1127-8), as the playwright extends the passage toward the moment of recognition—Agamemnon's—that they know what he knows and thinks they do not.

Wife-mother finally demands an answer to a question—husband-father says that he is willing to answer—and she blurts it out, at last:

Your child and mine—do you intend to kill her? (1131)

He cannot answer at first, tries to dodge that straight shot, but she persists and he, then, in anguish, ejaculates "Oh, what an evil daimon is mine!" (1137) to which she responds: "Yours? Mine and hers! One evil fate for three and misery for us all" (1138)! The line-by-line back-and-forth suddenly expands to a lengthy series of speeches by Klytaimnestra with small responses from Agamemnon—indeed, as she tells him that she knows the whole plot, he says that, rather than lie—because apparently he still cannot admit the truth regarding what is soon to transpire—he will remain silent (1140-45). The speech hardly seems designed to do what she and Akhilleus agreed that she should do—beseech him as a suppliant—because, of course, she has become so over-wrought (particularly, one might suppose, given his continued profession of ignorance that anything is awry with their daughter's situation).

She begins by reminding him in an exceedingly unflattering manner of how he won her, against her will, as his wife. Nonetheless, she continues, she adjusted and became an exemplary wife to him—and bore him a son and three daughters. And now he would kill one of these daughters. Why? Why can't you answer, instead forcing me to answer for you?

> I kill her, you must answer, that Menelaos
> may win Helen back. And so our child,
> in her beauty, you pay as price for a woman
> of evil. So you buy with our best beloved
> a creature most loathed and hated. (1167-70)

We may well recall at this moment that Helen is Klytaimnestra's sister, so the eristic framing of the hierarchy of love here adds another level, for it includes not only father-daughter versus brother-brother love (or hate), but parent-child versus sister-sister love (or hate)—albeit in Agamemnon's case this refers to his actions and in Klytaimnestra's case it refers to her words. And she warns him, moreover, that if he does this and then goes off for who knows how many years, to war, "from what heart shall I keep your halls in Argos?" (1173), particularly as "I sit down with tears of loneliness and for a mourning that will have no end (1176-7)."

> Here am I and the children you have left me. Oh, only
> a little more do we need of pretext
> and provocation so that upon your
> homecoming we give you the welcome that
> is wholly due. No! by the gods, do not
> force me to become an evil woman! (1179-83)

—and we, the audience, are well aware of what all these words will come to mean, although Klytaimnestra herself doesn't yet know what we know, so the irony is intensified. She continues

> ...When you return at last
> to Argos, after the war, will you embrace
> and kiss your daughters and your son? Heaven forbid!
> It would be sacrilege! (1191-2)

She comes full circle to a rhetorical question that functions, really, as an insult, and puts front and center the real love-focus that competes at this moment with his love for his daughter—have you thought about any of this, she asks, "or is your thought and need only to brandish scepter and lead armies? (1195)—his self-love, an *eros* that is centered in the *eris* of warfare.

At least insist that lots be drawn among the Akhaian leaders to choose who shall have to sacrifice a daughter, she insists—or better still, have Menelaos sacrifice *his* daughter since it is for him and Helen that this crisis has evolved. Why must Klytaimnestra, who has been a loyal wife, lose a daughter, while Helen, who has sinned against her husband's bed, be allowed to "return to prosper, and bring her daughter home?" (1205). Euripides has offered an extraordinary twist to the story by raising what seems to be an obvious question—and at this moment in the play, if we pretend that we do not know its outcome, we might ask how the literature that we have engaged would have had to be otherwise composed, had it been Menelaos' daughter—Hermione—instead of Agamemnon's daughter, who ended up on the altar dedicated to Artemis. How would the plots have had to adjust—from the depiction of Menelaos and Helen that we are given in Book Three of the *Odyssey* to Aiskhylos' *Oresteia* trilogy to the various plays by Sophokles and Euripides that focus on Elektra, Orestes, and— including this one, here—Iphigenia.

The Argive queen's long agonized speech culminates with the words "do not kill the girl—who is your child and mine" (1208). That specific nuance—the reminder of how they share in the parentage of Iphigenia, as opposed to emphaisizing her being the daughter of one or the other of them—punctuates an argument that is very different from what we have encountered in Apollo's speech in the *Eumenides*, in which the hierarchy of love distinguishes father from mother to the detriment of the latter: here they are co-equal—although one is begging for the child's life and the other is preparing to end the child's life. What in Aiskhylos' trilogy was necessarily a strife-ridden view of husband-wife-child relations is here desperately articulated as love-centered—the very centerpiece of loving—and thus something that must be preserved.

The chorus briefly affirms this notion—and then Iphigenia herself speaks up, and the narrative's denouement twists and turns from yet another angle. She speaks first as an eloquent suppliant, she

> ...who was the first to call you father,
> you first to call me child. And of your children
> first to sit upon your knees. We kissed
> each other in our love... (1220-22)

—she whom he promised to see married and who promised him to receive him in her home in his old age to recompense him for all the years of caring for her: she remembers all this but he apparently has forgotten it, having "willed it in your heart to kill me" (1233).

She turns next to her baby brother, Orestes, who "even without speech... begs you, father, pity and have mercy on my sister's life" (1244-5)—so that the claims of parent-child love are multiplied by those of brother-sister love. The chorus damns the name of Helen for bringing this crisis about. And Agamemnon responds to both his daughter and his wife (he places them in that order in his comment), offering his own agony to this *agon*. Unlike the Agamemnon whom we have seen elsewhere (particularly in the *Iliad*), he does not respond to what had been, in large part, antagonistic words from Klytaimnestra by emoting with anger, but rather with anguish and pity. For

> ... I know what calls
> to me for pity and compassion, and
> what does not. I love my children!
> Did I not, I would be mad indeed.

> Terrible it is to me, my wife, to dare
> this thing. Terrible not to dare it. (1255-8)

But the army, all assembled, awaits and cannot sail unless he sacrifices his daughter—and here he has embraced the Menelaos assertion that we recognize from earlier in the play: that this is about the protection of Hellas and its values; we must crush these barbarian Trojans,

> that they may halt the plunder of marriage beds
> and the rape and seizure of Greek women...(1266-7)

—thus turning the impending voyage away from being an effort on behalf of his brother and toward being an effort on behalf of The Nation itself. "Hellas lays upon me this sacrifice of you beyond all will of mine" (1270-1). More to the point, "Hellas turns to you, to me, and now, as much as in us lies, she [Hellas] must be free" (1272-3). So she is invited to martyr herself—to die for her country, (as opposed to dying for her father's ego).

It is of more than passing interest that the emphasis placed by Klytaimnestra on Helen as the one culpable for the murder about to take place—on an individual woman, that is—has been eclipsed by Agamemnon's turning the issue around to center not only on national honor but on an act viewed as having been accomplished by an entire nation. His view might be understood as a standard Greek male view: a woman cannot, by definition, be a major factor in the workings of the world; it takes another woman to arrive at the "radical" view that Helen is the power behind the *eros*-induced *eris* in which they find themselves embedded. Agamemnon's twist is, indeed, a back-handed insult to Helen: she has been reduced to a pawn, as if Paris/Alexandros forcibly carried her off, rather than her having been taken from her husband willingly. That ambiguity of perspective has been present since Book Six of the *Iliad*, but Euripides torques it further than before.

And the still further twist imposed on the traditional story by the playwright is that, as we shall see, Iphigenia agrees. Again, however, the playwright arrives slowly, gently, at that place. Agamemnon leaves the stage—Klytaimnestra suggests to her daughter that "your father, betraying you in death, has fled away" (1277) and Iphigenia offers an eloquent soliloquy, in which she reminds us that this tale has multiple beginnings. Among the earliest such beginnings was the birth of Alexandros and his having been cast out and appointed to be the herdsman of Priam's flocks on Ida, where those three goddesses notoriously appeared one day. She abruptly shifts to her own birth and what has come later: the involvement of a goddess, Artemis (who is not one of the three who engaged Alexandros to choose the most beautiful among them) that has led to

> [a] first sacrifice [for Ilion]!
> He who began my life
> has betrayed me in misery
> to a lonely dying.
> Oh, my wretchedness,
> as I see her,
> Helen, doom-starred and evil;
> bitter, bitter
> is the death you bring me!
> murdered by my own father... (1312-19)

Three men approach, and her mother, hopeful, recognizes that it is Akhilleus (with two armor-bearers). Off-stage the Argive troops are heard shouting, threateningly. That the shouts are threatening we know because Akhilleus tells the ladies that the men are screaming about Iphigenia, demanding that she be slaughtered in sacrifice. Akhilleus claims to have spoken to the yelling crowd "and so was in danger" of death by stoning (1348). Even his own beloved Myrmidons, caught up in the strife-directed fury, have threatened him—they before all others. "I answered that they would never slaughter my bride... whom her father had pledged to me" (1355-6).

So the greatest of the warriors to head to Troy—who, we know from a different thread in this tapestry, had been reluctant to participate from the beginning, but was pushed hard by Odysseus to agree to do so—is mocked: that he has "become a slave of this marriage" (1353). Those bent on war's strife assail the great hero for what they take to be his love—for the daughter of the very man with whom, in the early pages of the *Iliad*, the hero will engage in an explosive strife-ridden *agon* that will pull him out of the war, only to return when his best friend, object of his most intense love, is killed. Akhilleus' pledge to fight against all the Akhaians, alone, to protect Iphigenia, resonates forward, too, to the reason for the Iliadic *agon*: Khryseis, whom he protects by demanding of Agamemnon that he return her to her father, a priest of Apollo, and Briseis, his own honor-prize, whom he can but cannot protect from Agamemnon's depradations—as he could but could not have chosen never to have come to fight at Troy. This interweave of ironies is indeed woven by intertwined threads of human and divine actions, intersecting within the tightly-knotted skein of *moira*.

Akhilleus prepares to stand against the thousands—who are led by none other than Odysseus—who is referred to, oddly enough, not as the son of Laertes, but as the son of Sisyphos, who in one thread in the tradition is said to have seduced Antiklea, Laertes' wife and Odysseus' mother.[116] Akhilleus—who had been pushed by Odysseus to join the forces heading to Troy as the greatest of the Akhaians, asserts that he will not allow his opponents to take the girl away.

This is the point, however, at which Iphigenia steps forward to embrace her martyrdom in stages. She turns to her mother, imploring her not to have her "soul in anger against your husband. This is a foolish and an evil rage" (1368-9). Nor should they allow Akhilleus to be compromised and be "blamed by the army. Such a thing would bring us nothing but would bring him utter ruin" (1372-3). Rather, "I shall die—I am resolved—and having fixed my mind, I want to die well and gloriously, putting away from me whatever is weak and ignoble" (1375-6). She transforms her victimization—her being at the passive mercy of others, like Khryseis and Briseis and Elektra and like Iphigenia herself in non-Euripidean contexts, (and like Helen, implicitly, in Agamemnon's previous speech), to the extent that they spend any ink at all on her situation—into a heroic action, one that will earn *kleos aphthiton*. Stated otherwise, she has trumped her father and Akhilleus and any others among the Akhaians heading to Troy in search of *kleos*, gathering it all in for herself! How appropriate she would have been as a bride to Akhilleus—and how fit she is as a daughter to the assertive—manly—Klytaimnestra whom we have met in the *Agamemnon*.

She, too, embraces the national, rather than personal narrative spun by Menelaos and taken up by Agamemnon: that through her sacrifice,

> ...never more will
> Barbarians wrong and ravish Greek women,
> drag them from happiness and their homes
> in Hellas. The penalty will be paid
> fully for the shame and seizure of Helen. (1379-80)

Love of country trumps love of self and justifies her death as much as it does the *eris* of the war to come that is made possible by her death. It is, as we shall later discuss (below, chapter seven) a very Roman and much less a Greek ethos that she expresses, placing the needs of the community so distinctly above her own needs—unless we count *kleos* as a need for this beautiful young woman.

And indeed, it is not the case that she herself is not a part of her calculus—she is, after all, a Greek, like Akhilleus, Odysseus, Menelaos and her father, Agamemnon—for she envisions that "I, savior of Greece, will win honor and my name shall be blessed" (1384-5). But she pushes heavily on the issue of the Nation—even as she argues to her mother that "you bore me for all Hellas, not for yourself alone" (1386-7). So, too, in a more Roman than Greek tone, she argues for the propriety of her *pietas* (*hosiotes*): "if Artemis wishes to take the life of my body, shall I, who am mortal, oppose the divine will? No—that is unthinkable!" (1394-6)

We may recognize, too, the historical context in which Euripides is writing—in the very late fifth century BCE—perhaps with irony. In fighting against the Persians three and four generations earlier, the Greeks had specifically coined the term *barbaros* to refer to their adversary. While its origin was onomatopoetic, intended to convey how non-Greek, specifically Persian, language sounded (like giberrish: *bar-bar-bar-bar-bar*) to Greek ears, the term included the connotation, in a war-setting, of a distinction: between the mercenary/slave armies of the (barbarian) Akhaimenids and the free, Athenian-led armies fighting for Hellas.

Chapter Four   187

This is echoed in the last words in Iphigenia's speech, that "[i]t is a right thing that Greeks rule barbarians, not barbarians Greeks" (1400-1). But given the time of the play, 26 years into the Peloponesian Wars, does Euripides still see things that way? More precisely, does he view Athens as the bastion of freedom (that Sparta is presumably not)? This play follows ten years after Athens destroyed the Melians when they sought to remain neutral in that long-lasting intra-Hellenic conflict; that tyranical act renders the protestation of being the consummate freedom-championing polis more than a little bit ironic for us if we think not of the Akhaian/pre-Trojan War setting, but rather of the Athenian/late Peloponesian War performance setting—a setting of which Euripides was surely quite conscious.

But I digress... Akhilleus is inspired by Iphigenia to assert envy that she belongs to Hellas and not to him—and envies her that "Hellas has chosen you, not me, to die" (1407). He, too, is a far cry here from the Akhilleus about whom we know from the *Iiad*, the *Odyssey* and elsewhere; his self-love is not completely gone, but it has been subverted by admiration for Iphigenia's *kleos*-worthy words and thus his love for her. As with the twisted turnings of perspective to which Euripides treated the audience early in the play with regard to Agamemnon and Menelaos, here at the opposite end of the drama, analogous turning twists with regard to Iphigenia and Akhilleus take place: inspired as he is by her nobility, he expresses an even more firm desire not only *for* her but to *save* her—calling his goddess mother, Thetis, to witness, no less (1413).

To this Iphigenia responds that he must not sacrifice himself nor kill any Greek to protect her. To which Akhilleus responds that truly he won't fight here against all comers, but that he will go and wait at the altar (like a groom waiting at the altar for his bride to approach) and there will prevent her being killed. He leaves the stage and a mother-daughter version of the Akhilleus-Iphigenia conversation ensues: that Klytaimnestra ought not to weep or cut a lock of her hair—in short, ought not to mourn—for a daughter who is "not lost but saved! And you too, through me, will be remembered gloriously" (1439-40). As for her sisters, simply say good-bye to them and do not dress them in mourning clothes; and as for Orestes: "do this, nurture him and see that he comes to strength and manhood for my sake" (1450-1). Given the future that we already know from Aiskhylos and elsewhere, this could hardly be more poignant or more ironic. The overflowing of love in all directions from the fountain of Iphigenia will, we know, dry up, scorched by the sun of inescapable anger and incontrovertible fate, leaving nothing but strife where this family is concerned—but particuarly where Orestes and Klytaimnestra are concerned.

So, too, Iphigenia's love-filled plea: "do not hate him. Do not hate my father who is your husband" (1454), she begs—although at this moment, Klytaimnestra is still soaking in the cool waters of her daughter's love for her family and her country, and so recognizes that "your father must run a course of agony and terror for your sake" (1455). In her wisdom—wasted in the end, in spite of her hopes for her family's future—Iphigenia forbids her mother to be present at the sacrifical ceremony, fobidding even the shedding of further tears, and in the culmination of her long penultimate speech, cries out that she be drenched in waters of purification, that

> about the altar of Artemis,
> about her Temple,
> dance!
> Let us dance in honor of Artemis,
> goddess, queen and blest
> with my own blood
> in sacrifice
> I will wash out
> the fated curse of the god. (1478-84)

As she exits the stage—offering as her final words: "And now, and now, beloved light, Farewell!" (1508-9)—the chorus intones a paian of praise to her, crying out: "All hail to Artemis, goddess queen, ...you who joy in human blood..." and calling for her guidance toward Troy and glory for Agamemnon. The audience may be at once uplifted by love for this lovely girl and her self-sacrifice, and sympathy for the web in which her family has been caught, but also by questions, or even distate, for gods who demand such sacrifices to atone for human assaults on divine self-love. Indeed, astute members of the audience, aware of the entire Trojan War cycle might turn away from this play with large questions regarding what Fate is, what the gods are, what humans are who so thoughtlessly confuse and intertwine contradictions like *eros* and *eris*.

Chapter Five

Eros and *Eris* in Sophokles and Euripides Beyond the Trojan War

The Trojan War cycle, magnificent and diversely directed as it is, is not the only narrative in which Greek tragic playwrights found contradiction and paradox, in general and particularly with regard to *eros* and *eris* as those ideas specifically pertain to (dysfunctional) families. Sophokles is best-known, in fact for a trio of plays—not conceived as a trilogy, but written over the course of 35 years—that focus on the royal house of Thebes. The three plays were not written in the order of the narrative: he wrote the *Antigone* first—it was produced in 441 BCE—which focuses on the generation following that of Oedipus himself. He subsequently wrote the work *Oidipos Tyrranos* (Oidipos the King) (in ca 427-6 BCE); and in his old age, perhaps past 90, wrote the *Oidipos at Kolonnos*, (produced in 405 BCE), the narrative placement of which falls between the other two.

I Sophokles and the Oidipos (Theban) Cycle

If nonetheless, as a matter of what one might call coherence convenience, we might follow the order of the story and not the order of the writing of the plays, then we begin with the knocking on the palace door of Oidipos, king of Thebes, by a priest and a chorus of suppliant children. Oidipos asks them what they are doing there—and refers to himself as one "whom all men call the Great one" (9). The priest responds that he, Oidipos, is aware of the plague that has infested their city, and that they hope that he, with his god-aided wisdom and his penchant for bringing luck, might be able to figure out why they are being victimized thusly. It turns out that Oidipos has in fact just sent off Kreon, his brother-in-law—that is, brother of his wife, the queen, Jocasta—to the oracle of Apollo at Delphi to find out how he might be able to save the city.

As the play unfolds, its investigatory action largely pushed by Oidipos himself, who has a compulsion to know the answers to riddles (as we, the audience, already know), the reason for the plague—for the offense to the gods—slowly and increasingly painfully unfolds. It is Oidipos himself who has inwittingly committed the offense by committing acts that the gods find unacceptable, even if committed without the knowledge of the one committing them that s/he is doing/has done so.

Kreon returns with orders from Apollo, that they drive pollution ingrained within the land out of the land (97-8), "by banishing a man, or expiation of blood by blood, since it is murder guilt that holds our city in this destroying storm" (100-102). And what this truly means is gradually unravelled by Oidipos' questions and Kreon's responses: that Oidipos' predecessor as king, Laios, had been murdered at a crossroads—but that they were so preoccupied by the problem of the sphinx and its solution that the Thebans never really fully investigated that murder—but "I will bring this to light again, King Phoebos [Apollo]" (133), Oidipos promises... for "helping the dead king I help myself" (140). We who know where this is driving, cannot miss the pregnant irony of Oidipos' words, which only deepens the more he speaks about who he is, and what he will do to save the city of which he is king,

> for I am now the holder of his [Laios'] office,
> and have his bed and wife that once were his,
> and had his line not been unfortunate
> we would have common children—(fortune leaped
> upon his head)—because of all these things,
> I fight in his defense as for my father... (259-64)

In one little knot most of the threads are tightly bound: father-wife-(who is mother)-children-(who are siblings)-son-(who is murderer)-husband-(who is son)—and Oidipos is the great unraveller of knots, and therefore "called the Great one." All of these inherently loving relationships have been undone by one unwitting eristic act—the murder of his father—that led to the erotic relationship of the unwitting son with his unwitting mother that yielded offspring who are also his brothers and sisters. This is more profoundly disastrous than merely dysfunctional.

The plot must thicken slowly, however, aided by the playwright in bringing Teiresias, the blind seer—the one who sees what others cannot as he cannot see what others can—onto the stage in an increasingly eristic dialogue-become-*agon* with Oidipos. Teiresias underscores that "with those you love best you live in foulest shame unconsciously and do not see where you are in calamity" (366-8). But when in his long-winded rant (before the chorus intervenes with a few lines in the midst of the *agon*) Oidipos asserts, regarding the sphinx and her theretofore death-dealing riddle, that "I solved the riddle by *my* wits alone! *Mine* was no knowledge got from birds!" (398-9) (as opposed to the sort of knowledge gleaned with avian instruments by seers), he may be said to have pronounced his own doom. For his hubristic statement is fully conscious—and dangerously reflective—of excessive self-love: that self-love that, before the play is over, will have turned to self-hate and self-pity.

In between, Oidipos will accuse Kreon of plotting against him; Jocasta will enter onto the stage for the first time during the increasingly angry *agon* between her husband and her brother—intervening almost as a mother might intervene between two 10-year-old sons who are squabbling—and Oidipos, almost out of nowhere, will accuse Kreon of essentially requesting "my death or banishment" (659), a phrase that is, as an increasing number of phrases are, as the play hurtles forward, pregnant. So the loving relationship between these two has turned eristic, as Oidipos—his temper not unfamiliar to those who already know the circumstances in which, in a fit of anger, her murdered his father—is beginning to be paranoid: he simultaneously fights off the truth that is careening toward him as he pursues it, eager to possess, to *know* it.

But he is already coming closer to the unhappy knowledge that will yield the catastrophe of which banishment will seem an almost afterthought component. For as Jocasta remains on the stage with Oidipos and the chorus, after Kreon has exited, he queries her regarding details of Laios' death—and of Laios himself—and the audience recognizes that he is coming close to the truth regarding himself and his relationship both to Laios and to Jocasta. The dagger of perception finds its deep, sharp-edged mark when, in response to the question "How did he look?" (741), Jocasta in her remarkable, innocent ignorance, responds, in part "—and in form not unlike you" (743).

If he sees what he had never had a reason for seeing, how is it that she still is blind, given that her current husband who is her son is by now closer in age, and presumably in looks, to the age and looks of her deceased husband, who is his father, just before the latter's demise? She offers such a paradigm of the skill with which humans can remain blind to ugly truths dancing before our eyes—her particular case strikes me as sibling to the case of a wife/mother who remains blind to the sexual abuse being enacted by her husband on their daughter, even when the evidence is staring her in the face.

Jocasta's first family, deconstructed by the sudden death by murder of her first husband, led almost organically to the shaping of her second family, which is about to be deconstructed by heroic memory—by human actions, divine actions, and Fate that not only overtakes them all, but that, in retrospect, had already overtaken them all when the first decision was made by Jocasta and Laios to dispose of the infant Oidipos in order to avert a prophecy that, it turns out, could not be averted. As Oidipos slowly crumbles before his still-unaware wife/mother, he notes his fear "that the old seer had eyes" (748). Indeed, that blind man could see what nobody else could. It turns out that there was a survivor from Laios' retinue—who had *seen* what transpired at that crossroad; the others had perished with their master through the ferocity of his murderer. And now, hearing this, Oidipos wants to speak to him—to finalize his knowledge of what he didn't see and understand back at that time, just before he solved the sphinx's riddle and became king of Thebes.

But even before this wish is fulfilled—it will take some time for that servant who now works as a shepherd in the most distant of the fields of Thebes, can be brought forward—Oidipos shares with Jocasta the understanding of the family history to which he has tentatively arrived. Her last, desperate ploy to avoid the conclusions of that understanding, is to suggest sending gifts to the Temple of Lykaian Apollo: but we and surely even she must know that such pious gestures are futile, too little and certainly too late. And yet—as Sophokles extends the time until the inevitable moment when all shall see and know—a messenger arrives from Corinth, announcing that Oidipos has been chosen king there, in the aftermath of the death of Polybos the Corinthian king, clearly because Oidipos is believed by them to be the son of Polybos.

In a manner parallel to the reprieve that we have observed for Iphigenia at Aulis in Euripides' version of that story—a temporary reprieve that could not ultimately prevent its unhappy conclusion—there is a brief reprieve for the tragic characters enwrapped in diverse layers of love, but who will be torn apart by the eventual and inevitable recognition of Oidipos' once-upon-a-time eristic act at a crossroads along the way between Corinth and Thebes. For if Oidipos' father is dead, now, of natural causes, then Oidipos cannot have been and cannot be the cause of his father's death: the oracles were wrong (964-72)!

But of course the next in the ongoing series of types and twists of irony spills forth, as Oidipos explains that he won't return to Corinth, since his "mother" is still alive and thus he still fears that second part of the prophecy—that he will bed her somehow—although he has already apparently dodged the first part, that he will kill his father. The old messenger from Corinth, having brought what he (and everyone else) already thought was good news, now adds to it—and unknowingly turns that news into the penultimate articulation of the Oidipian disaster: "Do you know that all your fears ar empty?... How is that, if they are father and mother and I their son?... Because Polybos was no kin to you in blood..." (1014-16). "Why then did he call me son?... A gift he took you from these hands of mine" 1021-22)—and the other details, of the childlessness of Polybos and Merope, and the gift from one royal shepherd to another (so this messenger was the very Corinthian royal shepherd who received the infant Oidipos from the Theban royal shepherd and presented him to the Corinthian royals to raise and love as their own) are out. Even his swollen ankles—from which his name, Oidipos, ("swollen foot") derives—are part of this rendition.

We need only a few more letters to complete the mystery word, "tragedy" and bring it from past to present/future: one, that fellow from the field whom they await—who, the chorus already recognizes, is the very shepherd who handed over the infant years ago. Jocasta still tries desperately to push the surging denouement away from the palace steps, but Oidipos has become relentless in his pursuit of the knowledge of who he is, regardless of the outcome. She who can no longer avoid that knowledge, yells: "O Oidipos, unhappy Oidipos! that is all that I can call you, and the last thing that I shall ever call you" (1071-3)—who at the outset of the play had been called both happy and great—before she exits the stage for the last time.

The old herdsman arrives onto the stage, led by Oidipos' servants and only under duress and very slowly, in a rapid-fire *agon* with the King of Thebes, fits into place the last piece of the horrific puzzle of the past: that, he handed the infant (who now stands before him as an adult and his king) to the Corinthian royal shepherd:

> I pitied it [the baby], and thought that I could send it
> off to another country and this man [the Corinthian messenger/
>   shepherd]
> was from another country. But saved it
> for the most terrible troubles. If you are
> the man he says you are, you're bred to misery. (1178-82)

None remain on stage but the chorus—to receive and transmit to us, from a pair of messengers, the last elements of the horrific chemistry of the present: that Jocasta has hanged herself. And that Oidipos, coming upon her, crying out, cut her down and then took the brooch from her robe and stabbed his own eyes out: the eyes that have finally seen are blinded. Stated otherwise—because in an interesting grammatical peculiarity of the ancient Greek language, to say "I know: *oida*," is actually to use a past (aorist) tense of the verb "to see" and thus to say "I have seen"—Oidipos now knows all too well who he is. He has finally seen the truth with regard to his tragic story. He has become like Teiresias: blind to the everyday things and ways of seeing—he who, having fallen from most blessed to most damned has risen from most ignorant to most painfully knowledgeable.

And he appears on stage, blind, to lead us toward the solution of the terrifying mystery of the future. He acknowledges that, although "it was Apollo, Apollo, that brought this bitter bitterness, my sorrows to completion, ... the hand that struck me was none but my own" (1329-33)—although he might have added: *moira*. This final scene, like earlier ones leading to this point, is a long one. Oidipos' long speech and conversation with the chorus culminates with his concern: what can he say to Kreon, given their previous angry confrontation, the level of which anger had been engendered by Oidipos? But Kreon enters, far from gloating, with sympathy and, still, respect—he has not forgotten the importantly good things that his brother-in-law (who is also his nephew) has done for Thebes, just because of the revelation of his horrifying but unwitting acts. Kreon maintains his position as a loving family member, regardless of the strife that had arisen between them.

In their last conversation, Oidipos recognizes the role of Fate (1457-8) while on the one hand commanding—and beseeching—that Kreon bury Jocasta (twice-loved by Oidipos, one might say, as mother and wife) properly (1447-9); that he send Oidipos himself into exile; that while "you need not care about my sons; they're men and so, wherever they are, they will not lack a livelihood" (1460-2), he concern himself with Oidipos' daughters, Antigone and Ismene. He needs to touch them one last time, they "whom I loved most!" (1474)—which in his continued sympathetic generosity, Kreon was already hastening to make happen.

As Kreon, Oidipos, Antigone, and Ismene leave the stage, we who know where this story ends—for this is not the end at all—understand that there are two directions in which the playwright will take it (but only one part of this double direction would have been known at the time to an Athenian audience). One, *Oidipos at Kolonnos*, in which the blind former Theban king will achieve resolution, will be written by Sophokles more than two decades later. That play was apparently recited by him in its entirety, from memory, before the court to which his own sons had brought him, asserting that their father had dementia so that they could take control of the family finances as their father pushed into his nineties.

Art and life interweave, although Sophokles' situation is hardly as severe as that of his hero. Oidipos, accompanied by his daughters, encounters Polyneikes, the older of his two sons, late in the play. Polyneikes has come as a pilgrim to the father whom he had not only abandoned but who, according to the accusation spat out by Oidipos, he had thrown into exile when he, Polyneikes, was in power (1355-7). He, too, is now an exile, however, since his younger brother, Eteokles, has forced him out of Thebes—so that an exiled son/brother meets up with his exiled father/brother, and whatever we might expect or hope for by way of a loving family relationship is subsumed into strife. Indeed, Polyneikes has been sent by Theseus, king of Athens, to find his father and get his advice as to how he can regain control of Thebes from his brother—but Oidipos has only a curse to offer to *both* sons:

…You'll go down
all bloody, and your brother, too. For I
have placed that curse upon you before this,
and now I invoke that curse to fight for me,
that you may see a reason to respect
your parents, though your birth was as it was;
and though I am blind, not to disonor me.
These girls did not… (1374-9)

… you shall die
at your own brother's hand, and you shall kill
the brother who banished you… (1388-90)

From this to the vow to attack Thebes—which Antigone tries to prevent—and her brother's departure from the scene, the play follows to Oidipos' quiet and peaceful death, the place of which, we are told, must remain secret, and the manner, too: "nobody of mortal men could tell but Theseus… for he was taken without lamentation, illness or suffering; indeed his end was wonderful if a mortal's ever was" (1656-7; 1663-5). But this, too, is not the end—and this time, the audience already knows well, since the second narrative "epilogue" to the story of Oidipos the king, explored in the *Antigone*, had been penned more than thirty-five years earlier.

Indeed, Aiskhylos had penned a play back in 467 BCE, *Seven Against Thebes*. That surviving play from an Oidipean trilogy tells how the two brothers agreed to alternate rulership of Thebes in alternative years, but that Eteokles, the younger, ruling first, refused to give up the throne when his brother came back from wandering at the end of that first year. So Polyneikes gathered an army (led by seven heroes each of whom directed himself toward one of Thebes' seven gates), but the matter is resolved by a one-on-one battle—to the death, as it turns out—between the brothers.

In the aftermath of the great popularity of Sophokles' *Antigone*, the end of the Aiskhylean play was apparently changed, many years after Aiskhylos' death (456-5 BCE): instead of the two brothers' bodies lying on stage and both being mourned, a messenger appears on the stage to announce that there is a decree against mourning for Polyneikes and Antigone asserts that she will abrogate that decree. This leads, narrative-wise, directly into Sophokles' play, as does *Oidipos at Kolonnos*, albeit by a slightly different path. For here the play opens with Antigone and Ismene before the palace of Kreon—who has become king of Thebes in the aftermath of the deaths of all the other males in the Theban royal family. Antigone is discussing with her sister the fact that their brothers are both dead, but that the royal decree has led to the proper burial of Eteokles but not of Polyneikes. She notes the further decree that, should anyone abrogate the command to leave him unburied, the guilty party will be publicly stoned in the city.

When Antigone suggests that the two of them go out and accord some sort of burial to Polyneikes' body, Ismene is afraid to do so—as one of a pair of mere "women who should not strive with men" (61-2)—so Antigone decides to take on this task alone, "for I must please the dead below much longer than people here" (75-6). The love for her brother trumps the strife that will be inevitable with her uncle—and which may lead to her death; Ismene's love for both her brother and her sister are palpable but are less powerful than her fear of that of which Antigone is not afraid. As for Uncle Kreon, who arrives empowered by the gods and by Fate to what he now is—he briefly reviews the family history for the chorus, from Laios to Eteokles and his brother Polyneikes, who "sought to burn his fatherland, the gods who were his kin, who tried to gorge on blood he shared, and lead the rest of us as slaves…" (200-202). He decrees therefore that Polyneikes be left unburied, "his corpse disgraced, a dinner for the birds and for the dogs. Such is my mind. Never shall I, myself, honor the wicked and reject the just. The man who is well-minded to the state shall have his honor from me in death and life" (205-11).

We might notice two particular aspects of the new king's words. One, that—in a manner offering a very oblique echo of Menelaos' early words to Agamemnon in Aiskhylos' *Iphigenia in Aulis*—his primary focus is on the state and its needs, to the exclusion of individual needs. His love focuses on Thebes and not on his nephews, either of them, really. Two, that Sophokles has him emphasize how he is the one who has arrived at the conclusion: "my mind… I, myself… from me…" Is this reflective of a strong self-love, or might one wonder whether this bespeaks a certain fear: what is the level of his real, as opposed to feigned self-confidence as newly-reminted leader. Both of these linked issues will play out as the drama moves forward: Kreon's confidence and love(s) may run a course parallel to that in which Oidipos's need to see and to know pushed the drama forward when he was king of Thebes and Kreon was his advisor.

The chorus is Kreon's advisor here and reiterates that he—alone—can make (and has made) such rulings. The brief dialogue between them and him has just finished when word is brought that

> [s]omeone left the corpse just now,
> burial all accomplished, thirsty dust
> strewn on the flesh, the ritual complete. (245-7)

—which means that, barely has he articulated his ruling and it has been challenged, his decree abrogated, which also means that his will as ruler is already being tested.[117] The chorus opines that perhaps it was the act of a god (279), but Kreon will have none of that, and begins to grow increasingly annoyed with both the chorus and the guard—in a manner somewhat reminiscent of how Oidipos got increasingly angry and accusatory with Kreon and Teiresias in *Oidipos Tyrannos*. Kreon wants to know who did this thing and essentially threatens the guard with severe punishment if he cannot find out who it is.

It does not take long: the guards sweep the dirt from the corpse and sit on a hillock to see what happens, and after a whirlwind, they

> ...saw the girl. She cried the sharp and bitter
> cry of a mother bird who sees the nest
> bare where the young birds lay... (423-5)
>
> Soon in her hands she brought the thirsty dust,
> and holding high a pitcher of wrought bronze
> she poured the three libations for the dead. (429-31)

The girl, of course, is Antigone, whom the guard holds captive before Kreon. He leaves and the first *agon* between uncle and niece ensues. The basis of the *agon* is simple: he is astounded that she has presumed to disobey the law (that he has formulated), but she observes that such a man-made law cannot stand up to laws made by Zeus and by Justice: "...I did not think that your orders were so strong that you, a mere mortal, could overrun the gods' unwritten and unfailing laws. Not now, not yesterday, they always live, and nobody knows their origin in time" (453-7). So part of the issue is that of how man-made laws (*nomoi*; sing. *nomos*) compare with god-made laws, laws of nature (*physis*).

So, too, there is the issue of Kreon's insecurity that if he allows her abrogation to pass, his authority as a male will be undermined: "I am no man and she the man instead, if she can have this conquest without pain" (484-5). But there is, on the other hand, the fact that "she is my sister's child" — but that is not sufficient to let her (and her sister, Ismene, whom he also accuses of the treasonous act of helping plan the burial of Polyneikes; 489-91) get away with this. So Antigone challenges him to get it over with—her arrest and death (498)—for "what greater glory could I find than giving my own brother a funeral?" 502-3). Anticipating the kind of words spoken by Iphigenia at Aulis in Euripides' play, Antigone implies that love-induced *kleos* is every bit as important and powerful as that generated by the *eris* of warfare.

What *is* the hierarchy of love thus far? For Antigone, brother-sister and human-divine are more important than what stands front and center for Kreon: city and self. These contending perspectives will become further complicated as Ismene returns to the stage, eager to embrace the accusation against her: "Sister, I pray, don't fence me out from honor, from death with you, and honor done the dead" (544-5)—to whom Antigone expresses more than a little hostility, eager, it would seem, to be alone in her martyrdom: "Love Kreon; he's your kinsman and your care…for you chose to live when I chose death" (549; 555). The complications are exponentially expanded first with the question posed by Ismene to Kreon as to whether he will "kill your own son's promised bride" (568) and then after Haimon, that fiance, Kreon's son—his one surviving son, according to the chorus—himself arrives on stage. For the conversation between them begins with Haimon's assertion of a hierarchy of love: "Nor shall a marriage count for more with me than your kindly leading" (637-8), to which Kreon responds, delighted, that "for this men pray: to have obedient children grow up around them in their homes…" (641-2).

    We have thus returned to the matter of love between parent and child versus that between spouses (which, given the story in which this is embedded, offered its own particular irony). Kreon encourages his son's thinking, of course—"do not" he asserts, "let your lust mislead your mind, all for a woman's sake, (648-9)" and further—circling back to that primary concern for himself and his own position: "if I allow disorder in my house than I'd surely have to license it abroad. A man who deals in fairness with his own, can make justice manifest in the state, but he who crosses law, or forces it, or hopes to bring the rulers under him, shall never have a word of praise from me" (659-65) and "…I won't be called weaker than womankind" (680).

    Except that, as Haimon realizes what his father is about to do, his obedience unravels and a true *agon* ensues—and another aspect of Kreon's insecurities reveals itself: if as a male he is fearful of the power of women, as an older man he is fearful of the power of youth: "Men of my age, are we to learn to think from men who are his age, from men so young?" (726-7)—to which Haimon responds: "yes, nothing but the truth. If I am young you should regard my merit and not my years!" (728-9). And further, as Kreon continues to unravel, he asks rhetorically, "shall the city tell me how to rule?"

(734): thus he who first argued as someone fighting for the city now argues against the city that, it seems, disagrees with the decree that he alone (and not the city's citizens) has promulgated. And in the hierarchy of love, his love of self stands above other forms—but *alone* and *isolated* above them—and engenders strife between him and his niece, his son, the chorus, the city itself, as well as bringing catastrophe beyond what he could have imagined.

The *agon* with Haimon intensifies, as Haimon's love for Antigone butts up against Kreon's insecurities—to the point that the father rages that "every word you say is for her!"—to which Haimon responds "and for you. And for me. And for the gods under the earth," and his father, in turn, bellows: "You'll never marry her while she lives" (748-50)—as the heat continues to rise. Haimon's ability to love both his fiance and his father, and to recognize that his father's proposed action will be at least as damaging to Kreon as to Haimon and to Antigone cannot overcome Kreon's fear of losing control of the situation—of which he, accordingly, loses control, climaxing with Haimon's torrid exit from the stage, with the words: "You will never see my face again. Go on raving as long as you've a friend to endure you!" (761-3).

In the ensuing interlude of dialogue between Kreon and his choral advisers, he relents from the more extreme position that he had earlier taken—to execute both of his nieces—which hardly solves the problem that he has engendered. What follows is a succession of ascending (or descending) rungs on this ladder of tragedy. Kreon exits; Antigone arrives (under guard) and speaks touchingly with the chorus regarding her fate—in which she is interrupted by Kreon's return, which leads to one last semi-*agon* (she speaks, he barely responds). She asserts that

> I stand convicted of impiety,
> with the evidence of my pious duty done.
> Should the gods think that this is righteousness,
> in suffering I'll know the truth. But if the guilt
> lies upon the others who are wrong, then, I pray,
> may their punishment be no greater than my own. (923-8)

Strong words—and we might recall that unwitting offence towards the gods runs in the family as a characteristic, which helps enrich the complication of an otherwise simple juxtaposition of gods and humans as sources of law and the question of whom one might offend.

As Antigone goes off under guard—presumably to be walled up in a cave with a little food and water, as earlier Kreon had asserted would be her fate—Teiresias enters, blind and led by a boy and (briefly put) tells Kreon that he is inviting a curse on the city by not offering proper burial to Polyneikes: what Oidipos had brought on and then figured out in his pain how to alleviate, Kreon is bringing back. The King's response recalls the initial reaction of Oidipos to what Teiresias had to say back then: angry, hostile, refusing to accede to the seer's suggestion—even as the latter arrives at a chilling prediction, that "the sun will not have rolled its course many more days, before you shall pay back corpse for corpse, flesh of your own flesh" (1066-8). For Kreon has (in a different way), like Oidipos, sinned twice: once in not properly burying his nephew and once in wrongly burying his niece alive.

And yet, like Oidipos, while stubborn, Kreon can and does begin to feel the truth seeping into his guts, even as he acknowledges to the chorus how "hard it is to yield! but it is worse to risk everything for stubborn pride" (1095-6), after Teiresias exits. In spite of his stubbornness, he is as he always has been, a good person, a good man, who did not seek kingship but found himself king by default and as such found the situation beyond what he could comfortably manage under such unusual circumstances. The chorus encourages him to hurry, to go free Antigone and he rushes to do so...but it will be too late. This we hear from a messenger, as so often in Sophokles, who notes that "Fortune raises up, and Fortune casts down the happy and the unhappy alike" (1158-9), referencing Kreon, now (as such words might have once referenced Oidipos).

For, one: Haimon is dead, having committed suicide. Enter the queen, Kreon's wife and Haimon's mother, Eurydice, still unaware of what we have just heard, but aware of some new sorrow. And the messenger continues, telling her and the chorus and us that he and Kreon hurried out to the shredded corpse of

Polyneikes and bathed and properly burned what was left of it, building a towering barrow up and around the urn in which they placed his ashes; and hurried on to the vault in which Kreon had had Antigone placed. There, horrified, they found Haimon weeping as he clung to her corpse, for, two: she had hanged herself. It was there, as Kreon begged for forgiveness that Haimon spat at his father, drew his sword and lunged for him, missing, and then stabbed himself. "Corpse on corpse he lies. He found his marriage. Its celebration in the halls of Hades" (1240-1)—what Kreon had angrily "predicted" in the last heated interchange between father and son.

Upon hearing this Eurydice exits wordlessly, worrying the chorus, who send someone in after her—as Kreon enters, bearing his young son's body and bemoaning the "crimes of my own blind heart, harshness that has brought death" (1261-2). But it is not yet final; there is more, as a messenger returns from within the palace with further news. For, three: the queen is dead, having stabbed herself before the altar of the god—with her last words cursing Kreon—not only for Haimon's death, but for the death of their older son, Megareus, who perished in the conflict between Polyneikes and Eteokles detailed in Aiskhylos' play, *Seven Against Thebes*. For "Fate has brought all my pride to a thought of dust" (1342).

From Laios and Jocasta to Antigone, the Theban royal house has been a criss-crossing of problematic and radically dysfunctional family relationships, loving relationships intertwined with and tragically overwhelmed by strife. Nobody is left, in the end, but Kreon, in charge of Thebes but isolated and lonely, a shadow of what he had been and a fulfillment of what his son had predicted he would become as he charted his hubristic—self-loving and ultimately misdirected—course.

II Euripides' Medea and Jason

We might take this interweave within the context of family dysfunction one place further, outside the Trojan War narrative as well as the Theban story. Euripides does this most emphatically in his play, *Medea*, first performed in 431 BCE This is another re-vision of a familiar heroic tale that the playwright transforms by looking at it not at the point in its narrative that is most familiar, but rather at a less-touted aftermath of that heroic account. This is perhaps the most intense among several of Euripides' surviving plays that most reflect his role as an iconoclast—one who breaks the images of iconic figures and ideas.[118] For the main male character is Jason—the renowned Jason who sailed his ship, the *Argo*, accompanied by other heroes to find and bring back the Golden Fleece that would properly put Jason on the throne of Iolkos in lieu of his usurping uncle, Pelias.

In the denouement of that adventure he is assisted by the sorceress, Medea, who, helped by Aphrodite through the pushing of Hera, falls in love with the heroic Greek, and not only helps him gain possession of the fleece guarded on her father's behalf by a dragon-like creature. When her father pursues them, she delays that pursuit by cutting up her own brother and tossing the pieces into the sea so that her father will keep stopping to pick them up. Of course, she induces the daughters of Pelias to do the same to their father, convincing them that his body parts, boiled in a cauldron into which she has added some special herbs and over which she utters certain incantations, will both spring back together to life and be youthful again.

The subsequent death of Pelias (Medea never adds those herbs and incantations to the mixture) leads to the expulsion of Jason, Medea and their two sons. It is in Corinth, where they have taken refuge, that Euripides takes up his narrative, exploring the consequences of Jason's decision to marry the young princess, Kreusa, daughter of the Corinthian king Kreon (not to be confused with the Kreon of the Theban story) without bothering to imagine what might be Medea's reaction to such a plan. The opening soliloquy falls to the Nurse, who sums up how things have gotten to where they are, and evinces upset that this once united, loving couple is now divided by angry strife and hatred (16), thanks to Jason's desertion decision, after Medea had done so much to help him,

> And poor Medea is slighted, and cries aloud on the
> vows that they made to each other, their right hands clasped
> in eternal promise. (19-21).

That said, she expresses concern that Medea "may think of some dreadful thing, for her heart is violent. She will never put up with the treatment that she is getting…" (37-9).

Even before we have ventured forty lines into the play, at least two things might occur to us: one, that Jason's decision smells of a mid-life crisis, in which at one and the same time he has tired of the wife who, perhaps, like him, is no longer as young as she was when they fled Kolkhis together, so, like many men before and since, he seeks a situation with a younger woman. However, in the world in which he lives it is apparently possible to keep his older wife while enjoying his younger wife, as we shall see—but that presupposes that both wives are agreeable to such an arrangement.

Two, particularly given what transpired in Iolkos, we might further suppose that Jason's Medea-fatigue is in part his fear of what she might do next and how to manage the damage that might ensue from the combination of her sorceress skills and non-Greek ethnicity. Of course, in that case, he is perhaps doubly foolish to be embarking on this new romantic adventure, since there is no reason to suppose that she will accept the new arrangement (as the nurse notes) and if she does not, her response, while unpredictable with regard to specifics, is predictably dangerous.

As the Tutor enters onto the stage and discusses things with the Nurse, it becomes still clearer that the skies ahead will be stormy. Medea has been weeping, and the tutor suggests that the grounds for shedding tears are more serious than she yet knows, for he has heard "that Kreon, ruler of the land, intends to drive these children [i.e., the two sons of Jason and Medea] and their mother into exile from Corinth" (70-1). When the nurse questions whether the tutor thinks that Jason would allow his children at least, to be driven forth, the tutor sanguinely replies: "Old ties give place to new ones. As for Jason, he no longer has a feeling for this house of ours" (76-7). When the Nurse expresses dismay (she wishes Jason were dead), the Tutor responds—again in an almost casual manner:

> …Have you just now discovered
> that everyone loves himself more than his neighbor?
> Some have good reason, others got something out of it.
> So Jason neglects his children for the new bride. (85-8)

A kind of hierarchy of love is once again at issue, and, at least in the Tutor's estimation, self-love and a new-found infatuation stand above not only husband-wife love (particularly when the wife has become an "issue" for the husband) but father-children love. The Nurse sends those children, with the Tutor, into the house—warning him to keep the boys away from their mother right now. Indeed, we hear Medea off-stage, screaming to herself regarding her situation, and including in her rant words that we may recognize as possessing an inherent fateful irony: "I hate you, children of a hateful mother. I curse you and your father. Let the whole house crash" (112-14)—even as the Nurse, responding from on stage asks, rhetorically, "How can your children share in their father's wickedness? Why do you hate them?" and adds "Oh children, how much I fear that something may happen!" (116-18).

A kind of trialogue ensues, as the chorus—of Corinthian women, come to inquire after Medea and to console her—and the Nurse, on stage, converse, as Medea's ongoing soliloquys off-stage offer a third voice. The chorus asserts: "Suppose your man gives honor to another woman's bed. It often happens. Don't be hurt" (155-7)—words that are hardly likely to console Medea in her feverish mood who, in her next words commenting on how hateful her husband is and how she would love to see him and his bride and all their palace shattered (162-3), rues what she had once done for Jason—in a love hierarchy that had, for her, placed wife-husband over daughter-father or sister-brother, or love of native land: "Oh, my father! Oh, my country! In what dishonor I left you, killing my own brother for it" (165-6).

Eventually the Nurse retreats into the house, and a moment later Medea exits it, coming onto the stage. Her long speech to the chorus includes her assertion that

> what they [men] say of us is that we have a peaceful time
> living at home, while they do the fighting in war.
> How wrong they are! I would very much rather stand
> three times in the front of battle than bear one child. (248-51)

The Euripides who developed a reputation as a misogynist would hardly seem to be one—at least to those in his audience capable of listening well to Medea's words and who thus might question the standard attitude of/toward males and females. This is, albeit differently angled, a viewpoint 180 degrees opposed to that articulated by Apollo in Aiskhylos' *Eumenides* regarding the importance of men versus women in the child-creating process. (I refer, of course, not only to the process itself but to the underlying attitide regarding mothers versus fathers as expressed by the god).

Moreover, only a deliberately misogynistic audience member (although no doubt there would have been many of these—perhaps *most* of the predominantly male audience) could deny the truth of her words that, while the chorus has a country and family here, in Corinth, she is

> ...deserted, a refugee, thought nothing of
> by my husband—something he won in a barbarian land.
> I have no mother or brother, nor any relation
> with whom I can take refuge in this sea of woe. (255-8)

Nonetheless, the ax of the narrative's culminating disasters is being sharpened, as Kreon enters and does what the Tutor had heard that he would do: barely arrived on stage, he turns to her, virtually spitting out: "You, with that angry look, so set against your husband, Medea, I order you to leave my territories an exile, and take along with you your two children, and do not waste time doing it. This is my decree..." (271-4). In the *agon* that ensues, he admits that he is afraid of her, for "you are a clever woman, versed in evil arts" (285). Within her long response to him she asserts that "there is no need. It is not my way to transgress the authority of a king" (307-8)—an odd claim for someone who certainly transgressed the authority of the king who was her father (on behalf of Jason who would become her husband), and even, one might say, a former king, Pelias. We in the audience know all this, as we also know that her claim only to hate her husband and to think that "you [Kreon] have acted wisely" in giving his daughter to Jason to wed (310-11) rings false (even if we did not already know the final outcome of this drama). It seems to be part of the playwright's strategy of developing psychological tensions and contradictory feelings in his audience: he is slowly building that side of a two-sided case that will be anti-Medea.

Indeed, at the same time, Kreon comes off as rather harsh, doesn't he, when she begs him to rescind his decree of exile "by your knees, by your new-wedded girl" (324) and he cannot be moved — even if the issue is the worries resulting from that hierarchy of love. For he will not relent because "I love my family more than you... [and] I love my country, too — next after my children" (327, 329), to which she responds "Oh what an evil to men is passionate love!" (330). So the strife between Medea and Kreon — and it is more intense than appears from this excerpted part of the exchange between them — is, as it were, all about love and how and whither it directs us.

On that basis, really, in the end she is able to convince him to give her a day to figure out where she should go in her exile, and to "look for support for my children, since their father chooses to make no kind of provision for them" (342-3). Kreon's last words do threaten that she will die if she and the children are there beyond that day-long reprieve, during which — his last words — "you can do none of the things I fear" (356). He has barely exited when the chorus expresses its sympathy and Medea in a long speech has made it clear that they should save their moans, for "there are still trials to come for the new-wedded pair, and for their relations pain that will mean something" (367-8): the victim of Jason's abandonment and Kreon's decree is announcing how that tide will be turned.

And Jason himself, after her long exchange with the chorus, arrives onto the stage, almost as if in the middle of a discussion he had been conducting with her before the play began. For he starts right in, saying that, if she had only cooperated, "you might have lived in this land and kept your home" (449). But the first time she said anything about a desire to get back at Jason was just prior to Kreon's arrival on the stage — she spoke to the chorus and they agreed to keep silent about her words. And then there was her conversation with Kreon — but it was non-threatening. So either Jason is simply assuming, jumping to conclusions and/or prevaricating, or Medea said things before the play began that have neither been included in it up to this point nor referenced by the Nurse, the Tutor or Kreon, even if all of them have expressed concern or, in Kreon's case, fear that the aggravated sorceress might do something dangerous.

In fact, given the just-previous conversation between Medea and Kreon, it is hard to imagine that, even if she had never opened her mouth in protest against being deserted by Jason, she would have been welcome to stay in Corinth. Seriously? The rejected ex-wife who also happens to be a sorceress with a fairly dangerous track record? Maybe only a minority in that mostly male audience would have wondered about how seriously to take Jason's claim that "in spite of your conduct, I'll not desert my friends, but have come to make provision for you, so that you and the children may not be penniless in exile… for even if you hate me, I can never think of you except with kindness" (459-64). Surely some of them, at least, might have scoffed. What provisions would suffice? Who does not desert his friends—has he not already done that? Of course he should still think kindly of her, given all that she has done for him in the past! "Kindly"—of his savior, his presumably once-beloved wife, the mother of his sons? *Kindly*?!

Medea, for one, is having none of it. On the contrary, she barks at him appropriately: "Oh coward in every way!" She reviews all that she did for him, saving his life, killing that dragon for him, killing her brother, betraying her father, and tricking Pelias' daughters in order to slaughter him—all in order to protect Jason. She culminates her speech with the stunning optative:

Oh Zeus, you have given to mortals a sure method
of telling the gold that is pure from the counterfeit;
why is there no mark engraved upon men's bodies,
by which we could know the true ones from the false? (516-19)

And in this, which is truly the central *agon* of the play—concerning which one can imagine members of the audience cheering one or the other of them on in accordance with preconceptions or new perceptions—Jason responds that it was Kypria (Aphrodite) alone who saved his life, that it was "Eros with his inescapable arrows who forced you to save my life" (530-31). So even the validity of her positive emotions about Jason is discounted by him in his desire to destroy her position. He continues, insisting that she gained more than he did from their relationship:

> Firstly, instead of dwelling among barbarians,
> you live in the land of Hellas and know our ways,
> living under law instead of brute force.
> Next, all the Hellenes consider you a clever woman
> and honor you for it. If you were living on the far
> borders of the earth, nobody would have heard of you. (536-41)

He is, of course, expressing a standard Greek view: that since Greece is inherently superior to any other place—and within Greece, which had hardly thought of itself in such unifying terms until the Persian wars, Athenians would have said the same about Athens vis-à-vis other Hellenic *poleis*—then to be among Greeks is an immeasurable boon, particularly if one is honored by Hellenes for one's skills, and even if its laws make it reasonable for a husband to abandon his sons and wife in middle age in favor of a young bride, and even if honor also includes the fear that marginalizes, isolates, and ultimately exiles such a barbarian.

Indeed, Jason next defends his decision to abandon her, arguing that he could hardly have had a better piece of fortune than "to marry the king's daughter—I, a refugee" (554). He claims that Medea is wrong to suppose that he had become bored with her and sought a younger wife to have more children. "My greatest intention was that we might live well, and not be short of anything" (559-60), and, indeed, if there were to be further children with his young bride, he waxes idealistic about "begetting more offspring to be brothers to our own, and, uniting the families so that we would all be happy" (563-5). He concludes by complaining that a woman—like Medea—thinks that she has everything if her marriage runs smoothly, but if her husband no longer shares her bed "she considers what are her best and truest interests most hateful. It would be better if men could have children some other way, and women not to have existed" (569-75).

No doubt most members of the mostly male audience would have shaken their heads in affirmation of Jason's words, as he elaborated one argument after another that champions the supremacy of male Hellenes—while there may have been at least a few who thought his words sophistic. In fact, the chorus responds before Medea does, suggesting that, although his argument is clever, he is still in the wrong for having betrayed and abandoned his wife. And certainly some would at least question his claim that he would have, with more sons, created one big happy family. While the time of these events might or might not follow or predate the story of the House of Thebes, certainly everyone in Euripides' audience would have been aware of that story—and Sophokles' successful *Antigone* pre-dated this play by a decade, with its embedded account of Polyneikes and Eteokles—so that casually idealistic vision of Jason, his two wives and three or more sons (which he repeats a second time; 595-6) must have struck some of them as at least foolish if not altogether cynical.

In any case, the denouement of their argument is that he asserts that her current position of exile-to-be is her own fault because she started the arguments against his actions and the threats to Kreon's family; and she asserts that he is the one who, betraying his family, has brought about this disaster. Each ends by invoking the gods; he as witnesses that his intention was to help her and their children in every way (619-20) and she, not to witness but to assist, so that "you will make the sort of marriage that you will regret" (626). Given that the gods must have been called to witness when Medea and Jason were married—when they swore eternal vows to each other—there is an additional soupcon of irony to other ironies within this last exchange.

Euripides takes a familial version of the *eros-eris* theme that was first explored in some depth in Greek literature by Aiskhylos in his *Agamemnon* (although it had been alluded to earlier, in the *Odyssey*, as we have seen). That is, a radically dysfunctional husband-wife relationship that, were it a functional relationship might be expected to be dominated by *eros* turns, instead, to an *eris* that culminates with the murder of one spouse by another. But Euripides (who chose not to follow that particular thread when he came closest to it, in his *Iphigenia in Aulis*, as we have also seen), will offer his own outcome to this version of *eros-eris*. Neither spouse ends up dead, but both end up cut off from familial connections and bereft of real human relationships.

The remainder of the play follows a succession of three paths. First, after Jason leaves the stage followed by a choral interlude, Aigeus, king of Athens and apparently an old friend of

Medea, enters and the conclusion of their exchange is this: that he will provide her with refuge as an exile from Kreon's Corinth and she will supply the *pharmaka* (medicines or drugs, depending upon context) that will make it possible for his wife and him, unhappily childless up to this point, to have children.[119] Interestingly, she wants a pledge from him, noting that words alone can be too weak when confronted by people with strength and strong hostility, such as the houses of both Pelias and Kreon possess toward her. One might suppose, too, that she has learned from her mistake: after all the marriage vows of Jason, as strong as they may have seemed years earlier, proved weak indeed when circumstances changed. He agrees that it will be safer for him, as well, so that, if push comes to shove he will have an excuse for abiding by his oath to her—and he swears, at her behest, "by the plain of earth, and Helios, father of [Medea's] father, and name together all the gods" (746-7) that he will never cast her from his land.

The second course—after Aigeus has departed, and Medea has invoked Zeus, personified Justice (*Dike*, daughter of Zeus), and the light of Helios—is that she confesses to the chorus that she intends that Jason, for whom she will send a messenger to bring him to her, will never see his sons "alive again, nor will he on his new bride beget another child, for she will be forced to die a most terrible death by these my poisons (*pharmaka*)" 804-6)—and when they ask whether she can really kill her own flesh and blood, she responds: "yes, for this is the best way to wound my husband" (817).

Put another way, her plan is to deprive him of his ties to anything familial and to his legacy. The price she is willing to pay to do that is to do the same to herself—a kind of spiritual suicide—when one considers that, as a woman in this Greek world her identity is contoured by the men who are the perimeters of her being. She has already cut herself off from her father and her brother and she is now being cut off not only from her husband but, by her own act, from her sons. Aigeus may shelter her as a refugee, as a practical matter, but he will be finally beginning his own family, so she will ultimately become less than tangential to him.

But Euripides' Medea is a fearless feminist, one might say, who is not only willing to cut herself off from a male-dominated society as surely as she cuts Jason off from his future, but has consistently done so by deceiving men—certainly in this culmination of her career she emphatically deceives Kreon, Jason, and even Aigeus—using children as pawns in this deadly game. To repeat, though—again, ironically—in the end, she and Jason will be tied together at an unbridgeable distance by their co-isolation from family units and the completion of the transformation of their one-time passionate *eros* to confirmed and irremediable *eris*-shaped hatred for one another.

So what remains of the drama is to see exactly how this plays out, which is the third path that the story takes after that recent Medea-Jason *agon*. For Jason arrives, and Medea calls their sons out of the house, claiming (pretending) to have softened and become reconciled to exile. She bids the boys say farewell to their father, and weeps—but not for the reason that Jason supposes, who speaks rather more tenderly to her, asking after her tears after the words he utters. For these words still, yet again, a third time, articulate the future vision of

> a time [that] will come when you [their sons] will be
> the leading people in Corinth with your brothers.
> You must grow up. As to the future, your father
> and those of the gods who love him will deal with that.
> I want to see you, when you have become young men,
> Healthy and strong, better men than my enemies. (916-21)

Medea's tears underscore her momentary hesitation at these beautiful words and the pain that undergirds her terrible decision. One might also note a certain ambiguity in the playwright's text—deliberate one might suppose—as when she says that she is just weeping about the children, and Jason responds that he will look after them well (926), as if to suggest that only Medea will be leaving and they staying with their father in his new house and his new household. And in fact, this leads Medea to beg Jason that he indeed importune Kreon to allow the boys to stay—or better, still, ask his bride to ask this of her father.

To sweeten the pot of possible success for this embassy, she gives the boys the robe and diadem that she offers as wedding presents to that bride—"beautiful things that Helios of old, the father of my father, bestowed upon his descendants" (954-5): Helios the sun, made of fire. Jason, chivalrously begs her not to give up such beautiful things when there are so many garments to be had in the palace, but Medea insists, arguing that even the gods can be moved by gold—and these garments are golden through and through, designed to capture the fancy of a young girl's heart—and further insists to her sons that they be sure to give these things directly into Kreusa's hands, returning back to their mother with the news of the success of their mission.

It takes only a choral interlude for the tutor to return with the children and relate that the gifts are in the young bride's hands—and again Medea struggles with her conviction to complete the rest of her own mission: she asserts to the tutor that in a kind of craziness ("evil mindedness") she—and the gods—have planned a terrible thing. So she concerning whom Jason argued that she had been controlled by Aphrodite and *eros* is now controlled by madness and *eris*—or, as she will finally, say: fury (*thumos*; 1079). Her last long soliloquy, leading up to that word and its implications, is directed to her children who, she says, will never see their mother again (1038), and who keep looking at her with their beautiful eyes and their sweet smiles (1040-1). We might suppose that those eyes and smiles, alas, remind her—too much—of their father, but more to the point, were she to take them with her, now, to Athens, while they might cheer her up by their presence, yet "this shall never be, that I should suffer my children to be the prey of my enemies' insolence" 1060-1).

Of their fate and that of Kreusa we learn from a messenger, as so often is the case, since the acts take place out of our view—and that of the immortal gods who preside over the theater and prefer not to be present at moments of human death—and we can only hear the news, not see the action. The messenger tells Medea and us how overwhelmed with happiness and relief the royal household had been by the apparent reconciliation between Jason and Medea, how some courtiers kissed the children's hands and some their golden hair (1141). He reports how the princess could not restrain herself when she saw the gorgeous garment and the golden crown, throwing them on and twirling before the mirror—until she began to twist and turn as if gripped by a seizure, the white foam breaking through her lips and the pupils of her eyes rolling (1173-4); how the garment was tearing the flesh from her bones as from beneath the diadem smoke billowed out. By the time Kreon got to her she was lying on the ground, a corpse, and as he put his arms around her he was himself sucked into the flames that tore his own flesh—so that father and daughter (rather the opposite of Medea and her own father) died together in a passionate embrace.

There is no time for Medea to rejoice in this news of her successful horror, for she cries to the chorus after its brief response to this narrative, that that now her

> task is fixed: as quickly as I may
> to kill my children, and start away from this land,
> and not, by wasting time, to suffer my children
> to be slain by another hand less kindly to them.
> For every way will have it that they must die, and since
> this must be so, then I, their mother, shall kill them. (1236-41)

Is it inevitable that they must die? That they will be assumed complicit in and thus guilty of the murder of the king and his daughter? Or is this just her rationale to validate her decision—to punish Jason by their deaths, as opposed to protecting them somehow by that act—and imagining that their deaths will somehow be sweeter, more pleasant, more *acceptable* when committed by their loving mother than by someone else, in any case? Is this, indeed, *Medea* acting or the *thumos* that has enveloped her—and if the latter, was Jason correct in his sophistic speech in giving the credit to Aphrodite and not to Medea when, loving him, she helped him?

She rushes into the house and as the chorus holds forth, we hear the cries of the children from off-stage. The chorus is paralyzed with indecision: shall we go in and intervene to save them? They ruminate, even as they—these Corinthian women, mothers and grandmothers, we must suppose—note that Medea's heart "must be made of rock or iron, you who can kill with your own hand the fruit of your own womb" (1279-81). Jason arrives—too late—all caught up in the horror of what has just transpired in the palace to his bride and her father, only to be told by the chorus that a still worse act has just been committed in his own former house.

One might pause to reflect on this: that often—for example in Sophokles' *Philoktetes*—a narrative that required a resolution not reasonably possible at a human level would find that resolution delivered in some concluding statement by a god or goddess. The actor playing that role would arrive at the end of the play not onto but over the stage, hoisted there by a kind of crane—a machine. So such a figure would be referred to as the *deus ex machina* (in Latin): the god out of the machine. Euripides the iconoclast exposed the questionability of such a mechanism to achieve a divinely-imposed resolution by using the *deus ex machina* questionably—in the *Hippolytos*, for example, at the end of which the goddess Artemis—a *dea ex machina*—appears over the stage but offers a resolution the validity of which any *thinking* theater-goer would internally challenge.

So: the greater disaster that awaits Jason as the doors of his house open wide is the sight of his two dead sons—held by Medea in a chariot drawn by dragons—a chariot that has been supplied by Helios to his grand-daughter. She is, practically speaking, in that very *machina* used by gods and goddesses to offer true or false solutions and resolutions to the problems shaped by the human drama one slice of which has just been played out on the stage. She is no goddess, however, and she offers no solution or resolution from above the stage, only her own salvation from Jason's wrath and that, perhaps of the Corinthians. Jason's last long speech to her regards the monster that she is who has slain her own children and left him childless—who had, he now sees clearly—betrayed her own father and her native land, and slew her own brother, who now, "for the sake of pleasure in the bed killed [their sons]. There is no Greek woman who would have dared such deeds" (1338-9).

Her response is brief: that Zeus knows all that I did for you, that "no, it was not to be, that you should scorn my love, and pleasantly live your life through, laughing at me" 1354-5). So those culminating words suggest that, when all is said and done, like other key figures whom we have encountered, the highest rung on her ladder of love is for herself—which is what we might also say of Jason. The last, rapid-fire, back-and-forth between them is an exchange of agony (pun intended), and of blame for the deaths of their children—and of prophecy. The place of Medea, is to be hanging—literally—between heaven and earth, neither among humans nor among gods, in that chariot that is her salvation but offers no real resolution to her pain or Jason's. Her prophecy of demise for him—that he will die alone, struck on the head by a timber from the rotting Argo that was once the source of his *kleos* and of their glorious passion for each other—and her refusal to let him even touch the bodies of his sons one last time, underscores the overwhelming sadness with which this stunning tangle of *eros* and *eris* arrives at its conclusion.

Chapter Six

Comic, Platonic and Visual *Eros* and *Eris*

Euripides is certainly not the only iconoclast of his generation. His much younger contemporary, Aristophanes (ca 446-ca 386) chose to turn his dramatic genius in a comedic direction—which essentially means that his narratives end on some sort of a high note, without the demise of the main character, but that does not mean that the subject matter could not be and was not serious. On the contrary. If, for instance, in his *Frogs*, the issue is that, after the deaths of Sophokles and Euripides there are no great tragic playwrights left, that is certainly a serious enough issue for a culture-hungry *polis* like Athens—particularly in the midst of the last phase of the unhappy Peloponnesian War (431-404 BCE).[120]

I From Aristophanes' *Lysistrata* to Menander's *Dyskolos*

So while there is a masterful range of deliberately comic elements— from the descent into Hades by Dionysos, ridiculously attired to look like Herakles, in order to bring back one of the great three tragedians; to the chorus of frogs (chanting *brekekekex-koax-koax*) croaking from within the muddy shallows of the River Styx; to the mock *agon* between Aiskhylos and Euripides to determine which of them will be brought back to life in Athens (Sophokles had bowed out of the competition, ceding primacy to Aiskhylos)—the underlying cultural crisis is a serious matter.

Certainly as serious as the demise of tragic poetry is the matter of the Peloponnesian War itself, that on-again, briefly off-again, but then on-again catastrophe punctuated by the Great

Plague that decimated Athens, by the strategic disaster of the attack on Syracuse by Athens and the moral disaster of the destruction/enslavement of the population of Melos—and culminating with the humiliating defeat of an Athens that had begun the war with, it had seemed, all of the necessary elements to make victory over the Spartans inevitable. So the taking on of that topic comedically would have been a challenge in the first place.

Aristophanes chose to approach it through the issue of male-female relations—not the only time he played with that sort of topic—and in his play, *Lysistrata*, (411 BCE), specifically presented the women of Athens and the women of Sparta (and those of smaller *poleis* allied with one or the other) as agreeing to deny their husbands any sexual activity until the men work out an end to the war. It is a very funny, but very poignant (and were Aristophanes a child of the mid-twentieth century CE we would simply call it tragicomic), what-if kind of narrative.

So not only is the overall theme contrived of an *eros-eris* interweave: love and sex within the context of war, and war within the context of love and sex (and love as much as sex is at issue). Throughout the play there are any number of instances in the actions and the dialogues, particularly the mocking *agones* between men and women, in which the tone and verbiage both build on that interweave.

For Lysistrata's plan isn't easily agreed upon. First the women need to be convinced—and the ancient Hellenes thought that women enjoy sex more than men and thus have less ability to do without it—so Aristophanes' women are at first horrified at having to give up that activity. Lysistrata's angry (eristic) response is that her fellow women are

> utter sluts, the entire sex! Will-power:
> none. We're perfect raw material for Tragedy,
> the stuff of heroic verses. "Go sleep with a god
> and then get rid of the baby"—that sums us up! (137-9)[121]

We're doomed, she sighs, to unhappy endings (tragedy), to be raped and left behind... Fortunately, Lysistrata's Spartan colleague, Lampito, stands with her from the start, giving them the platform from which to draw the others to their cause. Having gotten all the women to swear the oath of temporary chastity, they split up, Lampito to set things in order in Sparta, and Lysistrata and her women to assist the older women who have commandeered the Parthenon and the whole acropolis and thus to set things in order in Athens.

Aside from the obvious importance of the acropolis and its temple as a symbol of the city and its patron goddess, for the purposes of this play the added significance—that Athena is both a goddess of war and also wisdom, and also a virgin goddess, born through a parthenogenesis process herself—is part of the Aristophanic tongue-in-cheek. The cry of one of the men, as they seek to retake the acropolis, that "the goddess needs our aid"—and the men's prayer for assistance to Athena (to re-assert male supremacy)—all has an ironic ring to it, given the context.

And we suddenly find ourselves in the first extended eristic moment: the battle for the acropolis, between the men and the women, each group seeking and expecting divine support—an intra-Athenian war begun in order to bring peace within the Peloponnesian War; a battle of the sexes that hasn't yet arrived at the instrumentation of sex and sex-refusal that the women (as we know, but the men do not know—not yet) have planned. This interior battle is certainly not without its symbolic logic: the men attack with torches, to burn their way into control of the acropolis, but they are defeated, their fires doused by water thrown over them by pitcher-wielding women—anticipating how the men will burn with desire and be doused by the oath-sworn women.[122]

The Commissioner of Safety appears on the scene, recognizes the trouble as women-made but also that it is men who enabled the development of such female freedom of action—with a few bawdy, pun-filled accounts of husbands leaving their wives open (pun intended) to craftsmen and their tools (yes, pun again intended). Then Lysistrata and her troops appear out of the temple precincts and four attempts to arrest her are emphatically thwarted, the police force is routed by the women—and the Commissioner finally gets to the question: why have you taken over the temple with its treasury? What do you want?

They want to budget the money—but the war needs that

money, he responds. But who needs that war? Every freedom-loving patriot… and Lysistrata reviews the reality of things up to this point: the men make all the decisions, expecting the women to be silent and just stick to their spinning and that male hegemony with its stupid decision-making has led to one war-soaked process after another. But now the women are going to assume a position of leadership and save all of Hellas from being—well, man-handled. The Commissioner, in shock, finds himself veiled and spun around and re-attired—as a woman, compelled to listen. The women of the chorus, led by Lysistrata, recite their talents and their ambitions, culminating with Lysistrata's words: "We'll wait for the wind from heaven. The gentle breath of Eros and his Kyprian mother will imbue our bodies with desire, and raise a storm so intense and tauten these blasted men until they crack…"

Love and desire will be the weapons with which they shall fight to end war. Like knotted yarn untangled with a spindle they will wind up and untangle the conflict. The Commissioner's objection is that women have not participated in the war—to which she responds: we gave up our sons to Sicily (that debacle in which so many Athenians perished) and we gave up our youths, waiting husbandless for years while our men were away. First the Commissioner and then—after he has been banged on the head by the women and sent packing—the chorus of men turn out toward the audience, begging for help. A particularly interesting moment, one might imagine, given that the audience would have been almost entirely made up of men.

This last observation might provoke another one, before moving forward—just, as it were, *by the way*. One convention that Aristophanes did not break is that all the actors in ancient Greek theater—all of them—were men. This means that Lysistrata's role was played by a man. And now think back: Medea, Klytaimnestra, Iphigenia—all of these extraordinary roles, each with different powerful aspects to it—would have been played by men. This offers yet another layer of irony—to the horror that men in that audience would have had at the dominating, "male-like" position asumed by Kytaimnestra for Aiskhylos, or the eloquently angry words delivered by Medea for Euripides. It surely would have added both to how disturbing and how hilarious Lysistrata would have appeared to her (his!) audience.

Lysistrata and her group withdraw within the acropolis gates. The two choral groups and their leaders tussle back and forth, mostly verbally, albeit with some physical violence. Lysistrata bursts back out onto the stage, distraught—because women in her group are sneaking out, for sex, unable to keep their oaths of abstinence. One by one various women exit the citadel, coming around to Lysistrata with various excuses as to why they must leave it—and she says: it's because you want your men—but they want you, too, and if we can hold out for a few more days we shall have victory!—and reads a "prophecy" that seems to offer just that: victory, if they stick together.

In the distance, a man approaches, who "seems to have suffered a seizure. Broken out with a nasty attack of love," Lysistrata observes. It turns out to be Kinesias, (his name punning on "move"—in this context, in the sexual sense) the husband of Myrrhine (one of Lysistrata's two main Athenian associates). He has arrived with an unmitigated erection, carrying their baby boy, hoping desperately to entice his wife into love-making, and she agrees—if and after he votes for peace. But of course he wants sex first, and she agrees, and then drags out a cot, then a mattress, then a pillow, then a blanket, taking off this piece of clothing and that—in short, driving him slowly mad, until, reminding him of his promise to vote for peace, she disappears back into the citadel, leaving him bereft and emphatically unsatisfied.

Kinesias leaves and a Spartan herald arrives—in a similar physical condition. He is looking for the Commissioner, who returns to the stage—in a similar condition—and after a pun-filled dialogue the center of which are their priapic problems, the Commissioner instructs the herald to go back to Sparta and sue for peace, as he is certain that he can convince the Athenian council to agree to one.

The two leaders of the choruses and the choruses themselves, reconcile—bringing an end to the internal war provoked by the women's revolution that sought to end the Athenian-Spartan war, but which had the obvious side consequence of also bringing an end to the "men are inherently superior" mindset of those males and thus creating a new, even playing field for both genders. Strife is resolved with a new mode of loving.

And meanwhile, a delegation of Spartan men arrives, all clearly—clearly—suffering from a painful priapic condition. They are greeted by the master of the chorus; they are ready to sue for peace at any cost—and when an Athenian delegation soon arrives in identical shape, all anyone wants to know is: where is Lysistrata, clearly the key to their communal cure.

The gates of the citadel open and she appears, accompanied by her handmaiden—her name is *Dialagge*, which may be translated as "reconciliation," or by extension, "peace"—who is completely naked and seen by the audience but not by the characters on the stage. In a moment Lysistrata calls for her, though, and instructs her to lead the two delegations to her, each group lined up to either side. While the men are struggling to concentrate, their eyes glued to Dialagge, Lysistrata gives her speech, point by point.

One, that we are all Hellenes, worshipping all the same gods, and here we have been killing each other while our real enemies, the Persians, watch and wait for the chance to pounce on us. Two, she reminds the Spartans how fifty years earlier the Athenians under Kimon came to their aid and saved their state; and reminds the Athenians how a century ago the Spartans saved Athens from the tyranny of Hippias and his Thessalian allies.

They agree on terms—territories that they will exchange, and Lysistrata promises them a banquet with the signing of the peace treaty in the citadel, and that they can then go home with their wives. The delegations follow Lysistrata and Dialagge up into the acropolis citadel, the choruses of men and women sing thinly-veiled lascivious songs before also begging entrance. When they all come out, an Athenian flautist plays and a Spartan dances and sings a song recalling the glorious success of both *poleis* against Persia a few generations back, and Lysistrata presides over a distribution of all the wives, released to their relieved husbands—or soon to be relieveed. A final song from the Spartan performer and they all exit singing and dancing. The outcome is not only sex, but festivals with singing and poetry—all of which is better than war.

So the poet embraces in a straightforward manner the intertwining of *eris* with *eros* in a unique and uniquely light-hearted manner. His focus is topical not mytho-historical (although this is the only one of his extant plays in which not a single character is actually someone who can be historically identified) but alas, the lens through which he sees the event—the Peloponnesian War—in question offers an idealized possibility for positive human transformation. That possibility is through the injection of *eros*, tied up and twisted by a clever woman and her allies with the ambition of saving her men and her *polis*—and all the men and all the *poleis* embroiled in the conflict. It yields a happy ending, very different from the history that would play out over the seven years after the play was first performed. The audiences may have applauded, but were apparently not driven to return home from the theater and change their lives.

Nearly a century after the Aristophanic plays, referred to as "Old Comedy," and passing through a period associated with the phrase "Middle Comedy"—except that we have no real material from that middle period—Greek theater arrived at what is commonly referred to as "New Comedy." Mostly fragments of the plays of Menander (ca 342-ca 292 BCE)—perhaps the greatest of the New Comedy playwrights, along with Philemon and Diphilos—and his associates have survived. One play by Menander, however, has managed its way into modernity more or less intact: the play called *Dyskolos* ("The Grouch/Misanthrope/Bad-Tempered Man"), and it gives us some sense of the prevailing style and content of that early Hellenistic form of Attic theater.

It is a far more slapstick/soap opera kind of theater than was Old Comedy. The standard formula offered an everyday reality with certainly nothing phantasmagorical as is so often the case with Old Comedy. Boy (upper class) in love with girl (from the wrong side of the tracks), boy's father unhappy with this and boy loses girl but in the end gets her back, largely due to the machinations of his very clever slave. In other words, the real hero is the slave: a far cry from Akhilleus, Odysseus and their colleagues. Among the most emphatic socio-psychological conflicts and contrasts which shape the drama are urban and rural sensibilities (typically expressed in a pseudo-*agon* involving a city slave and a country slave); and, of course, *eros/eris*: intergenderal and, even more so, inter-generational. Thus there are often low-key lover's spats and a father caught between anger and resentment at his son's behavior and love for him.

First performed at the Lenaian Festival in 317-16 BCE, the *Dyskolos* garnered the playwright first prize. Like many other works from antiquity, however, the play only survived in fragments until the discovery of a nearly complete manuscript from the third century CE was discovered in the excavations at Oxyrinchos, Egypt, in 1952. It was first published six years later. Menander offered particular original elements: most obviously, the real paternal obstacle is the poor girl's father, because he is such a misanthrope, rather than the rich boy's father. And it is really fate—*tykhe*, "fortune," a less grand-scale concept than *moira*—or perhaps the machinations of a non-Olympian god, Pan—more than a clever slave who functionally solves the problem of negotiating a final union between the boy and girl, between whom there is no time for lovers' spats.

The grouchy misanthrope in question is Knemon, who lives alone with his daughter and two slaves—since shortly after his daughter's birth Knemon's wife left him thanks to his unbearable treatment of her: she left husband and daughter thanks to his eristic nature and not some erotic attachment. She went to live, in fact, with her son by her first marriage (she had been widowed when she met and married Knemon). Meanwhile, the god, Pan, (a lesser, non-Olympian god, also called a *daimon*), whom we first encounter in the play's prologue and who operates beyond the scenes—and has a fondness for Girl (for that is the name of Knemon's daughter, presumably underscoring her generic symbolic value for the story)—facilitates her discovery by Sostratos, a wealthy Athenian boy out hunting in the vicinity of Knemon's rural homestead. Sostratos falls in love with her at first sight.

So the divine hand has pushed the drama toward love—but it will be problematic, at least at the outset, because Knemon is such an inherently eristic personality. When Sostratos sends one of his slaves Pyrrhias to talk with Knemon, the old grouch responds by hitting him in the head with a farm tool, chasing him off his property. When Girl's half-brother, Gorgias, finds out through his own slave about Sostratos' interest in Girl, he warns his urban friend not to mistreat her due to class differences—so protective fraternal love intercedes, at least temporarily, to obstruct boyfriend-girlfriend—or potential husband-wife—love.

Sostratos convinces Gorgias, however, that he is truly in love with Girl and has the honorable intention of marrying her. The second manifestation of the problem of Knemon's misanthropy manifests itself when they and we learn that Knemon will only allow his daughter to marry someone like himself—so that Sostratos will need to act like a grouchy, angry young man, a country bumpkin and not the kindly, happy-go-lucky city slicker that he really is, if hs is to win her father's permission to marry her. He sets out to do this with Gorgias' guiding assistance.

It is not clear how effective this trick will be—which is when *tykhe* (or is it Pan?) steps in to influence matters. The audience hears a cry: it is one of Knemon's servants crying out that her master has fallen into a well while trying to fetch a bucket that she had accidentally dropped into it earlier (but "accidents" can be and are in such contexts typically construed as the result of *tykhe*'s intervention in human affairs). Gorgias jumps in to save Knemon while Sostratos comforts—and compliments—Girl, as she weeps about her father's misfortune. Then the "mighty" Sostratos pulls the rope up that brings Knemon and Gorgias out of the well.

The outcome of this little sequence of events is that Knemon has had a partial change of heart: having been so close to death he instructs Gorgias to find Girl a husband, since he recognizes that he will never manage to find one himself who will be sufficiently pleasing to him. Mortality's stare has partially melted Knemon's unabashed eristic personality toward seeking love for his daughter in a more reasonable way than before. So, problem solved: Gorgias introduces Knemon to Sostratos, whom he betroths to his half-sister—and Knemon does not object, but remains rather indifferent. (Is *eris* the opposite of *eros*, or is indifference its opposite?)

The story doesn't quite end yet, anyway. When Sosastros, full of excitement and enthusiasm, tells his father, Kallipides, about his hoped-for impending marriage—and further suggests that they marry off Sosastros' sister to Gorgias—his father hesitates. To bring two "beggars" into the family seems a little bit much. But Sosastros argues to his reluctant father that wealth should not be an issue; money is, after all, an "unstable business" that can disappear at any moment—for it really belongs to *tykhe* and not to the one who thinks he possesses it. Kallipides ultimately agrees—that "a visible friend [is a better investment] than invisible wealth that one keeps buried away."

So the denouement—with almost everyone living happily ever after—is a double wedding. *Almost* everyone, since it would not be in Knemon's nature to be happy. But when Sikon and Geta (the first a cook and the other a slave in the employ of Sostratos'family) go over to Knemon's house to mock and torment him (who has stayed away from the wedding celebration) they succeed in teasing and tricking him into joining the wedding festivities. So, under the mischievously loving eye of the *daimon*, Pan, everyone does end up happy, even, within his emotional means, Knemon. His eristic nature has been overcome by too much love for him to be able to fend off happiness (in Greek: *eudaimonia*, which literally means "well-demoned").

II Love, Strife, and Plato's *Symposium*

Ironically, perhaps, in the aftermath of the time of Aristophanes' *Lysistrata* and, seven years later, Athens' defeat, the philosopher Sokrates (469-399 BCE) would be executed by an Athenian *polis* licking its wounds from that humiliation at the hands of Sparta and the succession of oligarchic governments put into place between 404 and 399. Sokrates would be accused of having offended the gods and therefore having invited their wrath onto Athens—and thus for having engineered the demise of the *polis*.

At quite the opposite end of the humor spectrum from Aristophanes and his sex-driven characters, and certainly profoundly different from the New Comedy of Menander and his colleagues a century later, the father Western moral philosophy—a younger contemporary of Euripides and an older contemporary of Aristophanes—is, in a fortuitous and appropriate historical turn, located chronologically between these embodiments of tragic and comic theater in that brilliant and tragic generation. In an even more direct manner than do these iconoclastic playwrights, Sokrates assailed some of the fundamental ways in which Hellenic thought had been pushing itself forward for the previous several centuries as, besides poetry and historiographic prose writing it had come to nurture the evolving forms of discussion that eventually acquired the label of *philosophia*: "love of wisdom."

The earlier Greek philosophers concerned themselves with the physical universe and eventually some of them directed their focus toward metaphysical matters. But it fell to Sokrates to seriously introduce the question of ethics into the analysis of the human condition and of what and how we should be as a species. His method, of discussing ideas with all kinds of people, typically centered around the issue of definition: what do certain terms, which represent concepts that usually offer significant ethical connotations, really *mean*?

His path to the ethical area of intellectual enterprise was strewn with the empty husks of all the standard thoughtless knee-jerk responses of his contemporaries regarding words reflecting important aspects of day-to-day life in a world such as that of mid- to late-fifth century BCE Athens: What is justice? What is friendship? What is piety? What is love? And other abstract concepts the ultimate meaning of which others really never bothered to consider. Sokrates himself never wrote down any of the many words that he must have spewed out and elicited from others.

His disciple, Plato (428-348 BCE) and, to a more limited extent, a second follower, Xenophon (430-354 BCE), wrote down the things about which Sokrates queried others, yielding, in Plato's case, an extensive series of "dialogues." I place the term in quotation marks since what we have are Plato's creations—his dramatic renditions—of conversations not all of which Sokrates necessarily had, or if he did, not necessarily exactly as Plato recounts them. For our purposes the question of where Sokrates ends and Plato begins—what within the Platonic corpus is genuinely Socratic thinking or Socratic verbiage and what is really Plato's own thoughts and/or words on a given matter?—need not concern us. It is the ideas rather than their progenitor that interest us.

The *Dialogues* of Plato cover a wide range of territory. For instance, the *Euthyphro*, named for the sophist of that name with whom Sokrates is talking, focusses on what *hosiotes*—"piety" or "holiness"—is.[123] The *Gorgias*, named for a second, even better-known sophist who serves as Sokrates' main interlocutor, concerns itself with the definition of "justice." The *Phaedros* is primarily devoted to analyzing and defining "friendship." The *Phaedo* wrestles with the question of the immortality of the soul, and by extension, how a true lover of wisdom—a philosopher—who is devoted to the truth, and who understands that his chances of arriving at an understanding of the truth and of the Good are improved without the distractions imposed upon the mind/soul by the body, should embrace death eagerly, (as Sokrates is shown to do), rather than fear it.[124]

There are actually several Platonic works in which the issue of love is the subject, but none for which it is as front and center as in the *Symposium*.[125] This is the story of a drinking party—*symposion* means, literally, a "drink-with"—at which Sokrates was said to have been present with a bunch of others, and in which he proposed that, for entertainment, instead of flute players or dancing girls moving before them, they provide their own after-dinner fun by having an all-hands-on-deck discussion of what love is and where it comes from. The narrative reaches its culminating presentation—the conceptual center of this central dialogue—with Sokrates' own speech on the topic, concerning which he asserts that all that he knows about love he learned from a wise woman, Diotima. He quotes her as describing love—*eros*—as "halfway between mortal and immortal" (202d12), whose function is "to interpret and convey messages to the gods from men and to men from the gods" (202e3-4)—a *daimon*. Moreover:

> He is always poor, and, far from being sensitive and beautiful, as most people imagine, he is hard and weather-beaten, shoeless and homeless, always sleeping out for want of a bed, on the ground, on doorsteps, and in the street… he schemes to get for himself whatever is beautiful and good; he is bold and forward and strenuous, always devising tricks like a cunning huntsman; he yearns after knowledge and is full of resource and is a lover of wisdom all his life, a skillful magician, an alchemist, a true *sophos*… what he wins he always loses, and is neither rich nor poor, neither wise nor ignorant.
>
> The truth of the matter is this. No god is a lover of wisdom or desires to be wise, for he is already [wise], and the same is true of wise persons, if there be any such. Nor do the ignorant

love wisdom and desire to be wise, for... a man who possesses neither beauty nor goodness nor intelligence is perfectly well satisfied with himself...

Who, then, I said [to Diotima], are the lovers of wisdom...? Clearly, [she responded], they are the intermediate class, of which *Eros* among others is a member. Wisdom is one of the most beautiful of things, and Love is love of beauty, so it follows that *Eros* must be a lover of wisdom, and consequently in a state half-way between wisdom and ignorance. (203c6-204b5)

...love is love of immortality as well as of the Good (207a2-4)

...This mechanism, Sokrates, enables the mortal to partake of immortality, physically as well as in other ways... it is in order to secure immortality that each individual is haunted by this eager desire and love...Do you suppose that Alkestis would have died to save Admetos, or Akhilleus to avenge Patroklos...if they had not believed that their courage would live forever in men's memory, as it does in ours? (208b26; 208d2-6)

This small part of the much longer discourse from Diotima reported to the assembled symposion participants by Sokrates might suggest to us at least three interlocked issues with respect to our discussion of *eros* and *eris*. One is the way in which love is said to connect to the matter of immortality and, specifically, undying glory: *kleos aphthiton*. That issue, as we have already considered it with regard to Akhilleus, is directly referenced by Diotima.[126] She may not be right, by the way, in her assessment of Akhilleus. He may be said to have come to Troy, in spite of the inevitability of his own death that coming there brought with it, for the purpose of gaining *kleos aphthiton*—and because Odysseus shamed him into choosing that form of immortality over a long, obscure life on his father's farm. When, having withdrawn from the conflict he re-enters the war after Patroklos' death, however, it seems to me that it is purely love for his friend that brings him to strife with Hektor (and in a distinct way, as we have noted, strife with himself); at that point, *kleos aphthiton* is the farthest thing from his mind.

So the relationship between love and immortality is not shaped in the manner that she proposes. It is rather the fact that, if there are those who love us and remember us, we achieve a kind of immortality; if we are, as Akhilleus and Hektor are, characters bigger than life—about whom poets and playwrights write poems and plays, then our loving "fans" who preserve our undying name and thus our immortality can go on, generation after generation, *ad infinitum*.

Two—and much more significant both for the Platonic dialogues and for our own discussion—is the way in which an astute auditor or reader would recognize a direct resonance between Sokrates' Diotima-sourced description of love and Sokrates himself as he is described both in the frame of the dialogue and within its body. Thus the idea of love as a creature that is between gods and men, who functions as a conduit between *sacer* and *profanus* (to translate Diotima's words into our own) is very much what Sokrates has always been for Plato's corpus: someone whose wisdom seems preternatural, and whose incessant inquiries with diverse kinds of people are designed to make them think and rethink—to examine without preconception—important issues and ideas in order more effectively to function as citizens of Athens and, by implication, bring the blessings and not the curses of the gods upon the city.[127]

Although Sokrates is not, per se, poor, he wanders around as if he were, little concerning himself with material comforts (or plying his trade as a sculptor to earn a real living); he is depicted as typically being barefoot (this is noted right at the beginning of the *Symposium*, at 174a, in fact) and, if need be, can sleep just about anywhere. Not only sleep, but can and often does pause in a standing yet sleep-like condition. This also happens at the beginning of the dialogue, when Apollodoros—narrator of the *Symposium*, tells us how he heard from Aristodemos, who reported the whole thing to Apollodoros (who is telling it to an unnamed friend)—showed up embarrassed at Agathon's door, because Sokrates, who had invited him to join the dinner party, was no longer with him, having paused on a neighbor's porch to think about something. He is, it turns out, notorious for doing that—standing sometimes for hours considering a problem: or it would seem that he has epilepsy or catalepsy, the sort of conditions that his contemporaries would consider divinely imposed. In any case, in his own reported explanation of what he does, in the *Apology*, he refers to an inner voice that guides him—a "divine voice"—suggesting that he himself understands his task as that of serving as a kind of guide for his fellow citizens, himself divinely guided.

If Love is a lover of wisdom there is surely no more enthusiastic lover of wisdom in all of Hellas than Sokrates, and his ongoing—and often, to his victims, annoying—pursuit of the Truth through continuous questions, is bold and forward and strenuous. He is, in his discussions, particularly with pompous, know-it-all self-proclaimed sophists, an inveterate deviser of tricks like a cunning huntsman, and somewhat of a magician and alchemist in how he seems to snare both his victims who resent him for it and his followers who love him for being drawn into his snares, "a true *sophos*."

He contrives to capture beautiful things—and wisdom is the most beautiful of things. But in a more banal sense, part of his interest (it is why he is at Agathon's house in the first place, whom at the outset of the dialogue he is reported by Apollodoros to have referred to as a handsome man for whom he has uncharacteristically bathed and put on shoes) is to seduce beautiful young men—their minds, that is—but is often shown in the *Dialogues* to be forced into conversations with them, not the other way around.[128] One might say of him that he solves the seducer's paradox: he often manages to find himself seduced into conversation by those whom he wishes to seduce to engage in just that sort of intercourse.

Indeed—and this is the third particular issue that Plato's dialogue, filtering Diotima's words through Sokrates by way of Apollodoros' report to "a friend" over whose shoulder we listen, so to speak—the most stunning concrete example of this process is arguably Alkibiades, a young, particularly handsome, wealthy and rather profligate adorer of Sokrates. And the resonance between what Sokrates has said about love and what he *is* proves to be only one conceptual shoe dropping within the center of the dialogue. For barely has Sokrates finished when Alkibiades, already quite drunk, crashes the party and, picking up the conversation, redirects it slightly, informing his audience that he would love to join in, but that his topic will be Sokrates himself. It is his recitation that, dropping the other shoe for the audience, twists the idea of love around that of strife most strongly: *eros* is interwoven with *eris* both in the lead-up to and in the delivery of his oration.

For Alkibiades at first, when, he is seated by Agathon at one of the tables of three and he realizes that Sokrates is one of his table-mates, evinces shock and surprise to find him there—and Sokrates, in mock fear and consternation, warns Agathon "the handsomest person in the room," according to Alkibiades, that he must be prepared to protect Sokrates, "for I find that the love of this fellow has become no small burden...his falling into a passion of jealousy and envy... makes him behave outrageously and abuse me and practically lay violent hands on me... I am really quite scared by his mad behavior and the intensity of his affection" (213c7-d6). So to begin with, the love relationship between Sokrates and his admirer are tinged with violent strife—whether truly or not is less important than the representation offered by Sokrates of it as such. This repartee: "there can be no peace between you and me" Alkibiades responds to Sokrates' comments, before settling down, gulping down a large quantity of wine and beginning his pained encomium of Sokrates by noting that he (Sokrates) can drink all that he wants and never be drunk (214a4-5). Then, pushed by Eryximakhos, he stops his random babbling and begins a systematic verbal depiction of Sokrates.

He notes—and consider Sokrates' Diotima-sourced words regarding Love's ugliness, because it pursues beauty that, if Love were himself beautiful, he would not need to seek—that Sokrates resembles Silenos. More precisely, he resembles "those figures of Silenos in statuaries' shops, represented holding pipes or flutes; they are hollow inside, and when they are taken apart you see that they contain little figures of gods. I declare he is like Marsyas the satyr" (215a7-b4). So not only is he likened to one of those lesser, woodland gods, just as Love had been depicted by Diotima through Sokrates as a lesser god, but he is represented as ugly on the exterior but with extreme—divine—beauty on the inside, accessible in layers.

Alkibiades clarifies: that Marsyas can charm men with his flute, "throwing men into a trance... [whereas] you, Sokrates, are so far superior to Marsyas that you produce the same effect by mere words without any instrument" (215c5-7). That is, he manages to seduce men's minds, entrancing them to "yearn to enter by initiation into union with the gods" (215c5-6). He is thus both an intermediary between gods and men and one who entrances men into a particular desire. The union that he induces them to desire is a union with philosophy, truth, and the Good.

The problem for Alkibiades is that, once he gets away from Sokrates for a while he reverts to succumbing to the temptations of popularity—doing what people want him to do or think he should do, or that he thinks will make him more popular, which is invariably other than noble things—rather than remaining directed to the more elevated, ethical behavior that Sokrates induces in him. He himself, Sokrates (like Love as Sokrates' Diotima had described him) "has a tendency to fall in love with good-looking young men, and is always in their society and in an ecstasy about them" (216d2-3), yet at the same time he despises good looks and while he himself looks ugly, "I doubt whether anyone has ever seen the treasures which are revealed when he grows serious and exposes what he keeps inside" (216e5-6).

Alkibiades likens his own condition, thanks to Sokrates, to that of one suffering from a snake-bite. He proceeds to tell the story of how he once spent the night with Sokrates and, having delivered to him a speech about how he wished to come as near to perfection as possible, failed completely to seduce the older man who presumably loves him and therefore should be trying to seduce *him*.[129]

Alkibiades describes the heroic behavior of Sokrates on the battlefield at Potidea, where he could go without food and drink more easily than anyone but who enjoyed drinking as much as or more than anyone and—yet again, he repeats this: "no human being has ever seen Sokrates drunk" (220a4-5). He notes how

> a problem occurred to him early one day and he stood still on the spot to consider it… by the time it was midday people noticed him, and remarked to one another with wonder that Sokrates had been standing wrapped in thought since early morning. Finally, in the evening after dinner, some Ionians brought their bedding outside—it was summertime—where they could take

up their rest in the cool and at the same time keep an eye on Sokrates to see if he would stand there all night as well. He remained standing until it was dawn and the sun rose. Then he made a prayer to the sun and went away. (220c3-d5)

Further, in battle nobody was braver or more oblivious to being shot at by the enemy—in fact, when Alkibiades received a decoration for valor, "it was entirely to Sokrates that I owed my preservation; he would not leave me when I was wounded, but succeeded in rescuing both me and my fighting gear" (220d7-e2), but because of Alkibiades' connections, he notes, the generals gave him, rather than Sokrates, the commendation for valor. And Sokrates' valor was even more obvious in the disorderly retreat from Delion, where he rescued a rather terrified Laches from the battle.

This long encomium concludes with three comments of particular note. One, that "he is like no other human being, living or dead—with no parallel [as opposed to Akhilleus or Perikles, both of whom have other historical figures to whom one might compare them]: "our friend here is so extraordinary, both in his person and in his conversation, that you will never be able to find anyone remotely resembling him either in antiquity or in the present generations, unless you go beyond humanity altogether, and have recourse to the images of Silenos-figures and satyrs that I am using myself in this speech" (221d3-5).

Moreover, while at first Sokrates' speech may seem utterly ridiculous, since "it is clothed in curious words and phrases… [and] he repeats the same ideas in the same language over and over again, so that any inexperienced or foolish person is bound to laugh at his way of speaking… [yet] if a man penetrates within and sees the content of Sokrates' talk exposed, he will find that there is nothing but sound sense inside, and that his talk is almost the talk of a god…" (221e2; 221e5-222a5). So his place as somehow between gods and men, as an interpreter and intermediary, is reiterated—and should recall in form Sokrates' own description of Love—and of course comes, not coincidentally, from someone who is himself both in love with and frustrated by Sokrates.

The third concluding comment of particular note is, indeed, that this lover, Alkibiades, includes a

> ...grievance against him, and [I have] told you how he has insulted me. I may add that I am not the only sufferer; Charmides the son of Glaukon and Euthydemos the son of Diokles and many others have had the same treatment; he has pretended to be in love with them, when in fact he is himself the beloved rather than the lover. So I warn you, Agathon, not to be deceived by him... (222a8-b8)

That warning closes the parentheses, one might say, opened when Sokrates had begged Agathon to protect him from Alkibiades just after the latter had entered the room! In any case, clearly sobered up by now—if rather drunk in a different way, with angry and frustrated love for Sokrates—Akibiades concludes. An exchange begins between Sokrates and him, and others might have started to become involve in the follow-up conversation, had not a band of revelers come pouring through the door at that point so that the entire discussion abruptly ended.

Given the way in which Plato has presented the image of Sokrates through Alkibiades as an echo of Sokrates' own description of Love as a paradoxic figure, and given the manner in which Alkibiades'own speech is fraught with *eros-eris* tensions— and given the unwitting but important albeit indirect role that Alkibiades will play in leading to Sokrates' demise—it is not surprising to see Sokrates as we see him at the end of the dialogue.[130] For Aristodemos reports through Apollodoros that Eryximakhos and Phaedros and some others went away at this point; and that he, Aristodemos, himself fell asleep for some time, as did everyone else who did not leave; and that he awoke to note that Sokrates was still wide awake (of course; he who can sleep anywhere can also go without sleep as long as necessary to complete a philosophical inquiry!) and seated between and discoursing to Agathon—the tragic playwright whose victory in the recent dramatic competition prompted the drinking party that he hosted—and Aristophanes, the renowned comic playwright, in one of whose plays, *The Clouds*, Sokrates is parodied. Sokrates is dominating them both in this last conversation of the long evening, "compelling them to admit that the man who knows how to write a comedy could also write a tragedy" and vice-versa (223d3-6).

So Sokrates, a comic figure (in the physical description of him, with his bulging eyes, satyr-like countenance, and roundish body) and a tragic figure (because we all know what his fate will be), in his position and commentary between comedy and tragedy, as it were, offers a metaphor for what he is as one positioned between divinities and humans, and for the tension centered on him between *eros* and *eris*. Soon after the last point in their conversation has been made by Sokrates, each of his two interlocutors fell asleep—first Aristophanes and then Agathon—we are told. At that point Sokrates simply left, went off, followed by Aristodemos, to the Lykeon to make his morning ablutions, and went off to conduct an ordinary day's affairs.

He who sits and perorates between tragedy and comedy is himself the embodiment of that paradoxic interweave: the comedic character described by Alkibiades who is also the most tragic for all of these friends who will lose him to the political machinations and scapegoating requirements of Athens in the aftermath of its disastrous loss of the Peloponnesian Wars, and with it the collapse and subsequent tainted resurrection of its democracy. The faux eristic tone of Alkibiades in his lovelorn description of the figure who is Plato's ultimate hero (who wrote the dialogue, after all—and since we don't know exactly how many words were actually Alkibiades' or anyone else's and how many of them Plato's, we can at least in part see all of this as Plato's loving description of Sokrates) offers an *eros-eris* tension parallel to that between comedy and tragedy.

III The Visual World of Love and Strife

One might also note, albeit for our purposes, only briefly, that the *eros-eris* theme and its analogues find their way into Greek art and not only Greek literature and philosophy. Not surprisingly, there are many themes not only from the Trojan War but from still earlier mythology that reflect the Greek obsession with antitheses that co-exist in dynamic tension with each other. Thus, for instance, *eris* is well represented in the depiction of Herakles battling the Nemean Lion—the first of his 12 labors that brought *kosmos* (order) out of *khaos* in this or that corner of Hellas. The eristic scene centers on a subtle but pronounced contrast between *ethos* and *pathos*: between the kind of calm, cool approach to reality that one associates with the Olympian gods with their distancing ability to see any given moment or event as part of a larger cosmic framework; and the emotional restlessness reflecting standard human involvement in the problems of the world around us and the limits of our perspective. The most obvious aspect of the image that conveys this is the juxtaposition of the faces of the two protagonists. Herakles has the sort of calm expression on his face that suggests a sweatless effort at combatting his foe, whereas the lion is snarling fiercely, all roar and complaint [FIG 1].[131]

Within the ever-popular context of the Trojan War narrative, the so-called Euphronios Vase, a red-figure Kalyx-Krater (for mixing wine with water; such a vase would have been in use at Agathon's symposion) dating from ca 515 BCE, presents the moment in *Iliad* XVI after Sarpedon has been killed by Patroklos. His body, with its wounds still gushing blood, is being lifted gently from the battlefield by the gods *Hypnos* (Sleep) and *Thanatos* (Death), as Hermes watches over the process. The viewer is expected to remember not only the eristic moment of the Lykian hero's death from *Iliad* Book Sixteen, but the conversation between his loving father, Zeus, and Hera that precedes that fatal battle and the outcome of which is this soft aftermath of the immortal god's mortal son's demise **[FIG 2]**.[132]

More overtly suggesting the interplay of *eros* and *eris* is the red-figure kylix dated to ca 500 BCE (Altes Musuem, Berlin), on which Akhilleus is depicted binding up the wounded arm of Patroklos. There is a logic to this, since Akhilleus was said to have been tutored by Kheiron, the centaur, who was renowned for his medical skills and thus Akhilleus, among his other more frequently referenced talents, mostly, of course, as an athlete-warrior, would also have had medical skills. More to the point of our own narrative, the moment that is depicted suggests a calm within the storm of the Trojan War and focuses not only on a skill of Akhilleus other than that of being the pre-eminent athlete-warrior on either side of the combat zone, but on the loving aspect of his personality that is only hinted at by the end of the *Iliad* as one moves through Book Twenty-three and its funeral games for Patroklos presided over by Akhilleus, and through Book Twenty-four and the encounter with Priam that leads to Akhilleus' return of Hektor's body to his father.[133] Moreover, the tender care being shown to Patroklos reflects the acknowledged fact that this is the main figure with whom Akhilleus has a strong and loving relationship: that tender love is expressed in this quiet moment in the midst of the strife-based war [FIG 3].

By contrast, the name-vase of the so-called Penthesilea Painter shows an even more emphatic *eros-eris* moment that, like the depiction of Akhilleus wrapping up the wound of Patroklos, derives from sources outside the extant canon of epic poems recounting the Trojan War. It reflects the thread in that tapestry that asserts that the Amazons, led by their princess, Penthesilea, came to fight as allies of the Trojans. The tradition further asserts that Akhilleus ends up fighting against Penthesilea in a one-on-one combat and that he slays her—but that at the moment in which he kills her he falls in love with her for her valor and skill.

The red-figure kylix (470-60 BCE; Munich Glyptoek) shows the two of them, their bodies cleverly posed to conform to the frame of the space—the interior bottom of a flat, bowl-lke vase—in which they are placed. Most importantly, as he plunges his sword into her breast—no heavy need for Sigmund Freud to assess the significance of this particular physical act of love-emulating strife as the center of the composition—their eyes meet. This is the first instance in Greek vase-painting in which two characters who interact are shown making direct visual contact with each other—and the expression in her eyes in particular could hardly be more gently loving. In this case, given the story and the obvious intention of the vase-painting to reflect it, there is tremendous poignancy in their loving ocular interaction at this moment marking the culmination of their eristic, death-dealing physical interaction [FIG 4].

While this last image emphatically wraps *eros* and *eris* around each other, one can see that sort of interplay more subtly and indirectly—embedded in other antithesis-pairings of both content and style—in certain sculptures. And one can further turn the wheel of this issue by continuing toward Roman sculpture—which also offers an appropriate segue toward Roman epic and lyric poetry as it reflects the *eros-eris* issue.

Thus for instance, the renowned ca 450-30 BCE sculpture by Polyklitos known as the *Doryphoros* (the "Spear-bearer," of which we currently possess only Roman copies, for the original is long gone). There are three interesting and relevant directions in which the *Doyphoros* can lead our discussion. One is its stylistic demonstration: a concise and well-articulated example of the innovative Athenian approach to balance: *symmetria*. This last word, from which our English term, "symmetry", derives, rather than referring to perfect, symmetrical balance, describes a dynamic balance made up of imbalances.

Thus the *Doryphoros*, rather than standing with one leg slightly in front of the other and his arms symmetrically posed at his sides, with his head facing front and all of the figure's components perfectly even and balanced, left-to-right—a style consonant with eternal and unchanging gods, such as the Egyptians depicted and Archaic Greek statuary emulated—is shown in the process of striding forward and thus shifting his weight from one foot to the other. One leg (the right leg) is straight, and bears the weight upon it, as evidenced in the muscles bunched around the patella, while the other, left, leg is bent but relaxed, as the weight has come off of it. By contrast, the right arm is straight, like the right leg, but relaxed to the side of the figure, whereas the left arm, bent like the left leg, is tensed, carrying the spear (that is missing in extant Roman copies).

This sort of chiastic balance is accompanied by a subtle series of diagonals as one views the work from the front: a diagonal from the viewer's lower left slightly up to the right at the line of the feet, which is reversed by the knees that offer a slightly down-on-the-right and up-on-the-left appearance. That diagonal is gradually subsumed into horizontality, as one's eye works its way up from the waist to the pectorals to the shoulders. And the head, finally, turned slightly to the viewer's left and tilted, offers a series of diagonals that echo those presented by the feet [FIG 5].

So stylistically, the entirety is a dynamic contrast between tense and relaxed, bent and straight, and diagonal directions—and ultimately a contrast between stasis and action, as the figure is at once dynamic yet stable. These visual ideas offer analogues to the conceptual dialogues between *ethos* and *pathos*, mortality and immortality, and between *eros* and *eris*. When, moreover, one considers that later Greek writers saw this figure as a portrait of Akhilleus, pre-eminent athlete-warrior and exemplar par excellence of the mortal-immortal tension to which all humans are subject at some level, it serves an exponentially important role together with the previously-mentioned vases in addressing these conceptual issues in a non-verbal manner.

But this work also leads in a second direction by virtue of the way in which in its original form it became a model for subsequent statuary, both to emulate and from which to diverge in specific ways. Thus while the *Doryphoros* was created in accordance with what, at the height of the classical period, were regarded as ideal athletic proportions—in terms both of musculature and the ratio of head to body—over the next century that sensibility began to change. Athletic figures became longer, more attenuated in the ratio relationship of body to head, with their muscles less overbearing. But other things were happening, as well. From the time of the unexpected defeat of Athens by Sparta that marked the end of the Peloponnesian War in 404 BCE to the time when all of Hellas was swallowed up by Philip II of Macedon, by way of the Battle of Khaironia, in 338 BCE, to the domination by Philip's son, Alexander the Great, in turn, from 336 BCE forward, a succession of *poleis* experienced brief periods of hegemony in the region. As Philip brought the era of Hellenic family-feuding, so to speak, to an end, so did certain perspectives regarding how to understand and depict heroes and gods.

In retrospect, iconoclasts like Sokrates and Euripides were already raising questions before the Peloponnesian War was even over. Sokrates did this in dialogues like the *Euthyphro*, which ends in *aporia* (literally "no way out": *poros* means "passage" and *"a"* means "un-"), as the sophist's proposal that *hosiotes* ("piety"/"holiness" is what is pleasing to the gods butts up against the realization that the gods often disagree about all kinds of things. Euripides did it in plays like *Hippolytos* that implicitly ask what kinds of gods these are whom we worship so unquestioningly; and *Medea*, which skewers a traditional, iconic hero—knocking him off his pedestal, at least for some of the audience. The evidence is scanty that the questions that these two raised were being addressed broadly in the visual arts, but it is there.

A sense of crisis near the end of and after the Pelponnesian War—especially, of course, for Athenians—is certainly reflected in the frenzied work in much of the visual art of the late fifth-early fourth century, and the increased emphasis on *pathos* rather than *ethos* also reflects the distress occasioned by the events of that time-period. There are particular political and cultural changes that arrive later, around the time when Philip and Alexander arrive, that engender more intense visual responses, and no sculptor more emphatically reflects this than Praxiteles.

One of his works, called *Apollo Sauroktonos* ("Apollo the Dragon-Slayer") reflects the move to front and center of the question as to whether the traditional Olympian gods were correctly understood by tradition. The Far-Darter—depicted, for instance, in the *Iliad*, as the marksman who single-handedly brings down the Akhaians with illness when their leader insults the god's priest— also possessed a back story focused most particularly on the heroic athletic-warrior skill with which he slew the gigantic serpent/ dragon that had made the region around Delphi so dangerously symptomatic of *khaos*. The god brought *kosmos* to that corner of Hellas, and his oracular shrine was therefore embedded there: the priestess/*sacerdos* was referred to, sometimes, as the Pythia, commemorating the god's slaughter of the great beast, Pytho, (from which our word, "python," is derived).

In Praxiteles' work there is scant evidence of these narratives. On the contrary, the sculptor has taken the proportions and muscles of the *Doryphoros* and extended the one and all but eliminated the other so that what stands before the viewer is a rather flaccid boy, almost effeminate in the softness of his flesh. Nor does he really stand—or stride—for the artist has also distorted the principles of *symmetria* and balance so that the boyish god leans against a tree, rather than standing or striding freely. It is on that tree that the object of his interest rests: a very small, surely very harmless lizard—a far cry from a ferocious and terrifying dragon/ serpent—at which Apollo pokes rather lazily with a stick. That is: the great serpent/dragon-slayer has been transformed into a barely pubescent boy poking at a lizard with a stick: he has been reduced to a far-from-heroic divine level indeed [FIG 6].

The transformation of Polyklitean sculptural canons—as applied to and with reference to a god-like hero such as Akhilleus was—into new canons applicable to a human boy-like god reflects the growing doubt for everyday Greeks as to whether the Olympians are the kinds of gods to protect us from the increasing chaos of our world. Praxiteles' even more strident statement came with a commission from the citizens of Kos to sculpt an image of Aphrodite for their temple devoted to the goddess of love and beauty.

What Praxiteles did, shocked and horrified them sufficiently so that they rejected the work that they had commissioned. He did two related things. He depicted the goddess, whom everyone understood to be "foam-born," thanks to Hesiod—born out of the sea-foam (*aphros*) that resulted from the castration of Ouranos by his son, Kronos—as if she were a beautiful maiden rising not from the sea, but from the bath. Again he transmuted the principles of *symmetria* to offer a more extreme version of tense-relaxed, bent-straight-limbed motion, captured not in a dynamically stable forward motion, but as if simultaneously moving from crouch to full stand and becoming suddenly aware of an intruder and thus hurrying to try to shield her breasts and her pubic area from view with her two antithetically disposed arms/hands. One might imagine this as a kind of ironic reference to familiar stories—the best-known, perhaps, that of Aphrodite's antithesis, the virgin hunter-goddess, Artemis, who was famously seen bathing by a mortal, Aktaeon. In her anger, she transformed him into a stag that was then chased down and torn apart by his own dogs **[FIG 7]**.

So the implications of this moment could be said to be subtly but distinctly other than flattering for how divinities treat humans, and thus it is an odd composition for a shrine designed to adulate a goddess. This was, however, the least of it. Far from subtle was the fact that was apparently familiar to everyone, that Praxiteles used his girlfriend, Phryne, as his model. So in a literal manner he transformed the girl into the goddess and the goddess into the girl: transgressing boundaries that, Akhilleus and other exceptions notwithstanding, can never be transgressed—or shouldn't, as far, at least, as the Kosians were concerned: the boundary between divinity and humanity. They ended up rejecting the sculpture.

Fortunately for the artist, the citizens of Knidos thought differently. So the *Knidian Aphrodite*, as she has come to be known (and of which, once again, we possess many Roman copies and/or variations, but not the Praxitilean original) found a home in a different shrine to the goddess of love, at Knidos. Put otherwise: the statue of the goddess of love, which served in part as a statement of love for his girlfriend by the artist and led to such strife with those who originally commissioned it, ended up embraced and loved by a different community—and the fame of her beauty apparently brought male tourists from far and wide to gaze unabashedly at her.

The world of which the two Praxitilean works we have discussed were part was becoming only more disturbing through the success of Alexander, between ca 330 and 325 BCE, in bringing Hellenic ideas to places as far away as India—and diverse foreign ideas back to Hellas—thus expanding the Hellenic sense of "our world" (*oikoumene*: "homeland", from *oikos*, meaning "home") beyond the comfort zone of most. The sense of discomfort would have increased exponentially in the aftermath of Alexander's sudden death by fever in 323 BCE, with the struggle for power among his best friends and most reliable generals, the eventual shaping of large kingdoms and within them large cities that offered an excess of anonymity rather than the continuity of familiar neighbors and friends, and a general sense of alienation from the *kosmos* and the distant, *ethos*-bound gods of Olympos who had once seemed so reliably concerned about human affairs.

In the course of the period that followed, called—from a Euro-centric and certainly Helleno-centric perspective—the Hellenistic ("Greek-like") period because of the spread of Hellenic cultural ideas and values far and wide (and in a kind of denial of how two-way the street of expanding the *oikoumene* was), Olympian gods found increased competition from the sorts of gods who are embodiments of the transgressing of that divine-human boundary. The cult of figures like Herakles, Dionysos and Aisklepios all grew immensely in popularity. They all share, with whatever diverse variations, a distinct and fundamental feature, that of being god-connected. Herakles' father was a god (Zeus) and his mother a mortal; Dionysos the same; Aisklepios was fully mortal but, in his skill as the consummate physician—and thus someone perceived to have a kind of power over life and death—was elevated to divine status. Added to this growing amalgam was an embrace, by some, of cults imported from elsewhere—particularly Egypt, Anatolia, and Mesopotamia. Religious traditions from these places and from Judaea (with its odd concept of a single, invisible God) were perceived as exotic and, in many cases, attractive.

All of this would end up transferred to the Roman world, as it gradually swallowed up the Hellenistic Greek world in the course of the last few centuries BCE. And all of this also leads to the third direction relevant to our discussion that one might take with the *Doryphoros* as a starting point. And that is the particular manner in which that statue is emulated in the most famous of its Roman counterparts: the *Augustus of Prima Porta*, so named because it was originally located in the back garden of the Villa belonging to Augustus' wife, Livia, at Prima Porta [FIG 8].

The same basic position as that of Polyklitos' sculpture is emulated, with four notable differences. One, the placement of the feet is wider and, with this, the proportions offer a figure broader relative to its height; two, the straight right arm/hand is upraised rather than resting against the side. These two differences in turn relate to a third one. The statue, rather than nude, is dressed in a military uniform—underscoring Augustus' position as commander-in-chief of the Roman armies, and offering a specific opportunity to assert that role's particularized significance by way of the low-relief-carved imagery across the breastplate. Indeed, that image shows the handing back of the Roman standards by the Parthians. The Roman leader, Crassus, notoriously led his army into a disastrous encounter with the Parthians in 53 BCE, losing both the Roman standards and his life in the process in the Battle of Carrhae; Augustus was able to win them back decades later. The fact that the scene offers a sky-god—presumably Jupiter—and the chariot of Helios sweeping across the heavens above the scene implies the imprimatur of the gods that Augustus asserts for himself and through him, for the Roman world that he protects.

Thus the reason for the difference in body proportions in comparison with the *Doyphoros* is clear: whereas the primary purpose of the first work was to adulate an idealized athlete-warrior in his naked-muscled glory, the main purpose of this work is to educate the viewer—to propagandize—regarding the important accomplishments of Augustus, and a wider "canvas" is needed to encompass the message. This in turn relates to the fourth obvious difference: that the work is designed to be seen only from the front, where the *Doryphoros* was intended to be viewed from any and all angles. Indeed, the *Augustus of Prima Porta* was placed in a niche (as were most Roman statues not intended for placement in a fountain, or against a wall), and from it, with his upraised right arm he commands the space before him: the space that includes the viewer within it. So, coming out of the back of the villa into that garden, the viewer would see the statue gesturing as an imperator who governed the entire garden, including the viewer.

There is more. Although wearing a military toga and breastplate, the *Augustus of Prima Porta* is barefoot, rather than wearing sandals—a detail that some historians of Roman art have asserted means that the figure depicted is dead.[134] Thus Augustus, who died at age 77, is shown posthumously as if he were not only the commander of armies but a young man in his early twenties. Moreover, at his feet there cavorts a dolphin—symbol of Aphrodite (Venus, in Roman terms), who was born in and from the foam of the sea, and thus is often symbolized by a dolphin. And on the dolphin's back rides a plump baby: *eros*/cupid, son of Aphrodite/Venus, holding onto the edge of Augustus' garment. The viewer is therefore reminded of the emperor's lineage: the descendant of the consummate Roman hero, Aeneas, Trojan prince of Troy, who was the son of Aphrodite/Venus. The emperor dressed for war—and with the reminder of his eristic success vis-à-vis the Parthians as the primary décor of his breastplate—is at the same time depicted with multiple reminders of his relationship to love as attributes.

This work brings us full circle back to the Trojan War—and to the Roman tradition that the ancestry of the Roman world was Troy—more precisely, that ancestry was shaped by the Trojan warrior, Aeneas, who, at the behest of the gods and fate, left the burning city in its destruction, leading a group of Trojan refugees to Italy. Embedded in that story (about which there will be more detailed discussion in the following chapter) was the account of what precipitated the destruction of Troy: not a straightforward military assault, but a trick, fashioned by Odysseus.

The trick was the building of the great wooden horse in which Akhaian soldiers remained silently hidden. The horse was dragged into Troy by the Trojans themselves, under the illusion that it was intended as a gift to the god Poseidon left by the Akhaians as they ended the ten-year siege and headed home empty-handed—thanks to a lie to that effect told to them by the sole Akhaian, Sinon, whom they found wandering on their shore, left behind by the others who had apparently departed for home. The Akhaians, however, had merely sailed around a nearby promontory, out of sight, to Tenedos, and sailed back, at night, as their fellow-warriors came out of the horse, opened the gates and began the destruction of Troy and the slaughter or enslavement of the Trojans.

The story within this story, however, that offers an irony and the paradox of *eros-eris* interweave so endemic to Greek and Roman thinking, hangs on the debate among the Trojans as to what to do with the horse. Laokoon—and in one version, also Kassandra, the prophet cursed by having nobody ever believe her prophecies, as punishment for having spurned Apollo—urge(s) the Trojans to burn the horse, suspecting the subterfuge; others clamored to bring it into the city. When the gods intervened—in one version, Athena, in another, Poseidon—by attacking Laokoon, the Trojans wheeled the horse into their city.

Thus in one version, Athena causes a minor earthquake where Laokoon stands, and makes him blind; in the better known version, his attacker is Poseidon. The tragic irony is that Laokoon is a priest of and therefore beloved by Poseidon. This we understand from the poem, of which only fragments remain, known as the *Iliou Persis* ("Sack of Troy") ascribed to Arktinos of Miletos and dated to the eighth century BCE. Moreover, Poseidon is is also a patron god of Troy, in the line-up of divinities that favor one side or the other in this conflict, so his eristic act, leading to the destruction of the city contradicts his love for it—but as with all of the gods, in the end, he, too, must ultimately bow to fate.

Poseidon's active participation in the destruction of Laokoon and his sons adds another layer to the tragic irony of Zeus' passive plaint regarding the death of Sarpedon in Book Sixteen of the *Iliad*. The mode of that participation is that Poseidon sends a gigantic serpent (or two, in the Roman version of the story) up from the sea, that head(s) directly for the priest and his sons, enveloping them in its scaly muscles and strangling them. This destruction of Poseidon's priest by Poseidon himself is logically enough taken by the Trojans to be a sign that they should indeed take the horse into the city and place it before Poseidon's temple.

There is surely no sculpture that is more exemplary of *pathos* than the one that depicts this horrific moment, dating from perhaps 200-175 BCE (and found in the Vatican Museum collections). This anonymously carved marble work, typically referred to as Hellenistic—although I believe that a case can be made for it as begun by a Hellenistic artist and completed, with the adding of a second base, by a Roman artist—offers a series of dynamic textural and compositional contrasts that serve as visual metaphors for the fundamental *conceptual* contrasts embodied by the story. The virtually rectilinear angles formed by the twisting of the human limbs contrast with the curvilinear coils of the serpent; the smooth human flesh contrasts with the scaly serpentine flesh, the intense musculature of Laokoon contrasts with the soft-muscled limbs of his sons, his thick hair and beard contrasts with the less overwhelming hair and beardlessness of those sons **[FIG 9]**.

The overall conception of the figures describes a series of heroic diagonals that were nonetheless broken by the twisting of the limbs. At the same time, the sense of agony is conveyed by the expression on the face of Laokoon, with his eyes and eyebrows drawn up in extreme diagonals—an expression said to have been first used by one of Praxiteles' contemporaries, Skopas, so that it is referred to as a "skopatic expression"—underscoring the *pathos* that the viewer is intended to observe and with which the viewer is intended to sympathize, sharing vicariously in the intense death-dealing experience through the suffering of these humans caught in a web contrived of Fate and gods (but also of humans).

The knowledge that the perpetrator of such suffering is a god who loves the sufferer upon whom he foists that pain twists the ideas of tragic irony and *eros-eris* in an unprecedented visual direction. Whether or not the work was completed by a Roman artist, the story of this event is recounted in a far more detailed manner by Vergil, through his Aeneas—in Book Two of the *Aeneid*, as we shall shortly see—than in any Greek literary source. As such it serves, as well, as an appropriate segue to a discussion of the *Aeneid* and Roman literature, in which both the epic and lyric—as well as comedic and satiric—forms of Roman literary expression offer a continuation and transformation of the Greek interest in intermingling *eros* and *eris*.

Fig. 1 Black-figure amphora: Herakles and the Nemean Lion
(Munich Glyptothek; ca 510 BCE)

Fig. 2 Red-Figure Kalyx Krater by Euphronios: Death of Sarpedon
(Archaeological Museum of Cerveteri; 515 BCE)

Fig 3. Red-figure Kylix by Sosias Painter: Akhilleus Binding the Wound of Patroklos (AltesMuseum, Berlin; ca 500 BCE)

Fig. 4 Red-figure kylix by Penthesilea Painter: Akhilleus and Penthesilea (Munich Glyptothek; ca 470-460 BCE)

Fig. 5 Polyklitos: Doryphoros (ca 450-40 BCE; Roman copy)

Fig. 6 Praxiteles: Apollo Sauroktonos (ca 340-30 BCE; Roman copy)

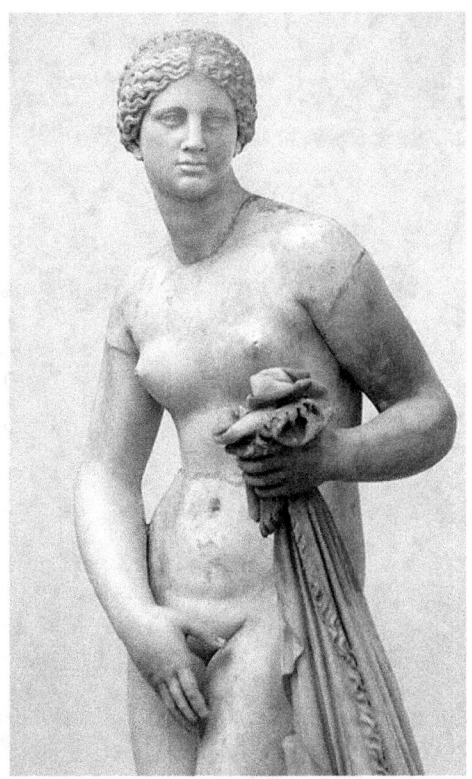

Fig. 7 Praxiteles: Knidian Aphrodite (ca 340-30 BCE; Roman copy)

Fig. 8 Augustus of Prima Porta (Vatican Museums; ca 20 BCE/15 CE)

Fig. 9 Laookon (Vatican Museums, ca 200-175 BCE))

Chapter Seven

Greek Epic Becomes Romanized: Vergil's *Aeneid*

There are many ways in which the Roman world, swallowing up the Hellenistic Greek world politically, began to be swallowed by it culturally. The political shift took place gradually, between 196 and 31 BCE—from the first time the Romans were invited to intervene and adjudicate among squabbling Hellenic *poleis* (after which first intervention, the Romans went back home; fifty years later they returned to perform the same task, but stayed to govern) to the absorption of the last Hellenistic state, Ptolemaic Egypt, into the Roman Imperium, with the defeat of its last Greek-descended ruler, Kleopatra VII and her Roman lover, Marcus Antonius, at the Battle of Actium.

In the course of that century and a half, the Romans were increasingly exposed to and interested in Greek art and literature. The outcome was that in some cases they imitated or simply copied it—literally: thus in the visual arts, works by Polyklitos, Praxiteles and many other Greek sculptors, as we have seen, yielded Roman versions (which in many cases remain the only extant versions of those originals). In others, they emulated but, adopting ideas, adapted them: this one sees, for instance, in the so-called *Capitoline Venus*, a variation on the *Knidian Aphrodite* of Praxiteles, and even more significantly in the *Augustus of Prima Porta* in its visual and conceptual relationship to the *Doryphoros*.

At times the Romans synthesized Greek with Italo-Etruscan ideas, as, for example in the architecture of their temples. Thus whereas Greek temples (like Greek statues) were typically intended to be visually and conceptually accessed from all directions—one might think, for instance, of the Parthenon in Athens, with columns all around it and resting on a low, multi-level platform with, in effect, "stairs" all the way around: there is no visual "front" but rather the edifice commands the space around it in all directions. By contrast, Italo-Etruscan temples were elevated on a distinct, high platform, accessed from a clear front—they command the space before them—by stairs leading up to a front porch held up by columns; there were no columns around the sides and back. Such temples also tended to be proportioned differently from their Greek counterparts: not nearly as long (deep) or as tall relative to their width as were Greek temples.

If one examines what is left of the Etruscan temple at Veii, one may certainly see this. And if, by comparison one looks at, say, the Roman (so-called) *Maison Carree* in Nimes, one can see how it has synthesized both sensibilities. It is raised on a platform with a set of front stairs leading to a front porch held up by columns. Like most Roman statuary, the building commands the space before it. But around the sides and back are embedded columns—pilasters—giving the illusion of being Greek-like with regard to the idea of columns all around; and its depth-to-width proportions are much closer to those of a Greek temple.

The Romans, however, innovated as well, particularly in architecture. Thus they developed the free-standing arch through their innovative use of the keystone, yielding dozens of them in and well beyond Rome. Such arches were typically decorated with imagery and inscriptions the purpose of which was to assert the Roman presence in a given location or the accomplishment of an individual—usually, an emperor, like Titus, Septimius Severus or Constantine (each of whom, not by coincidence, has an arch built and named for him in the heart of ancient Rome itself). But the Romans multiplied and piled up arches, in order to create structures like aqueducts, that could transport water over considerable distances from the mountains to some city. The most famous of these, the *Pont du Gard*, in what is now the south of France, carried water twelve miles from its source to the city of Nimes in a very carefully calibrated and graduated incline that both soared on its path over deep valleys and burrowed its way through hills that would otherwise have required problematic ascents and descents.[135]

The Romans also used the technology of piled-up arcades woven in curved formations to liberate the Greek Theater from being embedded as a half-moon in a hillside (although they continued to emulate that pattern for the production of both Greek and, eventually, Roman plays). Taking the theater out into the open and doubling it, thereby creating a free-standing elliptical configuration, they created amphitheaters (from the Greek root, *amph*, meaning "both" and the word theater, and thus meaning "both theater.")[136] Such a structure was designed for a different sort of entertainment: athletic competitions fought in pairs usually by prisoners of war and slaves, most often to the death—and also for animal fights, for humans hunting animals, as well as for the executions of prisoners—designed to entertain large audiences with diverse modes of blood-spilling in the course of a day.[137]

Arguably the most spectacular Roman transformation and innovation with regard to the arch was their success at three-dimensionalizing it in order to produce free-standing domes. The structure that most impressively demonstrates this is the Pantheon—the temple to all (*pan*) of the gods (*theon*)—which, in its present form was built under the Emperor Hadrian around 120 CE in the heart of the city. One can see, however, that more than a century earlier, the first version of this temple was built through the patronage of Agrippa—best friend, as far as we know, of Octavian/Augustus, the latter's eventual son-in-law, and the one who actually won the battle of Actium for Octavian in 31 BCE. For the dedicatory inscription may still be seen emblazoned (albeit the bronze outcropping letters are long gone) across the base of the triangular fronton that shapes the roof line of the front porch.

And here's the thing: what was done both for Agrippa and for Hadrian is clear. The earlier version had a front porch held up by Corinthian-capped columns (a Roman borrowing and continuation from the Greeks) accessed by a staircase; the porch gave entrance to the body of the temple, which no doubt continued its line back toward the rectilinear long-house form that, again, emulated the Greeks—and perhaps offered pilasters along the sides and back to further the illusion of being "Greek-like" while commanding the square before it, in the Italo-Etruscan style. We cannot be certain of the side and back pilasters, because that bodily structure no longer exists. Hadrian's architects presumably removed it, keeping the porch and appending to it a new body, an enormous one that is round, like the Roman amphitheaters were (but circular, not elliptical, unlike these other structures).

The interior offers a breath-taking dome, huge and perfectly circular, its apogee left open to the sky, creating an enormous eye—an *oculus*, in Roman/Latin terms. Not only have the Romans innovated in this free-standing domed structure (for there were rounded and beehive-shaped domes in earlier times and places, such as the tholos tombs at Mykenai dated to the time leading into the Trojan war (and the most famous of which is, in fact, traditionally associated with Agamemnon's family) or those in central Italy, at the Etruscan necropolis of Cerveteri. But those were all both smaller and, more importantly, built up within and supported by the earth around them. The pantheon was huge, with a perfectly shaped, free-standing sphere on the interior.

The pantheon's purpose was not merely to honor "all the gods." It sought to connect the Roman world to the world of the gods. As the eye of heaven (the sun) moved across the dome of the sky—the dome of the divine-governed macrocosmos—in the course of the day, its light would tumble through the *oculus* of the human-made microcosmos and work its way across the dome's interior. Indeed, that ceiling, sheathed in bronze, would surely scintillate with that light passing gradually across it. Moreover, as there were niches for statues of the Olympians around the lower periphery of the dome, the entire interior was constructed so that, from ground to *oculus*, a series of seven concentric circular levels carried the eye up to the top and/or down to the bottom. These represented the seven planetary divinities—an idea that the Romans learned from the Greeks who inherited it from earlier peoples: Egyptians, Mesopotamians, Persians and the like.[138]

In a nutshell, this amazing structure, sitting at the center of the city that was the center of the empire that had brought order—*kosmos*—to the known world was connected by the *oculus* and the light that comes through it to the greater *kosmos* and the gods associated with establishing and maintaining it—often with help from the sort of pious sacerdotal people that, as far as the Romans were concerned, defined them. For *pietas* was first and foremost, the attribute with which they identified, and identified their heroes. *Pietas* was defined by them as rendering to all the gods their due—not only to some, as poor Hippolytos had done, his failure to adore Aphrodite leading to his eventual demise in spite of his adulation of Artemis—but also properly honoring one's parents and ancestors, one's contemporaries, colleagues and friends, perhaps even enemies; and also one's children and heirs and descendants.

So where the Greeks obsessed about tragedy, irony and nobility within the human condition, the Romans, as much as they were also very interested in these ideas, placed greater emphasis on piety—and on *communitas* and that double system that ties a community together: *lex* ("law") and *religio* ("religion").[139] All of this leads to the question of the Roman relationship to Greece in the literary arts. If chronologically speaking this discussion should begin with the theater (since Plautus and Terence operate in the third and second pre-Christian centuries, respectively), there is a logic to coming to that subject last, as we shall see, and instead, we shall begin with epic poetry, following the Greek model of initiating its literary history with that style of poetry.

As far as the Romans were concerned, at any rate, the greatest literary achievements were those composed following the Greek model, formally speaking, of dactylic hexameter, and with it, heroic subject matter. However, the outcome was Roman in ideology and principles, not Greek. We see this most distinctly in the magnificent epic, the *Aeneid*, by Vergil. As a technical matter, whereas with the *Iliad* and the *Odyssey* we deal with two poems the authorship and precise dating of which offer several questions, in the case of the *Aeneid*, we are dealing with a definitive author not only whose precise dates of birth and death we know (70-19 BCE) but concerning whose process of shaping the epic we have some interesting details, to say nothing of being well aware of other works that he wrote and that have also survived—and earlier epic works by other that did not survive.[140]

The other Vergilian poems include a dozen short poems, the *Eclogues*—emulating and differing from a combination of earlier Greek lyric poetry and later Greek Hellenisitc pastoral poetry—and the *Georgics*: four medium-length works that focus on living and working in the countryside, parts of which bear a relationship to

Hesiod's *Works and Days*. So the principle of emulating but stepping in new directions vis-à-vis Greek models is apparent in these works as well as in the *Aeneid*. As for his epic masterpiece, it was supposedly composed in prose, first, and then converted into its poetic form, at the rate of two lines per day, over a period of twelve years. Vergil also apparently did not feel that it was completely done, since in his will he requested that the imperfect manuscript be destroyed.

Fortunately, his patron—none other than the Emperor Augustus (and one of Augustus' inner circle, the wealthy patron of poets, Maecenas)—refused that posthumous request, and so we possess it, albeit with a few issues here and there which may indeed reflect the not-quite finished status of the text at the time of the poet's death. One of the first things we might note about the poem is that the hero it features bears the epithet, *pius* ("pious"). This underscores both how that quality is so essential to Roman thinking and also how strikingly different Aeneas is intended to be, both in comparison with his primary Greek models, Akhilleus (whose epithet is "swift-footed") and Odysseus (whose epithets are "swift-witted" and "long-suffering")—and as a model for Vergil's #1 audience member: Augustus.[141]

As we shall see, the *pietas* exhibited by Aeneas has an additional nuance wrinkle in the context of Vergil's Augustan world view. As Cyril Bailey notes, "in its most fundamental manifestation, Aeneas' *pietas* lies not in his family relations, not in his conventional worship of individual gods, not even in his obedience to his divine mother, but rather in his whole-hearted acceptance of the position assigned to him as 'the man of destiny'."[142] The most obvious practical consequence of this is that we shall see in Aeneas a hero who tends much more to passivity than do Akhilleus and Odysseus: from the beginning of the poem, when he and his crew are being battered and tossed about by the stormy sea, through to the very end of the poem when his language distances him from his own hand as he slays Turnus, Aeneas most often responds to and is moved along by events rather than making them happen.[143]

The work is loosely structured as a combination of the two "Homeric" epics: in the first half of the *Aeneid* (the first six of twelve books in all), Aeneas wanders, battles storms, and has adventures most of which directly or indirectly recall the voyage and adventures of Odysseus. In the second half, battling in Italy to gain inhabitation rights on its central western shore, he and his fellow Trojans resemble, to an extent, the Akhaians at Troy—and he, therefore, Achilles—which offers its own appropriate irony, since that makes the native opposition to their settling there a conceptual echo of the Trojans at Troy, while the besiegers, actual Trojans, are, to repeat, a conceptual echo of the Akhaians. This is, however, one of the more brilliant things that Vergil does: he creates echoes that are oblique, not direct—even at times turned completely around from their Homeric models—as part of the strategy of creating an epic that is Roman and not merely parts of two Greek epics cobbled together and translated into the Latin language.

The *Aeneid* is rich in many ways, none more interesting than in the way it interweaves the concepts of *eris* and *eros*, virtually from the beginning of the poem. The very first verses suggest this, with Vergilian subtlety. The first words are *arma virumque cano*: "arms/weapons/war and the man I sing." The poet continues: (referring to that man) "...who first left the coast of Troy and came, as a refugee, to Italy and the Lavinian shore: *Laviniaque...litora*." Lavinian? Lavinia is the daughter of Latinus, king of the Latins whom Aeneas first approaches when he and his people first arrive on that Italian shore seeking hospitality—who doesn't merely accept the Trojans, but offers Lavinia as a wife to Aeneas (through which union part of the Roman future had already been predicted to Aeneas by his dead father, in their conversation in the underworld).

So "Lavinia" is, one might say, *eros* personified: she will be the *eros*-endpoint of the epic (the eventual union in fact not actually taking place until after the epic is done, but we finish the poem knowing that that marriage is now inevitable), but who arrives at the endpoint both through a protracted war—*eris* personified—into which Aeneas is forced by Turnus, the local prince who has been soliciting Lavinia's hand and who is stirred up to a violent defense of his prerogative by Aeneas' arch-enemy among the gods, Juno. Lavinia is the endpoint of many years of Trojan wandering that have been filled with strife at different levels—and strife—*arma*: "weapons"—is the poem's very first word. So we understand from the get-go that these two ideas, love and strife, will intertwine each other throughout the poem.

At the outset of its narrative we find Aeneas and his crew besieged by powerful winds and stormy weather, as he wonders and worries whether this is the end of the line for his fellow refugees and him. It turns out that the storm has been brought about by Juno—the queen of gods (Roman equivalent of Hera) who hates Aeneas because, like Athena/Minerva, she hates all Trojans ever since Paris/Alexandros chose neither of them as the most beautiful:

> ...deep in her heart
> Paris' decision rankled, and the wrong
> offered her slighted beauty; and the hatred
> of the whole race... (I: 39-41)

In her eristic frame of mind, Juno has induced the god of the winds, Aeolus, to blow the sea into a froth, hoping at least to bring intense discomfort to Aeneas, if not outright destruction. Aeneas moans in his storm-frozen desperation, refering back to one of the key eristic moments depicted in *Iliad* Book Two, when he fought one-on-one with Diomedes: why could he not have died then and there, in battle, rather than to be swallowed up by the sea? At that time, he was beaten by Diomedes, but rescued by Aphrodite. And here, too, the *eris* of Juno/Hera is counterbalanced by *eros*, which saves the hero.

First, Neptune (Poseidon), who has a particularly soft place in his heart for the goddess who was born of sea foam (*aphros*; see above, 20) arrives onto the scene and scolds the wind gods, sending them on their way, and bringing calm to the waters and succor to Aeneas. Next, Venus (Aphrodite)—the embodiment of love but more than that, as Aeneas' mother, mother-love personified, begs Jupiter (Zeus) to intervene to assure the success, and not merely the survival, of her son. The king of gods smiles—and previews briefly the history that will extend from Aeneas' soon-to-come arrival onto Italian soil and the rise of Rome to greatness—before sending Mercury (Hermes) down from Olympus to help prepare a hospitable welcome for Aeneas in the north African city of Carthage near where his ships will come to rest.

Here in Carthage the *eros-eris* plot will thicken with regard to both contemporary and, one might say, past and future contexts.

Within the contemporary context, Venus cons Juno into allowing a romance to develop between Aeneas and the Queen of Carthage, Dido. One might suggest that the moment of their first meeting is anticipated in a manner that would bring a smile to Freud's face: the concavely formed port in which those phallic ships arrive safely anticipates the port that Dido will offer on a more personal level to Aeneas.

The beginning of the process that will interweave *eros* and *eris* is the appearance of Aeneas before the Carthaginian queen—after he and Achates have noted how their own story is being carved on the walls of the temple being built to honor Juno, which reminds them and us that their *fama/kleos* already resonates world-wide—out of the mist in which Venus had enveloped him, and illumined "like a god, light radiant around his face and shoulders, and Venus also gave him the bloom of youth... Nobody saw him arriving until he spoke: 'here I am, whom you seek, Trojan Aeneas, saved from the Libyan waves... a remnant left by the Greeks, Dido'... And Dido marveled at his appearance, first, and all that trouble he had borne up under..." (I: 589-91; 594-6; 598; 613-14). We cannot miss the details that recall—and yet are different from—the account in the *Odyssey* of Odysseus arriving into the town and central palace of the Phaiakians concealed in a mist provided by Athene, and the nascent romantic thoughts toward him on behalf of Nausikaa by her father.

The culmination of this first contact is the glorious series of gifts that Aeneas gives Dido—including a golden, bejeweled crown—except that their history suggests a serious unhappy aspect to them that anticipates the tragic denouement of this initially promising relationship. For "the mantle stiff with figures worked in gold [and] the veil with gold acanthus running through it, once worn by Helen, when she sailed from Sparta toward that forbidden marriage... and the scepter that Ilione, Priam's eldest daughter, had carried once..." (I: 648-52; 653-4)—as magnificent as they must have looked, in reflecting on the diversely unhappy fates of these two women, they hardly seem designed by the poet to suggest that the Aeneas-Dido story is going to have a happy ending.

Nonetheless, the seeds of romance are being planted. And Vergil carefully articulates how perfect they are as a couple: both refugees, both widowed—he with a son and she desirous of children—she with a city and he desirous of one. All of this fuels the *eros* side of what will culminate with an *eristic* conclusion (so very different from that between Odysseus and Nausikaa). That beginning is, moreover, followed swiftly by the substitution of Cupid—Eros—himself, son of Venus, for Aeneas' son, Ascanius, at the dinner held on the first evening of the Trojans' arrival. It is a dinner at which the disguised divinity continues to shoot his arrows at the queen, who becomes increasingly smitten with the Trojan warrior who is her guest.

The eristic threads that interweave that evening are found in the narrative of the Trojan War offered by Aeneas in response to Dido's questions, as well as in the account of how Dido had arrived here in flight from Tyre, her husband Sychaeus having been murdered by her brother, Pygmalion (I; 340-56)—both of which events connect us to the past. On the other hand, some of the questions she asks him that evening ("How big was Achilles? And Diomedes: what were his horses like?" (I: 751-2)—the one who slew Hector and the other who defeated and nearly killed Aeneas himself)—and the sort of toast that she offers (to Bacchus, a god notorious for leading humans in dangerous directions when they consume too much of his liquid; I: 734); point toward the eventual unhappy—eristic—outcome of the romance. More than that, from the perspective of Vergil and his audience, it all points to the catastrophic relationship between the Roman and Carthaginian descendants of Aeneas and Dido who will fight three wars nearly a millennium after these events, in the two centuries before Vergil's birth, resulting in the destruction of Carthage. So the evening's festivities interweave past, present and future in its intertwining of *eros* and *eris*.

More specifically, as Book I yields to Book II, the story of the Trojan catastrophe is told, beginning with the story of the gigantic horse and the assistance to the Greeks (Akhaians) from Minerva (Pallas Athena, who, like Juno/Hera, hated the Tojans) in contriving a gigantic horse that could be misconstrued as an offering (by implication, to Neptune/Poseidon, god of the seas) for the Akhaians' (Greeks') safe return home.[144] That viewpoint was teased out in detail by Sinon in a lengthy, Odysseus-devised lie, and the most vocal in opposition to it was Laokoon—Neptune's priest. As Laokoon was making an offering at the altars devoted to that god, slaying a great bull,

> ...suddenly over the tranquil deep
> from Tenedos—I shudder even now,
> recalling it—there came a pair of serpents
> with monstrous coils, breasting the sea, and aiming
> together for the shore... [II: 203-5]

> ... they went on
> straight toward Laokoon, and first each serpent
> seized in its coils his two young sons, and fastened
> the fangs in those poor bodies. And the priest
> struggled to help them, weapons in his hand.
> They seized him, bound him with their mighty coils,
> twice around the waist, twice around the neck, they squeezed
> with scaly pressure, and still towered above him.
> Straining his hands to tear the knots apart,
> his chaplets stained with blood and black poison,
> he uttered horrible cries, not even human,
> more like the bellowing of a bull, when, wounded
> it flees the altar, shaking from the shoulder
> the ill-aimed axe... [II: 212-24]

Vergil fills his Latin verses with "s" sounds here, so that one can hear the hissing of those slithering monsters. And the priest of Neptune, sacrificing a massive bull to the god who sometimes assumes the form of a bull from the sea—and who loves the city of Troy—is sacrificed for the fulfillment of Troy's *moira*, attacked by serpents from Poseidon's own sea, and dies with his sons, bellowing as he is destroyed, like a sacrificial bull.

Aeneas tells how Cassandra, the prophet to whose words nobody hearkens, was dragged from the Temple of Pallas, and, in the midst of a broad description of the slaughter, spends a good many verses describing the vicious and impious behavior of Pyrrhus/Neoptolemus, son of Achilles who, recently arrived at Troy and untouched by the ten long years of siege and battle, revels— indeed, glories—in the destruction, slaying Priam himself as the aged king of Troy clings to the god's altar (II: 535-58). That description that concludes with the frightful image of Priam's headless, unidentifiable body lying on the shore somewhere, offers a particular, powerful contrast to the image of Aeneas, fighting and wishing to fight more, to his death, in defense of the doomed city, but not permitted to do so by his own *moira*, which directed him otherwise.

He seeks his father's house and his father within it, who is also preparing for his death. Along the way he sees Helen, cowering near the altar of the Vesta—an irony, for sure, as Aeneas himself notes it in the telling: she whom both Akhaians (Greeks) and Trojans were surely seeking out—the one group in vengeance and the other in anger—who might now go home to the comfort of Sparta, she who is the human equivalent of Venus, and whose beauty was the reward for Paris's erotic choice that led to all of this eristic violence. Aeneas' inclination to slay her is allayed by the sudden vision of his divine mother, telling him both to leave Helen to the gods and fate—pointing out, here and there, where gods are in fact arrayed against Troy at this point, not only Hera/Juno and Athena/Minerva, but even Zeus/Jupiter—and to think, if not of himself, then of his father and his son: in so many words, to think in *pius* terms and not self-centeredly (II: 589-623).

Indeed, it is in the midst of all this destruction that the enduring image of the hero as a man of *pietas* is articulated, for rather than stay and fight, he is visited suddenly by a vision instructing him to leave. It is that departure that marks him out for what he is in one concise image. For he is self-described by Vergil as leaving Troy with his father on his back, his son holding his hand (II: 705-11)—the *lares* and *penates* (household gods) in his father's hands (II: 717-20), at Aeneas' behest, since his own hands are polluted. Important, too, is the moment when, realizing that his wife, Creusa, is no longer with them, and he turns back to find her and encounters her ghost, already bound for the Other World. For she tells him that he must go on, and fulfill the fate that is both his personally and that of the community that he leads—the Trojan-that-will-eventuate-as-Roman community—that lies beyond the sea-voyage before him (775-91).

This moment with its snapshot of one of the often painful imperatives of *moira* will resonate later on, in the final, painful *agon* between Aeneas and Dido. For now, simply, the hero wept, as

> ...she left me,
> vanishing into empty air. Three times
> I reached out toward her, and three times her image
> fled like the breath of a wind or a dream on wings... (792-95)

—as Book II ends with the dramatic recounting of the destruction of Troy and Aeneas's god-and-fate-ordained flight from the burning city, leaving behind the ghost and the memory of his wife. The description of that last moment will have conjured, for the astute reader, the image of Odysseus in *Odyssey* 11, reaching out three times to embrace his mother's ghost, thus underscoring Vergil's genius at evoking his epic models in unusual and oblique and not only straightforward ways.

It also adds further poignancy to the way books three and four will unfold and unravel in turn: the young widower, leading his people from destruction to a divinely-guided but unclear future and the young widow, having led her people from disaster to a solid and clear present-future, are poised for an *eros*-centered meeting—but which will end in *eris*. In Book III Aeneas continues his narrative—and it seems that everywhere he stops, one or more of three events transpires. Either he finds the ghost of some dead, improperly buried Trojan, for whom *pius Aeneas* celebrates the proper rites; or he starts to build, as if thinking that *this* is the place for the future of his people—but soon a divinely-sent vision explains that this is not the place; or he encounters creatures and places like or unlike those that Odysseus encountered in his wanderings.

The experience with the Harpies is unique to Aeneas' voyage, for instance—after which he and his ships actually sail by Ithake, cursing Odysseus, who most singularly of the Akhaians turned these Trojans into refugees, and about whose current fate as a wandering refugee like them Aeneas and his crew know nothing. They spend time in Phaeacia—but of course Odysseus would not yet have arrived there, so the reference merely reminds the auditor/reader of different ways in which the paths of the two antithetical heroes unwittingly criss-cross. They encounter Andromache, widow of Hector, on land governed by the Trojan, Helenus, another of Priam's sons who managed to survive the debacle and now rules some Greek territory.

Andromache, it turns out, is now married to Helenus; she briefly tells the tale of her eristic marriage to Pyrrhus (Neoptolemus), son of Akhilleus, who ended up murdered at the altar of his ancestral home by none other than Orestes, maddened by the Furies—after having given her up to Helenus in boredom, in order to marry one of Leda's daughters.[145] So we are reminded of how the *eros-eris* knot within the Trojan War context remains tightly tied within the younger generation—and are perhaps struck by the irony that Andromache ends up married to one of Hector's brothers after having been married and borne children to the son of Hector's killer; and in turn of the double irony of that son's death: he who sacrilegiously slaughtered Priam at an altar is slain at an altar— by the son of the Agamemnon whom his own father, Akhilleus, once wanted to kill but who was later killed by his wife (Orestes' mother), who was a more renowned daughter of Leda than the one he married.

Helenus receives them warily, and here, too, they remain awhile, until Aeneas is reminded, by an oracle at the temple of Apollo, that he has much farther, still, to journey—to Italy's western coast, beyond Sicily; how he will encounter—and how to evade—Scylla and Charybdis; and how he must stop at Cumae, where the Sibyl will lead him to foreknowledge of his people's glorious future. Another poignant moment accompanies the time of departure, as Andromache, giving a scarf as a gift to Ascanius, notes how he reminds her of her own son—Astyanax, whom we all remember from the end of *Iliad* VI and who, still a small child, was slain by the Akhaians: "your face, your eyes, remind me of him so; he would be just your age..." (490-91).

They continue on past the east coast of Italy and Sicily, and do successfully avoid the double danger of Scylla and Charybdis (more successfully than Odysseus, who lost six men to the double monstrosity), arriving unwittingly onto the shores of the Cylopes. There they pick up a refugee—an Akhaian (Greek), Achaemenides—left behind, accidentally, by Odysseus, coming out of the woods, starving, and more than willing to be killed by them. But *pius Aeneas* takes him in, and he and his crew get away with only an observation of, rather than a confrontation with, the blinded Polyphemus, stumbling around with a tree trunk as a staff (and again, Vergil's Latin text offers phonemes that underscore the clumping cadence of the monster's footsteps). They pass Ortygia—an island off the coast of Sicily, associated with the nymph, Arethusa (and later, Syracuse). And in Derpanum, the hero's father, Anchises, who has been Aeneas' frequent and most important advisor along the journey, dies—bringing Book III to an end, in a manner analogous in its sense of loss and loneliness to the mood with which the previous book had ended.

What more effective combination—heroism together with loss and loneliness, to go with his rugged good looks and a clearly reported capacity to care for others—could there be to draw the Carthaginian queen in toward desiring a relationship with him (even *without* the conspiring roles of Venus and Juno by way of Eros/Cupid)? And indeed, Dido is increasingly inflamed and disturbed, as Book IV opens, by the thought that anyone could make her forget her much-beloved and long-lamented dead husband, Sychaeus, even for a moment. Her sister advises her not to fight against a pleasing passion—for the gods must have willed it so, and even Juno has helped to bring the Trojan ships to Carthage. She echoes what Venus had suggested to Juno, in fact, two books earlier: that together, an even greater, more glorious city could result from a union between these two peoples and their leaders than what might eventuate from Dido's efforts alone.

Book IV is both the heart of the *Aeneid* with regard to *eros* and the foundation stone for the history-long stretch in which *eros* becomes *eris* that will carry to the end of the poem and, by implication, continue for more than nine hundred years beyond the actions of its divine and human characters. The love-relationship between Dido and Aeneas develops quickly—but the crescendoing prelude to it offers a theme that, as we shall see subsequently, is common in Roman poetry, more so than for the Greeks: the negative, destructive power of love (or at least of lust, since lust and love are not distinguished with any clarity). Thus in the early continuing infatuation with Aeneas, Dido takes him all around the city-in-process to show him its ambitions, by day, and in the evening, feasting, continues to drink in his stories, becoming increasingly smitten. But the culmination of this incipient phase of the romance, the poet intones, is that

> the towers no longer rise, the youth are slack
> in drill for arms, the cranes and derricks rusting,
> walls halt halfway to heaven… (86-9)

The relationship seems to be destroying the ambition necessary for creating the magnificent future toward which both Dido and Aeneas wish to lay claim, for the queen, alone in her bed at night, languishes with ever-accumulating and unfulfilled *need*. Juno becomes aware that Dido is "held by this disease, this passion that makes her good name (*fama*) meaningless" (90-1). She rushes, all riled up, to Venus—but proposes, in a clear demonstration of the limits of divine foreknowledge, that they facilitate the furthering of a formal finalization of the Dido-Aeneas liaison, yielding a Tyrian-Trojan bond of peace and love. Her idea is that this will cure Dido of the fever of her unfulfilled desire and allow her to return to the broader national ambitions that the goddess wants to see fulfilled. Juno is willing to abandon her hatred of Aeneas and all Trojan refugees in favor of what she deludes herself into imagining: a happier future for Dido and her heirs than Fate or Jupiter have planned.

There is irony, to be sure, that the Queen of Heaven, who feels such eristic hate toward Aeneas and love toward Dido is the one who directly shapes the short-term success of their *eros*-relationship (it's the kind of plan one might have expected, instead, from Venus, as goddess of love) that will lead to long-term *eris* and for Dido, disaster—while yielding for Aeneas another piece in the puzzle of his own ultimate success. Not surprisingly, "Venus assented, not ungraciously" (127-8), aware that Juno thinks that she is winning by short-stopping the Italy-directed plans of Fate and Jupiter for Aeneas, but confident that her fellow goddess is merely effecting a short delay in the inevitable future domination of North Africa by Italy—of Carthage by Rome.

The following morning, Juno's misguided plan goes into effect. They all go out hunting when she provokes an enormous thunderstorm, sending the group in sudden search for shelter. Dido and Aeneas, by divine design, end up in the same cave, separated from everyone else,

where primal Earth and Juno, as bridesmaids, give the signal,
and the mountain nymphs wail high their incantations —
first day of death, first cause of evil. Dido
is unconcerned with name (*fama*), with how
how it seems to others (*specie*). This she calls marriage
and not some secret love; she covers
her folly with that name... (166-72)

The poet, for the second time, more emphatically, warns the reader that this moment of passion will lead to catastrophe. Rumor flies far and wide, at breakneck speed, that these two have become a couple.[146]

The immediate consequence of this is that the neighboring king, Iarbas, whose eager hand in marriage Dido had refused, comes running — to the temple of Jupiter — in anger: "She rejected me as a husband, but takes Aeneas to be her lord and master... that second Paris... his chin tied up in ribbons, with millinery on his perfumed tresses, takes over what he stole..." (211-17). Aside from the fact that the *eros*-bound relationship that has flourished between Dido and Aeneas almost instantaneously begets an eristic consequence, Vergil couches that *eris* very cleverly in familiar, Trojan War terms. Iarbas has the temerity to equate his position vis-à-vis Dido to that of Menelaus vis-à-vis Helen in order to justify his equation: that once again a Trojan — a perfumed, fancy-dressed Trojan whose rugged masculinity is mocked — has absconded with the "wife" of a straightforward, trusting, and very rugged, masculine "husband." North Africa is Achaean (Greek) Sparta in this equation — but the outcome of this story will be radically different from that of Helen, Menelaus and Paris! (On the contrary, of course: Troy — or its Roman descendants — will end up conquering and/or destroying all of North Africa).

Dido is hardly Helen; she is not the wife of Iarbas, except in his domineering male mind; on the contrary, she is the one who spurned his request for marriage. Aeneas, although a Trojan like Paris — who has Aphrodite/Venus as a powerful divine ally (but as mother, not as the grateful winner of a beauty contest) — is hardly the impious wife-stealer that his fellow Trojan was. Much less is he the unrugged fighter, Paris, for whose actions others — including

Aeneas—ended up having to shoulder the responsibility. So Iarbas' confusion between having been spurned by Dido and Menelaus' having been betrayed by Helen is a significant one: they share certain qualities of interweaving *eris* and *eros*, but his equation is off.

Most profoundly for Vergil's audience, Paris' abduction of Helen will result in a war that yields the eventual return of Helen to Menelaos, and the destruction of Paris' own city, whereas Aeneas' affair with Dido will lead in a very different direction: the destruction of Dido and three wars, many centuries later, between her descendants and those of Aeneas, that will result in the destruction of the great city she is building, the unequivocal domination of the Western Mediterranean by the city founded by Aeneas' descendants—and the only role that Iarbas will play in either catastrophe is that his anonymous descendants will be part of the territory that Rome swallows up by means of the Punic Wars.

Nonetheless, in the very short term it might appear that the neighboring king's plaint will yield an outcome that is at least satisfactory to him, for Jupiter hears that plaint and immediately summons Mercury, the Olympian messenger, and instructs him to swoop down to Carthage—"to Libya's sandy shore...[where he] sees Aeneas founding towers, building homes for Tyrians..." (257, 260-1)—to instruct Aeneas in no uncertain terms that it is time for him to move on. So the field will, in theory, be clear for Iarbas to gain (not re-gain, since he never had her in the first place) Dido. Again, though, either demonstrating divine ignorance, or perhaps simply due to the divine decision to respond to Iarbas less because of Iarbas than because of the Aenean fate of which the god does have knowledge—and in the end without Iarbas' impossible desires being fulfilled, really—the outcome, rather quickly, takes its own unhappy shape.

Mercury hurries down from above, where he sees Aeneas building new houses—for Carthaginians—which is what he does best, but again he is building in the wrong place, not the one marked out for him by fate. We not only recognize the irony of this misdirected urge to shape a new home. In the arc of the Dido-Aeneas subset tale within the longer narrative, as Aeneas arrived and observed from his invisibility cloud how the Carthaginians were building—noting specifically his own exploits on their temple walls—the situation's crisis crescendo was subsequently articulated by the poet as Dido's ceasing to build as she languished in unfulfilled passion for the Trojan hero. Now they are building again, and it is the Trojan object of that now-fulfilled passion who is shown taking the lead in supervising the building process. Yet that process moves forward at the expense of the Trojan future that is *supposed* to be progressing—but now with a divine intervention impelled by Iarbas, Dido will end up paying the bill for that expense, and Aeneas will simply continue his journey. Mercury barely pauses for breath and delivers Jupiter's message:

> …What are you doing,
> forgetful of your kingdom and your affairs,
> building for Carthage—for a woman?!
> The ruler of the gods, through whom turn
> the heavens and earth, has sent me from Olympus
> through the air with these words: what are you doing,
> with what ambition wasting time in Libya?
> If your own fame (*gloria*) and affairs count as nothing,
> nor do you think of the praiseworthiness of your own labors,
> consider Ascanius at least, whose kingdom
> in Italy, and whose Roman land, are waiting,
> owed to him! (265-76)

This is the first explicit mention of Rome itself. The ever-pious Aeneas, ever-respectful of the gods and fate—and in this case, of his son's future and that of his descendants—nonetheless always requires reminders to keep moving forward toward his ultimate goal. He is always, (to repeat), impelled by others rather than asserting his own initiative—from the departure from Troy to the stops and continuations along the way to Carthage, to the romance that unfolded with Dido, to the present new crisis (how to tell Dido that he must leave?). Terrified at the knuckle-slapping reminder from Mercury, he is quick to respond but not certain how to do so. He decides that the smartest course is simply to do it quietly and without warning the queen, so he instructs his now-joyous crew to ready everything for a swift departure.

It is not, as it turns out, so easily accomplished. The problem, of course, is what to say to unsuspecting Dido, so wrapped up in love for Aeneas—and, for that matter, for the Ascanius who is the most direct reason for the impending departure of the Trojans. Yet Rumor quickly flies through the city, and in any case, Dido's female sixth sense alerts her that something radical has changed and so, raging through the city like a crazed Maenad (300-303)—we may recall how twice before she had toasted Bacchus; now she is drunk, but on grief and anger and *eris*, not on wine and simple *eros*—she confronts Aeneas, pointing out the depths of his betrayal, who plans to leave, now, during the stormy winter season, no less. The argument and his response is the great, painful *agon* that one could easily imagine on a stage, cried out before a large audience. And while it bears formal comparison most obviously to that between Medea and Jason[147]—a hero become betrayer of his wife and accused by her—everything is not only substantively and tonally different, beginning with the fact that here the hero is leaving the woman behind and not sending the woman away (and there is no younger woman here, only a young son and the Roman future that is causing him to leave).

She argues that "our love (*amor*, which = Greek *eros*; it is also an anagram for *Roma*) means nothing to you, our exchange of vows (*data dextera*: "our right hands given"), and even the death to come of Dido could not hold you?" (307-8). (He does not even notice that hint of her immanent self-administered demise—or maybe he doesn't take the assertion seriously). She notes the odd season for his departure—and thus how desperate he must be to get away—and, again referencing the "beginnings of marriage, wedlock" (316) and how, on account of him, "I am hated by Libyans and Numidian kings and Tyrians alike; on account of you I am shamed, my honor, once high as the stars, is gone" (320-3). And where can she turn now: wait for her brother to come from Tyre to destroy her? Get carried away by Iarbas as a captive? Had he at least hung around long enough to leave her with a son, a little Aeneas, the whole thing might seem less dismal (325-30).

Her arguments do not fall on deaf ears, but on ears that, one might say, do not belong to Aeneas as an individual with his own desires and hopes, but to *pius* Aeneas whose *pietas* obligates him first to many others. And that is, in a nutshell, his counter-argument in this *agon*. He offers that he "will not regret remembering Elyssa, as long as there is breath in my body" (335-6). He calls her by her Tyrian name, Elyssa, rather than Dido, in this rather strange way of putting his future memory of her. On the one hand he asserts that he never claimed to be a husband, having taken no such vows (338-9)—technically true, as Vergil had warned us back on that stormy afternoon in the cave, although then and now it might seem strange to some to consider human-made marriage rules more important than those shaped by goddesses. To some the argument might recall the *agon* between Kreon and Antigone that hinged on the distinction between man-made and god/nature-made laws. On the other hand—and this is really the heart of his argument and the heart of the epic's story—

> ...If I had fate's permission
> to live my life my way, to settle my troubles
> at my own will, I would be watching over
> the city of Troy, and caring for my people,
> those who remained alive, and Priam's palace
> would still be standing; for the vanquished people
> I would have built the town again. But now
> it is great Italy that I must seek, Apollo's orders,
> to Italy the oracles call me.
> There is my love (*amor*), there is my fatherland... (340-7)
>
> I see my father, Anchises, or his ghost,
> who warns me in my sleep, and I am frightened;
> I am troubled for the wrong I do my son,
> cheating him of his kingdom in the west,
> and lands that Fate assigns him... (351-5)
> ...I saw the god [Mercury] myself, in full daylight,
> enter these walls, I heard the [warning] words he brought me.
> Cease to inflame us both with your complaints;
> I follow to Italy not because I want to. (358-61)

The passionate *eros* become *eris* drives the queen's words forward: "No goddess was your mother, no Dardanus the founder of your tribe! Liar!" (365-6) And she turns, really, from even addressing him directly, but more toward the gods—or to an imagined audience, such as we readers are—to recall how the gods fail to look at this and to operate with justice; and how she took Aeneas in, an outcast, a beggar, and rescued his fleet (373-5). She turns to him again and simply tells him, then "Go! Follow Italy on the wind and seek the kingdom across the water" (381), but "I hope for vengeance; I hope to hear you calling the name of Dido, over and over, in vain. Oh, I shall follow in blackest fire, and when cold death has taken the spirit from my body, I shall be there to haunt you, a shade, in every place" (382-6). Again she anticipates her own soon-to-come death, and again that idea passes over him unnoticed.

Aeneas is, nonetheless, stunned, and stammers, seeking an answer; *pius Aeneas* (as Vergil specifically refers to him once more) is "longing to ease her grief with comfort, to say something to turn her pain away, moved deeply by this great love (*amor*) (393-4)—but there is nothing he can say, and in any case, the gods command and he obeys them.

The *agon* has ended, the verbal *eris* contending with the still-present emotional *eros* has led back to where the argument began. Dido is distraught, Aeneas is gods-impelled to move forward regardless of his personal feelings. There are perhaps subtle elements that some members of the Roman audience would have noted. Whereas Dido had, during that first, fateful evening of feasting, asked some indiscreet questions, Aeneas is discreet to a fault: when he talks about the "what ifs" regarding staying and rebuilding Troy rather than setting out at the command of the gods and fate, he doesn't mention his wife, with whom presumably he would be enjoying that Trojan renaissance had he been able to control any element of his fate. That subtle discretion would have tag-teamed with the more overt distinction between the Dido-Aeneas romance and a real marriage—and between what is permissible to a swashbuckling heroic male and a female, even a people-leading and city-building queen.

The most obvious Homeric models would seem to be an oblique combination of Odysseus' relationships with Kirke and Kalypso. In both cases the hero stayed and moved on. In both cases, it was Odysseus, out of his own, self-focused needs, and not, per se, those of fate, who wished to leave—and in both cases, the one he left was a goddess, who could herself move on, and even help the hero move forward. Very different conditions from those for Aeneas, impelled to move on by forces beyond himself, and leaving a grief-struck and humiliated mortal woman behind, in order to come home not to his wife but to his new land. Vergil, as so often, uses little details, embedded within the big ones: it was really Odysseus' crew who demanded, after a year of his carousing with Kirke, that they continue their journey—analogous but not identical in detail to the enthusiasm shown by Aeneas' crew when he informs them that they are going to move on, as if they have been awaiting this moment eagerly.

Kirke's response is not eristic in the least, but rather offers Odysseus—aside from a terrific farewell party—direct advice on what he must do next and how to do it, in order to complete his voyage as it should be completed. It is rather Kalypso who is—a bit—upset when Hermes comes from Olympos to tell her that she must allow Odysseus (after seven years of cavorting with the goddess, and after having rejected an offer from her for him to become an immortal) to move on, so that her response is somewhat closer to that of Dido vis-à-vis Aeneas. But in the end Kalypso helps the hero on his way.

The end of Book IV will further the separation between this narrative and either of those within the *Odyssey*. She is still driven by love (*Amor*; 412) and—coming full circle to where this romance began with her confiding in her sister, she begs Anna to beg him at least to wait a bit, for better weather, to depart (424-36). But torn by the cries of his crew and his obligation to his people in contention with that toward his lover, he will not—cannot—delay. No last-night love-making as Odysseus had had with his goddess lovers. At last, in desperate straits, Dido instructs her loving sister to build a pyre in the palace courtyard, on which a bridal bed, together with Aeneas' armor (the bed of *eros* and the garments of *eris*) will be burned, following a prescription she alleges comes from a priestess from far-off Ethiopia—the purpose of which is to win back the heart of one whose heart has been lost, or assist the one who still loves to let go of that love. The queen stands with offerings at the altar, she suffers through the long night, playing over and over again her non-options ("go back to my Numidian suitors? Be scorned by those I scorned? Pursue the Trojans? Obey their orders?" 534-8).

Meanwhile Aeneas is sleeping soundly in the stern of his ship, everything having been prepared for the impending voyage—until once more, Mercury appears to him and warns him to get up and get going:

> this is no time for sleep! The wind blows fair
> and danger rises around you. Dido,
> certain to die, however else uncertain,
> plots treachery, harbors evil...
> get going without delay! Shifty and fickle always
> is woman. (560-4, 569-70)

Irony again—although I doubt that Vergil thought of this as ironic—for who proved shifty and fickle in this relationship, Dido or Aeneas? Even if we blame it on Fate or the gods, that inconstant quality came from the man and not the woman. Indeed, when dawn comes, and Dido realizes that Aeneas' ships are gone—the poet's image is strong with the queen's seeing that once-swarming, now-empty harbor that resonates with the once-full and now-empty bridal bed (that rests, waiting, on the unkindled pyre). She cries out for his perfidy: he who, she notes, carries with him now the *penates* as he once carried on his shoulders his aged father, yet who had given her his right hand (*dextra*) in faith (*fides*) that proved so false (597-9)—whom once perhaps she might have had at her mercy and torn to pieces, she now curses.

It is a lengthy curse, somewhat reminiscent of that from Polyphemos to his father, Poseidon, regarding Odysseus: that his journey be as painful as possible, since it seems that Jupiter ordains that it will be completed. The most significant part of it, because of the irony built into it, is her cry that the

> Tyrians, hate, now and forever
> the Trojan stock. Offer to my dust this funerary gift.
> No love (*amor*), no peace, between these peoples, ever! (622-4)

For this is the part of her prayerful curse that the gods and Fate will hear and bring to fruition—enmity for as long as Carthage shall exist—but not with the outcome that Dido would have wished. The end of the enmity will be the end of Carthage, as Aeneas' descendant Romans are not even to the midpoint of their imperial expansion in time and space by the end of the third Punic War.

This extraordinary tale within the tale of the *Aeneid*—love and strife interwoven with personal and communal obligations; with individual and national hopes, desires and aspirations; and with different modes of irony; reaches its tragic climax after this, Dido's last speech, as she ascends the still-unlit pyre and stabs herself with a sword that had not so long ago been a gift from Aeneas—an eristic instrument (an instrument that could hardly be more phallic) as a gift of *eros* is now used when that love has gone awry for a self-administered death (an act at once eristic and *eros*-bound). The servants are there, but see what is happening too late to stop it, a cry roars through the house, her loving sister comes running, rushes up the pyre steps to hold her dying sister in her arms—trying to staunch the flow of blood to no avail.

Sisterly love cannot save Dido, although her death is slow—three times she tries to raise herself up—until Juno takes pity on her pain and sends Iris down from Olympus to lead her soul away. The poet notes how Iris' intervention was needed since Dido died before her time, driven to her death by madness (*furor*). That detail, as we shall shortly see, offers another delicate thread scintillating from the Greek tradition woven so adeptly within Vergil's Roman fabric. For Aias was the only significant Akhaian to die at his own hand—after having been driven temporarily mad by Athena.[148] When Aeneas journeys to the Underworld, in Vergil's expansion of the analogous experience of Odysseus, Dido, in her response to Aeneas, echoes Aias in his response to Odysseus—as we shall see.

But meanwhile, Book V opens up with an Aeneas unaware of any of this, and his fleet sailing smoothly across the sea. Indeed, he looks back—we might suppose, with more longing than Vergil asserts for him—toward the walls of Carthage, glowing in the flames, although he does not know it, of Dido's funeral pyre. Indeed "what cause had kindled so high a blaze, they [the Trojans, who certainly recognized the flickering reds along those walls as derived from fire, and certainly saw the smoke rising up to heaven] did not know," yet had some foreboding as to what it might be, given "the way of a woman with frenzy in her heart" (4-7). But they sail on—we might imagine them sailing rather silently, even brooding, each enveloped in his (and her?) own thoughts—as the skies gradually begin to darken and Aeneas suggests that they not attempt a crossing all the way to Italy just now, but rather take harbor in a place not far—Sicily—where his friend, King Acestes, son of a Trojan mother and Crinisus, a river-god, rules.

Acestes, watching from a hilltop, sees the ships approaching and recognizing them as friendly, comes down to greet them warmly. They have barely landed and Aeneas calls his people together to announce that, since a year has passed since his father's death and burial here in Sicily, it is time to do what they could not do at that time: celebrate him and complete what amounts to a ritual to help accompany the soul of the deceased to its proper place in the Underworld. So nine days from their arrival they will engage in the sort of funeral games that we recall organized by Akhilleus for Patroklos in Book Twenty-Three of the *Iliad*, albeit with some variations—of course, we should expect nothing less from Vergil— between the sorts of competitions in the two poems. These will be a ship-race, rather than a chariot-race—logically, since they have ships but no chariots under the present circumstances—a foot-race, a javelin-throw or archery, and a boxing match with rawhide gloves (45-71).

There are four particularly interesting elements, for our purposes, in the games that take place. One, that Aeneas' role as disengaged and friendly-to-all master of ceremonies, in emulating Akhilleus in the *Iliad*, reminds us of how Aeneas-like Akhilleus had become by that point in the Homeric narrative and might cause us to wonder whether Aeneas could ever be Akhilleus-like—showing the kind of *menis/furor* that defined the Akhaian hero throughout most of the *Iliad*. This issue will have important implications later on, as we shall see. Two, as in the *Iliad*, the gods are involved, but far less directly and overwhelmingly—the opposite of what we might have expected in shifting from a Greek to a Roman context—again reminding us of how Vergil handles his literary models obliquely rather than directly, most of the time.

Three—perhaps symptomatic of the not-quite-finished, not finally proofread nature of the poem—that when the competitions take place, boxing precedes the archery contest (there is no javelin-throwing contest). This, however, allows King Acestes to have the last competitive word, as his arrow soars into the heavens and takes flame (519-28). Fourth, and completely different from the games in the *Iliad*: when these competitions are finished, Aeneas calls upon his son and the other young lads to come out in full—miniature—battle regalia, on horseback, and, breaking up into three squadrons, fight a mock battle, weaving in and out of each other in well-calibrated patterns (545-95).

This last component of the funeral games for Anchises offers at least three features that either underscore how the past and the future are held together by the present moment or further restate ironies that have accompanied the *eros-eris* theme since the arrival of Aeneas into Carthage. Thus the procession and performance of the youngsters led by Ascanius emphasizes the focus on the future that has led Aeneas from Troy in the first place and, most obviously and directly, from Carthage a brief while ago. For in the end, this story about Aeneas is less about Aeneas than about the future of his Roman descendants.

Moreover, that future is built on important connections to the past—these games are, after all, in honor of the memory of Aeneas' father—and so the observation by the poet that the idea of the youth engaging in mock-battles derives from a custom practiced at Troy that Aeneas remembers from childhood underscores that connection to the past. And the further statement that Ascanius would later establish this custom at Alba Longa, whose descendants at Rome would in turn continue to keep this ancestral rite, still further underscores that *pius* past-future relationship (596-603). Every Roman reader would recognize this particular activity as part of a larger, more general interest in being always concerned about *mos maiorum*: precedents in law and custom that are understood to be derived from and based on "the custom (*mos*) of our ancestors (*maiorum*)."

This past-future element, is most obviously enveloped in irony through the description of Ascanius as the most handsome of all the boys, astride a Carthaginian steed that had been a gift from

Dido (570-2). We are reminded suddenly both of her and perhaps of the dire Carthaginian future at the hands of the Roman descendants of Aeneas and his people—and perhaps also reminded that Aeneas and his people are so fully pre-occupied with the present rites and games that they have all but forgotten about Dido and her people (both the *eros* part and the *eris* part of that intersection with her life and their lives), and are still unaware of her demise. In Aeneas' case, he has been transformed in this first part of Book V from the passionate lover—think *menis/furor* with regard to love, rather than war—into the one who calmly and lovingly remembers his father and plays his role as father of Ascanius and also father of his people—he is referred to when he sends for Iulus, (545), as *pater Aeneas* ("father Aeneas")—analogous to (but different from) the Akhilleus who was becoming transformed from the man of *menis/furor* directed against Agamemnon, Hektor, and himself into the one who calmly and lovingly remembers his best friend and plays his role as father of the Akhaians in their funeral games. For both heroes, this will prove to be a lull before they return to the battlefield, the one at Troy (where he will die while achieving undying glory) and the other in Italy (where he will live and lay the foundations of the future greatness and undying glory that define Vergil's Rome).

Indeed, in the midst of this feast celebrating son-father and father-son love, strife arrives, in the form of the goddess Iris, goddess of the rainbow—but also Juno's usual personal messenger, as Jupiter usually sends Mercury--dispatched by the ever Aeneas-hating queen of heaven. Disguising herself as an old woman, Iris talks the other older women into setting fire to the Trojan ships, so that they can go no further—this is when we first find out that they have been actually travelling for seven years up to this point—in an attempt, once more, to prevent Aeneas' arrival onto the western coast of Italy. The discussion about whether or not to set fire to them evokes the discussion regarding the Akhaian-built wooden horse—and as with that disastrous denouement, the old women end up kindling the ships in a terrified frenzy that is virtually maenad-like in its intensity (620-63).

Appropriately enough, given the future emphasis that is accelerating throughout this book, Ascanius is the first on the scene to try to calm the old women and to quench the flames (667-74). But ultimately it is Aeneas who, praying to Jove, receives the immediate divine response in the form of the cloudburst that saves all but four of the ships (685-99). A worried but wise Aeneas makes a decision, in consultation with Acestes: that those too tired to continue the journey to Italy may stay behind in Sicily, to build a city here—and honor Acestes by calling it Acesta—and the rest will go forward with Aeneas. That decision was forged, moreover, through a dream at night experienced by Aeneas, in which his loving father, Anchises, speaks to him, suggesting this plan of division, and invites him, along the way, before they arrive at Latium, to visit him, first, in the Underworld—with instructions as to how to accomplish that visit. Those instructions recall Kirke's instructions to Odysseus, albeit, as we shall see, different, of course (721-40).

As nine days preceded the funeral games, now nine days follow between this vision and the departure from Sicily. These are nine days filled with farewell feasting—again reminiscent, in its way, of the night-long farewell feast accorded to Odysseus and his crew by Kirke before their departure and journey to the *profanus-sacer* edge of reality. And again, Aeneas' experience may be said to outpace that of Odysseus—one night versus nine days—and take things in a different, more familial and communally-focused direction. Both the feasting and the immediate pit-stop after they leave Kirke's island are Odysseocentric (a last night of love-making with the goddess and a journey to find out his own fate and future)—but Aeneas' instructions come from his loving father and the emphasis regarding the feasting is that, for the last time they are all one whole tribe: *gens omnis* (762).

Meanwhile—balancing the father-love that has set Aeneas in this last pre-Latium part of his journey—the hero's mother, Venus, worried that Juno may once more intervene to harm her son, comes to Neptune to assure that the Trojan ships have smooth sailing. This is the moment when Neptune's particular affection for Venus (and the reason for it) is stated explicitly, for he responds to her plaint beginning with the statement that "nobody has a better right to trust my kingdom than the goddess born near Cythera of sea-foam" (800-1). And he assures her that Aeneas will be under his protection and will reach Avernus (the point of entry into the Underworld) safely—albeit "one [individual] must be lost in the waters, one soul alone shall be given for the many" (814-15).

We note two obvious issues of interest: first, that the Poseidon who was Odysseus' enemy is Aeneas' friend—in spite of retaining a residual anger against the Trojans, who, he claims, in passing, betrayed him, which is why he helped destroy the walls he raised (810-11; this is the only justification we ever receive regarding Poseidon's role in Troy's destruction, (other than the assumption we might make that he had had to bow to fate, as all the gods ultimately do). This brings Vergil's oblique handling of his Homeric sources to another level (or back to where we first saw it in Book I).

The other issue of note is that, in the demand for a single human sacrifice, there is no real explanation of why Neptune insists on this—except that it will provide another oblique counterpart to an analogous event in the *Odyssey*. That is: Elpenor fell from the roof on the dawn of the departure from Kirke's home, broke his neck, died, and remained unburied—until Odysseus, having encountered his soul at the entrance to Hades, stopped back at Kirke's island to bury his crewman before moving on. And here, Palinurus, Aeneas' helmsman, will be forced into sleep by the god of sleep, who will then push him into the water, out of the hearing of his fellows. But the book ends with Aeneas starting up from sleep, somehow suddenly aware that there is nobody at the helm of the ship, and he realizes that Palinurus has fallen into the sea, and mourns for the friend who will be lying somwhere unburied on an unknown shore (870-71).

In the end, regardless of the reasons for this relatively gentle divine eristic act, the death of Palinurus is construed as a sacrifice by Neptune—of an individual on behalf of the community—which is the mood of Aeneas' epic journey within the epic journey that fills Book VI and pushes the Odyssean envelope from the edge of Hades into its depths. There Aeneas will learn less about himself than about the future of his people. Book VI in fact begins with Aeneas mourning Palinurus as he leads his small fleet up the coast toward Cumae and the grove of Diana, sister of Apollo, in the cave below whose temple the Sibyl dwells. It is she who will guide the Trojan hero into the Underworld by way of one of the hundred portals into the vast rock, facilitated, as she cries out in reminder and warning to him, by his fervent prayers. These are repeated by the poet, the central element of which is to bring his Trojan refugee community safely to Latium, where they can at last rest, and where he will build a great temple in honor of both Apollo and Diana.

Vergil offers a lengthy description of the Sibyl's wrestling in in-spiritation from and with the god—an altogether different angle from which to consider the tight interweave of *eros* and *eris*, as she rages fiercely and lovingly toward, against, beneath Apollo (98-101). The Sibyl warns Aeneas that getting down into that other world—the *sacer*—is not that difficult; it is getting back out that is the real challenge. Only a few have managed—have managed to be favored by Jupiter to do so (and while she doesn't mention anyone in particular, surely Vergil's audience, with its awareness of the Greek religious/literary tradition, would have thought of the difficulty that the hero Theseus, slayer of the Minotaur in its labyrinth, had in doing so; and how Herakles managed to do so (twice: once to rescue Theseus, in fact, and once to bring back Alkestis); and how Orpheus managed to do so, but lost his beloved Eurydike in the process and with her, his mind and shortly thereafter his life—all of whom, together with Pollux, brother of Castor, Aeneas has in fact mentioned in his plea to be allowed merely to *enter* the dark realm (119-23). Such thoughts would have expanded significantly the audience's perception of Aeneas' journey into Avernus as heroic, in general and in comparison with Odysseus' more limited journey to the mere edge of that *sacer* reality.

The Sibyl instructs him (a little bit of Kirke in her, then) that he must pluck a golden bough, sacred to Proserpine, in a sacred grove that protects it; only if Fate is willing will he (or anyone) be able to pluck that bough to bring as a gift to Proserpine, Queen of the Underworld, and thereby receive permission to come into and return back from Hades (142-8). She also tells him that one of his men—would this be Palinurus?—lies on the shore, unburied and thus a pollution to his entire fleet; that he must find and bury him with honor and offer black cattle slain in expiation for him before he can enter the Stygian kingdom (149-54). So: a further double twist that carries the Aeneas story beyond its Odyssean model with regard to this part of the adventure: he must perform this burial before he enters the Stygian-path cave again; and there will, in the end, be two unburied comrades (for it turns out that the referenced unburied man is *not* Palinurus) with whose funerary rites he will need to deal.

He returns out of the cave and confers with his comrade, Achates—and it turns out to be Misenus who is lying on the beach unburied and unmourned. He, a beloved trumpeter whose sounds would inspire men for battle—and a first-rate warrior with a spear, as well, who had once been Hektor's man-at-arms and then, after Hektor's death, a close follower of Aeneas—who had, in a fit of what can only be called madness, challenged the sea-gods to a martial musical duel. Vergil's audience might have thought of Marsyas and Apollo—with a partial sense of irony, given that Apollo is the god guiding Aeneas toward this particular adventure—as they heard/read how

...Triton, jealous, caught him,
however unbelievable the story,
and held him down between the rocks, and drowned him
under the foaming waves. (172-4)

So in great grief—none greater than that of Aeneas—they bury Misenus and slaughter four black bullocks as an expiating offering, resolving the pollution brought about by Triton's eristic act with loving care. Aeneas finds that golden branch and, praying for help from his loving goddess-mother, is able to pluck it, return to the final rites for Misenus and the erection of a mighty tomb, and then hasten back to the Sibyl.

The poet indulges in a powerful description of the horrifying realm into which Aeneas enters, guided by the Sibyl—and the first among the dead who pre-occupy the Trojan hero, even before he crosses the River Acheron, is Palinurus, who tells the story of his death. He is clear that neither Apollo nor any other god had betrayed him, but that he suddenly at some point lost hold of the tiller and plunged into the sea, where he managed to stay afloat for three days. On the fourth, he sighted land—Italy—and swam for the shore, but the locals slew him as he struggled to gain a foothold on land. Human, not divine *eris* destroyed him.

And this, too, yields to a more communal than personal history. For Aeneas may not help Palinurus across the river while the latter remains unburied, the Sibyl explains, but she also comforts him: that those who slew him will recognize their wrong, and make expiation for it by building a tomb for him, bringing annual offerings, and naming the place Cape Palinurus (377-81). So the Elpenor story bifurcates for Aeneas into that of Misenus and Palinurus, and the latter, more obvious analogue to the Akhaian figure will not actually end up buried by Aeneas, but by Italians who will someday be neighbors of Aeneas' descendants—and who will eventually be swallowed up by those descendants, as Rome expands in Central Italy, centuries before Vergil's birth.

The golden bough causes Charon the boatman to take them across the River Acheron[149]—his boat creaking with the weight of a heavy, living warrior in full regalia—after his initial challenge to them; the three-headed dog, Cerberus, becomes somnolent from a drug-soaked honeyed sop tossed to him by the Sibyl; they encounter the souls of wailing infants, and coming to the Field of Mourning, "where those whom cruel love had wasted were hiding in secluded pathways, under myrtle, and even in death were anxious" (441-4) —among whom Aeneas suddenly saw Dido.

> Weeping, he spoke to her with tender love:
> "unhappy Dido, so they told me truly
> that your own hand had brought you death. Was I—
> alas!—the cause? I swear by all the stars,
> by the world above, by everything held sacred
> here under the earth, that unwillingly, O queen,
> I left your kingdom. But the god commands,
> driving me now through these forsaken places,
> this deepest night, compelled me on…" (455-63)
>
> but the queen, unmoving
> as flint or marble, turned away, her eyes
> fixed on the ground… (469-71)
>
> …where Sychaeus, whose bride she had once been, took her
> with love for love, sorrow for sorrow.
> And still Aeneas wept for her, troubled
> by the injustice of her doom… (473-6)

We may immediately recognize that in the kaleidoscopic shifts with regard to Homeric reference points, Dido plays the role for Aeneas that Aias had for Odysseus (as had been, one might suppose, anticipated back in Book IV when Dido committed suicide): the one who turns away from him. We also recognize Vergil's desire to suggest that Aeneas still loves Dido—and how enslaved he is to his obligations, as *pius Aeneas*, to his community, past, present and future.

As a technical question, we may wonder at the suggestion that someone has told Aeneas that Dido is dead. Since it is highly unlikely that someone followed to Sicily from Carthage with that news, might this be, rather, a supposition such as was arguably implied when, sailing away and looking back at the fire-reflecting walls and the smoke, and knowing how passionate Dido was, someone astute in Aeneas' crew—like Achates, for instance—could have suggested that possibility to Aeneas, who now finds it confirmed as an actuality? Or could this be a Vergilian slip that, had he had time, he would have corrected before publishing his poem?

This interchange—his unquenched *eros* for her, resonating from her pregnantly silent *eris* as a final moment to the interaction, that will have as its ultimate outcome the *eris* between their descendants—leads Aeneas toward many others. These include Deiphobos—brother of Hektor and Paris, who, after the death of the latter, married Helen. She, he explains to Aeneas—his body and face so badly mangled by his killers' knives that Aeneas cannot at first recognize him—betrayed him to Menelaus and Odysseus, hiding all of Deiphobos' weapons and then leading the Akhaians to him, hoping to put herself back into her original husband's good graces through that betrayal (495-534). So: Aeneas encounters a fellow-Trojan destroyed through the eristic behavior of his lover, Helen, as by Menelaus and Odysseus, the latter of whom at this moment is, like Aeneas, trying to get home—to a wife who has not only been patiently waiting for him for more than seventeen years, but who at this moment and in the nearly three years following this moment is fighting and will continue to fight off the suitors for her hand, rather than betray Odysseus.

But the Sibyl hurries our hero forward, past assorted other denizens of the various levels of Hades, arriving finally to a deep green valley—the groves of the blessed—where they finally find Anchises. Seeing Aeneas coming toward him, "his hands reached out with yearning, he was moved to tears, and called: 'at last, my son—have you really come at last? And the long road nothing to a pious son who loves his father?'" (685-8) Anchises is, to Aeneas, a combination of what his mother and Teiresias were to Odysseus in their respective Underworld experiences. For on the one hand—although at the beginning, not the end of their conversation, he tries to hug him, reaching out for his father—as Odysseus had for his mother—the tears streaming down his face, "and three times the image fled like the breath of the wind or a dream on wings" (700-02), as had been the case with Odysseus' mother's spirit. And on the other hand, it is Anchises, who like Teiresias to Odysseus, guides the hero through the future that awaits.

There are three most obvious differences between the two encounters. The first is that Aeneas, to repeat, is *in* the Underworld where Odysseus had, as it were, stood at its edge; he less peered in than the spirits flitted out to converse with him. So Anchises points things out to his son which it would have made no sense for Teiresias to point out to Odysseus. Perhaps most important is his account of the process through which souls go after death. He explains how souls endure punishment and cleansing, by fire, wind, or water, to purge them of whatever guilt they possess, until the day comes

> when we are sent through wide Elysium,
> the Fields of the Blessed, a few of us, to linger
> until the turn of time, the wheel of ages,
> wears off the taint, and leaves the core of spirit
> pure sense, pure airy flame; a thousand years pass by
> and the god calls the countless host to Lethe
> where memory is annulled, and souls are willing
> once more to enter into mortal bodies. (743-51)

This discourse—with nothing like it in Vergil's Homeric model (so this constitutes a second important difference between the two Underworld narratives, and perhaps most overtly offers a positive-mood distinction from the straightforwardly unhappy view of death expressed by Akhilleus in his brief discussion with Odysseus in *Odyssey* 11)—among other things, reflects the poet's interest in Pythagorean-Orphic theology and its rather specific doctrine of long-term reincarnation.[150] This will have implications for an important moment in the conclusion of this Underworld journey, as we shall shortly see.

The third important difference is the content of the prophetic discourse offered by Anchises to his son. Where Teiresias had spoken to Odysseus about himself, his own future, up to his death, in fact—albeit with some obscure elements that have had classicist-interpreters scrambling mentally for generations—Anchises says virtually nothing about Aeneas himself. His words are all about the "illustrious spirits of Dardanian lineage, Italian offspring, heirs of our name, begetters of our future" (756-8). Aeneas' story is not as much about Aeneas, to repeat, as about the Roman descendants of Aeneas; he is merely part (admittedly an important part) of a narrative that began well before him and will continue to its climax more than a millennium after him—which radically separates him from Odysseus and his tale of personal, self-driven adventure.

The future does *begin* with Aeneas, of course—literally: Silvius/Alban will be the first offspring to mix Trojan with Italian blood: the son of Aeneas in his later years with Lavinia, a local princess; and that offspring will rule Alba Longa (763-6). Details and other names that are unknown to Aeneas but which would have been familiar to Vergil's audience lead to Romulus—referred to as a son of Mars; a counterpart to Aeneas himself as a son of Venus. Through him Rome will be founded and reach a climax—in Vergil's own generation—with "the son of a god, Augustus Caesar, founder of a new Age of Gold, in lands where Saturn ruled long ago; he will extend his empire beyond the Indies (792-5). Between these two figures, Romulus and Augustus, Vergil's Anchises lays out a concise version of the entire history of Rome, noting its key figures—Numa, Tullus, the Decii, the Drusi, Torquatus, Camillus, Pompey, Julius Caesar, and others—and their roles in the shaping of the great imperium of the Aeneas-Vergil future-present.

Consistent with Vergil's brilliant attention to details of mood and the reincarnational basis for the indication of this array that Anchises first asserted, the poet does not have Aeneas' father follow a simple linear chronology of these individuals. They are being pointed out—here and there, and yes, over here and over there, in no particular order, as it were—in the form that they currently occupy, as dead spirits within the large gathering that father, son, and Sibyl observe from a kind of hillock, who will subsequently be reincarnated as the individuals whom Anchises notes. He includes a few who pertain specifically to the Trojan-Roman future in its connection to the Trojan War past—as, for example, one who "will strike down a king descended from Akhilleus, revenge for Minerva's ruined temple, on behalf of his Trojan ancestors" (839-40).[151] What would have no doubt been a breathtaking review for Vergil's audience, would have been a fascinating if obviously somewhat confusing preview of his people's saga for Aeneas.

And thereafter,

...through the whole wide realm they went together,
from airy fields surveying all.
After Anchises had led his son through everything
and fired his soul with love of future fame and glory,
he spoke of wars to come, the toils to face or flee from,
of the Laurentine peoples, and Latinus' city. (886-92)

—even in this small summary, Anchises weaves love and strife, articulated as the love *of* strife that yields fame and glory.

When the time for them to part ways arrives, as Aeneas is ready to return to the upper world—our *profanus* world—the poet describes the passage out in terms that recall the words spoken by Penelope in *Odyssey* 19.560-9, when she is speaking to Odysseus, still disguised as an old beggar, and asking his opinion regarding the truth-value of a dream that she has had, regarding the immanent return home of Odysseus, in which an eagle, that begins to speak and reveals itself as Odysseus, has conversed with her. There she mentions two gates that lead to and from dreams, one of horn and one of ivory. The first is for true dreams and the second for false dreams (see above, Chapter Three, 119).

This same idea is referenced by Vergil—"two portals, twin gates of Sleep, one made of horn, where easy release is given true shades, the other gleaming, flawless white ivory, whereby the false dreams issue to the upper air" (893-6). It is interesting to note that the experience that Aeneas has just had is likened to that of a dream—acknowledging that sleep, dreams, and death are all co-aspects of the same phenomenon (in our terms: the *sacer*). More interesting is the statement that "Aeneas and the Sibyl part from Anchises at the ivory gate" (897-8), where he rejoins his comrades and the book comes to an end.

In leaving through the ivory portal, he exits through the gate of false dreams—hardly appropriate for a hero who has come all this way to encounter his father posthumously and gain truthful information about the future of Rome. And hardly appropriate for the review offered by Anchises, of personages and events that Vergil's audience would all recognize as part of the history extending between Aeneas' era and their own. Might one suppose that this is another Vergilian slip that he would have caught and corrected, had he lived a few years longer and had time to run through his manuscript one last time? Or could it be intentional? Is it, as at least one commentator has suggested, simply to indicate that he left the Underworld before midnight?[152]

Or could there be a different, more subtle, intention? Given Vergil's Pythagorean-Orphic inclinations and the account that he presented Anchises offering to his son, and to us readers, with regard to the thousand-year cycle of transmigration for certain souls; and given his reference to Augustus Caesar in the millennial future as the son of a god who will usher in a new golden age; could it not be his intention to suggest that what emerged through that gate of ivory, portal of false shades, was not the true Aeneas, but rather a false image—an *eidolon* of Aeneas? Could it be that the true Aeneas, son of a goddess, was waiting to be (re-)born eleven centuries later, as Augustus—adopted son of his uncle, the "Divine" Julius Caesar, who was said to have been gathered up among the immortals when a comet appeared during the time of the funerary events following his assassination—carrier of Troy/Rome toward a new golden age?

There is no certainty here, of course, but what could be more directly flattering than this to the main reader/audience of the entire poem, the Emperor Augustus himself, than to suggest that he is *pius Aeneas* reincarnated? And this certainly would be consistent with the most famous portrait we have of the Emperor, the so-called "Augustus of Prima Porta." In that statue the figure is in full battle regalia except, oddly, as we have earlier noted, in bare feet—that are typically construed as the feet of a dead man, making it a posthumous portrait, yet, like all Augustus portraits, depicting the Emperor in the full bloom of youth—and attended by the dolphin and cupid that remind the viewer of his connection to the sea-born goddess of love, Venus.[153]

This notion would also help solve a problem that comes at the end of Book XII—at the very end of the poem, as we shall see—which, as we move on at this point into Book VII, shifts from its "*Odyssey*-adventure" aspect into its "*Iliad*-war" aspect, and thus carries Aeneas from his Odysseus aspect toward his Akhilleus aspect. For Book VII initiates the Trojan arrival along the western Italian shore into Latium, where the Trojans will have to fight to establish their foothold. The narrative arrives to this new phase gently. Book VII begins with the noted death of Caieta, loving nurse of Aeneas, and her honor-shaped burial along this coast; it continues with the Trojan ships skipping past the shores of Kirke's island— from safely off shore they can hear the howls of those transformed into animals and kept in cages. There is a certain irony in this drive-by, since Odysseus' visit to Kirke ended with his redirection far out toward the edge of the sea's *sacer-profanus* reality to encounter the dead at a border, where the portal to actually enter the realm of the dead—from which Aeneas has just come—was, it would seem, much closer to hand.

They find harbor up the coast in the realm ruled by King Latinus, with his only daughter, the beautiful Lavinia with her many—rejected—suitors. "Most handsome, most blessed in his ancestry, was the prince Turnus whom the queen mother favored, but the portents of the high gods opposed" (55-8). We are not all that far from the catastrophic denouement of the Dido story— that had included in Iarbas a rejected suitor of some consequence, (particularly where the interplay between *eros* and *eris* is concerned)—so, like Vergil's audience who, unlike the audience of the *Iliad* and the *Odyssey*, doesn't necessarily already know the outcome of this story—we might wonder what these verses portend with regard to Aeneas and his crew, particularly as we recall Anchises' words regarding the birth of a son to Aeneas by a

Lavinia who would have been completely unknown to Aeneas at the time of that prophecy.

There had, moreover, been other prophecies—to Latinus—regarding a stranger who would come to rule his people, and another regarding the glorious future of his daughter, who would nonetheless doom her people to war in the course of gaining that glorious future. Troubled, Latinus turned to his father, Faunus—who, although alive had, like Aeneas' father, Anchises, after death—the capacity to prophesy. Faunus asserted to him that he ought

> not seek a Latin husband for the princess,
> oh my son; distrust such a marriage;
> stranger sons are coming, who will raise our family name
> high as the stars, and from that marriage offspring
> will see, as surely as the sun looks down on the ocean,
> the whole world ruled at its feet. (96-101)

Meanwhile, Aeneas and his son and the other Trojan leaders, lunching on shore near the mouth of the Tiber River, in the shade, end up eating the hardtack that they had used upon which to spread the rest of their food. As Ascanius jokingly and rhetorically asks, "are we eating our tables?" (116), alluding to an earlier prophecy given by Celaeno, one of the Harpies (III. 253-7)—oddly, Aeneas remembers it as coming from Anchises—that when they are at a place where they are gnawing their own tables in their hunger, there they should build; for there will be the beginning of the end of their hardships. The following morning, while Aeneas is already marking out the outlines of his new city he sends emissaries with gifts to Latinus. Latinus receives them warmly—already knowing who they are and what they have been through, and recalling the idea that the Trojans' ancestor, Dardanus, had been born here, in Italy, long ago.

The Trojan leader dispatched by Aeneas, Ilioneus, responds to Latinus' welcoming and also questioning speech—what has brought you here?—with equal warmth. He tells the king that they have arrived to this place not by accident but by intention, and are asking permission to install themselves in the region: "a little home, a harbor" (229-30). An astute listener/reader might have noted that, when observing how justice-prone his Latins are, Latinus references their descent from Saturn (Kronos; 201), and that Ilioneus references the Trojan descent from Jove (Zeus; 219). Given how Zeus and the Olympians overthrew Kronos and the Titans before the beginning of human time in order to establish the gods' rule over the *kosmos*, one might well understand the poet's intent to foreshadow the outcome of this peaceful encounter, which will ultimately yield more than a "little home, a harbor" to the Trojans, at the expense of the Latins. The presentation of scepter, diadem, and robes from the Trojan royal house, which might seem generous, could also seem portentous, given what Priam's fate and that of his city had been (246-8).

Indeed, Latinus' initial physical response is stillness, with eyes downcast—not because the gold mesmerizes him, but because of the prophecy of Faunus regarding his daughter's future marriage. And this thought prevails, as he responds gladly, asking that they bring Aeneas to meet him in person, telling him, in fact, that

> I have a daughter; prodigies from heaven
> innumerable, and my father's warnings,
> delivered through his oracle, forbid me
> to give my daughter to a native husband.
> They tell me that my son-in-law is coming
> from foreign shores, to raise our name to heaven. (268-72)

With such a speech of welcome—virtually already a proposal of marriage that would unite their two peoples—the story could end by the end of this book. But then there would be no epic battles that could give the audience an Aeneas who is both a Romanized Odysseus and a Romanized Akhilleus and also less opportunity to connect the events of the epic to the future leading toward Vergil's Roman world—to say nothing of missing the chance to intertwine this *eros*-based moment with the eristic events that it, in part, engenders, furthering the parallel between this moment and those events on the one hand and the marriage-feast beginnings of the Trojan War on the other.

So as the Trojans ride back to Aeneas, happily laden down

with gifts and riding the best steeds that Latinus can provide for them, Juno is coming back from Argos—whatever her business had been there, who can say? perhaps recovering from the death of Dido—and sees the Trojans building homes, comfortable in yet another land. Reviewing the times, places, and ways in which the hated Trojans might and could and should have been destroyed, she cries out: "I am beaten by Aeneas!" (310), in great frustration. She bellows that, if he will ultimately gain Lavinia and Latium, she can at least make the road to that conclusion slow and painful (313-16). And "as for the bride, bloodshed shall be her dowry... a funeral torch for Troy re-born" (317-22). She can guarantee an eristic shape to this immanent triumph of *eros*.

Juno dispatches Allecto, a Medusa-like, gorgonesque goddess, to wreak the necessary havoc that will "break up the peace, sow seeds of warfare, let arms be what they want" (339-40)—in short, infect the *eros*-filled moment with *eris*. Indeed, the first stop on Allecto's poison-strewing journey is to the palace in Latium, "where the queen, Amata, brooded, after the arrival of the Trojans, and Turnus' cancelled marriage, with womanly care and anger burning her blazing heart" (342-5). Allecto lets one of her hairs—an invisible serpent—slither onto the skin of the queen, beneath her garments, becoming a collar of gold and then intertwining her hair, sliding all over her and infecting her with its poison.

This leads, first, to Amata speaking to her husband, Latinus, quietly but weepingly, begging him to back out of the marriage plan with Aeneas—doing a variation of what Iarbas had done: comparing this Trojan to that other one (Paris) who had absconded with Helen, and who is therefore not to be trusted; begging her husband not to forsake Turnus due to some oracle. But Latinus' mind is made up, and now the queen gradually becomes enraged, flying around the city and out to the mountains and woods—where she tries to hide her daughter—stirring up the other Latin women. Meanwhile, Allecto continues on, to the palace of the Rutulian prince, Turnus, disguising herself as Calybe, an old priestess from Juno's temple. She stirs the prince up out of his sleep, yelling at him to fight for what is his.

The outcome of these two incursions of the gorgon is a call to arms and the end of the peaceful arrangement that had persisted since the Trojans first arrived onto the Latin shore. And meanwhile Allecto makes her way to the Trojan camp, where Iulus is hunting. She drives his hounds mad, who pursue a deer that, it turns out, was a pet to Tyrrhus and his children. Ascanius shoots the deer and when the poor beast limps wounded and dying into his stall, Tyrrhus grabs an ax and sounds the alarm so that all the farmers come running; young Trojans come running from the other side to help Ascanias. The fight that ensues leaves several people dead, with no definitive victory for either side: the victory is Allecto's (which is to say: Juno's), for "she had soaked the war in blood, had made the beginning of death in battle" (542-3).

Allecto soars up to Olympus where Juno receives her happily and gratefully, adding the final touches to shaping the larger battle that she has rendered inevitable: wedding has become war; *eros* will now be *eris*. The people clamor for violence and Latinus cannot overcome their will—he withdraws into his palace and relinquishes the reins of power. We may recognize certain developments or issues that pertain both to the matter of *eros-eris* and the matter of Vergil's use and transformation of his Homeric models, as the scene is now set for violent conflict.

One is that the first half of the *Aeneid*, the "Odyssean" part, is mainly—as the *Odyssey* is thought by many to be—centered on *eros*, thanks to the Dido story (as opposed to the Penelope story, and the goal of reunification between her and Odysseus that causes this epic to be perceived as centered on love), although that central narrative ends eristically (as the penultimate and even final moments in the *Odyssey* are eristic). But as the second half leads us quickly into *eris*, the cause of that *eris* is *eros* (the pending marriage between Aeneas and Lavinia), twisting around *eris* (the unquenchable hatred of Juno for Aeneas).

A second issue is that there is no real precedent for the Lavinia-Turnus-Aeneas story in the Homeric works. There is a false equation suggested, in order to help provoke the *eris*, with Helen-Menelaus-Paris. More legitimately, there are echoes of the Odysseus-Nausikaa story, given the ages of Nausikaa and Lavinia relative to those of Odysseus and Aeneas and of course the insider-outsider position of the two girls relative to the two men. But where both of Nausikaa's parents are quite taken with Odysseus, and her father even hints at a marriage possibility, he lays off quickly when he realizes that the Ithakan wants nothing more than to get back home to his wife—and there is no real competing suitor; the closest one comes to that idea of a challenging Phaiakian is that young buck, Euryalos, who insults Odysseus but shortly thereafter makes amends for the insult. By contrast, Aeneas is formally approached by Lavinia's father with the marriage idea (and we know already that in the end it will happen, since Anchises discussed it when Aeneas was with him in the Underworld), but her mother— emotionally enhanced due to Juno's gorgon emissary, Allecta—is strongly opposed to that union, favoring the local hero, Turnus— and Turnus is Aeneas' genuine competitor for Lavinia's hand. And rather than the sports events played by the Phaiakians, in only one of which Odysseus "participates," it is war with the Rutulians and Latins—and in the end, as we shall see, Turnus will perish. It is a very different story, a Roman story, not a Greek story.

As Book VII continues forward, it is a story in which the eristic part offers strong echoes of parts of the *Iliad*, but ultimately moves in its own direction. In a rather interesting turn, Vergil describes the *mos mairoum* of opening the double gates of Mars to declare war—but bringing that custom to his own time, since he mentions that it is a consul who must do this, girt in the dress of Romulus (and both the political title, consul, and the figure of Romulus come well after the time of Latinus)—and when Latinus refuses, (he who would prefer love to strife!) choosing to hide, instead, in the temple's darkness, in his sadness, Juno herself, "coming from heaven, shoved them [i.e., the gates of Mars] open with her own hand; the turning hinges grated. The iron was torn open for war" (620-2).

What follows is a detailed description of the various individuals and their troops who arrived from near and far to participate in the impending struggle against the Trojans. On the one hand, this catalogue of the troops recalls the so-called catalogue of the ships found at the end of Book Two of the *Iliad*, referencing all those who arrived with the Akhaians to attack Troy. On the other, Vergil's clever obliqueness is clear, in presenting a catalogue of defenders, not attackers, but in presenting these as fighting against the Trojans—just as, at Troy, those listed in the catalogue of ships had arrived to fight against Trojans—but these are, as it were, very different Trojans, "Roman" Trojans who, between the time of Aeneas and that of Vergil, will extend their political control over vast territories, beginning with those Latin lands in central Italy abutting their own beginning territory. Here and later the outcome will be radically different, compared to that which involved those Trojans defending their citadel!

Of further interest is the fact that, included in that long list are some Akhaians, including "Agamemnon's son, Halaeus, a hater of the Trojan name; for Turnus he yoked his steeds, he brought a thousand people..." (723-5). Among all these heroic warriors, Turnus is finally introduced—and he stands out, "taller than any." And last of all, Camilla rode—a Penthesilea-like warrior maiden—leading her troops on horseback, "her columns bright with bronze, a soldieress, a woman whose hands were never trained for weaving, for working wool, for basketry, a girl as tough in war as any, in speed of foot swifter than the wind" (803-7). Perhaps the reference in the last two verses of Book VII to the Lykian quiver that she carries is intended to evoke that singular Lykian warrior, Sarpedon, son of Zeus, who perished at the hands of Patroklos, in spite of Zeus' preference for an outcome in which Sarpedon would have survived.

In any case—and apropos of Akhaians invited to the war party—Book VIII opens with the sending of a message to Diomedes, arguably the warrior who, aside from Akhilleus, starred most consistently in the *Iliad*, in effect serving as Akhilleus' surrogate during the many books when the son of Peleus and Thetis was sitting out the battle. The Latins ask Diomedes to come to their aid, since the Trojans are in Latium, and Aeneas is proclaiming himself a king—and who better than Diomedes would understand the implications of all that? Diomedes' answer won't come back until Book XI, as we shall see—and it will not be a positive one, for he will assert that he holds no grudge against the Trojans; he fought against them and destroyed their city as part of his obligation as a warrior, not out of personal animosity.

As for Aeneas, meanwhile, as he senses the approach of war, he tosses and twists in distress at the turn of events, but the Tiber River itself speaks to him, consoling and comforting him with the assurance that this place will indeed become the home which he has been so long seeking, and that his son will be founding Alba Longa not far from here within thirty years. It is the Tiber that suggests to Aeneas that he journey inland to forge an alliance with an Arcadian people, "a race descended from Pallas' line; their king is called Evander...[and] they wage continual warfare with the Latin people" (51-2, 55) — a suggestion that will have both Trojan-helpful and fateful consequences. So Aeneas chooses two of his ships and they sail up river, arriving while Evander, together with his son, Pallas, is making offerings to the gods, particularly to Hercules, in a grove by the city.[154]

It is Pallas who rushes to greet the incoming ships, inquiring boldly as to who they are and what their business is, and it is to Pallas that Aeneas initially states that they are Trojans, come to seek Evander and his people as allies against the Latins. Hearing this, Pallas immediately brings Aeneas before his father. Aeneas notes that Evander is a Greek (Danaan/Akhaian), related to Agamemnon and Menelaos, no less — but asserts that Evander and he are "bound together by the god's holy oracles, by the old ancestral kinship" (131-2): for the Trojans' ancestor, Dardanas was a grandson of Atlas and Evander is also descended from Atlas. Evander's response is enthusiastic: he recalls how Anchises once visited, as a very impressive young man — as Aeneas himself now seems to him to be — and how Anchises left Evander with a gift of "a fine quiver of Lykian arrows, a cloak embroidered with gold, and a pair of golden bridles that my son Pallas enjoys now" (166-8).

The upshot is that Evander happily agrees to the alliance and to the use of his resources, and invites Aeneas to join in the annual rites being celebrated. Put otherwise, this is a love-fest to precede the war that is poised to explode. Evander explains the purpose of the rituals: to honor Hercules, who, way back when, had saved their community from the plague of the Vulcan-born, fire-breathing, cave-dwelling Cacus, slaying him with his superhuman strength. On the way back to the city — with Pallas ever near to his loving, doting father — Evander tells the history of the landscape and its people. They arrive at a sanctuary later "restored by Romulus" (342) — thus Vergil jumps forward again toward the Roman era; he has been doing this increasingly as his narrative has arrived into Italy.

Aeneas spends the night as a guest of Evander, but Venus his love-goddess mother, meanwhile, is anxious and worried, too well aware of what the Latins are preparing. So she turns to her husband, Vulcan (Hephaestos)—the smith god—and "her words were warm with love" (373) and begs him, as one who never asked for his help when Troy was burning, although she owed it to the Trojans to have done so, but now comes to him as "a suppliant...a mother asking weapons for her son. If Thetis and Aurora could move you with their tears, behold what people unite against me..." (382-5). When he hesitates, she throws her arms around him and "fire ran through him," and he quickly agrees—even asserting that, had she asked him years ago, he would have provided all the Trojans with arms that might have held off the Achaians for another decade!

We would recall Thetis turning to the same god on behalf of her son, Akhilleus, even had Vergil's Venus not specifically alluded to her. The two most obvious differences, however, between the two situations are that Venus is Vulcan's wife and the goddess of love, after all, whereas Thetis is a mere non-Olympian sea-goddess; and that Akhilleus required new armor because his original human-devised arms had been lost when Patroklos, using them, got himself killed by Hektor and Hektor stripped off that armor and donned it himself. That led to an obvious but incidental advantage to Akhilleus when he faced Hektor, but here the goddess is consciously and anticipatorily seeking to shape the situation in the impending *eris*, in which Aeneas, goddess-born and god-armed, will have the advantage over anyone who comes up against him. Vulcan-Venus love-making that night leads to his smithy work before the night is done, and the final preparation of the hero for his upcoming battle.

Vergil is surely conscious, too, of the ironic twists and turns to this armor-preparing moment: that Venus comes to Vulcan while her son is sleeping as a guest of Evander, who has just sacrificed to Hercules for the latter's destruction of Vulcan's son, Cacus—a character most reminiscent, within this world of epic poetry, of Polyphemos, son of Poseidon, who, blinded by Odysseus, brings his father's deadly curse upon the Akhaian hero. Odysseus is both a kind of analogue to Hercules in the Cacus/Evander context and of course of Aeneas in the larger epic poetry context—albeit Aeneas is starting to shift from being an Odysseus analogue to being an Akhilleus analogue, and the culmination of that transformation, including his privileged Hephaistos/Vulcan-made weaponry, is ultimately going to center around Evander's son, Pallas.

Every bit the match for Homer in his Vergilian way, the poet delays the arrival at that battle, both by bouncing back from Olympus to earth and from divine discourse and action to human conversation and action as the book continues forward; and by a rich description of the weapons devised by the smith-god. In the first case, Evander asks Aeneas to take Pallas with him, Evander's "hope and solace. You are the one to teach him a soldier's duty, how to endure; let him learn from you in action, behold your deeds, and in his youth, admire them" (514-17).

As Aeneas takes to his ships, reinforced both by allies and by a Venus-sent sign—a trumpet-like blast of thunder in the cloudless heavens—Evander "holds his son by the hand, cannot release him, speaking through his tears" (558-9) of how he wishes he were young again, to fight again, and recalling his defeat of Erulus, whose mother gave him three lives so that Evander had to kill him and strip his armor three times—and calling upon Jupiter and the other gods to take pity on a father, and to preserve Pallas' life in the upcoming war, culminating with the words: "I pray for life as long as Pallas lives, I pray to see him if you will spare him; if he returns safely I pray to meet him once again" (573-7). These words resonate from Hektor's prayer to Zeus and the other gods regarding Astyanax, near the end of *Iliad* VI. This is a different context involving different personalities and circumstances, but the central issue, of a father's enduring love for his son—and the prayer for the son's success in the first case and survival in the second—share the sad attribute of remaining unhearkened to by the gods and by fate: both sons, albeit in different ways, will succumb to strife-shaped death.

If one considers, yet again, the obliquely twisting parallels imposed by Vergil on his Homer-resonating poem, then consider the further turns to the words of Evander. He is as Hektor and Pallas is as Astyanax; Astyanax will be killed by the order of Odysseus; Aeneas, to whose care Pallas in consigned, is both Odysseus and

Akhilleus, and Aeneas will end up killing Turnus as Akhilleus killed Hektor because Turnus will slay Pallas as Hektor slew Patroklos (as we shall see) so that Pallas will also become Patroklos and not merely Astyanax by the end of the poem.

The weapons that will accomplish this task are finally presented by Venus to Aeneas as he and his fellows rest in Caere's grove: a fatal sword (to Turnus, most significantly), the breastplate, the greaves, the spear, and—the final masterpiece—the shield.

> On it the great prophetic Lord of Fire
> had carved the story out, the heirs to Ascanius,
> the wars, each one in order, all the tale
> of Italy and Roman triumph. (626-9)

The description of Akhilleus' shield was the one significant passage in the *Iliad* in which the issue was not an individual but rather, a human pattern—of love and strife—as we have earlier seen.[155] Aeneas' shield is more narrowly focussed—the only time this may be said to happen in parallel Vergilian-Homeric passages—on the same subject that had appeared in Book VI with the words of Anchises to his son in the Underworld regarding the future: the story of the Romans (rather than of humans).

Vergil leaps forward to Romulus and Remus, and on to the rape of the Sabine women, the destruction of the Etruscan Tarquin kings and the establishment of the Roman *res publica*.[156] He references the early sack of Rome (in 390 BCE) by the Gauls and the recovery from that low point in early republican history; the conspiracy of Catiline and the arrival onto the stage of Roman history of Augustus Caesar, includng his Agrippa-engineered defeat of Anthony and Cleopatra at Actium. Indeed, the culmination of the description and of Book VIII overall—most off the last 50 lines—is a long encompium of Augustus and his far-flung conquests. The entirety concludes:

> Such things on the shield of Vulcan, the gift of his mother,
> Aeneas sees and, ignorant [of what all these future events and personnages are], he rejoices

> as he lifts to his shoulder all that fame and the deeds of his descendants. (729-31)

Yet meanwhile, while Aeneas has been away, gaining allies and new armor, his nemesis, the goddess Juno, has been busy trying to do her best to forestall the ultimate Aenean success that will be meted out by fate—which is how Book IX begins. She sends down Iris to stir Turnus to action, to attack the Trojan camp while Aeneas is gone. Inspired—in-spirited—by the divine emissary, the spurned suitor of Lavinia leads an insistent charge. Turnus pushes up against a defense that occasionally singles out individual Trojans—including the handsome pair, Nisus and Euryalus, who vie with each other to be valiant, volunteering to go out, sneaking past the enemy camp, to find Aeneas quickly. These pass through at night, and cannot resist the urge to glory that comes with large numbers of enemy dead. They slaughter the sleeping Rutulians in a manner reminiscent of the havoc wreaked on a sleeping camp of Trojan allies by Odysseus and Diomedes in *Iliad* X.

But this adventure has a very different outcome from that enjoyed by the Akhaian pair. Not deigning to rob his victims of the rich plunder that is available, Euryalus insists that they must take something, and it is the golden sword-belt of Rhamnes, their first-named victim that he seizes—and which will be his undoing, as a relieving retinue of 300 horsemen, coming from the Latin city, see that prize glittering in the shadows as the two Trojans try to escape through the woods. They capture Euryalus, but Nisus manages to kill a few of them before, in the end, both he and Euryalus are struck dead.[157] The short-term victors hoist the heads of these two on stakes and parade them within sight of the Trojan camp—and Euryalus' mother goes crazy with anguish.

All of this, however, is really a prelude to the expansive role of Turnus: this book emphasizes his *aristeia* above all. His acts of martial greatness sandwich the moment when Ascanius is shown in successful action with his bow and arrow—until the ultimate bow-and-arrow practitioner, the god Apollo, intervenes and tells him to desist from further participation in the battle. So as in the *Iliad*, the gods are involved in human conflict. Back, then, to "Turnus, far off, raging and rioting" (691-2), who storms back toward the walls of the Trojan camp, his weapons flying. He pushes into the camp, somehow unnoticed, among the retreating Trojan warriors, to wreak further havoc and mocking Pandarus with the boast: " 'I have a message for king Priam: Tell him that Achilles was here!'" (742).

Pandarus' response is a spear that misses its mark; but Turnus' return throw splits the head of Pandarus. Juno supplies her champion with fire and strength, but he revels in the slaughter that he wreaks so much that he does not bother to open the gates and let his fellow warriors in; had he done so, the poet tells us, the battle and the war might have ended with the destruction of the Trojans that very day—before Aeneas had returned. Instead, fighting alone, however gloriously, Turnus eventually tires and must withdraw, set upon by the Trojans, and he leaps into the Tiber to be carried by the rushing waters back to his comrades-in-arms.

There is irony, of course, in Turnus comparing himself to Akhilleus—and cruelty, perhaps, in invoking the old king of Troy, who, with most of his 50 sons, is dead, slaughtered in his citadel, clinging to the altar of a god, by Neoptolemos, son of Akhilleus. For Turnus is really the Hektor of this poem, as every reader eventually knows, and however spectacular his success in Book IX, Aeneas, the Akhilleus of the narrative, will arrive in Book X, take center stage, and eventually destroy Turnus.

Book X opens with Jupiter calling a council of the Olympians to ask why they have countermanded his orders in allowing the battle to burst out on the field below—a reminder of how far from limitless is the power of even the most powerful of gods. He notes that violence will one day suffuse that landscape—alluding specifically to the Second Punic War and Hannibal's arrival with troops through the Alps—but asks that now there be the peace between the Latins and Trojans that he had demanded. The first response to this condemnation of the present state of *eris* comes in a long speech by the goddess of *eros* and loving mother of Aeneas, Venus. Once again, she asserts, the Trojans are under assault, but without their high walls that once protected them: "once more the son of Tydeus attacks the Trojans" (28-9).

There is, again, some irony here: in the literal sense, we have not heard a word about or from Diomedes yet, in response to the message sent to him asking for his assistance against the Trojans (and when we finally do, (to repeat), in Book XI, it will be negative). As a metaphor, Turnus, referenced a few lines earlier, with Mars as his "second-in-command" is now being likened to the Akhaian who most stood out as a warrior in the *Iliad*, after Akhilleus. This was particularly so in *Iliad* V, where Diomedes' *aristeia* soars as he is briefly endowed with superhuman abilities by Athena, slays many Trojans—among them an earlier Pandaros, gunned down with Diomedes' spear (as opposed to the Pandarus recently gunned down by the spear of Turnus)—and even wounding Aphrodite when the goddess steps in to protect Aeneas. Diomedes goes so far as to challenge Apollo, although the god pushes him aside; he briefly desists when he discerns Hektor aided by Ares (Mars)—but with Athena taking control of his chariot, he flies into the fray and wounds Ares himself.

This culminating confrontation with the god of war, invoked by the goddess of love in plaint regarding Turnus' actions, again reflects the poet's brilliant transformative use of not just broad themes but smaller details from the Homeric works that inspired his own epic poem. Venus reviews all of the hardships inflicted on the Trojan refugees by divine interventions, from wind-churned fire facilitated by Aeolus and Iris, in Sicily, to Allecto, here. She begs Jupiter at least to allow her to shelter Ascanius, to forget about the future empire but to shelter her grandson safely, elsewhere, if he has decided to let his wife win out by seeing the Trojans, including Aeneas, destroyed.

Surprise: the goddess of love begets an intensely eristic response from Juno, who accuses Aeneas of fomenting the violence by having come to Italy and advancing against Latinus, at the fates' command (65-7). Her speech is even longer than that of Venus: the two diatribes together constitute the most serious *agon* shaped by Vergil since Book IV and the unhappy farewell *agon* between Aeneas and Dido. The gods sway back and forth in their sympathies, until Jupiter "all-powerful father, ruler of all the world" (100; which he is manifestly not, or this meeting and its *agon* would not need to be taking place) speaks up. His response is tamely ambiguous, asserting that there can be no accord between Ausonians (i.e., Italians aka Latins) and Trojans, that he cannot and will not judge who is to blame for the current conflict, but that in the end "the fates will find a way" (113)—presumably to bring this conflict to a conclusion with whatever their preferred outcome.

So the divine council gives sanction to the *eris* down below and leaves it to Fate to lead it where it will go. And meanwhile, "at every gate Rutulians drive, determined to bring down men with iron, to ring the walls with flame. The legion of Aeneas' followers is held within, blockaded, with no hope of flight" (118-21). A description of the key Trojan defenders follows, centered around the shining figure of Ascanius, as Aeneas and his men cleave the seas—and again particular note is taken of young Pallas at the leader's side, "asking questions: what stars are those? Which was the one to guide them through the dark night? What fortunes had he suffered on land and sea?" (160-2) The last person to ask these kinds of questions of Aeneas was Dido—and interestingly, Pallas is said by the poet to be standing always on the left (*sinister*) side, the unpropitious side, of his beloved and loving hero.

The poet indulges in another muse-inspired review of the allies sailing now with Aeneas, as he can barely sleep at all. They approach the place where the Trojan camp is under siege, "and high on the stern, seeing the Trojans and his camp before his eyes, he lifted high the blazing shield with his left arm, and the Trojans raised a clamor to the high stars from the walls; added hope envigorated their anger" (260-3). Turnus and the Rutulians are dumfounded to see this suddenly-arrived mass of ships coming to shore, but he never loses confidence, and rallies his men, reminding them that "fotune helps those who are daring" (284). Aeneas and his men clamor onto the shore and the renewed battle is on. True to his Iliadic inspiration, Vergil offers myriad details of the fighting, singling out figures on both sides, here and there—but above all, Aeneas. Even more than on Aeneas, however, the verbal spotlight shines slowly but relentlessly on Pallas. He spars with Lausus, like himself, the poet notes almost in passing, a doomed young fighter. But their confrontation has no outcome, because Turnus' sister yells to him that Lausus needs help and he comes charging across the plain "to battle Pallas; Pallas is my prize alone" (441-3), and leaps from his chariot to duel Evander's son.

And so, like a lion stalking a bull,

> ... came Turnus,
> came within a spear-throw; Pallas, watching, knew it,
> took a step forward, and, that chance might favor
> however uneven his strength, prayed to the heavens:
> "If ever my father entertained a stranger
> who proved a god, and gave him food and greeting,
> aid me O Hercules! Let Turnus see me
> taking the bloody armor from his body,
> and his dying eyes behold me, Pallas, victor!" (456-63)

The divine response is unusual: Jupiter's heart is moved, but he cannot help Pallas, and tells him so, noting, gently, that one's appointed death—by fate—cannot be pushed aside, for even his own son, Sarpedon, could not be saved when the time for his death arrived beneath the walls of Troy.

The outcome is pre-ordained in the duel between a young, inexperienced warrior—a boy, however brave—and the most successful warrior among the Latins, an experienced and full-grown man. Pallas hurls his spear with all his might and it pierces Turnus' shield and merely grazes his side. Turnus throws with a mocking comment and his spear blasts through every layer of protective armor worn by Pallas, who pulls the spear out, but collapses as the blood gushes from his chest wound. A second time, Turnus mocks a grieving father—this one very much alive, unlike the posthumously mocked Priam—"let Evander know, I am sending back Pallas as he deserved... a costly welcome of Evander to Aeneas" (491-2; 494-5).

The slowly accumulating verbal acts of impiety will help justify the mode of Turnus' eventual demise at the hands of Aeneas, in a manner perhaps analogous to the miscues of Dido—her questions, her toasts to Dionysus, and her union with Aeneas unsanctioned by formal man-made rituals—as justifications for her demise.[158] He mocks the dead and their loving survivors, in the midst of *eris*; she had said and done the wrong things, inadvertently, through being so emotionally entangled in *eros*—but they will both end up in Hades through their encounter with Aeneas.

Bold though Turnus' words may be, the death of Pallas

from Turnus' spear will guarantee the death of Turnus at the hands of Aeneas as surely as the death of Patroklos at the hands of Hektor guaranteed Hektor's death at the hands of Akhilleus. Moreover, as Hektor reinforced that certainty by stripping the arms of Patroklos—Akhilleus' arms—from his dead victim, and donning them, Turnus reinforces his demise by stripping Pallas of his glorious decorated sword-belt. He

> ripped loose
> the belt's great weight, with the story of a murder
> carved in its metal, the young men foully murdered
> on their bridal night, the chamber drenched in blood,
> as Clonus, son of Eurytus, engraved it.
> And Turnus gloried in the spoil, exulting... (496-500)

> ...a time is coming
> when Turnus would pay dearly, could he purchase
> Pallas unharmed again, would view with loathing
> these spoils and this day... (503-5)

So: an oddly grim choice of story—that of the Danaids, fifty daughters of Danaus, all but one of whom slaughter their husbands on the first night of their marriages to the sons of their father's twin brother, Aegyptus (talk of *eris* within *eros*!)—within the grim story of Pallas' death, within the grim story of the slaughter that finalizes the new Trojan settlement in Italy. There is something subtle, perhaps, in Vergil's choice of this particular story: the villain, Danaus, who demanded that his daughters commit the outrage (that would lead them, eventually, into eternal torment in Hades) has a name that word-plays on the name of Turnus' father: Daunus. Turnus' own destruction is already foretold by Vergil here—and through the remainder of Book X, after word gets back to Aeneas that Pallas, like a son to him, has been killed, he rages in a manner reminiscent of Akhilleus' rage after the death of Patroklos.

Among the details that one might suppose Vergil would have tightened had he lived another year or two is that the body of Pallas is immediately carried to his father (507), as if Evander were right near the battlefield, not a ship's journey away, back at home where he remained when Aeneas, Pallas and the others headed back downriver to the shoreline battlefield. So, too, Aeneas is said to have received news from a runner that the Trojans were being pushed back, but he is already depicted cutting through Rutulians in specific search of Turnus, as if he has also learned of Pallas'death (510-15). There is no reason that the one should preclude the other, it's just that one might expect a more direct statement of his having heard that most important piece of news.

In any case, his *furor*—like the *menis* of Akhilleus—leads him directly into a behavioral pattern typical of Akhilleus but not typical of *pius* Aeneas, not merely mowing down those who stand in the warpath that he follows in seeking out Turnus, but specifically, "seizing four young men, the sons of Sulmo, and four whom Ufens fathered"—suggesting that they are younger rather than more mature—"he takes them, living, for later sacrifice, to dye with blood the funeral pyre of Pallas" (517-20). When Magus begs for mercy at the hero's knees, the response is a sword-thrust up to the hilt. The list of those he slays is extensive, and, led by his success, Ascanius and the other penned-up warriors are inspired to break the siege and come storming out of the Trojan camp (604-5).

As in the *Iliad*, the scene bounces back to Olympus. While Aeneas and the other Trojans are turning the tide in no uncertain terms, Jupiter suggests to Juno that Venus is helping the Trojans (although there has not been the usual statement that this divine aid is in process)—and thus Juno asks one favor from her husband: not that she be allowed "to rescue Turnus from the battle, restore him safely to his father Daunus" (615-16)—that would be too much to ask—but rather that, since he will inevitably die, "that as he perishes this innocent morally punish the Trojans" (617).[159] The word rendered "innocent" here is *pius*. So Juno is deliberately transfering the epithet from Aeneas to Turnus as she continues to view the former as guilty of aggression and the latter as merely defending the just cause, so powerful is her love for the one hero and her hatred for the other.

Jupiter responds—as if she *had* asked simply to rescue Turnus—that she may remove him from the battlefield to delay his demise, but that the ultimate outcome will not change. Weeping, she descends to the battlefield in a storm and fashions a false and hollow cloud in the form of Aeneas: a false *eidolon* of the Trojan leader, and Turnus, seeing it, attacks it. As that moment the *eidolon* turns and flees, confusing the Rutulian, who pursues this phantom onto a conveniently moored ship, and Juno breaks the moorings, carrying Turnus away—while meanwhile the real Aeneas "kept calling Turnus to the fight; kept killing anyone who crossed his path" (663-5).[160] Turnus, hardly seeing this moment as one in which he should be grateful for salvation, is instead more than frustrated, three times considering suicide in what he sees as his humiliation, but three times Juno stays his hand, as the ship carrying him sails relentlessly on to Ardea, city of his father, Daunus.

With the temporarily rescued Turnus away from the field, the battle surges on, as others enjoy the *aristeia* suddenly denied the son of Daunus. The Etruscan ally of Turnus, Mezentius, father of Launus, slays left and right. A list of others is offered by the poet, but it is mainly Mezentius to whom he keeps turning—who seems in particular to pick out young, inexperienced victims—until Aeneas catches up with him, wounds him with his spear and approaches with his sword. But Mezentius' son, Lausus, is able to intervene to protect his father just long enough for others to gather around and bombard Aeneas, so that he must take shelter, and Mezentius gets away.

Not so Lausus—who, as we know but Aeneas does not, had in his conflict with Pallas put Turnus in a position to slay Pallas. Inspired by the moment, Lausus pushes ahead and not back, directly into the path of Aeneas, who at first tells him to stay back, "why are you rushing deathward, daring against grown men? Your filial love makes you crazy" (811-12)—and Aeneas plunges his sword too easily into the figure holding too small a shield and wearing armor that is too light for such a confrontation.

The phrase "filial love" renders the Latin word, *pietas*—so once again, but in a different context and manner from when Juno applied the adjectival form to Turnus, a victim of Aeneas wears the latter's epithet—adorned with it, this time, by Aeneas himself. As so often in such a poem, the love between father and son embeds itself within a prime eristic moment. That moment arrives as if Aeneas suddenly remembers who and what he is: he pauses after slaying Lausus, "he groans with pity, reaching out as if to touch him with his hand, in comfort, knowing, himself, what love for a father can be" (822-3)—again *pietas* is rendered as "love for a father."[161]

And so, too, the love of a *son* by a *father*: Mezentius, wounded but despairing that his son has been killed in his stead, raises himself painfully to his feet and climbs upon his horse to go back out against his son's killer. He comes on quickly, crying out Aeneas' name, and the hero hears him, rejoices to come and meet him. Aeneas is on foot, Mezentius on horseback, circling and throwing one, then a second, then a third spear—all of which lodge harmlessly in the divinely wrought shield. Finally, Aeneas casts his own spear—not at Mezentius but at his horse. The rearing and then falling horse comes crashing down, pinning his rider beneath him. Mezentius' last words are only to ask that Aeneas see to it that father and son are buried together—before the sword thrust ends his life and the book.

Thus the last moment in Book X embeds the power of parental love within a deeply eristic context. It also underscores a certain ambiguity with regard to Aeneas that has emerged in the course of this war. He has both seen *pietas* in an enemy and exhibited it in his heart, and acted at times as if that attribute has fled his soul with the advent of battle, in favor of the need to establish his people in this place at whatever cost to that soul, moral or otherwise. One might suggest, then, that even in that negative sense—of his abandoning a purer *pietas*, at times—it is because his focus and concern are, Roman *pietas*-style, on the community of those around him, and those who came before him and will come after him, rather than on himself, even on his reputation/*fama*/*kleos* as *pius* Aeneas.

These are issues that Vergil will push slowly but surely toward the front and center of the stage as he extends his epic toward its denouement. Book XI opens, however, with a thoughtful, mournful Aeneas, disturbed at all the deaths that have already occurred, but quietly exultant, certain that, with the death of Mezentius he and his troops will easily march through the cities allied to the Latins and complete the Trojan task of conquest. First things first, however: Pallas—whose body, it turns out, is still resting within the Trojan camp, and causes Aeneas to weep: "… fortune… refused me the joy of seeing you ride back in triumph to your father's house with news of our new kingdom. I have not kept my promise to Evander your father, whose arms went around me when I left, who sent me to win a great empire" (43-7).

There is no real equivalent of this in the *Iliad*. The closest parallels are the weeping of the women in Akhilleus' camp for Patroklos—or perhaps, ironically enough, the sympathy that Akhilleus comes to feel for Priam, son of his defeated enemy, Hektor, through his sympathy for his own father, Peleus, who will some day soon mourn Akhilleus' own death. In that case, Pallas becomes Hektor, rather than Patroklos, in this expression of sympathy. And the Iliadic context, of course, has nothing to do with empire-building, but is entirely a matter of restoring an unhappy relationship, that of Helen and Menelaus, and about personal *kleos*.

At the end of his long speech bemoaning the empty hope of unhappy Evander, loving father of a son who had become like a son to Aeneas—his last words directed specifically to his own son, Iulus—Aeneas

> gave orders
> to raise the pitiful body for its journey,
> and chose a thousand men to honor Pallas
> with this last escort, to share Evander's tears,
> poor comfort for so great a grief, but owed to a father. (59-63)

> And then Aeneas brought two robes, whose crimson
> was stiff with gold, robes that Sidonian Dido
> had made for him, happy in her labor,
> running the gold through crimson. Over Pallas
> the robes are cast, the sad and final honor,
> the hair is veiled for the fire, and many trophies
> are added, prizes from the Latin battles,
> horses, and weapons, captured from the Latins,
> and human victims, offerings to the shades,
> their blood to sprinkle funeral fire, are led forth,
> hands bound behind them… (72-83)

Once more Vergil is sensitive to the irony of his details: that the robes with their weave of gold and blood-color recall the other unhappy moment during Aeneas' journey from Troy in which, specifically, he had failed someone, who had died as a consequence—but also due to fate-bound circumstances beyond his control. It is as if the last hint of a memory of the happy time together with Dido will now be burned, its ashes buried with the remains of Pallas and the memory of the brief happy time with him before Turnus slew him.

One might say that there have been *three* particularly unhappy moments for Aeneas on this journey, the third being the death of his father—but these two share a more obvious untimeliness and provide the basis for a feeling of guilt that Anchises' death does not. Each of these two deaths, moreover, has had an oblique reference point in the *Iliad* or the *Odyssey* that the death of Anchises also does not: the death of Patroklos and the encounter with Aias in the Underworld.

By coincidence or not, as the very long procession starts its painful journey back to the city of Evander with the body of Pallas, his riderless horse, his weapons—*all except what Turnus had taken as spoil*, the poet notes—envoys arrive from the Latin city asking for a truce so that bodies may be cleared from the battlefield and funerals be celebrated. Aeneas'response is not surprising: what destiny, he asks rhetorically, impelled you to such a tragic war in the first place, when we could have been friends? Peace you ask for and I am glad to grant it—Turnus should have taken me up on my challenge for a duel, and then everyone else could have stayed out of the fight. But go, gather your dead and perform the funeral rites (100-21).

The envoys cannot look Aeneas in the eye, until old Drances, "resentful of young Turnus," speaks up and praises the Trojan leader lavishly for both his justice and his war skills. He commits his troops to join Aeneas (again) with King Latinus and to let Turnus seek other alliances for himself. Twelve days of peace and friendship follow. And meanwhile Rumor flies up to Evander's home and city, bringing word of Pallas'death to his father shortly before the long retinue arrives with the young man's body.

The weeping father bemoans his son's failure to keep his promise to remain safe; "I knew all too well how much new glory and the sweet fresh pride in the first battle could overpower you"

(154-5). As Pallas is the *Aeneid*'s version of the Iliadic Patroklos, the role of grief-struck Akhilleus, and the words spoken in grief to the dead loved one is, appropriately enough, divided by Vergil: while as we shall see, the anger on the battlefield directed at Pallas' killer will fall to Aeneas, of course, the main role as mourner and verbal interlocutor with Pallas falls to Evander. Evander is also really the equivalent of Priam, then, who suffers the fate of outliving his son (Evander even notes how happy Pallas' mother is, already dead before the death of their son), whose comments echo those of Priam when the latter faces Akhilleus to beg for the body of Hektor.

Of equal importance for the *communitas* and Rome-anticipating emphases of the poem is the fact that Evander is clear that

> it is not your fault, oh Trojans; I do not blame you,
> the treaties joined, the hands we clasped in friendship.
> No: this was owed
> to my old age. An early death
> took away my son; I shall rejoice, hereafter,
> knowing that he slew thousands of Volscians
> as he led the Trojans into Latium. You were worthy,
> Pallas, my son, of such a death,
> as *pius* Aeneas and all the mighty Trojan
> and Etruscan leaders acknowledge… (164-71).

And the last part of Evander's mournful speech is directed as a message to Aeneas: that he owes Evander—and the shade of Pallas—one thing only: the death of Turnus. We cannot miss the number of times at which and angles from which the doom of Turnus is both forecast and justified!

Indeed, in the midst of the account that follows of all the funeral pyres burnt on both the Trojan and Latin sides during the truce, the call gets louder that Turnus end this war through a single combat with Aeneas, since after all the war was really being fought for the sake of his claim on Latinus' daughter. So we are reminded that, just as in the eristic *Iliad*—centerpiece of the Trojan War narrative—the eristic centerpiece here, within the epic of Aeneas' carrying his community and his home from Troy to Italy, revolves around *eros*: there is a woman at stake in both cases, albeit under admittedly different conditions, the first involving the treachery of a Trojan, Paris, the other not. So in another oblique twist of his inspirational sources, Vergil has cast Aeneas and Turnus not only as Akhilleus and Hektor but as Menelaus and Paris—but again, differently, since Aeneas never stole Lavinia from Turnus the way Paris stole Helen from Menelaus, although woman-theft was no doubt Turnus' view of things.

As if recalling such a twisting back toward his sources, Vergil chooses this moment in which finally to bring the response from Diomedes, the great Akhaian warrior, to the Latins: that no volume of gifts or pleading and reminding him of his past relations with Trojans will convince him to turn up for this battle. Diomedes' reported response is not a brief one, mind you; the envoys repeat a long message reviewing the Trojan War and the reason it took place, his own role in it—including his wounding of the goddess of love in a spontaneous act of madness—and the fate of the key Akhaians, in its aftermath, concluding by asserting that he holds no grudge against the Trojans, and has no desire to fight them, the war having ended. He adds, moreover, that the main reason the Akhaians were held at bay for ten long years of siege was the fighting skills of Hektor and Aeneas, so he concludes by recommending that they seek a treaty with Aeneas, not a fight: "beware, beware, of facing them in arms" (293).

Latinus speaks from his lofty throne, stating the obvious: whatever hope you had that Diomedes would join us, forget about it. And he recommends ceding a piece of land to the west to the Trojans, out of friendship, so that they may build and settle near the Latins—or if they prefer to go elsewhere, that our people build ships for them to help them onward. So the story of Aeneas and the Trojans in Italy has come full circle to where it began, before Juno and Allecto interefered, with a proposed alliance between the local Latins and the Trojans. To this Drances, speaking up again, adds a challenge to Turnus, that if he is so bound on having Lavinia for his wife that he accept a combat with Aeneas to resolve that matter— offering a direct resonance from the Menelaus-Paris duel in *Iliad* Book Three, with Helen to be definitively acquired by the victor.

Not surprisingly, Turnus responds with a violent blaze of

invective against Drances, Drances' words, and Drances' alleged cowardice. It is a fiery and powerful speech intended to stir up his troops to eagerness for the battlefield—and in which he notes, sarcastically, that the Trojans now make Diomedes tremble, and would presumably make Akhilleus tremble now, too, but not so Turnus! Indeed, when he culminates his speech with the words to bring on the great Trojan! he adds, "Let him surpass Akhilleus, and wear armor made by the hands of Vulcan!" (438-40), I will defeat him: "Aeneas calls? Well so do I! No Drances may take away my honor and glory" (442-4).

The reader understands the irony of these words, since Aeneas is indeed using arms made by Vulcan and, whether or not he surpasses Akhilleus in skill, Aeneas will equal his Akhaian counterpart's *furor* and with it, Turnus' Hektor-like doom. But the poet delays the arrival of that moment as a good epic poet should. While the Latins and their allies argue, Aeneas and his Trojans are approaching the city in battle formation—the truce obviously having ended, as far as they and we know. This offers Turnus an opportunity to regalvanize his troops: for "while you are arguing, they are preparing to attack us," he asserts in so many words. All is action within the city walls again—as Latinus broods that he should have been more hospitable to Aeneas in the first place, and Lavinia moves about with downcast eyes, feeling guilty for being the "cause" of all of this—with the digging of trenches and the bringing of offerings and prayers to the temple.

Lavinia's self-presentation is somewhat reminiscent of Helen's thoughts and words in *Iliad* VI:345-51—except that Helen *was* the cause of the Trojan War to the extent that she willingly (ignoring Euripides' later transmutation of this detail) went along with Paris/Alexandros' plan to be stolen away from her husband, whereas Lavinia is the completely innocent victim of two men's conflicting desires for her and of Turnus' misplaced sense that Aeneas is "stealing" her from him as if she were already his (Turnus') wife.

Turnus happily dons his armor and runs down to the main city gate, where he is met by perhaps the most unique figure in the epic, Camilla, and her Volscian troops. She has no real equivalent in the Homeric literature, although in the larger scope of Trojan

War narratives that have or have not survived, her equivalent would surely be Penthesilea, the Amazon princess who, as we have earlier noted, Akhilleus is said both to have slain and to have come to love at the very moment he was killing her, overwhelmed by admiration for her skill and particularly her courage as a warrior.[162] Camilla's appearance would certainly have offered an opportunity to interweave *eros* with *eris* in an obvious way, by suggesting a romantic connection to Turnus (or even a fatal encounter with Aeneas that emulated that between Akhilleus and Penthesilea), but the poet does not bother with that—as a practical matter, both Aeneas and Turnus are committed, in any case, to Lavinia, so Camilla merely remains a figure who is extraordinary, one that the poem's audience would not have anticipated: a warrior, and an outstanding one at that, who is female.

When she meets Turnus at the gate, they at first debate over who should go out and fight Aeneas—she suggests that she should fight the Trojan, while Turnus stay and guard the walls as Captain. Turnus has a different strategy planned—an ambush for Aeneas' troops in which he asks her to participate along with Messapus and other captains of Latin squadrons. Meanwhile, as once more the scene bounces back and forth between earth and Olympus, high in the halls of heaven, Diana, sister of Apollo, goddess of the moon and also of the hunt, expresses worry to a fellow divinity, Opis, over Camilla, her favorite mortal. Through Diana's long speech we get an account of who Camilla is, her family and her own accomplishments—and the fact that, wooed by many, she rejected all suitors in favor of her weapons and love (*amor*) of her virginity as an acolyte of the virgin goddess (582-4).

Diana sends her handmaiden Opis down to the battlefield with the goddess' own bow and arrows, to kill whoever wounds (or kills) Camilla—whose life, it seems, Fate has already committed to its end in the upcoming battle. The goddess describes how, when Camilla falls, she will waft her body in a cloud home to her own country—thus also making of her a parallel to another figure in the *Iliad*: Sarpedon, Lykian ally of the Trojans and son of Zeus for whom the god performs the same sort of service while unable to fend off the death decreed to Sarpedon by Fate, that comes at the hand of Patroklos.[163]

Enormous numbers of Trojan soldiers and their allies draw near the city walls, quickly met by squadrons of defenders, foremost among them, Camilla. Vergil sweeps his verses across the descriptive plain, detailing this duel and that, this death and that. His lens zooms in on Camilla, raging in the thick of the fight, "wearing her quiver like an Amazon, one breast exposed: she showers javelins, she plies the battle-axe; she never tires; her shoulder clangs with the golden bow, Diana's weapon," flanked left and right by well-chosen warrior maidens, all of them like Thracian Amazons (648-59). So the poet explicitly connects her and her squadron of maiden-warriors to the Amazons, as we might have expected him to do. Camilla's *aristeia* is presented by Vergil in bloody detail, making ample use of the sorts of similes that call the *Iliad* to mind. Alas, her death won't come at the hands of an Akhilleus.

Jupiter, meanwhile, watches the entire scene from on high, as often he seems to do—and reminding us, again and again, of how the *sacer* and *profanus* realms of divinity and humanity run on parallel but very separate tracks. He in-spirits Tarchon, the Etruscan ally of the Trojans, to resuscitate and rouse his troops, who are falling back before the fury of Camilla. The tide seems not yet to turn fully, until it falls to Arruns—albeit not by straightforward confrontation, but through stealth—to take Camilla down. "In hiding, he takes up his spear and prays: most high Apollo..." (784-5), asking for success, not to gain spoils or even glory for himself, but simply to remove this scourge of his fellow-soldiers from the battlefield and to get home alive. A unique sort of prayer before the cast of a weapon, in its disinterest in self-glory and emphasis on community—but consistent with the Roman ethos at its theoretical best.

And as often happens, Apollo hears and grants half the prayer. The hope for a return home, even without glory, will be denied, but the hope that his spear find its mark will be granted. Vergil presents the moment as if in time-lapse, as that spear flying swiftly yet in slow motion toward its target is somehow seen and heard by all the Volscians—except the Volscian who *is* the target; for Camilla hears and sees nothing until the spear is lodged in her bare breast. As Arruns slinks off—so his death will come not at this moment, from her enraged companions, for they are too focused on her to worry about the source of her demise—her maidens gather around their leader, hopelessly; Camilla orders Acca, her closest companion, with her last breath, to hurry to Turnus so that he can pick up the fight where she has left it.

Opis, meanwhile, has observed these events from high in the mountains, and, expressing mournful thoughts toward Camilla—asserting that she will be long remembered and honored, both by her patron goddess, Diana, and by human posterity—she pauses, and draws an arrow from the golden quiver of her mistress, letting loose a long, divinely true shot that finds its mark in the fleeing Arruns, who lies in the dust virtually unnoticed by his companions as the goddess soars back up to Olympus. The troops of Camilla, however, scatter and retreat, devoid of their bold leader; they are pushed back toward the city and the slaughter is pitiful—as mothers in their desperation fling weapons, as well as they can, from the walls down onto the Trojan attackers.

Book XI ends on a double note that sounds the doom of the defenders and the victory of the Trojans. The culmination of Camilla's *aristeia* is her death and the scattering retreat of her troops; this is followed in the last twenty verses by focus on the last, most ferocious defender, Turnus, who in his forest ambush, awaiting Aeneas, receives the unhappy report of Camilla's death, from Acca—so that he abandons his ambush and the woodlands his intimate knowledge of which would have given him some advantage over his foe, allowing Aeneas to go through the pass in safety and to come out of the dark woods.

> Both Turnus and Aeneas
> were striving to reach the city, swiftly, in full
> column and nearly side by side:
> simultaneously, Aeneas perceived the dust rising above the plain
> and saw the long Italian column,
> and Turnus saw Aeneas, fierce for battle,
> and heard the stamping and snorting of the horses. (906-11)

The long-delayed duel appears finally immanent—although the poet still delays a bit further, as night comes on to end the book in darkness, with the two armies camped before the city.

A Trojan victory and an Italian defeat have become inevitable, as the tone of Book XII's opening makes clear. For its first verse notes that "Turnus saw the Latins falling, broken, with Mars against them, and all eyes upon him"—for he knows that he must fulfill his vow to face Aeneas one-on-one. He boldly asserts that he shall do this, *now*. "...I will send him down to Tartarus, that renegade from Asia, (let the Latins sit and watch)—with one single sword—or we are beaten and he takes Lavinia as wife" (14-17).

The response from Latinus to the young warrior's bold declaration is quiet and calm: he reiterates that gods and men alike had prophesied that he ought not give his daughter to any local suitor; but that, when his wife, Amata, had been so upset—and because "I loved you, Turnus," he had given in, broke his initial promise to Aeneas, and allowed the taking up of arms to follow, with catastrophic consequences for the Latins. We have been beaten twice and barely hold the city;

>...the streams of the Tiber
> are warm with our blood and the broad fields
> white with our bones...
>
>...if, with Turnus dead,
> I stand prepared to join them as allies,
> then why not, while he still lives, break off the conflict?
> What will they say, all of your Rutulian kinsmen,
> all of Italy, if I betray you to death—may fortune keep
> such words from coming true!—the suitor of my only daughter?
> Consider war's uncertainties, and pity
> your aged father, far from us and grieving
> in Ardea, his homeland.

So Latinus remains true to his original convictions since the time when Aeneas first arrived, remains sorrowful that his inability to sway his wife and others has led to such destruction, and clearly considers it a foregone conclusion that, if Turnus goes out to battle

Aeneas, he—Turnus—will perish. His view of Turnus is somewhat paradoxical: he loves him as a son but remains unwilling to contradict the gods and so cannot accept him as a son-in-law, but his death is the last thing Latinus wants.

The words with which he ends—the reference to Turnus' father—recall at an oblique angle the sentiments that led Akhilleus to return Hektor's body to Priam, providing a—loving—resolution both to Akhilleus' anger and to the *Iliad* as an eristic epic. The oblique resonance might be seen to underscore Turnus'doom: Priam had come to Akhilleus to ask for his dead son's body back; Priam-like Latinus is trying to turn Turnus from the confrontation with the Akhilleus-like Aeneas that will kill Hektor-like Turnus.

Thus the outcome can, alas, not go in the positive direction that followed Priam's words to the real Akhilleus. The question, however, might be asked: what can Turnus possibly do at this point? Has he not painted himself into a corner? If he desists, will he appear cowardly in the shame culture of which he is part? Could he live in this general realm any longer—or would he need to go off, far away, gather a serious series of Odysseus-like, Aeneas-like adventures (and perhaps some exotic, far-away wife to love) before coming back, if he were to come back home at all? His situation is fraught with choice but without the perspective, perhaps, to consider the possible range and variety of choices that he might make. His response, unmoved by Latinus' plea, his anger only expanded, managing, at least, a loving rejection, is to address Latinus as "best of men" and to assert: "the care you have for me lay down, for my sake; let me have permission to trade death for renown/praise (*laus*). I, too, dear father, toss no mean spear, swing no mean sword, and blood follows the wounds I give. His goddess mother will not be there, this time, to hide him..." (48-52).

So Turnus—acknowledging a father-son/son-father love for and from Latinus—articulates the relationship between death and glory along lines that extend back into the Trojan War cycle and in particular to the figure of Akhilleus, who famously traded a long life/early death for undying *kleos*. He specifically alludes, within that cycle, to the moment in *Iliad* V, when Aphrodite rescued Aeneas from the battlefield at a critical, life-threatening moment in his duel with Diomedes.[164] The question of how and why Turnus knows, or thinks he knows, that she won't be there this time, sits in the air pregnantly—she has already assisted her son by providing him with divinely-wrought weapons, in any case—and is implicitly addressed by Amata, Latinus' wife, for whom Turnus has always been the favored would-be son-in-law: "He was the son she wanted," the poet notes.

"Clinging to him, she, [too,] made her plea: 'Turnus, our only hope, our only comfort in our sad, old age, the pride and honor of Latinus' kingdom, rest in your keeping... I implore you, I beg one favor: do not fight the Trojan!" (56-60). Even Lavinia, "listened and wept and blushed" (64-5)—which had the opposite effect on Turnus from what Amata might have wished. For seeing the girl's white cheeks turning crimson, he "burned more for battle" (71) and responded to Amata: "do not, oh mother, follow me with tears or any such omen as I go into battle. Turnus cannot delay his death" (72-4).

This outpouring of love and affection toward Turnus from all directions, is reminiscent, in its way, of the scene at the end of *Iliad* VI, when Hektor, Hekabe, Andromakhe, and Astyanax are gathered together on the walls of Troy, briefly viewing the battlefield below, just before, in spite of Andromakhe's plea, the Trojan hero returns to the battlefield and his eventual doom. The expressions of love and concern cannot, alas, contend successfully with Turnus' own pride and the exigencies of Fate—and Vergil's narrative, which demands a dramatic ending. He sends his friend, Idmon, as a herald, to offer the challenge to Aeneas for the following morning: one-on-one, with all the troops on both sides standing down, and Lavinia as the prize.

The poet shows us both heroes readying themselves—Turnus does have a Vulcan-forged sword, it turns out—and in another small detail that his final editing would no doubt have altered, Vergil seems to present him putting on his armor now, the evening before, rather than the following morning (87-8). Or is Turnus so eager for battle that he sleeps in his armor, or does he not sleep at all on that fateful night, perhaps the last of his life?

When dawn arrives, the drama of the poem calls for one more twist and one more delay before the narrative arrives toward its denouement. Juno (who else?) observing the spreading of troops out onto the field, pulling one last metaphorical arrow from her quiver, calls upon Juturna—Turnus' own sister, whom Jupiter had previously turned into a Naiad, (after he had raped her!), giving her tendance over pools and rivers—noting that she, Juturna, is the only one "of all the Latin girls who have made their way to big-hearted Jove's ungrateful couch" whom Juno has favored, giving her, gladly, a place in heaven (142-5). She bids her hurry down to the battlefield to help her brother, whom Juno cannot bear to watch engaging Aeneas—"and if there is some way, snatch him from death" (157).

On the battlefield below, that very Aeneas—*pius Aeneas*—utters both a prayer and, more than that, a statement—including, among the divinities to whom he directs his words, "Queen Juno, now, I pray, a kinder goddess" (179)—culminating with an oath that,

...if victory be granted,
(as I expect, and may the gods confirm it),
in this martial moment, I will not have Italians
be subject to the Trojans; I seek no kingdom
for myself: let both, unbeaten nations,
on equal terms enter eternal concord.
I shall establish rituals and gods;
may father Latinus keep his weapons, his sceptre.
The Trojans will build walls for me; Lavinia
shall give the city her name. (187-94)

Thus ever the *pius* leader, Aeneas addresses both gods and men, and reiterates the stance that he had originally taken when he first approached Latinus, but also initiates what the Romans would understand to be their approach to neighbors whom they have conquered or anticipated conquering: that, in theory, at least, non-Romans could aspire to become part of the *res romana*—the Roman thing—and not remain a conquered, downtrodden enemy. For the most part, this was true of Rome and a secret of its success: one could move from enemy to allied status and from that, gain "Italian" rights and then, perhaps "Latin" rights and even, eventually, full rights as a Roman citizen. Certainly one's place within the political firmament of Rome was not ethnocentrically determined—contrary to the norm throughout most of antiquity for most of its kingdoms and empires—but one could aspire to rise all the way to the top, theoretically, if one could and did contribute to the state.[165]

Latinus responds by swearing that no violence will erupt again from the Italian side, regardless of the outcome of the upcoming duel. The two leaders affirm this covenant between them, with sacrifices and altars high with offerings. And yet again, the Rutulian followers of Turnus remain restive and unsure of this commitment—and Juturna moves among them, disguised as Camers, a noble young warrior, seeking to stir them up, yet again. And once more a sign from heaven seems to point away from a simple Aeneas-Turnus confrontation and back toward full-out battle. The augur, Tolumnius, comments on what they all observe: an eagle by the shore capturing a fleeing bird in its talons, but then, when the entire flock wheels and turns back on the eagle, he drops his prey and flies back up into the clouds (245-56). The seer encourages the Rutulians to take up arms again, causing Aeneas to take flight—and lets fly his spear, which hits one of nine brothers, causing the others to take up their swords in anguish and anger.

This moment is no doubt intended to resonate from that moment in *Iliad* IV when the Trojan archer, Pandaros, is encouraged by a disguised Athena to let fly an arrow during the ceasefire in which Menelaos was defeating Paris in a duel; the arrow wounds Menelaos and causes the truce to fall apart.[166] Again, and typical of Vergil's cleverness, that resonance is made more complex. As the fighting gradually begins to pick up, the altars stripped—and one Etruscan leader, Aulestes, slain on the altars by Messapus; another, Corynaeus, snatches up a firebrand from an altar and thrusts it in the face of the attacking Ebysus before stabbing him with a sword; Podalirus is slain by the battle axe of Alsus—Aeneas, head bare, unarmed, calls out, hoping to check his men, and from an unidentified hand, (whether divine or human remains unknown), an arrow flies and wounds him, forcing him from the field (311-23).

The ultimate outcome of this moment must be different between the two epics, since both the dictates of Fate and of the poetic genre necessitate a difference. The broken truce in *Iliad* IV must spread like a flood from a broken dike: had the duel been allowed to play out, the war might have ended and Troy in the end might have been saved—and twenty more books of the epic would have not been composed. The break in *Aeneid* XII can only be temporary, on the other hand, since the epic is nearing its end and that end requires as its culminating eristic event the final duel between Aeneas and Turnus who are, when all is said and done, not as much the Latin-language equivalents of Paris and Menelaos as they are of Akhilleus and Hektor.[167]

This extended moment leading from oaths to broken oaths serves an important purpose with regard to that final duel. Once again, we are reminded of the *pietas*—the essential honesty, modesty and goodness—of Aeneas. And once again the eventual demise of Turnus is being anticipatorily justified: as he sees Aeneas leave the field, instead of adding his voice to the Trojan leader's call for a restoration of calm and a fulfillment of the agreement that the two of them would duel—and that peace would ensue regardless of who was the victor—he "calls for arms, for horses, leaps proudly into his chariot, plies the reins, drives fiercely, gives death to many brave heroes, rolls many, still half alive, under the wheels, crushes the columns in his vehicle, and showers spear after spear at those who try to flee him" (326-30)—in short, he exponentially expands the problem of a major broken truce, engendering eristic chaos rather than helping to limit it.

Somehow this final expression of Turnus' battle prowess feels less like a final *aristeia* than a hollow expression of brute force devoid of honor. But that is no doubt how it is intended to feel to the reader/listener. While Turnus is slaughtering Trojans left and right, Achates, Mnestheus, and Ascanius bring Aeneas back to camp, "bleeding, leaning on his long spear with every other step, struggling, angry, to pull the arrowhead from the wound, for the shaft had broken off" (385-8). They try to extract it by digging around it with a sword point, without success. Iapyx, with his Apollo-inspired medical knowledge, tries to get it out with herbs and also a forceps, but it is stubborn. Finally, Venus arrives, disguised in a cloud, with a plant—dittany, with its downy leaves and purple blossoms; a plant familiar to wild goats, that use it to cure arrow wounds—mixes it with river water, adding some ambrosia. Iapyx, not really aware of where this mixture had come from or what it could do, nonetheless washes the wound with it—and suddenly the pain was gone, the blood stopped flowing, the arrowhead was easily extracted from the flesh, and Aeneas felt entirely restored. Divine mother-love prepares him anew for battle.

As Aeneas quickly attires himself in his armor, his embrace and words are for his son: that he watch how skill and not mere luck determine the outcome of a battle—that he remember, in later years, the inspiration of his models: "your father Aeneas and your uncle, Hektor" (440). There is the usual kind of double irony in these last few words, since Hektor was defeated, in the end, by Akhilleus, who possessed both greater skill and superior arms—to say nothing of obliging gods and Fate—and because, in this case, Aeneas will be playing the role of Akhilleus (with superior armor, obliging gods and Fate, and perhaps superior fighting skills) and Hektor's role will go to the doomed Turnus.

As he rushes from the gates, indeed, "it is Turnus alone whom he summons" (466-7). In her panic, as she realizes that the delayed confrontation can be delayed no longer, Juturna tosses Metiscus, Turnus' charioteer, far from her brother's vehicle, assuming Metiscus' form and voice herself to take his place. She keeps steering in a manner that makes it impossible for Aeneas to catch up to his foe. Both Aeneas and Turnus leave victims in their wakes as they storm around the battlefield, never arriving before each other. The poet continues to delay that meeting, describing other confrontations, and including an assault on the gates of Latinus' city itself, demanding that they open them.

The situation of the Latins grows grimmer. Amata, believing Turnus dead, in her great grief—and crying out that she is "the guilty one and the source of all these evils (600)"—hangs herself. As the women learn, and then Lavinia does, the halls ring loud with lamentation. Meanwhile Turnus, down on the battlefield, feels less and less exultant—and turns to his sister, saying that he has known all along that it has been she, in disguise, who not only is driving his chariot, but was instrumental in breaking the treaty. Why, he asks her, have you come from Olympus for such labors? "Was it to see your brother in pitiful cruel death?"

It is a poignant moment, as he tells her that he knows and

she knows that he cannot be saved, but that he will die with honor—and barely has he finished speaking when a messenger, Saces, himself badly wounded in the face, comes with the news that Aeneas is tearing the field apart, that the Trojans are at the gates, that the queen has committed suicide, and that they all wait for him as their last hope. The audience understands that this hope is a function, really, of Aeneas' earlier vow and thus depends on Turnus' decision to call a halt to the fighting and to confront Aeneas, alone. He can only save them if he assents to his own demise. All of the delays, and with them, the myriad side-deaths, have followed the inexorable thread of Fate to this moment. Indeed, if at first Turnus is silent, staring with "shame and sadness boiling up in his great heart" (666-7), he speaks up and observes that "Fate is the winner now; keep out of my way, my sister: now I follow as the god and fortune (*fortuna*—which in Greek would be *tykhe*) call. I am ready for Aeneas, ready to bear whatever is bitter in death" (676-9).

No amount of sibling love can any longer prevent the inevitable, final moment of *eris*. Turnus rushes toward the city; Aeneas, perceiving his foe's approach, leaves the city gates and hurries out to meet him. The field is all but empty now, except for these two heroic antagonists, "and Jupiter holds the scales in balance with each man's destiny as weight and counterweight" (725-6). Full of confidence, "Turnus, rising to his full height, attacks swiftly, striking with his sword..." (728-30), "but the sword is treacherous; it is broken off with the blow half spent" (731-2)—it turns out that, in his hurry to return to the battlefield, Turnus had grabbed the wrong weapon, not the god-made blade left for him by Daunus, but that of Metiscus. So now, essentially weaponless, he flies across the plain in circles—Trojans all around him, a swamp to one side and the city walls on the other—trying to avoid the pursuit of Aeneas, who is not so fast, the arrow wound still hurting him: "his knees protest and impede his running, but he keeps on, footstep after footstep, hot after his anxious enemy..." (747-8).[168]

Five times they circle before the city, and Turnus yells for someone to bring him his proper sword, but nobody is willing to enter the field to do so. Aeneas, who cannot outrun his adversary, pauses to yank his spear out of the fractured trunk of an olive tree sacred to Faunus, where it had lodged. Turnus cries out to the woodland god in his panic, begging him not to allow Aeneas to pull out the weapon, and Faunus hears him; the tree holds the spear fast—while Juturna, still disguised as Metiscus, rushes forward with her brother's sword. Venus, angry at the double divine interference, forces Aeneas' spear out of the tree and now the two warriors face each other again, one with a sword and the other with a spear.

The churning of the waters of this confrontation with respect to the interweave—forgive the mix of metaphors—of human and divine action together with that third thread, Fate, begins a final surge as Juno, looking down on things, hears Jupiter's voice asking her whether she will continue to interfere in order to delay what she knows must be the ultimate outcome here: that Aeneas is destined for a divine sort of immortality. Was it proper for Juturna to intervene—who could not have done so without you!?—and give back to Turnus the sword that will delay the outcome? "Things have come to an end" (803). You were given license to do so many things to the Trojans to make them suffer and to delay their ultimate success here—"even to mix wedding hymns with mourning—but I forbid you from going any further" (805-6).

Indeed, most of the last five books of the epic have featured mourning over the dead killed in the strife engendered through divergent views of how Lavinia's wedding should proceed; that symbol of love has been submerged in ongoing strife and its aftermath. Juno responds to Jupiter that, knowing where he wished things to go she had left the field below for the Olympian heights, and thus abandoned Turnus. She admits to having urged Juturna to help her brother. She swears, though, that she did not grant her license to take up weapons herself, admitting by implication that the wounding of Aeneas from afar had been Juturna's own work; for the goddess specifically mentions *arcum*—"bow"—along with the more generic *tela*—"weapons" (815)—rather than merely referencing the bringing to Turnus of his sword.

Here, too, Juno underscores the sort of promise that Aeneas himself had made earlier: she asks of her husband that when, afterwards, peace is made, and the marriage between Aenas and Lavinia is celebrated, the Latins not end up required to change their language, to be known as Trojans. Let Troy, fallen, be forgotten

(823-5). Thus the poet ascribes to Juno credit for the carrying forward of a Latin-Italian essence into what will evolve as the *res romana* of which he himself is part. For Jupiter readily assents to this: Latin language, and Latin rituals and sacred laws will apply to the descendants of both contending groups down there on the battlefield—and Juno, happy, finally gives up her anti-Aeneas anger.

But on that battlefield below, the duel has not yet reached its outcome—and Juturna is still trying desperately to save her brother. Jupiter dispatches one of the Furies, who takes the form of a tiny screech owl that beats against the shield of Turnus. He suddenly feels his limbs tire, his hair rises in terror, his voice abandons him. And Juturna, perceiving this from afar, cries out: what can a sister do to help you now, poor Turnus?" (872)—and laments the fact that Jupiter had rewarded her for his taking of her virginity by granting her immortality, who now must outlive the beloved brother whom she will see slain before her helpless eyes. She sinks into the greyness of the river.

Aeneas yells to Turnus at this point that it is time to stop running; Turnus yells back that it is Jupiter and the gods whom he fears, turned against him—not Aeneas—and he sees a huge boulder. He lifts it—and the turn of phrase echoes the sort that appears in the *Iliad*: that a dozen men in our own era could barely lift it, but that he lifts it easily and throws it with speed and power. It falls short of its mark, nonetheless—"his knees shake and his blood runs ice-cold" (905), and he has nowhere to go: the chariot and the charioteer are gone (we recall how Hektor looks around and finds that the figure he thought was his brother, Deiphobos—whose guise Athena had taken—there to help and support him, had suddenly disappeared at the fateful moment)—and the fatal spear, huge as a tree, from Aeneas' hand, comes flying fast and furiously, piercing Turnus' seven-fold shield and his armor, and wounding Turnus in the thigh. He crumbles to the ground.

As he falls, the Rutulians rise to their feet; they groan aloud and their voices echo through the woods around. Turnus,

> humbled, a suppliant, lifts his eyes and his beseeching
> right hand—"I have indeed deserved this, nor do I beg for myself;

make use of your luck," he says, "but if feeling for an unhappy parent is able to touch you, pity old Daunus (as I would Anchises, your father): I ask only that you send my body back to him…" (930-6)

"…Lavinia is yours to wed.
Let hate continue no further." (937-8)

What might we expect of Aeneas at this moment? How will his renowned *pietas* translate into action? "Aeneas stood fierce in his arms, dropping his eyes and pulling back his right hand" — so Vergil repeats the words "*oculos dextramque,*" used of Turnus' action as a suppliant, but he flanks the phrase by very different verbs. Turnus' right had been extended in entreaty; Aeneas pulls his back with ambiguity: pulled it back, away from contact with Turnus' hand and/or pulled it back from its no doubt raised, aggressive position, with his sword held within it, about to strike?[169]

Indeed, this gesture more clearly bespeaks a pause as we follow into the next verse, in which "he hesitated, for the speech began to bend him" (940-1; *cunctantem flectere sermo coeperat*)" back from his anger and his murderous intention. So, more than merely agreeing to send the body back — which, Akhilleus' wrath at Hektor notwithstanding, as an exception to the rule — was not a particularly unusual request of a warrior about to die at the hands of his enemy, in this world in which high-born opponents most often retained a distinct respect for each other and for the gods and Fate. Aeneas *feels* to us as if he might even desist from administering the *coup de grace* to Turnus, overwhelmed by that part of his *pietas* that includes a sense of empathy.

Alas, the word that follows this phrase, *infelix* ("unhappy"), sets in motion the sudden surge in Aeneas' anger and the tumble downhill of Turnus' fate to the bottom of the poem, beneath the shadows. "Unhappy, accursed" — the beginning of a pouring out in the sort of fragmented syntax of which Latin is so uniquely capable, thanks to its grammatical forms — "on the shoulder, when there appeared, high, the swordbelt and with the familiar, glistening, very belt, studs, of Pallas the boy" (941-3), more coherently translated and continuing as

> ... he hesitated, for the speech began to bend him,
> when there appeared high on the shoulder the unhappy/accursed
> swordbelt—the very belt, with its familiar studs glistening,
> of the boy, Pallas, whom Turnus had wounded and killed—
> that enemy token that he now wore on his own shoulder. (940-44)

The interesting thing about that word, *infelix*, is that it can really attach itself to so many nouns in these lines: not only the sword belt, but Turnus as well as Pallas and also Aeneas are all encircled by the studded belt of unhappiness.

This is a moment that brings all four of these elements together as a reminder of how fundamental the human condition simply *is* as *infelix*, with its brevity—even if *kleos/fama/laus* can offer a kind of enduring length to it—and its constant tension between *eros* and *eris* elements. While Aeneas will not be doomed, per se, by the action that follows, the way Akhilleus was by his last eristic act in the *Iliad*, to perish before the war can come to an end—on the contrary, the immediate fate of Aeneas after the poem has ended will be to marry Lavinia (after the presumed appropriate time for mourning all the dead, including Lavinia's mother, Amata, has passed). His post-Turnus destiny is to set in motion a long and glorious history leading all the way forward to the time of Augustus and Vergil—yet, like Turnus and Pallas, he, too, will eventually die. His divine mother's love cannot change that fate any more than Turnus' fate can be altered through the intervention of his own divine sister's love.

Perhaps all of this is both part of what causes Aeneas to hesitate, and then—aside from the glint on Turnus' shoulder that sets his raw emotions back in motion—the realization that given the brevity of our time here, we need to act decisively, suffuses his mind and his limbs. For

> once he saw with his eyes that relic, reminder of
> his savage sadness, he felt his terrible anger surge with *furor*,
> [and screamed]: 'do you, clad in the spoils torn from one of mine
> really imagine that you will escape from me?!? Pallas with this wound,

Pallas slaughters you and exacts the penalty for your criminal blood!' (945-9)

It is an emphatic symptom of the irrational angry passion that has enveloped Aeneas that he rhetorically asks Turnus whether he imagines "that you will escape me?!?!?"—when all that Turnus had requested was that his body be returned to Daunus, not that he be spared death or shown some other mercy. Even at this penultimate moment, filled with the Akhillean wrath of Aeneas, the hero's words and the poet's syntax remove the responsibility for administering the final blow from Aeneas himself, transferring it rhetorically to Pallas; Aeneas might be viewed as the instrument through which the shade of Pallas works—that Aeneas who, from the first scene of the poem has again and again been moved along by forces larger than he, rather than pushing himself and events forward out of his own action.

The ultimate moment follows in two contrastive parts, in the last three lines of the poem. "Saying this, burning, he buried the iron blade in the chest before him, but as for the limbs of that other [Turnus], they relaxed with icy cold and with an indignant moan his life fled to the shadows below" (950-2). So Aeneas blazes with heat at this last moment as Turnus freezes with cold. The beginning of the *Iliad* was *menis*—the fiery wrath—of Akhilleus, which he had managed to quench in favor of empathy for others, by the end of that poem. Aeneas had begun the *Aeneid* freezing cold in that stormy sea. At the end of this poem he is on fire and his antagonist has turned cold.[170]

Many critics have been disturbed by the apparently un-*pius* conduct of Aeneas—or at least Turnus' sense of indignation at it—in these last eight lines. The words are often used as another example of something that Vergil would have fixed had he lived a little bit longer. If one might argue that all that Trunus asked for was that his body be returned to his father, and that there is no necessary indication that Aeneas will not do that, still on the other hand, the sudden rage with which he slays his foe seems somewhat out of character. And perhaps Vergil would indeed have altered the tone as he fine-tuned his masterpiece.

What, however, if that tone were *intentional* on Vergil's part? What if this ending deliberately connects to the apparently off-target ending of Book VI, when Aeneas returns through the "wrong" gate from the underworld—the gate of ivory, of false dreams, rather than that of horn, of true dreams? As noted previously, Vergil is known to have been drawn seriously to the Pythagorean/Orphic religion—a mystery religion that included among its beliefs the notion of the reincarnation of souls. It is clear that Augustus saw a direct connection between himself and Aeneas (and through Aeneas, to Aphrodite—as is evident from the small dolphin and Amor pairing at his feet in the renowned, full-fledged portrait of the emperor in the garden of Livia's villa at Prima Porta, as we have seen).[171]

I have earlier proposed, speculatively, that it was the poet's intention to suggest not that Aeneas came through the wrong *gate* but that the *wrong Aeneas*, so to speak, came back through that gate: that it was an *eidolon* of Aeneas. So the eristic Aeneas that carries through the second half of the epic, and culminates his eristic actions with the stabbing of Turnus who, surprised and dismayed by that act, flees indignantly to the shades below—is not the true Aeneas. His unexpectedly un-*pius* action reflects that reality. The *true* Aeneas is waiting to be reborn—a thousand years later, as *Augustus*. Augustus is—to repeat—Vergil's primary audience, the primary student for the didactic elements in particular strewn throughout the poem: he is being constantly reminded that, like his ancestral hero, he must be *pius*, with all that that term connotes in Roman ethos at its best. But perhaps Aeneas is intended by Vergil to be more than a mere model for Augustus.

There is a fundamental paradox for Anchises' *pius* son. He is modelled in part on Odysseus and in part on Akhilleus, but his *pietas* separates him from both. Yet the woman he leaves, Dido, self-destructs, whereas the goddesses left by Odysseus— Kirke and Kalypso—do not; and more problematic, the anger at his primary foe concludes Aeneas' epic whereas Akhilleus is given time to resolve his anger toward his primary foe in his epic. Even the profoundly merciless *eris* with which Odysseus deals with the suitors is followed by epilogic narrative elements that are allowed to culminate with an endnote of resolution and almost reconciliation. Vergil's Aeneas' most pressing difficulties will be resolved through an Augustus more able to exercise love, (in particular, *clementia*—

clemency), towards others—as the Emperor claims to have done in his *Last Will and Testament* (*Res Gestae*), (where he also asserts that his *pietas* was noted by the Roman people)—than Aeneas can at the end of his poem.[172]

The *Aeneid* ends on an unexpected and perhaps unsatisfying eristic note, but because Vergil has so directly connected it to the Roman future leading to his own time—most obviously in the prophecies provided to Aeneas by Anchises in the Underworld, in Book VI—the audience knows that the primary aftermath moment of this ending will be the wedding of Aeneas and Lavinia, and the resolution of the conflict between Latins and Trojans that will lead to the forging of a new people that will one day rule the world. In the end, *eris* will yield to the *eros* that engendered it—and the Trojan War cycle that began with a wedding on Olympos that led immediately and directly to the *eris* at Troy engendered by the goddess, Eris, herself, will come full circle in its final turn to a wedding, one that leads from the gates of Troy—back—to the new gates of Dardanian Rome.

Put differently, the *Aeneid* ends with the end of the Greek-emulating cycle of poetry and the last, very Akhaian-like act of its protagonist. The death of Turnus-Hektor is, one might say, the death of that cycle—and the end of Aeneas-as-Akhilleus/Odysseus. Its understood aftermath will be the birth out of those funerary ashes of the Roman cycle, which will culminate with the birth of Aeneas-as-Augustus. Aeneas' descendant and alter ego is the primary patron of the poem, and the consummate symbol for the poet and his larger audience of the *res romana* at its most magnificent and august (pun intended).

Chapter Eight

From Latin Epic to Lyric

The interweave of *eros* and *eris* in Roman poetry is by no means limited to Vergil's magnificent epic. On the contrary, it wends its way through Latin lyric poetry and resonates within Roman comedy and satire and is even noticable within the most singular of Latin-language philosophical works—itself composed as an epic poem, in six books of dactylic hexameter—the *De Rerum Natura* ("On the Nature of Things") by Lucretius.

Latin-language lyric poetry, like its epic counterpart, looks back to the Greeks; it resonates, in part, from Greek lyric poetry but then transforms it into something uniquely Roman. Occasionally, a Roman lyric poet will make a point of suggesting that his subject is more significant than that of war—more *epic* than epic, which is thus viewed as the articulator of *eris*—for his subject is *eros*.[173]

The last two generations of Roman elegists in particular will also be influenced by another development in Greek poetry—much later than the time of Sappho, Pindar and the other lyric poets. During the Hellenistic period—in the third-second centuries BCE, when, as we have noted above (247-8, 251), Greek art is evolving toward Roman art, there developed an important trend in Greek poetry to reject the urge to write epics modelled after and seeking to compete with Homer. Among the key figures in this movement was Kallimakhos,[174] an important and hugely erudite figure in the Alexandrian library but also a writer known for his short poems and epigrams. It was he who urged poets to "drive their wagons on untrodden fields," rather than following those well-worn tracks of Homer.

Kallimakhos (310-240 BCE) admired brief poems, carefully formed with well-chosen words. Although he did write poems in praise of his royal patrons—the Ptolemaic rulers of Egypt—he mostly stayed away from epic and heroic subjects and their standard dactylic hexameter form, trying different styles and different metrical schemes, as well as diverse subjects. Among these was a collection of elegiac poems organized in four books. One extended part of one of his longer works, the *Aitia* ("Sources") has been reconstructed—it is known as the *Koma Berenices*—from papyrus remains and from the renowned Latin adaptation by Catullus (Catullus 66). While Catullus (ca 84-ca 54 BCE) was the first Latin poet to make use of a work by Kallimakhos, the later poets to whom we will subsequently direct ourselves referenced him occasionally, usually to justify their not writing epic poetry. Even Vergil echoes him with regard to this issue in his pre-*Aeneid* writing, specifically *Eclogue* 6.3-5. And Propertius in particular refers to him a number of times, as we shall see.

Love is not the only subject of Latin lyric poetry, but it is certainly the subject best remembered down through the ages. But just as Vergil's *Aeneid*, as we have seen—and its Homeric antecedents—interweaves *eros* and *eris* both broadly and in myriad detailed ways, so the love focus most endemic to the poetry of Catullus, Horace, Tibullus, Propertius, and Ovid offers more than an occasional eristic aspect.

I Catullus

One of the unifying features found in the Roman lyric poets is that each has a particular girlfriend, who goes by what is typically a made-up name. Thus Catullus (87/4-54 BCE), for instance, devotes many poems to Lesbia—almost certainly the historical figure, Clodia—wife of the Roman aristocrat, Metellus Celer, and sister of L. Clodius Pulcher, supporter and agent of Julius Caesar. Clodia was a decade older than the young poet who arrived from his native city of Verona into Rome in his early twenties, still unknown as a poet. It took some time for her to return his affection, which in the end was insufficient to gain him the marriage to her that he wanted (Metellus died in 59 BCE), and eventually the bitterness of rejection—an eristic tone—enters into his words.

At first, though, things were sunnier. As it was never appropriate to direct one's poems to a clearly recognizable individual, given that the poems would be publicly consumed (and what would be the point for them to remain private: *self*-love demanded a desire for fame, just as the object and subject of one's love demanded beautiful lyrics). So he called her Lesbia—the meter of that name is identical to that of her real name, Clodia—as a kind of homage to Sappho, perhaps, since that Greek lyric poet came from the island of Lesbos. In fact, one of his presumed first poems (51)[175] dedicated to her is, in its first three stanzas—its rhythmic pattern is, in fact, called Sapphic meter—virtually a translation of a famous verse by Sappho that we have previously quoted:[176]

> He seems to me equal to a god,
> —he is, if it may be said without blasphemy, *above* the gods—
> who, sitting opposite you,
>   stares and hears
>
> you sweetly laughing, that tears
> all the senses from wretched me: for as soon as
> I saw you, Lesbia, [no voice]
>   was left to me,
>
> but my tongue is numb, flames course
> all through my weakened limbs, my ears
> ring with a sound all their own, my eyes
>   are covered with double darkness.

These three stanzas follow fairly closely the words of Sappho, translating Greek into Latin, and adding a few changes of detail. But just as Sappho's poem had four—if not five—stanzas, a case can be made that Catullus did not limit his poem to these three. His fourth, however, demonstrates again the truth that Roman poets, when they emulated Greek models, did not merely translate the language, but transformed the subject matter along Roman lines:

> Leisure, Catullus, is a disease for you,
> you exult and delight too much in leisure,
> leisure has destroyed kings of yore and
> > happy cities alike.

So the final stanza, if it is indeed part of this poem, redirects the poet's emotions away from the personal in a more communal sort of direction—consistent with evolving Roman principles. The element of strife is employed in the suggestion that the leisurely mood that supplies, and is supplied by, love, is ultimately destructive—albeit with less focus, in the end, on the poet himself than on prior kings and entire cities. Of course, one could say that self-love is still front and center through the self-aggrandisement of presenting himself on a par with kings and entire cities.

To whatever extent one might see this poem, like its sapphic model, as offering a tension between love as a positive experience and love as a negative (so not, then, necessarily "strife" per se, but one of its bitter siblings), other early poems more straightforwardly reflect the passion with which the romance with Clodia/Lesbia was developing. In one (2) he writes of playing with the little bird, his sweetheart's pet, held in her lap—and would seem to be punning on who plays with whose little bird thusly situated, "with her fingertip." In another, (5), he calls to her to "live and let us love, my Lesbia—and let us count the gossip of overly strict old men as worth a single penny"—their disapproval will fail to inject a mood of strife into their love, who must get lost in so many kisses that they cannot keep count of them.

Within two or three years, while he still believes in her love for him, there is a clear trace of less conviction (109): "You resolve to me an eternal pleasant love, my precious…may the great gods grant that this promise be true and that such a pact of eternal love be able to lead through our lives"—for it would seem not to be a given that the promise and resolution that she offers have the kind of shelf-life for which he would hope.

Sooner than later other poems reflect the disappointment and then growing bitterness that arrives after the death of Metellus in 59 and Clodia's freedom to marry Catullus; while she continues to profess her love for him—"my lady says none other than me would she marry, not even Jupiter himself"—the marriage is not going to happen, and "what a woman says to a desirous lover ought to be written in wind and fast-flowing water" (70). Within another year the situation has worsened: Clodia transfers her passion to Caelius Rufus—a close friend of the poet, no less. Catullus writes both regarding Caelius, of his betrayal of the friendship, (this is *eris* as it pertains to the destruction of love between friends), and of Clodia—placing the conflict between the two sides of his emotions front and center—to wit: "*Odi et amo...*"; I hate and I love. Perhaps you may ask me how I can do this. I don't know, but I feel it and I agonize" (8). With this couplet we arrive at the juxtaposition of love and strife as a self-conscious interweave within one tiny work.

Latin is particularly rich in its ability to convey emotion by the use of well-chosen phonemes—as we have seen in Vergil[177]—and the rhythmic patterns derived from and building on those of Greek poetry. Catullus has tended, up to this point, to end his poetic lines with the light mooded rhythm of iambs (ŭ —). As he pens the first of his poems that reflect his turn toward heavy despair, he uses a slow, limping sort of meter known as scazon, in which every line ends in a spondee (— —) or a trochee (— ŭ). He is torn between recognizing Clodia's fickleness and his own insanity at not being able to free himself from her emotionally (8):

Wretched Catullus, you must stop your craziness,
and let perish what you see is lost.
Once you were accustomed to bright, sunny days
when you wandered where that girl led you,
—she who was loved by me as no other shall ever be loved.
Then when those many pleasures were being enjoyed,
which she wanted as much as you did,
truly you were used to bright sunny days.
Now she no longer wants them: you, too, powerless, must cease to want them,
must cease pursuing her, cease living wretchedly,
but must be resolute: make your heart hard.
Farewell, beloved girl. Now Catullus is hard,
and will no longer seek you out nor beg you, unwilling one, to love.

But you will regret it when you are asked by no one for nothing.
Poor thing, alas for you, what sort of life remains for you?
Who, now, will come near you? To whom will you seem beautiful?
Whom now will you love? Who will call you his?
Ah, but you, Catullus, be hard and endure.

His words are bitter and sad—and filled with wishful thinking, given that she has already taken on another lover—his close friend—by the time that he is writing these words. Under other circumstances, perhaps—she is a decade older than Catullus—the idea that he is her last chance for love might make sense, but not as the situation was really playing out at that point in time.

Wishful thinking, as well, that he could remain hard and let her go from his mind and heart. For although he went abroad, to Bithynia, in 57, no doubt at least in part in order to forget her—during which journey, she and Caelius split up—when he came back to Rome he found himself still unable to keep her out of his mind.

Was it easier or more difficult, knowing that she and Caelius were no longer together—but that, apparently, there were others, still, who shared her bed? Not a single lover replacing him, but more than one—or so the stories flew regarding her lifestyle, although we lack her viewpoint, so can only see her through the lens that Catullus holds up for us. The idea of her taking on multiple lovers is as bitterly stated in a kind of epilogue to their affair (58)—addressed to Caelius, no less—in which he notes that "Lesbia, that Lesbia whom Catullus loved more than any and all others; now in the crossroads and alleyways, she robs the nephews of great Remus." That is: how the descendants of that noble Roman ancestor have fallen, paying for the services of Lesbia, who hangs out on street corners and side alleys—a cash-hungry prostitute.

He wrote a longer poem (76), a bit later—still her image tortures him, although he no longer wants to rebuild the relationship, should it be feasible—the centerpiece of which was his invocation to the gods to help him:

> It is difficult, so difficult, to give up that long-lasting love,
> but truly you must [help me] do it, in whatever way you can…
>
> Oh gods, if ever you could have pity, if ever
> you might give help at the end to one on the brink of death,
> look upon me, one filled with misery and, if you see a life of
>   purity,
> tear this pernicious plague from me…
>
> I no longer ask that she love me,
> or even be chaste—something she cannot do—
> but only that you remove this foul disease.
> Oh gods, give me back myself for the sake of my *pietas*.

So, embedded in his ongoing bitterness and interwoven with his incapacity to let go of his passion for Clodia is his sense of having been victimized by her wiles, he the innocent, *pius* one! (How very Roman of him; although *pietas* in this context most likely simply means that he was loyal to Lesbia, never straying toward other women…)

The last poem that seems to relate to Lesbia/Clodia—written a year or two before his death—was directed not to her but to two friends, Furius and Aurelius. To them he consigned his last message for or about her (11), still calling her (no doubt sarcastically, at this point), *mea puella*—"my girl"—and asking them, apparently in response to her asking them to convey the offer of a reconciliation to Catullus, to "say a few unkind words" to her. Those words that follow in the poem are cruel and bitter insults flung at her—that "she live and be well, who holds three hundred lovers in her embrace at once" and who murdered his love, like a scythe cutting down a wildflower that can bloom no longer.

The love that resonated through light-hearted poetry as the relationship began has ended in strife-driven words. Disinterest is the opposite of love; strife and hate are merely redirected continuations of it. It does not seem that the poet ever got over Lesbia—whether she actually was Clodia or someone else unknown to us. More to the point of this discussion, the "model" offered by Catullus in his life and his poetry—of intense *eros* that gradually yields to *eris*—will be followed and amplified by subsequent generations of Roman poets.

II Horace

We have side-stepped Vergil's *Eclogues* since they offer less to our theme (and space is limited) than does Catullus—or do other poets who are somewhat younger contemporaries of Vergil. Unlike Catullus and his Clodia/Lesbia, Horace (65-3 BCE), the first of these, directs those of his poems that are love-centered to several different women. His *Odes* ended up in four separate books—the first three were published together in 23 BCE and the fourth a decade later. There have been any number of discussions and theories regarding the organization and its relationship either to content or to the order of composition. For our purposes, we can simply examine them by following the edited order, but we must recognize that this will mean either that our poet experiences a good number of ups and downs, inconsistencies, and shifts in romantic mood between his first and last *Odes* or that the order offers no reflection of the biographical order of his heart.

Thus, early on in the sequence of the first collection of *Odes*—that begin with an invocation to Maecenas, the renowned patron of poets (I.1); and a second (I.2) to Augustus; a third (I.3) to the much-admired Vergil; and a fourth (I.4) to his wealthy friend, Sestius—this last is about winter's turn to spring, and the inevitability of death—he addresses Pyrrha (I.5). This may or may not be an ode that was written early, but the relationship has apparently already ended. The first three quatrains of the four that comprise the poem ask and comment, sarcastically, on her new relationship—with a boy—presumably considerably younger than she, but in any case, not a real *man*:

> Which graceful boy, soaked in perfumes,
> embraces you now among the roses,
>   in some pleasant grotto, Pyrhha?
>   For whom are you tying up your golden hair

in simple elegance? Alas, how often he shall
weep over changed faith and gods and will come to
    marvel, unaccustomed to difficult
        waters and dark gales,

who now enjoys you, believing you golden,
who hopes that you are always empty of love for another,
    so unaware of deceitful
        breezes.

It is difficult to convey the brilliance with which the poet structures his verse, scattering words here and there as Latin's declensions make possible. To whatever extent, like Catullus, he followed Greek models—particularly Alcaeus, Sappho and Pindar. He not only transformed their metrical schemes but played with word order in a manner befitting the glories of the Latin language, which are different from those of Greek. Important, too, is the motif he is beginning to introduce, of connecting love to the unpredictable sea, its waves and its winds—that can be warm and caressing at one moment and at another can turn into a dark instrument that can drown one. That idea is further fleshed out at the very end of the third quatrain and throughout the fourth:

    Wretched are they to whom

    untried, you seem to shine so! As for me, the sacred temple
    wall with its votive tablet shows that I have
        hung up my soaking garments
            to the powerful god of the sea.

There are four particular issues that we might note here. One, that again, the Latin syntax reenforces the meaning: the words are hung here and there like the dripping clothes one can imagine hanging from the branches of some tree after a sailor has survived the sea and a shipwreck. Two: this idea of surviving love as surviving the dangerous sea and a shipwreck will, as we shall see, be used elsewhere in Latin poetry. Three: votive tablets nailed to temple walls, detailing thanks to a god for surviving some potential death-dealing event—from pregnancy to plague to shipwreck—were common in Horace's world.[178] Four: what I have rendered as "sacred temple" is actually *sacer*—just in case the reader has forgotten the importance of that word and its inherent positive-negative ambiguities for our discussion.

Horace diverges from the Catullan precedent most obviously in that there is no one particular woman to whom he directs his poetry, but several, and so one finds no progression from a specific love to frustration, anger, strife, or hate, per se. His organizationally early *Ode* I.5 already speaks of the end of his relationship with Pyrrha—even, it might seem, the end of his interest in love and women altogether. Well, probably not women altogether. A second ode (I.13) is directed to Lydia: "When you praise the rosy neck and waxen arms of Telephus, Lydia, alas, my burning liver swells with jealous bile." He follows this with further details describing how eaten up he is with rage at seeing her being kissed by that frenzied boy (*puer furens*)—recalling, in its detailed way, the Sapphic-Catullan poem for which the passion described reads like a disease process. He ends:

> had you listened to me enough you
> wouldn't be hoping for constancy from one
> who strikes savagely with sweet kisses those lips
>   that Venus herself imbued with the quintessence of her own
>   nectar.
>
> Three times happy and more
> are those whom an unbroken tie holds and whom
> no tearing apart of love by evil arguments
>   can separate sooner than life's final day.

Again we have already arrived at the resentful crisis—precipitated by Lydia's betrayal of the poet's love—without having first heard about that love. The implication of this last stanza is that there had previously been a relationship—a tie—between Horace and Lydia that she has snapped, in her new infatuation for Telephus, but we can only infer the *eros* that has left *eris* in its wake.

And then there is Glycera, about whom we do hear of the poet's passion for her (I.19):

…the gleam of Glycera burns me,
   more purely dazzling than Parian marble.
Her graceful insolence burns me
   and her incredibly smooth face as I stare at it.

I am completely destroyed by Venus
   as she leaves Cyprus, nor allows one
to sing about the Scythians and about the sweeping
   horses of the Parthians, nor things that concern nothing.

Here, [slave] boys, place a living, grassy altar, on it
   aromatic branches and incense
and a bowl of unmixed, two-year-old wine:
   the goddess will be kinder when she arrrives if I sacrifice a
   victim.

The goddess of love forces him to write about his beloved's beauty, rather than about manly, epic, strife-centered subjects, like the Scythians or the Parthians. Love is more important, really, than war and its concomitants—a motif that Roman lyric poets will come to often make in justifying their words, and for which we have seen the first suggestion coming from Sappho.[179] The poet is both infatuated with Glycera and aware of how that passion is deadly dangerous; even at the outset of the *eros* that he expresses he recognizes that he must assuage the goddess of love if he is not to be destroyed by her.

By *Ode* I.23, the focus is on Chloe, whose affection he has not yet managed to gain. For she "shuns me like a fawn, clinging to its fearful mother" in her presumed shyness—or maybe she simply does not like him. "Yet I am pursuing you not as a savage tiger or a Gaetulian lion, to break you: cease following your mother, at last, for you are ripe for a man."

We don't know how long it took him to be successful in wooing the unwilling or not-yet-ready Chloe, but that *he* is ready for *her* is reflected shortly in his further, far from flattering, comments regarding yet another woman, Lydia (I.25)—again, (the same as in I.13?), in the published sequence. And those comments underscore how much she has become *yesterday's* affair. Indeed, he suggests that Lydia is now beyond charming any men at all:

> Less often now do wild youths bang
> > on your window shutters
> nor do they steal away your sleep, and the door
> > that hugs its threshhold
>
> that previously so easily moved
> > its hinges. Less and less now you hear
> 'while I who am yours am perishing through the long night,
> > are you sleeping, Lydia?'
>
> The time will soon arrive when you, a hag
> > all alone in a deserted alley.
> will weep over your proud lovers' disdain…

—and so on. Far from the object of love that she apparently once was, Lydia has become an object of the poet's deep and bitter distaste, the focus of his prophecy of her old age, ugliness, and abandonment.

We also recognize another motif that will become not uncommon among the Roman elegists: the window and the door as metaphors for the woman's pubis—shuttered or guarded when one cannot gain entry, shutters open or hinges well oiled for easy opening and access when she allows one in. As here, the use of this pair of metaphors is typically found in either lovelorn poems begging entry when it has been refused, or eristic poetry slandering the former girlfirend as a slut.

And then there is Terentia, whose charms are articulated, in *Ode* II.12, against the backdrop, in the first four of eight stanzas, of the epic subjects that the poet brushes aside as implicitly less interesting or worthy of his efforts: Numantia's fierce wars, the tale of Hannibal or the Sicilian sea, purple with Punic blood—two significant moments in Roman republican history when substantial enemies had been defeated. He goes further back in time to mytho-historic incidents: to the battles between Lapiths and wine-drenched Centaurs; and still further back, to Hercules' powerful labors; or still further back, to the war to order the universe between gods and Titans and giants.

Such war-torn, strife-ridden subjects—including the more recent stories of Caesar's battles and the barbarian kings whom he led in triumphs through Rome—he suggests to Maecenas, his patron, "you yourself can better treat, and in prose." More emphatically than in I.19 he asserts the importance of love lyric over againt war epic:

> Me the Muse has wished to proclaim
> the sweet singing of mistress Licymnia,
> her brightly flashing eyes and her
>   faithful heart embedded with love;
>
> she who gracefully steps among the dancers
> and vies jest for jest and links arms
> playing among the shining young girls on the sacred
>   day that celebrates Diana.

There is some irony here: he praises Licyminia in her virginal purity, invoking the celebration of the virgin goddess. Or is there no intended irony: is his infatuation chaste and distant, far from the myriad kisses and bird-petting invoked by Catullus for his Lesbia? In either case, his last two stanzas turn his praises back out to comparison with the sorts of things that others champion, but which cannot compare to championing her: a lock of Licymnia's hair is worth everything that wealthy Achaemenes once owned, or the riches of fertile Phrygia, or the well-filled houses of the Arabs— each of these an ever more distant and exotic person or place—for can any of these compare to

> when she turns her neck toward your ardent
> kisses, or denies them to you with playful cruelty,
> who delights in having them snatched rather than giving them
>   unprompted,
> and sometimes takes over snatching them?

We have finally arrived—here in *Ode* II.12—at a poem by Horace that takes us to the beginning, rather than the end, of an *eros*-inspired relationship! And the object of his affection is both pure and virginal and yet capable of heating up the erotic moment aggressively.

In terms of edited order, there is no more on this sort of subject for awhile, however. Naught on the subject, really, until *Ode* III.9, in which the poet twists the screw of the *eros/eris* issue another turn. He frames the ode as a dialogue between two lovers: Lydia and himself—arriving at a reconciliation after a break-up, during which break-up each of them has taken on another lover. So in spite of the nasty things he wrote to and about her in I.25, he still wants her back—or the published order of the *Odes* is completely disconnected from the order of the poet's actual life experience and writing.

He starts, in stanza one, by saying that, when she still loved him and no other, better favored, youth was throwing his arms around her dazzling neck, "I thrived, happier than the king of the Persians," to which she responds in the second stanza that, when he was enamored of her, so that Lydia ranked not after Chloe, "I, Lydia, thrived more gloriously than Roman Ilia."[180]

So we understand that this is a dialogue for which the time of writing coincides with a time when he had moved on to Chloe (and we now know for sure that he succeeded with Chloe, however long it may have taken)—after Lydia (and later, perhaps, to others, or were they all before Lydia?)—but it was written before the definitive end had arrived between Lydia and him. Yet in the third stanza he not only admits to Lydia that Chloe, "skilled in sweet ways and knowledge of the cithera, rules me," but that for her sake "I would not fear to die, if Fate would let her live"—to which Lydia responds (in stanza four) that her current lover is Calais, son of Thurian Oryntus, "for whom I would suffer dying twice, if Fate would let him live." Such proclamations hardly seem the material from which reconciliation could proceed—except that suddenly in the next, fifth quatrain, the poet asks

"What if ancient Venus[181] were to come back again
  joining those pulled apart with her brazen yoke—

if flaxen-haired Chloe were cast out and
   the doors thrown open for rejected Lydia?"

And Lydia responds to this, in the last quatrain:

"Though that other be more beautiful than
   the stars, and you lighter than a cork and
more furious than the insatiable Adriatic,
   I would love to live with you, with you I'd gladly die!"

So they *are* reconciled—for now at least, for whether it will indeed be until death that they do not part, we do not know. For now, the sea of their love resumes its calm and warm flow.

Horace has also added another thread to his weave: death. Each protagonist repeats virtually the same line about willingness to die for his/her lover and Lydia returns to that theme in the end with regard to living with Horace. The thing about love is that it is a kind of death—and rebirth. For the you who was before dies and a new you is born and this poem is about just that kind of dual resurrection.[182]

Yet in the very next ode (according to the published order) he is begging and complaining at the door—at least metaphorically—of yet another woman, Lyca: at her cruel portals with their cold north winds, at which he lies stretched out. Before her door "the trees that are planted moaning in the gale winds" and before which "Jupiter with a pure cloud freezes the fallen snow." It does not take an excess of Freudian thinking to see the expanding of these metaphors: not only her portals as the openings into her body, but the piled snows suggesting a frigidity about which men have complained for millennia, especially regarding women who are not interested in them.

While importuning her, he at the same time warns or even insults her: "You are no Penelope unyielding to patrician suitors"—as surely she and his readers would understand the reference to Penelope's unique situation: waiting twenty years for the return of Odysseus, without, it would seem, really aging, and managing to put off the accumulating suitors during the last few years before her loving husband's return to massacre them all. That ain't you, Lyca.

She is, it turns out, married, but her husband is having an apparently well enough known affair with a Thessalian mistress, so why should Lyca be loyal to him?[183] The end of the poem demands that she bend her heart, which is more rigid than an oak and less gentle than Mauritanian serpents. For, he warns her, he will not wait forever: "not forever will I stretch my body by your theshhold suffering celestial downpours." His wooing, in brief, is a good deal more eristic than erotic.

In the last ode that deals with love—last, that is, in the organization in which the first three books were edited and published, Ode III.26—he returns once again to the understanding of love as a kind of war whose battles are preferable to a poet to those fought by military men: "now this wall that guards the left side of sea-born Venus will have my arms and my lyre…." And he returns, it seems, to Chloe: "O goddess queen who holds happy Cyprus and Memphis free of Sithonian [Thracian] snows, touch just once the haughty Chloe with your upraised whip! " So she who is the only woman among those addressed in the Odes as an unachieved object of early, unrequited desire, is also the last to be referenced as not responding to his erotic overtures, to the point that he feels too battle-weary for continuing to try.

Between the time of the first three books and the fourth, a good deal had changed in the poet's world. Most importantly, perhaps, there had been a conspiracy against the life of Augustus in late 23 BCE, and if Maecenas was exonerated of having had a role in it, nonetheless there was something in his role that caused his relationship with the Emperor apparently never to be quite the same again, and thus the circle of which he was the center, that included Horace, diminished in stature.[184] Horace's stalwart friend and his most careful critic (in the positive sense), Quintilius Varus, had died just before, in 24 BCE, and the much-beloved and admired Vergil died in 19 BCE, as did Tibullus (about whom more, shortly). Horace's world seemed to be collapsing around him.

Interestingly, Augustus continued to admire him and honored him by asking him to write the central poem to mark the celebration of the *Ludi Saeculares*—the Centenary Games— in 17 BCE. When Horace died nine years later, a few weeks after Maecenas did, the emperor saw to it that he was buried, at his request, next to his long-time patron.

III Tibullus

The golden literary age of Augustus would be marked by other important lyric poets. A decade younger than Horace, the just-mentioned Tibullus (ca 55-19 BCE) wrote several books of elegies: he may be grouped with Ovid and Propertius—and Gallus, whose work is lost—as the leading poets to adopt elegiac meter as their medium. Two books of Tibullus' poetry have survived (the so-called third and fourth books are almost certainly not his; they are different in style and inferior in quality to the material of the first two). He would seem to have published these in a scant four years—between 23 BCE (given references in Book I to the campaign of Messalla in 23 BCE) and the poet's own death in 19 BCE. And his entire certain extant output consists of sixteen poems within these two books.

We know little about his life, but as for his poetry, for our purposes two issues are of particular interest. The first, of course, is that he directs so many of his poems toward a woman—well, one in the first book and in the second, a different one. Delia is the focus in Book One; her name a pseudonym for a certain Plania, if we can accept as fact the later comment by Apuleius (125-170 CE) in his *Apologia* 10. In the second book the odder pseudonym is Nemesis. Tibullus also devoted several poems in Book One to a boy, Marathus, who captured his fancy. The second issue of interest is that he follows the lead extending from Sappho to Horace of proclaiming that love as his subject is preferable to war—in our terms, *eros* is a better subject than *eris*.

Both these issues appear from the first lines of I.1—one might say that he announces his professional poetic intentions:

> Let him who will heap up the yellow gold
> and till his mighty acres of rich soil,
> his labor wrought in terror of the foe,
> his slumbers banished by the trumpet's blast.
> For me, my frugal fortune shall support
> a quiet life beside a welcoming hearth.
> And so may I, content with little, live
> free from the curse of constant journeying.

He continues to describe the pleasures of relaxing by his own tree by a stream and performing the chores of a farmer, giving offerings and pouring libations to divinities like Ceres, Priapus and the Lares. In the first 52 lines the poet rejects the plundered wealth to be gained from war in favor of being a homebody—and if it may not be too extreme to recognize the image of "a welcoming hearth" as also symbolic of the female pubis, and "constant journeying," perhaps, of going from woman to woman rather than keeping to one. By lines 53-60 he has made it clearer both that it is love as much as farming (for which the plowing of a field is, in any case, a metaphor for love-making) that he prefers to war and wandering, and who might be the object of that love:

> For you, Messalla, wars by land and sea
> to hang its trophies on your palace front;
> for me my bondage to a lovely maid,
> lying as watchman at her fast-barred door.
> I crave not glory, Delia mine: if I am yours
> the world may brand me sloth and sluggard, too.
> Let me but look on you as I face death
> and dying, clasp you with my failing hand.

So the nominal object of the poem's dedication is Messala, but in the end instead of providing the general with a poem glorifying war, its attendant strife, and Messala's heroic role in all of that, Tibullus is offering a love ode to Delia, whose door is barred but not to him and the relationship with whom enables him to face death without a quiver.

The role of death is not to be casually passed over, either. He uses that same motif that we have seen Horace use in III.9, of the willingness of the lover to face death if the object of his love is there with him—so his preference for love over war/strife is not due to fear of death on the battlefield but to a particular sense of the conditions under which death might be meaningful and not meaningless. We might, moreover, see the relationship between love and death in both Horace and Tibullus as an oblique comment on the relative value of lyric versus epic writing with their respective meters, images, and foci, if we think back to Odysseus and his desire to leave Kalypso's cave and isle: growing never old by the goddess' side, as we have earlier noted, is to be functionally dead, a condition the hero cannot abide. These two poets would welcome death if their lovers are by their side.[185]

One might note, further, that a partial consequence of the combination within the Greek world of its shame culture identity and its *erastes-eromenos* relationship concept—that is understood to offer the most mutually healthy and gratifying outcome for both individuals—is that one is expected to be considerably braver in warfare if one's doting *erastes* or admiring *eromanos* is present. One does not want to be shamed by cowardly behavior on the battlefield and one would certainly be willing, even eager, to sacrifice one's life for one's partner. So the Horace/Tibullus expression of willingness to die if one's mistress is present transfers that "motif"—the self-sacrificing motif—from a battlefield context to a bedroom context.

Tibullus continues, noting how he will be a good soldier of love and enjoy its quarrels—and delights—rather than those of real war. As that good soldier he follows in his second poem with an elegy, directed to his commanding officer, Delia, which he stuffs with virtually all of the standard love lyric motifs. He begins by presenting himself as the shut-out lover—"a savage guard is stationed over my girl and with harsh bolts her sturdy door is closed" (I.2.5-6)—and a suppliant: "you ought to remember my many suppliant prayers brought with the flower garlands that hung upon your doorposts. And you, too, Delia, you must dare to help fool your guardian: Venus herself assists those who are courageous!" (13-16)… "My lover's effort will not wound, if only Delia unseal her doors to me and call me silently to her side" (31-2). And so, further on, he asks of Delia that he hold her in his arms… "if so, I'll gladly, at her temple's door, lay down to kiss her sacred threshhold, and as a suppliant crawl the earth with bended knees."

The same sort of imagery, revolving around the doors into Delia's sacred temple of Venus, (her *mons veneris*) is placed before the reader. An important little detail in this second poem is the mention of her husband, (67-70) off at war, leading victorious troops of Cilicians and gathering silver and gold, while the poet tends his cows and is harnessed "to you, my Delia." So the warrior husband whom he replaces in her bed, and to whom he is "superior," is a stand-in for the war poetry that he does not write and to which his own love poetry is superior. But the poet slightly shifts his gears in poem three, where he imagines himself having gone off to war following Messala, but ill and left behind in some distant clime, worrying over the fact that Delia will not be present to weep for him—she who when he sailed is said to have consulted all the gods on his behalf. Love and death once more: he writes his own epitaph in the context of this painful, dying distance from Delia, whom he begs to remain faithful to him.

Faithfulness would seem not to be a simple story, however. In elegy #5, written during a phase of estrangement (*discidium*) from her; and #6—written after Delia's husband has returned from war and she has apparently betrayed both the husband-warrior and the farmer-lover-poet with some other lover—helps us recognize how little we really know about the substance of their relationship as opposed to his fantasies regarding its substance. In the sixth poem we also learn, incidentally, that the poet's pursuit of Delia was approved by her mother, for he writes of her, in affectionate terms (I.6.57ff). If the poet never turns to invective against Delia, what is either odd or not is that, although Tibullus continues to write poems to her, #4 takes him in a completely different direction: a poem to Marathus, his favorite boy. It ends: "oh how Marathus twists me with slow love! My arts and my tricks both fail. I beg sparingly, boy, lest I become a shameful tale, when they laugh at my empty controls."

So Tibullus has added another wrinkle to the matter of love: the objects of his affections are not only more than one but more than one gender. Marathus is again the object of the poet's address in poems 8 and 9—so Delia is the focus only five times to Marathus as the focus three times, and actually, after poem #6 he is silent regarding her (so her "punishment," if that is what is going on, is not invective but silence). The last poem of Book One is a strong statement against war and on behalf of peace, praised for how it makes the struggles, joys and quarrels associated with love possible. Indirectly, then, the book ends where it began, with a statement of love's place as above that of war, *eros* over that kind of *eris*.

Book Two, much shorter than Book One (only six poems long, totalling 428 verses) follows a similar trajectory—except that Delia has altogether disappeared, to be supplanted by Nemesis. She appears in poems 3, 4, and 6. Where Delia is apparently the pseudonym of an upperclass woman like Lesbia/Clodia and Lydia, Nemesis is apparently of a coarser grain and more interested in the lucre to be gained from her lover(s)—it is obvious that Tibullus was merely one among any number of her clients—than other, less material satisfactions. While he complains of his bondage to her and of her hard-heartedness, it doesn't seem that he was able to let go of his infatuation for her before his death at barely age 36. Ovid, (about whom more, shortly), writing in praise of Tibullus after the latter's death, asserted in *Amores* III.9.31, that "thus Nemesis and Delia will be long remembered (*longum nomen habebunt*), the one a recent obsession, the other his first love (*altera cura recens, altera primus amor*)."[186]

IV Propertius

In pure chronological terms, Sextus Propertius (ca 57/50-15 BCE/2CE) falls next in this extraordinary series of closely linked elegists. It seems that he was less well regarded than the others—in his own world, the rhetorician, Quintilian (35-100 CE), estimating poets of the Golden Age, certainly found him of less significance than Vergil, Horace, or Tibullus (*Inst. Or.* 10.193)—but for our purposes he could hardly be more emblematic of the *eros/eris* interweave. The tension between these two ideas is more emphatically present than with any other poet as that theme virtually defines the poet's relationship with his lady love. With Propertius more than with the others, the theme presents itself in a double frame, the two aspects of which interweave each other. There is both the continuous and emphatic assertion that the poetry of love and the actions it reflects contend with, and are ultimately superior to, the poetry that reflects on the actions of war and strife, and those actions themselves; and within the relationship trumpeted by the poet, love and strife form a tight knot.

This second element in particular is apparent—albeit subtly so—from the very first line of the first of his four books of elegies.

On the one hand, it is love at first sight. *Cynthia prima suis miserum me cepit ocellis...*: "Cynthia first captured miserable me with her eyes..." On the other hand, he has already identified himself as *miser*—miserable, wretched—by the beginning of the relationship. If she snatched him she simultaneously made him wretched: the slavery to which he will be subject is already clear to him and should be to us. But there is more. *Ocellis* is a diminutive form of the standard *oculis*, meaning "eyes," of course. However, particularly in this diminutive form, the term is a pun, in Latin slang, for testicles—eye balls can simply be balls. And given the declentional case (dative/ablative; the nominative singular would be *ocellus*), the preposition with which the noun may be preceded in translation may either be "with" or "by" (among others). So we might also render this opening line as "Cynthia first seized wretched me by the balls."

The poet is off and running—from where to where? Whence: as with Tibullus, we know little of the poet's life aside from what we glean from within his poems. He was born in Umbria, somewhere in the neighborhood of Assisi.[187] His father died while Propertius was a boy (IV.1.120ff) and his mother in his early manhood (also IV.1.120ff as well as II.20.15). We infer his birth year as somwhere between 57 and 50 BCE since, also in IV.1.120ff it seems that when he assumed the *toga virilis* he had already lost much of his patrimony through the confiscations of 41-40 BCE and the assumption of the *toga virilis* would not have been much later (and possibly earlier) than his seventeenth birthday.[188]

Most importantly for our own discussion, he was captivated by Cynthia no later than by 30 BCE—and her real name (our source is again Apuleius' *Apologia* 10) was Hostia. She was, like Tibullus' Nemesis, a *meretrix*—a courtesan—who *semper amatorum ponderat una sinus* ("she always weighs the laps of her lovers [as opposed to weighing power or honors]"; II.16.12) and who is compared by the poet to famous *meretrices* such as Lais, Thais, and Phryne (II.6.1-6). Their relationship lasted about five years (III.25.3)—although the referenced terminus may have been a pause-break, rather than a definitive end. He may himself either have married or adopted an heir, since Pliny the Younger (61-113 CE; *Epistles* IX.22.1) refers to one Passennus Paullus as a descendant of Propertius.

Once they have met, where does the relationship go within his poems? The first volume is almost entirely focused on her, and was apparently circulated separately even when all four were available and in circulation together. Of the 22 poems in that book, commonly referred to by a Greek nickname as the *Monobiblos* ("Single Book"), the first 19 are either directly adressed to Cynthia (2, 8, 11, 15, and 19) or are mainly about her—only the last three are not. Among recipients of those others in which she figures, but that are addressed to others, a friend named Tullus seems most important: the first and last (and the sixth and fourteenth) are addressed to him. So the words regarding Cynthia's eyes with which this part of our discussion began are intended for his eyes and ears.

The first eight lines of the poem continue:

Cynthia first captured miserable me with her eyes,
who had no sort of contact with love before this.
Then Amor/Cupid [*Eros*] threw over my unwavering, prideful glance,
pressing on my head with his firmly placed foot,
and taught me to hate chaste girls,
cruel one, and to live without a plan.
And now for a whole year this madness has not left me
as even now I have been pressed by hostile gods.

So these first eight lines set a tone of intensely interwoven *eros/eris* reality. Love—the god himself—is the weight that will not let him rise up. He plays on words for eyes—her *ocellis*, and his *lumina*—that are puns: her eyes are his balls, his eyes are lights that had been blind to love before and are now blind to the world beyond love for Cynthia. She is a *meretrix*, so hardly chaste (*casta*)—and he despises *castae puellae* (chaste girls) now—except that *"puella"* is the kind of term that he can and will use to refer to her, and her name is Cynthia, which is a name for Luna, the moon. The moon goddess is the virgin goddess, Diana (Greek: Artemis): a *casta puella* if ever there were one. (She is also the goddess of the hunt and protector of the hunted, as we have earlier noted). So Cynthia is the object of his love, but Amor has taught him to hate *castae puellae*, and by way of her *name* she is one of those. Love has taught him to hate Cynthia—whom he loves and whose love is such a crushing burden on his neck.

Mind you, this is apart from the attributes of the moon itself as a celestial orb: that it drives people crazy (they become lunatics) in its fullness; that, in its constantly and slowly shifting phases, it may be construed as fickle—never, so to speak, showing the same face twice; that that face is, particularly when full, beautiful (as noted by Sappho—in 34 and 96.6ff), among others; that, as a celestial element, it partakes of, and separates, lower and upper realities: the sublunar and eternal, heavenly realms. All of these features will sooner than later be asserted by Propertius to be attributes of Cynthia: she drives the poet mad, she is fickle, she is beautiful, and she partakes, as it were, in mortality and immortality.

Given Propertius' interest in obscure figures and mythic beings, it might not be too much to suppose even further regarding Cynthia and her name. Two female deities preside within the underworld. Proserpine (Persephone) is, of course, that daughter of the earth who was torn away from her mother and her playmates by Pluto (Hades) and carried off in his chariot into his world of darkness. (*Eros* and *eris* again, by the way: the lover-who-will-be-husband's first encounter with the object of his affections is to force her into his chariot and carry her away from the light—i.e., to rape her.) The other key goddess among the shadows is Hekate—and she came to be associated with Diana/Artemis. So from an oblique angle, Propertius is also noting that his Cynthia-Diana-Luna is/can be a Hellish creature: a veritable princess of Hell.

One might wonder, too, if the year-long *furor* ("madness") to which the poet refers is intended to call to the reader's mind the *furor* that was the basis for the *Iliad*—the *furor* of Akhilleus—and that perhaps Propertius intends to suggest his role is one that is as heroic as that of the premier Akhaian warrior.

I would only reach for these last two possibilities because the poet is so intent, always, on showing off his *doctus* ("learned") qualities, usually through his use of myth and his carefully complicated syntax and sometime neologisms. The poem, divided into sections of 8, 8, 8, 8, and 6 verses each, shifts gears in its second octave to a story from mythology that helps underscore that the poet is *doctus*—reinforced by his use of an obscure name for Atalanta; she is called Iasis by him—as these verses also end in love as conqueror. That is, with its hero, Milanion, dominating that athletic *puella*. If Milanion can also be seen here as a stand-in for the poet, then this is wishful thinking, isn't it?

The love god is again referenced, immediately invoked beginning in the third set of 8 lines and is begged for assistance: "you who do that trick of drawing down the moon and perform rites on magic altars" (19-20), help me win Cynthia's love. This should be no challenge for Amor, since if he habitually performs *fallacia lunae* ("a trick with the moon") and Cynthia, by her name, *is* the moon—Luna—then the outcome should be a successful one. But having used myth as a stepping off point to invoke Amor's help to get his girl, he turns around in the following 8 lines and asks her friends to help cure him of his madness.

By the beginning of the last six lines he has noted how Venus has imposed upon him bitter nights and Amor—her son, lest we forget—has at no time left him empty. If the nights have been made bitter by Venus, then love's constant presence has not been good. And so, "I warn you" addressing his reader(s), "avoid this evil; stick to a familiar place for love, for whoever has ears slow to hear my warning, wow, will he recall my words in pain."

This poem sways back and forth between expressions of desire—of *eros*—for Cynthia and references to the unhappy aspects of the relationship, embeds a mythological tale within it—one in which the woman, Atalanta, has been responsible for the deaths of many would-be husbands, by the way, until one finally conquers her—and twists and turns between asking for divine help and asking for help to escape what is madness, finally suggesting, however, that love that is grounded in a constant relationship is preferable to flitting from one relationship to the next.[189] Even at that, the slang that would have been understood by Propertius' audience—the "familiar place," for which *locum* means "place" but is also a term used to refer to female genitals—suggests an objectification of the beloved, rather than a warm, loving relationship with her.

One might say that the situation does not improve as one follows the poetry forward through the *Monobiblos* and into the other books of his elegies. There will indeed be reflections of mutual love, but then also suspicion and jealousy—and with gradually increasing vigor, vituperation, infidelity, and then the definitive break. His angle of focus can shift: in the second elegy he essentially criticizes Cynthia (this is a direct address to her, not a poem about her, as the first had been) for wearing too much make-up and clothes that are too fancy—the natural look is best for someone as beautiful as she (so it is a back-handed compliment). One notes in this poem both a very distinct echo of Tibullus' "lecture" to Delia in his I.8.9-16—reminding us of how a handful of these poets were part of a well-rounded Maecenan circle—and the repeat of a particular Propertian affectation that tends to separate him from Tibullus: referencing mythological analogues the point of which is not just their analogic value but the showing off of his *doctus* qualities.

The third poem begins with such mythological allusions—using three of these to analogize the languid look of Cynthia, lying gently sleeping, her arm behind her head as the poet comes in from a heavy bout of drinking. His choices of imagery are deliberate. Ariadne lay there abandoned by Theseus, (and would be swept up by Dionysus), and Andromeda lay there exhausted, having been rescued by Perseus, and the third reference is to a Bacchant—who serves Dionysus—lying there exhausted after dancing,[190] which last image segues directly to the poet's arriving into Cynthia's bedroom in step with Dionysus. He approaches her bed, doubly fortified and inspired—by both the God of Love, Amor, and the God of Wine, Liber (another name for Dionysus/Bacchus), "each of them a hard god" (I cannot imagine that "hard" is not a pun, here, too, even if both these gods are known for soft limbs and not hard muscles—but that's not the aspect of anatomy to which the poet's adjective directs itself, methinks).

Indeed, his inclination is to lift her up in his arms, his weapon in hand (for *arma manu* can certainly mean that, and under the circumstances, I suspect his desire is to ply that weapon—to place his sword in its scabbard, for which the Latin term is *vagina*) and and steal many kisses, but doesn't dare disturb her, fearing her well-directed savage outbursts, and so he remains transfixed, like Argus (another mythological allusion, to a thousand-eyed giant whose story ends with all of those eyes being torn out)—and shifts to the direct voice: "I tore the garlands from my brow and placed them on your temples, Cynthia." He further describes what amounts to his gentle fondling of her: re-arranging her hair, placing fruit in her sleeping hands (are *poma* merely some sort of apples, or perhaps the poet's two own somewhat smaller fruit?), worried about disturbing, even frightening her, until the moon, slipping through the window lattice, caused her to open her eyes and speak. This is at first a sweet and sexually charged description of a moment in the poet's loving relationship with Cynthia.

But the mood between them can change quickly. When her eyes and mouth flit open, it is not to welcome him but to criticize him—he's spent half the night out drinking, after all, and perhaps (at least in her mind) has been having his way with other women, for now "at long last you would come insult my couch when the closed doors of another shut you out?!" The Latin is a bit richer here, since *nostro*, as almost always in these poems, can both mean "our" and "my" (in the sense of the "royal we"), so that the insult is deeper: he is accused of profaning their joint bed and not just her bed.

> Where have you spent the long hours of my night
> to come wearily to me with the setting of the stars?
> Would that you, cruel one, could suffer such long nights
> As you always force upon wretched me!

And Cynthia rages gently on, describing the long, lonely suffering of separation while he goes out partying, ultimately crying herself to sleep. The last 12 lines are all hers, in fact, and as much as they are condemnatory of the poet, one recognizes here, still, her love for him as the source for that condemnation and can imagine that the epilogue to the poem is his comforting her, stealing those many kisses that lead beyond kissing and caressing to full-fledged sex and satisfyingly exhausted sleep in each other's arms.

There is that question of other women, still, and in the fourth poem, Propertius restates his singular devotion to Cynthia. That devotion is couched as an address to Bassus, whom he represents as trying to interest Propertius in other girls—the two that are specifically mentioned as models to be compared to Cynthia in beauty are, once again, from mythology or at least proto-Greek history — Antiope and Hermione — but the point of it is that not only is the poet loyal to Cynthia but that if Bassus keeps this up Cynthia — may she remain ever graceful — will demand that Propertius stay away from Bassus.

The fifth poem moves in virtually the opposite direction: Gallus is addressed — not the poet, Cornelius Gallus, but some other Gallus — and warned to keep his hands off the poet's girl.[191] For thirty lines he spells out less the danger to himself or the threat by him to Gallus than the danger to Gallus, who has no idea what he would be getting himself into were he to succeed in wooing her:

> She won't let you sleep, she won't let you out of her sight:
>   She alone binds the spirits of fierce men.
> Oh, contemptible one, how often you will come running to my door,
>   when your heroic words have collapsed with sobbing
> and trembling horror will rise up with mournful tears,
>   and fear will leave an ugly mark on you face...

Once more we may recognize that the first quoted verse (11) puns: *non illa relinquet ocellos* can both refer to her keeping her eyes (*ocellos*) on him and — thinking back to the first line of the first elegy — never letting go of his balls. And he continues these words of warning, telling Gallus that he will come to understand why he, Propertius, is often so pale — and don't come looking to me for sympathy.

But we will in the end cry on each other's shoulders. In the last couplet Cynthia is mentioned by name as the subject of this elegy, for Gallus is told, at that point, that he does not want to know the things of which Cynthia is capable (a pun, again: Gallus wants to know the sexual skills of which she is capable; Propertius is warning him of the cruelties of which she is capable): she does not come without punishment as a price. Ambiguities, then: is he warning Gallus by exaggerating the dangers because he fears losing Cynthia to him or is the relationship really that difficult — which he nonetheless does not wish to give up, supreme masochist-lover that he is?

That he is crazy about her is evident in poem six, in which he chooses not to go abroad with Tullus—the same Tullus to whom the first poem was addressed[192]—because of his enslavement to Cynthia: "the words of my girl who embraces me prevent me" (5). After a lengthier description of how Cynthia becomes upset when he talks of departing on a long trip, he tells Tullus to go on without him, adding that Tullus never had time for love in any case, (so he wouldn't really understand, perhaps)—"and may love never snare you the way it has me."

And embedded in his final comments is a turn to a familiar motif, that "I wasn't born suitable for praise or arms: the fates wanted me to undergo *this* military service" (29-30)—that is, the armed service between the sheets. He is a poet about love and a lover, not a poet about war or a warrior! This is, of course, a completely different angle with regard to *eros* and *eris*, referring not to the emotions or actions but to the poetry regarding them.

This last subject moves front and center in the next poem (#7), addressed to Ponticus, who is engaged in writing an epic poem to rival the Homeric works. Propertius defends the validity of his own writing, of love poetry: while you are writing about glorious heroic subjects and, frankly, can rival Homer, I am stitching together and stirring up works about love. That's what makes me famous, and neglected lovers in the future will read me carefully for guidance—I who am the only one to have pleased that difficult woman. If you get hit by love's arrows, then you'll suddenly find your poetic voice silenced, and you will admire me (whom now you might consider insignificant as a poet). Indeed

> Young lovers won't be able to keep silent, though, before my tomb:
> 'There you lie, oh great poet of our passion.'
> So beware when you condemn my poems with scorn:
>   often love arrives late but charging a large interest.

As with Catullus, Horace, and Tibullus, (particularly Tibullus II.4.15-20)—but more straightforwardly, perhaps, or at any rate more emphatically—Propertius turns the issue of *eros* and *eris* in the direction of poetry and the subjects to which it best accords, (love rather than strife/war), reminding us, too, that beneath the surface of his work, the love that resides above all is self-love, and the desire for his own immortality: it is the *poems* about love and *their* value that concern him more than the girlfriend about whom or to whom they might be directed and either her value or the value of their relationship.

One sees this in poem #9, which functions as a kind of companion piece to this one (#7), and is also addressed to Ponticus. It begins: "I told you what it would be like when love came upon you, and you mocked—but now your words don't flow so freely." There is, as so often with Propertius, an important pun, too. *Amores* is the word that I have rendered as "love" but in its plural form it underscores the idea that it is a synonym for "poems," since his poetry is about love. So it is not just that Ponticus has been conquered by love, but that his poetry is being conquered by Propertius' verses. The first eight lines are mainly devoted, however, to grinding Ponticus' nose in the servitude to love to which he has succumbed, and Propertius' skill at having prophecied this—alas, due to his own excessive personal experience with such a condition.

One might note that "me" appears with emphasis in both lines 5 and 7—and with regard to the matter of poetry, line 11 sums it all up: "one verse of Mimnermus on love is worth more than all of Homer." Mimnermus was, of course, a lyric poet, from Kolophon, who wrote in the mid-seventh century BCE. The poem references mythic love poets like Amphion, while letting Ponticus know that his suffering is really just beginning. It will only get worse. The twofold point, from the perspective of our topic, is that the love that Ponticus has found—or rather, that has found Ponticus—far from being described in terms that are in any way positive, is treated as a kind of painful, fatal disease, while at the same time the *writing* about love in elegiac poetry is being adulated. This is to say—this is the other shoe dropping after #7 with respect to this issue—that Propertius' ultimate point in all this is to adulate *himself*, the great poet.

Sandwiched between these two poems (#7 and #9), #8 reminds us of the ostensive source of Propertius' praeternatural skill, his muse and tormentor: Cynthia. Muse because she inspires him; tormentor, in this particular poem, because she is leaving—or threatening to leave, with some nameless lover, to go on a voyage to a cold clime (1-4):

> So are you then crazy, nor does my anxiety delay you
>   or am I worth less to you than frozen Illyria?
> And is—whatever his name is—already more to you
>   so that without me you wish to go wherever the wind blows?

And he both worries about and warns her (5-8):

> And are you strong enough so that you can listen to the violent sea's
>   crash, and can you lie on a ship's hard bunk?
> Can your tender feet endure the frosts?
>   Are you able, Cynthia, to bear the unaccustomed snows?

Interestingly—and presumably symptomatic of his genuine love for her—he is less angry about her going off with someone else than about her welfare. As much as he will keep begging her not to leave, and calling to her to return when she leaves, and regardless of

> whatever you deserve from me for your lies to me,
>   may Galatea not be hostile to your path;
> may you sail easily past Ceraunia
>   and reach Oricos on placid waters.
> For no woman will be able to corrupt me, in fact,
>   my true life; I shall make my plaint on your doorstep.

So, frustrated and upset though he may be by the prospect of her journey and its role in her betrayal of him, he wishes her a safe journey—with help, not harm from the sea nymph Galatea, one of the 50 Nereids, daughters of Nereus; and a successful passage past the dangerous promontory on the coast of Epirus, in northwestern Greece; and a comfortable arrival into the Illyrian port of Oricos, on the border of Epirus—she, who is his true life, his true love. He will be waiting, mournfully, tearfully, hopefully, for her to come back. His last words in the last line of the last couplet, regarding Cynthia, are: *illa futura mea est*: "she is my future."

Although in the manuscripts that we possess there is no break after that line (line 26) and the next, modern editions tend to break poem #8 into 8a and 8b because of the change from the direct address to Cynthia to a third-person discussion of her. (Then again, strictly speaking, that change comes in the middle of line 26, doesn't it?) In any case, the first line of 8b, (which is, to say, line 27 of #8 overall), rejoices in her agreement to stay, and in the poet's victory over his damned enemies (so that this love ode's imagery starts out with a martial tone, interweaving *eris* with *eros*). But really, the overall tone is simply that of ebullient and joyful love:

> My Cynthia has ceased going along new paths.
> She calls me beloved and through me, Rome is most precious,
>   and without me she refuses sweet kingdoms.
> Indeed, she prefers to lie with me on a narrow couch
>   and to be mine in whatever manner
> than to be in the ancient kingdom of well-endowed Hippodameia,
>   and those riches that Elis once obtained with his horses. (30-36)

He not only has her back, she would rather lie with him on a narrow couch to be his *quocumque modo*—"in whatever manner," but more specifically meaning both "on my own terms" and also "in any sort of sexual position"—than to see exotic places and be wined and dined by that unnamed other suitor for her favors. Hippodameia was, of course the wife of Pelops, so, as so often, he uses myth—this time to succintly describe a foreign locale—and it is a rather interesting choice: we know well how disastrous was the narrative of which Pelops and Hippodameia were part in terms of family relations, both parent-child and husband-wife. About as eristic a series of events within the context of *eros* as one could hope for.

But: Cynthia prefers a clearly loving outcome with Propertius than an exotic relationship with such negative potential. And Propertius has defeated his unnamed rival: "Rare Cynthia is mine!" (42)—and one might wonder, all things considered, whether *rara* refers to her uniqueness or to the fact that she rarely operates as the virginal moon goddess... Well, maybe not the latter this time, in this moment of exultation, for:

> now I can touch the highest stars with my soles:
> whether day or night shall come, she is mine!
> My rival cannot carry off such certain love:
> that glory shall know my old age. (43-6)

He turns a poetic twist to reverse the more normative turn of phrase ("my old age shall know that glory"). More importantly, "love" is actually *"amores"* — a plural — because it ultimately refers (once again) to his poems (his *love* poems) and thus the *gloria* to which he refers in the last line that will remain his into old age is the *gloria* that he will gain for his poetry (and that his poetry will gain for him). As we move forward it becomes increasingly clear that Propertius is a paradigm of a love elegist whose primary focus is really himself: his work is about self-love more than about any other sort of love.

The very first line of Poem #9, as we have seen, addressed to Ponticus, echoes the penultimate line of #8a, in using the term *amores* to refer both to the love that has now captured Ponticus and to Propertius' poems that will outlive the epic poetry of Ponticus. Poem #10 is, like both #7 and #9, not addressed to or focused on Cynthia — this one is to the same Gallus, presumably, who had been addressed as an unwelcome rival in #5, but here he is being observed as Ponticus was in #9, as one who has become infected by love — "when I saw you dying, Gallus, intertwined with a girl" (5-6) — so love is still the topic.

And any time love is his focus, so is his poetry. One might ask whether in the first line, when Propertius notes that, *primo cum testis amori* — it is the poet's intention that we we understand that phrase only to mean "when I was a witness of your first love" or also to intend "when I read your first love poems"? In which way is Gallus more of a competitor? So, too, given both love and love poetry, Cynthia cannot be and is not far away from his thoughts. Then while this poem is to and about Gallus and his love, nonetheless, the poet notes, he understands these things because

> Cynthia always taught me what sorts of things to desire
> and which to avoid; love has not led me to nothing. (19-20)

With that footnoting of his source, the poet uses the last ten verses to impart instructions to Gallus regarding how to treat his girlfriend. The lesson expands in the somewhat lengthier poem #13. The tone shifts, however, to one that is profoundly hostile—the poet is not welcoming Gallus into the realm of the happily in love, he's mocking his arrival into the realm of those severely oppressed by love, and suggesting that such suffering is his due. One may taste this (it is a rather sour taste) by perusing the first ten verses:

> Insofar as you are often accustomed to rejoice in my fall,
> > Gallus, that I am abandoned, alone, love torn away,
> yet I won't imitate your voice, dishonestly:
> > may no girl ever wish to deceive you, Gallus.

—a generous enough beginning.[193] But Propertius quickly catches up with his more hostile feelings:

> While your fame increases regarding deceived girls
> > and you steadfastly avoid any lasting love attachment,
> doomed one, at last there is a love for whom you begin to grow pale,
> for the first time you have slipped and begun your fall.

This one will be punishment for the despised pain of those others:

> One woman offers wretched payback for so many.
> This one will hold you back from those common affairs of yours;
> > you'll no longer be a companion to those looking for new adventures…

He goes on, saying that

> I saw you conquered, your whole neck down,
> > weeping for a long time, Gallus, your face in your hands
> willing to give up your pride for those desired lips
> > and what followed modesty conceals, my friend.

—and instead he switches to elaborate analogies with mythological figures, the sum total of which is simultaneously to compliment him on the beauty of his girlfriend and insult him for his past sins, his lust, and for being a weak captive of his current situation.

Which should bring us back to Cynthia, should it not? It does, if we backtrack to the two poems sandwiched between #10 and #13, which are far from happy. In #11 he asks Cynthia right at the outset what she is doing in Baiae, that summer beach vacation ground for well-heeled Romans. The poem begins:

> While you lie inactive in the midst of Baiae, Cynthia,
>   where the path lies along Herculean shores,
> and you marvel at how the seas near aristocratic Misenum
>   have recently been brought under Thesprotus' rule,
> do your memories conjure love of me as you lie (alone) during those nights?
> Now that I am lodged at the edge of your love, has some enemy—
> I know not who—stolen you away from me,
>   and thus stolen you from my songs, Cynthia?

Another crisis, it would seem: Cynthia has gone off to Baiae, (not far from Naples, just to its north), and although *cessantem* translates as "lie inactive," there is at least the possibility that she has been anything but inactive while down there. So his concern pertains to both adandonment and betrayal.

Mythologically, Herakles is said to have created the path along that shore, but Propertius uses a more poetic locution to express that. He again uses *cura* (more usually, "care") to mean "love" in line five, and *subit*, translatable as "[she] lies" (from *subeo*) also puns on a similar verb (*subo*) meaning "to be in heat." For of course he hopes that she is lying alone thinking of him, and not behaving as a female dog does when she is in heat. He feels himself dislodged from her love and feels her dislodged from her place as the muse of his poems. Thus his poetic voice is stilled; his poems are synonymous with his love, and that love is first and foremost for his poems that, inspired by Cynthia, *are* Propertius.

Oh, to be sure, however, he still loves and wants her. He ends his poem:

> You alone are my home, you alone my parents, Cynthia,
>   you are all my times of joy.
> Whether I come sad or happy among friends,
>   whatever I will be, I shall say: 'Cynthia was the cause.'
> So just leave corrupt Baiae as soon as possible:
>   those shores that bring divorce to many,
> shores that were hostile to chaste girls:
>   oh may they perish, those waters of Baiae, crime against love!

We cannot fail to remember *castae puellae* from the first poem, can we? That Cynthia is and is not, whom he loves and, according to that remembered verse, he has learned to hate... Then "were" (*fuerunt*) plays, too, perhaps, on its own indirect object, *castis puellis*: girls who were chaste, and are no more. Corrupt Baiae's waters, a crime against love, are also a crime against his poetry, as *amoris* can, of course, also refer to his poetry. So if they (his poems) and they (he and Cynthia as a pair) are to survive, she must come back to Rome.

In his brief poem #12, it appears that she has, on the contrary, receded further from their relationship. There is a sadness to this elegy—interestingly, addressed to Roman society itself, with its eyes and its gossip, referring to Cynthia in the third person—that we have not felt before: not anger, not frustration, not sarcasm, just sad resignation:

> Cynthia no longer nurtures my usual love with her embrace,
>   nor whispers sweet sounds in my ear.
> Once I pleased her: it was given to nobody at that time
>   to be able to love with such intense faith. (5-8)

> I am not what I was: the long road changes girls. (10)

> For me it is not fated that I love any other or stop loving her:
>   Cynthia was the first, Cynthia will be the last. (19-20)

Again the word in line five that translates as love—*amores*—may be taken also to refer to his poems: she no long nurtures the usual verses. The rest resonates with similar sentiments. Her interest has evaporated—the long road must mean that her travels, perhaps specifically to Baiae (or maybe it is merely the long road of a relationship that has lasted too long)—have brought about a change, away from Rome and away from him. But he will never stop loving her. That final line encapsulates what Propertius' poetry-articulated life is all about—and also what his love-life-articulated poetry is all about. "Cynthia," as the main topic of his poetry, is a synonym for that poetry; so it is his poetry—songs of himself—that was the first and will be the last—as we shall see ever more clearly, in continuing to move forward with him.

Elegy #14 is, like numbers 1, 6, and the 20, addressed to Tullus. Where in #6 he had contrasted the lover with the man of action, here the lover is contrasted—to his advantage—with wealth and its pleasures. He refocuses on Cynthia in #15. The fact that it echoes, somewhat, the second elegy, makes us realize how far the relationship has come in its slow, degenerating spiral. For here his criticism of her make-up and jewelry is in the dual context of his apparent illness—"look at me, how good fortune has snatched me away from such danger!" (verse 3; presumably, then, danger to his health, but he has survived that danger)—and the inappropriateness of her visit to him so dolled up while he is so ill; and his suspicion that she is already preparing herself for, or rather, betraying him with, another man. She who has "shown up so slowly to me in my terror" (4).

He adduces four different mythological females, from Calypso to Evadne, to offer images of how those who really love their men at least weep for them for weeks when the men are lost to them or at most, in the last case, throw themselves onto the burning funeral pyre of their husbands—and excoriates Cynthia for not being guided by such models in her behavior vis-à-vis the poet. Instead she lies to him. He arrives, in verse 32, to a perfect ambiguity: *sis quodcomque voles*—"be you whatever you want"—*non aliena tamen*: "just not alien." That second clause, and its central element, *aliena*, can be understood either as "don't leave me for some other" or "you cannot cease to be mine."

And he mentions those beautiful eyes that had, in poem 1 first snared him, as: "those little eyes... through which so often you have betrayed me!" (33-34)—she had "sworn by her eyes," presumably, regarding her fidelity: that "if you ever told a lie they would fall out into your own hands" (35-36). One might wonder, thinking back to poem 1, whether we might also understand her to have sworn to him by her eyeballs which is to say by his balls falling out of his toga by her hands: she swears to him as she fondles him. Such sexually punning innuendo would certainly not be inconsistent with other passages in these poems. His last words are to those who survive him, not to trust a flattering word she offers—but *blanditia* ("flattering words") can also mean "caresses."

Things continue in the same sort of vein in the following poem, one might say; but the voice that speaks is that of the doorway of his mistress—presumably Cynthia, albeit not actually named. And as eyeballs can be testicles, an entrance into a house where wild conduct takes place can also be an entrance into her body, as we have earlier noted. That entrance asserts that it is "battered so often by unworthy fists that I complain... he never allows my posts to have a rest who argues to me with flattering/caressing poems: 'oh deep inner doors, even crueler than my mistress herself, why are you silent, your hard gates closed to me?'" (6, 15)

And the doors continue to report the words of the excluded lover: I lie out here freezing at midnight with no response from your hinges... "My mistress is harder than Sicilian stone" (29)—which, given the domination of Sicily by Mount Aetna, could refer well enough to lava, which at first gushes out of the volcano hot and fiery, but eventually cools and solidifies into a hard stone; she lies in someone else's arms, the door to her chamber remains closed to me; "you remain untouched by my impudent tongue" (37)—which is both his poetry and whatever else one might suppose he does with his tongue, verbally and physically.

The last words are those of the door, complaining of being "defamed, thanks to its mistress' vices and the tears of her lover, by never-ending insults." Well, complaining seems to come in different flavors from our poet. In #17 it is he who is on the high seas, having left on a journey, away from Cynthia—although he cannot get her out of his mind, even as he stares up at the stars, "even the absent winds favor you, Cynthia" (5). He worries and wonders whether he will die in the storm, his body swept ashore in some foreign place, and whether it

> would not have been easier to conquer my mistress' moods
>   (however hard, she was a rare girl)
> than to look for a safe bay with unknown woods around it,
>   and hope for help from Castor and Pollux?" (15-18)

We have seen the stormy sea compared to love by Horace, and here that image is slightly re-angled so that the sea and the girl are comparable modes of storminess. Of course one cannot help wondering whether that is all that it is: the poem as a fantasy, not a report of an actual event. One can easily suppose that the poet never left Rome, but if he has left Cynthia's graces' even temporarily, then he is adrift at sea emotionally, and the storm he is experiencing (and that he imagines as having been caused by her anger at him and her curses to the elements as he sails away) is indeed occasioned by her presumed stormy slamming of her door in his face (see the previous elegy!). He strings out the whole self-pitying story: that he will die, but that—no doubt in belated grief over the loss of him—she will preside over his funeral somehow (will they bring the washed-up body back to Rome for burial?). He concludes his ode:

> If ever gliding Love has touched your waves
>   may you be gentle to this friend with tame shores.

—addressing the Nereids, and thereby really addressing the sea itself, and also thereby addressing his stormy Cynthia, still.

That fantasized flight into empty spaces beyond the crowded craziness of Rome as a metaphor—everything else about the poet that we derive from his writing and whatever scant information is available from others militates against such adventures as real— spills into the next poem, as well. And with it comes a more distinct articulation of his "flight" as occasioned by Cynthia's anger at him. The beginning reads simply like a pastoral poem—until by verses 5 and 6, when we quickly begin to know by a double-barreled statement not only that Cynthia is the real subject, and the one to whom he is addressing his words, but why he is alone out in this pastoral setting rather than in Rome partying with her:

> This is a quiet, deserted place, for one who protests,
> 	and Zephyr's air possesses the empty forest.
> Here one may bring forth one's hidden sadnesses without restraint,
> 	if only the rocks are able to keep a faithful silence.
> Where can I first recall your scorn, my Cynthia?
> 	What beginning of weeping do you give me, Cynthia?
> Somehow once I was counted among happy lovers,
> 	now in your love I am branded as disgraced.
> What did I do to merit this? What poems of mine changed you?
> 	Is my supposed new girlfriend the cause of your sadness?
> If so, return to me, capricious one, as no other
> 	has placed her beautiful feet across my threshold.
> However much my cruel hurts are owed to you
> 	my savage rage will not come forth so that
> I stay ever angry—although merited—at you... (1-15)

Her anger at him has driven him away, but he is not even sure why she is so angry. What were his crimes? And while the better-preserved manuscripts read *carmina* (which could translate as "songs" but also as "spells"), many editors amend that word to *crimina*, which they feel makes more sense.[194] Given that he is always obsessing about his poetry and about his poems to and about Cynthia and other matters, I am not so sure that *crimina* is better than *carmina* as a reading. Anyway, *he* is the one who should be angry, since she has done so many (unnamed) painful things to him! But he is not.

Be that as it may, he notes by the end of the poem that

> ...whatever my complaints may tell,
> 	I am forced, alone, to talk to the cunning birds.
> But however you may be, let the forests echo 'Cynthia' to me,
> 	nor let the deserted rocks cease resonating with your name. (29-32)

Poem #17 might be said to yield two particular offspring. Poem #18 furthers the idea of the poet writing, as we have just seen, from some distant place. That particular part of the darkness that has been ever-present throughout the love poems—the part that looks toward his own death with a kind of morbid self-love—also resonates from poem #17, but takes fuller form in #19. Its opening verses address the subject:

> Now I no longer fear the sad *Manis*, Cynthia,
>   nor at last need I delay what Fate demands;
> but that my funeral might be, perchance without you
>   this I fear far more strongly than the funeral procession itself.
> That boy is not stuck so lightly to my eyes
>   that I could forget my love when I lie as dust.

There are several particularly interesting features of these six verses. The first is the ordering of the words in the first line. "Cynthia" is placed as the penultimate word in the Latin, just before *Manis*. That position is typically reserved for the name of the deceased in Greek grave epigrams—in which the term "Manes" is used to refer to the gods/spirits/shades of the underworld (most specifically, referring to the dead themselves, now residing there). So it is her funeral, not his, which is to say, his death will be Cynthia's funeral, as far as her tyranny over him is concerned.

Moreover, such inscriptions are nearly always directed to the Manes.[195] But oddly, Propertius has used the singular form, which may be taken as masculine or feminine, nominative, genitive or vocative in case. It seems not unreasonable to view this intention as referring to Cynthia as if she is the deceased while at the same time addressing her as already deceased—hence "*Manis*," placed in the singular, feminine, vocative form.

So while he observes to her that he does not fear death, he may also be saying to her: you are already dead to me. It has been a long erotic journey shot through with *eris*, and we seem to have been arriving with the poet toward its end through the last few poems. Moreover, the dead are blind to our world and its events, so associating her with *Manis* and placing that word at the very end of this first line offers a perfect opposition to where in the first line of the first poem in the *Monobiblos*, the word *ocellis*—little eye(ball)s that see and grab (or are grabbed!) had appeared. And indeed, this is the last poem to address or focus on Cynthia in the *Monobiblos*, so if there were to be a final dropping of the other shoe after the dropping of the first in the first poem, this would be it.

If death and love can be—and we have seen them be—co-associated in both a standard positive way (the lover and the beloved both die and are reborn with the efflorescence of the new relationship that transforms both of them) and a Propertian negative way (that enslavement to love is enormously onerous); then on the other hand, he can be free of love and its death elements in two ways. One is that he dies—then he is free of everything in this world, including his oppressive mistress and including death and the fear of death, since the dead cannot fear death—and the other is that she dies.

Of course, he can still fear, somehow, that he won't have the last word—what could be more deadly for a poet?—which would be the case if she doesn't mourn him, in not showing up for his funeral. In the third verse, what I have translated as "be without"—*careat*—can also be rendered as "be free from," and if he is playing with the idea that she rather than he is actually "dead" then the pun contained in that verb underscores that play.

Puer—the "boy"—refers to *Amor/Eros*, who is love personified; so it is this time the poet's eyes (*ocellis*, coming at the end of that line) upon whom love does not rest so lightly that he would forget his love even beyond the grave—beyond his grave, yes, but perhaps if she is dead to him, who yet cannot get her out of his mind, then beyond her grave he cannot and will not forget her and their one-time love. As we page down the remaining verses, that twisting around—from *his* death as the subject to *her* death as the subject—is continually reinforced. He offers another allusion to myth, referencing Protesilaos—the first Akhaian to die at Troy, whose shade was permitted to visit his widow, who then killed herself rather than go on living without him—ostensibly to suggest how Cynthia should and hopefully would feel at the poet's death: suicidal.

But he immediately turns the words backwards: "Wherever/ whatever I am, I shall always be devoted to your image: great love pierces the shores of fate" (11-12) sounds a good deal more like his remembering her when she is dead than her behavior when he is dead. *Fatum* at the end of verse 12, "fate," can also be rendered as "death" and should be, given the context. So love transcends death. It is not only the god, *Amor/Eros* who is immortal, but one of the ways in which humans may achieve immortality is by being remembered by those who loved them when they were alive. Of course, that can only last a few generations at most, but someone about whom enduring poetry is written can be remembered forever, if the poetry is read forever.

So Cynthia, the object of Propertius' love and the subject of his poetry, is immortalized by his love-poems. And of course, so is he, whose real subject is himself and his combination of didactic *doctus* qualities and clever, sometimes neologistic lyricism. And both of them and neither of them is dead yet anyway. Having referenced a whole chorus of heroines—beauties taken as booty by the Akhaians after the conquest of Troy—he adds that:

> none of these, Cynthia, was more beautiful in shape, to me,
>   than you; and (may the Earth justly thus allow)
> however long the fates delay your old age
>   your dear bones will be washed by my tears (15-18).

Line 15, past tense, suggests that she is already dead, but then he shifts her death not only to the future but a hopefully distant future (*tellus*, "earth," is being referred to as the goddess of the dead)—when he, outliving her, (no matter how long she lives), will mourn her. This entire discussion is embedded—to use terminology with which our own discussion began—within a *sacer* context, both in playing between mortality and immortality and in ignoring the *profanus* logic of linear past-present-future time.

He does add: "and may you, living, be able to feel this way for my ashes"—i.e., if you outlive me—"then death will not be bitter to me wherever it happens" (19-20). He still worries "that an unfair love may drag you from my grave" (22)—there are always those competitors for her favors whose existence cannot be ignored—

"and force you unwillingly to dry your falling tears. The most faithful girls can be turned by constant threats" (23-24). We have come full circle back to the primary concern of the first quatrain, but upped the intensity: not that she not be at his funeral, but that she abbreviate her time by his grave under duress—although, of course *minis*, translated as "threats" can also refer to money, a specific Greek weight of silver. We are thus reminded that Cynthia's love may, perhaps, be purchased with other coin than poetry.

So Propertius concludes with simple advice in the face of the brevity of life and the inevitability of death—coming back to a straightforward *profanus* consideration of things—to have a good time together as long as we can:

> Let us enjoy ourselves as lovers while it is permitted by fate:
> Love is never long enough at any time. (25-26)

The penultimate line recalls Catullus' line to Lesbia, that we live and love—but is yet different. Where Catullus, fresh toward the outset of his relationship, mocked the frowns of conservative old men, Propertius, given the context of both this and his other poems and their timings, would seem to be at the other end of his relationship. Perhaps his last lines are as much a plea and even a eulogy as they are a casual suggestion at the end of an elegy.

This is, in any case, the last poem in the *Monobiblos*, as noted above, that is addressed to or focused on Cynthia. The last three that follow this one are: a long poem to Gallus—warning him about protecting his love, with the story of Hylas embedded within it, in order to make his point—a second, very short poem addressed to someone who remains unnamed; and one addressed to Tullus. In the three subsequent books of Propertius' elegies, Cynthia more than periodically reappears, however. In Book II, (published about five years after Book I), in the very first elegy, addressed to Maecenas, which begins with "You ask me why so often mine are written as love poems…it is not Calliope, nor does Apollo sing through me. That girl herself makes my talent" (1, 3-4)—"that girl" is clearly Cynthia.

She inspires me to sing such songs, he tells the renowned patron of poetry. Had the fates directed me instead to write of heroes, I'd write "about wars and the memorable deeds of your Caesar, and you, after Caesar, would be my second concern" (25-26). "Concerns" translates *cura*, otherwise meaning "care" but also, particularly in Propertius, "love." So you, Maecenas, would be my second love—indeed as a beloved and loving patron, perhaps Maecenas *is* second—to Cynthia, not to Augustus. But ultimately, "I keep turning to the battles within the narrow bed: let each devote his day to the art of which he is capable" (45-46). And so, in Book II Cynthia is associated with every elegy except the tenth, which *is* (at last) devoted to Augustus.

And even then, early in that tenth elegy, although he claims in lines 3-4 that "now it is pleasing to record mighty squadrons turned toward battles and to tell of the Roman campaigns of my prince," a mere four lines or so later he asserts:

Young age celebrates love, old age war's tumult:
 I shall celebrate wars, as soon as my girl is written up (7-8)

—and indeed, is he not still young and not yet old, although he is lightly and prematurely trying his hand at a war-ish theme? But he isn't really writing about war yet; he's still writing about writing about it. And as the poem moves forward, he keeps pushing the actual writing about it further away, into the hoary future. By line 12, he informs the "Muses, [that] now will be the work about greater limits" (although *now*, yet *will be*, not *is*), and he claims—after oh so briefly alluding to Augustus' post-Crassus success against the Parthians, and noting how the (nonetheless unconquered) Arabs tremble before Roman power, as no doubt those yet further away also do (oh *really, do* they?)—he asserts that "I shall follow these campaigns; as a poet singing about your battles I shall be great" (19-20)—but this is still all in the future tense, to which he adds the exclamation point in the remaining part of verse 21: "may the fates preserve that day for me!" a phrase that could hardly be exceeded with regard to wishful future thinking as opposed to present actuality.

And by the end of the short poem—all of 26 lines long—he confesses, that he is

helpless, now, to ascend the heights of songs of praise,
    I offer mine like worthless incense on impoverished altars.

My poems do not yet know the fount of Hesiod's home,
    but *Amor* bathes them only in the river of Permessus. (23-26)

Even here, his mythological allusions are delightfully *doctus*: what I have rendered as "Hesiod's home" is *Ascraeos*—Ascra being an ancient town in Boeotia regarded as Hesiod's birthplace—and *Permessos* is mentioned in verse five of Hesiod's *Theogony* as a river on Mount Helicon in which the Muses bathe themselves. But the point is that, even when Propertius wants to stray from *eros* and lyric to *eris* and epic—which he almost needs to, if he really wants the patronage of Augustus—he cannot. Cynthia, and with her, love in one form or another, remains his real subject.

As we wander through Book II the aspects of the relationship wander, too, each poem offering a particular situation or mood—and most often the mood is one of complaint or vituperation rather than adoration or adulation, and in the end (literally) his real devotion is not to her as much as to his own poetry, which uses her as a source of inspiration and as a vehicle for showing off his beautiful mind. The second and third elegies speak of her beauty and grace, but the fourth emphasizes her harshness and the fifth her perfidy: "is it true that all of Rome, Cynthia, is aware of how you carry on, living your iniquitous life?" (1-2) The ninth bemoans her betrayal as she has taken on a new lover (the requisite mytho-historical allusion is, by ironic or exemplary comparison, to loyal Penelope and thus to himself as Odysseus).

The one that follows the "failed" Augustus poem, #11—six lines long—even while speaking to Cynthia (without mentioning her name), tells her that he will not praise her: "Let others—or none—write about you as it is permitted: let him praise who sows seeds in barren soil," for one day those passing by your grave "will scorn your bones." All of a sudden, #15 rejoices in their love—and in an exultant tone reminiscent of Catullus at the height of his passion for Lesbia, sings sweetly that "even if you give me all your kisses, you will give me too few!" (50)—but in #16 she is being excoriated again for her faithlessness with some wealthy praetor who buys her favors with clothes and jewels. He even once or twice tries to taunt her by suggesting that he, too, can be and has been disloyal—as in #22, which begins "you know how many girls have pleased me equally."

And so on. Book II contains many more poems than does the first; thirty-four elegies, a number of them traditionally broken by editors into two or more parts, many of them very short and some—particularly the last—very long. The summing up of his place within poetry and of his immortality in this last elegy, #34, arrives—by way of Socrates and Aeschylus, Callimachus and Homer—at Vergil, who can write about epic events (Propertius references Actium and Augustus, careful to recognize the parallel between Aeneas and Augustus—and thus, by implication, between Turnus and Marc Antony): "yield to him, Roman writers, and yield to him, you Greeks! Something greater than the *Iliad* is being born" (65-66); Vergil, who can also write lyrical eclogues and Hesiodic (referring to *Works and Days*) Georgics. Yet, my learned songs of Cynthia will not be unwelcome to one who can sing them, whether he's expert in love or a total novice (79-83).

He references Varro, and "the writings of Catullus, whose Lesbia is now better known than Helen herself" (87-88). And he mentions Calvus and Gallus. A range, then, of poets, epic and lyric, scholarly and simple. The poem is as loosely constructed in terms of the chronology and type of figures mentioned as the entire second book of elegies is with regard to Cynthia—a symptom, in part perhaps, of his confused emotions. Like that second book in which it is literally the last word, the poem leads in the double direction we might expect, ending with the idea that, like the women immortalized by these other poets,

> so indeed will Cynthia, who is praised in the verse of Propertius, if Fame decides to place me among these poets.

His poetry will immortalize her as it will immortalize him.

This remains true—maybe even more true—in Book III. In general, the poems are scattered across different subjects, regarding and addressed to various friends—including mourning the death of one of them Paetus (#7). There is one long one asking Maecenas for support (#9), and even one cheering on Augustus and Roman arms (#3). Love is still often a main topic, whether advice to others or comments about his own life—even, yes, perhaps eight poems devoted to Cynthia. One of these (#10), acknowledges that it is her birthday; it is simply sweet and wishes her and her beauty well and a long continuation. Suggesting how she might begin and spend her day, he proposes that she wear the beautiful clothes with which "you first captured the eyes of Propertius" (15)—consciously or not evoking the first line of the *Monobiblos*. In another (#15), he asks Cynthia not to be jealous of Lycinna, the girl with whom he first learned about love several years earlier—thus giving the lie to the second line of the *Monobiblos*, in which he asserted that he had not known love before Cynthia (or does this confirm that line: he had had sex before Cynthia, but not love, which is part of the reason that Cynthia should not be jealous of Lycinna...?). Several others are no doubt directed to her but don't mention her name.

The penultimate elegy in book III (#24) does so, however, and looks toward a break or a terminus in their relationship: "your faith in your beauty is falsely placed... my love has paid such tribute to you, Cynthia: it shames me that you are famous through my verses" (l, 3-4)... my wreathed boats reach harbor... and I cast anchor. Now at last I have come to my senses, exhausted by my surging passion, and my wounds are healed... (16-18). (Again: if the wild seas are love with its potential dangers, he has come in from those seas to calm emotional safety). And the last elegy in the book (#25—in the first line of which he notes that he has served her for five years, thus giving us that explicit demographic of their relationship) suggests the end of the affair, of his anguish and his tears—and with a warning to her regarding that instrument, her beauty: "learn to fear the outcome of your beauty"—i.e., that it fades, leaving you with nothing, particularly given that your other possession, me, is now gone. These are the very last words of the poem.

What *he* has, on the other hand, is the immortal beauty of his poems. The most certain of the works in which he references this love of his words and song of himself comes in the third elegy in Book III. There he describes a dream he had, of finding himself on Mount Helicon, that mountain sacred to the Muses and to Apollo, patron of poetry. There Calliope informs him that his fate, as a poet, is not to write about war and the blast of Roman trumpets, but about love and the carrying off of girls—with which words the goddess moistens his lips with the water of Philetas—the famous Greek lyric poet from Kos—from her fountain. And so, indeed, as he says back in the first poem in Book III, (invoking Philetas, as well as Callimachus, in its first line): "I am the first priest, entering from the pure fount to lead with Italian revels the choirs of Greece" (3-4).

Since this third book was published after Horace's *Odes* I-III were published, we may recognize this beginning as a response to Horace's own assertion that he was the first to really present Greek lyric poetry in Roman verse, and declaring himself the priest of the Muses. Propertius' Book IV certainly adds to his own assertion of himself as "priest"—in a rather literal sense—since five of the eleven elegies within it offer focus on Roman cults. This is also part of his *doctus* persona being brought to the fore, and overlaps, too, with his attention both to early Roman history (in elegy #1) and more recent Roman history—specifically Actium (in 2.34)—showing his ability to write as a patriotic member of the *communitas* and not just as an individual infatuated with Cynthia or someone else.

Two other elegies in Book IV are spoken in the voices of two Roman women—one as a letter to her husband on the battle front (#4) and the other as the ghost of Cornelia speaking to her husband from the grave (#11)—and one (#5) offers a pile of curses directed at a procuress named Acanthis ("May the earth cover your grave with thorns, procuress..."—it begins). One could see this as another twist in the intertwining of *eros* and *eris*, given the manner in which a procuress and her clients refer to what she arranges for/with her "products" as love. All of these elegies are shot through with mythological references, of course, and there is a decided increase in imagining with regard to the dead.

In the first (#7) of the only two poems in this last volume that pertain to Cynthia this last idea plays out. The image of his dead and buried beloved is conjured somewhat horrifically, with her fingers rattling as bones, her lips eaten away by the waters of Lethe, standing over him as he had her in I.3—but whereas his thoughts regarding her and her beauty had been tenderly lustful there and then, hers here are wrathful—as she speaks with a living voice, a ghost who berates him for his infidelity. He has hardly mourned her, was barely at the funeral, she accuses him. Yet she acknowledges—of *course* she does, since this is *his* voice speaking through her imagined ghost, after all—that "nonetheless I shall not berate you as much as you deserve, Propertius: long was my reign in your books" (49-50). She instructs him regarding her servants and her possessions—and tells him to burn his poems about her, and what to write as her epitaph—reminding him that one day soon he shall be with her, bone rubbing against bone.

Cynthia reminds him that he ought "not to spurn dreams coming through the sacred gates" (87)—which opens wide the gate to understanding this poem as no more than a dream. That would help explain the second Cynthia poem, immediately following, (#8), which depicts the poet partying with two ladies of questionable character, Phyllis and Teia, when Cynthia, very much alive, arrives onto the scene and, outraged, her eyes flashing lightning, breaks up the party; the entire street reverberates with this midnight madness. Her rage is spelled out as are her conditions for restoring the relationship—and when all is done, and terms agreed to, the place purified with sulfur and water, "we resolved our war across the entire couch."

Just in case elegy IV.7 by itself hadn't been enough to do so, the juxtaposition of #7 and #8 reminds us that we must always be wary of what the poet describes as taking place as having really taken place: the relationship between autobiography and imagination is even more blurred than for ordinary people. But then, the point for him is neither the facts nor even his subjects, love and otherwise, but the success with which he depicts that which he presents, in the singular poetic voice that will earn him immortality.

In the interests of space, I have not reviewed all of the love-related poems in Books II-IV in all that much detail, (as compared to those in Book I). That I have invested so many words in Propertius over all is intended to serve four inter-related purposes for our narrative. First, to demonstrate how he is unique among these lyric poets in the obsessive consistency with which so much of his work is directed to one woman—real or imagined, or whatever her true name was. Second, his uniqueness as a writer of elegies that fall between simply being love lyrics and being didactic poems. Thus he consistently uses myth and its concomitants to educate his reader—and even more so, to show off how *doctus* he is. Third, one can recognize how much his poetry, ostensibly about Cynthia, is about himself: one might say of his work that it centers around three "m"s: myths, maxims, and me.

Fourth, and most important for our purposes, the ostensive *eros* focus of his elegies is rarely if ever disentangled from *eris* of one sort or another—from the eristic sense extractable from the *ocellis* pun in the first line of the first poem to the times and ways in which the relationship seems to be failing and his words to or about Cynthia ("Rome's prostitute") become vituperative to the last Cynthia elegy in Book IV, in which her outrage at him, conversely, is ultimately resolved through love-making.

This last Propertian book was no doubt published after 16 BCE, long after Maecenas had fallen from favor with Augustus and the Emperor had become increasingly wrapped up in his campaign to promote family values and old-style morality. This was not an atmosphere in which someone like Propertius would easily continue to find patronage.[196] An individual voice obsessed with an individual issue pushing back continuously against the stated communal values of the Empire calling itself a saved Republic[197] was in great danger of being stifled.

V Ovid

The ultimately unhappy combination of the increasingly astringent Augustan atmosphere and an even greater lasciviousness than was true for Propertius would lead the last of the great Roman elegists, Publius Ovidius Naso (43 BCE-17 CE), into an enforced exile by the Black Sea (on the western coast, in what is today Romania), in 8 CE, banished by imperial decree. If, besides chronology, one may plot a course that carries from the more intimate and personal tone of Catullus through Horace and Tibullus to the more intellective and often remarkably detached tone of Propertius, then it is particularly appropriate to arrive at Ovid in this part of our narrative, who is not only chronologically the last man standing in this array—a generation younger than Horace (and Vergil) and a decade or so younger than Tibullus and Propertius (and he refers to all four of them as sources of inspiration to him in his *Tristia* IV.10.41-54)[198] — but in his approach to our subject, by far the most detached and light-hearted while also the most overtly wanton. Well, outright sexual.

What is implicit (and, yes, occasionally explicit) in the others is more explicit in Ovid from the get-go: that a different rhythmic pattern is needed for lyric poetry from what is used for epic. He renounces hexameter in favor of the elegiac couplet, as he points out in the first poem in his first group, which is also the work most relevant to our discussion, the *Amores*. Where Propertius starts off by telling us about Cynthia, and only much later brings up the matter of epic as an alternative to elegy, Ovid starts with the discussion of those two types of poetry, explaining and excusing why he is heading for the latter, although he began by trying to head for the former. Indeed, where the very first word of the *Monobiblos* is *Cynthia*, the first word Ovid offers is *arma*—evoking the first word of the *Aeneid*.

> Of arms and violent wars I was preparing to
>   to sing, with subject matching meter.

So we shall see the interweave of three elements in our *eros/eris* matrix—of course: the subject matter of love versus strife/war and the issue of love versus war/strife poetry and, shortly, the idea, found previously, but particularly in Propertius, that this poetry is about the author as a poet more than it is about either subject, per se. Where poetry is concerned, the first verse is dactylic hexameter, but a missing foot has left the second verse as pentameter, and the combination of the two yields an elegiac couplet. So one might say that Ovid began with an epic meter but had slipped away from it by the end of the second line of his poem. The poet also notices this, and explains in the following couplets how this transpired:

> The second verse was equal [to the first]: but Cupid
>   is said to have stolen away one foot.
> "Who gave you, savage boy, [I asked], the right over poems?
>   We bards are the Muses' crowd, not yours!"

Ovid uses an old Latin term, *vates*, (resurrected by the elegists) for "poets" (hence my somewhat antiquated "bards"). The question posed to Amor/Cupid not only places love potentially in tension with strife, since the epic meter has been subverted by elegiac meter, but also places Amor in a position superior to Apollo and the muses, who are traditionally associated with the arts and humanities, including poetry. Indeed, the poet continues his rhetorical objection to Cupid's domineering manner through a series of references to divine-realm what-ifs that might upset the order (*kosmos*) of things and turn the world into *khaos*.

> What if Venus seized the arms of golden-haired Minerva,
>   while golden-haired Minerva waved the flaming torches [of love]?

He then adds (9-12): what if Ceres took over the forests from Diana and Diana the fields from Ceres; and what if Apollo took up the warrior's spear and Mars the poet's lyre…? So three examples of potentially chaotic changes in who does what among the gods. And a question to Amor: you have your own realm, but why are you then interfering with poetry? Are you even interfering with Apollo's realm? (13-16)

There is certainly an intended irony in this last rhetorical question: for surely the reader would be familiar with that renowned competition between Apollo and Amor with regard to whose arrows are more powerful, that ended with Love's triumph over the Far-Darter. The golden god was smitten with a nymph, Daphne, who, hit by Cupid's lead-tipped arrow, was far from interested in her pursuer's affections.[199] So the god of love was victorious over the god of poetry—and in the end, the poet's love-guided poetry will triumph over love itself.

This in spite of the verses that follow shortly, in which Amor draws arrows from his quiver and fires them unerringly at the poet—"'take these, bard,' he said, 'as subjects for your work'… I, *miser*, burn, and Love reigns in my once empty heart" (24-26). But with Ovid, indeed, the victor is Love/Amor/Eros/Cupid—the god—and his poetry is about Love, rather than the victor or his subject being *love*. This is why he will be able to be light and jocular about it, rather than tortured, like the other elegists.

And his work will be epic, beginning odd line by odd line with six dactylic feet, even as it is ultimately elegiac, ending, even line by even line, with five feet—rising and falling, (like a ship on the waves of the sea of poetry) and so: "Farewell you iron wars with your metrical style. Garland your fiery temples with myrtle from the shore, oh Muse who will be measured in eleven-foot lengths" (28-30). Sea tales to be told by the fire—brandy glass and pipe in hand, with humor—are what will follow.

In the second poem he repeats the idea of being victimized by love, referring again to those thin arrows: "fixed in his heart, as brutal Love twists the breast that he occupies" (7-8). This was, interestingly, the fate of Apollo after he mocked the capability of Amor's little arrows to do anything, as compared with his, Apollo's far-darting arrows. One of Cupid's arrows was fixed and twisted in the god's heart, while a different kind of arrow was fixed into the heart of Daphne.[200] To the extent that one recognizes this, one also understands an intention on the part of the poet to equate himself with Apollo—the god of poetry.

In any case, the poet admits to being Cupid's latest victim (19)—the word, *praeda*, more literally, means plunder or loot and is derived from military terminology, offering another small angle of interweaving the idea of *eros* with that of *eris*. Indeed, the poet goes on to describe the great triumphal procession that Cupid, in his chariot—drawn by doves (*columbas*; 23), birds associated with Venus—will experience, with a train of captives and a soldiers' escort, like a Roman general returning from the battlefield. Those captives are lovestruck young men (*capti iuvenes*) and maidens (*captaeque puellae*); he plays on the double meaning of *captus* as both captured in war and overwhelmed by love (27).

Whereas the first poem was about the poetry of love, this one places more emphasis on love itself, but—again—underscores the happy, rather than tortured nature of the poet who has been defeated by it: for the last two couplets, yet again twisting love around war and epic around elegy, proclaims to Cupid that

> since I can be part of your sacred triumph,
>> desist from wasting your efforts on me [since you are already] the victor.

> Look at the successful wars of Caesar, your relative:
> those he conquered he protects with the hand with which
> he conquered them.

He is a happy victim of these wars of love. He nonetheless begs for the sort of *clementia* that Augustus (whose image at Prima Porta reflects the tradition, we recall, that Eros/Amor is part of his Aenean ancestry) claimed to have exacted on his former enemies. And he has not, incidentally, named the girl who is associated with his delightful new servitude, yet. Only by the third poem does he begin a slow dance in that direction—first by immediately shifting slightly, in the very first couplet:

> I beg for justice: let the girl who has just plundered me
> either love me or say why I should always love her.

He is the victim/plunder not of the god of love, this time, but of the girl with whom he has fallen in love: the metaphor, somewhat more precisely, is of a huntress who has trapped her prey. As usual with the elegists, however, the metaphors mix casually: by verse five he asks her to accept him as her slave, as he promises to love her with perfect faith (*pura... fide*). He underscores that he doesn't take pleasure in a thousand girls, jumping from one love to the next, but "you will be my everlasting love-focus" (15-16). Moreover, he presents the god of love himself, Amor—together with Apollo, the nine muses, and Bacchus—as his "backers": they present him to her, compensating for his limited level of noble ancestry (7-14). So he who shot him through with arrows in the first poem is now his mentoring ally.

All of his words are ostensibly directed toward the girl, although the reader might be expected to raise one or even two eyebrows at the poet's protestations of purity and blameless modesty and absolute fidelity, thanks to puns here and there. To her he concludes by asserting that, if she were to "offer yourself to me as fruitful material for poetry, poems will pour forth worthy of you, their inspiration" (19-20)—following this direct beseeching address with no less than three references to women made famous through poetry. Each of them—Io, Leda, and Europa—was raped or at least seduced by Jupiter, king of gods, in one animal form or another. So he does conclude that, like these couples,

>we, also, shall be equally sung throughout the entire world
>and our names shall always be joined, mine and yours.

Anyone, however, who pauses for a moment to consider that Jupiter is the ultimate adulterer—the opposite of a pure, blamelessly modest and absolutely loyal lover (neither to his wife, Juno, nor to any one of those females with whom he constantly betrays her)—and that the poet is boldly comparing himself to Jupiter by implication, must think at least two thoughts while shaking his/her head. One, that the references are hardly designed to polish the poet's innocent image in any serious way; and two, that in the end, this *is* all about himself: the king of poets compared to the king of gods in pure, blameless immodesty and absolute elegiac dominance.

Mind you, if with this poem we have finally arrived at a direct address to the poet's girl, he has still not actually named her, has he? So if he shares with the other elegists, particularly Propertius, two obvious attributes—the frequent, diversely asserted greater importance of his elegiac love poetry than epic war poetry, and the greater importance of his poetry of love and thus of himself than of the beloved, ostensive object of his poetry—he is different from the others, and in particular, again, from Propertius, in taking his time about getting to the actual indication of who the theoretical object of his affections and his writing *is*. So, too, to repeat, he is distinguished by his ongoingly light tone. Even when he invokes the image of his beloved mourning him after his death—"may the thread of the sisters [i.e., the Fates] give me many years to live with you, and may it come about that I die amid your painful sorrow" (17-18)—there is such a casual tone to it as compared (yet again) with Propertius, as we have seen the latter suffering in many ways, including his twisted and torn images of his own death (see above, 385-6).

We can follow these issues through the *Amores* along varied paths. In the fourth poem, he begins by noting that his girlfriend's husband is going to be at the same dinner-party "which we will attend." This is a new wrinkle of straightforwardness; if Lesbia or Cynthia have husbands, those men don't enter into the poetry about or directed to their wives. Most of the poem is devoted to instructions as to how she (still unnamed) ought to behave, so that she and Ovid can express their thoughts about each other through signs—and he warns her not to accede to fondling or kissing her husband, or Ovid will reveal himself as her lover! And try to get him, the husband, as drunk as possible. Of course, this *is* her husband, which means that, at the end of the evening, she will go home with him, be locked in the house, while the poet pines away by the door, hoping, at least, that the husband is too drink to have sex with his wife—and demanding of her that, should sex occur, she not report it to Ovid the next day.

We finally learn what she is actually called in the fifth couplet of the fifth poem: Corinna. Her name is embedded between the opening description of a sultry afternoon, as he awaits her in his bedroom; and a briefer yet lush description of her, in which she is compared to Semiramis, the Assyrian queen, and to Lais, the renowned Corinthian courtesan (two exotic, beautiful figures of yesteryear and distant elsewheres). He tears her garment off, furthers his wrapt description of her naked body—offering us a kind of verbal Playboy centerfold—and hurries, pun intended, to the climax of his poem, for

Who doesn't know the rest? Tired out, we both relaxed.
May my afternoons always be so successful! (25-26)

The journey between clasping her naked body to his—this is daring description, not likely to find favor with someone of Augustus' prudish mien—and the post-coital state of relaxation is either rapid, beyond even Ovid's willingness to be explicit, or both. One of the more interesting elements of this short poem is that it so strongly evokes an actual experience, as opposed to so much else within the elegists' corpus, which can seem the outcome of imagination. And Ovid, above all, tends, as we have noted, toward flights of fancy rather than records of experience.

In any case, the next several poems are much, much longer. In terms of our own particular focus, #9, addressed to Atticus, brings us back explicitly to the matter of love and strife in other than the elegists' *odi at amo* kind of theme with which we are by now very familiar.

> Every lover fights as a soldier, and Cupid has his own army camp;
> Atticus, believe me, every lover fights as a soldier.

Castra, which I have translated as "army camp" can also mean "warfare." Either way, the point is clear: that love is its own kind of war in which every lover is a soldier—a half-line repeated at both the beginning and the end of the couplet. Moreover, the pentameter is actually reversible metrically. So the notion that love and war, Venus and Mars, *eros* and *eris*, are opposed is presented as false. More to the point, the lover victimized in the first poem, having assumed a position of willing partner rather than victim by the second and aggressor by the third, underscore the idea here that he serves not as a captive but as a *warrior* in Amor's army.

Nor does Ovid leave the idea after the first couplet. He notes how youth is the time of life appropriate for both war and Venus, following with an extended array of comparisons between the two professions in which what the soldier experiences the lover metaphorically experiences, from obstacles to inclement weather to well-fortified cities and their mighty gates and guards. "Mars wavers, and Venus is uncertain: and the conquered rise again, and those who, you assert, can never be brought down, fall" (229-30). So don't call love idle; it is active, he argues, and then reviews warriors whose greatness in war was inspired by love: Akhilleus, Hector, Agamemnon—even Mars himself, who was caught in Vulcan's chains because he could not resist the beauty of Venus.

This last is obliquely connected to the other three, and not only because Mars is a god and not a man like the others. This god is the god of war who was passionately involved with the goddess of love, but not, per se, inspired by her to great deeds. On the contrary, he was humiliated by her husband, captured in a net of chains from which he, god of war and warriors indeed, could not escape.[201] That datum merely adds fuel to the fire in which war and epic are being incinerated by the love-poet. I, too, he ends, was once idle but then love for a beautiful girl stimulated me to enlist in her *castra*—so that I am very active now, in fact, waging wars by night.

But then #10 begins with an implied series of mythic comparisons to Corinna (unnamed but presumably the one to whom the poem is directed), beginning with Helen, whose departure from Sparta and her husband, for love, with Paris, led to the war of wars—and continuing with Leda, seduced by Jupiter in the guise of a swan; and Amymone (the only one of the 50 Danaids who did not slay her husband on their wedding night). How exactly these all offer comparison to Corinna emerges by the fourth couplet:

> Just so were you: I feared the eagle and the bull
> and whatever shape love has made of mighty Jupiter.

So the poet who compared himself to Jupiter back in the third poem fears that somehow the god, in some disguise, might carry off Corinna the way he did other mortal women. But this turns out to be merely a prelude to the main body of the poem, which is directed to criticism of women selling their favors, apparently including Corinna, who has become ever more demanding of gifts—but it is a long poem, elaborating his theme and interweaving it with references to various mythological narratives. He all but calls Corinna a prostitute (line 42)—and it would seem that, as with the other elegists, Ovid is beginning to sour here and there on his sweet relationship—*eros* is shifting toward *eris*—except that his tone is different from that of his predecessors (again): more detached and lighter, less long-suffering, less intense.

For he is one who has ultimately been deputized rather than tortured by Amor, becoming a key officer in his army, as we have seen in #9—a far cry from when he referred to himself, as Propertius had, as *miser*, at 1:23. Even the paired #11 and #12, if they fail to yield the outcome that he wishes in terms of time with his girl, cannot slow his march toward poetic glory.

In the first of these two poems he addresses Nape, Corinna's servant, who has apparently helped facilitate their liaisons before, and he concludes his request for further intermediation through transmitting a written message by promising a crowning with laurel of the writing tablet itself on which his beloved writes back to him: "come"—and which he will dedicate at the temple of Venus. He will even make writing tablets famous, which "not long ago were cheap maple wood." And it is, conversely, the tablets that he addresses in #12—that inform him that Corinna cannot see him this day. These, that have betrayed him, shall indeed become firewood.

Yet another light-toned strife-ridden poem follows in #14. It is a kind of companion-in-condemnation of #10, entirely devoted to a direct-address criticism of Corinna's decision to dye her hair— the process seems to have caused some of it to fall out—and use of imported tresses, specifically from Germania. It is a somewhat nasty lecture that yields, finally, tears on her part, as she holds tufts of her hair in her hand, to which he responds that she should cheer up: her hair will eventually grow back. Most noteworthy for our purposes is his use of the phrase *me miserum* in verse 51, introducing that end sequence that begins with her tears. He is *miser*, moved by her tears. For if on the one hand this poem is part of a mounting series of strife-toned addresses to Corinna (or her writing tablets), on the other it underscores the more amused atmosphere that shapes the *Amores* in comparison with that of the other elegists, Propertius, of course, in particular. We have travelled quite some distance from the *me miserum* of Ovid's 1.25 and an even greater distance from Propertius' *miserum me* in the first line of the *Monobiblos*.

Like the others, his goal is *fama*—perhaps even more straightforwardly stated than by his fellow-elegists—and thus the epic hero who will be made famous is himself. So the last poem, #15, in Book I, comes full circle back to that theme that was introduced in the first book: "I seek eternal fame, forever sung throughout the whole world" (8). This statement comes on the heels of his comment—addressed directly toward *Livor*, (Envy personified), as a response to criticism that he has endured—that he has chosen not to pursue "the dusty rewards of military life" (4), or other "approved" (but as he puts it, merely mortal) professions: verbose law (5) and/or politics with its prostitutional mode of life (6). So within the familiar formula of asserting the value of love and its poetry over strife-based verses there is, however, a somewhat heavier, strife-sourced *feeling* of being stung by these criticisms over the years—*Livor* is described as *edax* ("devouring, voracious")— than was true in the opening poem. Perhaps he doth protest, a bit strongly, that he is achieving his own *kleos aphthiton*.

He flies, then, through a list (a tendentiously long and scatter-shot-organized list) of previous literary greats, both Greek and Roman: Homer, Sophokles, Aratus, Menander, Ennius, Varro, Lucretius, Vergil, Tibullus, and Gallus, (emulating Propertius by sometimes offering these figures in an obscure form—thus Homer is Maeonides, for instance, meaning "a son of Maeonia," which is Lydia, where Homer is said to have been born)—and ends by noting that poetry is immortal, and

> Golden-haired Apollo
>   Shall serve me cups filled with water from the Castalian spring,
> And I shall adorn my hair with cold-fearing myrtle
>   and shall be much read by anxious lovers.
> Envy feeds on the living; after death it is silent
>   When each man's glory safeguards him as he deserves:
> So, even when the final fires have consumed me,
>   I shall live on, and the great part of me shall survive. (35-42)

Ever the cheeky one, he is not only inspired by, and functions as a partner or a subordinate to Apollo, but will be *served* by the god from the spring on Mount Parnassus. If one thinks back to Ovid's reference in #9 (see above, 397-8), to the Amor-Apollo-Daphne story, then this couplet becomes still clearer: the poet who writes of love is equated with the god of love, (as he had once equated himself with Jupiter), victorious over Apollo himself; so the latter not only inspires but also serves the former.

His poetry, and its focus on love, shall achieve immortality for him, the writer—no mention here of characters within it who shall be immortalized, albeit characters there are. And also, as with the other poets, one woman in particular who seems to be his focus, Corinna, who appears at times and is reflected in the usual images of bolted doors and cruel door-keepers. But her name, amazingly, dispassionately, does not appear until the fifth poem—and then not again until the eleventh poem—within the first book of the *Amores*.

Book II spends more time with Corinna—at least her name appears more often (in the end, her name appears in nine of the 19 poems of Book II and is implied in two others)—but Book II is also where he notes that, really, every girl of whatever type appeals to him (in #4), even observing (in #10) that he is equally in love with two girls simultaneously (this is all so anti-Propertian)—because he is really in love with *love*. And given the almost standard play between "love" and "poems on love" he is (also) really in love with his poems—which is to say, with *himself*, the author of those wonderful poems. They *are* wonderful, and varied in subject matter and stylistic affectation.

We can certainly recognize a furthering of some of the same sort of strife that resonates through the other elegists. In II:7 he defends himself from Corinna's criticism that he had been fooling around with her maid: "How could a sordid slave invite my lust? By Venus and the arrows of her son I swear that I am not guilty of that charge" (26-28). The maid is named Cypassis in the poem—and in the very next ode (#8) he addresses her directly, asking accusatorily "What was the sign that gave our love away? From what did Corinna know that we two had loved?" (5-6). So I guess he *was* messing around with Corinna's maid. But since he has outright denied the relationship with Cypassis to Corinna, then Cypassis had better not betray him by doing other than also denying the relationship or he will confess to Corinna just how often he and Cypassis have been together, which will be a disaster for the maid far more than for him. Even in these poems there is a lighter, more distantly amused tone than we find in the previous elegists.

By III.11—a long poem usually broken by editors into 11a and 11b—he has ended the relationship with Corinna, in any case.

> Yield, ugly love, to my wearied heart.
> For certain now I am freed and have escaped my chains,
>   and what I was not ashamed to bear, it shames me to have
>   borne.
> I have won and trampled my vanquished love with my feet…
> (2-5)

We may indeed recognize that, as usual, the poet puns here, twice: the love (*amorem*) that he tramples, who is also the god of love, can also refer to his poetry, and the feet with which he tramples victoriously are also the feet of his verses: so he has conquered love and love poetry with his poetry. He continues, bitterly—and it is a bitter victory, not a sweet one—noting that he has observed her (he who has always been an observer) with her new, unnamed, lover:

> So I don't know whom you were holding in an embrace,
> as I watched like a slave before your closed door.
> I saw when your lover came through those doors all worn out,
> noting a weakened and discharged veteran. (11-14)

Whoever the poet's successor is, he has been damned to obscurity and scorned as worn out from his exertions with Corinna—but we are surely not deceived by the poet, who, we can be fairly certain, would welcome the exhaustion brought about through just those sorts of exertions. One might note, tooo, the pun on *emeritum*—"discharged veteran"—which, in carrying the same military connotation that is present in its English-language equivalent, reminds us that the field of love is a field of war and that both preoccupations are manned by soldiers who can be victorious but who can also be worn down or wounded or even killed.

The obscurity of the new lover is also contrasted, as we move forward, with the *fama* brought to Corinna through Ovid's verses, both in that others (including us) know her "name" and in that the relationship between Ovid and Corinna has already become a guide for others:

> Certainly through me you have achieved a popular following;
> our love has taught others how to love.
> And yet what can I say of the base lies of your vain tongue,
> and the god, perjured through my loss?
> the silent nods and secret conversations shared
> with other young men at parties? (19-24)

Her renown and his pain and suffering—of having been betrayed and lied to, as well as of seeing her with others, from which he cannot look away, it seems. So the poet as an observer, even a peeping tom, follows her with other lovers and her flirting to gain other lovers at parties—so that we may read his suffering as embraced not only because sometimes people embrace their pain and gain pleasure from it, but because it has added fuel to the fire of his poetry. He asserts his determined farewell:

> Find another now, instead of me, to suffer so. (28)

Yet even then he remains torn between love and hate—albeit perhaps with less genuine feeling than was true for Catullus when he shouted *odi et amo* to the rooftops. Poem #11b, immediately following, observes—observes of hmself—that "in my chest her love and her hatred battle, pulling in opposite directions, but, I think love wins. I shall hate, if I can; if not, I shall love unwillingly" (1-3). So he's done, but he's not quite done.

To the extent that he *is* done, it is not only from her but from this particular kind of elegiac poetry that he is parting ways. He has already, within the *Amores*, as we have noted, turned elsewhere, at times—but then Propertius, most single-focused of them all, also turns to other subjects than Cynthia and love from time to time. Ovid ends Book III with a reminder regarding what the project has been about, anyway.

> Find a new bard, mother of tender love-poems!
> The last goal of my elegies has been turned. (15. 1-2)

> Mantua boasts her Vergil and Verona her Catullus:
> I shall be acclaimed the glory of the Pelignian tribe. (7-8)

> And so, some stranger seeing the walls of
> watery Sulmona....
> ...shall exclaim: 'You were able to produce quite a poet;
> however small you[r poems] be, I call them great!'
> Elegant boy, and the Amathusian parent of that elegant boy,
> pluck up the golden traces from my field:
> the horned Lyaeus with his potent thyrsus chides.
> With mightier steeds I'll steer a greater course.
> Peaceful elegy, pleasure-giving Muse, farewell,
> but may my work remain beyond my fated end. (11-20)

It *is* time for him to move on in new directions—having with these three volumes won his race with *fama* and made himself the equal of Vergil and Catullus with his love poetry.[202] Farewell to love (that "elegant boy," Amor) and to love-poetry—Amathusia is one of the more obscure names for Venus, who was worshipped at Amathus, a city in Cyprus where she was washed ashore and born out of the sea—he is called now by Bacchus.²⁰³ If he will now become carefree, since Lyaeus' vintage beverage will release him from cares—on the other hand he has referenced Bacchus often enough in the *Amores* for us to know that he always had a connection to that god, and that therefore, perhaps, he is not following him *away* from the gods of poetry and love.

This sort of ambiguous message would certainly not be inconsistent with Ovid in his complex intellective cleverness. After all, Apollo is most often seen as opposed to Dionysos—as reason is opposed to unbridled emotion—but they have been intertwined in the *Amores*, as surely as Apollo and Amor have been, or, more importantly for our own purposes, Mars and Venus—which is to say: *eros* and *eris*—have been. Morover, the poet's choice of farewell imagery—pluck my golden traces (my poetry) from the field—might well be understood this way: that the golden traces may be visualized in a literal manner as golden stalks of grain. Dionysos, we may recall, is not only a god of the vine but also a god of grain, so the poet would be leaving Bacchus for Bacchus and not only leaving Apollo and Amor for Bacchus. Which is to say: he will continue what he has been doing, albeit shifting slightly his mode. Surely, young as he still is, Ovid does not imagine himself to have finished the race with *fama*; he's just completed another turn around the racetrack and, breathing lightly as he outdistances his competitors, he shall—and must—race on.

He was not, in fact—surprise!—quite finished with the subject of love. His epistles in elegiac meter are known as the *Heroides* ("Heroines") and are devoted to mytho-historical women abandoned by their lovers—Ariadne, Medea, Dido, and the like, and differently, Helen ("abandoned" by Paris/Alexandros), Leander and Hero, Cydippe and Acontius. If one may read the reference in *Amores* II.18.19-26 as a reliable allusion to this collection, as many do, then the *Heroides* were in fact written before at least the second edition of the *Amores* (2 BCE) or even before the first edition of 16 BCE.²⁰⁴ For our purposes the precise dating (of either of these works) is less important than the contents. Some of these heroines are renowned, some more obscure. The epistulary statements from and occasional dialogue between those abandoned and those who abandoned them share in common a tragic, crisis-driven seriousness completely different from the light-hearted tone of the *Amores*.[205] This is a very different thread in the lyric-elegiac *eros/eris* interweave.

From the perspective of our own discussion, the seventh of these poems, Ovid's handling of Dido—in the form of Dido's last (her only) letter to Aeneas, after he has affirmed his intention to set sail and explained why and whither—is perhaps most intriguing. It is certainly revolutionary when placed against both the *Aeneid* and what we can well assume was the party line regarding that story. For the Carthaginian queen points out that nobody in the Italy for which he heads will receive him with the kind of hospitality that she had offered—and predicts that "there will be another Dido, there, and another pledge being given, you'll again deceive." Hardly the Aeneas that Vergil—or Augustus—would have us embrace as the quintessence of Roman virtue: an Aeneas whom Dido—or rather, Elissa, which is the more historical name for Vergil's Dido, and the one that Ovid uses—admits, nonetheless, she still loves with an unbridled passion.

Indeed, she asserts that whereas, as Venus' son, Aeneas is Amor's half-brother, in her sincere love for the hero, it is she, Elissa, for whom Amor is the full, *true* brother. There is an appropriate irony to this comment, given that her human brother, in a display of pure *eris*, had murdered her husband, the rightful king of Tyre, forcing her to flee for her own life with her loyal followers—which is why she ended up in North Africa in the first place. So, her biological brother, embodying *eris*, stands opposite her spiritual brother, who is *eros* itself.

Her words are shot through with a powerful *odi et amo* sensibility—wishing the winds to overwhelm Aeneas and wishing him to change direction like the winds do, wishing him destruction on the high seas and wishing him survival. Resonating from sentiments directed in the *Amores* toward Ovid's own beloved regarding both death and the immortality afforded by poetry, she notes that, surviving, he would be "more widely known as the cause of my death": his *fama*, his *kleos* will expand only if he does live—or else nobody will know or care either about him or about her death.

And death crescendos as her real subject. Not just the ambivalence for him—to die or not to die—but by way of accusing him of being a liar, she sees herself as the second one he abandoned. Creusa, she asserts, did not perish the way he described any more than he carried his father and the *lares* on his shoulders in his tale (in *Aeneid* II): she merely "died alone, abandoned by a hard-hearted husband," as Dido has just been abandoned by the same hard-hearted husband. Her own demise, she says, began on that day in the cave during the rainstorm: she thought it was the nymphs whose voices she heard, but it was "the Furies giving warning of my fate."

All of which leads toward the main death being shaped by this epistulary poem: her own. She who betrayed the memory of her husband, Sychaeus—but really did not; he was already dead, after all, and she thought that *pius* Aeneas, son of Venus, would be a real husband; her error was honest. She reminds Aeneas that, as a refugee from her brother who murdered her husband, she had already built a city and fought off a thousand suitors when he arrived and received such hospitality from her. He is the wicked betrayer, abandoner—of a pregnant Dido. Yes, she drops this bombshell in Ovid's poem: that she is pregnant. So her death will not be the only one that he occasions by his precipitous departure: his unborn child will perish, too.

Her further words are, yet, again, a plea that he transform the city she has built rather than go seeking a place in which to begin a new one. Build peacefully *here* rather than having to fight *there* in order to establish a foothold. She even offers not to be his wife "if it is shameful," but just his friend. Or at least wait a bit: give your men a rest, and give me time to get used to the idea of your going away. But... the letter sways back and forth in its argument, like a ship tossed by the high wave of a stormy sea, in the specific directions of its subject and in its love-and-strife-ridden tone, reflecting the intensity of her emotions and the layered confusions that they bring upon her.

The Trojan sword (that fateful and fatal gift from Aeneas himself) sits on her lap as she writes and weeps, her last words for her sister, Anna, regarding her tomb inscription, are that it not follow convention—"wife of Sychaeus"—but "Aeneas provided both a reason to die, and the sword with which Dido died by her own hand." Another ambiguity of sorts: is Aeneas her true love and not her well-loved husband? The only non-ambiguity is her impending self-inflicted death, the consequence of the sudden wreck of a love-affair that had been sailing so smoothly.

Neither these nor the *Amores* are Ovid's last words on love, either. He writes an entire guide—a textbook—for the lover: the *Ars Amatoria* ("The Art of Love")—a didactic poem that reflects what the years have both given to and taken from the light-footed author of the *Amores*. It is a three-volume work; the first two directed toward men (the first, how to find a woman; the second, how to keep her), and the third toward women (how to win and keep a man).

Published around 2 CE, the *Ars* was, like the *Amores* and *Heroides*, written in elegiac couplets, rather than dactylic hexameter, and it also, like the *Amores*, nonetheless does not ignore war: in a manner we would recognize, here, too, he likens love to military service, necessitating the strictest obedience on the part of the man to his woman. Conversely, he advises women to make their lovers artificially jealous so that the latter do not become neglectful through complacency. When a slave is guarding a lovers' tryst and, say, the husband is suddenly sighted, he is to shout: *perimus!* ("We are lost")—a military kind of locution, so that the lover can hide. If the tone of the entire work is typically Ovidian in its sense of bare seriousness, on the other hand, he never becomes even ribald, much less obscene—although he does discuss sex (orgasms here, preferred sexual positions there) so that, even without ribaldry and obscenity, the work presumably found little favor with Augustus and his circle, who would have still read it as pornographic and filled with anti-family values—about which issue, more in a few paragraphs.

There is one more work the title of which indicates its focus on love—the *Remedia Amoris* ("Cures for Love")—to add further whimsy to the previous work. A kind of companion piece to the *Ars Amatoria*, the *Remedia* offers adivce regarding both how to avoid being hurt by strong feelings of love and how to fall out of that state. He writes from a virtual stoic perspective, never, however, permitting seriousness to achieve solemnity or his irony to arrive at bitterness.

The opening pair of couplets brings him to territory familiar to our discussion of his work as well as that of the other elegists.

> Amor, having read the name and title of this little book,
> said: 'It's war against me, I see, war is being declared.'
> 'Cupid, spare the condemnation of your bard for a crime, who has
> so often raised the standard given to him by you as his commander.

Love is suffused with the vocabulary of war, once again, from the very beginning. And strife-ridden elements play their way lightly though the love-cure guide—that concludes with gastronomic advice, the final notes to those intended readers who will visit his tomb in veneration, he says, for having healed them.

Ovid is best known, of course, for his *Metamorphoses*, a long work of fifteen books that he wrote between around 1 and 8 CE, and he wrote it in hexameter verse—from which we can infer the poet's intention to present it as a kind of epic poem. The array of tales of transformations of various and sundry sorts—and the most direct source through which later readers, including ourselves, encounter the various Greek myths that pepper our early educations—includes the previously noted story of Apollo, Amor, and Daphne, for example.

If the connection to the poet's overall theme in this last-mentioned tale is the final fate of Daphne, saved from the god's passion by being transformed by her river-god father into a laurel tree, the tale most directly connects to the theme of love and strife by its contours from beginning to end. The outset points out quickly that, while Daphne was the "first love" of Apollo, that love came about through the wrath of Amor. The specific context was that Apollo was feeling full of himself after having just slain the enormous serpent, the Python, at Delphi—the eristic act that, on a smaller scale, echoes the large process whereby the Zeus-led gods defeated the Titans and established the *kosmos*, the order of things: the culmination of effectively graduated phases since incipient *khaos*. Noticing Amor stringing his own bow, Apollo mocks him and—the rest is then told in poetic detail, until the final paean of the god establishing the evergreen condition for the laurel leaves and the laurel as his tree.

The heart of the tale is the interweave of *eros* and *eris*, of course: Apollo's love for Daphne and her hatred for Apollo—both simultaneously facilitated by the love-god who is the son of Aphrodite, goddess of love, and who engaged in his mischievous act because of the low-scale *eris* between Apollo and Amor. Other tales within the *Metamorphoses* also resonate with the *eros/eris* theme, but this one will suffice to help us recognize how, virtually throughout Ovid's work one can identify myriad instances, observable from varied angles, in which that interweave is significantly present.

For our purposes, all of this is wonderful. But the increasingly priggish mood of the imperial court was, to repeat, one that was decreasingly receptive to the sorts of things that Ovid was creating. Within the *Ars Amatoria*, for instance, he points to the splendid opportunities offered to the adventurous lover in temples and theaters—this was not likely to bring a smile from the Emperor whose rebuilt, marble-clad city, filled with temples and theaters, was supposed to be a model of decorum and, well, a certain kind of *pietas*. And the Emperor was no doubt growing continuously more frustrated with the lack of success of family values within his own family: with his daughter, Julia, and her reputation for having worked her way through half the army's beds, on the one hand, and with his own failure to produce a proper successor on the other.

So did Ovid merely offend Augustus with his poetry, or did he in some more active and less merely verbal way defy the Emperor's strictures on decency/indecency, or did he know of some corrupt activity in the Imperial court that Augustus was fearful would become known? We don't know. We have nothing from Augustus explaining his anger and nothing really from Ovid explaining it, but he was exiled by imperial decree in 8 CE—a pretty unusual event, although two interesting others were exiled at the same time: the emperor's grandchildren, the adopted grandson, Agrippa Postumus and Julia the younger, apparently due sto a conspiracy against Augustus in which they were involved (Julia's husband was executed, in fact; did Ovid know about this *conspiracy*, perhaps?)—and both he and his exile outlived the Emperor's own death (by three years).[206] The exile was finally revoked by Rome's city council in December, 2017—a few millennia too late for the poet to return to the city, at least in his original incarnate form.[207]

In any case, he had already begun a work called the *Fasti*—a poetic discussion of Roman religious festivals and therefore a work overtly asserting itself as *pius*, but that obviously didn't help. In exile he completed the *Fasti*, although only parts of it have survived. He also wrote the work previously noted, called *Tristia*—a lament for his exile and an importunement to be allowed to return to Rome, which fell on deaf ears—and a series of letters. So his life as an adult, most of which he devoted to love and love poetry, eventually brought him into strife with Augustus that would follow him to his grave. His large and diverse poetic legacy underscores the interweave of *eros and eris* across the poetic landscape of Rome within particularly its historically central epoch: the last pre-Christian century and the first few decades CE, which period marks the end of the republic and the first generation or two of the Empire.

Other poetic media both before and after this era flesh out our understanding of this theme in Latin literature, however, as we shall see.

Chapter Nine

From Roman Philosophy to Comedy and Satire

While Vergil and the elegists mark the most emphatic and continuous exploration of the interweave of *eros* and *eris* within Latin literature, other poets, both earlier, during and after that extraordinarily lush period, should be acknowledged for their contribution to this theme. Given the duly noted vehicle used or not used to express the elegists' obsession with not writing epic poetry—the dactylic hexameter vehicle—it behooves us to take note of a slightly older contemporary of Catullus, the philosopher, Titus Lucretius Carus (ca 99/4-55 BCE), who expressed the entirety of his Epicurean thinking in a six-book-long poem written in that metrical mode. His *De Rerum Natura*—"On the Nature of Things"— was intended to be perceived as an epic poem, but not about war. It was designed, above all, to explore and explain life and death as articulated in the thought of Epicurus, one of the key Hellenistic philosophers to emerge, along with Zeno the Stoic, Pyrrho the Sceptic, and Diogenes the Cynic as progeny of, responses to, and reactions against the philosophical schools derived from Plato and Aristotle.

I Lucretius

Lucretius' initial invocation as a poet is not to the Muses but to Venus, "Mother of Aeneas' clan, delight of men and gods, nurturing Venus... for you the checkered earth pours forth its lovely flowers; for you expanses of the sea do smile, and tranquil sky does gleam when bathed in outpoured light" (I.1, 7-9)—so love makes the world go around. Love is the beginning and the end of the order of things. He addresses the goddess further—in verses written "for Memmius, my friend" (26), the patron to whom this poem is dedicated—in asking for an era of peace in which to complete his task. And Venus is in a position to grant that wish, "since Mars, in arms all-powerful, rules the fierce works of war, your lover, Mars, who often sinks upon your breast, completely overcome by love's eternal wound..." (32-4)—so love can bring about peace by being intertwined, limb for limb, with strife's sibling, war.

The beginning of the poem thus sets the stage for all of reality by observing this fundamental intertwining of vernacularly opposed elements. It is after this invocation that the poet turns to his source of understanding of the nature of things: "A man of Greece" (66)—Epicurus—who first recognized certain issues, first among these the falseness of traditional religion: it is not we, the poet opines, who are impious (as he fears Memmius might think), but "rather religion has itself begot impious and bloody deeds" (83). The reference he adduces to support this radical contention is the slaying of Iphigenia by her own father at Aulis at the behest of the goddess—a story as familiar to Lucretius' audience as it is to us—which story he summarizes at length, culminating with the observation that, instead of love and marriage accompanied by wedding hymns, she ascended the altar accompanied by funeral chants and her sacrificial death.[208]

> ...a clean maiden become
> A sad and sacrificial victim at a father's blow,
> so that a fair and fortunate release be given to the fleet.
> So religion was able to persuade such monstrous acts. (99-101)

And religion is aided and abetted by its *sacerdotes*: "how many things can priests invent, vain myths to sap a lifetime's reasoning and muddy fortune's goods with fear" (104-5)? And since the basis of religion is fear, "this darkened terror of the mind must be dispelled, not by the rays of sun or gleaming shafts of day, but by the look and laws of Nature's laws" (146-8). Opposed, then, to the falseness of religion is the truth of nature—of science—all out there for humankind *on its own* to uncover. There is a logic and an order to the nature of things—nothing is arbitrary—to the cycle of the seasons and the growth and decay processes of plants. It merely requires investigation and the understanding that comes from careful query. And—which is the essence of the theory of Nature that he then expounds—it all starts with infinitesimal paritcles: *atoms*.

By about verse 215 we recognize that all of these first 214 verses were really a prelude to the setting forth of the poet-philosopher's theme: the so-called atomic theory, which reduces reality to two fundamental physical elements. These are the tiniest of material substance particles, *atomoi*—*atomos* (in the singular) is a Greek word meaning "uncuttable," so in other words, as small as it possibly can get—and the void, empty space, through which the *atomoi* are constantly falling downwards. He will expand on this in Book II, explaining that the atoms have different shapes (333-380) and how, falling straight downward due to their own weight they sometimes, somehow, by chance, swerve and in so doing knock into and stick to each other; some of them glomming together in large numbers making denser, heavier objects, some of them in more scattered and fewer numbers making lighter objects (216-262).

He introduces this discussion at the beginning of Book II by observing how sweet it is "to occupy the high, serene, embattled eminence, the ivory tower, whose battlements are thought and high philosophy, the wisdom of the wise" (II.7-8). He asserts, that is, that once one has realized that the fears that unhinge humankind due to religion are fears based on something that does not exist, then one can relax and calmly think about what *really* makes the world function, which he then proceeds to expound upon: a simple theory of physical elements, with no gods and goddesses or thread-wielding fates behind it.

Book III brings Lucretius to a fuller praise of Epicurus as his teacher and a step further into the issue of fear, as it pertains specifically to death: we fear death because we fear what comes afterwards—the sort of pain and deprivation exemplified (this is my illustration, not Lucretius') by the encounter between Odysseus and a very unhappy Akhilleus at the entrance into the Underworld in *Odyssey* 11 or (on a more positive note) the long discussion between Anchises and Aeneas in *Aeneid* VI. These fears he seeks to banish by arguing that death is really nothing but the disconnection of the globs of atoms held together while alive. Simply put:

> …when we will no longer be [alive],
> when soul and body out of which we're one entity are torn apart,
> then clearly nothing can happen to us who will no longer be,
> nothing will be able to move our senses to feel,
> even if ocean were commingled with earth and sea with sky.
> (III. 838-42)

> …there's nothing to be feared in death
> nor can one who no longer *is* be miserable (*misreum fieri*), nor is there
> a difference, then, whether he had never been born,
> when death immortal has snatched away his mortal life. (866-9)

We are contrived, body and soul, of nothing but atoms and void—the denser agglomeration of atoms comprising our bodies, the much lighter agglomeration our souls—and at death both sorts of agglomeration dissipate, leaving nothing but scattered atoms that resume their slipping through the void. So why fear or mourn it? Besides, he adds, much greater men that you have died, including Homer—and including Democritus and Epicurus, the shapers of the atomist theory.

This brings his discussion, in Book IV, to focus on the senses—vision, touch, thought, and also on bodily functions—which focus leads up to an intense (eristic, one might say) discussion of and condemnation of the uncontrolled passion associated with love. He describes how, once love is in play, then "though what you love is far away, yet pictures of her haunt the eyes; her lovely name, the ears" (IV.1061-2)—in other words, the different senses are engaged, even from afar. But Lucretius does not see this as a good thing. On the contrary,

> …it is best to flee from love's images
> and abstain from the food of love; turn the mind elsewhere,
> indulge your liquid lust with anyone at hand… (1063-5)

> The sore will grow and fester if you feed it.
> Day by day the madness (*furor*) and the tribulation grow graver,
> unless you confuse love's wounds with new blows,
> and cure them by loitering after ladies of the streets,
> or turn your thoughts in some other direction.
> He who shuns love does not lack the fruit of Venus,
> but rather picks pleasures less alloyed with pain,
> for surely purer pleasures come to those who are healthy
> than to the miserable (*miseris*). Indeed, even in the time of possessing [love]
> [love's] ardor tosses about storm-tossed, uncertain
> what first to enjoy with eyes (*primum oculis*) and hands.[209] (1068-78)

His view of love is entirely negative: he is singularly eristic in his discussion of *eros*. Reading through the elegists, one can understand why: everyone of them includes among his *eris/eros* interweaves the idea that the experience of love very quickly becomes either intertwined with pain and/or leads entirely into pain, and the whole point of Lucretius' Epicureanism—implied at the beginning of Book II and later more overtly stated as a goal of this philosophy—is tranquility, peace of mind: *ataraxia* is the Greek word, referring to a state of complete relaxation (in the largest sense, I completely relax because I am no longer churned up by fear of death because I understand that death is meaningless). Clearly *ataraxia* is impossible in love as the elegists describe it— Ovid comes closest in his sometimes clinical detachment from what he describes, but some would say of him that this is a weakness in his poetry—and as Lucretius understands it.

In any case, virtually the entirety of Book IV is devoted to exploring and explaining why love should be avoided. He describes the physical pain-pleasure aspects of the lovers' experience:

> What they have pursued they tightly squeeze, and cause
> the body pain, and often fasten teeth on lips, crush mouth
> with kisses; the pleasure is not pure,
> and secret stings lurk there, bidding them to hurt that very thing,
> whatever it is, from which those seeds of frenzy grow.

> But Venus lightly breaks these pains in the midst of love;
> sweet pleasure intermingled curbs back the bites. (1079-85)

—and so on. And the physical wraps around the emotional: "as in a dream, while he seeks to drink but no water comes forth…just so in love, Venus mocks the lover with these images [of the beloved]; he cannot sate his lust through gazing on love's frame" (1096-1106). No matter how tightly lovers press against each other, and intermingle moisture from their mouths, it's all in vain; he cannot shave away a fragment from her beloved flesh—whatever one has is fleeting, there's nothing that one can permanently possess.

Moreover, enthralled to love, the lover wastes his life, cannot work, cannot focus on anything else, ignores the dictates of *fama*, lets his fortune slip away in gifts for the beloved… and in a moment things can go awry; a casually dropped word from the beloved becomes the source of immense torture (1121-40). Torments abound. So

> … it is better to shun entanglement in the snares of love,
> as I have explained, and to beware lest you be enticed.
> For to avoid being caught in the snares of love
> is not as difficult as, once you are enthralled in its nets,
> to get out and burst the strong knots of Venus. (1144-8)

So: Lucretius does not as much interweave *eris* and *eros* when he writes about love—although parts of his description do indeed do that—as he simply excoriates *eros*, spewing his own *eris* on the subject. This intensely eristic position vis-à-vis *eros* may or may not be the source of the tradition about his own personal relationship to love: that he was driven mad by a love-philtre and in moments of lucidity between long bouts of insanity composed this work.

In any case, the remainder of his work is devoted, first, to praising Epicurus and his achievements in morally enlightening the world around him—the intellectual model that Lucretius is trying to emulate in his own epic overall, including within Book IV and his negative, cautionary discussion of love—and describing the evolution of humankind and why and when we began to imagine that there are gods (Book V). In the final book he discusses the causes of meteorological phenomena and then offers a detailed discussion and explanation of the great plague at Athens that occurred early on during the Peloponnesian Wars—the importance of which is that even a great and pious city, one concerned and careful about the worship of the gods, as Athens was, could be brought down by such a natural event. So why worry about that sort of "greatness" and that sort of worshipful "piety" rather than about the life of the moment and the search for calm *ataraxia*?

It is an odd and somewhat horrifying ending: not just death, but with it the image of people hurrying about and desperately fighting for proper burials for their beloved dead. If the point is that all the religion in the world could not fend off the disaster when it came, through natural causes, it is also an interesting choice of end-subject for a poem that began with a long evocation to the goddess of love. The love-death theme, seen several times among the elegists, becomes a kind of frame, rather than a center or overt subject for the poem—and if prayers and offerings to the gods are useless because gods either don't exist or don't care, then what of the invocation to the goddess that sets the entire work in motion? The mother of Eros, having been invoked, is in fact denied as an extant element of consequence in human experience. Chapter IV's passionate plea to stay away from or to rid one's self of love is obliquely repeated at the end, then: no amount of love could save those devoured by plague anymore than invocations to gods could save them.

II Plautus' *Haunted House*

Whereas with Lucretius we encounter deadly serious poetry as a vehicle for a particular philosophical perspective, within which the discussion of love is engaged with an eristic tone, to say the least, the theme of the *eros-eris* interweave is also expressed in specific ways in the comic theater that emerges well before this period in the plays of Plautus (ca 254-184 BCE) and Terence (185-159 BCE), toward the beginnings of Roman literature.[210] It is, by the way, interesting indeed that the oh-so-serious Romans, with their ideal of *pietas* as in part an articulation of that seriousness, should have, when it came to theater, so clearly preferred the comic—and the more soap-opera-shaped so-called New Comedy style of comedic theater, rather than the high-flying Old Comedy of Aristophanes, with its underlying serious issues—to the tragic and serious.

It is as if, so almost oppressed by their own *pietas* and its seriousness, they were desperate to escape from themselves when they could—whether it be in the array of intense life-death games that they witnessed, godlike, from above the upper seats in Roman amphitheaters; or the escapist theater in which the serious, issue-laden tragedies of the classical Greeks (and the issue-laden high comedies of the classical era at Athens) were eschewed in favor of Romanized variations on the light-hearted comedic efforts of Hellenistic playwrights like Menander (ca342-290 BCE).[211]

Among Plautus' more renowned plays, for instance, was *Mostellaria* ("The Haunted House"), which follows a familiar Hellenistic formula: a rich young man is in love with a young woman not of his "class"—something his slightly scowliing father would not approve—and finds time to be with her behind his father's back, who finds out or is in danger of finding out, but the young couple end up rescued from the father's potential wrath through the cleverness of the young man's slave. In other words, the real hero of the play, the brains behind its happy ending is not the kind of upper-crust figure who is the centerpiece of serious tragic or high-end comic theater, but the lowest one on the socio-economic totem pole, and the subject is an everyday one that involves no gods or mythic beings.

In *Mostellaria* there is the dissolute young man and his courtesan girlfriend, there is a credulous old man and a hen-pecked husband. The language is colloquial, frequently racy and certainly full of puns that even the probably not overly cultivated majority of his audience would have gotten, and the humor is almost slapstick. Most of it was sung, not said, often accompanied by a flute. The setting—as is typical in Roman comedy—is Athens, since that's where the sort of questionable moral behavior that is enacted is understood by Romans to take place: never in pious Rome!

Contrasting issues are aired from the start—between country bumpkin and city slicker, in this case personified by two slaves, Grumio (country) and Tranio (city), both of whom answer to their elderly master, Theopropides, who is out of town at this moment.

The two slaves' comedic *agon* both sets the mood and suggests the problem that will emerge as the narrative moves forward: that the dissolute son of Theopropides, Philolaches, has been allowing his father's wealth to dissipate, endangering all of them.

The two slaves leave the stage and Philolaches arrives onto it, singing out a long soliloquy to the audience. His words offer part of the reason why the play has its name: an extended simile of what a son is: like a house, well built by the father as the son is growing up, but which begins to go to ruin if that son is or becomes dissolute. The winds break off roof tiles and the rains come through and soak the walls.

> The builder's masterpiece is wrecked, and you really must confess
> that the builder is not to blame…
>
> The father is the builder of his son:
> He lays the foundations with the greatest care…
>
> > He teaches him letters
> >   and then ancient history
> > and math and law and government
> >   and plane geometry,
> > so that he'll be a model for
> >   the whole community…
>
> Now look at me: as long as I was under the builder's eyes,
> I was a very decent lad whom none would criticize.
> When I moved into my own control
> and took possession of body and soul,
>   I ruined—oh so fast!—
> the builder's work…[212]

Embedded within the allegory of this long, pseudo-philosophical meditation is the assertion that—he arrives at the issue within the issue—"then love seeped in, like rain, to drench my heart. It soaked my very soul. I began to fall apart." If one thinks back in our narrative and well forward chronologically to Horace in particular, among the elegists, then the image of love as a storm evolves from this Plautine image to the fiercer, more destructive image used two centuries after this comedic whimsy.[213]

So love has ruined him. To whatever extent he rues that situation, the eristic attitude is really momentary and effectively false, because he wouldn't give up love or his beloved for anything. Indeed, barely has he finished listing all the skills he once had that have gone to ruin and stated his realization that "I'm just no earthly good" and his beloved, the prostitute, Philomedia, together with her elderly maid, Scapha, enter onto the stage, albeit unaware of his presence—so that he is able to share asides with the audience (beginning with his note that this is indeed *she*, "the windstorm that swept away all my modesty, which was my roof, so that Love and Desire rained into my heart, and I never can repair it any more. The walls of my heart are soaked through and this house is a complete ruin."

His conversation with the audience sways back and forth between adoring and detesting Scapha, depending upon what comment she makes to Philomedia either with reference to Philolachus or that he construes to be in reference or failed reference to him. Thus his smiles turn to frowns when she swears "by Philolaches' love for you" instead of swearing by your (Philomedia's) love for *him*. After a very lengthy double dialogue between mistress and maid and between lover and audience, Philolaches reveals himself to the women, sends Scapha off-stage, into the house, and the two lovebirds are alone before us. Briefly alone, since shortly, Philolaches' buddy, Callidamates—well into his cups and singing loudly—together with his girlfriend, the prostitute Delphium, enters.

Well it is clear that a party is in the offing as Act One ends. But a problem emerges almost immediately as Tranio runs breathlessly back onto the stage at the outset of the second act—with the news that Philolaches' father, Theopropides, is unexpectedly back in town. This is where, of course, not only does the plot thicken, but the second and more direct reason for the play's name comes into play. With the agreement of Sphaerio, one of Theopropides' slaves—the one who was apparently given charge of the house when Theopropides went off on his business trip—and having shooed him and the four young people inside the house and locked it up from inside and outside, Tranio, keys in hand, greets his master's father when he arrives home after three years in Egypt.

The plan cooked up by Tranio on the spot, for the salvation of the son against the expected wrath of the father, begins rapidly to unfold—and reflects the underbelly of Roman *pietas*: the belief not only in the Olympians, but in myriad gods, goddesses and *daimones*, both propitious and nefarious, all around us. This is not just a matter of lesser and great powers and categories of the *sacer* such as we've seen Kirke and Hermes represent, but a matter of more immediate and not always friendly spirits of which one must be aware.[214]

In brief: Tranio convinces Theopropides that the home he left three years ago when he began his journey has become infested with an unhappy *daimon*—that by merely touching the house (for Theopropides banged on the door, annoyed that it should be locked in the middle of the day) he has endangered himself.[215] He cooks up a tale about a host within it having murdered his guest years ago, stolen the guest's gold and buried him in the house; that while Theopropides was gone, Philolaches came back from dinner one evening, they all went to sleep, and the ghost of the murdered man came to Philolaches in the middle of the night and terrified him. The problem is, the people inside keep making noise and Tranio is afraid that their noise will ruin his plan—as Act Two ends.

Complications multiply: Act Three opens with the arrival onto the stage of a money-lender, Misaryrides (meaning: "hate-money"), from whom, it emerges, Philolaches has borrowed a good deal of cash as his allowance dissipated, and the money-lender, come to collect his interest, is surely going to complain to Theopropides when he sees him—which will expose the wreckage that Tranio is trying to hide. Quick on his feet, Tranio convinces Theopropides that the money was borrowed for the down payment on a brilliant real estate deal: the purchase of the house next door. Well and fine, if not for the fact that the neighbor, Simo, is not only in town but at home and steps out of the house at the next moment.

Simo is exclaiming—singing—over the great meal that he has just enjoyed. He further tells us that he has fled the house because his wife, having served him the meal now wants him in bed, which is not what he wants after such a full meal. (Simo may not be eristic toward his wife exactly, but he certainly is not erotically inclined toward her). To this, Tranio responds in song—to the audience—that Simo's wife is going to be seriously pissed off, to which Simo in turn responds. The two are not singing to each other but to us (Tranio) or to nobody in particular (Simo), yet in a kind of antiphony that mocks the idea of an *agon*. Simo's "response" is that:

> If a man gets married to a wife that's rich
> and old as the hills, he'll simply dread
> the hour when he has to go to bed.
> > In such a wife's arms
> > sleep loses its charms...
>
> [and turning to the audience]:
>
> You folks out there, what kind of wives
> > you have I cannot guess;
> But this I know and know right well:
> > I've drawn a sorry mess.
> She's a pain in the neck, a plague, a curse,
> and day by day she's getting worse and worse.

A more detailed, light-hearted play with with *eris*—hardly at the intensity level of the love-smitten sort of emotion expressed by Philolaches in Act One, but both share the quality of being light-handed—twisting against husband-wife *eros* that, for Simo, at least, is as erotic and passionate as a pile of coins is soft.

Seeing Tranio, Simo asks how things are going in the ongoing party in the house of Philolaches, and Tranio confides that he is terrified because Theopropides has come back—although Poppa doesn't know a thing about what's been happening in his absence. Tranio convinces Simo, moreover, that Theopropides is considering some renovations on his home—an added woman's apartment, for he means to marry off his son quickly, now that he is back—and has heard great things about the interior design of Simo's house. So he asks if Simo would mind taking them through a tour of his house (that Theopropides thinks that he is buying at a bargain price and therefore believes that he is looking it over in order to evaluate his purchase-in-process).

Surely one of the great moments of the play is when, just before they enter the house interior, standing in the vestibule, Tranio points out a non-existent wall-painting scene—kind of like an early Roman version of "The Emperor's New Clothes"—to the two old men, describing a "picture of a crow making fools of two old buzzards... There's a crow standing between two buzzards and it's nipping away at the two of them in turn. Look in my direction, please, so that you can see the crow.... Then look over there toward the two of you and since you can't see the crow, you might be able to see the buzzards."

Simo needs to go do some business in the forum, so only Tranio and Theopropides actually enter the house as the act ends. Act Four opens innocently enough, with two slaves of Callidamates come to fetch their master from the partying at Philolaches' house, and Theopropides and Tranio coming by and discussing the great real estate "deal" that, guided by his slave, Philolaches has managed—except that Tranio doesn't notice the slaves banging on the door and leaves to go around to the back and let his master know how well things are going. Theopropides, seeing the two slaves, engages them in a conversation—they have no idea who he is, except some nosey old man—the outcome of which is that the loving father is beginning to see the truth: that his son spent all his money to buy the freedom of his girlfriend, not on some real estate deal. Our rain-soaked house may have ruined the house-builder, it would seem.

And along comes Simo, back from the forum. It doesn't take too much of a conversation between these two for Theopropides to realize how badly he has been had—and he asks Simo to help him as the act ends. This is a comedy, after all, so the last act cannot end in disaster, can it? And the last act opens with Tranio's soliloquy: proud of himself, pushed aside once he had gotten all the partyers out of the house, aware that his deception cannot go on much longer and hopeful that he can think his way out of the mess. His soliloquy may be seen as the second shoe dropping: the first was the soliloquy of his young, profligate master, in Act One. The non-heroic master and the mock-heroic slave are book-ends. More to the point, Tranio is a comedic Odysseus: a "hero" from the opposite end of the social spectrum (less prominent a social figure than even Thersites).[216]

Eris emerges from Simo's house in the form of Theopropides, accompanied by two of Simo's slaves, loaned for the purpose of helping him to chain up Tranio—who, in the midst of the brief dialogue with Theopropides, each talking across the other, quickly takes up a position on a conveniently nearby altar, where he will be safe from the chains that he anticipates.[217] Ever the clever one, when Theopropides asks him why he has taken that spot, he replies that it is so that Simo's slaves cannot take it, whom he has proposed be cross-examined (by torture) to find out whether Philolaches has in fact given any money to Simo.

Enter the *deus ex machina*, to solve the problem and save the hero, in the form of—of all people—Callidamates. Tranio casts him as an arbitrator—which means that the assertions that Tranio and Theopropides make constitute an *agon* (of sorts).

> Theo: You corrupted my son.
> Tranio: He did do wrong—but was his behavior any different from that
> of other boys from the best families?
> Theo: The main thing that bothers me is that you made a fool of me.
> Tranio: True, but you should have more sense at your age!

He adds that, if he is friends with Diphilos and Philemon, Theopropides ought to tell them how his slave made a fool of them, giving them the best lot in comedy. At least some of the audience would have enjoyed that sort of interior joke: these two are, with Menander, considered the great playwrights of Attic New Comedy—so it is a way for Plautus to pat himself on the back, through words spoken by his hero, as the continuation and the equal of these luminaries.

In any case, Callidamates is able to convince Theopropides to forgive his son—who, he says, is really and truly ashamed of his behavior, (so ashamed that he couldn't face his father himself), which *was*, after all, behavior not unexpected from someone of his age and class. Besides, his behavior had been under the influence of his friends, including Callidamates—and they have aall agreed to raise the money amongst them to pay back what was spent liberating Philomedia. Far more reluctantly, Theopropides is induced to forgive Tranio, who not only also claims to be ashamed, (ha!), but more honestly suggests that he will no doubt get into some more mischief by tomorrow—"and then you can punish me really good and proper for both things at the same time!"

III Terence's *Woman of Andros*

So all is well that ends well: the anger provoked in the father and the *eris* between him and both his son and his son's slave yields to his love for his son—and even to his embracing his son's love affair with both his friends and his girlfriend. This sort of light-hearted handling of our theme and others is to be expected in Roman comedy, and continues into the generation of Terence, from whom only six plays survive—but of course, he died by the age of 26. One of these, *The Woman of Andros*—in which the playwright explains in his prologue that he has combined elements from two of Menander's plays—exemplifies that continuity particularly well.

The key elements are as familiar as ever: an Athenian setting, a boy and a girl in love, a clever slave who provides the solution to the drama's expanding problem(s), inter-generational conflict (strife interwoven with love)—and a light-hearted, happy ending, of course. The complications do not involve a father being gone but on the contrary, too present, and eager to push his son into a marriage with the proper girl, daughter of a proper Athenian, an old friend going back to the father's childhood—the very day on which the action is set.

There are other complications: that the son not only doesn't love this girl, but he loves another—and that information accidentally becomes public with the sudden death of her presumed older sister, Chrysis, the two of them having come as immigrants—non-citizens—from Andros some time earlier. Pamphilus had thrown his arms around Glycerium to hold her back when in her grief she teetered too near to the funerary pyre. Since everyone saw that, including the proper Athenian, Chremes, he withdrew the wedding proposal on behalf of his daughter that he had proferred earlier, back when he had seen Pamphilus as a model of unexpected youthful probity.

The plot thickens. It turns out that Charinus, a buddy of Pamphilus, is crazy in love with the daughter of Chremes—and that Glycerium is pregnant and soon to bear Pamphilus' child, whom he has promised to accept and acknowledge as his offspring. So Pamphilus has no interest or intention in marrying the daughter of Chremes. But his clever and devoted personal slave, Davus, suggests that he throw his father off when the latter tells him that he must marry that very day and to whom, by simply saying "yes, father, whatever you wish"—because Davus sees no preparations at either the house of Chremes or that of Pamphilus' father, Simo, so he is certain that there is no danger of the wedding taking place.

There is a further complication: Byrria, devoted slave of Charinus, overhears the conversation between Pamphilus and his father and thinks that his master has been betrayed by Pamphilus— that he lied to Charinus regarding his intentions toward Chremes' daughter. More overhearing opens Act Three: the midwife, Lesbia,[218] and Mysis, handmaid to Glycerium, enter onto the stage—with the comment that "you'll rarely find a man at all who is faithful to a woman, but this man Pamphilus has kept his word that, boy or girl, the baby's to be kept"—overheard by Simo and Davus, which means that Simo now knows his son's huge little secret, "a *foreigner's* child!" He immediately relieves himself of this concern by believing that it's a false story intended to push Chremes away from those wedding plans.

The intertwined matrices of concern that become obvious as the play moves to and beyond this point include not only the concern of the father that he be properly respected by his son and thus that his word be treated as law; and not only the socio-economics of who is and who is not an appropriate wife for that son; but the ethnocentricity that characterized most of antiquity. In the Greek context—and this, we may recall, was an an issue addressed by Aristophanes' Lysistrata at the end of the play named for her—it was not merely an issue of us Hellenes versus those non-Hellenes, but us Athenians versus those Spartans or Corinthians or

Boeiotians. So perhaps the most horrifying feature of Glycerium to Simo is that she is a foreigner.[219]

As Davus realizes that Simo has talked himself into this belief, he pushes it—to suggest that Glycerium is out to deceive Pamphilus, not Simo. As Davus heads inside, and Simo is about to seek out Chremes to finalize the wedding details, Chremes happens along, looking for Simo—having heard that Simo, a crazy man, is planning a wedding today, of their respective son and daughter. It turns out, though, that they both want the wedding, but that Chremes, for good reasons, doubts the wisdom of it for his daughter, while Simo is convinced that he can pull his son away from Glycerium, because he believes that she and Pamphilus have quarreled seriously—he believes that *eris* has driven itself into the heart of *eros*—and he is certain that Davus has told him this. The long and short of it is that, by the end of the act, the wedding has been agreed upon and Davus realizes that his plans on behalf of his master have backfired.

So… Act Four opens with Charinus and Pamphilus (along with Davus) both on stage—the first feeling betrayed, the second trying to explain that things are not as they seem, as Davus begins to concoct a new salvational plan. He has Mysis place the baby on Simo's doorstep, just as Chremes appears—and begins to argue with Mysis about whose baby it is, as if not noticing Chremes' presence, but thereby, of course, not only revealing the paternity of the baby but referencing what had been told as if it were some wive's tale back in Act One: that the "woman of Andros"—Glycerium—is in fact an Athenian citizen (shipwrecked near Andros, years earlier, together with her father, who later died, at which time she had been taken in by Chrysis and brought up like a younger sister) who therefore has rights with respect to the father of her child, i.e., that he marry her.

The last act opens with the arrival onto the stage of Crito, an elderly traveller from—Andros. He is, in fact, the cousin of the deceased Chrysis, come to claim her property—and asks after Glycerium: specifically, has she been in contact with her family yet?—but makes it clear that he won't take the property if Glycerium remains without family contacts and thus resources, since she has always been treated as the sister of Chrysis. Crito and

Mysis, followed by Davus, enter Glycerium's house and Simo and Chremes come out of Simo's house, arguing. The key words spoken by Chremes are that "you pushed me into giving my daughter to him—to a life of domestic discord and a most precarious marriage. You expect me to cure your lovesick son no matter what it costs my daughter!"

Where Chremes reference's Glycerium's citizen rights, Simo is still convinced that the whole thing—from her alleged Athenian identity to her post-natal condition—is false. His anger mounts to a rage after Davus comes out to tell him what is really going on—he calls to his overseer to tie Davus up and carry him off; he is more outraged as Pamphilus come to the door of Glycerium's house and responds in the affirmative to the question of her Athenian citizenship. The crux of the matter, from Simo's viewpoint, is his frustration with a son who has "found yourself a home, a wife, regardless of your father's wishes" and from Pamphilus' viewpoint that he confesses "that I love her and if I've done wrong, I confess that, too. I put myself in your hands, father. Punish me as you choose."

Pamphilus runs into Glycerium's house to bring out Crito who, in the face of the stormy winds of anger still blowing in all directions from a disbelieving Simo—but recognized by Chremes as an old friend—tells the tale of the shipwreck and what followed, adding the important detail that the father's name was Phania. Except it was not her father, but rather, her uncle, as Phania had noted before he died—which, it tunrs out, means that she is the daughter of Chremes!

The denouement is as poignant as it is happy: that Phania left Athens to avoid the war, following his brother to Asia Minor, but endured shipwreck along the way—something that, until now, Chremes had not known: this is the first he is hearing about the fate of his brother, and of his daughter. So in the end, Pamphilus will indeed marry the daughter of Chremes—Glycerium (who had originally, we learn, been called Pasibula)—which also means that the never-named daughter loved by Charina can become his bride. And, of course, Davus will be exonerated. Things end happily for everyone and the flute-playing musician enjoins the audience to applaud the play and its presentation.

Otherwise put, the outcome is love all around, after the resolution of a range of eristic moments, brief and extended—between Simo and Chremes, Simo and Pamphilus, Simo and Davus, and Simo and Crito, but not in fact, between Pamphilus and Glycerium. One can recognize the relationship between this play and those New Comedy plays like Menander's *Dyskolos*, in which most of the *eris* revolves around one angry person—who is, in his own way, as potentially loving as he is actually angry, and is therefore able to cross to the other side of his emotional being with just a little push from one or more of the other protagonists.

IV Women, Love, and Strife in Juvenal's *Satires*

At the opposite end of the chronological sweep of Roman literature, Decimus Junius Juvenalis—more simply known as Juvenal—(ca 55-130 CE), a key figure within the period usually referred to as the Silver Age of Roman literature, is the last of those poets who transform the comedic palette of Plautus and Terence and their fellow playwrights, taking humor off the stage and turning it into a different kind of instrument. The satires of poets like Juvenal—the heir to Lucillius, Horace,[220] and Persius—are almost long sermons recited by a single voice on serious topics that are sifted through his sarcasm and irony. The form is uniquely Roman, as opposed to having been directly developed from and following along the lines of Greek models.

Juvenal composed sixteen *Satires* that we know of, organized into five books. They are written in dactylic hexameter, offering a specific *gravitas* association with epic poetry, as we have seen for Lucretius, and all of them are focused on aspects of Roman vice and folly. They present no narrrative structure, but function as a kind of stream-of-consciousness rant. The *Sixth Satire* focuses on women: objects of love whose habits he consistently skewers with an eristic spear. The poem-sermon, directed to Postumus, begins by taking up the matter of chastity and placing it at its most prominent, way-back-when time frame, in the era of Saturn—in other words, he emulates the sort of model first expressed in Hesiod's *Works and Days*, of an early golden age from which conditions have degenerated for humans, age by age.

There is a rapid push in a direction at least unfriendly to contemporary women—it might not be fair to label the beginning as fully misogynistic, but certainly by the end of the poem it would be difficult not to apply that word to the poet. Wives in that long-ago era were very different from, and implicitly both more chaste and better over all "than you, Cynthia, or you whose bright eyes were dimmed by the death of the sparrow" (7-8)—alluding to the love-objects/subjects of Propertius and Catullus respectively. As Jupiter and the Olympians took over, some chastity remained, but gradually "Astrea (Justice) retired to the heavens with Chastity as her companion, and the two sisters fled hand in hand" (19-20). And so, the Iron Age led to other crimes, but the Silver Age saw the first adulterers—by which he means women adulterers.

With these conditions in mind, why would anyone get married? Suicide is a readily available and preferable option—or if that is not what you want, why not share your bed with a young lad, who won't scold you, demand gifts, or complain that you are not performing as you should. Really decent wives are rare, he asserts. Say you want to comply with the Julian Law—passed in 18 BCE to encourage matrimony and the production of children (with a financial reward for those producing more than two offspring), and related to the push toward family values that were increasingly obseessing Augustus—where might you find a woman of chaste repute?

He shifts the gears of his insult-mongering—to begin a long litany that follows a rather scatter-shot order, as opposed to some logical progression, through to the end of the poem—by next suggesting that women are crazy for actors, musicians, and gladiators: all low-life types for Juvenal and his audience. He offers a specific story to support this notion—that of Eppia, the wife of a senator, who ran off with a troupe of gladiators, all the way to Egypt, forgetting about her husband and her family, and about Rome, her community, braving the high seas that would ordinarily terrify her (82-94).

> If there is a good and honorable reason for the hazard,
> a well-born woman is afraid; her frightened bosom
> grows cold at the thought; she cannot stand

on her trembling feet. But they show a valiant heart
when their daring is in a base cause... (95-7)

...What youth so captivated
Eppia? What beauty set her all aflame? What
did she see that made her willing to be called
a gladiator's wench? Why, her little Sergius
had long since been scraping his chin; he hopes
that they will allow him to return with his wounded arm;
there were plenty of scars on his face; there was a
huge wart on the middle of his nose where the helmet
rubbed it; his sweet little eyes ran continually with
a chronic inflammation. But he was a *gladiator*!
That makes a man as handsome as Hyacinth. (103-10)

The poet then moves on to love potions and charms concocted by women—such as are used by a step-mother trying to seduce her stepson. Conversely, husbands who put up with unfit wives do so for money—or are blinded by the physical beauty that will not last: "If you will shake the truth out of him, it is a face, not a wife, that he's in love with" (143).

He offers a sweeping panoply of insulting comments, from the haughtiness of upper-class women (he uses Niobe as an example, from mythology, following the elegists in that sort of *doctus* or quasi-*doctus* direction, as we have seen—whose pride led to the deaths of all of her sons and daughters) to the snotty show-off tendency to use Greek: "For what is more nauseating than the fact that no Italian woman considers herself charming until she has made herself into a Greek instead of a Tuscan, a pure-bred Athenian instead of a lass from Sulmo" (185-7)? And a devoted husband, kind to his wife and completely loyal ends up victimized and abused by her. Have we found Juvenal's attitude toward the act of loving women sufficiently eristic yet?

And then, of course, there is the mother-in-law and her nefarious influence on the wife: "You may give up any hope for harmony as long as your mother-in-law is alive" (231)! Women love litigation—"there is hardly a lawsuit that some woman didn't begin" (242)—and what about female athletes? Nothing but negativity about that subject (246-67). On the other hand, "any bed that contains a wife is always the scene of arguments and mutual recriminations" (268-9)—and it is impossible to win an argument against a woman, even when she is dead wrong, for "there is nothing like female audacity when you catch them in the act; their guilt just makes them angry and bold" (284-5). So embedded within this long eristic poem regarding objects and subjects of *eros* is this particular reference to the impossibility of having a love relationship without *eris* entering into the equation with frequency.

He continues—returning, in tone, to the opening verses of his poem—that only in the frugal and more innocent past were Roman women vrituous: "it was poverty that kept Latin women chaste in days of old…all was work and hours of sleep were brief" (287-9). But now we suffer the travails of long peace and luxury has descended upon us—"avenging the conquered universe." This last twist turns interestingly on—or really back *against*—the normative imperial pride of Rome as orderer of the known world, emulating and in partnership with the gods who order the larger universe: the sort of self-conception symbolically expressed in the architecture of the Pantheon, built in its current form late in the lifetime of Juvenal (ca 120 CE). These passages also resonate with the sort of sneering downward look reflected in the ambiguous attitude toward the Greeks—respect for their culture but contempt for their morals—reflected from early comedy forward (although the view of the "other" who are not equal to "us" is broader than just the Greeks): "It was filthy money that first brought in foreign wars, it was dissolute wealth that has enervated the age with shameful luxury" (298-300).[221]

And he continues: the extravagance and whims of women, their fanatical enthusiasm for musicians (another synonym, like gladiators, for rock-star low-life types), their passion for gossip, their brutality toward their neighbors and their inherent discourtesy toward guests: visitors wait and wait, hungry and thirsty, while she takes a nice, long bath, and then she finally shows up, drinking more and eating more than all of them—until she vomits,

> so her husband turns queasy and covers his eyes while
> he retches.

> Yet she is still worse when she takes her place at the table,
> praises Vergil and finds an excuse for Dido (432-5)

—so we understand that Juvenal's perspective is that the Carthaginian Queen was entirely in the wrong and deserved what she got through her illicit relationship with the swashbuckling Roman hero. Moreover, "the wife" (who "finds an excuse" for someone who was not a wife in the full legal sense) is so bombastic in her assertions regarding Vergil and Homer, that "teachers of literature yield the floor, professors of rhetoric retire in defeat, the whole crowd falls silent; neither a lawyer nor a town crier will say a word—not even another woman" (438-40)! (And she is a stickler for proper grammar and syntax, to boot—"a husband ought to have the right to use careless grammar" (456)!

A wealthy woman is intolerable, because she can afford to plaster her ugly face with all kinds of hideous powders and creams—"yet such a face, when it is coated and bathed with so many changing cosmetics and plastered with bits of damp breadcrust: is it a face or shall it be called a running sore" (471-3)? To which must be added her cruel behavior toward slaves: anytime she is in a bad mood she takes it out on those poor creatures. She applies her cold cream, chats with her visitors, and admires the gold border on her dress—while her hired torturer is busy whipping some slave into a bloody pulp.

Women are inevitably drawn to outlandish religious cults and superstitions, they are easily victimized (with their husbands' money) by charlatan fortune-tellers and sooth-sayers. Worse, still, are the women who claim that they themselves have powers of divination. And (circling back, in a way, to the issue of marriage provoked by the Julian Law of 18 BCE), rich women refuse to bear children to their husbands—these women are too skilled at abortion techniques—and if they do get pregnant, it may well not be the husband who is the father, anyway. Conversely, they pass off foundlings as their own. Yet they drive their husbands mad with love potions—so even love is treated by Juvenal as a falsely induced uncontrollable passion rather than a positive emotion. In all of these charactereistics, the poet returns to that ethnocentric sense of prejudice that he evinced earlier: outlandish cults are Egyptian or Judaean, fortune-tellers are from Armenia or Commagene, nefarious love potions are from Thessaly—nothing nefariuos is, he implies, native to Rome.

The culmination of all of this misogynistic vitriol—verbal *eris* at its best, in considering what, in the natural order of things might be expected to be a focus on objects and subjects of *eros*—is the poet's assertion that women kill their stepsons. This is of course the opposite of the sort of claim he made earlier on, that they seduce them with potions—which, apart from the overall crazyquilt organization of his comments, suggests how simply unchained from reason he is on this hateful subject. Women even kill their own children, he continues, if it is a matter of property and inheritance. Or out of revenge against a spouse. I am not making this stuff up, he insists—and references Medea's notorious slaying of her sons to get revenge on Jason (as in the Euripidean play) and Procne, wife of Tereus, who for similar reasons killed her children (as in the Senecan play). These models are emulated in our own, everyday world, he insists.

If we have observed the tendency by the elegists—particularly Propertius and Ovid—to use stories out of familiar (and occasionally unfamiliar) mytho-history to bolster their points and to show off their (often arcane) knowledge, for Juvenal such references are intended merely to bolster his argument—which is ultimately always the same: stay as far away from women and "love" as you can if you want to survive.

So: the first words in our overall narrative were given to the discussion by Slater of the social complications of husband-wife/mother-son/brother-sister relations in the world of classical Athens. We proceeded to Hesiod's view of the coming into being of our world as a processs that involved a good deal of inter-generational and inter-genderal strife among relationships that might, ought, and often were otherwise paradigmatically loving. From that double starting point we have considered a wide range of works of literature, and some of art, covering a period of roughly a thousand years, in which the issue of love and strife—*eros* and *eris*—has been considered from a range of different angles.

If in works like the Homeric epics, the Greek tragedies, and Vergil's *Aeneid*, the interplay between these two forces is exemplified by the narratives and the characters within them, in turning to writers like the Roman elegists, we noted how the poets themselves, focusing on various women, *exhibited* rather than *illustrated or described* that interplay: they constantly swayed between love-borne passion and strife-ridden anger. The pendulum swung back to descriptive illustration of love-strife ambiguities, albeit in a lighter vein, in turning to the diversely conceived Old and New Comedy in Athens and the comedies of the expanding Roman republic.

Other aspects of the *eros-eris* interweave resonate out of Plato's Sokrates and from Lucretius, where the subject is love itself, considered from a philosophical perspective. And the last word on the subject, chronologically speaking, in being delivered by Juvenal, offers the most emphatic example of a poet exhibiting a virtually unalloyed *eris* in his discussion and description of women—as the objects and subjects of many men's love and desire, but of his own profound animosity.

By Juvenal's time, as we have noted, the Roman empire has expanded to its greatest historical geo-political extent. By that time, too, the Hebrew-Israelite-Judaean ethno-religious tradition has reached an important watershed, bifurcating to yield Jewish and Christian streams. Over the next few centuries, these two siblings of a common spiritual parent will engage in their own versions of *eris* and *eros*, as they contend not only with each other regarding who offers the most "correct" understanding of the divine *sacer*, but also competing with the vibrant forms of paganism that continue not only to prevail but to proliferate in new variations.[222]

By the time the empire has definitively collapsed, in the late fifth century, and one can slowly begin to abandon the word "antiquity" in favor of the phrase "medieval world," Christianity has achieved religious and political hegemony across its extent; within a few more centuries, the various kingdoms and empires that shape the medieval world will have all embraced one form or another of Christianity. Our world is largely the legacy of both the Greco-Roman ancient pagan world in which we have spent all of our narrative up to this point, and of the medieval and post-medieval Christian world that forms the context of Rome's extended epilogue—with regard to the *eros/eris* matrix as well as in so many other ways.

Chapter Ten

An Epilogue of Sorts: From the Bible to the *Baghavad Gita*

While the point and purpose of this narrative has been primarily to examine Greek and Latin literature—and more broadly, Greek and Roman culture—through the prism of the *eros-eris* interplay, one cannot leave that prism without noting how much more chronologically ubiquitous it is across Western thought, (and across non-Western thought, as well). Slater's discussion, which I have used as a take-off point, leads not only, as I have suggested, into the *eros-eris* matrix, but does so because that matrix reflects a profound aspect of the human pysche and of inter-human (and human-divine—and for the Greeks and Romans, divine-divine) relations, and not only in ancient Greece and Rome.

If for the Greco-Roman world, Hesiod and Homer offer the evidence that the gods themselves are exempla of this interweave, then an obvious question might be: how is it evidenced when we move beyond that world into the medieval and modern Western reality not only chronologically but with a different concept of divinity: one God, all-powerful, all-knowing, all-good, all-merciful, and coninuously interested and involved in human affairs?

I Love and Strife in the Hebrew Biblical Family

Our primary text with respect to that changed spiritual sensibility in the West—and the other foundation stone for Western thought alongside that of Greco-Roman thinking—is the Hebrew Bible. From the virtual beginning of the text we are engaged in human relations—family relations, to be more specific: inter-genderal, inter-generational, inter-spousal, and sibling relations. Even a cursory look at some of the most critical moments in the narrative sweep of the Hebrew Bible offers myriad instances in which aspects of the *eros-eris* matrix that suffuses Greek and Latin literature is in evidence.

In Genesis we encounter an all-encompassing God that creates the first male, Adam, out of a clod of earth (Hebrew: *adamah*), and breathes Its spirit into that clod (Gen 2:7), thus be-souling or animating it.[223] Oddly, God instructs Adam not to eat from the Tree that seems to be able to provide him with what he will need to survive (Gen 2:17): it is a "tree of the knowledge of good and evil" which phrase can be and has been construed both to mean "moral knowledge," and also to mean "knowledge about all things" (for reasons beyond this discussion).[224]

This interchange provides us with at least three complications within the context of a God understood to be both all-good and all-powerful. One: why does God instruct Adam not to eat from this tree, threatening him with death if he does so (Gen 2:17 ends with the words, "for on that day you shall surely die")—and then, moreover, when Adam abrogates that direct commandment from an all-knowing God (who must, therefore, have known that Adam would go ahead and do what he did), why doesn't God immediately fulfill the promise/threat of death?[225] Was it, rather, intended to mean *eventual* death—that in the Garden of Eden, Adam would have remained immortal, but once outside it, he became mortal?

Two: where does Eve fit into this story?[226] The text of Genesis presents her as created (from Adam's rib—Gen 2:21-2— but that is another issue for another day) *after* God commanded Adam regarding the Tree. Adam is also presented as not relaying God's command exactly as he had received it from God; he did what anyone in an any culture knows to be a foolish thing: he *edits* God's words (adding the injunction not even to touch the fruit from that tree—Gen 3:3), and it does not take much to see that when the serpent ("cleverest of the creatures that the Lord God has made"—no more, no less) invites Eve to touch that fruit and nothing happens, then it will be easy for her to be induced to taste it—and then to offer it to Adam—which double act does indeed have consequences.

Adam and Eve are thrown out of the garden, he to work hard for his food and she to bear children in pain (Gen 3:16-19). We realize, moreover, that a third interpretive possibility regarding the identity of the Tree is that it offered *sexual* knowledge, since virtually the first act of the first human couple when they are out of the Garden is that "Adam knew his wife Eve" (Gen 4:1)—the same Hebrew root (*y-d-'*) is present in that verb as in the noun translated as "knowledge."

If we turn this narrative over a bit, we see that, after Eve was created, Adam clung to her—as "flesh of my flesh"—which relationship plays out by Genesis 3 and the exit from the Garden as a clinging in a distinctly sexual manner (that produces offspring, in fact). Between these two events, however, the confrontation with God comes. That all-knowing, all-good God, that presumably loves Its creation, is yet sufficiently exercised over having been disobeyed that, in a distinctly eristic conclusion to the discussion, It metes out strong punishments to both Adam and Eve (as well as to the serpent). Moreover, that discussion resonates with a distinct *eris* between Adam and Eve (and the serpent): rather than taking responsbility, Adam blames Eve and she in turn blames the serpent (Gen 3:12-13).

We clearly cannot know what God's original or ultimate plans were or are for Adam and Eve and for humanity—after all, God is the ultimate *sacer* and we are *profanus* creatures. We can only "know" what God chooses to reveal to and through selected *sacerdotes*, and the text understood by traditional members of the Abrahamic faiths to be revealed does not offer distinct information on this issue. Could it have been the intention of the all-knowing God that is also all-good that Adam and Eve assert themselves, and eat from the tree that gave them a measure of knowledge so that they would be prepared for the outside world into which God intended all along to send them? Was God merely offering tough love to these apogetic consequences of Its creative inclinations—and not merely being eristic toward them in the punishment that they endure?

In any case, there is a dstinct flavor of *eris/eros* in the way in which this narrative moves forward, on both the human-divine and human-human levels. And if the human-human level is husband-wife, by the next generation the issue has come to encompass siblings. Cain and Abel compete for God's love—and Abel wins that competition, presumably because his offerings to the Lord reflect a greater sincerity than do those of Cain—and the eristic outcome of that situation is that Cain, in his anguish and his anger, slays Abel (Gen 4:2-8). Sibling love is crushed by sibling strife.[227]

One might, by the way, ask whether Cain's "sin" was to have killed his brother, or something else? No human death of any sort had yet occurred before Abel's death, and surely, as boys growing up, Cain and Abel must have wrestled and boxed and thrown each other down and hit each other any number of times. So it is arguable that Cain's smashing of Abel in great anger was not intended to *kill* him—and even, when Abel did not get up this time, that Cain may not have understood that his brother was "dead." But like his parents, when he is confronted by God, instead of owning up to his act—even, perhaps, stating that he had not meant to permanently hurt his brother, but that Abel never rose again after being hit, and expressing worry or sorrow over this—he famously abdicates any responsibility: Duh, I dunno where Abel is... "Am I my brother's keeper?" (Gen 4:9) he intones, rhetorically—and that is the moment when God metes out his punishment.

It is a punishment of marked exile, but also mitigated by that mark, so that he is simultaneously cast out and protected (Gen 4:14-15)—for could God simply respond in unmitigated *eris* to a creature that God is understood to love? This leads, in turn, to the third complication engendered by the initial story of the Tree in the Garden. And that is, if we understand the Tree as a tree of the knowledge of good and evil, then what eactly is *evil*? If Adam and Eve sinned in disobeying God and/or in denying responsibility for their act; and if Cain sinned in killing his brother and/or in denying responsibility for his act; what is it that all of the humans who have populated the earth by Genesis 6 and the beginning of the story of Noah and the flood done in order to merit wholesale destruction?

The text of Gen 6:1-4 notes that they had all become evil, which is why God purposes to destroy them—all that is, except for Noah ("a righteous man in his generation") and his family. But nowhere does the text specify what it is that they did that was evil. Unlike Adam and Eve, their descendants—humanity—

are not represented as having disobeyed God, whose only other commandment, to Adam and Eve, to "be fruitful and multiply" has clearly been fulfilled, or there would be no humanity to be destroyed by flood. What, to repeat, did they do that was so evil? Why, if Adam and Eve ate from that tree of knowledge of good and evil do we not get a clear idea from the text as to what constitutes evil?

Or is it *because* they ate that we don't find it in the text, but are expected to figure it out for ourselves—eventually—because the tough-loving God wants us to grow up as a thinking species that asks questions rather than making knee-jerk assumptions about such matters (which, within the Greco-Roman context, is where Sokrates comes in, as we have noted). Once more, this discussion would carry us beyond the parameters of our narrative—except to remember that the *sacer* is by definition beyond our understanding, and that narratives and commandments transmitted from the *sacer* to and through *sacerdotes*, to the extent that they may be intelligible as revelations when the *sacerdotes* are still around, become subject to the problematic of interpretation once time and history have moved forward.[228]

With respect to the focus of our own narrative we take away from these opening chapters of Genesis a sense of ambiguity along the *eros/eris* axis both where the divine-human relationship is concerned—as it should be, given the fundamentally ineffable, unknowable, unpredictable nature of God (the *sacer*) and the question of whether we can even apply these human-sourced terms to God in the first place: what do "love" and "strife" *mean*, what does "all-powerful" or "all-good" or "all-knowing" *mean* in God's terms?—and, more intelligibly, perhaps, where human-human relations are concerned.

We can follow these issues forward, of course. We come to what are known as the Patriarchal Narratives, beginning with the story of Abraham and Sarah and Hagar and the two sons of these two women, Isaac and Ishmael, and we realize that there are certain basic dysfunctionalities in this family—a dynamic tension between the role of Abraham in particular as a hero of Genesis 12-23, engaged in unique conversations with God, and his everyday, down-to-earth, unexalted status as a human being: a husband and father.

He loves Sarah but is represented as willing to see her enter the harem of the pharoah when they are in Egypt due to drought in Canaan (Gen 12:10-20)—and again with King Abimelekh of Gerar (Gen 20:1-7)—but most significantly, that adoration continues in spite of her inability to produce an offspring (which has not been the norm acros history, has it?).[229] It is then she who proposes her Egyptian handmaiden to him to provide an heir (Gen 16:2-3). Hagar bears Ishmael, and apparently begins to treat the childless Sarah with less and less respect—but then, miraculously, well beyond the age of child-bearing, Sarah bears Isaac (Gen 21:1-3). In brief, tension grows as the two boys grow, Ishmael, the elder, dominating and perhaps threatening his younger half-brother until, at Sarah's insistence, Abraham (assured by God that Ishmael will prosper; Gen 21:9-23) sends Hagar and Ishmael away.

Within this loving family, dominated by a patriarch who is both God-loving and presumably family-loving, there is a good deal of strife, to say the least—certainly between wives and between brothers. And father-son love is gradually being strained with increasing tension. First the issue of sending his first-born son away—albeit, okay, his mother is merely a concubine and not the beloved wife that Sarah is. But the matter intensifies when we arrive at the crux of the story with respect to the transmission of the unique Covenant between Abraham and God, intended to extend from one generation to the next. For that crux explicitly presents God as approaching Abraham with respect to "your son, your only son, whom you love, Isaac…"

And what about that son? Here, at the outset of Genesis 22, Abraham is called upon by God to sacrifice him—and without a scintilla of hesitation, the loving father takes the lad up Mount Moriah to do just that. Not a word to Sarah about this, mind you—but at the last moment, he is turned aside from his purpose by divine intervention in the form of a being that instructs him not to harm his son—now that God knows that Abraham loves God more than he loves even his own son, and the timely entanglement of a ram in a nearby tree, which Abraham sacrifices instead. Two further related issues for our purposes derive from this moment: first, that Abraham never sees Sarah again alive—for if one reads Genesis 22-23 with any care one realizes that he did not return home—was perhaps afraid of the wrath of Sarah and so moved elsewhere, to Beersheva (Gen 22:19), returning later to Hebron, where Sarah continued to dwell, only after her death, to bury her (Gen 23:2-20).

And second, one might wonder what kind of conversation Isaac and his father had on the return journey down from the mountain, and later, when Sarah is dead and Isaac is living with his father. How does the father explain in human terms what he almost did? Except that Isaac is, like Abraham, what Kierkegaard will one day call a "knight of faith" in the moment when he defies ideal human norms regarding parental love and does not hesitate for an instant to fulfill God's command.[230] Isaac is also caught up in this paroxysm of profound and profoundly irrational faith who, after all—at least by the time his father has bound him and laid him on the altar, the fire is warming his back, and his father stands over him with a large knife—might have piped up and asked Abraham if he was sure that he knew what he was doing.

All of the relationships contained within these chapters of Genesis are fraught with a tension between the loving aspects of husband and wife, and father and son and mother and son—and the strife that populates all of these same relationships: between Sarah and Hagar, obviously, and between Ishmael and Isaac, but more subtly between Abraham and both of these women and between him and both of his sons. Nor do these issues—largely, in the long run, centered around the covenant with God and the question of how and to whom that Covenant should be transmitted from one generation to the next—achieve a satsifactory resolution at an ordinary human level, for the most part, in the company of so much silence between pairs of protagonists, at least until the next generation.[231]

And that central covenantal matter and its dysfunctional family-derived basis for the interweave of *eros* and *eris* continue into that next generation: yet again two brothers (full brothers)—Jacob and Esau—contend for the covenantal blessing from their father, Isaac, and again the intervention of their (shared) mother, Rebecca, in contention with the preferences of their father, pushes that covenantal blessing in the direction of her preferred son (or at least the son who she believes will be better psychologically equipped to carry forward that Covenant): Jacob. The murderous *eris* of Esau toward his brother after the deception that yields Esau's loss of his birthright blessing forces Jacob to flee back to the place, Haran, from which his mother (and much further back, his grandfather) had come (Gen 27:1-28:5). Once again, then, love and strife entangle the relations between husband and wife, parents and children, and siblings.

The epic continues as Jacob meets up with his uncle, Laban, falls in love with his cousin, Rachel, and is tricked by Laban into marrying Rachel's sister, Leah, after seven years of hard work, thus requiring a second seven-year period of work, in order to marry Rachel (Gen 29:16-30). In brief, after twenty years as part of the extended family of his uncle, (with whom he has a rather distinctly strife-ridden relationship), Jacob eventually returns home to Canaan with two wives, two concubines, twelve sons and a daughter and lovingly reconciles with Esau—although it is notable that, when Esau, having come out on the road to greet his brother then offers to accompany him and his family to their parents' settlement, Jacob rather insistently suggests that Esau instead go ahead and let their parents know that he is coming.

He suggests that with his wives, concubines, all those children, servants, and baggage, his flock will move slowly, and he will follow—slowly (Gen 33:4-14). One wonders whether this is not a bit of wisdom on Jacob's part: that he recognizes that, if he and Esau walk and talk togther, they might turn to reminiscing and that could end up turning back to the reasons that Jacob left home in the first place, and get ugly. Loving reconciliation could revert to strife. Jacob also loses his beloved wife, Rachel, shortly before this moment, who dies in giving birth to their youngest son, Benjamin. The older of Rachel's two sons—all of the rest came through Leah or the wives' handmaidens—is Joseph, and his resemblance to Rachel makes him by far his father's favorite.

The balance of the book of Genesis, centered around Joseph and his brothers includes, first, their decision in their eristic jealousy of the one whom their father loves best, to sell him into slavery (Gen 37:18-28). Second, Joseph ends up in Egypt where, through a very different kind of series of love-strife experiences, (most notably that which involves Potiphar and Potiphar's wife in a tangled triangle with Joseph) he ends up as the vizier to the pharaoh, and oversees the strategy of gathering grain in anticipation of a long famine (Gen 37:36; 39:1-41:46). When indeed that famine arrives, seven years later, and lasts for another seven years, among those who come to Egypt asking for grain are none other than Joseph's own brothers; he recognizes them, but they don't recognize or understand him as he is attired as an Egyptian nobleman and of course goes through the pretense of speaking to them in Egyptian, through an interpreter. He certainly plays with them—it is a relatively light-handed eristic sort of behavior, compared with what he might have done in revenge for what they had done to him—contriving through that game to bring first his beloved younger full brother, Benjamin, and then eventually his beloved elderly father down from Canaan into Egypt, before he is reconciled with them all and they all settle happily in a border territory within Egypt graciously provided by the pharoah (Gen 42:6-47:27).

Love is again interwoven with strife—albeit the emphasis has shifted more fully onto the siblings—and given the fear that his brothers express, when their father dies, that now Joseph will truly avenge himself on them, and his response—that, on the contrary, he understands that it had all been part of God's plan—we may once more recognize that the relational core of the entire narrative pertains not only to the tensions within the human realm, but to that between God and these particular humans who have developed an ongoing covenantal relationship with God.

That relationship expands from a succession of individuals to their descendants as an entire people many generations later, in the context of Moses, with the book of Exodus and the other books that follow within the Pentateuch (Torah). There are periodic turns that intertwine *eros* and *eris* in that ongoing narrative, involving Moses and his Midianite wife, Tzipporah—most clearly, his near-fatal forgetting to circumcise his son, (God contemplated slaying his prophet for having neglected to fulfill this act, sign of the Covenant between God and Abraham's male descendants), at which time she essentially saves his life by remembering to do so (Ex 4:24-6). Later it involved the sister of Moses, Miriam, and his brother, Aaron, whose inappropriate disapproval of Tzipporah as a non-Israelite wife for their younger brother might have led to their deaths at God's hand had Moses not intervened on their behalf (Num12:1-15).

The expansion of the covenantal narrative from the personal to the ethno-national begins at Sinai, with the embrace by the People of Israel of the Ten Commandments and its concomitant injunctions mediated from God to them by Moses. That narrative leads, by way of a failure on the part of the People Israel to have complete faith in the protective efficacy of that Covenant, to the unhappy normalization of Israel into a kingdom, the formative moments of which are further fraught with *eros/eris* elements—"unhappy,' because everything in the story up to that point demonstrates the importance of their being abnormal in their unique relationship with a unique one-God-concept: women who are loved although they cannot produce male heirs, or do so with difficulty; younger sons, rather than older sons, inheriting the primary covenantal relationship; a people led by prophets and priests, rather than kings, their only tangible manifestation of God and Its presence a pair of stones kept in an elaborate box.

One sees the complications of this in the evolving relationship between the prophet Samuel and Saul, the king whom Samuel anointed at God's behest—culminating in I Samuel 15 and the strife-ridden final conversation between king and prophet after Saul's failure to obey God's commands regarding the Amalekites; and in I Samuel 28 and the poignant and desperate effort of Saul to avoid his demise at the hand of the Philistines on Mount Gilboa by conjuring Samuel's spirit from the dead—a passage reminiscent of and yet so very different in tone from that in *Odyssey* 11 when Odysseus conjures the shade of Teiresias from Hades. This Samuel-Saul, father-son mode of relationship ends with the tragic rejection of the "son" by the "father," through a more profound loyalty to God, and the passing over of the "son" with regard to covenant and kingship, by God Itself, as the mantle of political leadership passes from Saul's family (and the Tribe of Benjamin) to David and his family and tribe (the Tribe of Judah).

That father-son mode of tragic *eros/eris* tension evolves, moreover, sandwiched between these two just-noted passages in I Samuel, in the relationship between Saul and David—the boy who, as a man, will become the new king over Israel. David's successes against the Philistines both help save the Israelite kingdom and invite first the affection and then the anger of Saul; David's skill as a musician becomes about the only thing able to calm an increasingly despondent Saul (I Sam 16:23) — and Saul more than once tries to kill David and then repents such an action and such an emotion for one whom he loves like a son, while David, who loves Saul like a father, resists the opportunities to strike out at the king (I Sam 18:10-12; 19:9-10).

Meanwhile, Saul's real son, Jonathan, and David are closer to each other's hearts than brothers (I Sam 18:1-4) — Jonathan protects David on at least one occasion from Saul's irrational wrath, but Jonathan is doomed to die with his father on Mount Gilboa (I Sam 31:2). Saul's daughter, Michal, is also smitten with David, and becomes his wife (I Sam 18:20-21). That relationship sours when Michal criticizes David for dancing among the people with his legs exposed — she thinks it humiliating for a king; he responds by asserting that to rejoice with God and for God with wild abandon could hardly be considered humiliating — and it is clear from the text that their physical relationship as husband and wife ends from this point (II Sam 6:16-23). Thus within the royal house of Israel *eros* and *eris* contend from generation to generation and, in this last case, between formerly loving spouses.

One can find more details that express this interweave and contention both within these already-noted narratives if one examines them carefully, and further into the biblical text if one follows its narrative forward — but suffice it to say that, even with this handful of examples, *eros* and *eris* may be seen to mark out an enormously significant part of the territory carried within the biblical material, providing a counterpart to the Greco-Roman tradition as a shaper of the foundation upon which Western literature and thought continue to build throughout the centuries leading out of antiquity.

II The *Chanson de Roland*

The fusion between classical pagan civilization and the Israelite-Judaean culture — offering a stunning interweave of apparently antithetical forms of spirituality — yields a medieval Christian reality that, by the fifth and sixth centuries has become hegemonic across Europe and much of the Middle East and will push its geopolitical boundaries yet further over the centuries that follow. The confrontation of the Christian world (with a Jewish minority scattered across and embedded within it) first with waning paganism and then with emergent Islam (to say nothing of the internal crises of heresy and schism) helps shape some of the great epics that emerge in the 9th through 13th centuries.

As literature moves forward and takes on new aspects of both content and form, it also carries with it certain issues and ideas from ancient mytho-history. The *Chanson de Roland* ("Song of Roland"), the first significant work in that vernacular dialect of late Latin that is in the process of becoming French, focuses on the great Frankish Emperor, Charlemagne (*Carlus Magnus*: Charles the Great) and specifically his nephew Roland. It began as a series of troubadour poems—*chansons de geste*—sung across the southern parts of what is now France in the ninth and tenth centuries, as Islam was sweeping out of the *'arav,* across north Africa, and up into the Iberian peninsula.[232] The poem is written in stanzas of irregular length called *laisses*. The lines are ten-syllables each (decasyllabic) with a strong caesura (rhythmic break) usually after the fourth syllable. This is a far cry, formally speaking, from the dactylic hexameters with which the ancient Greeks and Romans expressed heroic epic.

The tale—that probably transforms a historical reality in which the Basques (Gascons) refused to submit to the rule of Charles the Great, and is based on a battle at Roncevaux (called Roncesvalles in Spanish) pass in the Pyrenees, in 778—shapes its narrative through the lens of the Christian-Muslim conflicts being played out with new vigor by the late 11th and 12th centuries at both ends of the Mediterranean. The Reconquista had begun in earnest with the collapse of the Umayyad dynasty in Spain, in 1031, and the First Crusade was declared at the Council of Clermont by Pope Urban II—a generation after the defeat of the Byzantine Christians at the hands of the newly Muslim Seljuks—in 1095.[233] The poem's final version was organized between 1040 and 1115.

What is most essential for our purposes are some of the details that structure the poem. The key villain is Ganelon. Charlemagne and his troops, having come through the Pyrenees and achieved success in battle after seven years—all but Saragossa has fallen to them—but having agreed to accept a peace offer from Marsile, King of Saragossa, (that includes gifts and an agreement to convert to Christianity), have begun their turn back home. The rear guard of Charlemagne's army, commanded by his nephew, Roland, is separated by many leagues from the main body of the Christian fighting force. Ganelon points out to Marsile how he can successfully ambush the Roland-led rear guard, as it passes through the Roncevaux pass, with a substantial body of Muslim troops.

But Ganelon is the step-father of Roland and Charlemagne's own brother-in-law (married to the Emperor's sister). So this most eristic of acts—betraying and virtually dooming Roland, but also committing treason against Charlemagne—is committed by someone who ideally should love the pious and heroic Roland, and certainly not want to break the heart of the Emperor to whom he is related and whom he presumably loves and reveres. Ganelon had proposed that Roland command the rear guard, as Roland had previously nominated Ganelon to go negotiate with Marsile for an end to hostilities, and Ganelon believed that he would be killed there, and that Roland had set him up for that death. So his act of treason was also an act of personal revenge.

Five times the far larger Muslim army attacks the Christian force, the latter led not only by Roland but by several confederates, most notably Turpin, a warrior-bishop who literalizes the notion of a cleric fighting in the name of the Lord; and Olivier, Roland's best friend—and the brother of his fiance, Aude. Four times the Muslims are turned back by the vigor and skill of Roland's knights—and each of those times Roland refuses to sound his ivory horn, the oliphant, to summon his uncle for help (and each time he chooses not to do so, that potential relieving army is getting farther and farther away). Olivier begs him to do so, asserting that if he does not, he won't allow his friend to see Aude again, whom Roland loves more than anyone—and even Bishop Turpin asks him to sound the horn.

But only with the fifth attack, when the Muslim force proves to be too much, does Roland blow the oliphant. As his army is slowly but inevitably being overrun, he finally sounds it, (blowing so hard that the veins in his temples burst) and Charlemagne, well beyond ordinary hearing distance, somehow hears the sound. Even then, Ganelon attempts to trick the Emperor, suggesting that he is hearing things, that the oliphant blast is an illusion.

The great king nonetheless swoops back through the Pyrenees into the mountain pass of Roncevaux where the battle has been taking place—too late, alas, to save his nephew and the other heroes. He who loved Roland as a son, (whereas—quite the opposite—Ganelon did not), manages only to hold him in his arms right after Roland breathes his last. But Charlemagne is able, in short order, to attack and take Saragossa, capturing Marsile's queen (who will subsequently convert to Christianity), and to find out who the traitor was—and to put him on trial. Ganelon is found guilty of treason (his defense had been that it was merely an act of appropriate revenge—but the defeat of his own best friend in a duel with the good knight, Thierry, proves that Ganelon is guilty in the eyes of God, and he is drawn and quartered. Aude weeps copiously over the death of her fiance—and ultimately the epic ends with Charlemagne recognizing, through a dream, that he must go back into Iberia and continue the war to subdue its unrepentant Muslim populace.

So, embedded within a black and white tale that pits good guys against bad guys on both a single (Roland and Ganelon, for starters) level and a group level—Christians versus Muslims, (who are also referred to as pagans; there is no distinction between these two religious categories of non-believers/infidels in the poet's mind)—love and strife among key protagonists play an essential role.

III Between Worlds: Dante's *Divine Comedy*

By the time a version of this story has reverberated into Italian literature in the fifteenth and sixteenth centuries, the medieval world has begun to shift toward modernity by way of what would later be called the Renaissance. One of the most signal works of Western literature, and an important transition poem between medieval and renaissance sensibilities takes shape between ca 1308 and 1320 at the hands of the Florentine poet, Dante Alighieri (1265-1321). It is known as the *Divine Comedy*—in the first part of which,

The Inferno, Ganelon is included deep down in Cocytus, in Antenor, the second round of the ninth and lowest circle of hell, where those who betray their country are located by the poet.

Like the *Chanson de Roland*, *The Divine Comedy* can be seen to continue the epic tradition that begins in Western Literature with the *Iliad*.[234] Among the most obvious broad differences are that *The Divine Comedy* has a known author, that it has a happy ending—which is why it is referred to as a "comedy" and not because there is anything humorous about it—and that it may also be seen to continue the lyric poetry tradition, particularly as that tradition evolved among the Roman elegists.

Dante's poem is, with the exception of the introductory two cantos, set entirely in the Underworld—so where Odysseus arrived at the border and conjured those with whom he spoke out of Hades in that unique, goddess-instructed, ritually contrived border territory; and whereas Aeneas, one might say, one-upped Odysseus by actually going down into and through Hades, guided first by a *sacerdos*-sibyl and then by his father; Dante may be seen to out do both of them in a way: his entire journey carries him through the various parts of the Underworld. Anchises describes to Aeneas the place and position of different kinds of individuals in Hades; Dante—led by the shade of Vergil himself, poet of the *Aeneid*—travels through three distinct regions: *Inferno* (Hell), *Purgatorio* (Purgatory), and *Paradiso* (Heaven).

Moreover, Dante the poet is one and the same as Dante the hero (both adventurer and pilgrim) who makes this journey—so in a manner reminscent of material written by the Roman elegists, but in a more direct manner, the entire triple poem is a song of himself, devoted to self-love (or at least self-aggrandisement, which may be functionally the same thing). It is obsessed with numerological symbolism, medieval style. The most prevalent number is three and variations on three, echoing the all-important Christian understanding of God as triune. Thus the three books are made up, each, of 33 cantos (chapters)—yielding a threefold multiple of eleven: which offers three times three plus the remaining two that signify the dual nature of Jesus as human and divine. Except that the *Inferno* offers an introductory canto that presents the setting, so that the actual total number of cantos is 100. In Christian medieval thought, ten is the perfect number because it is three times three plus the one that underscores God's unity; if there is a yet more perfect number it is 100—ten times ten.

For that matter, each of the three Underworld realms follows this numerological pattern: Hell has nine circles and beyond these a tenth is the realm in which the Satan is imprisoned in ice; Purgatory has nine rings crowned by the Garden of Eden as a tenth level; Paradise is comprised of nine celestial bodies and beyond them is the Empyrean containing the very essence of God.

All of these cantos are made up of hendecasylabic (eleven-syllable) lines, organized into three-line stanzas—tercets—following an aba, bcb, cdc, etc rhyme scheme. Dante is not the absolute first to do this—in Italian it is called *terza rima*—but he is the first to use that format in such an extensive way. So on the one hand the work is steeped in aspects of medieval thinking, both in form and in its rich descriptive and symbolic content. On the other hand, that the language is not the Latin still typically in use in academic, cultural, and clerical circles, but is the street dialect that is in the process of becoming Italian (specifically, the Tuscan sub-dialect of that Latin dialect that is becoming Italian) is symptomatic of a push forward out of the medieval world into the Renaissance.

The language indeed offers subtleties that exponentially expand the sort of play in which Vergil sometimes engaged in the *Aeneid*. Thus a careful analysis of the *Inferno*'s language shows it to be rougher than that of the *Purgatorio*; the language of the *Paradiso* is lightest. Each in turn represents a qualitative aspect of the Trinity: the heavier style of the *Inferno*, and its contents, of course, represents the eartbound Son, who suffered as one of us—and because of who he was and what he endured for humankind, it represents Divine *Caritas*: Charity/Love. The slightly lighter language style of the *Purgatorio*, and its cleansing content, intermediating between punishment and redemption, represents the Holy Sprit and Hope; the *Paradiso*'s style is lightest in language, and its salvational essence represents the Father and the purity of absolute Faith.

Moreover, the fact that there is such a constant correlation, particularly in the *Inferno* where sinners are punished, between the actions of an individual while alive and the torments that he or she now suffers posthumously, and for all of eternity, suggests the importance of human action over and against the pre-determining will of God—embracing a more modernist than traditional medieval perspective.

The setting is splendidly *sacer*: kind of the dark side of Odysseus' experiences when, journeying through the unknown *sacer* with all of the positive and negative creatures and adventures he encounters, he travels, as it were, deeper into and yet to the further, outer edge of, the *sacer* when he arrives on Kirke's island and yet both further into and further out to the edge of the *sacer* within the *sacer* when he comes to the island of the dead where he opens up the portal into Hades. In Dante's case—both Dante the poet who contrives this poem and Dante the hero who stars in it—he awakens to find himself, without quite knowing why, in the midpoint of his life (meaning, 35 years old, midway through the normative biblically-mandated human life span: three score years and ten; Psalm 89:10) alone in the middle of a dark wood. The time proves, by his description, to be as *sacer* as the space; it is a non-existent—in *profanus* terms—dawn:

> …at the first widening of the dawn
> as the sun was climbing Aries with those stars
> that rode with Him to light the new creation. (I.37-9)[235]

The last phrase reflects a medieval triadition that the sun was in Aries at the time of Creation. So astronomy and religion coincide perfectly here: he was awakened and/or arrived to this place just before dawn on Good Friday in the year 1300 (since he was born in 1265). So the new life that will emerge from this adventure, beginning under Aries—zodiacal sign of creation—at dawn, which symbolizes rebirth, takes place also during the season of Easter. This implies both death (crucifixion) and, more importantly, rebirth (resurrection). The further description presents the moon as full and the sun at its vernal equinox---but this pair of conditions did not fall together on *any* Friday in 1300. This is a perfect, idealized *sacer* Easter weekend of resurrection and rebirth.

That Dante the poet is also Dante the hero both extends the epic idea in a particular way beyond Homer and Vergil, and also obliquely shifts toward the elegiac lyric poets of Rome. For as we have seen, again and again they send the message that the ultimate subject of their poetry is not Lesbia or Cynthia or any other woman; the subject of their poetry is their poetry, which is to say that the subject of their poetry is themselves, embedded within their poetry: it is, really, all about *me*. Dante the hero-adventurer is also Dante the pilgrim—who will return from his pilgrimage goal profoundly refreshed in spirit—and he is also a mystic, seeking the innermost recesses of the Divine, (the *mysterion*). That is, he seeks enlightened esoteric knowledge inaccessible to everyday worshippers, but returning from that ineffable experience burdened with the obligation to somehow describe it in order to improve the community around him: for not to enlighten others, hoarding one's new knowledge for one's self would be selfish and yield a failed mystical mission.

At the edge of the woods and the beginning of his journey, our hero is suddenly aware of the approach of a trio of wild beasts—a leopard, a lion, and a she-wolf—drawn no doubt from Jeremiah 5:6,[236] but also symbols of Florence (lust for earthly pleasures), France (violent and ambitous pride), and the papacy (incontinence and greed). He backs slowly away from them, deeper into the wood, when a shade appears—able to rescue him from these enemies. The shade is that of Vergil—so we understand that the poet has overtly looked to Vergil and the *Aeneid* as a foundation upon which he is building his own literary edifice. And Vergil explains that, to avoid these beasts one must take a round-about path—through an eternal place through which the ancient poet will guide the hero.

Vergil, who will serve most broadly as a symbol of reason, will lead Dante in a far more complex journey than, but reminiscent of, that journey through Hades along which Aeneas was led by Anchises. He will only be able to lead Dante so far, however—through Hell and up the mountain of Purgatory. He informs the traveller-adventurer-hero-mystic that, if he wishes to climb further, to witness the blessed choir,

> a worthier spirit shall be sent to guide you.
> With her I shall leave you, for the King of Time,
>
> who reigns on high, forbids me to come there,
> since, living, I rebelled against His law... (I.116-119)

We shall come to understand that the "her" in question is Beatrice—symbol of faith: so reason can only lead so far toward Christian paradise; reason is important (the more so in a renaissance rather than a purely medieval world, toward which this poem helps push western literature) but faith extends well beyond reason. Beatrice is both faith in the context of faith-reason and the paritcularized embodiment of divinely-sourced love in the context of faith-hope-love.

That we are, therefore, in a distinctly Christian world, different in important ways from the pagan world of Homer and Vergil and their epics, is also clear—even clearer as we move through Canto II, entering the *sacer* within the *sacer* where the poem began, and reference is made to the advent of Peter and Paul as heroically-scaled advocates of a new spiritual order; and when the poet/hero asks Vergil rhetorically, regarding the impending journey:

But how should I dare? By whose permission?
I am not Aeneas; *I* am not Paul.
Who could believe *me* worthy of the vision? (II.31-33)

—it is yet more obvious that this heroic journey, intended to be a spiritual allegory as much as or more than it is to be understood as physical, interweaves Christian concerns with classical sources.

While we might understand how Vergil, as a righteous pagan, might be consigned to the Limbo that he describes shortly thereafter, we might wonder why he would stand accused—or accuse himself—of "rebelling against His law" if we assume that that law refers to the commandments leading to true belief in the true God that only gradually become dominant in the Roman world well after Vergil's own time (between the time of the Crucifixion under Tiberias in the 30s CE and the declaration of Christianity as the offical religion of the Empire under Theodosius, around 380 CE). For Vergil, as we know, was dead by 19 BCE, a generation before the birth of Jesus. Perhaps Dante's understanding of this chronology is limited. In any case, this little mystery is an analogue of the mysteries left behind by Vergil himself in the *Aeneid*, some of which we have noted.

What we further understand, as Canto II goes forward, is that Beatrice had come to pluck Vergil from Limbo so that he might perform the task of fetching Dante from the misguided direction that his life has taken up to this point and to bring him on this journey that will transform him and bring him salvation. Beatrice says to Vergil:

> My dearest friend, and fortune's foe, has strayed
> onto a friendless shore and stands beset
> by such distress that he turns afraid
>
> from the True Way, and news of him in heaven
> rumors my dread that he is already lost.
> I come, afraid that I am too-late risen.
>
> So fly to him and with your high counsel, pity,
> and whatever need be for his good
> and soul's salvation, help him and solace me.
>
> It is I, Beatirice, who send you to him.
> I come from the blessed height for which I yearn.
> Love called me here... (II.61-72)

Indeed, as Vergil reports to Dante and to us, Beatrice references an even higher source for the poet-hero's salvation: "a Lady in Heaven so concerned for him"—who is the Virgin Mary herself, who, breaking precedent, has suggested to Beatrice that she rescue Dante's soul from perdition. These two female presences, together with a third—the divine light called Lucia (which is "light" in Italian); so that the three beasts of Canto I are "balanced" by the three ladies of Canto II—offer a continuation of "threeness" resonating throughout this extended prelude that marks the start of a spiritual rebirth for the poet-hero. He is led, in turn, with the beginning of Canto III, to the vestibule of Hell with its renowned doorway inscription culminating with the words: "Abandon all hope, ye who enter here" (III.9)

By addressing the question of who Beatrice is, we can underscore both how the *Divine Comedy* is both epic and lyric poetry and how *eros* and *eris* undergird its narrative. She is presumably Beatrice Portinari, a woman whom Dante had many years before idealized. He apparently met her—saw her, perhaps from a distance—in childhood (he—and she?—was apparently 9 years old at the time) and continued to admire her from afar, seeing her with much greater frequency after age18, following the mode of the then-fashionable courtly love tradition. That tradition—whose practitioners referred to themselves as *fideli d'amore* ("those loyal to love")—offered certain prescribed elements: the beloved is *only* admired from afar—she is usually married to somebody else—and is idealized by poetry (to which the *fideli* are also loyal, as they are loyal to their feelings and their visions, as well) that adumbrates her perfections.

Dante apparently continued his long-distance infatuation with Beatrice into his early adulthood as he started to become a poet, even after he was himself married—to the daughter of a key player in the political party opposite his own. (When he went into exile in 1302, neither his wife, Gemma, nor any of their four children seem to have joined him). Beatrice, one might say, had upped the intensity of the unrequited love syndrome by dying young—in 1290, at the age of 24—the outcome of which was that her death inspired Dante's first major poetic work, the *Vita Nuova* ("New Life"), which appeared in 1295, in which he first used what was called the *dolce stil nuovo* ("sweet new style").[237] We recognize traces of the Latin elegiac poets in the *fideli d'amore* adherents and their poetry, but with a fundamental difference: from Catullus to Ovid, as we have seen, however idealizing may be their tone at the outset of addressing or describing their lady-loves, at some point there is either a sudden turn—or the beginnings of a gradual turn—toward anger: *amo* becomes *odi*.

For Dante, Beatrice was, is, and will be a yearned-for, much beloved ideal. This is understandable as a function of the conditions of courtly love: that the beloved not only remain distant but that the relationship never move beyond the spiritual toward the physical; the goal is never to sleep with her when her husband is elsewhere (whether or not she loves her husband is another matter—that question does not engage the courtly love poet). So, further idealized after death, Beatrice makes perfect sense as the one whose profound spiritual love causes her, in Dante's poetic construal, to send Vergil to rescue him from himself when he begins to set down the *Divine Comedy*, in exile from his beloved city, so many years after her death.

Eros—albeit in the spiritual sense—governs Dante's heroic journey, one engendered in a biographical context of pure *eris*: that when his own political party was pushed out of power (he was, at the time, away in Rome, negotiating on behalf of Florence, with the head of the Papal states, Pope Boniface VIII) he was forced into exile, never to return to Florence. (When he died, he was apparently buried in Ravenna). We understand, then, that the three wild beasts—symbols each in its particular way, of intense *eris* that will be balanced in Canto II by the three ladies offering spiritual *eros*—are reflections of three communal sources of his pain: his own city, the papal states, and the France that at that time offered particularly strong negative interference in the political affairs of Florence and other Italian city-states, and therefore in his own life.

So as Beatrice represents faith where Vergil does reason, she—together with the Virgin Mary and Lucia—also represents *eros* where Florence, Rome, and Paris and certain particular inhabitants of those locales represent *eris*. And the entire poem carries us from the consequence of individualized eristic behavior—particularly where individuals had acted toward Dante himself in a negative way; this text is his revenge on those individuals, as he places them in eternal suffering in different locations in Hell—toward and into the realm where loving behavior is rewarded with eternal spiritual joy.

Once we have crossed the threshold of that vestibule with its inscription, at the beginning of Canto III, then, we enter into an increasingly intense house of horrors, in which everyone incarcerated—including Dante's real or perceived enemies, mixed in with scores of historical and mytho-historical personalities (like the aforementioned Ganelon)—is suffering in accordance with crimes and sins she or he has committed: we are treated to a menu of sins that carry from gluttons to those who betrayed their masters. In this last category—regarded as even worse than that of those who betrayed their country (that would be Ganelon's category)—are individuals whom we have not encountered in our own literature-based narrative, but certainly could have, had our purview moved beyond literature and art. Brutus and Cassius are there, leaders of the assassination plot against Julius Caesar—Brutus in particular had been viewed by Caesar as a son, and the heartbreak of that betrayal of filial/paternal love is recounted literarily from Suetonius to Shakespeare—and Judas Iscariot is there, who betrayed his beloved master with a kiss.

If the *Inferno* is pure *eris*, (and these last examples in particular are inherently fraught with *eros/eris* tension, since the betrayers presumably loved and/or were loved by those whom they betrayed unto death), divine love makes it possible for those who were neither so bad that they deserve eternal damnation nor good enough to be in paradise, to choose their own punitive means of purging themselves (hence: Purgatory) and gradually, over a lengthy but not endless stretch of time, to work themselves up the painful mountain toward the Garden that offers a prelude to Paradise. And it is love in its fullest efflorescence into which those worthy of Paradise are gathered in that blessed and beatific realm. Into this realm Beatrice leads Dante. Its innermost precincts through which a river of light flows are shaped like a rose with an infinite number of petals—a white mystical rose, each frond symbolizing and occupied by or reserved for a different spiritually exquisite being.

Where Odysseus learned about his own future, together with the ambiguities attending his eventual arrival back to Hades through the natural process of death; and where Aeneas learned about the future of his people, down to the time of Augustus Caesar and Vergil himself; Dante learns about—and teaches his audience about—the possibilities for an afterlife that can either be terrible or wonderful (or in between) depending upon what one does with one's life.

Within the heart of the pure white rose the poet's poem becomes most clearly a work of love not only of himself but of and for humanity; here he most strongly resembles mystics who have managed to step outside themselves and become one with God, entering into the *mysterion*—the "hiddennesss" at the center of the center (which is also the outermost edge) of the spaceless *sacer*—and become eager to return from his vision to lead his reader through that multi-petalled flower toward the Empyrean, where

> my powers rest from their high fantasy,
> but already I could feel my being turned—
> instinct and intellect balanced equally
>
> as in a wheel whose motion nothing jars—
> by the Love that moves the Sun and the other stars.

That overall statement, regarding love as the essential feature that motivates the universe both encompasses and pushes back against the words inscribed over the portal into the *Inferno* that end with the admonition to beware, those who would enter there. For that statement had included the note that—regarding this way into the city of woe, of forsaken people, and of eternal sorrow—

> Sacred justice moved my architect.
> I [this gate] was raised here by divine omnipotence,
> primordial love, and ultimate intellect.

That architect of human *being* with its paradoxes and contradictions—*eros/eris* among them—has left us as instruments to respond to and encompass what we are as a species, as bodies and as souls, our literature and our arts.

IV Love and Strife within Love and Honor: Corneille's *Le Cid*

As one follows the literature of the west further forward one finds the interweave of *eros* and *eris* again and again. To be clear, this is not to suggest that this interweave is absolutely ubiquitous, nor that there are not also other aspects of how we are as a species that are reflected in literature and art, but simply—to repeat—to assert the frequency of this theme. (Nor does this epilogue to our narrative encompass anything near the totality of literary or visual instances where this theme appears). If, for instance, however, one moves forward another three centuries from Dante and arrives, say, at *Le Cid*, a play by Pierre Corneille (1606-84), one may see how the intertwining of love and strife shapes the backbone of the drama.

Corneille's play, first performed in Paris in 1637, is a take-off on the great Spanish-language medieval *El Poema de Mio Cid*, (also known as *El Cantar de mio Cid*: "The Song of My Cid"), composed between ca 1140 and 1207, which might be considered the other shoe dropping for medieval *chansons de geste*, if the *Chanson de Roland* is the first. Like *Roland*, *el Poema de Mio Cid* is a mythologized handling of a historical figure, Rodrigo Diaz de Vivar (ca 1043-99), placed within the context of the *reconquista* and thus of martial Christian-Muslim relations. Both the medieval poem and Corneille's play present Rodrigo as a heroic warrior based in Valencia who battles the Moors, whereas historically, he was a mercenary who fought for the highest bidder: sometimes Christian against Moor, sometimes Christian against Christian—and sometimes Muslim against Christian.[238]

In Corneille's version—in which the playwright follows his usual habit of pitting honor against love and then promoting honor as the ideally more dominant force—it is the *eros-eris* matrix that creates the tension between these principles. The five-act drama is written in rhyming couplets; the metrical scheme, popular in classical French poetry, is called alexandrine—thus each line is comprised of 12 syllables with major accents on the sixth and twelfth syllables and a caesura after the sixth.

The first act begins with Don Sanche and Don Rodrigue fighting for the hand of Chimene—so already *eris* envelops the issue of *eros*.[239] Chimene prefers Rodrigue, a preference, she is told by her nurse, corroborated by her father. Chimene is guardedly happy—she still worries that Fate could intervene to change her father's mind. The first complication emerges when it is revealed that the *infante* (the princess) is also in love with Rodrigue—but she cannot hope to marry him because of his lower social class, so she has decided to bring Chimene and Rodrgiue together as a means of quelling her own passion.

If that intitial potential problem is solved, a second one that emerges almost immediately thereafter is not so easily dealt with. Chimene's father, Don Gomes, learns that the king (Fernand of Castille—who historically ruled in 1035-65) has asked Don Diegue, elderly father of Rodrigue, to serve as the tutor for his son, the prince of Castille. Don Gomes believes that he is more worthy to serve in such a position and says so to Don Diegue. Don Diegue redirects that issue toward the idea that the two of them should be friends under any cirumstance, since their children wish to be marrried. (The eristic approach of Don Gomes is redirected by Don Diegue's reference to *eros*). But still piqued by the king's failure to choose him as tutor to the prince, Don Gomes refuses the hand of friendship and slaps Don Diegue, who draws his sword but is too old and weak to hold it, so that Don Gomes easily disarms him, insulting him before leaving the stage.

Don Diegue is of course humiliated by this event and asks his son, Rodrigue, to avenge him by fighting Don Gomes. This creates a conundrum for Rodrigue, since he realizes that if he duels the count and wins—meaning most likely that he will kill him—he will lose Chimene's love. The family honor, however (as opposed, per se, to filial love, interestingly enough, although it is arguably the love for his father that provokes his decision, since it is specifically his father's honor that he wishes to restore, not his own or his family's, really) trumps love for his fiance, and so the first act ends with his decision to fight his father-in-law-to-be.

So what began with strife over the love of a woman shifted to a crisis derived from Don Gomes' self-love, that produces strife and then the potential further follow-up to that strife causes man-woman love to take a back seat to love between father and son, opening the door at the end of the act, to further strife both between son-in-law-to-be and father-in-law-to-be and between husband-and-wife-to-be.

If there is someone who might be considered a villain of sorts in this court of courtly behavior, it is Chimene's father, Don Gomes. For it was his exalted sense of self-love and self-worth that led to the crisis at the end of Act I and as Act II opens, a courtier, Don Arias, informs Don Gomes that the king forbids a duel between him and Rodrigue, but with a splendid show of arrogance, Gomes not only prepares to disobey the king but taunts Rodrigue. With perfect ambiguity, he also commends Rodrigue for his fearlessness and asks him to stand down—but he has pushed the situation too far and Rodrigue cannot and will not do so.

Not surprisingly, Chimene is distraught about this fight, and confides her fears to the *infante*—who, we recall, possesses a love for Rodrigue that can never be consummated, except that, oddly, as Chimene hurries off the stage the *infante* thinks over the idea that if Rodrigue wins the duel and is therefore rejected by Chimene, she may be able to win him after all. Meanwhile, her father, King Fernand, expresses his anger at Don Gomes to Don Sanche and Don Arrias for the count's cruel and insulting behavior toward Don Diegue and his intention to accept the duel with Don Rodrigue. These strife-ridden complications while he (the king) is worried about a potential attack from the Moors—a large-scale potential *eris* to parallel the small-scale issues that have occupied the drama so far—and the act ends with the arrival onto the stage of Don Alonse, who announces that Rodrigue has killed Don Gomes in their duel.

Act III begins with Rodrigue coming to Chimene's home, proposing to—beseeching—Elvire (Chimene's nurse) that he die at Chimene's hand. But Elvire tells him to flee and so he hides as Chiemene arrives onto the stage. Chimene confesses to Elvire her conflicted feelings—caught between love for Rodrigue and her strife-induced obligations and feelings of family honor. She must make sure that Rodrigue dies—and she will kill herself after that—but when he appears out of hiding and offers her his sword as the instrument of his execution she finds that she cannot use it to accomplish that end.

The plot twists and thickens when Rodrigue returns home after this unresolved confrontation and his father informs him that the Moors are about to attack. Rodrigue, the pre-eminent warrior-knight in the kingdom, must go out to fight against them—but if he returns alive and victorious, the king will no doubt praise him so strongly that he will regain Chimene's love. This act in particular offers the rather strange phenomenon in which love is and then is not an uncontrollable, irrational emotion, but rather a rationally arrived at calculation. (Rodrigue never lost Chimene's love, just her ability to express it rather than expressing hate for him, right?)

The issue of Act IV is brief: Rodrigue goes off to fight and comes back a war hero. He is so splendid a warrior, in fact, that the captured Moors revere him and dub him *Al Sayyid*—that becomes hispanized (and unchanged from Spanish to French, except for the definite article) as "El Cid" ("Le Cid" in French)—meaning "lord".

Under the heroic war-strife-outcome circumstances, the *infante* herself—there is some irony here, given the *infante*'s own feelings for Rodrigue and her thoughts toward the end of the previous act—begs Chimene to end her quest to kill Rodrigue, but personal-family-honor-strife still overwhelms nearly forgotten love, and Chimene refuses the request.

King Fernand, however, allows Chimene to believe that Rodrgiue has been killed, and her reaction to that "news" makes it clear to everyone that she sill loves him—yet she still also feels the need to avenge her father's death, as also remains clear when the true news, of his very living victory, comes out. There is still strife within her own heart between filial love (and family honor) and love for her potential spouse. In any case, Don Sanche asserts his willingness to fight Rodrigue on her behalf, and she agrees to marry whoever is victorious in that duel. So we have come full circle, as it were, to where we began at the beginning of the play, with Sanche and Rodgrigue about to fight for Chimene.

The last act begins with Rodrigue coming to Chimene and telling her that he will not defend himself in the duel with Don Sanche—but she begs him to do so, to save her from an undesirable marriage to Sanche: so it is the combination of her admitted love for Rodrigue, her strong antipathy for Sanche, and above all, Rodrigue's love for her that will combine to prevent Rodrigue from allowing his otherwise-directed, honor-laced love for Chimene to cause him to throw the fight—and throw away his life.

The ever-selfless *infante* offers a monologue to the audience in which she underscores the idea that Rodrigue must truly belong to Chimene, if so little hatred has managed to wedge its way between them in the aftermath of his slaying her father. Indeed, when Don Sanche enters onto the stage with a bloody sword, and Chimene believes that Rodrgiue has been killed, she cries out that she loved and still loves Rodrigue and pledges to enter a convent—to grieve there, forever, for both her father and Rodrigue—rather than to marry Sanche; leaving him, instead, all of her possessions. When King Fernand informs her, however, that Rodrigue is not only alive but had disarmed Don Sanche but chose not to kill him, Sanche responds by being the one who now says that Chimene and Rodrigue should marry given how clear their love is for each other.

One individual after another exudes both honor and love for others in this idealized chivalric court of Corneille's imagination. Indeed, the king in the end virtually commands Chimene to desist from her full-hearted/half-hearted "kill Rodrigue" campaign: she has served her father well enough, he suggests, by putting Rodrigue in danger and no longer needs to feel obliged to avenge Don Gomes. It is time, he concludes, for her to do something for herself—by marrying Rodrigue—but, recognizing that she still needs time to mourn her father, he suggests that the marriage be put off for a year, while (conveniently for the needs of the king and his kingdom), Rodrigue will return to the battlefield against the Moors and, ever-faithful to Chimene, will only become more worthy of her love as that year progresses.

One might yet wonder—in a manner somewhat analogous to the question of Abraham and Isaac after the near-sacrifice and in particular after Sarah's death, and analogous to the question of Jacob and Esau after Jacob's return—whether there will be moments in the the married life to come of this exemplary couple when somehow the death of Chimene's father at the hand of Rodrigue might haunt them? Or shall we leave it at the idea that "they will live happily ever after" (at least if he doesn't get killed in the following year—contrary to the play on this play that was shaped by Hollywood with Charlton Heston and Sophia Loren, in which he dies). Corneille clearly understood some of the comic ambiguities with his tragedy—or the tragic elements of his comedy (a serious play with sad elements but a happy ending still with some sad possibilities)—since he labeled it a "tragi-comedie." This was the first time that turn of phrase was used in Western theater.

V From West to East: God's Words in *The Baghavad Gita*

The interplay of these various issues, and entrenched within them, often anchoring them, the interplay between *eros* and *eris*, may be found spread across literature, from Miguel Cervantes' *Don Quixote* and Shakesepeare's *Hamlet* (in which the basic plot offers strong echoes of the *Oresteia*) to James Joyce's *Ulysses*—and, to repeat, beyond the West. This last point may be exemplified by the *Baghavad*

Gita ("The Divine Song"), a mini-epic embedded within the much larger Sanskrit-language epic known as the *Mahabharata*.[240] The very opening chapter of that poem presents the prince, Arjuna, having been blessed by having the god, Krishna as his charioteer, beginning a dialogue with the god in which the latter instructs the former on the *dharma*—the divinely-mandated laws of life—which instructive dialogue fills out the entirety of the *Gita*'s narrative.

The issue raised by Arjuna is his concern that he is about to fight against an army that includes those whom he inherently loves: cousins and neighbors—for his blind uncle has usurped Arjuna's throne, and naturally his uncle's sons and many of their friends and neighbors have sided with the uncle, Dhritarashtra.[241] In short, Arjuna is disturbed by what he sees as an unacceptable interweave of love and strife. Krishna's long and detailed response—which carries beyond the purposes of *this* discussion—designed to allay Arjuna's concerns has, at its heart, two principles: one, that according to divine *dharma*, to restore the proper order of things trumps the matter of familial love in tension with potential familial or communal strife; and two, that, in any case, he (we) must keep in mind the linked doctrines of *samsara* (cycling of the immortal soul from one incarnate form to the next); *moksha* (release from the cycle of *samsara* at some hoped-for point in a soul's existence); and *nirvana* (the state of perfection arrived at with *moksha*, in which the soul becomes one with—is restored to where it began, and is subsumed into—ultimate *Being*, which is Krishna Itself).[242]

Given these doctrines, Arjuna can never actually kill any of those in the army opposing him: all he will do is to destroy the physical carapaces in which the immortal souls reside—and who knows? he may even be helping someone he "kills" to move further along in the cycle of *samsara* to the next, higher incarnation (say, from being a *kshatriya*, a warrior; to being a *brahmin*, a priest), or even to *moksha* and to the condition of *nirvana* itself. So the young prince is encouraged by the god to engage in this extended act of strife on behalf of the order of things and on behalf of love—both of those, counter-intuitively, whom he will fight and, even more importantly, of the God who orders all things. While the point of the *Gita* is not *eros/eris*, per se, this matrix provides the context in which the God articulates all of his points.

The turn to a non-Western epic poem brings us full circle back, too, to the kind of literature with which this narrative began, with a series of Greek epic poems that presented the gods in action shaping the order of things and then in interaction with humans in the contouring of the great Trojan War and parts of its aftermath. Appropriately enough, we might move toward the conclusion of our narrative with reference to two very different modern responses to these epics—specifically the *Iliad* and the *Odyssey*—and then, (full disclosure), with a brief epilogue within this epilogue.

Chapter Eleven

The Western Return to Epic and the Epilogue of Music:
From Nikos Kazantsakis and Derek Walcott to *West Side Story*

I Kazantzakis' *The Odyssey: A Sequel*

The first of two modern poems that return this narrative full circle—or nearly—to where we began with the Hesiodic and Homeric epics and their engagement of heroic human characters within a larger world of gods and fate, is a long one. Written by the modern Greek writer, Nikos Kazantzakis (1883-1957), his poem raises the sort of question that we have noted within the contexts of the *Odyssey*; of the Abraham-Isaac and Jacob-Esau stories; and also of Corneille's *Le Cid*: what happens afterwards between the key protagonists of a heroic narrative? Can they possibly just live happily ever after? Kazantzakis' poem, *The Odyssey: A Sequel*, is designed to address just that question with respect to Odysseus and his loved ones. After having adventured out to the outer edges of the *profanus* and swashbuckled his way through diverse *sacer* realms, what will a still-vibrant Odysseus feel and do after his halls have been cleansed and a kind of divinely-ordained peace has been restored between his neighbors and him? What will Telemakhos do to assert himself as a man and an individual, now that he has started to come into his own but his bigger-than-life father has finally returned home in a blaze of bloody gore and glory?

Published in 1938 after nearly 13 years of compositional process, this work—twenty-four books long, like Homer's *Odyssey*, but three times the length of its ancient counterpart—served as a kind of summing up of the author's own life and thought. In brief, it is a poem seeking to define what human *freedom* is—a modernist twist to the Greek obsession with the relationship between free will and divinely ordained or Fate-mandated predetermination—and is written in iambic octameter (each verse 17 syllables long, so it's really "octameter plus"!) and might be seen in part as a response to the notion that we live "in an age when all scholars agreed that it was no longer possible to compose a long narrative poem based on myth."[243]

By comparison with the ancient epics, this poem invokes the sun, not the muses, in its prologue—and by comparison with Dante, each of whose three poems in the *Divine Comedy* ends up at the same place, beneath the stars, Kazantzakis ends his brief epilogue where he begins his prologue, addressing the sun. Indeed, the poet invokes the sun as well as fire and light in general throughout his poem, with their association, in Genesis ("let there be light!")—as well as with Helios and Apollo in the Greek tradition—with order and reason. Kazantzakis' Odysseus resonates from the Odysseus of a handful of previous poets also seeking to understand the great adventurer, beginning with Dante (the last three-quarters of *Inferno* 26—from verse 55 onward)—who is the first to imagine the fulfillment of Teiresias' prophecy regarding the hero's future, (that death will come to him from the sea, "in sleek old age"). Dante's Odysseus tells his visitor that

> I put out on the high and open sea
> with a single ship and only those few souls
> who stayed true when the rest deserted me.
>
> As far as Morocco and as far as Spain
> I saw both shores, and I saw Sardinia
> and the other islands of the open main. (94-99)
>
> ...Hercules' pillars rose upon our sight (103)
>
> ...we bore southwest out of the world of man;
> we made wings of our oars for our fool's flight. (116-17)
>
> At the fourth [crashing, swirling, spinning of their ship within a huge sea storm],
>   the poop rose and the bow went down
> till the sea closed over us and the light was gone. (130-31)[244]

Aside from Dante, Tennyson's poetically-conceived Odysseus, eager both for knowledge and to be free of the domestic drudgery that largely define his life back in Ithake, offered Kazantzakis a source of inspiration. And then, of course there was also the exquisite gem of a poem by the father of modern Greek poetry, Constantine Kavafis, whose poem, "Ithake" dwells on the magnificent journey of the hero as a gift to him from his home town—for it sent him forth on his adventures and brought him back.

Kazantzakis begins his own Book I with an emphasis on strife. Having in effect ignored the loving and reconciliatory parts of books Twenty-Three and Twenty-Four of the Homeric *Odyssey*, the poet begins with a description of Odysseus' bloody hands and body after the suitors' deaths—emphasizing the gore covering his groin as if to underscore crudely the relationship between sex/love and death. Penelope flees in horror, and quickly he is pre-occupied with subduing a revolt effected by the shades and families of the suitors, with wiles, though, and without more boodshed and with some help from Telemakhos—who is nonetheless represented as more than dismayed at the return of his gore-loving father, in spite of the tale Odysseus tells him of how he hopes that Nausikaa might become Telemakhos' wife.

At the feast that Odysseus organizes to celebrate his homecoming, he shocks everyone by offering a libation not to the gods but to the the intrepid human mind. But the court singer's song about Odysseus stirs up in him a fever of frustration that he is *here, home*, and not still engaaged in some fiery adventure. Athough he calms himself by walking by the sea, by Book II he is preparing to set sail once again. That book begins by the campfire the night after the feast where, gathered around him, his son, wife and father hear tales that he never shared with the Phaiakians. He puts things in an interesting manner: that death had approached him during his long homeward journey in three different guises. First as Kalypso, who offered him immortality, which tempted him until an oar washed up on the shore of her island, reminding him of what he needed to be doing—as we have noted earlier: immortality away from the *profanus* and its crazy business would be death for Odysseus, a man of constant, restless action. So he built a boat and sailed to within sight of Ithake, but was driven away by a storm.

In a delirious state he imagined himself visiting the immortal gods on Olympos, where they all in fact marveled at his mortal, aging body. In shifting the order of adventures from how they are presented in the Homeric epic, he next mentions Kirke, where he was tempted by passion for her—love/*eros*—to turn into a beast for her, to forget about human virtue and the importance of the soul, abandoning himself entirely to the delights of the flesh—and here, too, death-by-immortality was an option, but one that he rejected in the end, when he saw some simple fishermen, and a mother and her baby, all enjoying the basic human comforts of food and drink. This recalled him to everyday life—the *profanus*—with its joys and responsiblities.

So once more he built a boat, but was shipwrecked; washed up on the island of the Phaiakians, he was tempted to stay on with Nausikaa, living a normal but unassuming life—but came to recognize that kind of life, too, as a mask, a sweet one, for death. He left Nausikaa, then, but still hoped to return one day to her home and bring her to Ithake to be Telemakhos' bride, so that—even here we recognize the self-love that is emphatic for Odysseus—she might breed grandsons for him (not sons for his son, but grandsons for him).

It is, of course, a rather odd tale, given the audience. More intensely than in the Homeric epic, he may be seen to edit his experiences of women in Penelope's presence—although we might suppose that, as a child of his era, he might expect that she would assume that he had various women along the path of his travels. But to refer to his feelings for Kirke in terms that seem so strong shifts things somewhat from Homer's hero. One never has the sense that the Odysseus of Homer thought much beyond the physical satisfactions of being with either Kirke or Kalypso; and where Nausikaa was concerned he was never apparently even sexually interested, but was already fully focused on getting home to his wife when he met her.

In the *Odyssey*, the unalloyed joy and passion with which Penelope is represented as greeting her husband—once she is convinced that it is truly he—drowns out the questions that we might imagine her having about his relationships over the twenty years of his absence, just as it does the questions we might have about how old she has become in her husband's absence. Love dominates both that relationship and the one between Odysseus and Telemakhos; *eris* is reserved entirely for the relationship between Odysseus and the suitors (and their families). It is the unasked questions back in Homeric Ithake that, taken up by Kazantzakis, produce not only the manner of Odysseus' telling of his tales to his family, but their minimalist response and in particular the sense we receive of Penelope as a mere shadow of her Homeric counterpart.

The culmination of these tales of *eros* interwoven with thoughts of *thanatos* (death) and embedded within the *eris* that helped shape Book II and that will continue as the narrative moves forward is his realization when his tales have been told that Ithake itself is the most lethal mask of death of them all: a confining jail cell relationally dominated by an aging wife and an overly careful son. Soon thereafter, his father Laertes dies and he buries him, and he sends a ship laden with a substantial dowry to fetch Nausikaa — and decides to leave home forever: he is the wanderer who can never, ultimately, come home again. He gathers an odd crew of crusty veterans like himself (including Orpheus, whom the poet has transferred from an altogether different thread within the tapestry of traditional Greek mythology, to be the ship's singer).

Meanwhile, the women (and goddesses) whom he had bedded on his journeys, hearing of his return, send him the bastard sons and daughters whom he has begotten, and he puts them to work — the only one of them who provokes a sense of paternal love is his daughter by Kalypso. Meanwhile, Telemakhos, obviously frustrated with how things are going and not going, begins organizing a plot to assassinate his father. Summer arrives, however, and with it, Nausikaa, in her bridal ship, and a great wedding is celebrated.

It is during the wedding party — the feast of *eros* — that Odysseus detects signs of the assassination plot (*eris* in a serious vein) and confronts his son — rejoicing, however, to see him exercising such manliness. He promises to leave Ithake the next morning: so this most interesting twist to the *eros-eris* matrix offers a father who for the first time truly loves his son when he senses the eristic side of their relationship in an emphatic way: the son's murderous inclination toward him. When he leaves at dawn, he has looted his own palace of food and weapons and goes without sayng good-bye to either his son or his wife: so much for the compelling love that pulled Odysseus through ten (twenty, counting the war itself) years of experiences, (almost) always seeking home—the long-sought dream proved far less enticing once gained in reality.

As Book III opens, the hero is sailing for Sparta where, in his dreams, he imagines Helen as bored as he, longing to be adbucted again. And in Book IV, he will do just that, abduct Helen—recapitulating one of the beginning points of the Trojan War, of course—not to take her back to his home, however, but to take her along on the last and greatest adventure of his life. This he does after declaring his great love and eternal friendship for Menelaus at the feast organized to honor Odysseus' visit. In the early dawn after that evening celebration, at the end of which Menelaus is drunkenly asleep, Odysseus effects the abduction to which Helen readily assents; they are joined that morning by a brave shepherd boy who now constitutes the last member of Odysseus' small but skilled crew.

Love and strife are thus interwoven in the poem almost from its beginning and follows from book to book and adventure to adventure. Odysseus and his crew destroy Knossos (Book VIII) and foment rebellion in Egypt (Book X). They work their way south through Egypt and deeper into Africa, seeking the source of the Nile (Book XIII). In Book XIV, Odysseus communes with God on the top of a mountain; in Book XVI he becomes a renowned ascetic. He encounters diverse characters as we follow through Books XVIII-XXI and in Book XXII he builds his final boat and sets sail—by then, alone, having lost or left behind Helen and his crew—for the South Pole. We might here recall, as surely Kazantzakis intends us to, Teiresias' prophecy in Book 11 of the *Odyssey*, regarding Odysseus' eventual death, "in sleek old age," "from the sea"—as, one by one, all remaining landmarks disappear. He passes the antithetical limits of the world, the enormous, clashing mountains of Yes and No.

He gripped his tiller proudly, and his brave chest swelled,
for he knew these were Yes and No, Death's mountain peaks

that loomed at the world's end, that gaped and closed and smashed
all ships which dared to pass beyond the world's bound.
(XXII. 78-81)

—and his own life sweeps back to him through the portal of memory: the first woman with whom he had a liaison, when he first held his son, the first time he killed someone—as he reflects how on the question of questions:

What is this life, what secret yearning governs it?
There was a time I called its lavish longing God,
and talked and laughed and wept and battled by his side
and thought that he, too, laughed and wept and strove beside me,
but now I suddenly feel I've talked to my own shadow!
God is a labyrinthine quest deep in our heads;
weak slaves think that he's the isle of freedom, and more close,
all the incompetent ones cross their oars, then cross their hands,
laugh wearily and say, 'The Quest does not exist!
But I know better in my heart, and rig my sails:
God is wide waterways that branch throughout man's heart.
(409-19)

His real love affair has always been with life, even as, now, he prepares to face death. Indeed, his life-long struggle with death is subsuming less into a passive acceptance of death than as a paradoxically active embrace of it. This is Kazantzakis' own twist on love-death, in which turn *eros* and *eris* are *resolved* by death.

So: the poet opens book XXIII by invoking the

Great sun, O Father, Mother, Son, three-masted Good...(1)
Great Sun, you cast your warm wings on the nested eggs...(8)
O Sun, Great Son, profound joy of our earthen eyes,
hold us forever in your palm, hatch us, dear God,
turn all our feet to wings and all the earth to air. (17-19)

which invocation gradually angles itself toward an invocation of death:

> In a great blaze of wings and light, in salt embrace,
> make Death come riding down astride a gallant thought!
> Let Death come down to slavish souls and craven heads
> with his sharp scythe and barren bones, but let him come
> to this lone man like a great lord to knock with shame
> on his five famous castle doors, and with great awe
> plunder whatever dregs that in the ceaseless strife
> of his staunch body have not found time as yet to turn
> from flesh and bone into pure spirit, lightning, deeds, and joy.
> (25-33)

So: sun, fire, and light that are knowledge, wisdom—and life and love—and are the bringers of death: the end of strife and thus the beginning of love and life: of the spirit, sailing beyond the limits and limitations of the body. Through Death, all the hero's goods will have

> ...escaped you [the Archer; Time] in pure spirit, and when you come,
> you'll find but trampled fire, embers, ash, and fleshly dross. (36-37)

The shadowy form of Death appears on the prow of Odysseus' boat, assuming a diversity of shapes until settling into a very reocgnizable one: that of the hero himself, feature for feature—each of us carries death within ourselves, nourishing and nurturing him within our decaying bodies as we grow—who welcomes his long-term companion aboard.

> He gathered all his memories, held Time in his hands.
> like a thick ball of musk and smelled it in the wastes
> with flaring nostrils till his mind was drenched with scent....
> (234-6)

> And as Odysseus smelled the ripe and flaming fruit,
> A sweet swoon seized him, all his entrails came unstitched...
> (243-44)

Chapter Eleven 483

> The five tumultuous elements that strove for years
> to forge the famous form of the world-wandering man
> shifted and parted now and slowly said farewell—
> earth, water, fire, air, and the mind, keeper of keys… (248-51)

He invokes and praises the women—woman—in his life, for only with love are the barriers of the flesh broken and the source of life penetrated. He dozes and dreams—of his ancestors, and of his father (all, of course, dead); all the elements of the *profanus* world pour though his *sacer*-dreaming mind in a last farewell.

He awakes, joyful at seeing Death still sitting on the prow of his boat—awakened from *sacer*, death-like sleep he sees *sacer* Death as the sun-filled waking state of life—but the figure suddenly vanishes. He recognizes that his own end is drawing near, recalling the fires of burning Troy (for the strife-ridden dispute over the love of Helen) and of the Knossos that he torched *with* Helen, and he blesses those five elements that comprise his physical self. He dreams, again, of God creating and of the growing pride and power of humans—and in revolt and freedom he chases God away from earth and up into the sky. This is a post-pagan, post-Christian vision dreamed by an existentialist Odysseus.

An iceberg apporaches and crashes into his boat, and he leaps onto the cold glistening wall—it will be his final vessel—his hands bloodied, his weapons falling away; the cold wind strips him bare. Seven crows—note well the number! completion and perfection—lean crows, which have followed him since his birth, gather around his feet; his seven souls (an idea directly derived from ancient Egyptian religion) row about him on a cloud.[245] The five elements of his body begin to disconnect; only Love and Memory remain; the hero's consciousness, his robust spirit, leaps like a flame from its wick, glows for a moment, and disappears completely.

The fire of memory still blazes, though, gathering all the souls that it has loved on earth into itself: "O faithful and beloved, O dead and living comrades, come!" (1315)—both dead and living, because ultimately the boundary between those two realms has been eradicated, just as that between *eros* and *eris* has been dissolved. The problem of irony with regard to mortality and immortality with which ancient Greek literature begins is solved within this signal epic expression of modern Greek poetry.

This is how, in the last book, Odysseus, gone but not gone, his spirit having been reduced to a soul-flame that has disappeared, is yet *there*, alone and naked in the boat, sailing into his death, sinking into the earth even as he is dissoved into the sea. The four winds smash open the four gates of his head: plants rush in through the north gate; and animals, birds and insects rush in through the south gate; and thoughts and dreams and imagination's creations through the east gate, while through the west gate hordes of men of every race and type flow in—all lodged within the vast urban labyrinth of his memory. All of those who had mattered in his life, as well as sages from the West and the East—all those kept alive through the love embedded in his memory—in response to the hero's sky-cleaving cry that he will not give up his soul without his dying and dead companions, rise from their graves or their deathbeds to join him on that boat, helping to shepherd him into the realm of Hades.

Three "forefathers"—Fates in the form of Prometheus, Tantalos, and Herakles—root themselves on the deck of the boat, like three solid, soaring masts from which pomegranates, figs, and grapes are hung by the womenfolk, and the boat gows like a floating garden. The universe merges into a flame and mind soars like fire, longing to burn everything away into no-thingness yet again.

The hero's last gesture is to laugh—

> and his eyes cleansed and emptied, his full heart grew light,
> for Life and Death were songs, his mind the singing bird. (1382-3)

—and to thrust his hands into the three fruits hanging on his Fate-masts and to disappear:

> All the great body of the world-roamer turned to mist,
> and slowly his snow-ship, his memory, fruit, and friends
> drifted like fog far down the sea, vanished like the dew. (1387-9)

His mind "leapt to the peak of its holy freedom," and fluttering, "soared high and freed itself from its last cage, its freedom." (1391/93).

In the brief, 22-line epilogue, the poet again invokes the sun—that is setting, in the third verse—ultimate symbol of the transmutation of all matter into fire, light, and spirit. The sun and the earth lament: "today I've seen my loved one vanish like a dwindling thought." (22) The hero is the beloved child of earth and sun—and sea and sky—who, like all heroes and non-heroes, vanishes, but is still among us, sung in these many verses. The setting of the sun with the opening of the epilogue suggests that the entire gargantuan Kazantzakian narrative has encompassed only a day—albeit a *sacer* day that is as short as it is endless, in which love and strife and all other antitheses meet at an indefinable *sacer* point of timeless time and spaceless space.

II Derek Walcott's *Omeros* and the Common Man

As Kazantzakis translates the terms of the *Odyssey* into a heroic post-myth myth, Derek Walcott (1930-2017) translates the terms of the *Iliad* into the everyday world of poor Carribean fisherfolk—specifically on the island of St Lucia in the West Indies—in his own epic poem, *Omeros*.[246] His 1990 epic is written in a loosely-rhyming non-metrical (i.e., prose-like) version of *terza rima* and organized into seven books divided into 64 chapters with further subdivisions, offering as its key characters, not only the key figures with *Iliad*-reminiscent names—Akhille, Hector, and Helen, as well as Philoktete—but others, such as Ma Kilman, who runs the local food and herb and rum shop (and who, by the end of the narrative, we will understand, is a modern avatar of the Cumaean sibyl who led Aeneas into the Underworld to learn of Rome's destiny); the English officer, Major Plunkett and his wife, Maud; and also the blind man, Seven Seas, who represents Homer himself—and the narrator-author himself.

The work is conceived in a kind of lattice structure reminiscent of the *Iliad*. It interweaves the relational issues of humans and the elements (in lieu of humans and the fates or the gods), humans and humans—specifically men and men and men and women—and *eros* and *eris*, as well as mortality and immortality. Walcott's is a world far from Troy—although, as the narrative moves forward, more and more will seem obviously to be held in common with it—as is clear from the first tercet:

> "This is how, one sunrise, we cut down them canoes."
> Philoctete smiles for the tourists, who are taking
> his soul with their cameras.... (I.I.1-3)
>
> I lift my axe and pray for strength in my hands
> to wound the first cedar. Dew was filling my eyes,
> but I fire one more white rum. Then we advance." (I.13-15)

That last line hints at where the poem may go: the cutting down of trees for canoes, necessary in order to fish and therefore to eat, is spoken of in military terms: "we advance."

We are introduced to Achille in the second part of this first chapter: he is in fact trimming a tree, hoping to produce a canoe from it: "Tree, you can be a canoe! Or else you cannot!" (II.12) By the end of that section, the pirogues are lined up, "crouched in the sand like hounds with sprigs in their teeth" (II.52-3)—so we quickly recognize how adept Walcott is at performing one of Homer's most noteworthy feats: the use of interesting similes—the priest has sprinkled them, before they go out to fish. The priest smiles at the spelling of the name of Akhille's boat—*In God We Troust*—but

> "Achille said "Leave it! Is God' spelling and mine." (II.55-6)

We are also introduced to Hector. For at sunrise the canoes enter the sea, and their nodding prows

> agreed with the waves to forget their lives as trees;
> one would serve Hector and another, Achilles. (II.59-60)

In fact, the whole crowd of fishermen is noted by name (lightly resonating with the sounds of the *Iliad* Book II's "catalogue of ships") as Chapter II begins. Besides Hector and Achille, there are Theophile, Placide, Pancreas, Chysostom, Maljo, "Philoctete with his head white as a coiled surf"—and with a sore from a scraping, rusted anchor, on his shin, that remains unhealed—and all of them with only first names ("Christian names").[247]

We are introduced early on to the poet's play not only between names evoking Greek antiquity and those that do not and between the key characters and their Homeric counterparts, but also between the poet as a poet and as a chracter, Dante-like, (but also Latin elegist-like), within his narrative. Seven Seas, up before dawn at the outset of section II of chapter II is and is not the one who intones to the poet

> O open this day with the conch's moan, Omeros,
> as you did in my boyhood, when I was a noun
> gently exhaled from the palate of the sunrise. (II.II.40-42)
>
> ....Only in you, across centuries
> of the sea's parchment atlas, can I catch the noise
> of the surf lines wandering like the shambling fleece
>
> of the lighthouse's flock, that Cyclops whose blind eye
> shut from the sunlight... (II.46-59)

We taste the allusions to that Mediterranean antiquity like the salt spray: is "my boyhood, when I was a noun" the childhood of Seven Seas or is it the epic poem recited by the blind poet who was Seven Seas' antecedent by three millennia? Is the Cyclops just a colorful metaphor for the lighthouse light or that edifice's imagined ancestor who was blinded by Odysseus (and avoided by Aeneas)?

And Omeros? That ancient poet, his name pronounced as it would have been by his contemporaries? Or the poet of the poem called "Omeros"—addressed by his ancestor's conceptual descendant, Seven Seas? Indeed, (as the third section of chapter II begins),

> "O-meros," she laughed. "That's what we call him in Greek,"
> stroking the small bust with its boxer's broken nose,
> and I thought of Seven Seas sitting near the reek
>
> of drying fishnets, listening to the shallows' noise.
> I said: "Homer and Virg are New England farmers,
> and the winged horse guards their gas-station, you're right."
> (III.1-6)

"She" is a somewhat Asiatic-looking young woman, Antigone—another name claimed from Greek antiquity—and a guest in the studio of, well, Omeros, which is, presumably, to say, the poet/narrator, in which there sits a bust of Homer. The studio is in New England (mirroring the teaching location-experience of Walcott himself), and Antigone, the raven-haired beauty, both yearns to go back to Greece and evokes in the poet, Omeros, his own desire to return to St Lucia. Other desires are invoked, as well—of course. The context offers the first hint of *eros*, but as a frame outside the story of Achille, Hector and Helen down on that sun-swallowed island.

Eris introduces itself with the very beginning of chapter III, as an argument—that sways back and forth between English and the French patois of St Lucia—between Achille and Hector over a tin that Achille was in the act of borrowing, without permission, from Hector's canoe, to bail water out of his own. The villagers gather to see the face-off—Hector with a cutlass nad Achille apparently unarmed—that will explode at the edge of the water, mirroring the explosions of the surf itself. Hector charges Achille,

> his cutlass lifted. The surf, in anger, gnashing
> its tail llike a foaming dogfight. Men can kill
>
> their own brothers in rage, but the madman who tore
> Achille's undershirt from one shoulder also tore
> at his heart. The rage that he felt against Hector
>
> was shame. To go crazy for an old bailing tin
> crusted with rust! The duel of these fishermen
> was over a shadow and its name was Helen. (III.I.29-37)

The pieces are beginning to fall into place: the strife between the two male protagonists—the same two, by name, as in the eristic denouement of the *Iliad*—over the love of a woman. But the ancient woman by the same name was the bone of contention between Menelaus and Paris/Alexandros, not Ackhilleus and Hektor—both of whom were in conflict at Troy for others' reasons, but who ultimately faced off because of Akhilleus' love for Patroklos and love for and anger at himself. And while Hektor had no choice because Paris was his brother and the Troy that he was defending was his own city, Akhilleus had a choice—but had no choice, because he was *shamed* by Odysseus into coming to Troy.

So Walcott's *eris/eros* kernel resonates from Homer's, but at a number of oblique angles simultaneously. So, too, the other figures and their details—like Philoctete, whose wound won't heal and who

> ...believed the swelling came from the chained ankles
> of his grandfathers. Or else why was there no cure? (III.10-11)

For this is a tale about everyday people, poor black people, living on an island—the sort of people whom Odysseus and Agamemnon and the other Akhaian nobility would have thought of as beneath thinking about—less, perhaps, even, than Thersites[248]— and they are on this island not as the Trojans or Akhaians were at Troy, but because only a few generations back their grandparents or great-grandparents had been forced from their homes in Africa and deposited in this part of the world as slaves.

The community of the poem is, in fact, a more complex and odder one than that. For it includes the aforementioned Major Plunkett and his wife, Maud, whom we meet in the first section of Chapter V—Brits who have established themselves in retirement on this sunny isle, on a farm (she raises orchids)—and who stop in the straw-roofed bar every afternoon at the same hour for his Guinness and her ale. So they come from that race and culture particularly involved in the slavery process—although the Major and Maud, of course, were born far too late to have been part of that. On the contrary, he was part of the war to save the world from Nazism, and was wounded fighting the renowned German tank commander, Rommel, in North Africa. Sadness overwhelms him along with memory of those events—every afternoon along with his drink—and out of the silence that prevails between him and Maud, she reaches across the table

> and grip[s] his fingers. He knew she could see inside
> the wound in his head. His white nurse. His officer (V.I.74-5)

Their love, then, is a quiet one, intimately interwoven around his memory—and her sort of understanding of his memory—of the *eris* that he survived.

That eristic era, stretching back another generation and for too many generations, really, forms part of the backdrop for what is ultimately the heart of the narrative. At the end of Chapter V, the signing of a British-French treaty at Versailles—but wasn't that a different war? Does it matter? In any case the references to war are interspersed with the passing of Helen across the sight lines of Maud and Major Plunkett—wearing a dress that Maud had altered for her, tragically lacking a history (in the Major's estimation), and she tells lies too often (in Maud's estimation)—and then we learn, too, that the village has an Olympiad every year on St. Peter's Day in which the Major fires the starting flare gun.

...Hector

would win, or Achille by a hair; but everyone
knew as the crossing ovals of their thighs would soar
in jumps down the cheering aisle, or their marathon

six times round the village, that the true bounty was
Helen, not a shield nor the ham saved for Christmas;
as one slid down the greased pole to factional roars. (V.III. 93-99)

And so on. The real story is about Helen and Achille as troubled lovers tryng to make life work, mixing their *eros* with *eris*—as Hector competes with Achille for Helen's affections. It is, to repeat, about the struggles of men with each other interwoven with the struggles between a man and a woman, played out against the fierce and unforgiving forces of nature—all resonating with clarity and subtley from the world of Troy and Ithake and Mykenai and Sparta. Chapter IX, section III begins by describing

[t]he Cyclone, howling because one of the lances
of a flinging palm has narrowly grazed his one eye,
wades knee-deep in troughs. As he blindly advances,

Lightning, his stilt-walking messenger, jiggers the sky
with his forked stride, or he crackles over the troughs
like a split electric wishbone. His wife, Ma Rain,

hurls buckets from the balcony of her upstairs house. (IX.III.1-7)

And so — as these verses push into the next, and we move toward hurricane season — the charactars wrestle with nature, but Cyclone is also a pun on Cyclops, with his one eye poked out by Odysseus with a burning log, so that the classical background and the natural background merge.

The narrative spins around the everyday events that link all of these everyday people, coming back again and again to the Hector-Achille-Helen trio either directly or through their interactions with the others or the others' perceptions of them. Chapter XXIII, section III, within the Second Book — for instance — finds Maud watching a liner (she wishes she could go back to Ireland but Plunkett finds the prices for passage prohibitive) that periodically docks at the island harbor, in the midst of her gardening. She sees a girl approaching and recognizes her as Helen, as men one by one stop their work to watch her go by. Maud's perspective is hostile — eristic, one might certainly say — as she considers Helen's almond eyes and smooth face to be carved of arrogance, "then hated herself for her rage. Those lissome calves, that waist swayed like a palm was her island's weather..." (XXIII.III.32-33).

The center of the interaction that follows is Maud's anger that Helen, she believes, is there to seek employment from Maud:

come back looking for work after ruining two men,
after trying on my wardrobe, after driving Hector
crazy with a cutlass, you dare come, that what you mean?
(III.52-4)

But she is wrong:

"We've no work, Helen." "Is not work I looking for."
Pride edged that voice; she'd honed her arrogance
on Maud's nerves when she worked here, but there was sorrow
in the old rudeness. (III.55-8)

It turns out that Helen wants to borrow five dollars—and that she is pregnant—but how will she pay Maud back if she is not working? and

"It's none of my business, but what happened to Achille?

Hector not working?"
                  "I am vexed with both of them, *oui*."
What was it in men that made such beauty evil?
She was as beautiful as a liner, but like it, she

changed her course, she turned her back on her friends.
"I'll fetch my purse." Maud said. Helen turned her back
and stared out to sea. This is how all beauty ends.

When Maud came with the money, she was down the track
with the arrogant sway of that hip, stern high in the line
of the turned liner. Maud stood, enraged, in the sun.

Then she picked up the flower Helen had wrenched from the
    vine.
The allamandas lasted three days. Their trumpets would bend
and their glory pass. But she'd last forever, Helen. (III.63-75)

The lynchpin—as in the Trojan war—is Helen and her beauty. Helen who is the focal point of Hector and Achille, but neither of whom can provide her with the limited funds that she needs. Helen and her beauty will last forever—if not the beauty of this or any Helen in particular, yet the beauty of "Helen," as a concept, will. It's what Maud resents and admires; it's what hypnotizes her so that her eristic thoughts translate into a loving act—what else can one call that almost unquestioning response of going for her wallet?—that is not, in the end, accepted; Helen has already walked away, toward the sea.

The epic plays on, book to book, chapter to chapter, section to section, like the untiring roll of waves onto the island's beaches and the unchanging battle of the protagonists with those waves as they head out to bring in food from the sea. The fact that many have perished—and the names of a few of these, as well as those who perished in the Middle Passage—is part of the mental itinerary of Achille in section II of Chapter XXIV, the last chapter in Book Two, as he is some twenty miles away from shore, baking in the sun. He even "saw the ghost of his father's face shoot up at the end of the line" (XXIV.II.86-7)—all of which mental activity caused him, "for the first time, [to ask] himself who he was" (90). He "questioned his name and his origin" (III.7).

This question of self-knowledge and of identity—that carries back to Akhilleus and his decision to come to Troy in order to fulfill his fate of *being Akhilleus*; and to Odysseus' quest to find out who he is as much as to find his home, which double quest led him to the outermost edge of reality and Teiresias' prophecies—slips like Achille's pirogue into Book Three and its opening Chapter XXV, beginning with the description of

> Mangroves, their ankles in water, [which] walked with the canoe.
> The swift, racing its browner shadow, screeched, then veered into a dark inlet. It was the last sound Achille knew
>
> from the other world. He feathered the paddle, steered away from the grouping mangroves, whose muddy shelves slipped warted crocodiles, slitting the pools of their eyes...
> (XXV.I.1-6)

as the hero comes home, guided by the sea-swift.

> Women paused at their work, then smiled at the warrior returning from his battle with smoke, from the kingdom where he had been captured, they cried and were happy.
> (XXV.III.13-15)

Or is he still out to sea? He sees a man striding toward him: his father; "he was moving with the dead" and converses at *loving* length with his progenitor—about the meaning and import of their names, Afolabe and Achille. For without meaning to their names, meaning itself—and they themselves—are lost, at sea, lost to the white foam, lost to both past and future. Lost.

It is not until chapter XXIX that the narrative focus shifts from Achille—this combination of ancient Akhilleus and Odysseus, Willy Loman, and whatever he is that is beyond and apart from all of them—and turns toward Helen, and to Hector.[249] At noon, Helen is pulling dried sheets from the line strung in Hector's yard, her heart pummelled by the call of a dove:

> ...not Helen now, but Penelope,
> in whom a single noon was as long as ten years,
> because he had not come back, because they had gone
>
> from yesterday, because the fishermen's fears
> spread in the surfing trees... (XXIX.I.16-20)

She worries that he might not come back, this time—because every time he sails away that question must be asked, and not because of Kyklopes or Skilla and Kharybdis, but because of the simple and straightfoward forces of nature, the vast sea in which Akhille and Hector—and which of these two is the focus of her concern?—and the other fishermen pass in their small pirogues. She sprawls alone, stripped naked on her bed, remembering Akhille in that bed, and in her body, just yesterday. But he *does* return (by the end of Chapter XXX), and sees Helen, and watches her leave the beach with him in sight. (Has her sense of *eros* for him turned to *eris* in her anger at the fear his absence installed within her? Or is it because she is living with Hector?)

And in the last chapter (XXXII) of Book Three, the narrator interweaves himself among the other threads of his story: it is he—Derek Walcott—leaving the island, again, not to sail out in a carved-out canoe for fish but to return to the States for his teaching livelihood, and speaking to his old mother, "on the verandah with her white hair" (XXXII.II.1), sewing and ripping the stitches that she finds not good enough. There is that resonance of Penelope, weaving and undoing her weaving, isn't there? And whose heart, filled with love, is more likely to break, a mother's or a wife's (Odysseus' mother dies of heartbreak, we may recall; he saw her where he saw Teiresias and the others, and tried three times without success to embrace her), when that son or husband goes off? Is it an eristic break at being left behind with one's sewing or one's son and/or a gaggle of suitors?

The poet watches, he tells us, "enlarged by the lamp, a stuttering moth" (II.33)—the last image he offers before he turns away to leave—and in the next section, III, "the moth's swift shadow rippled on an emerald lagoon" in the Gors Ilet village where, in the last tercet of Book Three, we return to Achille, watching "our minnow plane melt into cloud-coral over the horned island" (III.8-9). The hero watches the inconceivable departure of the poet who is writing about the hero.

Book Four in fact begins by following the poet in his spare life lived up in New England and his travels through different parts of the States, out among the sites where Native Americans and Africans suffered—noting, almost in passing, in the midst of section II of Chapter XXXV, and in referencing his own son, how

... More and more we learn to do without
those we love. With my father it was the same. (XXXV.II.17-18)

—as his own journey of discovery—his own odyssey—across the continent, with references to its museum paintings (Homer's— *Winslow* Homer's—*The Gulf Stream*) and its literature (Melville's "great American novel," *Moby Dick* and its sea-swallowed protagonists) continues, always with a verse here or there that analogizes his own experience to that of one of his characters: Achille usually, or Philoctete once.

He journeys, still, and reaches the opposite shore of the wide Atlantic: to Lisbon's wharf, progenitor of the first modern-era European explorers on the high seas (and an early partner in the slave-trade triangle that involved Europe, West Africa, and the Americas). And on to England and then further, Ireland—the ancestral world of Maud Plunkett. He turns toward the heated south, the Aegean pocket within the large Internal Sea through so many parts of which Odysseus sailed, to Istanbul—and back to New England, his mind and imagination outpacing any and every ship, past or present. Once again the era of emerging North America, and the ground-under Natives are evoked, and "I walked like a Helen among their dead warriors" (XLIII.II.33)—that is: as the embodiment of *eros* among the aftermath of *eris* at its ugliest.

But look carefully at the text: the "I" is not merely the poet, it's the voice of an older Sioux squaw who has survived the massacre administered by white men to her people—and she continues into the third section of this chapter:

"This was history. I had no power to change it.
And yet I felt that this had happened before.
I knew it would happen again, but how strange it

was to have seen it in Boston, in the heath-fire.
I was a leaf in the whirlwind of the Ordained.
Then Omeros's voice came from the mouth of the tent:

'We galloped towards death wept by exaltation
of meeting ourselves in a place just like this one:
The Ghost Dance has tied the tribes into one nation.'" (XLIII.III.1-9)

As the poet—Omeros—speaks through the voices of his characters, the anonymous grey-haired Sioux woman speaks through the voice of Omeros, who is the voice of the tribes unified against the invader through a new dance ritual, in 1890,[250] but ultimately destroyed by him as Troy was destroyed by the Akhaians, at which time and place Helen of Sparta, Menelaus' stolen wife and the concubine of Paris/Alexandros—she the symbol of erotic beauty who became the symbol of consummate *eris* for that world—wandered among the dead she had come to know in the previous decade. This, just before she would be carried back, unscathed, to the Sparta where one day Telemakhos would meet her while searching for his unknown and beloved father, when the love between Menelaus and Helen would offer questions as to how real it is or ever was.

The poet is still wrapped in his own recollections—of his travels and of the dispersal of Native Americans before the oncoming Europeans—as Book Six (Chapter XLIV) begins. While a fierce storm pours out its wrath, he lay in bed

with current gone from the bed-lamp and heard the roar
of wind shaking the windows, and I remembered

Achille on his own mattress and desperate Hector
trying to save his canoe. I thought of Helen
as my island was lost in the haze, and I was sure

I'd never see her again. (XLIV.I. 26-31)

    We might suddenly wonder: is the poet in love with Helen? Has she become for him like the statue created by Pygmalion in the Greek tradition conveyed by Ovid?[251] The poet's own creation that he would embrace as surely as Propertius would Cynthia and Dante Beatrice—albeit each in such different ways, as the females in question offer such different kinds of questionable reality?
    Perhaps so. He returns, in any case, to Helen's world by way of Hector (Chapter XLV)—driving a vehicle, a Comet, ferrying tourists along the curvacious roads of his island, somehow, as the poet returns to visit, driven by another driver who tells him over his shoulder, (and tells us), that Hector was a real road-warrior.

"...He would drive like a madman when the power took.
He had a nice woman. Maybe he died for her." (XLV.III.11-12)

. . .

He'd paid the penalty of giving up the sea
as graceless and as treacherous as it had seemed,
for the taxi-business; he was making money

but all of that money was making him ashamed
of the long afternoons of shouting by the wharf
hustling passengers. He missed the uncertain sand

under his feet, he sighed for the trough of a wave,
and the jerk of the oar when it turned in his hand,
and the rose conch sunset with its slow pelicans.

Castries was corrupting him with its roaring life,
its littered market, with too many transport vans
competing. Castries had been his common-law wife

who, like Helen, he had longed for from a distance,
and now he had both, but a frightening discontent
hollowed his face; to find that the sea was a love

he could never lose made every gesture violent. (III. 31-46)

The fisherman gave up the sea and his canoe for a taxicab; he abandoned the village for the town—perhaps because he sought a better living (if not a better life), or perhaps because he sought escape from the love he could not achieve, Helen, even *if* he nominally *had* her, and the internal *eris* that churned his inner heart—and while he found a firmer economic base he lost himself and his soul, it would seem, and, never losing, merely redirecting, that inner churning, lost his life far from the walls of Troy or the crushing waves and rocks of the sea.

So the funeral for Hektor, breaker of horses, celebrated at the end of the *Iliad*, becomes the funeral for Hector the fisherman-turned-cab-driver in the opening lines of Chapter XLVI:

Hector was buried near the sea he had loved once.
Not too far from the shallows where he had fought Achille
for a tin and Helen... (XLVI.I.1-3)

. . .

...Crouching for his friend to hear,
Achille whispered about their ancestral river,
and those things he would recognize when he got there,

his true home, forever and ever and ever,
forever, *compere*. Then Philoctete limped over
and rested his hand firmly on a shaking shoulder

to anchor his sorrow. Seven Seas and Helen
did not come nearer. Achille had carried an oar
to the church and propped it outside with the red tin.

Now his voice strengthened. He said, "Mate, this is your spear..." (I.13-22)

And this is where love resides: within the profound friendship, the sense of common roots wrapped around whatever strife existed, between Hector and Achille. Hector is not Hektor but Patroklos to this Achille who is not Akhilleus but his own everday hero, in whose mind the poet puts the words that place his relationship with Hector "beyond vexation" and drenches it in admiration and mutual knowledge. His unstated words "I know how well you treat her" (I.28) cannot fail to raise the question: who is "her"? Is it Helen? Or is it the sea—*la mer*, female in the gendered grammar of both French and French patois?

Achille looks up, sees her, (Helen), reaches to the grave and lifts the tin toward her and she nods—and

> Pride set in Helen's face after this, like a stone
> bracketed with Hector's name; her lips were incised
> by its dates in parentheses. She seemed more stern
>
> more ennobled by distance as she slowly crossed
> the hot street of the village like a distant sail
> on the horizon. Grief heightened her... (II. 1-6)

—and she is pregnant, still, but with whose child? It is apparently Hector's. Achille learned, perhaps through Hector's death or perhaps through his relationship with Helen or perhaps through both relationships and still other relationships, "that there is no error in love, of feeling the wrong love for the wrong person" (XLVIII.I. 48-9).

But this chapter mainly belongs to Ma Kilman—and to Philoktete, whom she can cure of his uncurable wound: as

> [t]he wild, wire-haired, and generously featured
> apotheosis of the caverned prophetess
> began... (II.1-3)

and after the myriad processes of her method and methods of her process—including babbling in the language of the ants and of her great-grandmother, and brew of the root in which she bathed him,

> ...and the sun
> put the clouds to its ears as her screech reeled backwards
> to its beginning, from the black original cave
> of the sibyl's mouth... (II.39-42)

—he is cured.

That act of healing love brings us, like a boomerang, back to our question regarding the poet, who "felt the wrong love leaving me where I stood on the cafe balcony facing the small square" (XLIX.III.1-2), and who "imagined [the fine rain] cooling the bubbling pits of the Malbolge" (III.12-13—a Dantean vision that reminds us of the potential identity between poet and his hero—and who multiplies his relationship to Dante with his reference to drying roofs glittering "with an interior light like Lucia's" (III.21), punning within this context on the name of his West Indian island and on the name of the third female, together with Beatrice and the Virgin Mary, who shepherd the poet-pilgrim of *The Divine Comedy* into Paradise. Ah yes, that question: of whether he, the poet, is in love with Helen—who is in any case, the starting point of his inspiration, his Beatrice.

For as he felt the wrong love leaving him—perhaps because he has learned from his hero, Achille, that there is no such thing as the wrong love, so that concept will have left the now-better-informed poet—and felt an elation as the drying roofs glittered after the rain with an interior light like Lucia's

> and my joy was pounding like a stallion's hooves
> on a morning beach scattering the crabbed wrestlers
> near Helen's wall to this thudding metre it loves. (III.22-24)

—he adds:

> Of course we loved each other, but differently,
> as we loved the island. My braceleted Circe
> was gone, like the shining drizzle, far now, at sea,
>
> but the Caribbean ringed me with infinite mercy
> as did the island... (III.25-29)

Can it—must it—not be Helen-Beatrice about whom these last two statements are offered: that they loved each other *differently* (he loved her like one of the *fideli d'amore*...) but that she is now gone; and that she is a sorceress-goddess who kept him on her island for, say, a year, (so she is also Kirke), through the force of her beauty and her love? He, the poet, who—unlike Achille, who merely sailed and rowed bravely out in a canoe a distance of some twenty miles from the island's shore—travelled across America and across the Atlantic and around the Mediterranean, like a contemporary Odysseus?

But if the baby that Helen carries is Hector's where does that leave Achille and the poet—and if Hector is dead, (and what difference does it make whether he was killed in an auto accident, rather than having drowned somewhere out at sea, or been devoured by sharks?), where *does* that leave love and strife, with or without Helen as its focus? Nor—by the way—is he the only one to die in this war with island life. Maud died, in the morning, in her bed, of cancer (Chapter LII)—and the Major mourned piteously for all that she had been to him and for him for so long. "He rubbed their names against her stomach" as she lay there. "'Maud, Maud, it's Dennis, love, Maud.' Then he stretched beside her, as if they were statues on a stone tomb" (LII.I.21-3). No strife there, only love, at least at this point, reclining alongside death that begets no rebirth in the *profanus* realm.

It is at Maud's funeral (Chapter LIII), embedded within the incomprehensible eloquence of Major Plunkett's eulogy for his wife, that our poet sees Helen, in her mourning veil, and Philoctete together with Achille (the latter in a worn black suit)—both he and Helen still buried in mourning for Hector—and wonders what Achille and the other fisherfolk are doing here who surely cannot even understand Plunkett's words. "Could he, in that small suit too tight at the shoulders, who shovelled the pens in the rain at Plunkett's, love him" (LIII.I.36-38)? Is the latticed web of love that veils this magical island of memory and imagination composed of more threads than one might have supposed, hidden until death and poetry came and revealed them?

As for the poet, he

>...knew little about Maud Plunkett. I knew I was here
> because the Major had trained us all as cadets.
> What I shared with his wife we shared as gardeners. (II.1-3)
>
> I was both there and not there. I was attending
> the funeral of a character I'd created;
> the fiction of her life needed a good ending
>
> as much as mine... (II. 13-16)

He watches his other creations—Achille, Philoctete, and Helen—as the Major acknowledges them and as they watch the hearse being filled up with orchids and as "Helen, in that slow walk of hers" (III.12) comes over to Achille, and, lifting her veil, says "'I coming home.' Then he and Philoctete walked with her to the transports near the Coal Market" (III. 14-15).

The next morning, (Chapter LIV) he sees the Major at the bank who asks: "'Our wanderer's home, is he?' I said: 'For a while, sir'" (LIV.I. 25). The poet has come home to St Lucia as Helen has come home to Achille, drawn by love and driven by death, at least for a while. The encounter provokes a memory of a time, years earlier, apparently, when both Plunkett and the poet sought somehow to quell what they each saw differently as Helen's arrogance. But he wonders why he cannot simply see Helen "as the sun saw her, with no Homeric shadow's winging her plastic sandals on that beach alone, as free as the sea-wind?" (II. 24-7). Memory provokes the further rhetorical question:

> ...When would the sails drop
>
> from my eyes, when would I not hear the Trojan War
> in two fishermen cursing in Ma Kilman's shop?
> When would my head shake off its echoes like a horse
>
> shaking off a wreath of flies? When would it stop,
> the echo in the throat, insisting, "Omeros";
> when would I enter that light beyond metaphor? (III.6-12)

Did Walcott divide his narrative into seven books simply because he *did*—or was he thinking of the importance of that number across the history of thought as a symbol of completion and sometimes perfection? It is from the perspective of the beginning of this last, seventh book (and its first chapter, Chapter LVI) that he, the poet, stands at sunrise on the balcony of his white hotel and surveys the calm sweep of the January sea and the shifting of shapes in the foam. One of these assumes the form of Omeros, who then becomes the foam-haired Seven Seas.

Hurrying down to the beach, the poet follows that form and claims to him that he saw him in London, clutching his manuscript—and to have read part of it.

> I heard my mouth babbling as ice glazed over my chest.
> "The gods and the demi-gods aren't much use to us."
> "Forget the gods," Omeros growled, "and read the rest."
>
> Then there was the silence any injured author
> knows, broken by the outcry of a frigate-bird,
> as we both stared at the blue dividing water,
>
> and in the gulf, I muttered, "I have alwys heard
> your voice in that sea, master, it was the same song
> of the desert shaman, and when I was a boy
>
> your name was as wide as a bay, as I walked along
> the curled brow of the surf; the word 'Homer' meant joy,
> joy in battle, in work, in death… (LVI.III. 16-27)

When Omeros asks our poet—which is, to say, Walcott—who gave hm the correct name of Homer, he responds "a girl"—but cannot, or purports not to be able, to remember who she was or from where. And what's the difference, now?

> None, maybe, to you, but a girl . . . that's very nice.
> Her image rises out of every battle's noise.
> A girl smells better than a book. I remember Helen's

smell. The sun on her flesh. The light's coin on my eyes.
That ten years' war was nothing, an epic's excuse. (III.40-45)

Indeed. The book is a strife-ridden struggle, the wresting of its content and style out of the mind and the wrestling of its verbal colors into words. Better the undersanding of the poet's own name, at least, gotten from a girl, like Helen, a source of beauty and love, than from a dusty epic's pages:

Beyond these stone almonds [her eyes] I can see Comte de Grasse
pacing like horned Menelaus while his wife swings
her sandals by one hand, strutting a parapet,

knowing that her beauty is what no man can claim
any more than this bay. Her beauty stands apart
in a golden dress, its beaches wreathed with her name. (LVII. III. 7-12)

So if that ancient *Helen* is this *Helen*, then this contemporary *Hector* is that ancient *Menelaus*—bull-like but also horned-as-cuckolded into the Great War at Troy for the love and lust of her or perhaps, ego slighted, more for the love of himself, and the love of plunder. And she, like the beauteously curved bay of light, is a force of nature against which men may strive but which they can never conquer, like

…the ocean, [which] had

no memory of the wanderings of Gilgamesh,
or whose sword severed whose head in the *Iliad*.
It was an epic where every line was erased

yet freshly written in sheets of exploding surf… (LIX.I. 34-7)

. . .

…It never altered its metre
to suit the age, a wide page without metaphors.

Chapter Eleven 505

Our last resort as much has yours, Omeros. (I. 43-45)

. . .

Why waste time on Achille, a shade on the sea-floor?
Because strong as self-healing coral, a quiet culture
is branching from the white ribs of each ancestor,

deeper than it seems on the surface; slowly but sure,
it will change us with the fluent sculpture of Time... (II. 1-5)

That's why. Because the flow of mortals adds up to a kind of immortality that can compete with Time, reshaping it from Uruk and Troy to St Lucia. And from the shore of this last-named island, Achille, with and without Philoctete, sails and rows and sails, beyond the tourist liners, upended by a whale, bailing out the bilge with that rusty can once borrowed from Hector—sailing south as far as the Grenadines.

Major Plunkett seeks his Maud in the beyond, through Ma Kilman, the sibyl of the rumshop, in a séance in which he asks the medium to tell Maud that "no other wife would have borne so much" (LXI.I.96-7]. How much strife *was* there in their love that sought and never bore the son for which they ardently wished, among whatever other desires? He imagines her in the car next to him, for a moment, as he drives back to the now-too-quiet farm from the village, and "when he thought of Helen /she was not a cause or a cloud. Only a name for a local wonder" (III. 19-21).

For—as always with the human story, whether chanted or written down by a poet, of whatever color, whether in the Aegean or the Caribbean—it begins and ends with questions.

...And is she the Helen they love,
instead of a carved mouth with the almond's odour?
She walked on this parapet in a stolen dress,

she stood in a tilted shack with its open door.
Who gives her the palm? Did the sulking Achille grapple
with Hector to repeat themselves? Exchanges a spear

> for a cutlass; and when Paris tosses the apple
> from his palm to Venus, make it a *pomme-Cythere*,
> make all those parallels pointless. Names are not oars…
> (LXII.II. 13-21)

What are we, then, as a species, that interweaves and intertexts ourselves across time and space, so fiercely, and intertwines the intensity of love and the power of strife, contending with each other, with the gods and fate, with the forces of nature? How do we achieve immortality who are so mortal? By the stories we tell of each other, and by the offspring that carry our names slowly forward, generation by generation—if and when the next generations remembers the previous ones. And we are not, then like the leaves in *Iliad* VI or like the evanescent bubbles of froth in the vast sea, from which the goddess of love was once shaped.

Chapter LXIII, section II begins as

> Helen came into the shop, and she had that slow
> feline smile of a pregnant woman, the slow grace
> that can go with it… (LXIII.II.1-3)

. . .

> "She is making child," [Ma Kilman] said. "Achille want to give it,
> even is Hector's, an African name. Helen
> don't want no African child. He say he'll leave it
> till the day of the christening. That Helen must learn
> where she from… (II.10-14)

Identity, heritage, socio-culturally, linguistically, and otherwise, shape the various subsets of our species—although as time passes and migrations and invasions and changes of venue occur, fewer and fewer of us can identify ourselves by only a single line of that shape. How do we know *who* we are?

Chapter LXIV, section I, verse 1: "I sang of quiet Achille, Afolabe's son,"

> who never ascended in an elevator,
> who had no passport, since the horizon needs none… (I.2-3)

> ... I sang the only slaughter
> that brought him delight, and that from necessity—
> of fish, sang the channels of his back in the sun.
>
> I sang our wide country, the Caribbean Sea. (I.7-10)

Achille and his simple complex love affair with Helen, whom you can see

> ...at the Halcyon. She is dressed
> in the national costume: white, low-cut bodice,
> with frilled lace at the collar, just a cleft of breast
>
> for the customers when she places their orders
> on the shields of the tables... (II.1-5)
>
> ...holding a tray
> over her stomach to hide the wave-rounded sigh
> of her pregnancy... (II.8-10)

—Achille and his complex simple love for Hector, whose child is growing within Helen's belly. The poet's last image is of Achille, alone, on the beach, in from fishing and gutting his catch as night comes on—quite sure, really, who he is—putting "the wedge of dolphin

> that he's saved for Helen in Hector's rusty tin.
> A full moon shone like a slice of raw onion.
> When he left the beach the sea was still going on. (III.31-33)

—the tin with which the first argument between the two heroes emerged, and which Achille lifted gently from Hector's grave with Helen's silent, nodding approval. An ending every bit as poignant as that offered to us of that other Achilleus and that other Hektor, three millennia earlier, on the beach outside Troy—from which, today, the sea, silted up, has receded miles away, so that, even if they squint, tourists who climb the hill of archaeological ruins, cannot see the water from there.

III An Epilogue of Sorts: Words, Music, and *West Side Story*

The beach can no longer be seen from the site of Troy's ruins, but the songs of its protagonists are still chanted across Western culture. And epilogue to this epilogue: *eros* and *eris* are not, as the centuries and human-devised art forms evolve, limited in expression to literature and visual art. As the harnessing of verbal narratives to increasingly diverse musical forms eventually yields operas and operettas and as these in turn yield the varied forms of the musical, love and strife contend with and wrap around each other in new modes of gentle ferocity. One might consider just one of these: *West Side Story*—its flawless music by Leonard Bernstein and its equally perfect libretto and lyrics by Stephen Sondheim, gestating for nearly a decade before its first performance in 1957.[252]

Originally conceived as a story of conflict—*eris*—between Italian and Jewish immigrant communities in the late 1940s-early 1950s Upper West Side of NewYork City, by the time of its performance the two communities at odds with each other had long been re-imagined as Puerto Rican and Euro-American; the first as newly arrived immigrants and the second as already-resident on the island of Manhattan. The underlying idea—inspired by Shakespeare's *Romeo and Juliet*, which was, in turn, inspired by the Greek story of Pyramus and Thisbe—could hardly be more fundamentally grounded in *eros* and *eris*.

In both the Greek and Shakespearean versions, two families are intractibly inimical to each other, but one has a son and the other a daughter, who, against the odds, fall in love with each other. Their desire to be together—whether to run away together (Pyramus and Thisbe) or to get married (Romeo and Juliet)—leads, through one form or another of miscommunication, to the deaths of both young lovers. The only positive outcome of the drama, in both cases, is that the two families, recognizing both how their animosities had led to these tragic deaths and also how stupid, ultimately, those animosities were in the first place, are reconciled.

The bittersweet poignancy of the more complex Shakesperean version of the story inspired at least three major orchestral works—by Hector Berlioz, Peter Ilyitch Tschaikovsky, and Sergei Prokoviev, and the last two of these were composed to accompany full-length ballets—so instead of the verbal expression of the narrative's events, the motion of the human body in all of its potential majesty, became the centerpiece of these two dramas. All of this formed the artistic background for the Broadway masterpiece by Bernstein and Sondheim—together with balletic staging and choreography by Jerome Robbins.

But it is the story that interests us in this discussion, in which, rather than two families, two communities are hostile toward each other. Or strictly speaking, two sub-communities: the teen-aged members of the two, organized into two gangs, the *Sharks* and the *Jets*—whose main purpose seems to be to make trouble in and around the neighborhood and to rumble with each other. Tony, the erstwhile leader of the *Jets*, has in fact started to leave gang life behind, but his best friend, Riff, still very much involved, as the nominal head of the gang, induces him to consider joining them for one more rumble—he is, after all, the Akhilleus of the *Jets*. But a dance organized by the grown-ups at the gym, in which both groups are compelled to participate and which is to be strictly non-hostile territory, is on the agenda first.

Tony comes to the dance. So does Maria, the younger sister of Bernardo, leader of the *Sharks*—who is engaged to and impassioned with Anita. At the dance, Tony and Maria somehow see each other across that crowded gymnasium and are smitten with each other. So *eros* has somehow forced its way emphatically into the midst of all of this *eris*. Other threads interweave this one within the fabric of the story, (for instance the argument within the Puerto Rican community over loving Manhattan and hating Puerto Rico and loving and longing for Puerto Rico while hating Manhattan: a different sort of love-strife relationship) but the essential issues for our purposes that spill out after each other center on the Maria-Tony liaison.

Tony and Maria wish they could get away to some place not drenched in this kind of anger, hate, and strife. One of the sweeter among the many beautiful songs sung in the course of the musical is the articulation of that desire:

Tony:
There's a place for us,

Somewhere a place for us.
Peace and quiet and open air
wait for us
somewhere.

Maria:
There's a time for us,
Someday a time for us.
Time together with time to spare,
time to look, time to care,
someday!

Tony:
Somewhere.
We'll find a new way of living,

Maria:
We'll find a way of forgiving
Somewhere . . .

Both:
There's a place for us,
a time and place for us.
Hold my hand and we're halfway there.
Hold my hand and I'll take you there.
Somehow!
Someday!
Somewhere!

In love with a Puertoriquena, Tony recognizes more than ever the stupidity of hating Puerto Ricans just because they are Puerto Ricans—there is something amiss about an identity that is shaped by a sense of *eris* toward whatever and whoever the "other" is just because it is different. He realizes—his heart filled with love for one of those "others" and thus simply filled with love, for *humanity*—that he has to stop the scheduled rumble. His love must eradicate the strife. He arrives when it is just getting started, and when the duel with knives between Riff and Bernardo has begun, in his fervent desire to stop it, he stays Riff's hand—giving Bernardo the opportunity to stab and kill Riff. Tony is so overcome with the grief-fueled rage of a moment over the fall of his best friend—this is the Patroklos to his Akhilleus—that he grabs the knife extended to him by Riff with his dying gasp, and stabs Bernardo.

Tony is now even more distraught with what he has done; he runs to Maria and confesses his act, his shame and his horror; they re-affirm their love and their desire to somehow get away—but as a practical matter, Tony has to hide until the heat is off. In another, differently poignant moment, Maria convinces Anita—after a long and beautifully sung *agon* between them ("A boy like that who'd kill your brother, forget that boy and find another, one of your own kind. Stick to your own kind!" "Oh no, Anita, no! Anita, no! It isn't true, not for me! It's true for you, not for me! ...You should know better. You were in love, or so you say! You should know better...")—to take a message to Tony about where and when to meet to get away—but in the place she goes to find him, Doc's drugstore, half a dozen Jets are hanging out and abuse her severely enough that, in the end, frustrated and angry, she spits out a different message: that Maria is dead.

So, then: Tony, believing that Maria is dead, comes out of hiding and wanders the streets yelling for Bernardo's best friend, Chino, to kill him. At the same time, Maria, realizing how the message has ended up miscommunicated, has come out looking for Tony. They see each other—reminiscent of but so different from when they saw each other at the gym that first time, and as they approach each other, Chino appears from the shadows with a gun and shoots Tony. Dying in Maria's arms, he and she reprise the last verse of "Somewhere" before he expires. She rises from the ground in anger as much as in anguish, spinning around toward all of them with that gun that had been dropped on the ground by Chino—and, as in Shakespeare's play, the stupidity and the terrible price of their long-held *eris* is overturned by *eros* and *thanatos*, as members of both gangs jointly lift up the body of Tony to carry it off-stage as the curtain falls.

Ideas and questions that obsess the Greeks, which are in evidence from the beginnings of their literature and visual art, carry forward into Latin literature and Roman visual art but also follow across Western culture, eventually engaging other art forms as well. Many of these same ideas and questions are also evidenced across biblical and diverse non-Western cultures, because they are so fundamental as ideas and questions in *human* culture. Endless variations on the aspects of the relationship between *eros* and *eris* are evidenced as one courses through human history—as, in tension with our unique ability as a species to be destructive, we again and again express our creative side in diverse media. All of this helps shape a multi-valent immortality for our species, mortal though we may be.

This is far from a perfect immortality since, like its mortal counterpart, it is fraught with contradiction and paradox, involving love and strife and their analogues. This has been evident from the beginning—whether of *kosmos* born out of *khaos* or of heavenly lights spoken into existence several days after God had already declared the existence of—apparently some other primordial—light. It continues to be articulated—since whatever that beginning *was* and whenever it *happened*, whether by figures of heroic proportion, their deeds sung down the generations, or by small-scale characters struggling to be heard—and to be embedded as facts in human history or within the imaginations of authors known or unidentified.

Notes

1 Robert J. Littman, *The Greek Experiment*, 4.
2 Ibid, 11.
3 Ibid, 13.
4 In this he is repeating the original formulation offered by E.R. Dodds in his *The Greeks and the Irrational*.
5 Littman, 14.
6 Ibid, 14.
7 The title of his book is a rendering into English of the word/name "Herakles" (*kles* in Greek means "glory")—alluding to the idea that the great accomplishments of the Greek hero were occasioned by the hostility to him of Hera (who is a sort of stepmother to him, since his own human mother was destroyed by Zeus): her relentless persecution leads, among other directions, to his renowned Twelve Labors.
8 Philip Slater, *The Glory of Hera*, 4-5. Slater is quoting from Arnold Gomme's *Essays on Greek History and Literature,* and summarizes from H.D.F. Kitto's *The Greeks* and Heinrich Bluemner's *The Home Life of the Greeks*. Translated by Alice Zimmern.
9 Ibid, 7-8.
10 Ibid, 8.
11 Ibid, 8.
12 Ibid, 11.
13 Ibid, xx.
14 Ibid, xxii-xxv.
15 See Soltes, *The Problem of Plato's* Cratylus: *The Relation of Language to Truth in the History of Philosophy*.
16 Thus 1 o'clock is reliably followed by 2 o'clock and the distance from the Washington Monument to the White House is reliably different from that between the Washington Monument and the Empire State Building in New York City or the Eiffel Tower in Paris.
17 The term *"sacer"* is of course the ancestor of our word "sacred," as *"profanus"* is the ancestor of our word "profane." I use these Latin antecedents rather than their English descendants for three reasons: because they imply a greater range of analogic aspects; because

they underscore the potentially positive or negative but intrinsically neutral nature of the concepts; and so that the reader, not used to these terms, will necessarily pause for a millisecond each time they are used, rather than slipping swiftly and unthinkingly over excessively familiar terms.

18 There are other kinds of *sacerdotes*, as well. Poets and artists are inspirited by the *sacer* to do what they do, particularly, say, poets who write about the divine *sacer*—this is why Hesiod, for instance, spends the first 115 lines of his poem, the *Theogony* ("The Coming to Be of the Gods") invoking divine inspirational assistance, so that he may tell his tale accurately and effectively. Heroes (to repeat) are capable of acts beyond ordinary humans due to their divine connection, sometimes in the form of unique levels of support, and sometimes because the hero is actually part god. Pharaohs and shahs are—or wish their constituents to believe that they are—half-divine, or at least that they operate with specific divine imprimatur.

19 When we first encounter Odysseus weeping on the beach of Kalypso's island and eager to continue home to his wife—after a dalliance of seven years with the goddess—he is rejecting the immortality that she offers him in favor of returning to Ithake and a certain eventual death. Kalypso's name is cognate with the Greek verb, *kalyptein*: "to bury." Odysseus needs to get back to an existence that places him in the middle of all kinds of action, however complicated or disturbing that action might be, rather than remaining in isolation, cut off from human storm and stress—for to spend eternity in that condition, even if in the company of a voluptuous goddess, is to be functionally dead and buried. Thus mortality and immortality functionally contradict their respective meanings: to become an immortal with Kalypso is to die; to get back into the turbulent stream of life is to further his undying glory but arriving, at some point, at death. See below, 67 and fn 83.

20 The underlying intention has to do with cruelty: what could be crueler than to cook veal, say, in the milk taken from its own mother—something altogether conceivable in a sheep-, goat-, and cattle-herding community. The process of digestion is likened to the process of seething, so to drink a glass of milk—particularly in a *post*-herding reality, where I don't know exactly where the milk came from—that might conceivably have come from the mother of the animal whose delicate meat I am consuming, would be to abrogate God's commandment. This is connected (the connecting process itself an interpretive act) to the rabbinic interpretation (in *Pirkei Avot* 1:1) of the first clause in the verse from Deuteronomy—which is that one must

"build a fence *around the Torah*," which is in turn interpreted to mean that one must go beyond fulfilling a divine commandment a mere 100% (which is called a *humra* in rabbinic thought) to make sure not to abrogate it inadvertently—and leads to the decision not to consume milk and meat *products* together (hence, no cheeseburgers) or even one after the other (hence no post-steak ice cream). The discussion will eventuate, over time, to include the question of how *long* after my steak I need to wait before I have digested it, so that I can have that ice cream for which I have been eagerly waiting. (One to six hours, depending upon whom you ask—although the 12th-century French rabbi, Rabeinu Tam, asserted that if one merely recites the grace after meals, clears the soiled dishes away and removes the tablecloth, one may immediately drink one's milk, having fully abided by the commandment). His *interpretation*!

21 A note on spellings: I admit to a snobby prejudice regarding the transliteration of Greek words and names; we tend to follow Latin versions of these. Thus, for instance, we write "Democritus" or "Neoptolemus" when a more accurate transliteration of the Greek would yield "Demokritos" and "Neoptolemos." (A few key Greek names do end in "-us"—such as "Akhilleus" and "Odysseus," however). So I use what I think are more accurate transliterations, except under three conditions: if a name is so commonly used according to the Latinized transliteration (e.g., "Cleopatra") and/or likely not to be recognized if I change it, I leave it; when I am quoting Roman writers in Latin I abide by the Latinized forms of Greek words and names that they use; if I am quoting someone who uses the Latinized transliteration, I leave it. Therefore, I may even spell the same name two different ways on the same page, in the same paragraph or even within the same sentence, (theoretically), if, say, I am quoting a Latin-language writer but then refer to some Greek-named character to which he refers. By the way, a similar issue applies from a different angle to god-names: if the context is Greek, I use the Greek version, and if it is Roman, I use the Roman version—eg, Zeus vs Jupiter, Ares vs Mars, Hermes vs Mercury, Aphrodite vs Venus, et al. So it goes. May the gods of spelling and transliteration accept these little complications and not destroy my kingdom... and may the reader not get too annoyed!

22 There is scant definitive information regarding Hesiod outside what may be inferred from verses here and there in the poetry ascribed to him—"ascribed to him" although there are those who question his actual existence, in which case those poems in the Boeotian style have no specific author. Fortunately for this discussion the matter of authorship is irrelevant; it is the content that interests us.

23 Consistent with the other-than-all-fitting-neatly-together reality of the mythical tradition (as one might expect, since it deals with *sacer* reality), in the *Iliad*, Aphrodite is presented as the daughter of Zeus and Dione—without, incidentally, specifying when Dione had been his spouse (see *Iliad* V:131,312,374 and 820).

24 The divine food makes the gods what they are: *nek-tar* means "that which crosses over death" and *am-brosia* means "un-dying" or "immortal."

25 Strictly speaking, not all editors agree that these verses and the 15 that follow belong here or are even necessarily Hesiod's, but for our purposes that issue is not relevant.

26 The Greeks called themselves "*Helleines*" (anglicized as "Hellenes"). "Greek" is the term the Romans used: "*Graecus*" in Latin, derived from "*Graekos*" in Greek—which originally referred to a Hellenic tribe from Boeotia that migrated to Italy in the eighth century BCE.

27 "As things are, the Argives will take flight homeward /over the wide ridges of the sea to the land of their fathers/ and thus they would leave to Priam and to the Trojans Helen/ of Argos, to glory over, for whose sake many Akhaians/ lost their lives in Troy far from their own native country."

28 Richmond Lattimore, transl, *The Iliad of Homer*, 22.

29 "…but never to Hera/ nor Poseidon, nor the girl of the grey eyes, who kept still/ their hatred for sacred Ilion as in the beginning/ and for Priam and his people, because of the delusion of Paris/ who insulted the goddesses when they came to him in his courtyard/ and favored her who supplied the lust that led to disaster."

30 Glaukos presents the poignant assertion that "as is the generation of leaves, so is that of humanity./ The wind scatters the leaves on the ground, but the live timber/ burgeons with leaves again in the season of spring returning./ So one generation of men will grow while another dies…" This recitation leads to the story of Bellerophontes, the outcome of which is the realization that he (Glaukos) and Diomedes, to whom he is telling the story just before they are about to fight each other, have an ancestral guest-host relationship—and so should not, and do not, end up fighting, instead exchanging gifts. Phoinix, as part of his contribution to the attempt to convince Akhilleus to re-enter the fight, tells the tale of the Kouretes and Aitolians, "slaughtering one another about the city of Kalydon."

31 Photius (Photios) I (810-91 CE), Patriarch of Constantinople, wrote a work dedicated to his brother, called *Bibliotheca*, which was a review/summary of 279 books that he had read, including a *Chrestomathy* by Proclus (Proklos) that included excerpts from the "Epic Cycle." The

compiler who was known by that name was almost certainly not the famed 5th-century CE Neoplatonic philosopher of the same name (Proklos Diadokhos). He was either the 2nd-century CE grammarian, Eutykhios Proklos, or a different, otherwise unknown figure. The "non-Homeric" epics, ranging from 2 to 11 books in length, are said to have included: *Cypria* (encompassing events leading up to the war); *Aethiopis* (from the arrival of Trojan allies, including Penthesileia the Amazon queen, through the death of Akhilleus); *Little Iliad* (events after Akhilleus' death, including the building of the horse and the award of the arms of Akhilleus to Odysseus); *Ilios Persis* ("*Sack of Troy*": the destruction of the city); *Nostoi* ("*Homecomings*": the homeward voyages of the Akhaian heroes—except Odysseus—culminating with Agamemnon and Menelaos); *Telegony* (Odysseus' post-Odyssey visit to Thesprotia, his subsequent return to Ithake, and his death at the hands of an illegitimate son, Telegonos).

32 The discussion of this may be found in any number of places, such as in Lattimore, pp 22-28, or M.M. Willcock, "The Funeral Games of Patroclus," 4-5. For the purposes of this narrative, I am simply referring to Homer, as if there is no question that such an individual, by that name, not only existed but authored both the *Iliad* and the *Odyssey*. But these are important aspects of what is a long-argued authorship issue.

33 Most fundamentally, gods differ from humans in being immortal where humans are mortal—the gods don't grow ill, grow old, or die; humans endure all of that—and since one is either mortal or immortal, not both, then the two realms are inherently separate. The Greeks recognize that the issue is not that simple, not only in the exceptional case of an Akhilleus who is paradoxically both, but in the less exceptional case of a poet immortalized by his poetry or still less exceptional, a grandparent/parent immortalized by the fact that his children and grandchildren remember him—so that she "lives" somehow, in their memory, as surely as Akhilleus "lives" in our continual retelling of his story three millennia after that story unfolded.

34 See *Cypria* as quoted by Proklos: *Chrestomathy* I and as quoted by the scholiast to *Iliad* I.5; see also Apollodorus: *Epitome* III.1-2.

35 This is recounted by Hyginus, in *Fabula* 81; by Ovid in *Heroides* and by Lucian in *Dialogues of the Gods* 20.

36 One might note in passing how an important subset of the notion of divine immortality plays out here: that of divine (*sacer*) time frames. Akhilleus is presumably born after the wedding of Peleus and Thetis—however long after does not matter—and yet is old enough to have

already been one of the former suitors for Helen's hand by the time, in the fairly immediate aftermath of that wedding, she is offered, already married to Menelaos, as a prize to Paris. Akhilleus should at most be a mere babe in swaddling clothes by then, were we operating according to the linear *profanus* patterns of time as humans understand it—unless we assume that the judgment among the goddesses happened, say, two decades after the wedding feast, or that Aphrodite waited a very long time before fulfilling her promise to Paris.

37 We are offered yet another reminder of how the gods operate, as contradictory, paradoxic forces, from a human viewpoint. Artemis is both the patroness of hunters and the protectress of wild beasts from the depredations of hunters. There is some logic to this opposition, however. As with any process of engaging gods and goddesses, the result of the engagement—blessing or curse, help or hindrance—will be a consequence of whether or not the individual (or community) engages the divinity in a proper manner. So a hunter hunting what, where and when he should, with the proper invocations and perhaps offerings to the goddess, can reasonably anticipate her help; whereas one hunting what, where, or when he should not, as was the case with one of Agamemnon's men at Aulis, can anticipate an angry and potentially damaging reaction from her. But of course an everyday hunter may not know what, when and where is proper, and which invocations are the correct ones, so may inadvertently invite disaster. Ignorance of the goddess' laws is no defense.

38 About which subsequent doom we will hear from authors who come after Homer, such as Aiskhylos, in his *Agamemnon* and Euripides (see below, Chapter Four). Klytaimnestra and Helen share the same mother, Leda, but whereas Helen's father was Zeus (who, as noted above, in the form of a swan, seduced Leda), Klytaimnestra's father was Tyndareos.

39 I.6, 8: "since that time when first there stood in division of conflict (*diasteten erisante*)... What god was it then set them together in bitter conflict (*eridi... makhesthai*)? Twice, a form of the word *eris* is used.

40 This is Khryseis—whose name means "golden one."

41 I.29-31: The girl I will not give back; sooner will old age come upon her/ in my own house, in Argos... going/ up and down by the loom and being in my bed as my companion." And 112-14: " ... and indeed I wish greatly to have her/ in my own house; since I like her better than Klytaimnestra/ my own wife..."

42 See, for example, II. 354-6 ("...let no man be urgent to take the way homeward/ until after he has lain in bed with the wife of a Trojan/ to avenge Helen's longing to escape and her lamentations") and also

XVI. 97-100 and the discussion in Michael Nagler: *Spontaneity and Tradition: A Study in the Oral Art of Homer*, 45ff.

43 Thus:
"I for my part did not come here for the sake of the Trojan spearmen
to fight against them, since to me they have done nothing. Never yet
have they driven away my cattle or my horses, never in Phthia where
the soil is rich and men grow great did they spoil my harvest, since
indeed there is much that lies between us, the shadowy mountains
and the echoing sea; but for your sake,
O great shamelessness, we followed, to do you a favor,
you with your dogs' eyes, to win your honor and Menelaos'
from the Trojans. You forget all this or else you care nothing.
And now my prize you threaten in person to strip from me,
for whom I labored much, the gift of the sons of the Akhaians.
Never, when the Akhaians sack some well-founded citadel
of the Trojans, did I have a prize that is equal to your prize.
Always the greater part of the painful fighting is the work of
my hands; but when the time comes to distribute the booty
yours is far the greater reward, and I with some small thing
yet dear to me go back to my ships when I am weary with fighting."

44 This distinction has been noted by Willcock, Ibid.

45 Just as, prior to the *Iliad*'s events, Agamemnon had been willing to sacrifice his own daughter, Iphigenia, to his honor, lest he be supplanted by Palamedes as leader of the Akhaians.

46 Among recent and contemporary translators, both Lattimore and Fitzgerald rendered it as "anger," whereas Robert Fagles renders it as "rage" and Caroline Alexander as "wrath." All of these are justifiably highly regarded translations of the epic. For the most part, I am using Lattimore when I quote passages from the *Iliad*. Where I disagree with his rendering, I impose my own translation.

47 There is one moment that offers a sort of analogue in the Akhaian camp to the laugh moment engendered by Hephaistos on Olympos: when, in the discussion early in Book II, Thersites—described as chicken-chested, hunch-backed, pointy-headed, and lame—speaks up on the issue of continuing the siege or going home (212-42). Odysseus excoriates him for daring, as a common soldier, to speak up among the upper-crust officers (246-64). He then proceeds to beat him with his staff, causing the gathered troops to laugh heartily (265-77)—but even more than with Hephaistos on Olympos, the Thersites moment is symptomatic of a social structure that I would hope a modern mind would find cruel rather than amusing.

48 It is interesting that Menelaos' name means "wrath/anger/passion

of the people" (from *menis* and *laos*): one might say that the anger of the Akhaian people at the abduction of Menelaos' wife, Helen, set in motion the great war upon a slice of which the action of the *Iliad* is based, beginning with — its very first words focused on — and following the progress of, the *menis* of the greatest of the Akhaian warriors.

49 III.399ff: Oh strange goddess, why are you still so stubborn to beguile me?
... Is it because Menelaos has beaten god-like Alexandros
and wishes, hateful even as I am, to carry me homeward,
is it for this that you stand in your treachery now beside me? (403-5)
...[you] stay with him forever, and suffer for him, and look after him
until he makes you his wedded wife, or makes you his slave girl... (408-9)
... my heart even now is confused with sorrows. (412)

50 "...clearly the victory is with warlike Menelaos.
Do you therefore give back, with all her possessions, Helen
of Argos, and pay a price that shall be befitting,
which among people yet to come shall be as a standard." (457-60)

51 "*nek-tar*" comes from two Indo-European roots. "*Nek-*" means "death" (in Greek, for instance, "*Nekuia*" is a term referring to narratives in which heroes visit/encounter the (land of) the dead — and "*tar-*" means "transcend, cross over," as in the Sanskrit verb, "*tarami*," which means just that.

52 By the time "Homer" is "writing," of course, the very cities that are enumerated, with the exception of Sparta, will have experienced destruction.

53 Yet — a further irony — Ares as a warrior is not as invincible as Akhilleus, even as Ares can never die, being an immortal, whereas Akhilleus can and will die, but only by the less-than-straightforward attack that another thread in the tapestry associates with a cowardly Paris/Alexandros.

54 VI:431-2: "Please take pity upon me then, and stay here on the rampart,
that you may not leave your child an orphan and your wife a widow..."

55 VI:433-4: "...but draw your people up by the large fig tree, there where the city/ is most open to attack, and where the wall may be mounted."

56 VI: 476-81:
Zeus, and you other immortals, grant that this boy, who is my son,
may be as I am, pre-eminent among the Trojans,
great in strength, as am I, and rule strongly over Ilion;

and some day let them say of him: "He is better by far than his father,"
as he comes in from the fighting; and let him kill his enemy
and bring home the bloody spoils, and delight the heart of his mother.

57 See the further discussion of this in B.L. Hijmans, Jr., "Alexandros and his Grief," in Wace and Stubbings, *A Companion to Homer.*
58 185-6.
59 Such as Cedric Whitman, in *Homer and the Heroic Tradition*, 223ff.
60 The word knees is *"gounai'"* (in the genitive plural form)—derived from the same root that we might recognize in the English word, "gonad(s)." So she strokes his chin and grasps both of his…*gounat'*… And let us not forget that Zeus had once been quite smitten with Thetis.
61 It may be noteworthy that the two new figures highlighted in Book Nine—Nestor and Phoinix—are both older men: father figures. Nestor, in loving Agamemnon as a son, and Phoinix, loving Akhilleus as a son, seek to lead these "sons" away from strife with each other. If this would seem uncharacteristic of the fathers we have encountered thus far—leading sons away from strife—we must remember that they are doing this so that the two son-figures can re-unite to engage in the deadlier strife that their conflict has put on a kind of pause. The culmination for both "sons" in the long run, will be death—the one before the war at Troy has ended and the other upon returning home from that war.
62 See below, 72-3.
63 This irresistible garment is an
   …elaborate, pattern-pierced
   zone, and on it are figured all beguilements, and loveliness
   is figured upon it, and passion of sex is there, and the whispered
   endearment that steals the heart away even from the thoughtful (214-17).
64 See verses 315-28.
65 See, for example, D.S. Barrett, "The Friendship of Achilles and Patroclus," in *The Classical Bulletin*. 57.1 (1980), 87-93; W.M. Clarke, "Achilles and Patroclus in Love," in *Hermes* 106.3 (1978), 381-396; Manuel Sanz Morales and Gabriel Laguna Mariscal, "The Relationship Between Achilles and Patroclus According to Chariton of Aphrodisias." *Classical Quarterly*. 53.1 (2003), 292-326; and Manuel Sanz Morales and Gabriel Laguna Mariscal, "Was the Relationship between Achilles and Patroclus Homoerotic? The View of Apollonius Rhodius," in *Hermes* 133.1 (2005), 120-123.

66 See, for example, Gregory Nagy, "Achilles and Patroclus as Models for the Twinning of Identity," http://nrs.Harvard.edu/urn-3:hlnc.essay:Nagy.Acchilles_and_Patroclus_as_Models.2018.

67 Then in turn Thetis answered him, letting the tears fall:"Hephaistos, is there among all the goddesses on Olympos
one who in her heart has endured so many grim sorrows
as the griefs Zeus, son of Kronos, has given me beyond others?of all the other sisters of the sea he gave me to a mortal,to Peleus, Aiakos' son, and I had to endure mortal marriage though much against my will. And now he, broken by mournful old age, lies away in his halls…"
We might recall, moreover, that it was because of a prophecy from Themis—that Thetis, wed to a god, would engender *eris* in the form of a son who would be more powerful than his father—that Zeus (and Poseidon; for they were both in love with her) married her off to a mortal.

68 At least two false weddings are embedded in the Trojan War cycle: that between Akhilleus and Agamemnon's daughter, Iphigenia, which never took place nor was ever intended to (See below, Chapter Four); and more ironically and obscurely, given this first false wedding, the promise by Agamemnon to Akhilleus in Book Nine, if the hero returns to the fray, that he may choose any of the leader's daughters (remaining daughters, that is, although that is never mentioned) as a wife.

69 …was this the better way…
… that we, for all our hearts' sorrow,
quarreled together for the sake of a girl in soul-perishing hatred?
I wish that Artemis had slain her beside the ships with an arrow
on that day when I destroyed Lyrnessos and took her.

70 Especially verses 86-94.

71 Verses 282-30, which begin:
…she folded
him in her arms and cried out shrilly above him and with her hands tore at her breasts and her soft throat and her beautiful forehead…
—and continues by addressing Patroklos' corpse directly, as "far most pleasing to my heart in its sorrows" (287), commenting, too—with a recollection that resonates from the words of Andromakhe in Book VI, 414-28, but with different implications—how, when Akhilleus conquered her city, and her three brothers all perished, and Akhilleus himself slew her husband, but "you would not let me sorrow, but said that you would make me godlike Akhilleus' wedded lawful wife… You were kind always." (296-8, 300)

72 See above, 42: IV:440: "...Strife whose wrath is relentless, she is the sister and companion of murderous Ares..."
73 There is a peculiar poignancy to these verses. It is as if Andromakhe has heard the Trojan War cycle—as we have. She does not know what is happening out on the battlefield, and yet, since Book VI, she has somehow known what the outcome of the strife-ridden meeting between her husband and the one who had killed her family previously will be.
74 See verses 587-95.
75 See, for example, E.T. Owen, *The Story of the* Iliad, 235, where he touches lightly on this. A more extensive discussion comes up in Ori Z Soltes, *God and The Goalposts: A Brief History of Sports, Religion, Politics, War, and Art*, 46-8.
76 That is, to say: the wedding of Peleus and Thetis, which both yielded the conflict among the three goddesses induced by *eris* and yielded the offspring, Akhilleus, induced by the *eros* between Peleus and Thetis—to say nothing of the *eris* the cause of which was the *eros* between Helen and Paris/Alexandros and its interphase with the pact agreed upon by all those Akhaian men attracted by *eros* to Helen before she chose Menelaos as her spouse.
77 See I.364-430 and 500-16
78 See I.11-34.
79 She weeps:
My husband, you were lost young from life, and have left me
a widow in your house, and the boy is only a baby
who was born to you and me, the unhappy one. I think he will never
come of age.... (725-8)
...some Akhaian
will take you [i.e., Astyanax] by the hand and hurl you from the tower into horrible
death, in anger because Hektor once killed his brother.
or his father, or his son..." (734-7)
She anticipates the fate of her baby, but not the reason for it.
80 Such a perspective would have been known to both poet and audience from the much larger Trojan War epic cycle, of course, and in particular from the eleven-book-long epic *Kypria*, ascribed to Stasinos of Cyprus (or, by some, ascribed to Hegesias, and by still others to Homer).
81 The other *nostos*-type epics that we know of include a five-book-long poem. *The Returns*, (*Nostoi*, ascribed to Agias of Troizen—or to someone else, even to Homer); and perhaps the last part of the two-book-long *Sack of Ilion*, (ascribed to Arktinos of Miletos), which carried from the building of the wooden horse and the fall of Troy through the journeys home of the Akhaians (except for Odysseus).

82 The *Theogony* has not yet been written—at least theoretically—so the counter-weight to such an assumption, at least for the pre-human gods and their forebears is not sitting before the poet for his consideration.

83 The symbolism of the paradoxic condition in which Odysseus finds himself could hardly be more direct. He has been within the cave of the nymph, buried by a passion that pushes everything else out of his existence, for a time-period—years numbering seven—a number that in antiquity, among diverse Mediterranean cultures, was associated with completion and perfection. (See Ori Z Soltes, *Our Sacred Signs*, 31-4). For Odysseus the opposite is true: the passion has run its course and feels less and less complete and perfect. The sex was good, but not good enough to keep him Kalypso's love-prisoner forever. Returning to Penelope means returning to mortality—to illness, infirmity, old age, and the death that is inevitable for human life—but is means returning to *life*.

84 I am not ignoring Agamemnon's role in his own demise—from the young lover, Kassandra, whom he glibly expects his wife to embrace, to his abrogation of proper religious custom, soiling the god-appropriate pathway laid out for him by Klytaimnestra before he has purified himself from his long journey—but for the present discussion these actions are beside the point. For more on this, see Chapter Four.

85 For, as we shall see in Chapter Four, Orestes comes home from the childhood-long exile imposed upon him by his mother and her lover, when he hears that his father has returned from Troy. Finding his father dead and confronted with the imperative to avenge his father's death, he ultimately takes action—which, alas, means killing not only Aigisthos but Klytaimnestra, Orestes' mother

86   Telemakhos' speech extends from verses 40 to 79; the heart of the matter occupies 47-62:
"...A double evil has fallen on my house. First, my noble father is
   dead, who once
ruled among you, like a gentle father. And now
a far greater evil has come, one which will soon ruin
my house and destroy all of my substance.
For my mother is beset by suitors, against her will—
Our own sons of men who are of the highest birth here.
They are afraid to journey to the house of her father, Ikarios,
who might provide his daughter with a dowry and give her
to the man she wants, to whomever she finds most pleasing.
Instead they loiter about our house day after day,
killing our oxen and our sheep and our fat goats.
They make merry and drink the flaming wine

recklessly. Most of our substance is wasted. For there is no man here such as Odysseus was, to drive this curse from the house..."

87 I am deliberately not distinguishing "object of love" from "object of desire" because I do not believe that the Homeric literature is sensitive to that distinction. The difference between the two words/concepts will be considered later on, most obviously when we get to Sokrates/Plato, as we shall see. In any case, in the *Odyssey*, love *or* desire for the hand of Penelope—particularly given her likely age relative to that of the suitors—cannot be separated from their desire for her (Odysseus') property, so this strife-ridden process is focused on love of land and groves and vineyards and herds as much as or more than it is on love for a woman.

88 These first four books are often spoken of as constituting their own mini-epic, the *Telemakhy*.

89 I am using the phrase "in the direct sense" to mean that her abduction sets in motion the sailing of the ships to Troy to do whatever is necessary to get her back, but obviously one could argue (as I have in Chapter Two) that there are several inception points, from the falling in love of Thetis and Peleus and their wedding on Olympos, on the one hand; to the falling in love of Priam and Hecube and the birth of their son Paris/Alexandros in the face of a dire prophecy, on the other.

90 I say "perhaps" in order not to ignore the argument that Helen was *carried off* (in Latin: *rapta*—from which we get the English-language word, "rape") by Paris, as opposed to her having simply and willingly *run off* with him. Lest we forget, the same Euripides who made the "linguistic" observation regarding the relationship between *eros* and *eris* would come to write a play in which he supported the notion that Helen in fact spent the war in Egypt, her wifely honor intact, and that it was merely an *eidolon*—an image—of her that Paris unwittingly carried with him to Troy. This is a very different thread within the Trojan War tapestry from the one woven into Book Four of the *Odyssey*, of course. See below, Chapter Four.

91 Sophokles would write an entire play (*Philoktetes*) about how Odysseus and Neoptolemos, son of Akhilleus, managed to accomplish this task—not easy, given how angry at Odysseus in particular Philoktetes remained after he had been marooned on the island at Odysseus' suggestion and through his (Odysseus') trickery.

92 This might be more obvious were the *Odyssey* written in Latin, in which the word for "sheath" is *vagina*. See fn 94, and also the discussion of the *Aeneid* and the affair between Aeneas and Dido, below, 271.

93 As noted above, when in the *Iliad*, Thetis grasped/embraced Zeus' knees. See above, fn 60.

94 This is a Greek text, of course, not a Latin one, but I cannot resist again reminding the reader that the Latin word for "sheath" is *vagina*. Now go ahead and reread that line!

95 More about this story in Chapter Five.

96 See more regarding this story below, in Chapter Four.

97 Presumably Klytaimnestra, like Agamemnon, is dead, but either Hades is so large that he has not run into her, or perhaps, given her actions, she was immediately consigned upon dying to the Tartarean depths of Hades, and that's why he hasn't seen her.

98 The Homeric audience would no doubt have been familiar with that part of Neoptolemos' story and its intersection with Odysseus the strategist in bringing Philoktetes and the bow and arrows of Herakles to Troy to finalize the victory; that story will be told by Sophokles in this play, *Philoktetes*. They may not have been familiar with the direction in which Euripides would one day carry the Neoptolemos story—a much less flattering one, that shows him to be sacrilegious and cowardly—in his play, *Trojan Women*.

99 Thanks to Adrianne Pierce for reminding me of this. So, too, though the tale is not told here, the audience would have known that Aias went mad and slew his own flocks thinking they were his fellow Akhaian warriors, and when he realized what he had done, committed suicide. Sophokles would later present the story in his play, *Ajax*.

100 Homer's Odysseus neglects to mention that the rape was at the behest of Hera, who was no doubt angry for the affair that resulted in Tityos' birth; as usual, she cannot take out her frustrations directly on Zeus regarding his behavior—so she takes it out either on the woman whom he has seduced, or on her offspring.

101 The left side is negative, in virtually all cultures and traditions. One sees this most obviously in the linguistic sense when one turns to Latin, in which the word for "left" is *sinister*, as that term comes to be used in English.

102 If Telemakhos is about 20 years old, how old are the suitors? Young enough not to have sailed to Troy two decades earlier. If, let us say, they were more or less eight to twelve years old at that time—they could be a bit younger or a bit older, of course)—then they are all in their late twenties and early thirties, hence the disparity between them and Telemakhos and also, of course, between them and Odysseus, who is arguably in his mid-forties. Penelope, if we might assume, given the time and place, that she married Odysseus when she was, say, 14 years old, would therefore be in her mid-thirties—and therefore not much older than the suitors, which helps account for whatever sexual interest they have in her to supplement

the presumed fiscal interest: that she comes with Odysseus' property (or at least some substantial part of it, since much of it will go to Telemakhos if he survives into maturity (which survival they have tried to prevent, once confronted with the fact of his arrival at that stage of life).

103 Each man will have two spears, a shorter, lighter one, for throwing and killing from a distance, and a longer, heavier one for close-up stabbing.

104 See above, 45

105 I choose the word "opponent" rather than "enemy" deliberately, since part of what is important regarding Akhilleus' transformation in his newly developed empathy is the concomitant realization that ultimately neither he nor Hektor, was in the war for his own cause (except, of course the personal cause of *kleos aphthiton*). They are not real *enemies*, but are ultimately part of, sharers in, and symbols of humanity and the human condition, for which death is inevitable, except to the possible extent that anyone's *kleos can* become *aphthiton*.

106 That question will be brilliantly taken up in the twentieth century by the Greek writer, Nikos Kazantsakis in his *The Odyssey: A Sequel*, as we shall see in Chapter Ten.

107 This is, of course, part of what Kazantsakis takes up in his poem.

108 Although only the *Iliad* and the *Odyssey* have survived in complete form to our own time, we are aware, thanks to Hellenistic librarians, of other, shorter epics that dealt with aspects of the Trojan War not covered by these two works, such as the *Kypria*, the *Aithiopis*, the *Little Iliad*, and the *Telegony*, as previously noted. And apparently, one poet could perform in both epic and lyric style: consider Demodokos, whom we encounter at the Phaiakian court, reciting the epic of the Trojan War and then the story of Ares and Aphrodite, the latter tale accompanied by a lyre. (see above, 82).

109 Anne Carson, *Eros the Bittersweet*, 3.

110 D2, E2, LP 31, P 2

111 See below, Chapter Eight, 346ff, on Catullus, and the discussion of the other Roman lyric poets that follows.

112 This issue is brilliantly addressed in a both scholarly and accessible manner in the volume, *Greek Homosexuality*, by K.J. Dover.

113 We must keep in mind that Aiskhylos plays with and sometimes interweaves three different kinds of irony. The first is an irony of events: what might or might not have happened had something else happened or not happened. The second is when a character speaks words that are pregnant because neither s/he nor anyone else on the stage knows the outcome of events, but the audience does. The

third is when a character speaks words the real import of which s/he knows, (and the audience knows), but his/her on-stage auditor does not.

114 I say "for the time being," since elsewhere the tradition furthers the tale of Orestes, and his thread interweaves that of Neoptolemos, son of Akhilleus, with a not altogether happy *eros/eris* outcome. Neoptolemos was originally betrothed to Hermione, daughter of Menelaos and Helen, but while Neoptolemos was otherwise occupied (with Andromakhe, Hektor's widow), she was married to Orestes (her cousin). Neoptolemos showed up and demanded her, and Menelaos, in order not to abrogate his promise (the original betrothal), took Hermione from Orestes and gave her to Neoptolemos. Enraged and insulted, Orestes shortly thereafter slew Neoptolemos while he was making sacrifices at Delphi—as told in the *Fabulae* (*Fables*) of Gaius Julius Hyginus (64 BCE- 17 CE), Superintendent of Augustus Caesar's Palatine Library. See also the following footnote.

115 They do have one daughter: Hermione. She is already betrothed by her grandfather, Tyndareos—to Orestes, who at this juncture is still an infant. However, during the war she will be re-promised by her father, to Neoptolemos (also known as Pyrrhos), son of Akhilleus, which will end up leading to further *eris* between those two families. Shortly after settling into domestic life with Neoptolemos, Hermione finds herself in conflict with Andromakhe (widow of Hektor), the concubine Neoptolemos had obtained as a prize after the sack of Troy. Hermione blames Andromakhe for her inability to become pregnant, claiming that she has been casting spells on her to keep her barren. She asks her father to kill Andromakhe while Neoptolemos is away at war, but when he chooses not to go through with the murder, Hermione flees from Epirus with her cousin Orestes.

Hermione and Orestes marry, and she gives birth to his heir, Teisamenos. The stories do not mention Hermione after that, though it is said that Orestes later married his half-sister Erigone, daughter of Klytaimnestra and Aigisthos, who was Orestes' second cousin. See also the previous footnote.

116 It is an inieresting choice by the playwright: it would place Odysseus and Agamemnon on the same plane in an odd and unhappy way: each has an ancestor famously consigned (for different reasons) to the lowest level of Tartaros and subject to a unique torment.

117 In passing one might note that what is important is the fact of a ritual, allowing the soul of the dead to makes its transition to the underworld—from *profanus* to *sacer*—and not the particulars of that ritual: in order to do her duty as a loving sister for her brother,

Antigone has had to perform a funerary ritual which, in this case, includes a symbolic, not necessarily a literal, burial.

118 The other most strenuous example of this is the *Hippolytos*, in which the nature of the very gods we worship is brought into question; somewhat less strident is the *Alkestis*, in which both the figure of Herakles and even more so, the concept and image of loving parents, are both undercut.

119 By way of a different thread in the vast tapestry of Greek story, we know that Theseus will be the offspring in question.

120 *Frogs* was produced in 405 BCE—a year before the disastrous (for Athens) end of the Peloponnesian War.

121 I am using Douglass Parker's very modernized translation of the Greek. The range from one translator of Aristophanes to the next is delightfully broad.

122 Not to mention the phallic shape of the torches, and the womb-like, fluid-encompassing shape of the water-pitchers... Aristophanes is an absolute Freudian playground.

123 The word "sophist"—in Greek, *sophos*—means "(a) wise (man)." The term was used in Sokrates' day to refer to itinerant teachers or teachers/lawyers who claimed that, for a fee, they could train or teach a client almost anything, including how to defend one's self successfully in a court of law. It is because of the Platonic *Dialogues*, in which so many sophists are exposed by Sokrates in discussion as so lacking in wisdom and in clear knowledge that the term came to have a rather pejorative connotation. Sophistry and sophistic arguments are typically understood by us to be filled with logical holes even if they look very clever on the surface. A good example in what we have previously examined would be Jason's arguments in the *Medea*, as we have noted. (See above, 211-13).

124 The Greek word for "wisdom" is *sophia*, sibling to *sophos*. The prefix *philo-* pertains to love, so *philosophia* is "love of wisdom" and a *philosophos* is a "lover of wisdom."

125 Xenophon also wrote a version of this same event and its discussion.

126 I did not discuss, although with more space I certainly could have— the Admetos-Alkestis relationship, which is taken up by Euripides in his play, *Alkestis*. In that drama, Admetos had managed to dodge death because his loving wife, Alkestis, agreed to die in his stead. His own parents, in spite of their advanced age and presumed proximity to death, had both refused to take on that task. Herakles, a friend who comes as a guest and at first is too otherwise distracted to notice the state of mourning of Admetos' household (who is, in turn, too fine a host to impose his grief over his wife's death on his

guest), when he realizes what has happened, goes down into Hades and brings Alkestis back from the dead (to be brief). The hierarchy of love is very much explored in this play, albeit with much less interplay with strife than in other plays (although the relationship between Admetos and his parents offers a bit of that, to say the least).

127   That wisdom is reported in the *Apology* to have been validated by Apollo, who responded to Khairephon's query to the oracle at Delphi regarding who was the wisest man in Hellas, that it is Sokrates—which Sokrates interprets to mean that he is the only one wise enough to know that he does not know anything, whereas others whom he queries all think that they *know* things (like the definition of piety or justice, for instance) and they do not.

128   This is perhaps most emphatically exemplified at the beginning of the *Republic*, where Sokrates is coming up from the Piraios toward the city but is "forced" back to the house of Kephalos by a small gang of young men.

129   I might point out that the "norm" in the world of Sokrates and Alkibiades would be for an older man, as the lover (*erastes*) of a younger man—the beloved (*eramenos*)—both to be the aggressor and to serve as the tutor to the younger man who was learning his way through proper Athenian society. Sokrates limits his tutoring to moral issues while Alkibiades is so smitten by the older man that he finds himself frustratingly operating as a (failed) *erastes* vis-a-vis his *erastes*/mentor. For further detail on the *erastes-eramenos* relationship see the informative discussion in the earlier-noted K.J. Dover's *Greek Homosexuality*.

130   In a nutshell, Alkibiades convinced his fellow Athenians to undertake an absurd attack on Syracuse, Sicily, in 415-13 BCE, on the spurious grounds that Syracuse was aiding Sparta against Athens in the Peloponnesian conflict. (The distance of Sicily from the arenas of conflict is what most particularly made the attack absurd). While Alkibiades was sailing to Sicily as leader of the expedition, his enemies successfully mounted a court case against him, and, recalled to Athens to face trial, he instead headed to Sparta—to which he offered his services. (He was eventually tracked down and killed). When 14 years after the debacle, Sokrates was tried by his enemies as a corrupter of youth, Alkibiades was understood to offer a golden example of that corrupt influence, since Sokrates was blamed for Alkibiades' treasonous behavior.

131   There are several versions of this scene—one in the Boston Museum of Fine arts (black-figure kylix; 530-10 BCE); a second at the Louvre

(black-figure amphora; ca 510 BCE); a third in the Cleveland Museum of Art (Berlin Painter: black-figure neck amphora; ca 515-10 BCE); a fourth in the Munich Glyptotek (black-figure amphora, ca 510 BCE); a fifth in the University of Pennsylvania Art Museum (red-figure stamnos; 490 BCE) — to name a few. All of these are very similarly conceived, with strong emphasis on the dynamic diagonals assumed by the fighters' bodies, the scene placed in a stabilizing horizontal by vertical frame.

132   The vase appeared in the Metropolitan Museum of Art's collections with a good deal of fanfare in 1972, but the Italian government almost immediately lodged a claim that it had been plundered from an Etruscan tomb near Cerveteri in central Italy, and demanded a review of the work's provenance history from the Met. A thirty-year battle ensued, and the work was finally returned to Italy in 2008; it currently resides in the Archaeological Museum of Cerveteri. The tale of museums and plundered art is a story for another day.

133   See above, 63.

134   In the past few decades there has been some pushback against this interpretation of this detail; some have argued that his barefoot condition references his deification. He is in either case not depicted as an ordinary person.

135   For the better part of a century, at least, the aqueduct was believed to have been built in 19 BCE by Augustus' son-in-law, aide, and close friend, Marcus Vipsanius Agrippa, but more recent archaeological discoveries have suggested a later date, between 40 and 60 CE.

136   Think of the type of Greek vase known as an *amphora*. It means "both ears" — which name refers to the two large handles on the sides of such a vase, that can well suggest to an anthropomorphizing mind that the head-like vase has two large ears raising from its sides.

137   For more information on these contests and their significance, politically and religiously, see Soltes, *God and The Goalposts*, Chapter Five.

138   For more details about this, see Ori Z Soltes, *Our Sacred Signs*. For a more extensive discussion of the idea of the dome as it relates to this and other ideas, see Soltes, "The Emotive Power of an Evolving Symbol: The Idea of the Dome from Kurgan Graves to the Via Farini Tempio," in Fabrizio Ricciardelli, ed., *Emotions, Passions, and Power in Renaissance Italy*.

139   The root of the matter is *"leg-/lig-"* — which means "bind(ing)". Thus *re-lig-io* binds us back/again (*re-*) to the gods; *leg-es* (the plural of *leg-s* — that becomes *lex* over time) bind(s) us together as a community.

140   Both Lucius Livius Andronicus (ca 284-205 BCE) and Gnaeus Naevius (ca 270-201 BCE) wrote earlier epics, albeit in Saturnian verse (the

precise configuration of which is now somewhat uncertain). Livius' epic, *Odussia*, of which some fragments survive, was a translation or paraphrase into Latin of the *Odyssey*; Gnaeus' poem was an account of the First Punic War. The first Roman-authored epic in dactylic hexameter was the *Annales*, authored by Quintus Ennius, sometime in the second pre-Christian century. He composed it originally in 15 books and later added three more. Apparently the narrative carried from the destruction of Troy to the founding of the Republic in 509 BCE (books 1-3); continued from the early Republic to the First Pyrrhic War (281-271 BCE; Books 4-6); followed the events of the first (264-241 BCE) and second (218-201 BCE) Punic Wars—and contemporary events transpiring in the east (Books 7-9); focused on the Second Macedonian War up to the war against Antiokhos III (ca 192 BCE) in Books 10-12; and concluded with the events of that war against Antiokhos (192-188 BCE) with emphasis on the events of the Aetolian War (191-89 BCE). Sometime after publication he added three books that focused on the Istrian and Macedonian Wars (214-148 BCE)—but only fragments of all of this have survived.

141 Note that in the balance of this chapter, since it pertains to Roman and therefore Latin-language material, I will be using the more familiar, Latin-based forms and spellings of those named in the *Aeneid*. For that matter, since Vergil refers to Greeks rather than to Akhaians (he does refer to Danaans) for the most part, I will use that term whenever he does. Aren't you glad you asked?

142 Cyril Bailey, *Religion in Vergil*, 315.

143 As my colleague Adrianne Pierce reminded me in an email, "Aeneas' passivity is obvious in his first appearance in the poem, where his name is not even in the nominative case"—i.e., as the subject of the sentence, *doing*, but rather *being done to*. One of Vergil's exceptional features is his sensitivity to and use of various phonemic and syntactic features of the Latin language, and this is an instance of the latter. I might add that this first Aenean appearance doesn't occur until verse 92; all of the stormy action leads at length to his appearance in the text. I shall return to this verse toward the end of this chapter, for other reasons.

144 Troy's destruction will be born out of the belly of that horse, its temporary denizens slithering out of its womb by climbing down an umbilicus-like rope. If birth ideally (alas, not always, by any means) is the consequence of *eros*, here it is purely born of *eris*: not just the war but the ostensive reason for the war, which was fundamentally the consequence of a rape: Helen was *rapta* by Paris/Alexandros.

145 Presumably one of the other daughters of Leda, and not the dead

Klytaimnestra nor the already-accounted-for-and-still-married-to-Menelaus Helen. Of course, we understand from Odyssey 2 and its connections to other threads of story that Neoptolemos married the daughter of Helen and Menalaos—a granddaughter of Leda.

146 As so often, Vergil uses language to help contour the idea that he is conveying. He does not use the word *rumor*, as he might have, but rather, *fama*—twice within four words at the end of verse 173 and the beginning of 174—which was the word he also used in 170, thus also reminding us of the inherent ambiguity of that word: it can be the positive news of one's glorious name or, here, the dragging of one's name through the mud of public present and/or future opinion

147 Or, thinking ahead to Roman lyric poetry, the similarly-styled *agon* between Theseus and Ariadne in Catullus 64.

148 See above, 100.

149 Charon rows the dead across both the River Styx and the River Acheron, depending upon the particular narrative.

150 See Bailey, *Religion in Vergil*, especially 243.

151 This most likely refers to the defeat of Perseus, King of Macedonia, by Lucius Aemilius Paulus in 168 BCE, at Pydna, during the Third Macedonian War. It was not only a signal victory for Rome with regard to asserting its presence and power in the Hellenistic world, but—as far as the Roman historiographers were concerned—in establishing the superiority of its flexible Roman legions over the rigidly configured Macedonian phalanx.

152 This is the assertion made, for instance, by Charles Knapp, in his note on these lines in his Latin text, *The* Aeneid *of Vergil: Books I-VI, Selections VII-XII, with an Introduction, Notes, and Vocabulary*. Revised Edition. Knapp asserts that for both the Greeks and the Romans, dreams dreamt before midnight were accounted false and those after midnight, true, and thus the use of the ivory portal for Aeneas was intended to indicate the time of his exit—and although Knapp doesn't say so, if we take it as obvious that Aeneas is not dreaming but having a real experience, time-indication could be the only intention for the ivory-gate exit; the false-true issue need not apply. Maybe.

153 See above, Chapter seven. 314.

154 One might add that, topographically, if Evander's kingdom is up the Tiber River from the coast, it is arguably located more or less where Rome would subsequently be situated, and a Roman audience might be sensitive to that little datum, and able to take pride, as it were, both in being descendants of Aeneas' people and of the people who helped Aeneas against the Latins—with multiple implications, given

the role of Pallas in the last part of the *Aeneid*. Such a genealogical complication would not be inconsistent with the complications explicitly laid out in the text for the alliance between Evander and Aeneas, or the reference to a shrine that was later "restored by Romulus."
155 See above, 57.
156 "The People's (*publica*) Thing (*res*)" which is how the Romans viewed their government infrastructure, even in Vergil's time, although it had become entirely transformed by then from a democratic republic to a demagogic empire.
157 To be more precise, Nisus and Euryalus are clearly lovers (or at least best friends) who have gone out on and perish in this eristic adventure and when Euryalus is captured, Nisus—who could presumably have escaped—comes back out of love to try to save Nisus.
158 One might also recall—obliquely but very appropriately—the accumulation of small and large outrages inflicted on the household of Odysseus by some of the suitors, intended surely to build up the audience's anger at them and thus justify Odysseus' absolutist, death-dealing violence against them in the end.
159 They will be morally punished by being burdened with having shed his innocent blood!
160 There is some question regarding the correct order of verses in this brief passage, so it may be that we are reading 661-2, 665.
161 One might be reminded, in this moment of softness engendered by thinking of father-son/son-father love, of where Akhilleus arrived by the end of the *Iliad*: how, thinking of his own father, he arrived at his decision to return the body of Hektor to Priam. This is a twist within the twist: the *pius* Aeneas who has just been so very Akhilleus-like is restored for a moment to himself, and thus recalls the post-Akhillean Akhilleus.
162 See above, 242
163 See above, 55.
164 See above, 43.
165 Needless to say, it could and would not necessarily be so simple, but as a point of historical fact, when the Roman Empire is at its greatest physical extent, in the early second century, the two emperors who preside over it, Trajan (98-117 CE) and Hadrian (117-138 CE) are both from Spain (both born in Italica)—not Italy, much less Latium or Rome itself.
166 See above, 333.
167 One might also note that Vergil has adhered to a principle that Greek classical sculpture developed and that Thukydides used syntactically

in his prose: chiastic structure. Polyklitos' *Doryphoros* exhibited this with its bent-straight, relaxed-tensed arms and legs; Thukydides did it with sentences; Vergil is doing it with his two protagonists: Aeneas is, as it were, Paris the Trojan and Akhilleus the Akhaian; Turnus is Menelaus the Akhaian and Hektor the Trojan.

168 I honestly doubt that Vergil intended another oblique parallel here, but it is a nice one anyway: we may recall Odysseus among the Phaiakians; he could not compete in running contests, asserting that his legs had lost that capability due to his long travels at sea — and suffering *in* the sea.

169 So he apparently had a sword and not only a spear with him as he faced Turnus who was armed with his sword — or had he picked up Turnus' fallen weapon?

170 We now think back to the note regarding the first appearance of the hero's name, in verse 92 of Book I See above, 270): *extemplo Aeneae tendens frigore membra* ("immediately the limbs of Aeneas are dissolved by cold [fear]"). This not only offers to us an Aeneas not as a nominative case actor/doer, but as an oblique (dative) case to whom things are done, but underscores the cold that he feels at that moment at the beginning of the epic. Here at the end, he feels hot (and the limbs of Turnus go cold) — and his limbs (his sword hand) seem to operate beyond his control.

171 See above, 248-9, 301.

172 See *Res Gestae Divi Augusti (The Achievements of the Divine Augustus)*, P.A. Brunt & J.M. Moore, eds., 34:2.

173 One might add that Aristophanes also more than merely implied this in *Lysistrata*, the end of which suggests that not only are sex and love better than war but so are the accompanying arts of love and peace: singing, dancing, and religious festivals. See above, 226.

174 The common English-language spelling is Callimachus, but I am continuing my stubborn and snobby insistence on transliterations that are closer to the Greek letters when a name is Greek and not Latin.

175 The numbers attached to Catullan poems derive from the order in which they are offered in the first complete manuscript to appear beyond antiquity, in Verona, around 1300. That manuscript presumably reflects the previous 14 centuries of hand-written collections of varying lengths, and in any case led to several manuscript lines that continue until the first printed edition of 1472, which enshrined the traditional order. The first 60 of these are fairly short poems, the following eight are longer and the last 45 are epigrams. There are about 30 Lesbia poems scattered among the first

group, which also includes some poignant works referencing the death of his beloved older brother.
176 See above, 146-7.
177 See above, 273 and 277, regarding Vergil's phonemically charged presentation of the destruction of Laokoon and his sons, or of the blind Polyphemus.
178 Not only tablets, but sometimes, particularly if some body part had survived, a relief-sculpted image of that body part. One can still see arrays of these miniatures, often in silver, on the walls of small country churches in Greece and other Mediterranean climes: arms, hands, legs, feet, eyes, breasts, and so on. Conversely—and appropriate to the mood of this ode—curse tablets, also often specifying particular body parts to be harmed, were quite often placed, hanging (or sometimes buried), in *sacer* spaces.
179 See above, 148.
180 "Ilia" is another name for Rhea Silvia, mother of Romulus and Remus and thus the metaphorical mother of Rome itself.
181 He is punning between the name of the personified goddess and the abstraction of the old love between Horace and Lydia.
182 Later on, the French will refer to an orgasm as *"une petite mort"*—"a little death." All things considered I would hardly deny these Roman poets the same kind of sensibility.
183 The poet refers to that mistress as being from Pieria, which is southeastern Macedonia, which is Thessaly.
184 See the brief discussion of this in L.P. Wilkinson, *Horace and His Lyric Poetry*, 15-16, among others.
185 See above, 67.
186 Nemesis is oddly named, too: a Greek goddess of retribution, usually toward those who have exhibited hubris (overweening, arrogant pride); and as an everyday word, the inescapable agent of one's downfall. Is this truly her name, or is this the name that the poet has applied to her?
187 This datum is garnered from I.22 and IV1.120ff.
188 It strikes me as a bit ironic that these confiscations of property were made by Octavian (he would not yet be Augustus) in order to provide allotments of land to veterans who had served in his armies—given the frequency with which the *eris/eros* theme plays out as a disparagement of warfare, the soldier's life, and their concomitants (although Propertius among the elegists does this least of all).
189 Just to remind us all: Atalanta agreed to marry anyone who could outrun her—and speared those who tried and failed. It was not until Hippomenes beat her—by letting fall three of the golden apples of

the Hesperides, which she paused to pick up, one by one—that she married, and had physical relations with a man. Another tale of *eris* intertwined with *eros*.

190 And is he also thinking about how Bacchantes, under the influence of the god, have at times gone mad and torn apart any males within their reach? The most famous example in Greek and Latin literature is that in Euripides' play, *The Bacchae*, in which the main male character, Pentheus, is torn apart by such a group of females, led by his own mother, who tears off the head of the son she does not recognize in her god-induced state. Even more relevant, perhaps, is Orpheus who, like Propertius, was a poet-singer, who was also torn apart by maenads.

191 Since we don't know who Gallus was, really, we might consider at least the possibility that, like the name, Cynthia, "Gallus" is a pseudonym. An interesting one, since it means rooster or cock. Gallus is shown several times liking to crow, but Propertius ends up being able to crow more loudly, if one follows to poem 10 and particularly to 13.

192 Tullus' uncle was Lucius Volcacius Tullus, consul in 33 BCE and proconsul of Asia in 30-29 BCE. When he tells Tullus to go on without him, Propertius adds that he should surpass his uncle, to "restore ancient rights that our allies have let slip," so the plan must have been to go out to Asia and even join in campaigns against the Parthians who had defeated a Roman army led by Crassus in 53 BCE and taken the Roman standards. Augustus would famously get them back in a victory over the Parthians in 20 BCE.

193 And as often in Propertius, the music of the Latin cannot be easily conveyed in English: he plays with the sounds of *soles*—"you are accustomed" in the first line—and *solus*—"alone"—in the second line.

194 See the comments by W.A. Camps in his edition of *Propertius Elegies Book I*, 89. He argues for *crimina*—versus the standard Latin edition edited by E A. Barber, *Sexti Properti Carmina*, which is part of the Oxford Classical Texts series. Barber sticks with *carmina*, but acknowledges the *crimina* alternative in his notes.

195 Again and again: *diebus manibus*, often abbreviated as D. M.: "to the gods/shades of the underworld..." the deceased is consigned.

196 It is certainly interesting that in Book IV he writes so much about Roman history and Roman cults—as if to display his ability and interest in focusing on that old-morality essence of Rome—its *pietas*—and to underscore his "old-style" talent.

197 Let us not forget that the very word "republic"—*res publica*, meaning

"people's thing"—emphasizes a communal-values identity. So Augustus' claim (specifically articulated, later on, in his *Res Gestae*), to have saved the republic after a century of civil wars, coincided with his "family values" moral stance—the more so, one might imagine, given the failure of his own family to exhibit those values...

198 The *Tristia* are a series of poems—some of them really letters—written, while in exile, in elegiac couplets. The second book is particularly sad, in essentially being a plea to Augustus to recall him from that exile (to which there was no response).

199 Among the most effective tellings of that tale is the version found in Ovid's own *Metamorphoses* (Book I)—in which the nymph is saved from the god by her father, Peneus, a river-god, by being transformed into a laurel tree just as Apollo is reaching her. The god then takes that plant as his own symbol, and successful poets would for generations be crowned as "laureates" to symbolize their connection to the god of poetry. Ovid here, in the *Amores*, is seeking just such a crown.

200 See below, 413-14 and above, fn 199 for a slightly fuller review of that story.

201 Every reader would have recognized that famous story, the ultimate symbolic basis for this narrative, in fact. Aphrodite, married to Hephaistos, ugliest of gods, has an affair with Ares. Helios (or perhaps Hermes, the messenger god), eventually informs Hephaistos that he is being cuckolded, and the smith-god creates a metallic web that ensnares his wife and her lover in the bed. The other gods are brought in to see Ares and Aphrodite thusly caught and presumably humiliated. In one version one god notes that he would willingly trade places with Ares: capture in Hephaistos' net is a small price to pay for having lain with the goddess of love and beauty... The story is well told in *Odyssey* 8.267ff and Ovid himself retold it in his *Metamorphoses* 4.170ff.

202 Sulmona is the city in which he was born, in the territory of the Peligni.

203 Bacchus is a horned god in his physical capacity as a bull, and also called, among other epithets, Lyaeos, from the Greek verb, *luo*, meaning "to loosen," referring to his ability to free one from cares and anxieties through his beverage and his being.

204 For more of a discussion of this, see Peter E. Knox's introductory essay in his edition of *Heroides, Selected Epistles*; also see his article, (2002) "The *Heroides*: Elegiac Voices," in B. W. Boyd (ed.) *Brill's Companion to Ovid*, 117–39—and also the article by J. Farrell "Reading and Writing the *Heroides*," *Harvard Studies in Classical Philology* 98 (1998). 307–338.

205 The first fifteen of the *Heroides* are letters from the woman in question to the man; there is a smaller group that is often included and then typically referred to as the *Double Heroides*—epistles 16-21—which offers a series of dialogues.

206 In *Tristia* 2.207, Ovid mentions that his exile was the result of *carmen et error*—"a poem and a mistake"—but that still doesn't tell us what either of these actually *was*.

207 There have been some modern scholars (in particular, J.J. Hartman in 1923 and more recently, Fitton Brown in 1985) who have asserted that he actually never went into exile—that that part of his life and his writings were a function of his imaginative powers—but most scholars regard the exile as having been genuine and genuinely painful.

208 See above, Chapter Four, 155-7, 170-89.

209 A heck of a nice coincidence, this phrase, *primum oculis*—but surely a mere coincidence in its connection chronologically forward to the opening line of Propertius' *Monobiblos*! (see above, Chapter Eight, 366)

210 So I have deliberately continued to backtrack chronologically in moving from "serious" to "comedic" material; I will leap forward again in concluding this section of my discussion, in moving from comic theater to satire.

211 One is hard-put, in fact, to think of serious—tragic—playwrights in the Roman tradition. Seneca, the Stoic philosopher, wrote several tragedies, which seem to have been rarely performed, if at all, and which are quite boring. His *Medea* pales in comparison with the play of that name by Euripides, for instance.

212 I am using the translation by Harry J. Leon, who effectively captures the flavor, rhythm and sometime-rhyme scheme of Plautus, rather than providing my own.

213 Horace, *Odes* I.5; see above, 352-4)

214 For a fuller discussion of these categories and their consequences not only for pagan Greco-Roman civilization but, subsequently, for early Judaism and Christianity, see Ori Z Soltes: *Magic and religion in the Greco-Roman World: The Beginnings of Judaism and Christianity*.

215 The issue is, in the terms coined by Sir James Fraser, "contagious magic": transferring a positive or negative condition through touch. See ibid, 30-32.

216 See above, fn 47

217 There are, of course, ubiquitous altars in a *pietas*-ridden Rome, as today there are churches on every corner—almost.

218 To our eyes and ears there is certainly something inherently

humorous about the fact that the midwife is named Lesbia, but of course Catullus was several generations from being born, so the most that the name would have connoted to Terence's audience was that she came from the island of Lesbos.

219 At a practical level, by the time of Perikles, when Athens was at its political, military and cultural height, citizenship in the Athenian democracy was limited to adult, free-born Athenian males who were the offspring of two free-born Athenian parents—a closed franchise, except on the rare occasion that a non-Athenian might be honored with citizenship for having done something unusual for the *polis* (e.g, a very successful Olympic athlete). One could live in or around Athens for generations without acquiring the rights and responsibilities of citizenship. I might add that the Akhaemenid Persians first, possibly Alexander the Great after them, (depending upon how one reads his biographical information), and certainly the Romans, broke that pattern: one could gain Roman citizenship gradually (from allied status to Italian rights to Latin rights to Roman citizenship rights)—in theory regardless of one's parentage. When the empire was at its greatest extent, in the early second century CE, its emperors, first Trajan and then Hadrian, came from Spain, as previously noted.

220 Yes, the same Horace whose lyrical love poetry we examined in Chapter Eight.

221 In fact, the Greeks per se had little to do with the claim Juvenal makes. While one could say that the Roman taste for plundered riches began after their third and final war with Carthage (the Third Punic War, 149-146 BCE), the end of which coincided with their second military visit to Corinth, also in 146 BCE—after which they never left (as opposed to the first visit to Corinth, in 196 BCE)—if there were a moment that culminated this increasing taste, it was the death of the Hellenistic king, Attalus III of Pergamon, in Asia Minor. Lacking an heir, he left his very wealthy kingdom to Rome in his will, in 133 BCE; that moment, coinciding with the era of the Gracchi, set in motion a century of civil wars that only ended at Actium—by which time the shreds of the republic had been rewoven together into the empire that reached is greatest extent during Juvenal's lifetime.

222 For a detailed discussion of the interplay among paganism, Judaism, and Christianity in the Greco-Roman world, see Soltes: *Magic and Religion*.

223 The Hebrew term for that spirit, and for "soul" is *n'shama*; the Greek is *psykhe*, and the Latin is *anima*—hence "to animate" means "to be-soul."

224 Simply put, to "know the good and evil" of something is to know all

about it—in rhetoric, to use two opposed terms to refer to an entirety is called a merism—so if this is a tree of the knowledge of good and evil it is a tree of knowledge of moral totality. See Cyrus H. Gordon & Gary A. Randburg, *The Bible and the Ancient Near East*, 36. Also see the rabbinic discussion found in Midrash *Breshit* (Genesis) XXV.7. By felicitous coincidence for our discussion, in fact, *Od* 20.309-10 presents Telemakhos as saying "I know all things, the good and the evil."

225   For a more extensive discussion of this issue, see Alex Shalom Kohav, *The Sod Hypothesis*, 55-6.

226   For our purposes I am ignoring the complication—part of a much larger series of issues—that, while Adam eventuates as a male, the biblical text, when it first presents him as created from earth, notes that the Lord created the first human as "male and female." The Hebrew language casts every noun of whatever sort into grammatically male and female forms—there is no neuter as, for example, Greek and Latin both possess—and defaults to the masculine form. Thus *grammatically*, "Adam" is "male"—just as "table" and "tree" are, whereas "leg" and "picture" are "female". The rabbinic interpretive tradition ultimately suggests that an original female is being referenced in that phrase—before the creation of Eve; that she was, like Adam, made of earth (not from Adam's rib—another story for another day—as Eve was), and thus at the very least his equal. Her name was Lilith—and thereby develops an emphatically eristic story regarding the relationship between Adam and his first wife...

227   One might note that this is an all too common motif in the literature that we have just left behind: it sets in motion the problematic of Sophokles' *Antigone*, as we have seen, as well as the Romulus-Remus story to which we have alluded as one of the essential details in the narrative leading from the time of Aeneas to that of Vergil and Augustus. (See above, 199ff and 298-9).

228   Nonetheless, for a more detailed discussion of the problem of evil in Genesis see Ori Z Soltes, "Revelation, Interpretation, Language and Human Responsibility: The Problem of Evil from Genesis 6:5 to Contemporary Acts of Terror," in Aurelie Renault & Patricia Reynaud, eds., *La Question du mal: Ethique, politique, religion comparee*, 47-61; and also Soltes, "Ethics and the Problem of Interpretation in Sacred Scriptures," in Richard Penaskovic and Mustafa Sahin, eds., *Peacebuilding in a Fractious World: On Hoping against All Hope*, 30-43.

229   For the purposes of our discussion, other issues raised by the repeat of this process in two locations—and again in Gerar, with Isaac and Rebecca—that are addressed, in part, by the Documentary Hypothesis, are not relevant and I am therefore ignoring them.

230 See Soren Kierkegaard, *Fear and Trembling* and *The Sickness unto Death*, (transl with introduction and notes by Walter Lowrie, esp 69-82. Kierkegaard does not, however, include Isaac in his felicitous turn of phrase, reserving that absolute perfection of faith for Abraham alone.

231 By this I mean that there is no final dialogue of resolution between Abraham and Hagar, Abraham and Sara, Abraham and Ishmael, Abraham and Isaac—to say nothing of Sarah and Hagar or Sara and Ishmael or Isaac, or Hagar and Ishmael or Isaac. The closest we get—and it is still silent—is the statement that Ishmael showed up to bury his father together with Isaac (Gen 25:9).

232 The Muslims also took control of Sicily and occasional parts of southern Italy in 902 (the first conquest actually came earlier, in 827) and held that control until the advent of the Normans, gradually, between 1061 and 1091. Much later there is a two-part Italian "version" of the *Chanson de Roland*, as well, the first entitled *Orlando Innamorato*, written by Matteo Maria Boiardo, which appeared in 1495, after the author's death, and the better-known, *Orlando Furioso*, written by Ludovico Ariosto in 1516 and first published in a complete form in 1532.

233 The defeat at Manzikert in 1071 led the Byzantine emperor Romanos IV Diogenes to beg for support from Western Christendom—there had been a religious and political schism between west and east in 1054 that was far from healed—but that "support" took 25 years to materialize. By then Romanos' successor, Alexios I had restored some semblance of stability to the Empire—and the papacy was having ever more disturbing problems with heretics, spiritually aberrant and sometimes too powerful monastic orders, and restive and contentious secular knights (and occasional kings), requiring a major distractive and nominally unifying activity. The Crusades would try to offer that sort of activity for the next two centuries.

234 To split a hair: if we consider the Middle East to be part of the West in literary terms, then perhaps the *Gilgamesh Epic* would and should be considered the beginning point of Western Epic poetry.

235 I am for the most part using John Ciardi's translation with its strong effort to convey the feel of Dante's *terza rima*.

236 "Therefore, a lion from the forest will slay them [those who do not know the way of the Lord], a wolf of the deserts will destroy them, a leopard will watch over their cities."

237 He may have been inspired earlier to *begin* the composition of this work, after he chanced to see her, in the company of two somewhat older women, strolling along by the Arno River near where he

was—happened to be?—standing, and she is said to have greeted him; he was so taken aback that he did not respond but hurried back to his room to think about her, slept, and in a dream received the inspiration for the beginning of the *Vita Nuova,* in which case, it took him quite some time to complete the work. The style itself used in that early work and perfected in the *Divine Comedy* seems to have had its origins among the Provencal troubadours, been imitated and emulated in the court of Frederick II (1194-1250) in Sicily, and its development perfected—so he is regarded as the "founder" of the *dolce stil nuovo*—by Guido Guinizelli of Bologna (ca 1230-76); Dante would have been 11 years old when Guido died.

238 "Moor" is the most common word used in medieval and then modern English to refer to the Muslims in Spain. Derived from the Greek word *mauros*, meaning "black" it suggests a kind of skin-pigment/racial distinction in the mind of the user, between "us light-skinned Europeans/Christians" and "those darker skinned Middle Eastern/North African Muslims." Other terms would come into use, such as "Saracen," as well, and of course the term Arab was and remains in many cases confused with the term Muslim, so that too many historians incorrectly refer to the "Arab invasion of Spain," whereas it was a Muslim invasion in which the leadership—or some of it—was Arab, but most of the troops were Berber. And, of course, the term "blackamoor" is actually a redundancy.

239 Since the play is written, of course, in French, I am using the French, rather than Spanish (or English) versions of all the names, as well as of the word, "infanta."

240 The *Mahabharata* ("Great Bharata") is twelve times as long as the *Iliad* and *Odyssey* combined.

241 He was Arjuna's regent when Arjuna's father, the king, died, but refused to hand over control of the kingdom to his nephew when Arjuna came of age, so Arjuna's impending battle is to regain the throne and restore the proper order of things.

242 To clarify: *nirvana*, unlike heaven/paradise, is not a *place*, it is a *condition*—in which the individual soul loses its individuality in being subsumed into Brahman/Krishna.

243 I am quoting here from the introduction by Kimon Friar to his masterful translation—which transfers Kazantzakis' metrical poetic style from modern Greek to English iambic hexameter. See Nikos Kazantzakis, *The Odyssey: A Modern Sequel*, transl. into English verse, introduction, synopsis and notes by Kimon Friar, ix.

244 I am using the inspired translation by Kimon Friar both because it very accurately conveys the Greek of Kazantzakis and because its

lyrical qualities of sound and meter also handsomely resonate from the poet's original language—and why presume to try to improve on something so excellent?

245 And see above, fn 83.

246 Walcott was born and grew up on St Lucia but his far-ranging travels also resonate through the poem, which spends time in various places, including Achille's imagined journey on a slave ship from Africa to the Americas.

247 See above, 81-82, and fnn 91and 98, for a quick reminder of who Philoktetes was, with his unhealing wound, in the Homeric-Sophoklean world.

248 See Thersites in unhappy action in *Iliad* II. 212-77 above, fn 47.

249 My reference to Willy Loman is intended—in recalling that renowned "everyman" character in Arthur Miller's play, *Death of a Salesman*—to allude as well to Miller's 1949 essay on "Tragedy and the Common Man," in which he emphasizes the difference between Greek tragedy with its bigger-than-life and socio-economically gigantic heroes and the everyman heroes of his own (our own) era and writing.

250 The "Ghost Dance" reflected a new religious movement that incorporated diverse Native American belief systems. It was led by the Northern Paiute spiritual leader, Wovoka (aka Jack Wilson), whose prophetic teachings encompassed the idea that, properly performed, the Ghost Dance would unite the various Native American peoples in the region and also connect the living to the spirits of the dead. This would create a force that would push white colonists back, and bring peace and prosperity to the newly unified Native American peoples. It was first practiced by the Nevada Northern Paiute in 1889, but spread rapidly throughout the southwest, from California to Oklahoma; in each new location, local tribes usually synthesized particulars of their own customs to the general pattern established by Wovoka's teachings. Practice of the Ghost Dance movement is believed to have helped inspire resistance to forced assimilation, particularly by the Lakota; in the massacre at Wounded Knee of 1890, US Army forces killed well over 150 Minconjou and Hunkpapa from the Lakota people.

251 See Ovid, *Metamorphoses* 10.243-97

252 The musical made its debut at the National Theater in Washington, DC in August, 1957 and on Broadway in September of the same year. In 1961 a movie version of the musical was made which won 10 academy awards.

Brief Bibliography

Note:
There are scores of journal articles that have both fed into my reading over the years and that are available with regard to aspects of this narrative, but I am only listing a few of those that stand out as particularly useful to the reader or that I specifically reference in the notes. There are also at least three or four excellent translations of the *Odyssey, Iliad, Aeneid,* and *Divine Comedy*, but I am only listing the translations that were my primary reference points, since I was mainly reading the works I discuss in their original languages. Nor am I listing the various editions of these works in Greek, Latin, Hebrew, Italian, Spanish, Sanskrit, or Modern Greek, but only the translations that will be most useful to most readers—with a few exceptions, either where I have referenced the commentary in a particular edition or contrastive readings between two editions (eg Camps' edition of Propertius vs that by Barber) or in cases, such as Horace and Corneille, where I was not using any English translation at all, for one reason or another, when I was writing.

Aeneid of Virgil, The, A verse Translation by Rolphe Humphries. New York: Charles Scribner's Sons, 1951
Aeschylus I: *The Oresteia*, edited with an Introduction by Richmond Lattimore. New York: Washington Square Press, 1969
Aristophanes, *Lysistrata*, Douglass Parker, transl., New York: The New American Library, 1964
Bhagavad Gita, The, Translated and Interpreted by Franklin Edgerton. New York: Harper & Row, 1944
Bailey, Cyril, *Religion in Vergil*. New York: Barnes & Noble, Inc, 1935.)
Barber, E.A., *Sexti Properti Carmina*. London: Oxford University Press, 1974
Barrett, D.S., "The Friendship of Achilles and Patroclus," in *The Classical Bulletin*. 57.1 (1980), 87-93
Bluemner, Heinrich, *The Home Life of the Greeks*. Translated by Alice Zimmern. New York: Kessinger Publishing, LLC, 2007
Bradford, Ernle, *Ullysses Found*. New York: Harcourt, Brace & World, 1963

Brault, Gerard J., *The Song of Roland. An Analytical Edition*. Vol I (Introduction and Commentary); Vol II (Oxford Text and English Translation). University Park, PA: Penn State University Press, 2010

Boyd, B. W., ed., *Brill's Companion to Ovid*. Leiden: Brill, 2002; see in particular the essay by Peter E. Knox, "The *Heroides*: Elegiac Voices"

Butler, Samuel, *The Authoress of the Odyssey*. Chicago: University of Chicago Press, 1967

Camps, W.A. *Propertius Elegies (Books I -IV)*. London: Cambridge University Press, 1969

Carpenter, Rhys, *Folk Tale, Fiction and Saga in the Homeric Epics*. Berkeley: University of California Press, 1974

Carson, Anne, *Eros the Bittersweet*. Princeton: Princeton University Press, 1986

Clarke, W.M., "Achilles and Patroclus in Love," in *Hermes* 106.3 (1978), 381-396

Commager, Steele, *The Odes of Horace: A Critical Study*. Bloomington: Indiana University Press, 1967

Corneille, Pierre, *Le Cid*. Paris: Classiques Larouuse,1959

Dante, *Vita Nuova*, Mark Musa, transl. Oxford: Oxford University Press, 1992

Dante, *Inferno, Purgatorio, Paradiso* (3 vols), John Ciardi, transl. New York: The New American Library, 1970

Dodds, Eric Robertson, *The Greeks and the Irrational*. (Second Edition). Berkeley: University of California Press, 2004

Dover, K.J., *Aristophanic Comedy*. Berkeley: University of California Press, 1972

_____, K.J., *Greek Homosexuality*. New York: Random House, 1980

Euripides, *Alcestis*, Richmond Lattimore, transl. Chicago: University of Chicago Press, 1966

_____, *Hippolytus*, David Grene, transl. Chicago: University of Chicago Press, 1966

_____, *Iphigenia in Aulis*, Charles R. Walker, transl. Chicago: University of Chicago Press, 1965

_____, *Iphigenia in Tauris*, Witter Bynner, transl. Chicago: University of Chicago Press, 1956

_____, *The Medea*, Rex Warner, transl. Chicago: University of Chicago Press, 1966

Farrell, J., "Reading and Writing the *Heroides*," *Harvard Studies in Classical Philology* 98 (1998)

Finley, Moses I., *The World of Odysseus*. New York: The Viking Press, 1965

Fraenkel, Eduard, *Horace*. Oxford: Oxford University Press, 1970

Gomme, Arnold, *Essays on Greek History and Literature*, Oxford: Basil Blackwell, 1937

Gordon Cyrus H. & Gary A. Randburg, *The Bible and the Ancient Near East*, (4th edition). New York: W. W. Norton & Co,1997

Hesiod, translated by Richmond Lattimore. Ann Arbor: The University of Michigan Press, 1970

Hesiod, *Theogony*, translated, with an introduction, by Norman O. Brown. Indianapolis: The Bobbs-Merrill Co, 1953

Hijmans, Jr., B.L., "Alexandros and his Grief," in Wace and Stubbings, *A Companion to Homer*. London: MacMillan Co., 1969

Horace, *Odes and Epodes*, edited with introduction and notes by Paul Shorey. Pittsburgh: University of Pittsburgh Press, 1960

Iliad of Homer, The, translated and with an introduction by Richmond Lattimore. Chicago: University of Chicago Press, 1967

Kazantzakis, Nikos, *The Odyssey: A Modern Sequel*. New York: Simon & Schuster, 1958

Kierkegaard, Soren, *Fear and Trembling* and *The Sickness unto Death*, (transl with introduction and notes by Walter Lowrie. Princeton: Princeton University Press, 1968

Kitto, H.D.F., *The Greeks*. Baltimore, MD: Penguin Books, 1964

Knapp, Charles, *The Aeneid of Vergil, Books I-VI, Selections VII-XII, with an Introduction, Notes, and Vocabulary*. Revised Edition. Glenview, Ill: Scott, Foresman and Company, 1951

Knox, Peter E., *Heroides, Selected Epistles*. Cambridge: Cambridge University Press, 1995

Kohav, Alex Shalom, *The Sod Hypothesis* Boulder, CO: Makom Books, 2013

Lee, M. Owen, *Word, Sound, and Image in the Odes of Horace*. Ann Arbor: University of Michigan Press, 1969

Littman, Robert J., *The Greek Experiment: Imperialism and Social Conflict 800-400 BC*. Harcourt Brace Jovanovich, Inc., 1974

Menander, *Dyskolus*, Carroll Moulton, transl., New York: The New American Library, 1977

Morales, Manuel Sanz and Gabriel Laguna Mariscal, "The Relationship Between Achilles and Patroclus According to Chariton of Aphrodisias," in *Classical Quarterly*. 53.1 (2003), 292-326

_____, "Was the Relationship between Achilles and Patroclus Homoerotic? The View of Apollonius Rhodius," in *Hermes* 133.1 (2005), 120-123

Nagler, Michael, *Spontaneity and Tradition: A Study in the Oral Art of Homer*, Berkeley: University of California Press, 1974

Nagy, Gregory, "Achilles and Patroclus as Models for the Twinning of Identity," http://nrs.Harvard.edu/urn-3:hlnc.essay:Nagy.Acchilles_and_Patroclus_as_Models.2018.

Nelson, Conny, ed., *Homer's Odyssey: A Critical Handbook*. Belmont, CA: Wadsworth Publishing Co, 1969

Odyssey of Homer, The, translated and with an introduction by Richmond Lattimore. New York: Haper & Row, 1967

Owen E.T., *The Harmony of Aeschylus.* Toronto: Clarke, Irwin and Co., Ltd., 1952

_____, *The Story of the Iliad.* London: G. Bell & Sons, 1947

Page, Denys, *History and the Homeric Iliad.* Berkeley: University of California Press, 1959

Plato, *The Symposium,* William Hamilton, transl., Baltimore: Penguin Books, 1967

Podlecki, Anthony J., *The Poliltical Background of Asechylean Tragedy.* Ann Arbor: University of Michigan Press, 1966

Pollitt, Jerome Jordan, *Art and Experience in Classical Greece.* Cambridge: Cambridge University Press, 1972

Pomeroy, Sarah B., *Goddesses, Whores, Wives, and Slaves: Women in Classical Antiquity.* New York: Schocken Books, 1976

Poschl, Viktor: *The Art of Vergil: Image and Symbol in the Aeneid.* Ann Arbor: University of Michigan Press, 1970

Pucci, Pietro, *Hesiod and the Language of Poetry.* Batlimore/London: The Johns Hopkins University Press, 1977

Quinn, Kenneth, *Virgil's Aeneid: A Critical Description.* Ann Arbor: University of Michigan Press, 1969

Res Gestae Divi Augusti (The Achievements of the Divine Augustus), P.A. Brunt & J.M. Moore, eds. Oxford: Oxford University Press, 1973

Sheppard, J.T., *The Pattern of the Iliad.* New York: Haskell House, 1966

Sissa, Julia, *Greek Virginity.* Cambridge, MA: Harvard University Press, 1990

Slater, Philip E., *The Glory of Hera: Greek Mythology and the Greek Family.* Boston: Beacon Press, 1968

Soltes, Ori Z., "Ethics and the Problem of Interpretation in Sacred Scriptures," in Richard Penaskovic and Mustafa Sahin, eds., *Peacebuilding in a Fractious World: On Hoping against All Hope.* Eugene, OR: Pickwick Publications, 2017

_____, *God and The Goalposts: A Brief History of Sports, Religion, Politics, War, and Art.* Savage, MD: Bartleby Press, 2017

_____, *Magic and Religion in the Greco-Roman World: The Beginnings of Judaism and Christianity,* Boulder, CO: Western Academic Press, 2017

_____, *Our Sacred Signs: How Jewish, Christian, and Muslim art Draw from the Same Source.* New York: Westview Press, 2005

_____, "Revelation, Interpretation, Language and Human Responsibility: The Problem of Evil from Genesis 6:5 to Contemporary Acts of Terror," in Aurelie Renault & Patricia Reynaud, eds., *La Question du mal: Ethique, politique, religion compare.* Paris: Classiques Garnier, 2014

_____, "The Emotive Power of an Evolving Symbol: The Idea of the Dome from Kurgan Graves to the Via Farini *Tempio*," in Fabrizio Ricciardelli, ed., *Emotions, Passions, and Power in Renaissance Italy*. Florence: Villa LeBalze Studies, 2013

_____, *The Problem of Plato's* Cratylus: *The Relation of Language to Truth in the History of Philosophy*. Lewiston: Edwin Mellon Press, 2007

Sophocles, *Antigone*. Elizabeth Wyckoff, transl., Chicago: University of Chicago Press, 1976

_____, *Oedipus at Colonus*. Robert Fitzcerald, transl., Chicago: University of Chicago Press, 1976

_____, *Oedipus the King*, David Grene, transl., Chicago: University of Chicago Press, 1976

_____, *Philoctetes*. Translated and with an Intorduction by David Grene. Chicago: University of Chicago Press, 1957

Vrissimtzis, Nikos A., *Love, Sex & Marriage in Ancient Greece*. Athens: I Macris, 1995

Walcot, P., *Hesiod and the Near East*, Cardiff: University of Wales Press, 1966

Walcott, Derek, *Omeros*. New York: Farrar Strauss Giroux, 1990

Whitman, Cedric H., *Homer and the Heroic Tradition*. New York: W.W. Norton & Co., 1958

Willcock, M.M., "The Funeral Games of Patroclus," in *Bulletin of the Institute of Classical Studies*, (London), 1973

Wilkinson, L.P., *Horace and His Lyric Poetry*. Cambrdige: Cambridge University Press, 1968

Index

Note: When a proper name is also the name of or embedded in the name of a play, (eg, *Antigone, Medea,* or *Oidipos Tyrannos*) or a Platonic Dialogue (eg, *Phaedo, Phaedros*) I only indicate the unitalicized name of the individual, but a search will also yield the play of that name. Also a reminder regarding my decision regarding transliterated Greek spellings, most obviously that I almost always transliterate the Greek *kappa* ("k") as a "k" rather than as a "c" and the Greek *omikron* ("o") as "o" rather than as "u".

Aaron, 451
Abel, 446
Abraham(ic) 8, 15, 18, 445, 447-9, 451, 471, 475, 542
Acca, 328

Acestes, 288-9, 291
Achates, 271, 294, 296, 334
Acheron, 92, 151, 294, 295, 533
Actium, 263, 265, 311, 391, 393, 540
Adam, 444-47, 541
Aeneas, 249, 252, 268-282, 284-343, 391, 410-12, 417, 419, 457, 460, 461, 465, 485, 487, 525, 532, 533, 534, 535, 541
Aeneid, 143, 252, 263, 267, 268, 269, 277, 287, 305, 323, 334, 341, 343, 346, 396, 410, 411, 419, 440, 457, 458, 460, 461, 525, 532, 533, 534, 545, 547, 548
Aeolus, 270, 314
Africa, 278, 279, 410, 454, 480, 489, 495, 544
Agamemnon, 30, 36, 37, 38-42, 44, 47-9, 52, 55, 57, 58, 60-4, 66-8, 70, 73, 80, 97-101, 108, 126, 135-8, 148, 151-8, 160, 162-6, 169-83, 185-8, 200, 213, 266, 276, 290, 307, 308, 402, 489, 517, 518, 519, 521, 522, 524, 526, 528
Agathon, 234-6, 239-41
agon, 115, 119, 122, 132, 164, 165, 166, 171, 175, 182, 185, 193, 196, 201, 202, 203, 209, 211, 215, 221, 227, 274, 282, 283, 284, 314, 424, 428, 430, 511, 533
Agrippa, 265, 311, 414, 531
Aiaia, 89
Aias, 30, 47-51, 53, 54, 61, 73, 100, 107, 126, 135, 143, 168, 287, 296, 322, 526
Aigeus, 213, 214, 215
Aigisthos, 66, 67, 68, 70, 136, 151, 152, 153, 155, 156-7, 161, 162, 163, 524, 528
Aineias, 43, 58, 70
Aiolos, 88, 89, 94, 105, 134
Aiskhylos, 5, 152-3, 158, 160, 167,

175, 181, 182, 188, 199, 200, 205, 209, 213, 221, 224, 518, 527

Aisklepios, 247, 248
Akhaian(s), 24, 28, 36-40, 42, 44, 45, 47-51, 57, 59-61, 63-4, 65, 68, 70-3, 80-1, 87, 98, 100, 120, 125, 126, 133, 135-6, 139, 155, 169, 170-1, 175, 177, 181, 185, 187, 245, 250, 269, 272, 274, 275-6, 287, 288, 290, 295, 296, 306-8, 309, 312, 314, 324, 325, 343, 368, 386, 387, 489, 496, 516, 517, 519, 520, 523, 524,, 526, 532, 535
Akhilleus, 9, 28, 30, 32-3, 36-44, 46-50, 54-64, 66, 74, 80, 82, 90, 95, 98, 99, 100, 107, 126, 127, 135, 136, 137, 142, 143, 155, 160, 166, 167, 170-1, 175-8, 180, 184-7, 227, 233-4, 238, 241-2, 244, 246, 255, 256, 268, 276, 288, 290, 298, 299, 301, 303, 307, 309-11, 313-14, 317-18, 321, 323-7, 330, 334, 335, 339, 340, 341, 342, 343, 368, 402, 419, 488-9, 493, 494, 499, 509, 511, 515, 516, 517, 518, 520, 521, 522, 523, 525, 527, 528, 534, 535
Alba Longa, 289, 298, 308
Alexander, 244, 245, 247, 519, 540
Alexandros, 35, 36, 40, 41, 44, 45, 47, 72, 133, 143, 162, 169, 183, 184, 270, 325, 409, 488, 496, 520, 521, 523, 525, 533, 547
Alkibiades, 235-40, 530
Alkinoos, 78-86, 97, 105, 106, 115
Allecto, 304, 305, 314, 324
Amata, 304, 329, 331, 335, 340
Amazon, 326, 327, 517
Amores/amores, 365, 374, 377, 381, 396, 400, 404, 405, 408, 409-10, 412, 538
Anchises, 277, 283, 289, 291, 297, 298, 299, 300, 301, 302, 306, 308, 311, 322, 339, 342, 343, 419, 457, 460
Andromache, 275, 276
Andromakhe, 45-6, 58-60, 141, 168, 331, 522, 523, 528
Anna, 285, 412
Antigone, 191, 197-99, 201-5, 213, 283, 488, 529, 541, 549
Antikleia, 93, 94, 98
Antilokhos, 56, 60, 61, 137
Antinoos, 68, 113, 114, 122, 123, 124, 125, 139
Aphrodite, 20, 21, 26, 35, 36, 39, 40, 41, 43, 44, 52, 59, 63, 71, 82, 115, 141, 150, 206, 211, 216, 217, 246, 247, 249, 259, 263, 267, 270, 279, 314, 330, 342, 414, 515, 516, 518, 527, 538
aphros, 20, 246, 270
Apollodoros, 234, 235, 239
Apology, 235, 530
aporia, 244
arch, 264, 265, 269
Ares, 24, 26, 39, 40, 41, 42, 43, 44, 55, 59, 82, 152, 314, 515, 520, 523, 527, 538
Arete, 78, 79, 82, 96, 97
Argo, 206, 219
Ariadne, 96, 370, 409, 533
aristeia, 43, 50, 53, 54, 55, 58, 75, 80, 312, 314, 319, 327, 328, 334
Aristophanes, 5, 221, 222, 224, 230, 239, 240, 423, 432, 529, 535, 545
Arjuna, 472, 543
arma, 269, 370, 396
arrows, 81, 125, 128, 211, 272, 308, 326, 373, 397, 398, 399, 406, 526
Ars Amatoria, 412, 414
Artemis, 24, 37, 64, 71, 74, 101, 115, 120, 155, 169, 176, 177, 179, 181, 184, 186, 188, 218, 246, 267, 367, 368, 518, 522

Ascanius, 272, 276, 281, 282, 289, 290, 302, 305, 311, 312, 314, 315, 318, 334
Astyanax, 45, 59, 60, 64, 141, 276, 310, 311, 331, 523
Atalanta, 369, 536
ataraxia, 421, 423
Athene, 9, 24, 35, 36, 41, 42, 43, 48, 67, 68, 72, 74, 76, 77, 78, 79, 84, 90, 100, 106, 107, 108, 109, 110, 111, 112, 113, 114, 118, 119, 120, 121, 122, 126, 128, 129, 134, 135, 139, 140, 141, 142, 165, 167, 168, 271
Athenian, 3, 4, 167, 168, 186, 187, 197, 223, 225, 226, 228, 230, 243, 431, 433, 434, 437, 530, 540
atom/oi/os, 419-20
Atreus, 49, 61, 97, 110, 135, 151, 157, 160, 168, 169
Atticus, 401, 402
Augustus, 248, 249, 260, 263, 265, 268, 298, 300, 301, 311, 340, 342, 343, 352, 360, 361, 389, 390, 391, 395, 399, 401, 410, 412, 414, 415, 436, 465, 528, 531, 535, 536, 537, 538, 541, 548
Aulis, 37, 64, 155, 170, 172, 173, 174, 177, 195, 200, 201, 213, 418, 518, 546
Avernus, 291, 293
Azaz-El, 13

Bacchus, 272, 282, 370, 399, 409, 538
Baiae, 379, 380, 381
Bailey, Cyril, 268, 533, 545
Barbarians, 186
Bassus, 371, 372
Beatrice, 461-5, 497, 500, 501
Bible, 7, 5, 6, 443, 444, 541, 546
Bithynia, 350

border, 8, 12, 13, 92, 301, 375, 439, 451, 457
Briseis, 38, 46, 48, 49, 55, 58, 59, 63, 185
Bronze Age, 29, 30
Burning Bush, 14

Caelius, 349, 350
Caesar, 298, 300, 311, 346, 357, 389, 399, 465, 528
Cain, 446
Callidamates, 426, 429, 430
Carrhae, 248
Carribean, 485
Carson, Anne, xi, 146, 527, 546
Carthage, 270, 271, 272, 277, 278, 280, 281, 287, 289, 296, 540
Cassandra, 63, 250, 273
castra, 402
Catiline, 311
Catullus, xi, 346-52, 353, 357, 373, 388, 390, 391, 395, 408, 417, 436, 463, 527, 533, 540
Ceres, 362, 397
Cervantes, 5, 471
Chanson de Roland, 453, 454, 457, 467, 542
chaos, 18, 174, 246, 334
Charlemagne, 454, 455, 456
Charon, 295, 533
chiastic, 243, 535
Chimene, 467, 468, 469, 470, 471
Chloe, 355, 358, 359, 360
Chremes, 431, 432, 433, 434
Christian/ity, 6, 10, 15, 267, 415, 441, 453-6, 457, 461, 467, 483, 486, 532, 539, 540, 543, 548
Cid, Le/El, 466, 467, 469, 475, 546
Cilissa, *162*
Circe: see Kirke
Clodia, 346, 347, 348, 349, 351, 352, 365

Clouds, The,
Comedy, 7, 227, 230, 417, 423, 430, 435, 441, 456, 457, 462, 464, 476, 500, 543, 545, 546
Corinna, 401, 403, 404, 405, 406, 407
Corinth, 195, 206, 207, 209, 211, 214, 215, 540
Corneille, Pierre, 466, 467, 471, 475, 545, 546
Crassus, 248, 389, 537
Crete: see Krete
Creusa (Aeneas' Trojan wife), 274, 411
Croesus, 16
Cronus: see Kronos
Crusade, 454
Cumae, 276, 292
Cupid, 272, 277, 367, 396, 397, 398, 402, 413
Cyclone, 490, 491
Cynthia, 366-77, 379-95, 396, 401, 408, 436, 460, 497, 537
Cypassis, 406
Cyrus, 16, 541

dactylic hexameter, 30, 145, 267, 345, 346, 396, 412, 417, 435, 532
daimon, 179, 228, 230, 232, 427
Danaan, 53, 308
Danaids, 317, 403
Dante Alighieri, 5, 456-66, 476, 477, 487, 497, 500, 542, 543, 546
Daphne, 397, 398, 405, 413, 414
Dardanian, 151, 298, 343
Daunus, 317, 318, 319, 336, 339, 341
David, King, 452-3
Davus, 432, 433, 434
De Rerum Natura, 345, 417
death, 7, 12, 13, 14, 16, 28, 32, 36, 42, 45, 48, 50, 51, 53, 54-60, 62, 63-4, 67, 72, 92, 93, 94, 98-102, 105, 107, 114, 120, 130, 132, 135, 136, 137, 138, 141, 143, 147, 150, 155-8, 160, 163, 165, 166, 167, 170, 177, 178, 183, 184, 186, 193, 194, 195, 198-202, 205, 206, 214, 216, 229, 232, 233, 241, 242, 247, 248, 251, 265, 267, 268, 274, 276, 279, 282, 284, 287, 288, 292, 294, 295, 296, 297, 298, 300, 301, 302, 304, 305, 310, 316-18, 320-3, 326-7, 328, 329, 330, 331, 332, 334, 335, 336, 341, 343, 348, 351, 352, 354, 359, 361, 362-3, 364, 365, 385-8, 391, 400, 405, 410, 411-12, 415, 417, 418, 419-21, 423, 424, 431, 436, 444, 446, 449, 455, 456, 459, 463-4, 465, 470, 471, 476, 477-8, 479, 480, 481-3, 484, 496, 499, 501, 502, 503, 514, 516, 517, 520, 521, 523, 524, 527, 529, 530, 534, 536, 540, 542
Deiphobos, 51, 72, 296, 338
Delia, 361, 362, 363, 364, 365, 370
Delion, *238*
Delphi, 8, 15, 151, 163, 165, 192, 245, 413, 528, 530
Demeter, 21, 24, 28, 53, 74
Democritus, 420, 515
Demodokos, 79, 82, 83, 527
destiny, 21, 22, 44, 58, 97, 135, 163, 268, 322, 336, 340, 485
deus ex machina, 218, 430
Deut(eronomy), 15, 514
Dialagge, *226*
Dido, 271-2, 274, 277-87, 290, 295, 296, 301, 304, 305, 314, 315, 316, 321, 322, 342, 409, 410-12, 438, 525
Diomedes, 43, 44, 49, 52, 59, 72, 110, 270, 272, 307, 312, 313, 314, 324, 325, 330, 516
Dionysos, 24, 136, 153, 221, 247, 248, 409

Dionysus, 316, 370
Diotima, 232, 233, 234, 235, 236, 237
Divine Comedy, The, 457
doctus, 368, 369, 370, 387, 390, 393, 395, 437
dolce stil nuovo, 463, 543
Dolios, *139*
Doryphoros, 243, 244, 245, 248, 249, 257, 263, 535
Drances, 322, 324, 325
dream, 8, 9, 40, 76, 95, 119, 275, 291, 297, 299, 300, 392, 394, 422, 456, 480, 543
Dyskolos, 221, 227, 228, 435

Earth, 18, 19, 22, 24, 100, 279, 387
eclogue(s), 267, 346, 352, 391
Egypt, 14, 169, 228, 248, 263, 346, 426, 436, 448, 450, 451, 480, 525
eidolon, 74, 101, 169, 300, 319, 342, 525
elegies, 361, 365, 369, 388, 390, 391, 393, 394, 395, 408
elegist, *377, 487*
Elektra, 157, 158, 159, 160, 161, 168, 181, 185
Elpenor, 93, 97, 101, 292, 295
Elyssa, 283
Epic, 7, 11, 263, 345, 475, 516, 542
Epicurus, 417, 418, 419, 420, 422
Epimetheus, 25
Erinyes, 20 (See also Furies)
eris/eristic, ix, xi, 5, 6, 16, 21, 23, 26, 33, 35, 36, 37, 39, 44, 51, 53, 55, 56, 58, 62, 66, 67, 70, 75, 76, 88, 89, 91, 92, 97, 99, 111, 119, 122, 127, 131, 143, 145, 146, 147, 148, 149, 150, 152, 153, 155, 156, 158, 160, 169, 174, 177, 181, 183, 186, 189, 191, 201, 213, 215, 216, 219, 222, 226, 227, 229, 233, 236, 239, 240, 241, 242, 243, 244, 250, 251, 252, 269, 270, 271, 272, 275, 276, 277, 278, 279, 280, 282, 283, 284, 285, 289, 290, 293, 294, 296, 301, 304, 305, 309, 313, 315, 316, 317, 326, 336, 340, 342, 343, 345, 346, 349, 352, 354, 358, 361, 364, 365, 367, 368, 373, 376, 385, 390, 393, 395, 396, 398, 402, 403, 409, 410, 414, 415, 417, 421, 422, 423, 428, 431, 433, 435, 438, 440, 441, 443, 444, 445, 446, 447, 449, 451, 452, 453, 462, 464, 465, 466, 467, 469, 471, 472, 479, 481, 483, 485, 489, 490, 494, 496, 498, 508, 509, 511, 512, 518, 522, 523, 525, 528, 532, 536, 537
Eris, xi, 3, 7, 11, 21, 26, 35, 42, 43, 64, 74, 142, 191, 221, 343, 430, 488
eros, ix, x, xi, 4, 5, 6, 16, 21, 26, 33, 35, 36, 37, 44, 53, 55, 62, 66, 74, 75, 76, 79, 84, 85, 88, 89, 91, 92, 97, 100, 102, 111, 119, 122, 131, 133, 142, 143, 145, 146, 147, 148, 149, 150, 152, 153, 154, 155, 156, 160, 161, 169, 181, 183, 189, 191, 213, 215, 216, 219, 222, 226, 227, 229, 232, 233, 236, 239, 240, 241, 242, 243, 244, 249, 250, 251, 252, 269, 270, 271, 272, 275, 276, 277, 278, 279, 280, 282, 283, 284, 285, 287, 289, 290, 293, 296, 301, 303, 304, 305, 313, 316, 317, 324, 326, 340, 343, 345, 346, 351, 354, 355, 358, 361, 364, 365, 367, 369, 373, 376, 390, 393, 395, 396, 398, 402, 403, 409, 410, 414, 415, 417, 421, 422, 423, 428, 433, 438, 440, 441, 443, 444, 445, 447, 449, 451, 452, 453, 462, 464, 465, 466, 467, 468, 471, 472, 478, 479, 481, 483, 485, 488, 489, 490, 494, 496, 508, 509, 512, 523, 525, 528, 532, 536, 537

556   *Eros and Eris*

Eros, xi, xii, 18, 20, 21, 26, 35, 66, 146, 211, 224, 233, 272, 277, 367, 368, 386, 387, 397, 399, 423, 464, 527, 546
Esau, 8, 449, 450, 471, 475
Eteokles, 198, 199, 205, 213
Ethics, 541, 548
Ethiopia, 285
ethos, 186, 241, 244, 245, 247, 327, 342
eudaimonia, 230
Eumenides, 164, 168, 181, 209
Eupeithes, *139, 140, 141*
Euripides, 7, 10, 4, 5, 145, 168, 169, 170, 177, 181, 183, 186, 187, 191, 195, 201, 205, 206, 208, 213, 214, 218, 221, 224, 230, 244, 518, 525, 526, 529, 537, 539, 546
Euryalos, 80, 82, 306
Euryalus, 312, 534
Eurykleia, 68, 115, 117, 118, 120, 124, 129, 130, 132, 133
Eurylokhos, 89, 90, 103, 104
Eurymakhos, 69, 113, 114, 115, 121, 123, 124, 125, 127, 128
Eurypylos, 50, 54
Euthyphro, 231, 244
Evander, 308, 309, 310, 315, 316, 317, 321, 322, 323, 533, 534
Eve, 444, 445, 446, 447, 541
evil, 19, 25, 26, 27, 48, 50, 69, 91, 139, 140, 151, 172, 174, 179, 180, 184, 185, 209, 210, 216, 279, 286, 354, 369, 444, 446-7, 492, 524, 541, 548
Ex(odus), 14, 15, 451
Eyerdam, Pam, *xi*

fama, 271, 278, 279, 320, 340, 404, 407, 408, 409, 410, 422, 533
Fasti, 415
fate, 13, 32, 33, 38, 39, 45, 47, 54, 55, 60, 62, 66, 67, 73, 84, 85, 86, 93, 108, 109, 114, 125, 140, 152, 163, 164, 165, 167, 169, 173, 178, 179, 188, 203, 204, 216, 228, 240, 249, 250, 274, 275, 280, 281, 283, 284, 285, 291, 292, 303, 310, 312, 316, 322, 323, 324, 339, 340, 387, 388, 392, 398, 411, 413, 434, 475, 493, 506, 523
Fate, 32, 39, 41, 45, 76, 103, 104, 126, 163, 168, 177, 189, 194, 197, 199, 205, 251, 278, 283, 286, 287, 293, 315, 326, 331, 333, 335, 336, 337, 339, 358, 385, 400, 467, 475, 484
Faunus, 302, 303, 336, 337
fideli d'amore, 463, 501
fides, 286
Flores, Perry, xi
free will, 33, 127, 475
Freud, 3, 90, 242, 271
Frogs, 221, 529
funeral, 36, 60, 61, 63, 102, 136, 201, 242, 287, 288, 289, 290, 291, 304, 318, 321, 322, 323, 381, 383, 385, 386, 388, 394, 418, 498, 501, 502
Furies, The, 20, 114, 165-8, 276, 338, 411
furor, 76, 287, 288, 290, 318, 325, 340, 368, 420

Gaia, 18, 19, 21, 22, 23, 24
Gallus, 361, 372, 377, 378, 388, 391, 405, 537
Ganelon, *454, 455, 456, 457, 464*
Gen(esis), 444-51, 542
gender, 5, 97, 149, 364
generation, 5, 20, 21, 25, 30, 111, 139, 149, 155, 191, 221, 230, 234, 276, 298, 395, 415, 431, 446, 448, 449, 453, 454, 461, 490, 506, 516
gladiator(s), 436-8
Glaukos, 34, 44, 51, 516

gloria, 281, 377
Glory of Hera, The, 2, 513, 548
Glycera, 355
Glycerium, 431, 432, 433, 434, 435
Golden, 206, 365, 405
good (as noun or moral adjective), 14, 25, 26, 49, 62, 79, 85, 157, 175, 176, 179, 197, 204, 207, 232, 233, 278, 334, 363, 369, 381, 420, 426, 436, 443, 444, 445, 446, 447, 456, 462, 465, 494, 502, 541
Good, The, 232, 237
Gorgias, 228, 229, 231
gorgon, 304, 306
Great Dionysia, 170
Greece, ix, 4, 15, 171, 173, 186, 212, 267, 375, 393, 418, 443, 488, 536, 548, 549
Greek Experiment, The, 15, 513, 547
guilt culture, 15

Hadrian, 265, 266, 534, 540
Hagar, 447, 448, 449, 542
Haimon, 202, 203, 204, 205
Hanson, J. Arthur, xi, xii
Harpies, 275, 302
Heaven, 18, 19, 22, 24, 181, 278, 457, 462
Hebe, 101
Hekabe, 168, 331
Hektor, 30, 42-56, 58-64, 80, 90, 127, 136, 141, 157, 233, 234, 242, 290, 294, 296, 309, 310, 311, 313, 314, 317, 321, 323, 324, 325, 330, 331, 334, 335, 338, 339, 343, 488, 489, 498, 499, 508, 523, 527, 528, 534, 535
Helen, 34, 35-7, 38, 40-1, 44-7, 49, 50, 58, 64, 70-3, 96, 100, 110, 111, 133, 137, 148, 152, 156, 162, 169, 170, 172, 173, 174, 177, 180-6, 271, 274, 279, 280, 296, 304, 305, 321, 324, 325, 391, 403, 409, 480, 483, 485, 488, 490-2, 494, 496-502, 504, 505, 506-8, 516, 518, 519, 520, 523, 525, 528, 533
Helenus, 275, 276
Helios, 89, 94, 102, 103, 104, 134, 135, 214, 216, 218, 248, 476, 538
Hellas, 99, 177, 183, 186, 187, 212, 224, 235, 241, 244, 245, 247, 530
Hellenic, ix, 3, 4, 127, 145, 166, 187, 212, 230, 244, 247, 263, 516
Hellenistic, 227, 247, 248, 251, 263, 345, 417, 424, 527, 533, 540
Hephaistos, 24, 26, 39, 57, 59, 82, 136, 310, 519, 522, 538
Hera, 21, 24, 33, 35, 36, 39, 40, 42, 43, 48, 52, 53, 54, 62, 101, 147, 206, 241, 270, 272, 274, 513, 516, 526
Herakles, 24, 81, 95, 101, 167, 221, 241, 247, 248, 253, 293, 379, 484, 513, 526, 529
Hercules, 308, 309, 316, 357, 476
Hermes, 9, 24, 35, 62, 63, 74, 75, 90, 91, 92, 104, 135, 137, 165, 241, 270, 285, 427, 515, 521, 522, 538, 546, 547
hero, 24, 28, 45, 48, 49, 58, 61, 65, 66, 67, 69, 75, 76, 77, 78, 79, 84, 86, 87, 88, 90, 91, 92, 93, 94, 96, 98, 100, 102, 103, 104, 105, 106, 108, 109, 110, 111, 112, 114, 116, 118, 120, 123, 126, 127, 128, 129, 134, 138, 142, 150, 154, 158, 167, 184, 198, 227, 240, 241, 244, 246, 249, 268, 270, 274, 277, 281, 282, 284, 285, 288, 291, 292, 293, 294, 296, 297, 300, 306, 309, 315, 318, 320, 331, 341, 342, 363, 369, 404, 410, 424, 429, 430, 439, 447, 457, 459, 460, 461, 462, 469, 476, 477, 478, 480, 482, 483, 484, 485, 493, 495, 499, 500, 513, 514, 522, 535

Herodotos, 16
Heroides, 409, 412, 517, 538, 539, 546, 547
Hesiod, x, xi, 5, 17, 18, 25, 27, 28, 29, 73, 246, 268, 390, 435, 440, 443, 514, 515, 516, 547, 548, 549
Hieron, 149, 150
Hijmans, B.L. Jr., 521, 547
Hippodameia, 150, 151
Hippolytos, 218, 244, 267, 529
holiness, 15, 231, 244
Homer/ic, 5, 30, 34, 37, 46, 55, 79, 310, 345, 373, 374, 391, 405, 420, 439, 443, 459, 461, 475, 478, 485, 486, 487, 488, 489, 495, 503, 504, 516, 517, 518, 519, 520, 521, 523, 526, 547, 549
honor, xii 38, 39, 45, 48, 54, 55, 56, 60, 63, 78, 79, 151, 165, 171, 178, 179, 183, 185, 186, 188, 200, 202, 208, 212, 266, 271, 282, 289, 291, 293, 301, 308, 321, 325, 331, 334, 467, 468, 469, 470, 471, 480, 519, 525
honor-prize, 38, 45, 60, 185
Horace, 346, 352, 354, 358, 359, 360, 361, 362, 363, 365, 373, 383, 393, 395, 425, 435, 536, 539, 540, 545, 546, 547, 549
horn, *119, 299, 342, 455*
hosiotes, 186, 231, 244
hubris, 43, 54, 536

Iarbas, 279, 280, 281, 282, 301, 304
iconoclast, 206, 218, 221
Iliad, x, xi, 5, 28-31, 33-4, 37-9, 41, 45, 64-7, 75, 80, 82, 95, 98, 99, 110, 126, 127, 130, 137, 141, 142, 143, 153, 155, 160, 167, 170, 172, 178, 182, 183, 184, 241, 242, 245, 251, 267, 270, 276, 288, 289, 301, 306, 307, 310, 311, 312, 314, 318, 321-7, 330, 331, 333, 338, 340, 341, 368, 391, 457, 473, 485, 486, 488, 498, 505, 506, 516, 517, 519, 520, 523, 526, 527, 534, 543, 544, 545, 547, 548
insult, 48, 51, 181, 183, 306, 371, 379, 436
interpretation, 14, 15, 447, 514, 515, 531
Iolkos, 206, 207
Iphigenia, 37, 64, 151, 152, 155, 156, 157, 158, 161, 164, 166, 169-71, 173-5, 177-9, 181-8, 195, 200, 201, 213, 224, 418, 519, 522, 546
Iris, 43, 287, 290, 312, 314
Iron, 29, 30, 436
irony, 27, 31, 44, 46, 49, 60, 71, 75, 78, 87, 103, 104, 107, 109, 114, 127, 131, 153, 154, 161, 162, 174, 175, 176, 179, 181, 186, 192, 195, 202, 208, 213, 224, 250, 251, 267, 269, 274, 276, 278, 280, 286, 287, 289, 294, 301, 313, 321, 325, 335, 357, 397, 410, 413, 435, 470, 483, 520, 527
Iros, 114
Isaac, 8, 447, 448, 449, 471, 475, 541, 542
Ishmael, 447, 448, 449, 542
Ismene, 197, 199, 201, 202
Israel, 15, 452, 453
Italy, 145, 249, 266, 269, 276, 278, 281, 283, 284, 288, 290, 291, 294, 295, 302, 307, 308, 311, 314, 317, 323, 324, 329, 410, 516, 531, 534, 542, 549
Ithake, 24, 65, 68, 73, 84, 85, 89, 101, 105, 106, 107, 108, 111, 113, 131, 138, 142, 154, 275, 477, 478, 479, 490, 514, 517
Iulus, 290, 305, 321
ivory, 119, 299, 300, 342, 419, 455, 533

Jacob, 8, 449-50, 471, 475
Jason, 205, 206, 207, 208, 209, 210, 211, 212, 213, 214, 215, 216, 217, 218, 219, 440, 529
Jewish, 441, 454, 508, 548
Jocasta, 192, 193, 194, 196, 197, 205
Joseph, 450, 451
Judaea, 248
Julian Law, 436, 439
Juno, 269, 270, 271, 272, 274, 277, 278, 279, 287, 290, 291, 304, 305, 306, 312, 313, 314, 318, 319, 324, 331, 332, 337, 338, 400
Jupiter, 248, 270, 274, 278, 279, 280, 281, 286, 290, 293, 310, 313, 314, 316, 318, 327, 332, 336, 337, 338, 349, 359, 400, 403, 405, 436, 515
Juturna, 332, 333, 335, 337, 338
Juvenal, 435, 436, 437, 438, 439, 440, 441, 540

Kadish, Josh, *xii*
Kalkhas, 39, 170, 174
Kallimakhos, 345, 346
Kallipides, 229
Kalypso, 24, 66, 67, 73, 74-7, 79, 84, 85, 86, 104, 105, 113, 126, 133, 134, 162, 169, 284, 285, 342, 363, 477, 478, 479, 514, 524
Kassandra, 151, 154, 156, 524
Kavafis, Constantine, 477
Kazantzakis, Nikos, 475, 476, 477, 479, 480, 481, 485, 543, 547
khaos, 26, 241, 245, 397, 414, 512
Khaos, 18, 21
Khryseis, 38, 46, 185, 518
Khryses, *38, 62*
Kikonians, *85, 86, 133*
Kinesias, *225*
Kirke, 24, 85, 86, 89-93, 95, 101-3, 126, 133, 134, 162, 284, 285, 291, 292, 293, 301, 342, 427, 459, 478, 501

kleos, 28, 37, 85, 87-8, 98, 100, 109, 110, 111, 115, 134, 135, 136, 138, 159, 170, 174, 178, 185-7, 201, 219, 233, 271, 320, 321, 330, 340, 404, 410, 527
Klytaimnestra, 37, 63, 66-8, 70, 97-8, 108, 137, 138, 151-5, 157-8, 160-2, 163-4, 170-1, 174-3, 185, 187-8, 224, 518, 524, 526, 528, 533
Knemon, 228-30
Knidos, 247
knowledge, 17, 18, 22, 26, 28, 29, 32, 33, 113, 175, 192, 193, 194, 196, 232, 251, 280, 328, 334, 358, 440, 444-7, 460, 477, 482, 499, 529, 541
Kohav, Alex Shalom, xi, 541, 547
Kokytos, 92
Kolkhis, 207
Kos, 246, 393
Kosmos, 31
Kratylos, 6
Kreon, 192-3, 197, 199-205, 206, 207, 209-11, 213-15, 217, 283
Krete, 107, 109
Kreusa, 206, 216
Krishna, 472, 543
Kronos, 18, 19, 20, 21, 22, 23, 142, 246, 303, 522
Kyklopes, 78, 86, 87, 89, 117, 494
Kyklops, 88, 118, 133, 134
Kypria, 211, 523, 527
Kypros, 20

Laban, 450
Laertes, 68, 69, 75, 84, 94, 138, 139, 140, 141, 143, 185, 479
laisses, 454
Laistrygonians, 89, 133
Lampito, *222, 223*
language, 17, 18, 154, 186, 196, 238, 268, 269, 334, 337, 338, 345, 347,

353, 407, 424, 458, 467, 472, 500, 513, 515, 525, 532, 533, 535, 541, 544, 548, 549
Laokoon, 250, 251, 272, 273, 536
lapis niger, 10, 12, 13
lares, 274, 411
Latinus, 269, 299, 301-6, 314, 322-5, 329-33, 335
Latium, 291, 293, 301, 304, 307, 323, 534
Lausus, 315, 319
Lavinia, 269, 298, 301, 302, 304, 305-6, 312, 324-6, 329, 331, 332, 335, 337, 339, 340, 343
Leah, 450
Leda, 36, 96, 156, 276, 399, 403, 518, 533
Lemnos, 81
Lesbia, 346-8, 350-2, 357, 365, 388, 390, 391, 400, 432, 460, 536, 540
lex, 267, 531
Libation Bearers, 158
Licymnia, 357
Linear B, 29
Littman, Robert J., 1, 2, 4, 5, 547
Lotus(-eaters), 85-6
Lucretius, 345, 405, 417, 418, 419, 420, 421, 422, 423, 435, 441
Luna, 367, 368, 369
Lycinna, 392
Lydia, 16, 354, 356, 358, 359, 365, 405, 536
lyric, x, 5, 131, 145, 146, 147-8, 243, 252, 267, 345-6, 347, 355, 361, 362, 363, 374, 390, 391, 393, 394, 396, 410, 457, 459, 462, 527, 536, 549
Lysistrata, 222-226, 230, 432, 535, 545

Ma Kilman, 485, 500, 503, 505, 506
Maecenas, 268, 352, 357, 360, 388, 389, 391, 395

Mahabharata, 472, 543
Manes, 385
Manis, 385
Mannering, Caitlin, xii
Marathus, 361, 364
Mars, 298, 306, 314, 329, 397, 402, 409, 418, 515
Medea, x, 205, 206, 207, 208, 209, 210, 211, 212, 213, 214, 215, 216, 217, 218, 219, 224, 244, 282, 409, 440, 529, 539, 546, 551
Melanthios, 113, 128, 130
Melantho, 115
Melos, 222
Melville, Herman, 5, 495
Memmius, 418
Menalaos, 533
Menander, 5, 221, 227, 228, 230, 405, 424, 430, 431, 435, 547
menis, 38, 39, 44, 48, 49, 55, 57, 58, 59, 60, 61, 62, 63, 126, 127, 288, 290, 318, 341, 520
Mentor, 128, 129, 139, 140, 141, 142
Mercury, 270, 280, 281, 283, 286, 290, 515
Metellus, 346, 347, 348
Metiscus, 335, 336, 337
Mezentius, 319, 320
Michal, 453
Middle Passage, The, 493
Midian, 14
Minerva, 270, 272, 274, 299, 397
Miriam, 14, 451
Misenus, 294, 295
miserum, 366, 404
Mnemosyne, 18, 24
moira, 32, 33, 38, 44, 55, 58, 63, 103, 128, 163, 185, 197, 228, 273, 274
moly, 90
Monobiblos, 367, 369, 386, 388, 392, 396, 404, 539
Moors, *467, 469, 471*

mortal/s, 24, 28, 31, 49, 57, 75, 76, 90, 99, 132, 165, 167, 186, 198, 201, 232, 233, 241, 244, 246, 248, 285, 297, 326, 403, 404, 420, 444, 478, 506, 512, 516, 517, 522
mos maiorum, 289
Moses, 14, 17, 451-2
Mostellaria, 424
Mount Olympos, 23
Muse, 79, 83, 152, 357, 374, 398, 408
Mykenai, 148, 154, 158, 266
Myrrhine, 225
Myrtilos, 150, 151
mythoi, 34
mythos, 3, 96

nature, 15, 2, 9, 21, 32, 39, 46, 62, 66, 90, 108, 117, 201, 228, 230, 283, 289, 398, 418, 447, 457, 490, 491, 494, 504, 506, 514, 529
Nausikaa, 76-9, 82, 85, 271, 272, 305, 477, 478-9
nectar, 23, 41, 354
Nemean Lion, 241, 253
Nemesis, 361, 365, 366, 536
Neoptolemos, 100, 313, 515, 525, 526, 528, 533
Neptune, 270, 272, 273, 291, 292
Nestor, 48, 50, 70, 111, 136, 521
Night, 18, 21
Nimes, 264
Nisus, 161, 312, 534
Noah, 446
nomoi, 201
nomos, 201
nostos, 65, 84, 86, 101, 523
numerological, 457, 458

Odes, 352, 358, 360, 393, 539, 547
Odi et amo, 349
Odysseus, 9, 24, 25, 28, 30, 37, 42-3, 45, 48-50, 52, 58, 65, 67-143, 153, 154, 155, 159, 160, 162, 169, 170, 174, 184, 185, 186, 227, 233, 250, 268, 269, 271, 272, 275, 276-7, 284-7, 291, 292, 293, 296-8, 299, 301, 303, 305-6, 309, 310, 312, 330, 342, 343, 359, 362, 390, 419, 429, 452, 457, 459, 465, 475-80, 482-4, 487, 489, 491, 493, 494, 495, 501, 514, 515, 517, 519, 524, 525, 526, 527, 528, 534, 535, 546
Odyssey, x, xi, 5, 16, 33, 34, 50, 64, 65, 66, 75, 88, 96, 98, 127, 132, 136, 141, 142, 143, 153, 157, 160, 172, 175, 181, 187, 213, 267, 271, 275, 285, 292, 298, 299, 301, 305, 322, 419, 452, 473, 475, 477, 478, 480, 485, 517, 525, 527, 532, 533, 538, 543, 545, 546, 547
Ogygia, 79
Oidipos, 11-12, 25, 27, 95, 191-200, 204
oikoumene, 247
Oinomaos, 150
oliphant, 455, 456
Olympian, 24, 26, 40, 52, 74, 82, 149, 228, 241, 245, 247, 280, 309, 337
Olympos, 35, 39, 41, 43, 44, 53, 59, 63, 90, 134, 150, 167, 247, 285, 343, 478, 519, 522, 525
Olympus, 270, 281, 287, 305, 310, 318, 326, 328, 335
Omeros, 485, 487, 488, 496, 503, 504, 505, 549
Opis, 326, 328
order, 6, 11, 12, 15, 17, 18, 31, 36, 43, 44, 47, 48, 52, 56, 73, 76, 91, 93, 96, 101, 102, 111, 131, 132, 146, 150, 157, 166, 168, 176, 182, 191, 194, 209, 211, 221, 223, 233, 234, 241, 264, 265, 266, 276, 279, 285, 299, 303, 305, 310, 311, 337,

350, 352, 353, 357, 358, 359, 388, 397, 411, 413, 417, 418, 428, 436, 438, 440, 446, 450, 456, 460, 461, 472, 473, 476, 478, 486, 493, 525, 528, 529, 534, 535, 536, 543
Orestes, 66, 68, 70, 98, 151, 152, 153, 157, 158-69, 173, 179, 181, 182, 187-8, 276, 524, 528
Orphic, 298, 300, 342
Ortygia, 277
Ouranos, 18, 21, 22, 23, 246
Ovid, 346, 361, 365, 395, 396, 397, 401, 402, 403, 404, 405, 407, 408, 409, 410, 411, 412, 413, 414, 421, 440, 463, 497, 517, 538, 539, 544, 546
Oxyrinchos, 228

Palinurus, 292, 293, 294, 295
Pallas, 72, 142, 168, 272, 273, 308, 310, 311, 315, 316, 317, 318, 319, 320, 321, 322, 323, 339, 340, 341, 534
Pamphilus, 431-4
Pan, 228-30
Pandaros, 42, 314, 333
Pandarus, 313-14
Pandora, 23, 25
Pantheon, The, 265, 438
paradox, 2, 8, 13, 17, 26, 31, 69, 93, 136, 191, 235, 250, 342, 512
Paris, 34, 35, 36, 37, 40, 41, 45, 46, 47, 49, 51, 52, 72, 133, 141, 143, 162, 183, 270, 274, 279, 280, 296, 304, 305, 324, 325, 333, 334, 403, 409, 464, 467, 488, 489, 496, 506, 513, 516, 518, 520, 523, 525, 533, 535, 546, 548
Parthians, 248, 249, 355, 389, 537
passion, 20, 37
pathos, 66, 241, 244, 245, 251
Patroklos, 33, 42, 48, 49, 50, 54, 55, 56, 57, 58, 59, 60, 61, 62, 63, 64, 135, 136, 137, 167, 233, 241, 242, 255, 288, 307, 309, 311, 317, 321, 322, 323, 326, 488, 499, 511, 522
Peleus, 28, 35, 48, 57, 62, 63, 64, 74, 99, 100, 136, 307, 321, 517, 522, 523, 525
Pelias, 206, 209, 211, 214
Peloponnesian War, 221, 223, 227, 244, 529
Pelops, 149, 150, 151, 376
penates, 274, 286
Penelope, 65, 66, 67, 68-70, 73-4, 75, 78, 79, 82, 84, 91, 96, 98, 108, 112, 113-20, 122, 124, 126, 127, 130-4, 137-8, 140, 141, 143, 159, 162, 299, 305, 359, 390, 477, 478-9, 494, 524, 525, 526
Penthesilea, 242, 256, 307, 326
Perikles, 238, 540
Persephone, 92, 93, 97, 101, 368
Perses, 25, 27, 28
Persian, 166, 186, 212
Phaedo, 232
Phaedros, 231, 239
Phaiakians, 65, 76, 77, 78, 79, 80, 81, 82, 84, 86, 88, 96, 105, 106, 107, 108, 109, 110, 113, 115, 116, 118, 133, 134, 162, 271, 306, 477, 478, 535
pharmaka, 89, 90, 214
Philip II of Macedon, 244-5
Philoitios, 120, 123, 124, 128, 130, 133, 135, 139
Philoktetes, 81, 168, 218, 525, 526, 544
Philolaches, 424, 425, 426, 427, 428, 429, 430
Philomedia, 426, 431
philosophia, 231, 529
philosophy, 31, 230, 237, 240, 419, 421

Phoenicians, 30
Phoinix, 34, 48, 49, 516, 521
Phrygia, 357
Phryne, 246, 366
Phthia, 99, 519
physis, 201
Pierce, Adrianne, xii, 526, 532
pietas, 186, 266, 268, 274, 282, 319, 320, 334, 339, 342, 343, 351, 414, 423, 424, 427, 537, 539
piety, 130, 158, 231, 244, 267, 423, 530
Pindar, 145, 149, 150, 345, 353
pious, 27, 28, 195, 203, 266, 266, 281, 297, 423, 424, 455
pius, 268, 274, 275, 276, 282, 284, 289, 296, 300, 318, 320, 323, 332, 341, 342, 351, 411, 415, 534
plague, 11, 12, 191, 192, 308, 351, 354, 422, 423, 428
Plato, x, xi, 5, 6, 230, 231, 234, 235, 239, 240, 417, 441, 513, 525, 548, 549
Plautus, 267, 423, 424, 430, 435, 539
poleis, 145, 212, 222, 226, 227, 244, 263
polis, ix, 2-5, 29, 30, 145, 187, 221, 227, 230, 540
Polybos, 195
Polyklitos, 243, 248, 257, 263, 535
Polyneikes, 198, 199, 200, 201, 204, 205, 213
Polyphemos, 87, 88, 89, 93, 95, 107, 109, 110, 117, 162, 286, 309
Ponticus, 373, 374, 377
Poseidon, 21, 51, 53, 66, 73, 74, 76, 79, 84, 88, 93, 94, 95, 96, 101, 105, 106, 108, 149, 150, 250, 251, 270, 272, 273, 286, 292, 309, 516, 522
Potiphar, *450*
Praxiteles, *245, 246, 251, 258, 259, 263*

predetermination, *475*
Priam, 42, 46, 48, 49, 52, 62, 63, 135, 151, 184, 242, 271, 273, 274, 275, 276, 283, 303, 313, 316, 321, 323, 330, 516, 525, 534
Prima Porta, *248, 249, 260, 263, 301, 342, 399*
Prodikos, 6
profanus, 7, 8, 9, 10, 11, 13, 14, 16, 20, 75, 97, 102, 106, 142, 143, 145, 169, 234, 291, 299, 301, 327, 387, 388, 445, 459, 475, 477, 478, 483, 501, 513, 518, 529
Prometheus, *23, 25, 100, 484*
Propertius, 346, 361, 365, 366, 368, 369, 371, 372, 373, 374, 376, 377, 378, 379, 381, 385, 387, 388, 389, 390, 391, 392, 393, 394, 395, 396, 400, 403, 404, 405, 408, 436, 440, 497, 536, 537, 539, 545, 546
Proteus, 73
puella, 351, 367, 369
Punic, 280, 287, 313, 356, 532, 540
Pylades, *151, 152, 158, 161, 162, 163*
Pylos, *70, 107, 111, 139*
Pyriphlegthon, *92*
Pyrrha, *352, 354*
Pyrrhias, *228*
Pythagorean, 298, 300, 342
Pythia, *245*
Pytho, *101, 245*

Rachel, *450*
rain, *425, 429, 500, 502*
reconquista, 467
refugee, 209, 212, 214, 269, 275, 276, 293, 411
religio, 10, 11, 267
religion, 6, 10, 11, 14, 267, 342, 418, 419, 423, 459, 461, 483, 539, 541, 548
Remedia Amoris, 412

Res Gestae, 343, 535, 538, 548
res romana, 332, 338, 343
revelation, 10, 14, 15, 197
Rhea, 21, 22, 23, 536
Robbins, Jerome, 509
Rodrigo, 467
Rodrigue, 467-71
Roman, ix-xi, 5, 10, 143, 147, 148, 186, 243, 247-50, 251-2, 257, 258, 259, 263-9, 270, 272, 274, 277, 279, 281, 282, 284, 287, 288, 289, 290, 298, 299, 303, 306, 307, 308, 311, 320, 327, 332, 342, 343, 345, 346, 347, 348, 350, 351, 352, 355, 356, 358, 380, 389, 391, 393, 395, 398, 405, 410, 415, 417, 423-4, 427, 429, 431, 435, 438, 439, 441, 443, 447, 453, 457, 461, 512, 515, 527, 532, 533, 534, 536, 537, 539, 540, 548
Rome, ix, 11, 264, 270, 278, 280, 281, 289, 290, 295, 298, 300, 311, 323, 332, 333, 343, 346, 350, 357, 376, 380, 381, 383, 384, 390, 395, 415, 424, 436, 438, 439, 441, 443, 459, 464, 485, 533, 534, 536, 537, 539, 540
Romulus, 298, 306, 308, 311, 534, 536, 541
Roncesvalles, 454
Roncevaux, 454, 455, 456
Rumor, 279, 282, 322
Rutulian, 319, 329, 333

Sabine, 311
sacer, 7-13, 16, 20, 89, 92, 102, 106, 117, 169, 234, 291, 293, 327, 387, 427, 445, 447, 459, 461, 475, 483, 485, 514, 516, 536
sacerdos, 9, 12, 13, 15, 17, 103, 135, 245, 457
sacerdotal, 12, 14, 266

salvation, 90, 91, 134, 159, 218, 219, 319, 427, 462
salvational, 119, 433, 458
Sam(uel), Book of, 452-3
Sappho, 145, 146, 147, 148, 149, 345, 347, 353, 355, 361, 368
Sarah, 447, 448, 449, 471, 542, 548
Sarpedon, 33, 51, 55, 167, 241, 251, 254, 307, 316, 326
Satire, 7, 417, 435
Saul, King, 452, 453
Scapha, 426
Scheria, 105
Seljuks, 454
seven, 24, 53, 67, 75, 79, 89, 186, 199, 227, 230, 266, 285, 290, 338, 450, 451, 455, 483, 485, 503, 514, 524, 533
Seven Against Thebes, 199, 205
Shakespeare, 5, 465, 508, 512
shame culture, 15, 330, 363
shipwreck, 78, 137, 353, 354, 434
Sibyl/sibyl, 276, 292-6, 299, 300, 457, 485, 500, 505
Sicily, 145, 149, 224, 276, 288, 291, 296, 314, 382, 530, 542, 543
Silenos, *236, 238*
Simo, 427, 428, 429, 430, 432, 433, 434
Sinon, *250, 272*
Sirens, The, *102, 134*
Sisyphos, *101, 185*
Skopas, *251*
Skylla and Kharybdis, *102, 103*
Skyros, *100*
Slater, Philip, 2-5, 440, 443, 513, 548
sleep, 7, 9, 21, 40, 49, 52, 89, 96, 97, 103, 104, 105, 115, 130, 133, 134, 165, 234, 239, 241, 242, 286, 292, 299-300, 304, 315, 331, 356, 371, 372, 427, 428, 438, 463, 483
snow, 359, 484

Sokrates, 6, 16, 230-40, 244, 441, 447, 525, 529, 530
Sondheim, Stephen, 508, 509
Sophokles, 5, 11, 12, 33, 95, 168, 181, 191, 195, 197, 198, 199, 200, 204, 213, 218, 221, 405, 525, 526, 541
Sostratos, 228, 229, 230
Sparta, 4, 35, 36, 41, 42, 70, 72, 73, 109, 110, 132, 133, 137, 187, 222, 223, 225, 230, 244, 271, 274, 279, 403, 480, 490, 496, 520, 530
St Lucia, 485, 488, 502, 505, 544
storm, 76, 85, 101, 103, 104, 192, 224, 241, 270, 318, 335, 383, 421, 425, 476, 477, 497, 514
Stygian, 293
Styx, 92, 221, 533
suppliant, 59, 62, 78, 107, 112, 166, 178, 180, 182, 191, 309, 338, 339, 363
Sychaeus, 272, 277, 295, 411, 412
symmetria, 243, 245, 246
Symposium, x, 230, 232, 234, 548
Syracuse, 149, 222, 530

Tantalos, 101, 149, 150, 484
Tartaros, 24, 528
Taurians, 169
Teiresias, 92-4, 103, 133, 134, 143, 193, 196, 200, 204, 297, 298, 452, 476, 480, 493, 495
Telemakhos, 68-71, 73-4, 80, 81, 97, 108-15, 120-25, 128-33, 135, 137, 139, 140-41, 143, 475, 477, 478, 479, 496, 524, 526, 527, 541
Tenedos, 250, 273
Terence, 267, 423, 431, 435, 540
Terentia, 356
terza rima, 458, 485, 542
thanatos, 479, 512
Thebes, 11-12, 25, 27, 151, 191, 194, 195, 196, 197, 198-200, 205, 213

Theoklymenos, 111, 113, 121
Theopropides, 424, 426, 427, 428, 429, 430, 431
Thersites, 44, 52, 429, 519, 544
Thetis, 28, 35, 39, 48, 56, 57, 60, 62, 63, 64, 74, 98, 100, 136, 187, 307, 309, 517, 521, 522, 523, 525, 526
Thrasydaios of Thebes, *151*, *152*
thumos, 216, 217
Thyestes, *151*, *154*, *157*
Tiber, 302, 307, 308, 313, 329, 533
Tibullus, 346, 360, 361-5, 366, 370, 373, 395, 405
Titans, 19, 20, 21, 23, 24, 303, 357, 413
tragedy, 2, 31, 40, 157, 196, 203, 222, 240, 267, 471, 544, 548
Tranio, 424, 426, 427, 428, 429, 430, 431
Tristia, 396, 415, 538, 539
Trojan War, 24, 28, 29, 33-5, 37, 39, 40, 57, 65, 70, 74, 80, 81, 84, 85, 132, 133, 140, 147, 148, 152, 153, 168, 187, 188, 191, 205, 240, 241, 242, 249, 272, 276, 279, 299, 303, 323, 324, 325, 330, 343, 473, 480, 503, 522, 523, 525, 527
Troy, 25, 28, 29, 32, 35, 36-7, 39, 41, 42, 43, 50, 53, 54, 55, 60, 62, 63, 64, 65, 66, 70, 71, 80, 81, 83, 85, 87, 89, 97, 98, 100, 105, 107, 110, 118, 123, 136, 139, 143, 148, 153, 155, 157, 158, 160, 164, 169, 176, 177, 184, 185, 188, 233, 249-50, 269, 273-4, 275, 279, 281, 283, 284, 289, 290, 292, 300, 304, 306, 309, 313, 316, 322, 323, 331, 334, 337, 343, 386, 387, 483, 485, 488, 489, 490, 493, 496, 498, 504, 505, 508, 516, 517, 521, 524, 525, 526, 528, 532
Tullus, *298*, *367*, *373*, *381*, *388*, *537*

Turnus, 268, 269, 301, 304, 305, 306, 307, 311, 312, 313, 314, 315, 316, 317, 318, 319, 322, 323, 324, 325, 326, 328, 329, 330, 331, 332, 333, 334, 335, 336, 337, 338, 339, 340, 341, 342, 343, 391, 535
tykhe, 228, 229, 336
Tyre, 272, 282, 410
Tyrian, 278, 283
Tzipporah, 14, 451

Ummayad, 567
Underworld, The, 287, 288, 291, 292, 293, 297, 298, 300, 306, 311, 322, 343, 419, 457, 458, 485, 567
undying glory, 28, 32, 37, 233, 290, 514 (See also *kleos aphthiton*)

vagina(l), 19, 370, 525, 526
Venus, 249, 263, 270, 271, 272, 274, 277, 278, 279, 291, 298, 301, 309, 310, 311, 313, 314, 318, 334, 337, 354, 355, 360, 363, 369, 397, 398, 402, 403, 406, 409, 410, 411, 417, 418, 421, 422, 506, 515
Vergil, 143, 252, 267-9, 271-5, 277, 279, 280, 283, 284, 285, 286, 287-8, 290, 292, 293, 294, 295-301, 303, 305, 306-11, 314, 315, 317, 320, 321, 323, 324, 327, 331, 333, 339, 340, 341-3, 345, 346, 352, 360, 365, 391, 395, 405, 408, 410, 417, 438, 439, 440, 457, 458, 459, 460-3, 464, 465, 532, 533, 534, 535, 536, 541, 545, 547, 548
Virgin, 462, 464, 500

Volscian, 325, 327
Vulcan, 308, 309, 310, 311, 325, 331, 402

Walcott, Derek, 485, 486, 488, 489, 494, 503, 504, 544, 549, 567
West Side Story, 5, 508, 567
Woman of Andros, The, 431, 567
women, 2, 3, 24, 38, 46, 49, 58, 69, 71, 78, 95, 96, 97, 99, 118, 123, 129, 130, 132, 134, 158, 161, 168, 183, 186, 199, 202, 208, 209, 212, 217, 222, 223, 224, 225, 226, 271, 290, 304, 311, 321, 335, 351, 352, 354, 359, 371, 391, 393, 399, 403, 409, 412, 426, 435, 436, 437, 438, 439, 440, 441, 447, 449, 452, 478, 479, 483, 484, 485, 493, 526, 543
wooden horse, 50, 72, 73, 250, 290, 524
Works and Days, 18, 25, 27, 29, 268, 391, 435

Xanthos, 58, 59
Xenophon, 231, 529

Zeus, 21, 22, 23-5, 27-8, 33, 36, 39-40, 41-2, 43-4, 45, 48, 50, 51, 52-6, 59, 62, 64, 66, 67, 68, 69, 73, 74, 75, 85, 87, 95-6, 100-1, 103-4, 105, 109, 120, 124, 133, 135, 136, 140, 141-2, 150, 156, 159, 167, 168, 178, 201, 211, 214, 218, 241, 248, 250, 270, 274, 303, 307, 310, 326, 413, 513, 515, 516, 518, 520, 521, 522, 526

www.ingramcontent.com/pod-product-compliance
Lightning Source LLC
Chambersburg PA
CBHW060748230426
43667CB00010B/1478